NORTHERN HONSHU
Pages 260–279

HOKKAIDO
Pages 280–291

KYOTO CITY
Pages 154–185

CENTRAL HONSHU
Pages 128–153

NORTHERN
HONSHU

CENTRAL
HONSHU

TOKYO

KYOTO
CITY

Sapporo

Hakodate

Aomori

Morioka

Sendai

Niigata

Nagano

Takayama

Nagoya

TOKYO AREA BY AREA

Pages 60–113; for Street Finder map, see pages 114–23

CENTRAL TOKYO
Pages 64–75

NORTHERN TOKYO
Pages 76–87

WESTERN TOKYO
Pages 88–99

JAPAN

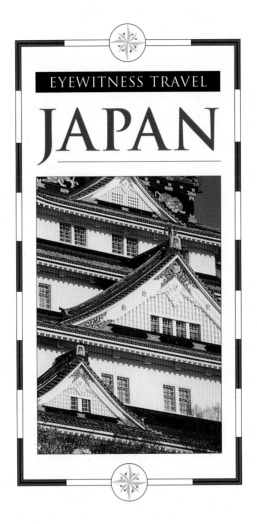

EYEWITNESS TRAVEL
JAPAN

DK

LONDON, NEW YORK,
MELBOURNE, MUNICH AND DELHI
www.dk.com

Produced by Blue Island Publishing Limited
London, England
EDITORIAL DIRECTOR Rosalyn Thiro
ART DIRECTOR Stephen Bere
SENIOR EDITOR Jane Simmonds
US EDITOR Mary Sutherland
ART EDITORS Tessa Bindloss, Ian Midson
PICTURE RESEARCHER Ellen Root

Dorling Kindersley Limited
MAP CO-ORDINATOR Dave Pugh
DTP DESIGNER Lee Redmond

CONTRIBUTORS
John Hart Benson Jr., Mark Brazil, Jon Burbank,
Angela Jeffs, Emi Kazuko, Stephen Mansfield,
Bill Marsh, Catherine Rubinstein, Jacqueline Ruyak

RESEARCHER
Mayumi Hayashi

MAPS
Era-Maptech Ltd

PHOTOGRAPHERS
Demetrio Carrasco, Clive Streeter, Linda Whitwam, Peter Wilson

ILLUSTRATORS
Richard Bonson, Gary Cross, Richard Draper, Paul Guest, Claire
Littlejohn, Maltings Partnership, Mel Pickering, John Woodcock

Reproduced in Singapore by Colourscan
Printed and bound in South China

First American Edition 2000

Reprinted with revisions 2002, 2003, 2005, 2007

08 09 10 9 8 7 6 5 4 3 2 1

Published in the United States by
DK Publishing, Inc., 375 Hudson Street,
New York, New York 10014

Copyright © 2000, 2007 Dorling Kindersley Limited, London

ISSN 1542-1554
ISBN: 978 0 75662 876 5

Throughout this book, floors are referred to in accordance with US
usage, ie the "first floor" is at ground level.

Front cover main image: View of Mount Fuji, Central Honshu

**The information in this
Eyewitness Travel Guide is checked regularly.**

Every effort has been made to ensure that this book is as up-to-date
as possible at the time of going to press. Some details, however,
such as telephone numbers, opening hours, prices, gallery hanging
arrangements and travel information are liable to change. The
publishers cannot accept responsibility for any consequences arising
from the use of this book, nor for any material on third party
websites, and cannot guarantee that any website address in this
book will be a suitable source of travel information. We value the
views and suggestions of our readers very highly. Please write to:
Publisher, DK Eyewitness Travel Guides,
Dorling Kindersley, 80 Strand, London WC2R 0RL, Great Britain.

◁ **Student monks at Mount Koya, Western Honshu**

Matsumoto Castle in the Japan Alps

CONTENTS

HOW TO USE
THIS GUIDE 6

INTRODUCING
JAPAN

DISCOVERING JAPAN
10

**Wall hanging of a geisha in a
museum in Takayama**

PUTTING JAPAN
ON THE MAP 14

A PORTRAIT OF
JAPAN 16

JAPAN THROUGH
THE YEAR 44

THE HISTORY OF
JAPAN 50

Makunouchi bento, a classic meal-in-a-box

TOKYO AREA BY AREA

Imperial figure at Yomeimon Gate, Tosho-gu Shrine, Nikko

TRAVELERS' NEEDS

Neon lights in the Roppongi district of Western Tokyo

JAPAN REGION BY REGION

Todai-ji Temple, Nara

HOW TO USE THIS GUIDE

This guide helps you to get the most from your visit to Japan. It provides detailed practical information and expert recommendations. *Introducing Japan* maps the country and sets it in its historical and cultural context. Tokyo and the eight regional sections describe important sights, using maps, photographs, and illustrations. Restaurant and hotel recommendations can be found in *Travelers' Needs*, together with general advice about accommodations and Japanese food. The *Survival Guide* has tips on everything from transportation to etiquette.

TOKYO

This city is divided into areas, each with its own chapter. The *Farther Afield* section covers peripheral sights. All sights are numbered and plotted on the chapter's area map. The information for each sight follows the map's numerical order, making sights easy to locate within the chapter.

Sights at a Glance lists the chapter's sights by category, such as Notable Districts, Historic Buildings, Modern Architecture, Parks and Gardens, and Markets.

All pages relating to Tokyo have red thumb tabs.

A locator map shows where you are in relation to other areas of the city.

1 Area Map
For easy reference, sights are numbered and located on a map. City center sights are also marked on the Street Finder on pages 114–23.

2 Street-by-Street Map
This gives a bird's-eye view of the key areas in each chapter.

3 Detailed Information
The top sights in Tokyo are described individually. Telephone numbers and public transportation links are given, along with other practical information. The key to the symbols is on the back flap of the book.

NORTHERN HONSHU

1 Introduction
The history and character of each region is outlined here, showing how that area has developed over the centuries and what it has to offer to the visitor today.

JAPAN REGION BY REGION

Following the Tokyo chapter, the country has been divided into eight regions, each of which has a separate chapter, including Kyoto City. The most interesting towns and other places to visit are numbered on a map at the beginning of each chapter.

Each region of Japan can be quickly identified by its color coding, shown on the front flap of the book.

2 Regional Map
This shows the road and rail network and gives an overview of the whole region. All the best sights to visit are numbered. There are also useful tips on getting to, and around, the region by public transportation.

3 Detailed Information
All the important towns and other places to visit are described individually. They are listed in order, following the numbering on the Regional Map. Within each town or city, there is detailed information on important buildings and other sights.

Stars indicate the highlights and most important features of Japan's top sights.

Story boxes explore related topics.

For all top sights, a Visitors' Checklist provides the practical information you need to plan your visit.

4 Japan's Top Sights
These are given two or more full pages. Three-dimensional illustrations reveal the layouts and interiors of historic monuments. Interesting districts are given street-by-street maps from a bird's-eye view.

INTRODUCING JAPAN

DISCOVERING JAPAN

I solated for so long by its position on the volcanic Pacific Rim, the Japanese archipelago retains an enigmatic fascination for visitors; the following four pages present many of its highlights. A curious mixture of ancient and modern permeates Japan's big cities, where futuristic towers and raucous karaoke bars

Buddhist monk at Senso-ji

jostle with ancient temples and teahouses. Diverse geography and climate lend the five main islands distinctive qualities. These beautiful and extreme contrasts are found throughout Japan, from the frozen peaks in Hokkaido to the tropical coral coast of Okinawa .

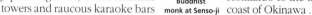

Busy shopping street in Ginza, Central Tokyo

TOKYO

- **Fashionable shopping at Ginza and Shibuya**
- **Buddhist rituals**
- **Sushi at world's largest fish market**
- **Exhilarating nightlife**

Swelling daily with the influx of hundreds of thousands of commuters, the population of Japan's capital city is made up of innumerable small communities. Upscale **Ginza** *(see pp66–7)* and fashionable **Shibuya** *(see pp96–7)* are meccas for shopping, while **Shinjuku** *(see pp90-93)* is the city's entertainment, karaoke, gastronomic, and business center.

The panoramic views from **Tokyo Tower** *(see p69)* enable visitors to get their bearings, with the Pacific-facing land-fill developments of Tokyo Bay visible to the southeast

and, on a clear day, the peak of Mount Fuji to the south-west. North of the center lies the beautiful **Imperial Palace** *(see p71)* and the hotchpotch of popular discount electronics stores and stalls of **Akihabara** *(see p73)*.

To get the best sense of Tokyo's juxtaposition of past and present, take a cruise along the Sumida River from **Hama Detached Palace Garden** *(see pp68–9)*. Visit the capital's oldest and most sacred temple, **Senso-ji** *(see pp86–7)*, to witness Buddhist monks going about their daily lives. The freshest sushi imaginable can be found at the largest fish market in the world, housed in a modern hangar at **Tsukiji** *(see p68)*, among a maze of tiny stalls.

Occupying a large swathe of Northern Tokyo, **Ueno Park** *(see pp78–9)* is a peaceful and serene oasis of pagodas, ponds, temples, and shrines. It is also home to the city's zoo and **Tokyo National Museum** *(see pp80-83)*, which houses a large and exquisite collection of Japanese antiquities.

CENTRAL HONSHU

- **Bustling Chinatown**
- **Sacred Mount Fuji and the Fuji Five lakes**
- **Takayama festival floats**

With an infrastructure that makes it easy to head in any direction, much of Central Honshu is used by Tokyo-ites as an antidote to daily life. The cosmopolitan city of **Yokohama** *(see pp132–3)*, only separated from Tokyo by the Tama-gawa River, has a distinctly different feel due to its long history as a port and large influx of foreign settlers. Packed with restaurants and ethnic stores, the city's bustling **Chinatown** *(see p133)* is built around a temple in classic Chinese style.

The picturesque seaside town of **Kamakura**, further down the coast, *(see pp134–7)* makes for a great day out; a medieval military capital scattered with Zen temples, it exudes a timeless quality.

Mount Fuji and the **Fuji Five Lakes** area *(see pp140-41)* attracts many pilgrims to its

Traditional Japanese houses in the foothills of Mount Fuji

Cherry blossoms at Kiyomizu-dera Temple, Kyoto

shrines, as well as more secular hikers and watersports enthusiasts, so gets very busy. Nearby, **Hakone** *(see pp138–9)* is equally popular for relaxation, with golf courses, hot springs, and an excellent collection of art museums.

The Zenko-ji Buddhist temple in **Nagano** *(see p151)* offers wonderful glimpses of old Japan. The marvelously preserved Edo-period town of **Takayama** *(see pp144–6)*, is full of character – lavish mechanical floats feature in its twice-yearly Matsuri festival *(see p42)*.

KYOTO CITY

- **Amazing religious sites**
- **Serene temple pavilions**
- **Geisha quarter in Gion**

It is hard to travel far in Japan's old imperial capital without stepping back in time. History, religion, and art and craft traditions combine to create pockets of awesome beauty and constant surprise, best explored leisurely on foot or by bicycle, bus, or subway.

The high drama of **Nijo Castle** *(see pp160–61)* offers amazingly ornate reception rooms with an ingenious 16th-century security system – the joinery of the floor-boards gives out a bird-like squeak when trodden on, to alert against intruders!

Kinkaku-ji *(see p174)*, an exquisite, gilded pavilion, and the more intimate **Ginkaku-ji** *(see p171)*, known as the Silver Pavilion, are symbols of a bygone imperial age. The skillfully crafted wooden veranda of **Kiyomizu-dera** *(see p168)* is on a grand scale. Views from here to the city and surrounding hillsides are resplendent with cherry blossom in April. The austere Japanese rock garden at **Ryoan-ji** *(see p174)* takes the Zen art of gardening to minimalist extreme. By colorful contrast, stunningly attired traditional geisha can be glimpsed on most evenings in the **Gion District** *(see p162)*. Farther east are the preserved stone streets of **Higashiyama** *(see pp166–7)*.

Geisha apprentice in Gion, Kyoto

WESTERN HONSHU

- **Monumental temple of Todai-ji in Nara**
- **Samurai castle at Himeji**
- **Sacred Miyajima Island**
- **Potters at work in Hagi**

This part of Japan's main island offers a wealth of cultural assets. The country's first recognized capital, **Nara** *(see pp190–95)*, is especially richly endowed, with six listed religious sites. These include the world's largest wooden building – immense Buddhist temple **Todai-ji** *(see pp192–3)*; the world-famous reconstructed Shinto site at **Kasuga Grand Shrine** *(see p191)*; and the imposing five-story Buddhist pagoda of **Kofuku-ji Temple** *(see p190)*.

Beyond the port of Kobe on the south coast lies the feudal samurai stronghold of **Himeji Castle** *(see pp206–9)*, its mighty donjon softened by undulating gables and white plaster walls. Modern warfare and the devastating effects of the atomic bomb which fell on **Hiroshima** *(see pp214–15)* in 1945 are memorialized in the twisted remains of the city's A-Bomb Dome.

Perched on stilts in the primeval forest of **Miyajima Island** *(see pp216–17)*, Itsukushima Shrine appears to "float" above the bay at high tide.

For less spiritual pursuits and to escape the crowds, go to the Ninja town of **Iga-Ueno** *(see p197)* to see the "art of stealth" in action, or to the pottery town of **Hagi** *(see pp218–19)*, famed for its delicate ceramic arts and teahouses. The residence of 19th-century Irish journalist, Lafcadio Hearn, in **Matsue** *(see pp212–13)* provides a refreshingly Western perspective on Japanese culture.

Bronze Buddha statue inside Todai-ji Temple, Nara

Awa-Odori dancers celebrating the Festival of the Dead in Tokushima

SHIKOKU

- **Ancient and modern bridge systems**
- **Epic 88-Temple Buddhist pilgrimage circuit**
- **Returning ancestral spirits at the Festival of the Dead**

Owing to its mountainous and rugged interior, Shikoku is still relatively unknown. This makes it a magical place for those who have the time and inclination to wander at will.

A marvel of modern-day engineering, the **Naruto suspension bridge** *(see p225)* spans the whirlpools of the Inland Sea to connect Shikoku to Honshu, and is predated by many more traditional bridge designs of wood and twisted vines, such as at **Shikoku Mura Village** *(see p224)*.

Those who travel the famed **88-Temple pilgrimage route** *(see pp222–3)* of sacred Buddhist sites which are dotted around the island may do so more devoutly, on foot. Walking the entire route takes six to eight weeks so is not for the faint-hearted; a bus

tour takes a week or less. Either way, the therapeutic waters of an *onsen* (spa) come as a blessed relief. The venerable hot spring at **Dogo** *(see p226)*, in use for over 1,000 years, is an especially fine example.

Local artisans can be seen at work in **Kochi** *(see p226)* producing hand-forged knives, and at **Uchiko** *(see p227)* making traditional Japanese paper and bamboo umbrellas.

At the height of summer, Shikoku celebrates with four days and nights of festivities as Japanese ancestors are honored at the annual Festival of the Dead (Bon Odori). The best place to enjoy the merriment is at **Tokushima** *(see p225)*, where you'll be invited to join the outdoor dancing.

KYUSHU

- **Traditional Japanese spa towns**
- **Cosmopolitan Nagasaki**
- **Fukuoka's lamp-lit *yatai* food stalls**

The large southern island of Kyushu is a land of extremes, with little rain in winter and frequent typhoons in late summer and fall. Active volcanoes such as at **Mount Aso** *(see pp244–5)* are also much in evidence here.

The "Nine Hells" of **Beppu** *(see pp234–5)* – rumbustious and rather kitsch bubbling hot pools containing mineral-infused waters of various hues – are balanced by the town's many curative *onsen* (public hot springs) for more serious bathing. Not far away

is the serenely beautiful thermal Lake Kinrin at **Yufuin** *(see p235)*, a quieter, more sophisticated spa town.

A magnificent harbor setting and record of foreign influence make **Nagasaki** *(see pp240–43)* a very special place, despite a history full of shadows in the relentless persecution of early Christians and the second horrific atomic bomb attack of 1945.

But little spoils Kyushu's determination to live life to the full. While *yatai* street stalls selling food and drink have been banished in other cities, they still enliven the streets of modern **Fukuoka** *(see pp236–7)*, one of the best places to eat in Japan.

Marine life in the aquarium at Ocean Expo Park, Okinawa

OKINAWA

- **Battle of Okinawa memorial sites**
- **Spectacular beaches and marine life**
- **Enchanting Yaeyama Islands**

Life on the chain of magical Okinawan islands is slow-paced, especially once you leave Okinawa main island, where many **World War II battle sites** *(see p255)* are preserved. The monument to American journalist Ernie Pyle, on **Ie Island** *(see pp256–7)*, is particularly affecting.

The coastal **Ocean Expo Park** *(see p256)* presents a microcosm of exotic marine life and native Okinawan culture. Ferries from lively **Naha City** *(see p254)* allow you to jump off at different ports to savor the unique character of each island and

Waterfront development in Fukuoka, Kyushu, seen at night

Library of Buddhist scriptures at Tosho-gu Shrine, Nikko, Northern Honshu

witness local artisans weaving and dyeing fine linens, or making lustrous black Okinawan laquerware.

The warm waters of these near tropical islands produce magnificent spots for swimming, diving, sailing, and fishing. **Kume Island** *(see p258)* is the quintessential coral island, with white-sand beaches, sugarcane plantations, and pristine waters; a causeway at low tide connects it to **O Island** *(see p258)* , with its intriguing mosaic of pentagonal stones.

Okinawa's most southerly islands, the **Yaeyamas** *(see p259)*, are also unspoiled and wonderfully varied: Ishigake Island has the world's largest reef of blue coral; Taketomi Island is a living museum, with ox-drawn carts trundling along streets of white coral; and Iriomote Island's dense rainforest, winding rivers and high waterfalls, are untouched.

NORTHERN HONSHU

- **The sacred Dewa Sanzan range**
- **Mausoleum-shrine of Tosho-gu**
- **Extravagant festivals**

Still predominantly rural and agricultural, Northern Honshu has much that is both monumental and awe-inspiring. Expansive rice-growing areas dominate Iwate Prefecture, where the remnants of historic **Hiraizumi** *(see p276)* and its Buddhist "paradise on earth" are located. The three sacred mountains of the **Dewa Sanzan** range *(see p274)* offer superb hiking and breathtaking scenery. In the far north, **Lake Towada** *(see p278)* is set in a deep caldera and encircled by prehistoric beech forest.

The rural landscape of Northern Honshu is awe-inspiring. Nowhere is this better demonstrated than in **Nikko** *(see pp264–71)*, where towering Japanese cedars dwarf visitors who climb to see the complex of **Tosho-gu Shrine** *(see pp266–7)*, its splendor a fitting memorial to the mighty Japanese warlord Ieyasu (1543–1616).

For festivals on a grand scale, it would be hard to beat the spectacular ostentation of the **Nebuta Matsuri** *(see p43)* in Aomori or the slightly more refined **Neputa Matsuri** *(see p46)* in Hirosaki, both in the far north of Honshu. Featuring enormous papier mâché figures and illuminated paper lanterns, these ancient festivals are possibly the most raucous in Japan, and are frequently televised. It was partly to see such sights that the venerated haiku poet Matsuo Basho made his five-month trek through Northern Honshu in 1869 *(see p279)*.

HOKKAIDO

- **Winter sports at Niseko**
- **Sapporo's snow sculptures**
- **Fire and ice in Hokkaido's National Parks**

There is a pioneering flavor to this most northerly, and mainly undeveloped, island of Japan. On the same latitude as Siberia, it lies under deep snow for much of the year. Prime, high-altitude slopes and abundant powdery snow in **Niseko** *(see p284)* draw skiers and snowboarders from as far away as Australia.

Sapporo's impressive **Yuki Matsuri** snow festival *(see p285)* also attracts international visitors to the capital's Odori Park, with its winter wonderland of elaborate snow sculptures and ice carvings. Hokkaido's second largest city and early treaty port, **Hakodate** *(see p284)*, features many Western-style buildings, including a Russian Orthodox church complete with onion domes.

Outside the two main cities, the island offers a huge variety of terrain and wildlife. To the east, rolling meadows reminiscent of Europe and New England are rich with dairy farms, sheep, and horses. In the southeast, the protected **Kushiro Wetlands National Park** *(see p290)* offers perfect conditions for roosting birds like the red-crowned crane.

Central and northeastern Hokkaido have both active and extinct volcanoes, including the sublimely beautiful volcanic calderas of **Akan National Park** *(see p287)*, home to large flocks of whooper swans, and the rugged, glacier-carved peaks of **Shiretoko National Park** *(see p291)*; *shiretoko* means "end of the earth" in the local language.

Fun in the snow at Sapporo's Yuki Matsuri festival, Hokkaido

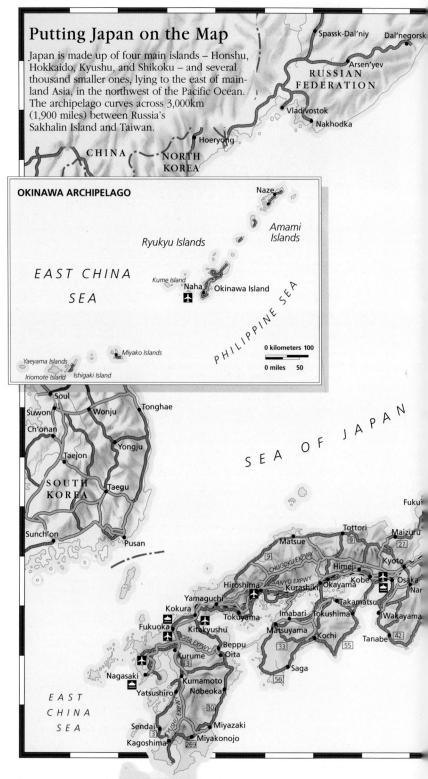

Putting Japan on the Map

Japan is made up of four main islands – Honshu,
Hokkaido, Kyushu, and Shikoku – and several
thousand smaller ones, lying to the east of mainland Asia, in the northwest of the Pacific Ocean.
The archipelago curves across 3,000km
(1,900 miles) between Russia's
Sakhalin Island and Taiwan.

Spassk-Dal'niy
Dal'negorsk
Arsen'yev

**RUSSIAN
FEDERATION**

Vladivostok
Nakhodka

Hoeryong

CHINA   **NORTH
KOREA**

OKINAWA ARCHIPELAGO

Naze

Amami
Islands

Ryukyu Islands

**EAST CHINA
SEA**

Kume Island

Naha   Okinawa Island

PHILIPPINE SEA

Yaeyama Islands

Miyako Islands

Iriomote Island   Ishigaki Island

0 kilometers 100

0 miles   50

Soul

Suwon   Wonju   Tonghae

Ch'onan

Yongju

Taejon

**SOUTH
KOREA**   Taegu

SEA OF JAPAN

Sunch'on   Pusan

Fuku

Tottori

Matsue   Maizuru

9   27

CHUGOKU EXPWY   Kyoto

Himeji   Kobe   Osaka

Hiroshima   Kurashiki   Okayama   Nar

SANYO EXPWY

Yamaguchi   Takamatsu   Wakayama

Kokura   Imabari   Tokushima

Fukuoka   Tokuyama   Matsuyama   42

Kitakyushu   Kochi   Tanabe

OITA EXPWY   Beppu   33   55

Kurume   Oita

3

Nagasaki   Kumamoto   Saga

Yatsushiro   Nobeoka   56

**EAST
CHINA
SEA**   10

KYUSHU EXPWY

Sendai   Miyazaki

Kagoshima   Miyakonojo

269

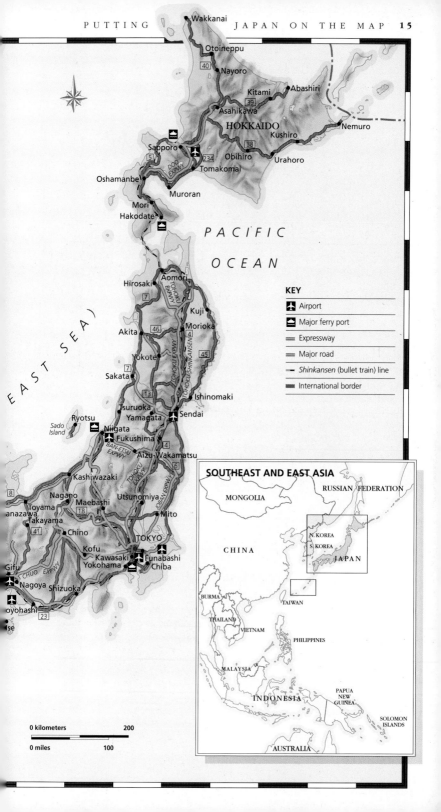

A PORTRAIT OF JAPAN

Few people in the modern world are not affected in some way by the ideas, culture, and economy of Japan, yet this country remains for many an enigma, an unsolved riddle. Westernized, but different from any Western country, part of Asia, but clearly unlike any other Asian society, Japan is a uniquely adaptable place where tradition and modernity are part of one continuum.

With over 3,000 islands lying along the Pacific Ring of Fire, the Japanese archipelago is prone to frequent earthquakes and has 60 active volcanoes. Much of the country is mountainous, while cities consume large areas of flat land and coastal plain. The Tokyo–Yokohama area is the largest urban concentration in the world, and 70 percent of Japan's 127 million people live along the Pacific coast stretch between Tokyo and Kyushu.

Fashionable teenager in Tokyo

The remaining slivers of cultivable land are farmed to yield maximum crops. Generous amounts of rainfall, melting snowcaps, and deep lakes enable rice to be cultivated in near-perfect conditions.

Each spring, the Japanese are reminded of their country's geographical diversity as the media enthusiastically tracks the progress of the *sakura zensen*, the "cherry-blossom front," as it advances from the subtropical islands of Okinawa to the northernmost island of Hokkaido.

The Japanese regard themselves as a racially integrated tribe, though different dialects and physical features distinguish the people of one region from another. Moreover, there are many minority peoples in Japan, from the indigenous Ainu to Okinawans, and an admixture of Koreans, Chinese, and, more recently, Southeast Asians and Westerners who have made Japan their home.

Buddhist monks gathered for a ceremony in the ancient capital of Nara

◁ Soft colors of an old temple garden given over to moss, one of many tranquil corners in Kyoto

Planting rice in flooded paddy fields, Fushimi

illustration of the Japanese belief in the transience of the material world. Nature, too, retains its key role in the national consciousness, in cities and rural areas alike, often ritualized in the annual cycle of *matsuri* (festivals).

A LAND OF CONTRADICTIONS

Appearances are often deceptive in Japan, obliging foreign visitors to keep adjusting their perceptions of the country. An exit at a large train station, for example, might deliver you to street level or just as likely funnel you through a modern, high-rise department store.

Businessmen bowing, Osaka

Here, among familiar shops, you might discover a whole floor of restaurants, some with rustic, *tatami*-mat floors and open charcoal braziers, others with displays of plastic food in the window. Closer inspection might reveal a fortune-teller's stall set up outside a software store, a moxibustion clinic next to a fast-food outlet, or a rooftop shrine to the fox-god Inari by the store's Astroturf mini-golf course.

Priest at Senso-ji, Tokyo

In this country of cherry blossoms and capsule hotels, of Buddhist monks and tattooed gangsters, the visitor finds that rock music, avant-garde theater, and abstract painting are as popular as flower arranging, Noh drama, or the tea ceremony. The Grand Shrine at Ise, torn down and rebuilt every 20 years in identical design and materials, exists not to replace tradition but to preserve and renew it – the ultimate

Wherever one looks, a stimulating fusion of East and West reveals itself: Zen priests on Hondas; the *salaryman* bowing deeply to a client on his cell phone; neon signs written in Japanese ideograms; ice-cream flavors that include red-bean paste and green tea. In one of the world's most energetic and industrialized nations, there are moments of carefully arranged beauty too, even tranquillity, with people who still find the time to contemplate the crack or glaze of a tea bowl, and burn incense for the dead.

SOCIETY, VALUES, AND BELIEFS

Although modern Japanese society developed from a feudal system, Japan today is astonishingly egalitarian. Hereditary titles were abolished along with the aristocracy after World War II, and members of the imperial family, the world's longest unbroken line of monarchs, now marry commoners. Class is defined by education and job status. The people employed by the top government ministries, large corporations, and other prestigious companies are Japan's true elite today.

Woman on a scooter passing a monk with his begging bowl, Kyoto

Burning incense and praying, Nagano

The Japanese have a practical, syncretic, and polytheistic approach to religion, often perplexing to outsiders. Religion is essentially an instrument for petitioning the gods to grant such requests as success in business or a school entrance exam, recovery from illness, or an uncomplicated birth. It is common in Japanese homes to find both Buddhist and Shinto altars. Confucianism is sometimes called Japan's unofficial, third religion after Buddhism and Shinto. More moral code and tool for social organization than religion proper, it has had a profound influence on Japanese thought since its introduction in the 6th century.

These beliefs, alongside family values and devotion to hard work, combined with a submission to the consensus of the group rather than the individual, have long been major binding elements in Japanese society. Most women regard child-rearing as their main objective. Men aim to climb the corporate ladder, seeing their work as integral to their identity, and many will socialize exclusively with their work colleagues.

Faultlines, however, are appearing in this monolithic structure, as younger voices question the benefits and value of self-sacrifice. A life outside the group, or in smaller, more intimate, groups, has increasing appeal. Young couples now prefer to live apart from their parents, and men are gradually disengaging themselves from a practice of after-hours socializing, in order to spend more time with their family. The steady increase in the divorce rate and the larger number of women who remain unmarried are other indications of changes taking place. The latter is often a decision on the part of Japanese women who cannot find partners with the right credentials. Thus, what might appear to be a contemporary Western-driven tendency, or an expression of feminist awareness, is a reflection, to some degree, of orthodoxy.

Lion mask to ward off evil spirits, Takayama

Japan's declining birthrate, now fewer than 1.5 births per family, is not enough to sustain current population levels, and the specter of an aging, more state-dependent population, looms. This is not just a result of women choosing not to marry. Cramped living conditions and the need for parents to provide offspring with a first-rate, costly education are among other factors.

Visitors dwarfed by the Great Buddha statue at Kamakura

The landmark Studio Alta screen and neon-lit streets of East Shinjuku, Tokyo

POLITICS AND THE ECONOMY

Through much of Japan's history, parallel with the institutions and prevailing ideologies of the day, there has been a distinction between power and office. The emperor had little power from the 12th century onward,

Car on display in Toyota showroom

being essentially a puppet under first the regents, then the shoguns, and, later, the military government before and during World War II. This distinction persists today in the relationship between bureaucrats, who are given enormous power to oversee the economy, and politicians, who merely co-opt, accommodate, or head off the opposition groups.

The existence of widespread political corruption was revealed in 1983 with the exposure of a scandal in which a former Prime Minister, Kakuei Tanaka, was implicated. Pressure then mounted on Japan's conservative regime. Contentious economic stimulus packages, an unpopular consumption tax, and more scandals connected to corruption, fund raising, and graft, further tarnished the party's image for consistency and reliability. The Liberal Democratic Party (LDP)

eventually lost its 38-year long grip on power in 1993, ending almost four decades of political hegemony. The government was forced into potentially unstable coalition arrangements.

In the 1980s the yen soared against the dollar, and Japanese companies made the headlines by buying up American film studios and over-priced works of art. Japanese tourists, long used to sightseeing in their own country, began to travel abroad in unprecedented numbers. Land prices in Japan, foreigners were confidently told, would continue to rise because "Japan was different from other countries." However, friction over a massive trade surplus with America, growing criticism of Japan's "checkbook diplomacy," and the recession that struck in 1992, bursting its "bubble" economy, have been sobering. Despite the hardships suffered by the unemployed and those

Door attendants at Gucci emporium, Tokyo

forced into early retirement, and the increase in homeless people evident in big cities like Tokyo and Osaka, the 90s recession brought back a degree of sanity that was missing during the decades of uninterrupted growth. It also prompted the Japanese government to make moves toward long overdue economic reform and a greater opening of its markets to international trade.

Baseball, now the most popular sport in Japan

and early novels of the Heian period, and in the screen painting and *ukiyo-e* woodblock prints of the Edo era.

Visits by geisha and their patrons to discreet hot springs in the mountains are the material for some atmospheric novels by writers such as the Nobel laureate Kawabata Yasunari (1899–1972).

Nature and aesthetics fuse in the national appreciation for cherry blossoms, a passion that both charms and perplexes the visitor. *Hanami* (cherry blossom) parties are held throughout the country. Because competition for the best viewing sites can be fierce, company bosses often send their younger scions ahead to claim a good patch under the trees. The cherry, as the Japanese see it, is a felicitous symbol but also a poignant reminder of the evanescent beauty of this floating world. Few nations have extracted so much refined pleasure and sadness from the contemplation of a flower.

The Japanese hunger for innovation and advancement has not devoured their spiritual heritage or the natural grace extended toward visitors. Most travelers return home with the impression, in fact, of an unfailingly generous and hospitable people, for whom politeness and consideration toward a guest are second nature.

LEISURE AND THE ART OF LIVING

The Japanese take their sports and leisure activities almost as seriously as their work. Traditional sports, in particular, often embody some underlying cultural, spiritual, or aesthetic principle, so that there is not only the method but "the way." This applies especially to ancient disciplines like kyudo (archery), kendo, karate, and aikido. Sumo, the national sport of Japan, originated as an

Sumo wrestler preparing for a bout

oracular ritual linked to prayers for a bountiful harvest. Having a similar appeal to sports audiences as Kabuki dramas do to theater-goers, sumo ranks many non-Japanese among its fans. Japan gained many soccer fans after the creation of the J-League in 1993 and its selection, along with Korea, as cohost for the 2002 World Cup. Professional baseball attracts an even larger and more devoted following.

Traditional leisure activities, such as the pleasures of summer fireworks, and seasonal maple, moon, and snow viewing, are much celebrated in literature and art, in the poetry, diaries,

Kabuki performance, a traditional entertainment

The Landscape of Japan

Japan lies on the intersection of four plates and is the world's most geologically active zone. The islands themselves were pushed up from the ocean floor by earth movements. Evidence of this activity can be seen in the sharply defined mountain ranges rising from the plains, in smoking volcanoes, and in hot mineral waters that well up from the ground. The Japanese take earthquakes, volcanoes, tsunamis, and typhoons in their stride, building and rebuilding their towns wherever they can find flat land. Modern cityscapes *(see pp24–5)* contrast greatly with the seasonal beauty of the relatively undeveloped mountainous interior, and the national parks, the largest of which are in Hokkaido.

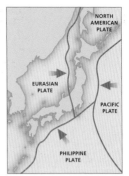

Plate movements, *as shown, force the sea-bed to be pushed underneath the lighter rocks of the Japanese archipelago. This causes nearly a thousand obvious earthquakes each year in Japan.*

The thickly forested hillsides are relatively undeveloped, though some remote peaks are used as the isolated setting for hill shrines and temples.

Maple, birch, cypress, and cedar trees *are among the most common woodland mixes on the hillsides, creating stunning fiery colors in the fall.*

TYPICAL VIEW OF THE LAND

This idealized representation shows the typical landscape features of central Japan. The plains next to the sea are densely populated, while farther inland thickly forested hillsides rise up steeply to snow-covered mountain peaks and the craters of both dormant and active volcanoes.

Freshwater lakes such as Lake Biwa in Western Honshu *(see p212)* are utilized for industry, irrigation, and recreation.

Faultlines run beneath the sea and land, showing up in some places as a rift in the landscape.

Bamboo groves *are found in the tropical and temperate zones of Japan. The fast-growing plant is both a foodstuff and building material.*

Paddy fields *may not be associated with Japan as much as they are with other parts of Asia; nonetheless rice-growing occupies a major part of the cultivable landscape. In suburban areas, small rice plots often take the place of gardens.*

Japan's 60 or so active volcanoes *are scattered along a line through the main islands. Many of these, such as Sakurajima (see p249), smoke and steam constantly. Explosive eruptions of lava and pyroclastic rock-flows take place every few years.*

Sulfur vents *are found in volcanic regions, staining the rocks yellow in such places as Hokkaido's Akan National Park (see p287) and releasing noxious fumes at Mount Aso (see pp244–5) and other craters.*

Dormant crater

Fruit and vegetable farming takes up what slivers of cultivable land are left after rice farming, but Japan is forced to import about half its food.

The high, snow-covered mountain areas, such as the Japan Alps near Matsumoto *(see p151)* and parts of Northern Honshu and Hokkaido, have been developed as skiing resorts.

Rising from the plain is the near-perfect cone of a dormant volcano, the supreme example of which is Mount Fuji *(see pp140–41).*

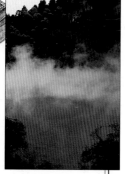

Dissolved particles of iron oxide *are responsible for the bright color of this natural steaming lake, one of the so-called "Boiling Hells" of Beppu (see pp234–5).*

Heavily built-up and industrialized plains

Most of the major Japanese cities, *such as Tokyo, Osaka, and Kobe, are working ports. Land suitable for building is at such a premium that artificial peninsulas and islands have been constructed.*

NATURAL HOT SPRINGS

Geothermal activity at thousands of sites in Japan has created natural hot springs either at ground level or just below the surface. The mineral content of the waters varies; some are declared to have therapeutic benefits for humans, especially for diseases of the nervous system and intestines. The Japanese have bathed in the springs for centuries and have also used them for purification rituals. Many have been developed as spas, or *onsen (see pp354–5)*; the Dogo Onsen in Matsuyama is over a thousand years old *(see p226)*. The water of some springs must be cooled before it is suitable for bathing.

Monkeys bathing in the geothermal waters of Jigokudani *(see p151)*

Modern Japan

Perhaps nowhere else does the modern world of high technology and constant change show itself more poignantly than in Japan. For some people, modern Japan is an anathema, a kitsch distillation of the Western world that destroys traditional culture. Others embrace the nation's fascination with invention and image, and praise it for often leading the West. Few urban buildings are more than 25 years old, and consumer trends may change in a matter of weeks in this economic powerhouse. In some ways, though, the liking for change is a manifestation of ancient religious concepts *(see pp26–9)* that emphasize the importance of impermanence and renewal.

The Japanese automobile industry *manufactures about ten million vehicles each year. In a land where space is at a premium, the small car is king.*

Tange Kenzo's earthquake-proof Metropolitan Offices *(see p92)* are praised by some and villified by others.

A forest of neon *characterizes the shopping and entertainment districts of cities that strive to be modern, such as Tokyo, Osaka, and here in Fukuoka. Vast television screens and public announcements over loudspeakers add to the audio-visual tumult.*

The Sony Corporation *has grown from 20 employees in 1946 to an electronics empire with assets of $52 billion. The Sony Showroom (see p66) displays the latest inventions before they reach the shops.*

The Yamanote train line connects Tokyo's main districts in a loop.

Department stores are accessed directly from the world's busiest train station.

HIGH-TECH TOYS AND GAMES

Japan has a proud tradition of video games and toys, beginning in the late 1970s with arcade classics like *Space Invaders* and *Pac-Man*. Today the industry continues to flourish, and companies like Nintendo, Sega, and Sony have developed generations of powerful home entertainment systems with sophisticated graphics and audio. Recent phenomena include robotic pets (such *Tamagotchi*) and motion sensitive devices, with more exciting innovations never far behind.

Tamagotchis for sale in Harajuku

Robot (robotto) *technology was exported to Japan from the US in 1967. Today, about half of the world's robots are found in Japan, used widely in industry. Some are delightfully zoomorphic.*

MODERN ARCHITECTURE

An eclectic mix of contemporary building styles can be seen in Japan. Tange Kenzo (1913–), who built the Olympic Stadiums in 1964 *(see pp94–5)*, still casts a shadow over younger designers. Foreign practitioners, too, have been influential.

Osaka's Umeda Sky Building *(completed 1993) was inspired by the 1960s' dream of a "city in the air." Hara Hiroshi's twin towers are linked by the Floating Garden Observatory, which hovers above the city* (see p202).

An amusing, almost cartoon-like building, *the Super Dry Hall was built in 1989 by French designer Philippe Starck for the Asahi beer company, near the Sumida River in the Asakusa district of Tokyo. International architects have designed some of their most ambitious projects in Tokyo.*

A modern house, *designed by Ando Tadao (1941–), allows light to seep through in unusual ways, such as through glass slots between ceiling and walls. One of the foremost contemporary Japanese architects, Ando's works include the Himeji City Museum of Literature (see p209).*

The oxygen bar, *in which customers inhale pure or scented oxygen for health and relaxation instead of imbibing alcohol, originated in Japan and is becoming popular in other countries.*

Mount Fuji   The Greater Tokyo conurbation

MODERN CITYSCAPES

Shinjuku district in Tokyo, shown here *(see also pp90–93)*, epitomizes the modern Japanese urban labyrinth. Buildings are constructed wherever land becomes available, using such materials as aluminum, steel, and concrete. Increasingly, flexible-frame technologies are used to withstand

Manga *("comic pictures") are immensely popular in Japan, especially the genre of narrative comics called gekiga, which emerged in the 1960s. The content is diverse – politics, baseball, romance, martial arts, and pornography are all popular.*

The Tokyo International Forum (see p71) *is a shiplike structure built by the South American architect Rafael Viñoly in 1996. Its glass-walled atrium, supported by elegant columns and bars, is widely considered to be a masterpiece of engineering.*

Shinto: the Native Religion

Shinto is Japan's oldest religion, the "way of the gods." Its core concept is that deities, *kami*, preside over all things in nature, be they living, dead, or inanimate. There are lesser and greater *kami*, worshiped at thousands of shrines *(jinja)* erected on hills and along waysides. From ancient times the emperor's rule was sanctioned by the authority of the greatest gods, said to be his ancestors. Shinto was the state religion from the 1870s to 1940s. Today, few Japanese are purely Shintoists, but most will observe Shinto rituals alongside Buddhist practices. Many Japanese habits, such as an emphasis on purification and an austere aesthetic, are derived at least in part from Shinto.

*The **torii** is the most recogniz-able icon of Shinto. These gateways mark the entrance to the sacred precincts of a shrine. Many are made of vermilion-painted wood; some are con-structed in stone, even concrete. All have two rails at the top.*

Miscanthus grass thatch

*The **shimenawa** is a rope made of twisted rice straw. It is hung over entrances within shrine precincts to separate sacred and secular places. It is also set above doors of houses to ward off evil and sickness. Izumo Taisha (see p213) has many examples of* shimenawa, *some of them immense.*

The treasuries, to the west and east of the main structure, house ceremonial regalia, silks, and paper.

Inari shrines, *identifiable by the bibbed stone foxes standing guard within them, are dedica-ted to the* kami *of cereal crops. The head Inari shrine is at Fushimi (see p179), just south of Kyoto, and 30,000 others are scattered throughout the country.*

ISE INNER GRAND SHRINE

The home of the spirits of all past emperors, the Grand Shrine at Ise *(see p198)* is the most venerated Shinto site. The inner shrine shown here is dedicated to Amaterasu, the sun goddess, and is said to house her mirror, an imperial sacred treasure. It is not open to the public. The complex is completely rebuilt every 20 years, most recently in 1993, following a tradition begun in AD 690.

The *Shinto priesthood* (kannushi) *tended to be transmitted through fam-ilies, and important families (shake) are still connected with some shrines. The* kannushi, *who usually wear white and orange robes, perform purifica-tion ceremonies and other rituals.*

In the main sanctuary (honden) *of a shrine is an object* (shintai) *believed to be the abode of the* kami *to whom the shrine is dedicated. Usually only the head priests enter the* honden; *the hall for worship* (haiden) *is often separate.*

Worshipers *stand in front of the* haiden *hall, pull on a bell rope, toss money into a box, clap three times to summon the resident* kami, *then stand in silent prayer for a few moments.*

Metallic caps cover the exposed grain of the timber.

Forked finials, chigi, are used in traditional Japanese joinery to secure timber frames.

Straight roofline

Posts are set directly into the ground.

Fertility *is a major concern of Shinto. Some shrines have statues depicting phalluses, lovemaking, childbirth, or milk-engorged breasts. Couples will ask the spirits for conception and good health for mother and child.*

Ise Shrine has its own style of architecture, called *yuitsu shimmei-zukuri,* which has been imitated at just a handful of other shrines.

About 13,000 cypresses are used to rebuild the shrine every 20 years on alternating, adjacent sites.

CHARMS AND VOTIVE TABLETS

Good-luck charms, called *omamori,* are sold at shrines across Japan. Common themes relate to fertility, luck in examinations, general health, or safety while driving. The charm itself might be written on a piece of paper or thin wooden board and tucked into a cloth bag, which can be worn next to the body or placed somewhere relevant. (Do not open the bag to read the charm or it will not work.) Prayers or wishes can also be written on *ema* boards and hung at the shrine.

Ema **boards wishing for success in examinations**

Charms for conception, safe childbirth, and safety while driving

Buddhism in Japan

Buddhism, founded in India, arrived in Japan via China and Korea in the 6th century AD. Different sects *(see p275)* evolved and were adopted over the centuries. The new religion sometimes had an uneasy relationship with Shinto, despite incorporating parts of the native belief system. Buddhism lost official support in 1868 but has flowered again since World War II. The complex cosmological beliefs and morality of Buddhism permeate modern Japanese life, especially in the emphasis on mental control found in Zen Buddhism.

Buddhist monk

Prince Shotoku *(573–621) promoted Buddhism in its early days in Japan* (see p196).

Senso-ji temple (see pp86–7) *is the site of some of Tokyo's main festivals* (see pp42–7). *Buddhist festivals honor events in the Buddha's life and the return of dead spirits to Earth* (bon). *They often incorporate Shinto elements.*

Memorial stones *are erected in cemeteries attached to temples. Called* gorin-to, *many are made up of five different-shaped stones. Plain, box-shaped ones are called* sotoba.

Worshipers remove their shoes and kneel before the altar in silent contemplation and prayer.

Pagodas, *found in some temple complexes, house relics of the Buddha, such as fragments of bone. The relic is usually placed at the base of the central pillar, hidden from view. Three- or five-story (see p196) pagodas are common, but access to the upper stories is rarely permitted.*

JIZO STATUES

Red-bibbed statues of Jizo are found at thousands of temples and along waysides in Japan. Jizo is the guardian *bosatsu* of those who suffer, especially sickly children and pregnant women. Children who have died young, including babies who have been miscarried or aborted, are helped into the next world by Jizo. He is often shown holding a staff in one hand and a jewel talisman in the other. The red bibs are placed on the statues by bereaved mothers and other sufferers.

Jizo, Toji Temple, Kyoto

Jizo and babies, Uwajima, Shikoku

Pilgrimages to Buddhist sites *are very popular. Pilgrims, typically dressed in white, walk from site to site, sometimes making epic journeys of many weeks' duration, such as for Shikoku's 88-Temple Pilgrimage* (see pp228–9).

The semi-enclosed area at the front of the platform has a burner for incense offerings. Beyond is a type of tabernacle containing a sacred object *(bonzon)*, hidden from view.

The Asuka Plain *of Western Honshu was the site of the earliest Buddhist worship in Japan* (see p197). *This bronze image of the Buddha dates from 609.*

Tatami mats line the floor of the *hondo*. The Zen temple *hondo* is characterized by its relative starkness and lack of ornamentation.

THE BUDDHIST TEMPLE IN JAPAN

Buddhist sites, identifiable by the suffixes *-ji* and *-dera*, are usually translated as "temples" (whereas Shinto sites are "shrines"). The temple complex includes a main hall *(hondo)*, shown here, maybe a pagoda, cemetery, buildings used by monks, and often a small Shinto shrine too. The layout of a typical Zen Buddhist temple is shown on page 137.

Meditation *is a cornerstone of Buddhism: clearing the mind of cluttered thoughts is the road to Enlightenment. In* zazen *sitting meditation, photographed here in about 1950, a nun uses a* keisaku *stick to slap meditators who seem to be losing their alertness.*

GLOSSARY

Amida The Buddha of Infinite Light, as venerated by the Pure Land sect.
Amida
Bosatsu Japanese word for *bodhisattva*, a figure that has attained Enlightenment and helps others.
Buddha Usually means the historical Buddha, who was born in India in 563 BC.
Butsudan Altar in house.
Enlightenment An expansion of mind as achieved by *bosatsu*.
Hondo Main hall of temple.
Honzon Principal object of worship in main hall.
Jizo A popular *bosatsu*.
Juzu Buddhist rosary.
Kaimyo Buddhist name awarded posthumously.
Kannon The goddess of mercy. Sometimes has 1,000 arms (Senju Kannon).
Karesansui A rock and sand garden inspired by Zen Buddhism and Chinese landscape painting.
Keisaku Stick used to slap shoulders during meditation.
Mahayana Major branch of Buddhism, emphasizing the importance of
Kannon
bosatsu. Practiced in Tibet, China, Korea, and Japan.
Myoo Deified king of light.
Nio Temple gate guardians (Brahma and Indra in India).
Nirvana Release from the cycle of rebirth and suffering.
Nyorai Epithet for the Buddha.
Pure Land Western Paradise of the Amida Buddha.
Sanmon Free-standing gateway to a temple complex.
Satori Sudden Enlightenment in Zen Buddhism.
Shingon Very popular Buddhist sect (see p275).
Takuhatsu The monks' practice of begging.
Tembu Type of heavenly being.
Tendai Major Buddhist sect (see p275).
Zazen Sitting meditation, popular in Zen.
Zen Major school of Buddhism (see p275).
Tembu

Japanese Gardens

Originating around early Shinto shrines, Japanese gardens have been influenced by the Shinto love of nature and the Buddhist ideal of paradise. Although classic Japanese gardens can be roughly divided into four types – paradise gardens, dry-landscape gardens, stroll gardens, and tea gardens – they share many components and principles, and have continued evolving through the centuries. The common aim was to create a microcosm: stones, water, bridges, and other elements were combined to form an idealized and symbolic miniature landscape. Paradise and dry-landscape gardens were designed to be viewed from a single point or side, while stroll gardens and tea gardens were made to be walked through.

Modern gardens *in Japan have altered as architectural styles have changed, but many still use traditional components, such as water, stones, and gravel, in a less sinuous, more geometric way than in the past.*

PARADISE GARDEN

Motsu-ji garden in Hiraizumi *(see p276)* is a beautifully preserved example of a paradise garden, designed to evoke the Pure Land, or Buddhist paradise. Use is made of "borrowed landscape" – trees or mountains outside the garden that appear to be part of it. Stones are arranged to create islands and rocky shores.

DRY-LANDSCAPE GARDEN

Attached to Zen Buddhist temples, these gardens of carefully chosen stones grouped amid an expanse of raked gravel provide an object for meditation. A classic dry-landscape garden is at Ryoan-ji temple, Kyoto *(see p174)*, where the plain, earthen walls enhance the abstract arrangement of the stones.

This waterfall, *at Iso Tei-en garden, Kagoshima, exemplifies the art of creating artificial features that look entirely natural.*

This sand mound, *like a flattened Mount Fuji, is at Ginkaku-ji temple in Kyoto. The raked sand around it resembles a silver sea by moonlight.*

The Phoenix Hall *at Byodo-in near Kyoto houses an Amida Buddha (see p29). The building is reflected in the pond in front, which represents the Western Ocean.*

The "Treasure Ship" stone *at Daisen-in, Kyoto (see p173), is one of Japan's most famous stones. Individual stones are not intended as symbols, but this is said to suggest a junk traveling through waves.*

SEASONS IN A JAPANESE GARDEN

The Japanese awareness of the seasons is an integral part of their garden design. A careful balance of shrubs and trees is one of the essential ingredients for a harmonious garden. Evergreen trees and bamboos are often planted for year-round greenery; deciduous trees are chosen for their shape when bare as well as when clothed with foliage to ensure year-round interest. In tea gardens, where every detail is symbolic, fallen blossoms or leaves may be arranged by the path to suggest the season. Some gardens are planned for a spectacular effect in one season; many are best visited in spring or fall.

Contrasting maple leaves in fall at Tenryu-ji, Kyoto

Winter in a Kyoto temple garden

STROLL GARDEN

The views in a stroll garden change with virtually every step, with vistas concealed and revealed. These gardens were popular in the Edo period when they were made by *daimyo* (feudal lords). Kenroku-en in Kanazawa *(see p148)* included four ponds and uses "borrowed landscape" skillfully.

TEA GARDEN

Dating from the Momoyama period (1568–1600), a tea garden consists of a short path, with trimmed plants on either side, leading to a teahouse. The path links the real world to the world of the tea ceremony *(see p169)*. In keeping with the simple ceremony, this Kyoto garden has rustic posts and a bamboo fence.

Murin-an garden *in Kyoto is a small stroll garden, designed to look highly naturalistic. A meandering stream, pond, and overhanging trees create a quiet and secluded enviroment through which to walk.*

Stone basins *were at first purely functional, for washing hands and mouth, but then came to symbolize purification before the ceremony.*

Pruning *is prized as an art, bringing out the inherent qualities of a tree. A beautifully pruned tree often forms a focal point in a stroll garden.*

Slightly raised *and spaced apart, the stones in the path are sprinkled with water before the ceremony to welcome guests; the Japanese thus call the tea garden* rojo *(dewy path).*

Traditional Japanese Houses

Known as *minka* or "commoners' houses," traditional dwellings vary widely in their layout and appearance from region to region, often in response to local weather conditions. Made largely of wood and paper, they were designed to be adaptable in their use of the interior space. Although *minka* in their original form are rarely occupied today, partly due to a move toward Western domestic architecture, partly through destruction (often by fire), they can still be seen around Japan and are sometimes open as museums. The way of organizing the living space is, however, still widely used, even in modern, Western-style houses.

Town houses *such as these in the Gion area of Kyoto are known as* machiya *and are the urban equivalent of* minka. *The layout differs as the width of the frontage is limited.*

The *irori (hearth) forms the heart of the house, often kept burning as the main source of heat. It is also sometimes used for cooking. In minka the hearth is usually sunk into a wooden floor; a* tatami *surrounding indicates a wealthy household.*

The *doma (area with a packed-earth floor) lies just behind the entrance. Here people take off their shoes before stepping up to the wooden surface.

The *engawa is a space outside, like a veranda, covered with a sloping roof. It may be enclosed by heavy wooden doors, or opened to allow air to circulate. This entrance is mainly used by visitors, who will stand on the stone step to remove their shoes.*

The main entrance to the *minka* is through sliding doors.

TYPES OF ROOF

Traditionally a *minka* roof is thatched, often with miscanthus reed, though the material varies according to what is available locally. Tiled roofs are also widespread as they are simpler to construct and fire-resistant; the ends of tiles may be decorated with an image, such as a devil, to protect the house. Shingles are also used, sometimes weighted down by stones. Roof shapes vary widely in design and complexity.

An intricate, gabled roof with decorated tile ends

A semi-gabled thatched roof of a *kabuto-zukuri* house

A thatcher at work replacing worn thatch

A Buddhist family altar (butsudan) *is found in many homes, usually along with a much simpler Shinto altar.*

Bedding of futon mattresses and quilts is rolled and stored in a cupboard in the day and unrolled on the floor at night.

Wooden ceilings above the more formal rooms double up as storage space.

Ramma – open and sometimes carved wooden lintels above the **fusuma** – separate the rooms.

The **tokonoma** *is a wooden-floored alcove in a formal room, used for displaying a scroll and ceramics. The scroll is often changed to reflect the season.*

Fusuma sliding doors of wood and heavy paper are opened or closed to alter the size of a room.

Vertical beams are sunk into foundation stones, which help to minimize dampness inside the house.

Tatami mats *cover the floor of the formal room or rooms. These straw-and-rush mats are a standard size within each region, and room size is often measured in* tatami *mats. Typically formal rooms are six to eight mats in size, and are used to receive guests.*

Shoji sliding doors open onto the **engawa**. A door consists of a wooden frame and Japanese paper, which allows light to filter through.

A ONE-STORY MINKA

This illustration shows features of the layout of a *minka*. The toilet and washing facilities were usually located outside the main house. The main variations on this basic design include the *gassho-zukuri* house *(see p147)*, the L-shaped *magariya*, used to house horses as well as people (found mainly in Iwate prefecture, Northern Honshu), and the *kabuto-zukuri* house, designed to allow in more light and air (found in Yamagata prefecture, Northern Honshu).

A kotatsu *is a heater combined with a low table. The heater (traditionally charcoal, now electric) may be situated under the frame, or inside a pit sunk into the floor. A futon is draped under the tabletop for extra warmth in winter. Individuals kneel on cushions or rest their feet in the pit.*

Sumo and the Martial Arts

Now more of a professional sport than a martial art, sumo can trace its origins back 2,000 years to Shinto harvest rites, and strong links with Shinto remain in many sumo rituals. There are six sumo tournaments in Japan every year *(see p358)*, broadcast live on TV and followed enthusiastically. Training is a way of life *(see p102)* for sumo wrestlers, and if a tournament is not on, it may be possible to watch practice sessions *(see*

A karate kick

p111). Martial arts are known as *budo*, or the "martial way." They aim to cultivate balance, control, speed, and accuracy in a spiritual, mental, and physical sense. Kendo and kyudo, the least changed since the days of the samurai, are seen as the purest of the martial arts.

Sumo wrestlers *were a highly popular subject for Edo-period woodblock prints.*

Throwing salt *to purify the ring and the fight to come is part of a complex pre-match ritual that the wrestlers undertake. They also stamp, clap, and raise their hands before crouching down in front of their opponent ready to start.*

The gyoji (referee) wears traditional court costume and uses a fan to signal when to begin.

SUMO WRESTLING

Despite their size – there are no weight restrictions – sumo wrestlers *(rikishi)* move quickly and with agility, and so matches are often short (10 seconds or so). The loser is the first to touch the ground with any part of his body, except the soles of his feet, or to step out of, or be pushed from, the ring. The referee *(gyoji)* declares the winner.

Grand champions (yokozuna) *perform pre-match rituals wearing a richly decorated ceremonial apron and a white hemp-rope belt hung with folded paper (as seen at Shinto shrines). This champion is performing shiko, lifting his leg and stamping his foot to banish evil spirits and intimidate his opponents.*

A referee pours an offering *of sake onto the ring as part of the dedication ceremony before a tournament. The ring is a platform of clay edged by a square of sunken rice-straw bales, with an inner ring (where the match is fought) also marked by sunken bales.*

Banners *announce a sumo tournament – here at the National Sumo Stadium in Tokyo (see p102). Each tournament lasts 15 days. The lower-ranking wrestlers fight early in the day, while higher-ranking ones appear from mid-afternoon onward.*

The wrestlers' hair is oiled and fastened into a topknot *(mage)*.

Only 48 winning techniques are commonly used, but many more have been identified.

A loincloth *(mawashi)* is worn for bouts, along with a thin belt *(sagari)* hung with threads similar to those seen at Shinto shrines.

The ring stands *under a suspended roof resembling that of a Shinto shrine. A different-colored tassel hangs from each corner of the roof, representing the four seasons.*

MARTIAL ARTS

Originally developed as arts of war by the samurai, the martial arts have evolved into forms of austere discipline *(shugyo)* aimed at spiritual improvement; some are also competitive sports. The modern forms of kendo and kyudo trace their origins to methods practiced in Japanese antiquity.

Kendo *means the "way of the sword." Origi-nating from samurai fencing, kendo now uses bamboo swords. Contestants wear extensive padding and protection. In a match, points are gained for hitting the head, torso, forearm, or throat.*

Kyudo, *or the "way of the bow," has close associations with Zen Buddhism. Although accuracy in hitting a target is important, the emphasis is also on concentration of mind and body.*

Judo *developed from jujitsu. A system of self-defense, it is well established as a sport in which throwing and grappling techniques are used to subdue an opponent.*

Karate *("empty hand") reached Japan in 1922 from Okinawa. A form of self-defense as well as spiritual and physical training, it has become a sport, consisting of explosive yet controlled kicks, punches, or strikes, and blocking moves.*

Aikido – *the "way of harmonious spirit" – uses an opponent's strength and speed against them. Training unites spiritual awareness and physical flexibility.*

Japanese Traditional Theater

Four major types of traditional theater are still performed regularly in Japan: Noh, Kyogen, Kabuki,
and Bunraku *(see p108 and p184)*. Originating in Shinto
rites, Noh was first performed by Kan'ami Kiyotsugu
(1333–84) and developed by his son Zeami. Adopted
by the *daimyo* (feudal lords), Noh became more
ritualistic and ceremonial. Gradually its farcical elements
were confined to a separate form, Kyogen. By the 17th
century, people wanted a more comprehensible and
entertaining form of drama, and Kabuki evolved from
Noh, starting in Kyoto. A form of puppet theater, Bunraku, like Kabuki, was aimed at the general populace.

A Noh play *is being performed
for the imperial household in
this 1863 woodblock print by
Taiso Yoshitoshi.*

The backdrop is a single pine tree,
epitomizing the simplicity of Noh staging.

Noh actors may be men
or women but the
majority are men.

NOH

An austere, restrained, and powerful theatrical
form, Noh is performed on a bare, three-sided
cypress-wood stage roofed like a shrine, with an
entrance ramp to one side. One or two masked
characters appear at a time. Their slow, choreographed actions *(kata)* are performed to music.

Musicians playing
traditional drums and
flutes sit at the back of
the stage and
accompany the actors.

A chorus of six to eight
people sit to one side and
comment on the action.

Kyogen *evolved from comic interludes
devised as relief from the demanding
nature of Noh. A down-to-earth, colloquial form, its characters highlight
human foibles and frailties. Masks are
rarely used, and costumes are plain.
The actors wear
distinctive yellow
tabi socks.*

Noh masks *are worn by the leading
characters; the greatest masks are
classified as National Treasures. The
mask on the right represents a samurai,
and on the far right, a demon.*

Noh costumes *are
usually richly deco-
rated and heavy. Many
layers are worn to make
the actors seem larger
and more imposing.*

Kabuki actors were popular subjects for Edo-era woodblock prints. The tradition can still be seen in this modern poster advertising a Kabuki play.

BUNRAKU

Bunraku puppets are about 1.2 m (4 ft) tall with carved wooden heads, movable hands, and elaborate costumes. The main puppeteer wears traditional formal dress; his two assistants, one on each side, are clothed in black. *Shamisen* music accompanies the action, and a narrator both tells the story and speaks all the parts. Many Kabuki plays were originally written for puppets; Bunraku has in turn borrowed a number of Kabuki dramas.

Bunraku puppet with his manipulator

Stage right is where less important characters are usually located.

Costumes and wigs are highly elaborate, indicating the status and personality of each character.

The pine trees on Kabuki stage backdrops are a reference to its evolution from Noh.

KABUKI

Kabuki is flamboyant and colorful with a large stage and cast. The major actors are stars, often from famous acting dynasties. Elaborate make-up replaced Noh masks, and a curtain allowed set changes. The musicians and chorus sit behind screens on either side or on stage.

Stage sets often incorporate special effects including trapdoors, revolving sections, and overhead cables for flying.

Stage left is usually occupied by characters of high rank or importance.

The *hanamichi* (flower path) *is a raised walkway running from stage right through the audience and is used for dramatic entrances and exits.*

Aragoto, or "rough-style" acting, is used in certain plays by male characters who move in exaggerated, choreographed ways and wear stylized makeup. Eye and facial movements are crucial to an actor's success.

Although Kabuki *was founded by a woman, Izumo no Okuni, female actors were soon banned as immoral. All actors are now male, and female roles are played by highly skilled* onnagata.

Traditional Arts and Crafts

Wood *netsuke*, used to secure a cord

In Japan there is no rigid distinction between arts and crafts; both have a long, distinguished history and are equally prized. Many techniques came to Japan from the Asian continent, especially China and Korea, and have since evolved and been refined. Early arts and crafts were dominated by Buddhist influences, but from medieval times onward they became increasingly secular and decorative. Today traditional arts and crafts are thriving, with thousands of practitioners making a living from their work. Artisans can be seen at work in many areas.

Metalwork *includes items such as samurai swords, temple bells, and tea kettles. This tea kettle is from Morioka (see p277).*

CALLIGRAPHY

Known as *shodo*, the way of writing, the art of calligraphy was introduced to Japan along with the Chinese writing system in the 5th century and came to be considered as an essential accomplishment for the cultured person. Traditional writing implements consist of a brush, ink, an inkstone, and a water vessel. Buddhist monks have often led the development of styles through the centuries. Modern calligraphy has been influenced by Western Minimalist and Abstract art.

A 17th-century example of calligraphy

Calligraphy today, still using traditional methods

PAINTING

Early paintings include religious mandalas, and scrolls illustrating works such as the *Tale of Genji (see p53)*. Ink painting thrived in the 14th century; its most famous practitioner was the Zen monk Sesshu (1420–1506). The Kano School *(see p161)* was most noted for its screens. *Ukiyo-e* woodblock prints *(see p85)* predominated in the Edo period. Modern painting in Japan is inspired by Western and traditional sources.

Screen by Shibata Zeshin (1807–91) depicting the four elegant pastimes of painting, music, the game of Go, and calligraphy

CERAMICS

Ceramics up to 12,000 years old have been found in Japan. Myriad styles have developed in different areas, fueled by the central role of ceramics in the tea ceremony and cuisine. Kyushu is renowned for its porcelain and stoneware *(see p239)*; Hagi *(see pp218–19)* and Inbe *(see p210)* produce stoneware for the tea ceremony; Mashiko *(p272)* is known for its folk pottery and as the birthplace of 20th-century potter Hamada Shoji.

Potter at work in Kanazawa, Central Honshu

Bowl from Naha, Okinawa

19th-century vase from kyushu

TEXTILES

Sophisticated methods of dyeing, weaving, and hand decoration have developed in Japan, resulting in an astonishing range of textiles. Relatively isolated islands and areas evolved their own techniques; for example, the Okinawans use the *kasuri* method to tie-dye threads before weaving. *Yuzen*-dyeing in Kanazawa (see p148) uses a paste for resist-dyeing to create complex and colorful designs, often using natural vegetable dyes. Indigo (*ai*) was the most popular dye, though it has largely been replaced by synthetic alternatives. Modern designers such as Issey Miyake continue to experiment boldly with fabrics.

Dyeing *bashofu* fabric in Kijoka village, Okinawa *(see p257)*

Complex design of samurai woven into silk

Hand-painting dyes onto fabric, part of the resist-dyeing process

WOODCRAFT, BAMBOO, AND LACQUERWARE

The Japanese admire the grain and color of wood as much as the artifacts that are created from it. Traditional buildings have been made from wood for centuries; some are still in existence as a testament to their makers' craftsmanship. On a smaller scale there are exquisite wooden statues, along with wooden vessels and utensils, and traditional dolls *(see p277)*. To produce lacquerware, for which Japan is famed worldwide, the wood is coated with many layers of lacquer (derived from tree sap) and burnished to a smooth, lustrous finish. Bamboo, being strong and flexible, is used for umbrellas, toys, and baskets.

An 18th-century wooden carving of Amida Buddha

Laquerware box from Aizu-Wakamatsu

Bamboo craftsman at work

IKEBANA AND BONSAI

Ikebana is also known as *kado*, or the "way of flowers," and originated from early Buddhist flower offerings. The tea ceremony required simple arrangements of flowers, while more avant-garde creations have been popular since the late 19th century. Today there are about 3,000 *ikebana* schools in Japan. Bonsai came from China and involves growing and training trees in miniature form; prize specimens are valuable heirlooms. Both *ikebana* arrangements and bonsai may be displayed in the *tokonoma (see p33)* of a traditional.

Demonstrating the art of *ikebana*, or flower arranging

An evergreen bonsai tree

Japanese Traditional Dress

Although most Japanese now wear Western-style clothes (*yofuku*), it is not unusual to glimpse a kimono-clad woman in the street or a man relaxing in a lightweight summer kimono (*yukata*). Kimonos are wraparound garments worn by men and women, usually on formal occasions and at festivals. Some people change into a cotton kimono to relax in the evenings. A good kimono can last for years, even generations – it is made to a standard pattern, rather than to fit the wearer; the fitting is done when dressing. The left side of the garment is always wrapped over the right; the opposite is done only when dressing the dead.

Kimono style *for women and men has changed little since the Edo period.*

The *haneri* is a replaceable neckband, just visible under the kimono.

A new, *formal kimono can cost tens of thousands of yen, but these garments become family heirlooms. Before cleaning, they are taken apart along the seams; for storage they are folded and wrapped in paper.*

A length of silk known as the *obiage* holds the *obi* in place.

The *obi* is a sash up to 4 m (13 ft) long.

The *obijime* decorative cord further secures the *obi*.

The *obi* *sash is usually made of silk and tied tightly at the back. The quality of material and the knot used vary according to the season and formality of the occasion.*

A tuck, or *ohashiori*, at the waist adjusts the length of a kimono.

Tabi socks have a split between the big and second toes.

Zori sandals usually have wedge soles.

WOMAN'S KIMONO

This woman is wearing a *furisode*, a formal kimono with long, flowing sleeves. These are traditionally worn by young, unmarried women on special occasions, such as Coming-of-Age Day in January, and are often made of brightly colored and extravagantly patterned materials.

Yukata *are unlined cotton kimonos worn by men and women, often at summer festivals or hot-spring resorts.*

The sumptuous fabric *used for women's kimonos is often hand-painted, woven, or dyed using one of the many traditional Japanese techniques to produce a complex design.*

Women's hairstyles *grew increasingly elaborate in the Edo period, reflecting a woman's age and social and marital status. Today, women wear traditional styles only on formal occasions.*

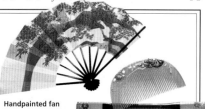

Handpainted fan

Comb and hair pin

Fans, *usually bamboo covered with hand-painted paper, are traditional accessories carried by women and men. Combs and hairpins may be tortoiseshell, lacquer, or ivory, and are often exquisitely decorated.*

The family crest is known as the *mon*.

The *montsuki* is a formal kimono (which can be worn by men or women) bearing a crest.

The *haori* is an outer coat worn over the kimono.

A pair of braided cords, known as *himo*, are used to tie the kimono.

Hakama are loose trousers, similar to culottes, which are worn over the kimono.

At a traditional wedding, *or* tomesode, *the man wears a formal kimono, while the woman wears a white kimono, known as* shiromuku, *and a special headdress.*

Men's sandals are known as *setta* and have a surface similar to *tatami* mats. The soles are made of leather.

Children wear *miniature versions – often rented – of the adult kimonos on formal occasions, and especially at the Shichi-go-san (Seven-Five-Three) Festival in November (see p46).*

MAN'S KIMONO

Formal clothing for a man consists of a black silk kimono; a man's kimono is shorter than a woman's, allowing greater freedom of movement. Over the top go ankle-length *hakama* and a long, loose jacket or *haori*, plain apart from the family crest embroidered in white.

TRADITIONAL SHOES

Since the Nara and Heian periods (from the 8th century on), the Japanese have worn variations on thonged rush or leather sandals (*zori*) and wooden clogs (*geta*). Both are highly practical for slipping on and off when entering and leaving houses. *Zori* are still worn with formal kimonos, and *geta* with *yukata*. *Geta* often tended to be raised off the ground to prevent the wearer's feet from becoming muddy; in the late 17th century the fashion for courtesans was for 30-cm (12-in) high soles, almost impossible to walk in. *Tabi* split socks are worn with both types of shoes.

Geta wooden clogs

Making wooden clogs

Japan's Festivals: Matsuri

Matsuri means both festival and worship, indicating the Shinto origins of Japanese festivals. Some are nationwide, others are local to individual temples and shrines. Matsuri are a link between the human and the divine, often marking stages in the rice-growing cycle (mainly planting and harvest) or historical events. The aim of the matsuri is to preserve the goodwill of the deities *(kami)*. All matsuri follow a basic form: purification (often by water or fire); then offerings; then a procession in which the *kami* is invoked at the shrine and escorted in a portable shrine *(mikoshi)* to a temporary dwelling where there is entertainment such as dancing or archery. The *kami* is then taken back to the shrine.

The basic form *of matsuri has changed little over the centuries. This print shows an 18th-century religious festival with men carrying a* mikoshi.

Omizu-tori *has been celebrated at Todai-ji temple, Nara (see pp190–93), since the 8th century to signal the advent of spring. Water is drawn from a sacred well and purified with fire from huge torches.*

The *mikoshi* is a colorful, ornate portable shrine in which the *kami* rides en route from and to the shrine.

Takayama Matsuri *takes place in spring and fall. Spectacular floats are escorted from the Hie Shrine through the town by people dressed in Edo-period costumes. The aim is to placate the* kami *of plague.*

Rice festivals *all over Japan were central to the matsuri cycle, but have declined as agricultural techniques have changed. Women plant the rice in spring, symbolically passing their fertility to the crop. Fall festivals give thanks for the harvest.*

Aoi Matsuri, *or the Hollyhock Festival, in Kyoto, originated in the 6th century. Participants in Heian-period costume parade from the Imperial Palace to Shimogamo and Kamigamo shrines, re-creating the journey of imperial messengers who were sent to placate the gods.*

Nebuta Matsuri, *held in Aomori in August, is one of Japan's most spectacular festivals, featuring huge paper lanterns. At the end they are carried off to sea as a symbol of casting away anything that might interfere with the harvest.*

Participants are dressed in short kimonos known as *happi,* and headbands, or *hachimaki.*

The bearers of the *mikoshi* tend to take it on a boisterous ride as the gods are said to enjoy revelry.

Bon, *the Buddhist Festival of the Dead, takes place in mid-July or mid-August. Ancestors are welcomed back to the world of the living and then bid farewell again. Bon Odori, hypnotic outdoor dancing, takes place.*

Tanabata Matsuri *in July is known as the Weaver, or Star, Festival. Based on a Chinese legend, it is said to be the only day when the two stars Vega (the weaver) and Altair (the herdsman) can meet as lovers across the Milky Way. People write down wishes and poems and hang them on bamboo poles.*

KANDA MATSURI, TOKYO

Held in May in alternate years, this festival is one of Tokyo's largest. Numerous floats and portable shrines are paraded through the streets of Tokyo to placate the gods of Kanda Myojin Shrine *(see p73).* In addition to communicating with the gods, the festival encourages a sense of community.

Equestrian archery *is a traditional test of martial skills at matsuri. Archery contests take place at Hachiman shrines as offerings to the god of war; the best-known is at Kamakura's Hachiman-gu Shrine (see p134).*

Jidai Matsuri, *or the Festival of the Ages, is a relatively new matsuri. It was initiated in 1895 to commemorate Kyoto's long history. Dressed in historical costumes dating from the 8th century onward, people parade from the Imperial Palace to the Heian Shrine.*

JAPAN THROUGH THE YEAR

The year in Japan revolves through five seasons: spring, rainy season, summer, fall, and winter. Though less reliable than in the past, perhaps due to global warming, the seasons are still clearly discernable and dictate many of the traditional, agricultural-based *matsuri*, or festivals. The country follows two calendars: the contemporary Gregorian, and to a lesser degree the ancient Chinese lunar system. Because Japan also has two main religions, Shinto and Buddhism, there are double the number of festivals found in most countries. In fact, the days, weeks, and months are marked by so many festive occasions and national holidays that the year speeds past in a colorful procession of official observations, historic commemorations, sacred rites, and wild celebration.

Puppet from a Takayama festival float

Cherry blossom along the Philosopher's Walk, Kyoto

SPRING

Although spring does not officially begin until the cherry trees bloom in early to mid-April, this is the time the elements begin to warm and thaw. Cherry-blossom parties take place throughout the country. In Golden Week (April 29–May 5) and adjacent weekends many Japanese take the time off to travel.

MARCH

Omizu-tori *(Water-Drawing Festival, Mar 1–14)*, Nara. At Todai-ji temple, water is ritually drawn to the sound of ancient sacred music at 2am on the 13th day *(see p42)*.
Hina Matsuri *(Doll Festival, Mar 3)*. Throughout Japan, dolls in Heian-period imperial costumes are displayed in homes with young daughters.
Kasuga Shrine Festival *(Mar 13)*, Nara. Shrine maidens perform a 1,100-year-old dance.

APRIL

Hana Matsuri *(Buddha's Birthday, Apr 8)*. Celebrated at temples nationwide. Sweet tea is poured over a small image of the Buddha to signify devotion.
Takayama Matsuri *(Apr 14–15)*, Gifu prefecture. A festival at Takayama's Hie Shrine, famed for its procession of richly decorated floats *(see p42)*.

Yayoi Matsuri *(Apr 16–17)*, Nikko, Tochigi prefecture. A festival at Futara-san Shrine including colorful floats.

MAY

Hakata Dontaku Matsuri *(May 3–4)*, Fukuoka. Costumed citizens escort legendary gods on horseback.
Hamamatsu Matsuri *(Kite-Flying Festival, May 3–5)*, Hamamatsu, Shizuoka prefecture. Amazing kites are flown.
Kanda Matsuri *(Sat & Sun before May 15, alternate, odd-numbered years)*, Tokyo. Portable shrines are paraded in the neighborhood around Kanda Myojin Shrine; there is also a gala tea ceremony *(see pp42–3)*.
Aoi Matsuri *(Hollyhock Festival, May 15)*, Kyoto. Magnificent pageantry at the Shimogamo and Kamigamo shrines, reproducing past imperial processions *(see p42)*.
Cormorant Fishing *(May 11–Oct 15)*, Nagara River, Gifu city. Start of the season of nighttime torchlit fishing with trained birds.

Seasonal vegetables on sale in Naha, Okinawa

Cormorant fishing in Nagara River, Gifu, between May and October

Tosho-gu Grand Festival
(May 17–18), Nikko, Tochigi prefecture. As the highlight, 1,000 men in samurai armor escort three *mikoshi* (portable shrines) through the local streets.

Sanja Matsuri *(3rd Fri–Sun in May)*, Tokyo. Locals parade *mikoshi* through the streets near the shrine of Asakusa Jinja, accompanied by music. Can be quite wild.

Mifune Matsuri *(3rd Sun in May)*, Kyoto. An ancient boat festival charmingly re-enacted on the Oi River.

RAINY SEASON

From the pleasant climate of late spring, skies cloud and there are torrential downpours which are often the cause of landslides and flooding. A blanket of humidity envelops the landscape. Only Hokkaido, being so far north, manages to steer clear of such discomfort. The rest of Japan finds beauty in viewing hydrangeas and other flowers through the mists of mid-June to mid-July.

JUNE

Sanno Matsuri *(Jun 16)*, Tokyo. Portable shrines are carried around Hie Shrine in the Akasaka area.

Rice-Planting Festival *(Jun 14)*, southern Osaka. Girls wearing traditional farmers' costumes ceremonially plant rice in the Sumiyoshi Shrine's fields, praying for a good harvest *(see p42)*.

Chagu-chagu Umakko *(Horse Festival, Jun 15)*, Morioka, Iwate prefecture. Decorated horses parade to Hachiman Shrine.

SUMMER

Technically summer begins in mid-July, as soon as the last clouds of the rainy season have left the sky. The heat and humidity continue to rise, mountains "open" for the season, and in mid-July, as soon as schools break for the vacations, the sea also "opens" for swimming. The air vibrates with the sound of insects; the rice grows fast; and people do what they can to keep cool. Even as the overheated landscape begins to sigh with exhaustion, frenzied summer celebrations break out, including spectacular firework displays that light up the night skies.

JULY

Yamagasa Matsuri *(Jul 1–15)*, Fukuoka. Climaxes with a race of giant floats over 5 km (3 miles).

Tanabata Matsuri *(Star Festival, Jul 7)*. Celebrated nation-wide to mark a Chinese legend *(see p43)*. Stems of bamboo are decorated with paper streamers inscribed with poems. The week-long Hiratsuka Tanabata in Kanagawa prefecture features Disney-style mechanical exhibits in competition.

Bon *(Jul 13–16; held in Aug in most areas)*. See under August, page 46.

Nachi no Hi-Matsuri *(Fire Festival, Jul 14)*, Nachi-Katsura, Wakayama prefecture. At Nachi Shrine, 12 massive torches are set alight and carried by priests in white robes.

Gion Matsuri *(Jul, esp 17 and 24)*, Kyoto. The city's biggest festival, dating from the 9th century, when the people were seeking the protection of the gods from a deadly pestilence that was ravaging the local population. The streets are especially crowded for the parade of fabulous ancient floats on the 17th.

Kangensai Music Festival *(mid-Jul–early Aug)*, Miyajima, Hiroshima prefecture. Classical court music and dance performed on beautifully decorated boats at Itsukushima Shrine.

Tenjin Matsuri *(Jul 24–25)*, Osaka. Celebrated at Tenman-gu Shrine. A flotilla of boats carries portable shrines down the Dojima River accompanied by the sound of drumbeats.

Hanabi Taikai *(last Sat in Jul)*, Tokyo. Spectacular fireworks on the Sumida River near Asakusa; a revival of Edo-era celebrations.

Carrying torches at Nachi no Hi-Matsuri

Fall colors at Sounkyo Gorge in central Hokkaido

AUGUST

Neputa Matsuri *(Aug 1–7)*, Hirosaki, and **Nebuta Matsuri** *(Aug 2–7)*, Aomori. These festivals are so spectacular they are televised. Massive illuminated and painted papier mâché figures are paraded on floats *(see p43)*.

Kanto Matsuri *(Aug 4–7)*, Akita. Men compete in balancing huge poles hung with lanterns on their shoulders, foreheads, chins, and hips.

Sendai Tanabata *(on the original date of the old calendar: Aug 6–8)*, Sendai, Miyagi prefecture. In Sendai's traditional version of the festival celebrated in July elsewhere, streets are decorated with colored paper streamers and hanging banners.

Awa-Odori *(Aug 12–15)*, Tokushima, Shikoku. The whole city sings and dances for four days and nights; the festival originally commemorated the building of the castle here in 1587.

Girls holding bamboo decorated with paper strips, Sendai Tanabata

Bon *(Festival of the Dead, Aug 13–16)*. Religious rites in connection with the Buddhist belief that spirits return to this world to visit loved ones in summer. A big family occasion, with everyone visiting, cleaning, and decorating tombs. Communal Bon Odori dance parties are held most evenings *(see p43)*.

Daimonji Bonfire *(Aug 16)*, Kyoto. Five large bonfires on the hills surrounding the city burn to mark the end of Bon, followed by dancing.

SEPTEMBER

Hachiman-gu Festival *(Sep 14–16)*, Kamakura. A procession of floats and horseback archery at the Hachiman-gu Shrine invariably draw a big crowd *(see p43)*.

FALL

Although the children are back at school and the sea is once again "closed," the heat goes on. Now is the time to start thinking about harvesting the rice. Apples flood the shops, leaves start to fall, and snow will soon begin in the north.

OCTOBER

Kunchi Matsuri *(Oct 7–9)*, Nagasaki. A dragon dance of Chinese origin winds between floats with umbrella-shaped decorations at Suwa Shrine.

Takayama Matsuri *(Oct 9–10)*, Gifu prefecture. Held at Takayama's Hachiman-gu Shrine, this harvest festival is most memorable for a procession with ornate floats.

Kenka Matsuri *(Oct 14–15)*, Himeji, Hyogo prefecture. At Matsubara Shrine, nearly naked youths carrying *mikoshi* challenge each others' skills in balancing.

Doburoku Matsuri *(Oct 14–19)*, Shirakawa-go, Gifu prefecture. A harvest festival with dancing and drinking.

Nagoya Festival *(Fri–Sun in mid-Oct)*. Long procession in Nagoya City with impersonations of historical characters.

Tosho-gu Fall Festival *(Oct 17)*, Nikko, Tochigi prefecture. Armor-clad samurai escort a portable shrine.

Jidai Matsuri *(Festival of the Ages, Oct 22)*, Kyoto. One of the city's big three festivals. Citizens in colorful costumes re-create 1,200 years of the city's history at Heian Shrine *(see p43)*.

Kuram Matsuri *(Fire Festival, Oct 22)*, Kyoto. Torches lining the route to Yuki Shrine, Kurama, are set alight, and children march through them holding more torches.

NOVEMBER

Karatsu Kunshi *(Nov 2–4)*, Kyushu. Celebrated at Karatsu Shrine and known for its colorful parade of floats.

Daimyo Gyoretsu *(Nov 3)*, Hakone. A re-enactment of a feudal lord's procession along the old Tokaido road between Edo and Kyoto.

Tori-no-ichi *(Rake Fair, mid-Nov)*, Tokyo. Stalls at the Otori Shrine near Asakusa sell ornately decorated rakes *(kumade)* for raking in the money next year.

Shichi-go-san *(Seven-Five-Three Children's Festival, Nov 15)*. Parents take children of these ages to shrines in appreciation of their health and to pray for further blessings. Wonderful photo opportunities of kimono-clad kids.

WINTER

The cold season begins in Hokkaido, Northern Honshu, and to the west of the Japan Alps in late fall, with the first snows. By contrast, the east coast – including Tokyo – rarely experiences more than a few days of snow a year. Southern Kyushu remains quite dry and warm through the winter; Okinawa even more so. The period around New Year is one of the year's peak travel times.

DECEMBER

On Matsuri *(Dec 15–18)*, Nara. Celebrated at Kasuga Shrine. A procession of courtiers, retainers, and wrestlers of ancient times.
Hagoita-Ichi *(Battledore Fair, Dec 17–19)*, Tokyo. Ornately decorated battledores are sold in the precincts of Senso-ji Temple.
Namahage *(Dec 31)*, Oga, Akita prefecture. Grotesquely masked men visit households with children, scaring them into being good.
Okera Mairi Ceremony *(Dec 31)*, Kyoto. A sacred fire is lit at Yasaka Shrine; people each take some embers home to start their own fires of the new year.

JANUARY

New Year's Day *(Jan 1)*. Japan's most important religious festival. Most people eat *soba* noodles the night before to bring long life. Witnessing the first sunrise is considered very lucky. The first few days are family-oriented, with visits to temples and shrines to buy lucky talismans for the year ahead.

Tokyo fireman at the Dezo-meshiki, or New Year's Parade

Dezomeshiki *(New Year's Parade, Jan 6)*, Tokyo. Dazzling display by Tokyo firemen in traditional uniforms, performing acrobatic tricks on top of bamboo ladders.
Usokae *(Bullfinch Exchange, Jan 7)*, Dazaifu, Fukuoka prefecture. Festival of Dazaifu Tenman-gu Shrine.
Toka Ebisu Festival *(Jan 9–11)*, Osaka. Celebrated at Imamiya Shrine. Ebisu is worshiped by those who pray for good commercial

fortune in the year ahead.
Yamayaki *(Grass Fire Festival, day before Coming-of-Age Day)*, Nara. Old grass is burned on Mount Wakakusa-yama to initiate new growth.

FEBRUARY

Setsubun *(Bean-throwing Festival, Feb 3 or 4)*. Nationwide. Celebrities at major temples throw dried soy beans into crowds of onlookers, symbolizing the casting out of bad spirits.
Lantern Festival *(Feb 3 or 4)*, Nara. Some 3,000 candle-lit lanterns attract huge crowds to the Kasuga Shrine.
Yuki Matsuri *(Snow Festival, early Feb)*, Sapporo, Hokkaido. Vast, intricate sculptures carved from snow and ice fill Odori Park.
Saidai-ji Eyo Matsuri *(Naked Festival, 3rd Sat in Feb)*, Saidai-ji, Okayama prefecture. Celebrated at Saida-ji Temple. Young male devotees wearing *fundoshi* (loin cloths) jostle for a pair of sacred wands thrown into the darkness by priests.

PUBLIC HOLIDAYS

If a public holiday falls on a Sunday, the following Monday is also a public holiday.

New Year's Day (Jan 1)
Coming-of-Age Day (2nd Mon in Jan)
National Foundation Day (Feb 11)
Vernal Equinox Day (Mar 21)
Greenery Day (Apr 29)
Constitution Memorial Day (May 3)
Children's Day (May 5)
Maritime Day (Jul 20)
Respect for the Aged Day (3rd Mon in Sep)
Fall Equinox Day (Sep 23)
Health-Sports Day (2nd Mon in Oct)
Culture Day (Nov 3)
Labor Thanksgiving Day (Nov 23)
Emperor's Birthday (Dec 23)

One of the snow carvings at Yuki Matsuri, Sapporo

The Climate of Japan

Japan's climate varies primarily with latitude, from cool, temperate Hokkaido to subtropical Okinawa. Most of the country is warm, temperate, and rainy; temperatures are cooler year-round in the mountains. The other key distinction is between the Pacific and Japan Sea coasts. Both have a lot of rain in June and July. The Pacific coast also has heavy rainfall and typhoons in September but is sunny in winter, while the Japan Sea coast has long spells of rain and snow in winter.

Subtropical Iriomote Island, south of Okinawa Island

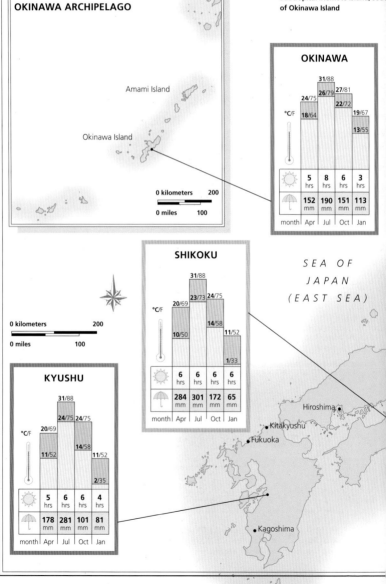

OKINAWA ARCHIPELAGO

Amami Island

Okinawa Island

0 kilometers 200
0 miles 100

OKINAWA

°C/F			
24/75	**31**/88	**27**/81	
18/64	**26**/79	**22**/72	19/67
			13/55

☀	5 hrs	8 hrs	6 hrs	3 hrs
☂	152 mm	190 mm	151 mm	113 mm
month	Apr	Jul	Oct	Jan

SHIKOKU

°C/F			
20/69	**31**/88	**24**/75	
10/50	**23**/73	14/58	11/52
			1/33

☀	6 hrs	6 hrs	6 hrs	6 hrs
☂	284 mm	301 mm	172 mm	65 mm
month	Apr	Jul	Oct	Jan

SEA OF JAPAN (EAST SEA)

0 kilometers 200
0 miles 100

KYUSHU

°C/F			
20/69	**31**/88	**24**/75	
11/52	**24**/75	14/58	11/52
			2/35

☀	5 hrs	6 hrs	6 hrs	4 hrs
☂	178 mm	281 mm	101 mm	81 mm
month	Apr	Jul	Oct	Jan

Hiroshima

Kitakyushu

Fukuoka

Kagoshima

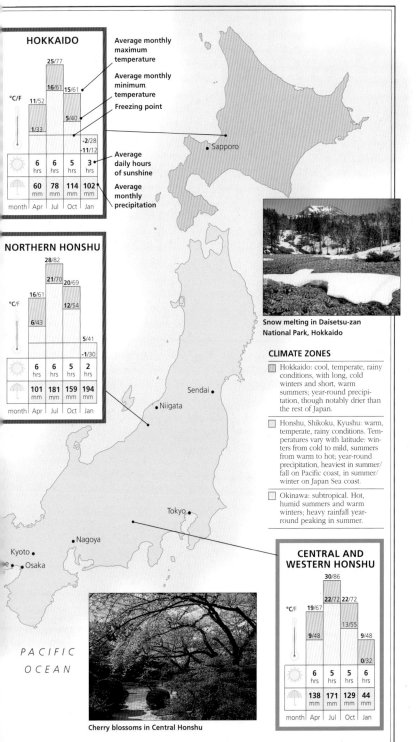

HOKKAIDO

Average monthly maximum temperature

Average monthly minimum temperature

Freezing point

°C/F

	25/77		
	16/61	15/61	
11/52			
		5/40	
1/33			
		-2/28	
		-11/12	

Average daily hours of sunshine

6 hrs	6 hrs	5 hrs	3 hrs

Average monthly precipitation

60 mm	78 mm	114 mm	102 mm
month	Apr	Jul	Oct	Jan

NORTHERN HONSHU

°C/F

	28/82		
	21/70	20/69	
16/61		12/54	
6/43			
		5/41	
			-1/30

6 hrs	6 hrs	5 hrs	2 hrs

101 mm	181 mm	159 mm	194 mm
month	Apr	Jul	Oct	Jan

Sapporo

Snow melting in Daisetsu-zan National Park, Hokkaido

CLIMATE ZONES

Hokkaido: cool, temperate, rainy conditions, with long, cold winters and short, warm summers; year-round precipitation, though notably drier than the rest of Japan.

Honshu, Shikoku, Kyushu: warm, temperate, rainy conditions. Temperatures vary with latitude: winters from cold to mild, summers from warm to hot; year-round precipitation, heaviest in summer/fall on Pacific coast, in summer/winter on Japan Sea coast.

Okinawa: subtropical. Hot, humid summers and warm winters; heavy rainfall year-round peaking in summer.

Sendai

Niigata

Tokyo

Nagoya

Kyoto

Osaka

PACIFIC OCEAN

CENTRAL AND WESTERN HONSHU

°C/F

	30/86		
19/67	22/72	22/72	
9/48		13/55	
			9/48
			0/32

6 hrs	5 hrs	5 hrs	6 hrs

138 mm	171 mm	129 mm	44 mm
month	Apr	Jul	Oct	Jan

Cherry blossoms in Central Honshu

THE HISTORY OF JAPAN

From the origins of the Japanese race to its military behavior in World War II, Japan's history is still subject to conjecture. What is indisputable is that the people of this archipelago were able to avail themselves of the fruits of continental civilization even as their isolation protected them from attack. As a result, Japan has one of the most distinct of all the many Chinese-influenced cultures in Asia.

During glacial epochs when the sea level was low, Japan's first inhabitants may have reached the archipelago overland from Sakhalin and Siberia, China and Korea, or the Okinawa islands. Crude stone tools found at sites in Aichi and Tochigi prefectures may date back 40,000 years.

Recent discoveries posit the emergence of the hunting and gathering society known as Jomon around 14,500 BC. Jomon pottery is among the world's oldest and includes vessels and figurines, particularly of women. Mounds of shells and other evidence indicate that the diet included fish, shellfish, deer, wild pigs, and wild plants and seeds. In the Kanto Plain (near Tokyo), the Jomon culture in its later stages included village-like groupings.

Rice agriculture and bronze, iron, and other crafts are believed to have reached Kyushu island via Korea during the Yayoi period. The Yayoi people spread from Kyushu to Honshu and Shikoku over time, pushing the earlier inhabitants north. Chinese histories record a visit by an envoy of Himiko, queen of Yamatai,

Clay figurine from the Kofun period

to the Chinese kingdom of Wei in 239, but Yamatai's location is still open to debate. Aristocratic orders emerged, including that of the emperor (a line unbroken to the present day), said to be descended from the sun goddess Amaterasu. Figures of high rank were buried in *kofun* (tumuli), along with clay sculptures, armor, mirrors, and jewelry.

By the late 6th century, tribes that had migrated to the fertile lands of Yamato *(see p187)* were engaged in a power struggle over the introduction of Buddhism. Prince Shotoku, appointed regent by Empress Suiko in 593, helped seal victory for the pro-Buddhist camp. The temple Horyu-ji *(see p196)* was completed in 607.

In 701, the Taiho code, a penal and administrative system based on the Chinese model, was in place. The temples of Nara *(see pp190–95)*, which became the capital in 710, epitomize this Chinese influence and are some of the best intact examples of their kind. With the completion of the *Man'yoshu*, the earliest known Japanese poetry, in 759, the culture began to establish a clear voice of its own.

PERIODS AT A GLANCE

Jomon	14,500–300 BC
Yayoi	300 BC–AD 300
Kofun /Asuka	300–710
Hakuho	645–710
Nara	710–794
Heian	794–1185
Kamakura	1185–1333
Muromachi	1333–1568
Momoyama	1568–1600
Tokugawa (Edo)	1600–1868
Meiji	1868–1912
Taisho	1912–1926
Showa	1926–1989
Heisei	1989–present

TIMELINE

300 BC–AD 300 Continental methods of farming, metalworking, pottery, and other skills reach southwestern Japan via Korea, and spread through islands

710 Heijo-kyo (Nara) made capital

701 Taiho code put in place, the basis of the first Japanese legal system

AD 1	200	400	600

Yayoi earthenware

239 Himiko, queen of Yamatai, sends envoy to kingdom of Wei in China

587 Power struggle over introduction of Buddhism from China

712 *Kojiki* completed, Japan's oldest historical account

◁ **Detail from a 16th-century screen painting, showing customs month-by-month in the Momoyama period**

COURT LIFE AND THE TALE OF GENJI

Court life in Kyoto focused on romance, aesthetic pursuits, and fastidious observation of precedent and ritual, as documented in the *Pillow Book* of court lady Sei Shonagon in the late 10th century. The *Tale of Genji*, written in the early 11th century by Sei Shonagon's rival, Murasaki Shikibu, a court lady of the Fujiwara clan, is possibly the world's oldest novel. It depicts the loves and sorrows of a fictitious prince, Genji, and, after he dies, the amorous pursuits of a man whom Genji mistakenly thought was his son. The story has been illustrated in countless scrolls and other media.

Tale of Genji scroll

HEIAN PERIOD

The powerful Fujiwara family and Emperor Kammu built a new capital, Heian-kyo, now Kyoto (*see pp154–79*), in 794. The new system, also based on Chinese models, held that the land and people were ultimately the property of the emperor. Tax-exempt status was granted to Buddhist institutions, large landholders, and settlers who would expand the state's frontiers. Meanwhile, the Fujiwara clan gained influence by acting as regents, and intermarriage with the imperial family. A pattern emerged in which emperors would abdicate, name a younger successor, enter a monastery, then exercise power from behind the scenes.

Buddhism's influence continued as proponents such as Saicho adapted it, launching the Tendai, Shingon, and Pure-Land schools (*see p275*). Powerful temples like Enryaku-ji (*see p178–9*) grew militant in faceoffs with other temples and the government, creating armies of warrior-monks.

Wooden statue of Minamoto no Yoritomo

Ironically, Buddhism's abhorrence of killing fed the nobility's contempt for the farmer-warriors – the early samurai (*see pp54–5*) – on the frontier, who battled the indigenous Ainu people (*see p287*) and each other. After 1100, the court could no longer control infighting, and tensions rose between two clans of farmer-warriors from the northeast: the Taira and the Minamoto. By 1160, ruthless Taira no Kiyomori was the most powerful man in Japan. But the Minamoto, led by the brothers Yoshitsune and Yoritomo, fought back to defeat the Taira and establish the first military shogunate at Kamakura (*see pp134–7*) in 1185.

Heian-period fan

KAMAKURA SHOGUNATE

Deliberately basing his government far from the imperial court in the village of Kamakura, Minamoto no Yoritomo carefully crafted a system that benefited his *bushi* (warrior) peers and brought 150 years of relative peace and stability. Yoritomo's direct heirs were shoguns only in name, however, as they were dominated by hereditary regents from the military Hojo family of Kamakura. The Hojo assumed the prerogatives of power while granting the imperial institution and nobility the privilege of signing off on policy.

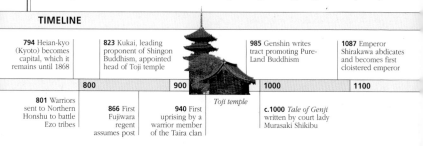

TIMELINE

794 Heian-kyo (Kyoto) becomes capital, which it remains until 1868	**823** Kukai, leading proponent of Shingon Buddhism, appointed head of Toji temple		**985** Genshin writes tract promoting Pure-Land Buddhism	**1087** Emperor Shirakawa abdicates and becomes first cloistered emperor
800		**900**	**1000**	**1100**
801 Warriors sent to Northern Honshu to battle Ezo tribes	**866** First Fujiwara regent assumes post	**940** First uprising by a warrior member of the Taira clan	*Toji temple* **c.1000** *Tale of Genji* written by court lady Murasaki Shikibu	

Portuguese in Kyushu – the "Southern Barbarians" who introduced firearms and Christianity to Japan

The *Tale of the Heike*, a chronicle of the war between the Taira and Minamoto clans, was first recited to lute accompaniment at this time. Temples and works of art were created in Kamakura, reflecting Yoritomo's warrior ideals of stoicism, self discipline, frugality, and loyalty. Zen Buddhism as imported from China was popular with the samurai, while the Pure-Land, True-Pure-Land, and Nichiren Buddhist sects promoted salvation to the common people.

Mongol invasions were repelled twice in the 13th century, but weakened the resources and command of Kamakura. The end came in 1333, when the Ashikaga clan, led by Takauji, toppled the Kamakura shogunate. However, the power systems instigated by Yoritomo and the Hojo influenced Japanese life for five more centuries.

Muromachi-period sword guard

MUROMACHI SHOGUNATE

With military power back with the imperial court in Kyoto, arts such as Noh drama and the tea ceremony flowered under the patronage of Shogun Ashikaga Yoshimasa. However, a succession dispute split the court into southern and northern factions. With leaders engaged in power struggles, chaos and famine were common. The nadir was reached during the Onin War (1467–77), when arson and looting destroyed much of Kyoto.

The Muromachi period, named for the Kyoto district where the Ashikagas built their palace, was a time of craven ambition that unleashed every class in society to vie for advantage. Warfare, once the exclusive business of samurai, now involved armies of footsoldiers (*ashigaru*) recruited from the peasantry, who could hope for promotion based on success in the battlefields.

In 1542 a trio of Portuguese from a shipwrecked junk emerged in Tanegashima, an island off Kyushu, and introduced firearms to Japan. Francis Xavier, a founding member of the Society of Jesus, established a Jesuit mission at Kagoshima in 1549. The contact with Europeans further destabilized the political situation and set the stage for the first of the great unifiers, Oda Nobunaga, who entered Kyoto in 1568.

1180–85 Minamoto clan defeats the Taira and establishes Kamakura shogunate

Great Buddha image at Kamakura

c. 1400 Zeami performing Noh dramas and writing

1467 Devastating Onin War begins. Vast sections of Kyoto are burned over the next decade

| 1200 | 1300 | 1400 | 1500 |

1160 Ascendant Taira clan under Taira no Kiyomori suppresses its rivals, the Minamoto, and dominates court life

1281 Second Mongol invasion

1274 First Mongol invasion

1242 Emperor Shijo dies without naming heir, setting off succession dispute

1560–80 Oda Nobunaga victorious in battles for hegemony of Japan

1428 Peasant uprising in Kyoto

1401 Formal relations with China reestablished

The Samurai

The samurai, also known as *bushi*, emerged in the 9th century when the emperor's court in Kyoto, disdaining warfare, delegated the overseeing and defense of far-flung holdings to constables and local farmer-warriors. Affiliated to *daimyo* (lords of noble descent), the samurai formed their own hereditary clans over time and became more powerful than the emperor; from their ranks emerged the shogunates (military dictatorships) of the 12th–19th centuries. Strict codes of loyalty and behavior, called *bushido* ("way of the warrior"), were inspired in part by Zen Buddhism and included ritualized acts of suicide *(seppuku)* to prove honor.

Castle towns *were built in strategic positions by powerful samurai. The most distinctive castles, such as at Himeji (see pp206–209) and Osaka, date from the 16th century.*

Seppuku, *also known less formally as harakiri, was the honorable method of suicide, whereby the samurai would disembowel himself in front of witnesses.*

On the wet and windy night of **October 20**, the armies massed in the hills around Sekigahara. At 8am the following morning, 100,000 samurai went to war.

Most military archers were mounted on horseback.

Oda Nobunaga *(1534–82) was the first of the "Three Heroes" of samurai history, who between them unified most of Japan. The other two were Toyotomi Hideyoshi (1537–98) and Tokugawa Ieyasu (1543–1616).*

BATTLE OF SEKIGAHARA

After Toyotomi Hideyoshi died, *daimyo* from eastern and western Japan fell into dispute and sent their samurai, led by Tokugawa Ieyasu and Ishida Mitsunari, to battle. Ieyasu won the battle, in a valley in Central Honshu on October 21, 1600, and subsequently founded the Tokugawa shogunate.

Saigo Takamori *(1827–77) was one of the last samurai. After helping to overthrow the Tokugawa shogunate and leading the Satsuma Rebellion he committed suicide.*

The daimyo *were the hereditary, landholding lords of the feudal era, to whom most samurai swore their allegiance. Under the Tokugawa shogunate the daimyo were forced to journey to Edo every two years with all their people.*

Steel swords *were first forged in Japan in the 8th century. The samurai wore pairs of swords, long and short, from 1600. They were banned after the Meiji Restoration of 1868.*

Every warrior took a musket, spear, or bow into battle, as well as a sword.

SAMURAI BATTLEDRESS

The samurai developed remarkably ornate and colorful armor from the 9th century on. The earliest style, *oyoroi*, was designed for archers on horseback. In the Muromachi period it was superseded by lighter armor, *domaru*, worn by foot soldiers, and later a style called *tosei gusoku*, shown here, which helped protect against firearms.

Kabuto (helmet)

Mempo (face defense)

Sode (shoulder defense)

Do (cuirass)

Kote (arm defense)

Kusazuri (upper thigh defense)

Haidate (lower thigh defense)

Suneate (shin guard)

Long vertical banners *(nobori)* were hung on poles to identify different military families and groups of warriors.

Heads were collected in the thousands and set by roadsides.

Ronin ("floating men") *were samurai without allegience to particular masters. In the 47 Ronin Incident of 1703, portrayed in the Kabuki play* Chushingura, *a group of* ronin *avenged the killing of their lord, then were ordered to commit suicide by the shogunate (see p103).*

Screen depicting the Battle of Nagashino in 1575, won by Oda Nobunaga's 3,000 musketeers

MOMOYAMA PERIOD

After Japan had been racked by over a century of debilitating, inconclusive warfare, Oda Nobunaga, who rose through military ranks in the provinces, set out to unify the nation under his rule. From 1568–76 Nobunaga defeated rival warlord Asai Nagamasa; burned down Enryaku-ji, where militant monks had long challenged the court and their Buddhist rivals; drove Ashikaga Yoshiaki into exile; and deployed 3,000 musketeers to massacre the Takeda forces at the Battle of Nagashino. In 1580, in his last great military exploit, Nobunaga obtained the surrender of Ishiyama

Momoyama-period detail at Nishi Hongan-ji, Kyoto

Hongan-ji, a nearly impregnable temple fortress in what is now central Osaka. Surrounded by moats and walls, the temple had been the power base of the Buddhist True-Pure-Land sect.

By 1582, when he was forced to commit suicide by a treasonous vassal, Nobunaga was in control of 30 of Japan's 68 provinces. Nobunaga's deputy, a warrior of humble birth named Toyotomi Hideyoshi, promptly avenged his lord and continued the work of unification, launching epic campaigns that brought Shikoku (1585), Kyushu (1587), the Kanto region (1590), and Northern Honshu (1591) under his control. He followed up by destroying many of the castles and forts belonging to potential rivals, confiscating weapons belonging to peasants, and devising a system in which peasants held their own small plots and paid a fixed tax directly to the central government.

In his later years, Hideyoshi ordered two unsuccessful invasions of Korea and persecuted the Portuguese missionaries and their Japanese converts *(see p234)*. Like Oda Nobunaga, however, Hideyoshi never actually claimed the title of shogun but became obsessed with ensuring the perpetuation of his line after his death. Two years after his death in 1598, however, dissension among his retainers led to the Battle of Sekigahara *(see pp54–5)*, in which Tokugawa Ieyasu emerged victorious.

THE TOKUGAWA SHOGUNATE

Named shogun by the emperor in 1603, Ieyasu split the population into rigidly defined hereditary classes. To end turf wars, samurai were forbidden to own

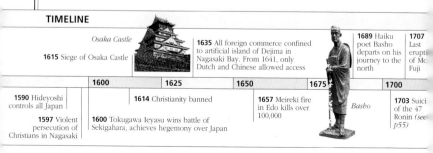

TIMELINE

Osaka Castle

1615 Siege of Osaka Castle

1635 All foreign commerce confined to artificial island of Dejima in Nagasaki Bay. From 1641, only Dutch and Chinese allowed access

1689 Haiku poet Basho departs on his journey to the north

1707 Last eruption of Mount Fuji

| 1600 | 1625 | 1650 | 1675 | 1700 |

1590 Hideyoshi controls all Japan

1597 Violent persecution of Christians in Nagasaki

1614 Christianity banned

1600 Tokugawa Ieyasu wins battle of Sekigahara, achieves hegemony over Japan

1657 Meireki fire in Edo kills over 100,000

Basho

1703 Suicide of the 47 Ronin *(see p55)*

land and could reside only within certain quarters of castle towns. Farmers were allotted small plots, which they were obliged to cultivate. Artisans formed the next class, merchants the bottom. Movement between regions was strictly regulated, and families or whole villages could be punished for crimes by their kin or neighbors.

The *daimyo* or lords who governed regions were subject to Tokugawa authority and shuffled to different regions if their service was not approved. After 1635, the *daimyo* and their samurai retinue were forced to reside every other year in the city of Edo (Tokyo), the new seat of the shogunate.

Fireman official's garment in Edo

ISOLATION AND THE RISE OF EDO
William Adams, an Englishman who reached Japan on a Dutch ship in 1600, served Ieyasu in various capacities over the next two decades (as portrayed in James Clavell's 1976 book *Shogun*). During this time, the English, Dutch, Portuguese, Spanish, and New World governments made overtures to the shogunate on trade. However, the increasingly xenophobic Tokugawa regime restricted all foreign shipping to Nagasaki from 1635; only Chinese and Dutch traders were allowed from 1641. This heralded 200 years of isolation from the rest of the world. Persecution of Christians intensified.

While Kyoto remained the official capital through the Tokugawa period, Edo eclipsed it in size and was probably the largest city in the world by around 1700. Edo also hosted an explosion of arts such as Kabuki and Bunraku theater *(see pp36–7)* and the *ukiyo-e* works *(see p85)* of Utamaro, Sharaku, Hokusai, and Hiroshige. Patrons included the merchant class and samurai.

In 1853 Commodore Matthew Perry steamed into Edo Bay leading a fleet of nine US vessels to challenge Japan's refusal to enter into international relations. Weakened by unrest from within its own and other ranks, the shogunate could only accede to Perry's demands. Samurai from the Satsuma, Choshu, and Tosa domains in Kyushu, Western Honshu, and Shikoku became the driving force behind a successful restoration of imperial power and a reorganization of the government carried out in 1868.

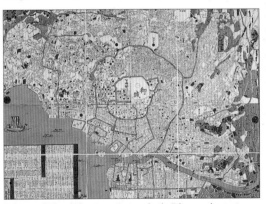

Early map of Edo, which outgrew Kyoto under the Tokugawa shogunate

1748 Kabuki drama *Chushingura* debuts, based on suicide by 47 Ronin

A Hokusai view of Mount Fuji

1831 Hokusai's *Thirty-Six Views of Mount Fuji* published

1725	1750	1775	1800	1825

1723 Love suicides *(joshi),* spurred by rigid customs and hierachy during the Edo period, reach a peak

1782 Tenmei Famine claims as many as 900,000 lives

1853 Commodore Matthew Perry anchors in Edo Bay; Kanagawa Treaty between US and Japan signed

Woodblock print of Sino-Japanese War of 1894-5

MEIJI RESTORATION

Emperor Meiji (1852–1912) was 16 when the restoration of imperial rule was declared on January 3, 1868. Tokyo was swiftly made the new capital.

A new centralized system pressed for changes that would render Japan capable of competing with the West. Military conscription and the elimination of the hereditary samurai class were undertaken to create a modern fighting force, provoking furious resistance from samurai in 1874–6. *Daimyo* domains were gradually transformed into prefectures, although *daimyo* and court nobles lingered in the form of a new class called *kazoku*. Universal literacy became a goal. By 1884, tax and banking reforms, and an industrial strategy aimed at exports were underway. The Meiji Constitution of 1889, promulgated by the emperor, allowed the military direct access to the throne while creating a house of peers and a lower house.

Following disputes over control of the Korean peninsula, the Sino-Japanese War of 1894–5 ended with Japan's victory over China, but showed that greater military strength would be needed

Women in traditional Japanese and 1920s Western dress

for the nation to contend as an imperial power equal with the West.

By the turn of the century, the transformation to an industrial economy, with textiles the chief export, was well underway. A second imperialist conflict, the Russo-Japanese war of 1904–5, ended with Japan aggrandizing its claims to Korea, which was annexed in 1910, and southern Manchuria.

During the final decade of Meiji's reign, the home ministry stressed reverence for the emperor, the family, the Shinto religion, and military and national heroes. Suppression of groups seen as enemies of the state became the government's prerogative.

WAR WITH CHINA AND WORLD WAR II

The attempt to transform Japan from a feudal to a modern industrial state caused severe dislocation. By 1929, when the stock market collapsed, resentment against those who had prospered from exports intensified. Young officers, chafing to restore national pride, began assassinating rich moderates, while militarists and oligarchs in the government believed that seizing land from China and Russia would secure raw materials and improve national security. At the same time, a Pan-Asianist movement, which saw Japan on a mission to lead Asia out of servility, construed the Chinese resistance to Japanese domination as an insult. By 1937, the country was embroiled in an unwinnable war with China that further estranged it from the rest of the world.

TIMELINE

1868 Meiji Restoration; Edo is renamed Tokyo and made capital

1869 Colonization of Hokkaido begins

1889 Imperial constitution promulgated

1890 Imperial Diet convenes for first time

Diet Building

1895 China cedes territory to Japan, ending war. Russia, France, and Germany force Japan to relinquish the territory

1910 Korea becomes Japanese colony

1932 In the May 15 incident, young naval officers assassinate prime minister and attempt coup

1904 Russo-Japanese war begins

1894 Sino-Japanese war begins

1905 Treaty of Portsmouth ends war. Korea becomes a Japanese protectorate

1933 Japan withdraws from League of Nations

1923 Great Kanto Earthquake

1865	1880	1895	1910	1925

Aftermath of the bombing of Tokyo in 1945

When the US cut off Japanese access to oil, Tokyo made the desperate decision to seize Pacific territory in a sneak attack on Pearl Harbor, Hawaii, in December 1941. A few months later, Japan took Southeast Asia.

By 1944, American bombers were decimating Japanese cities, but the Japanese army was determined not to surrender unconditionally, opting instead for a suicidal defensive strategy. In August 1945, the US dropped atomic bombs on Hiroshima and Nagasaki, and the Soviet Union entered the war in the Pacific. Emperor Hirohito ordered the cabinet to sue for peace.

Akihito, who was made emperor in 1989

JAPAN SINCE 1945

Although World War II ended in disaster, the experience mobilized the Japanese people toward instinctive self-discipline and cooperation. The Allied Occupation force under General Douglas MacArthur began arriving as millions of homeless Japanese returned to bombed-out cities. The emperor renounced his divine status; land reform was promptly implemented; and war-crimes trials were soon underway. Against the backdrop of escalating Cold War tensions, the reformist ardor of the occupation leadership soon cooled; a general strike was canceled and communists were purged from government jobs.

By 1952, when the occupation ended, the neighboring war in Korea had turned into a boon for the Japanese economy. Industrial production surged as the average household set its sights on obtaining a washing machine, refrigerator, and television.

In 1960, massive protests against the ratification of the US-Japan Security Treaty rocked Japan, leading to the cancellation of a visit by President Eisenhower. The prime minister resigned. His successors concentrated on economic growth. By the time of the Tokyo Olympics in 1964, annual growth was around ten percent and rising.

Prosperity based on exports like electronics, automobiles, and sophisticated technological products made Japan one of the world's richest nations and also helped keep the Liberal Democratic Party the dominant force in politics since its creation in 1955. The recession of the 1990s (from which Japan is now slowly recovering) along with significant changes in traditional roles in society (see p19), has created a climate for further change.

High-tech games in Roppongi, Tokyo

1937 Sino-Japanese war of 1937–45 begins; 140,000 Chinese massacred in Nanjing

1945 Atomic bombs dropped on Hiroshima and Nagasaki; Japan surrenders

1995 Great Hanshin Earthquake in Kobe; fanatical cult releases sarin gas on Tokyo Subway

1997 Economic recession in Southeast Asia, spreading to Japan

2001 Baby girl born to Crown Prince Naruhito

| 1940 | 1955 | 1970 | 1985 | 2000 | 2015 |

1964 Tokyo Olympics; first "bullet train"; government begins to promote computer industry

2006 Shinzo Abe succeeds Junichiro as prime minister

Prayers of a soldier

1989 Emperor Hirohito (Showa) dies; Akihito is new emperor

1941 Japan enters World War II

Shinkansen ("bullet train")

TOKYO AREA
BY AREA

Tokyo at a Glance

Japan's capital is situated on the banks of the Sumida River, by Tokyo Bay. As the fishing village of Edo it became the shogunate's center of power in 1590. The Shitamachi (low city) of merchants and artisans served the political and intellectual elite in the Yamanote (high city) on the hills to the west. Renamed Tokyo and made capital in 1868, the city was devastated by the Great Kanto Earthquake of 1923, followed by World War II bombing. It has since reinvented itself as one of the world's most modern, exciting, and energizing cities. Transportation is efficient: the easy-to-use Yamanote JR line circles the city, subway lines crisscross the center (*see* Back End Paper), and *shinkansen* lines link it with the rest of the country. It can be difficult to find individual buildings by their addresses *(see pp384–5)*. The Tokyo Street Finder *(see pp114–23)* locates all the sights, restaurants and hotels mentioned in this guide.

LOCATOR MAP

West Shinjuku (see pp92–3) *is an area of soaring skyscrapers, providing a visible manifestation of the corporate wealth of Tokyo. The most impressive buildings are the Tokyo Metropolitan Government Offices, designed by Tange Kenzo.*

WESTERN TOKYO
(see pp88–99)

Shibuya (see pp96–7) *is a mixture of large department stores and smaller shops, all catering to young consumers. Adjacent to Shibuya are the equally fashion-oriented areas of Harajuku and Minami-Aoyama.*

East Shinjuku (see pp90–91) *comes alive when West Shinjuku shuts down. It encompasses a red-light area, countless bars, and various forms of entertainment from movies to pachinko parlors.*

◁ The neon lights and busy streets of East Shinjuku

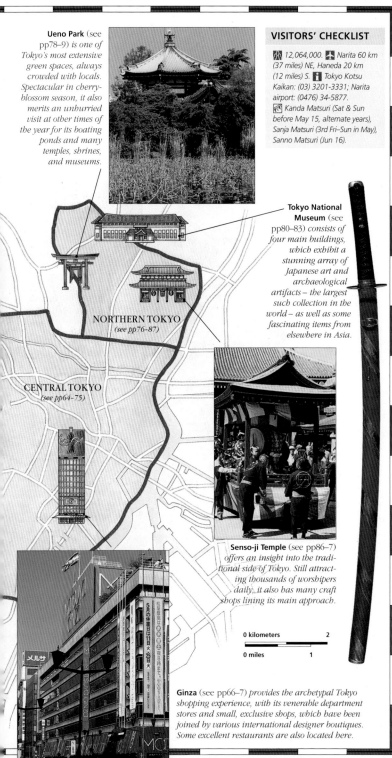

Ueno Park (see pp78–9) is one of Tokyo's most extensive green spaces, always crowded with locals. Spectacular in cherry-blossom season, it also merits an unhurried visit at other times of the year for its boating ponds and many temples, shrines, and museums.

VISITORS' CHECKLIST

🏠 12,064,000. ✈ Narita 60 km (37 miles) NE, Haneda 20 km (12 miles) S. 🛈 Tokyo Kotsu Kaikan: (03) 3201-3331; Narita airport: (0476) 34-5877. 🎎 Kanda Matsuri (Sat & Sun before May 15, alternate years), Sanja Matsuri (3rd Fri–Sun in May), Sanno Matsuri (Jun 16).

Tokyo National Museum (see pp80–83) consists of four main buildings, which exhibit a stunning array of Japanese art and archaeological artifacts – the largest such collection in the world – as well as some fascinating items from elsewhere in Asia.

NORTHERN TOKYO
(see pp76–87)

CENTRAL TOKYO
(see pp64–75)

Senso-ji Temple (see pp86–7) offers an insight into the traditional side of Tokyo. Still attracting thousands of worshipers daily, it also has many craft shops lining its main approach.

| 0 kilometers | 2 |
| 0 miles | 1 |

Ginza (see pp66–7) provides the archetypal Tokyo shopping experience, with its venerable department stores and small, exclusive shops, which have been joined by various international designer boutiques. Some excellent restaurants are also located here.

CENTRAL TOKYO

Situated to the north and west of the Sumida River, this area has been at the heart of Tokyo since the first shogun, Ieyasu, built his castle and capitol where the Imperial Palace still stands today. Destroyed by a series of disasters, including the Great Kanto Earthquake of 1923 and the Allied bombing in World War II, the area has reinvented itself several times over. Ginza and Nihonbashi were commercial centers and are still thriving and prosperous, offering a mix of huge

A kimono-clad woman at Kanda Myojin Shrine

department stores and well-heeled, side-street boutiques. For more down-to-earth shopping, there's the Jinbocho area for books, Akihabara for discount electronics and software, and the early-morning Tsukiji Fish Market. Central Tokyo's continuing political importance is evident in the Hibiya and Marunouchi districts, and the area is also home to two very different shrines: Kanda and Yasukuni. A selection of green spaces provides a respite from the frenetic bustle elsewhere.

SIGHTS AT A GLANCE

Notable Districts
Akihabara Electronics
  District **17**
Ginza see pp66–7 **1**
Hibiya District **10**
Jinbocho Booksellers'
  District **14**
Marunouchi District **8**
Nihonbashi District **7**

Historic Buildings
Diet Building **10**
Imperial Palace **11**
Kabuki-za Theater **2**

Shrines
Kanda Myojin Shrine **16**
Yasukuni Shrine **13**

Modern Architecture
Tokyo International
  Forum **9**
Tokyo Tower **6**

Parks and Gardens
Hama Detached
  Palace Garden **4**
Kitanomaru Park **12**
Koishikawa Korakuen
  Garden **15**
Shiba Park **6**

Market
Tsukiji Fish Market **3**

River Trip
Sumida River
  Trip **5**

KEY

  Street-by-Street map *pp66–7*
S Subway station
R Train station
🚌 Long-distance bus station
ℹ Tourist information

GETTING THERE
The best ways to get around are by Yamanote line or subway, or, for smaller distances, on foot. The Yamanote line stops at Akihabara, Kanda, Tokyo, and Shinbashi stations, while a number of subway lines crisscross the area.

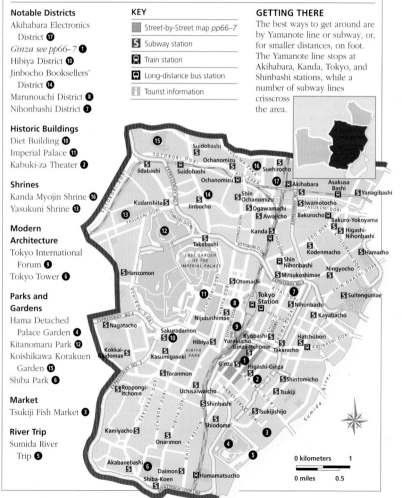

◁ **The San'ai Building at Ginza Yon-chome crossing**

Street-by-Street: Ginza ❶

銀座

When Ieyasu moved his military capital to Edo in
1590, Ginza was all swamp and marshland. Once
filled in, the area attracted tradesmen and merchants.
The silver mint that provided Ginza's name, "silver
place," was built in 1612. In 1872 fire destroyed
everything and, with the Meiji Restoration in full swing,
the government ordered English architect Thomas
Waters to rebuild the area in red brick. From then on
it was the focus for Western influences and all things
modern, and is still one of Tokyo's great centers. Tiny
shops selling traditional crafts mix with galleries, landmark department stores, and the ultra-modern Sony
showroom for an unrivaled shopping experience.

**Shoppers at the Ginza Yon-chome
crossing**

**Mullion Building, housing Hankyu and Seibu
department stores**

Hankyu and Seibu
department stores
focus on fashions,
with a mix of
Japanese and
international
labels.

Gallery Center Building

*On the second floor of this
modern building are a
number of exclusive
galleries showcasing
Japanese and West-
ern art. On the fifth
is an auction house,
and the sixth has
the Youkyo Art Hall,
with exhibits by
artists working in
different media.*

**Ginza Noh
Theater**

Sony Showroom

*Sony's latest technology and gadgets are on
display on several floors here, and many
can be tried out.*

**Namiki-Dori
and Chuo-Dori**
are now called
"Brand Street"
with boutiques
such as Gucci,
Dior, Louis
Vuitton, and
Cartier.

**The Asahi
Building** contains a
traditional kimono
shop, silversmiths,
and several
boutiques.

HARUMI-DORI

SOTOBORI-DORI

NAMIKI-DORI

MIYUKI-DORI

SUZU

KEY

– – –　Suggested walk route

▭▭▭　Train line

For hotels and restaurants in this region see pp298–9 and pp330-31

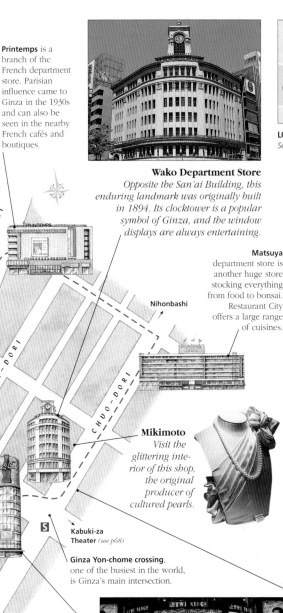

Printemps is a branch of the French department store. Parisian influence came to Ginza in the 1930s and can also be seen in the nearby French cafés and boutiques.

LOCATOR MAP
See Tokyo Street Finder map 5

Wako Department Store
Opposite the San'ai Building, this enduring landmark was originally built in 1894. Its clocktower is a popular symbol of Ginza, and the window displays are always entertaining.

Matsuya
department store is another huge store stocking everything from food to bonsai. Restaurant City offers a large range of cuisines.

Nihonbashi

Mikimoto
Visit the glittering interior of this shop, the original producer of cultured pearls.

Mitsukoshi Department Store
This classic Tokyo store retains an aura of glamour – some people still dress up to shop here. Don't miss the particularly sumptuous kimono department.

Kabuki-za Theater (see p68)

Ginza Yon-chome crossing, one of the busiest in the world, is Ginza's main intersection.

San'ai Building
Made of glass, this building is at its best at dusk when the lights and neon signs inside shine through the glass, creating a magical effect.

0 meters 100

0 yards 100

The curved gable at the front of the Kabuki-za Theater

Kabuki-za Theater ❷

歌舞伎座

Map 5 C3. 4-12-15 Ginza. **Tel** (03) 3541-3131. **S** Higashi-Ginza stn, Toei Asakusa & Hibiya lines. www.shochiku.co.jp/play/ kabukiza/theater/index.html

Tokyo's principal theater for Kabuki (see p37) opened in 1889 during the reign of Emperor Meiji – a part of Kabuki's shift from daytime entertainment for the Shitamachi masses in Asakusa to a more highbrow art form.

The building is one of the oldest surviving examples of the use of Western building materials and techniques in traditional Japanese styles. Its curved front gable was added in 1925 after earthquake damage in 1923. Almost destroyed by the Allied bombing of 1945, the theater was rebuilt in 1951. Performances take place most days (see p108).

Tsukiji Fish Market ❸

築地中央卸売市場

Map 5 C4. **S** Tsukijishijo stn, Toei Oedo line. **◯** 5am–noon Mon–Sat.

A visit to this bustling fish market, officially Tokyo Central Wholesale Market, is an experience unique to Tokyo. It moved to this location from Nihonbashi after the 1923 earthquake and its subsequent fires destroyed the old one.

Every morning except Sunday, auctions are held from about 5am to 10am (the busiest time is 5am to 8am). During this time 15,000 restaurateurs and food sellers from all over the city buy 450 types of sea produce from about 1,700 stalls. The market itself is a huge hangar filled with a maze of tiny stalls, each crammed with fish still dripping sea water. The best way to see it is simply to plunge in. In spite of the frantic pace most people are quite friendly and tolerant of casual visitors. On the same site is a large wholesale vegetable market.

A small bridge marks the entrance to the market. Just before the bridge is **Namiyoke Inari Jinja** (Wave-repelling Fox shrine), where fishermen and traders come to pray for safety and prosperity. Opposite is a street lined with shops selling everything from dried tuna to porcelain dishes. In the alleys to the right are more shops and stalls where excellent and cheap sushi, tempura, even curry, are sold.

When leaving the market, turn left before the bridge for a line of shops and small restaurants. The river wharf where boats unload is over the bridge to the left.

A box of fish from Tsukiji market

Hama Detached Palace Garden ❹

浜離宮庭園

Map 5 B4. **Tel** (03) 3541-0200. **S** Shiodome stn, Oedo line. **R** Shinbashi stn, Yamanote line. **≈** see Sumida River Trip. **◯** 9am–5pm. (Last adm 30 mins before closing.)

Situated where the Sumida River empties into Tokyo Bay, this 25-hectare (62-acre) garden was built in 1654 as a retreat for the shogun's family, who also hunted duck here. America's President Ulysses S. Grant stayed in a villa in the gardens during his visit in 1879 and sipped green tea with Emperor Meiji in Nakajima teahouse.

TUNA FISH SUPPLIES

Tsukiji market specializes in *maguro* (tuna) from as far away as New Zealand and the North Atlantic. Japan consumes about 30 percent of the annual global 1.7 million ton tuna catch, and eats 80 percent of its tuna raw, as sashimi, which requires the best cuts of fish. Suppliers can demand prices of up to 10–20 times that of the lower-grade tuna. The Pacific Ocean's South Blue Fin tuna, a favorite for sashimi, is endangered. The catch is managed and tuna numbers currently seem to be stable, although that may be due to the recession of the 1990s (from which Japan is now slowly recovering). If the economy in Japan starts to boom, South Blue Fin stocks could once again be put under pressure.

Rows of frozen tuna at Tsukiji fish market

The garden grounds surrounding the duck ponds are still a pleasant, uncrowded place to stroll and sit. All of the original teahouses and villas, trees, and vegetation burned down after a bombing raid on November 29, 1944. **Nakajima teahouse** has been faithfully rebuilt, appearing to float over the large pond. Green tea and Japanese sweets are available here.

Nakajima teahouse in Hama Detached Palace Garden

Sumida River Trip ⑤

隅田川の屋形船

Map 5 C4, 4 F3. 🚢 *about every 40 mins; from Hama Detached Palace Garden 10:20am–4:20pm; from Asakusa 9:45am–3:45pm.* 🎫

Tokyo was once a city that lived by its rivers and canals. During the Edo period almost all commerce came to the capital on waterways. As wheeled transport, particularly the railways, grew, the rivers and canals declined.

In recent years, the city's main river, the Sumida, has been cleaned up to an extent, and river traffic is on the increase again. A little-seen view of Tokyo is available on the river trip from Hama Detached Palace Garden to Asakusa in Northern Tokyo. The boat squeezes though a gate in the sea wall into the open water where the Sumida river meets the salt water of Tokyo Bay.

Hinode Pier is the first stop – it is also possible to start from here, and to take a number of other trips around Tokyo Bay. From Hinode the boat starts back up the river, passing first between Tsukiji and **Tsukuda island**, which escaped the worst of the World War II bombing and remains a center of old Edo culture. During the trip the boat passes under 12 bridges, each painted a different color. It is still possible to glimpse people in the narrow parks that line most of the banks beyond the sea walls.

Near Asakusa there are long, low boats that also take out groups for lantern-lit evening cruises.

Shiba Park and Tokyo Tower ⑥

芝公園と東京タワー

Map 5 A4, 2 F5. 🚇 *Shiba-Koen stn, Toei Mita line.* **Tokyo Tower** 🚇 *Akabanebashi stn, Oedo line.* **Tel** *(03) 3433-5111.* ⏰ *9am–10pm daily (to 9pm Aug).* 🎫 *(extra for higher viewpoint).*

Shiba Park is a rather fragmented green space. A large part of it is a golf driving range, but a portion in the east is pleasantly landscaped with woods and a water

The soaring Tokyo Tower, the city's highest viewpoint

course. The park used to be the Tokugawa family's graveyard. At its center is **Zojo-ji**, the family temple of the Tokugawas. It was founded in 1393 and Ieyasu moved it here in 1598 to protect his new capital spiritually from a southeasterly direction. The present-day building dates from 1974; nearby are the rebuilt Daimon (big gate) and the Sanmon (great gate, 1622).

To the west of the park is **Tokyo Tower**. Completed in 1958, at 333 m (1,093 ft) tall, it is higher than the Eiffel Tower in Paris, on which it is based. The ground floor has an aquarium and elevators to the observation deck. Other floors house amusements. You can visit two viewpoints – the main one at 150 m (492 ft) and a higher one at 250 m (820 ft), with more spectacular views. Be sure to go on a clear day.

Tokyo's skyline from the vantage point of the Sumida River

View of Mitsukoshi's central hall in Nihonbashi

Nihonbashi District **❼**

日本橋地区

Map 5 C1–2, 6 D1. **S** *Tokyo stn, Marunouchi line; Nihonbashi stn, Ginza, Tozai & Toei Asakusa lines; Mitsukoshimae stn, Ginza & Hanzomon lines.* **R** *Tokyo stn, many lines.* **Tokyo Stock Exchange** *Tel (03) 3665-1881.* ◐ *9–4pm Mon–Fri.* **Bridgestone Museum of Art** *Tel (03) 3563-0241.* ◐ *10am–8pm Tue–Sat, 10am–6pm Sun & public hols.* ✍

Nihonbashi was the mercantile and entrepreneurial center of Edo and Meiji Tokyo. Its name means "Japan's bridge" after the bridge over the Nihonbashi River that marked the start of the five major highways of the Edo period. After the destruction of the 1923 earthquake, shops, businesses, and banks started relocating to Marunouchi and Ginza; even the fish market moved to Tsukiji.

Although the area never regained its original importance, it is still a thriving commercial center, with dozens of bank headquarters as well as huge department stores and smaller traditional shops. **Mitsukoshi** has its main store here, on Mitsukoshimae. It started as a kimono shop in 1673. Head for the basement food market with its free samples, and the sixth-floor bargain counters where you can jostle with Tokyo's thrifty elite.

A robot trader exhibit, Tokyo Stock Exchange

To the west of Mitsukoshi, the **Bank of Japan**, built in 1896 and modeled on the Neo-Classical Berlin National Bank, was the first Western-style building designed by a Japanese architect, Tatsuno Kingo.

On the north bank of Nihonbashi River, just before **Nihonbashi bridge**, is the bronze marker from which distances to and from Tokyo are still measured. The bridge here today dates from 1911.

On the south bank of the river, east of the bridge, is the **Tokyo Stock Exchange**, which lists around 2,500 companies, making it one of the world's top five. During the "bubble" economy of 1980s, it was possible to watch the frenetic hand signals of the traders. In 1999 trading was completely computerized, but this is still a great place to see how important commerce remains in Tokyo. The visitors' observation deck overlooks the trading floor and has some interesting exhibits comparing stock markets worldwide, with French and English explanations.

To the south of Nihonbashi bridge, the **Bridgestone Museum of Art** holds one of Japan's best collections of Western art, including works by Manet, Picasso, Rouault, and Brancusi. To its north, the **Pokemon Center** is a shop devoted to the famous animation characters.

Marunouchi District **❽**

丸の内地区

Map 5 B1–2. **S** *Tokyo stn, Marunouchi line.* **R** *Tokyo stn, many lines.*

This district lies to the south and west of Tokyo Station. During the Edo era, it earned the name "Gambler's Meadow" as its isolation made it an ideal place to gamble secretly. In the Meiji period the army used it, selling it in 1890 to Mitsubishi. Many laughed at Mitsubishi's apparent folly in buying a barren wasteland. The arrival of the railway increased Marunouchi's desirability as a business site, and firms from elsewhere in the city moved here after the 1923 earthquake.

Tokyo Station, designed by Tatsuno Kingo and completed in 1914, is a brick

Tokyo Station's Western-style façade

building based on the design of Amsterdam station. Its handsome dome was terribly damaged in the 1945 air raids and subsequently replaced by the polyhedron there today.

A short walk west of the station up Miyuki-dori and over the moat via the gently arched Wadakura bridge leads to the **Wadakura Fountain Park**, which contains some interesting water features. Returning over the Wadakura bridge, cross Hibiya-dori and turn right. After about 500 m (550 yds) is the **Meiji Seimei-kan Building** (1934), with its huge Corinthian columns. Hiroshige, the woodblock print artist, was born on this site in 1797. Beyond, the **Imperial Theater** shows Broadway musicals and Japanese popular dramas.

Tokyo International Forum 9

東京国際フォーラム

Map 5 B2. **S** Yurakucho stn, Yurakucho line; Tokyo stn, Marunouchi line. **R** Tokyo and Yurakucho stns, many lines. ○ 8am–11pm daily.

Designed by the American-based Rafael Viñoly, and completed in 1996, the Forum is one of downtown Tokyo's most distinctive and enjoyable buildings *(see p25)*. A cultural center, it is made up of two buildings: a curved, glass atrium soaring 60 m (200 ft), and a cube-like, white structure housing four halls (the largest seating 5,012). A tree-shaded courtyard separates the two, while glass walkways provide an overhead link.

The interior of the huge atrium is filled with light and has a ceiling resembling a ship's hull. Inside the Forum are a number of shops, cafés, and restaurants, all supported by state-of-the-art facilities. You can also enjoy surfing the world wide web from internet stations in the lobby.

The imposing granite exterior of the Diet Building

Hibiya District and the Diet Building 10

日比谷地区と国会議事堂

Map 2 F3, 5 A2, 5 B2. **S** Kokkai-Gijidomae stn, Chiyoda & Marunouchi lines; Hibiya stn, Toei Mita, Chiyoda & Hibiya lines. **Hibiya Park** ○ 24 hours daily. **Diet Building** ○ 9am–5pm Mon–Fri. 🎦 (compulsory, by reservation)

Central Tokyo's only large, Western-style park, Hibiya Park is the focus of Hibiya district. Its location, east of the political centers of Kasumigaseki and the Diet Building, makes it a favorite place for protests, especially on May Day. The large bandstand is occasionally used for concerts.

Completed in 1936, the **Diet Building** houses the legislature of the Japanese government, originally established as the Imperial Diet in the Meiji era. Tours (in Japanese only) cover the well-worn inside, including the diet chamber, where you can see the deliberations of diet members, and the extravagantly decorated rooms used by the emperor for official functions.

Imperial Palace 11

皇居

Map 3 A5, 3 B5, 5 A1, 5 B1. **S** Nijubashi stn, Chiyoda line. **R** Tokyo stn, many lines. **Imperial Palace** ○ Jan 2, Dec 23. **East Garden of the Imperial Palace** *Tel* (03) 3213-2050. ○ 9am–4pm Tue–Thu, Sat, Sun (Nov–Feb: to 3:30pm).

Ieyasu, the first Tokugawa shogun, started building his castle here in 1590. In the Edo period his successors made this into the world's largest castle; now only the inner circle remains. The emperor and his family still live in the western part of the grounds in the **Imperial Palace**, rebuilt after the previous one was bombed in World War II. Public access is allowed twice a year: at New Year and on the emperor's birthday. The rest of the grounds, bounded by the moat, is divided into public parks.

The most famous landmark is the **Nijubashi**, a double-arched stone bridge, east of the palace. Completed in 1888, it was the palace's main entrance. The huge **Otemon** (Big Hand Gate), rebuilt in 1967, was the main gate before Nijubashi was built. Now it is the entrance to the **East Garden of the Imperial Palace**. Just inside is **Sannomaru Shozokan**, a collection of art and artifacts of the Showa Emperor. Beyond is the Edo-era **Hyakunin Basho**, where 100 samurai lived while standing guard in shifts. Behind is the **Honmaru**, the castle's main keep, now just massive stone walls with good views from the top. To the east of the Honmaru is the restful **Ninomaru** garden, landscaped by shogun Iemitsu in 1630.

A glimpse of the Imperial Palace over Nijubashi

The airy glass-and-metal interior of the Tokyo International Forum

Tokyo-ites enjoying a summer picnic in Kitanomaru Park

Kitanomaru Park ⓬
北の丸公園

Map 3 A5. **S** *Kudanshita stn, Hanzomon, Toei Shinjuku & Tozai lines; Takebashi stn, Tozai line.* **National Museum of Modern Art** *Tel (03) 5777-8600.* ⏰ *10am–5pm Tue–Sun.* 📷 www.momat.go.jp/english **Crafts Gallery** *Tel (03) 3211-7781.* ⏰ *10am–5pm Tue–Sun.* 📷 **Science and Technology Museum** *Tel (03) 3212-8544.* ⏰ *9:30am–4pm daily.* 📷 www.jsf.or.jp/english

Lying to the north of the Imperial Palace, Kitanomaru Park is reached through the massive **Tayasumon** (gate). A former ground for the Imperial Palace Guard, the area became a park in 1969. Before entering, walk past with Tayasumon on the left to reach **Chidorigafuchi** (the west moat), one of Tokyo's most beautiful cherry-blossom viewing spots. Row boats can be rented here.

Within Kitanomaru's pleasant grounds are a number of buildings. Near Tayasumon is the **Nippon Budokan** (*see p361*). Built for the 1964 Olympics martial arts competition, it is now used mostly for rock concerts. A short walk farther on is the **Science and Technology Museum**. Some of the interactive exhibits are

fun, including virtual bike rides and electricity demonstrations (explanations are in Japanese).

Five minutes beyond, over a main road and left down the hill, is the **National Museum of Modern Art**. The permanent collection comprises Japanese works from the 1868 Meiji Restoration to the present day; visiting exhibits are often excellent. Nearby is the National Museum of Modern Art's **Crafts Gallery**. Inside this 1910 Neo-Gothic brick building is an exquisite collection of modern workings of traditional Japanese crafts – pottery, lacquerware, and damascene (etched metal artifacts). Some pieces are for sale.

Yasukuni Shrine ⓭
靖国神社

Map 2 F1. *Tel (03) 3261-8326.* **S** *Kudanshita stn, Hanzomon, Tozai & Toei Shinjuku lines.* ⏰ *24 hours daily.* www.yasukini.or.jp/english **Yushukan** ⏰ *9am–5:30pm daily Mar–Oct (9am–5pm Nov–Feb).* 📷

The 2.5 million Japanese, soldiers and civilians, who have died in war since the Meiji Restoration are enshrined at Yasukuni Jinja (Shrine of Peace for the Nation), which was dedicated in 1879. Its history makes it a sobering place to visit.

Until the end of World War II Shinto was the official state religion, and the ashes of all who died in war were brought here regardless of the families' wishes. Unsettling for some of Japan's neighbors, the planners and leaders of World War II and the colonization of China and Korea are

also enshrined here, including wartime prime minister, Tojo Hideki, and eight other Class-A war criminals. Visits by cabinet ministers, even in a private capacity, are controversial.

Beside the shrine is the **Yushukan**, a museum dedicated to the war dead. Many exhibits put a human face on Japan at war: under a photo of a smiling young officer is a copy of his last letter home, and there are mementos of a nurse who died from overwork. Still, romanticized paintings of Japanese soldiers in Manchuria and displays of guns, planes, and even a locomotive from the Thai-Burma Railway may be troubling to some.

Jinbocho Booksellers' District ⓮
神保町古本屋街

Map 3 B4–5. **S** *Jinbocho stn, Toei Mita, Hanzomon & Toei Shinjuku lines.*

Three of Japan's great universities, Meiji, Chuo, and Nihon, started out in this area in the 1870s and 1880s, and soon booksellers sprang up selling both new and used books. At one time 50 percent of Japan's publishers were based here. Although only Meiji University is still here, dozens of bookshops, several selling *ukiyo-e* prints, remain, all clustered around the junction of Yasukuni-dori and Hakusan-dori. For English books on Oriental subjects try **Kitazawa Books** or **Issei-do**; for *ukiyo-e* prints, visit **Oya Shobo** – all are on the south side of Yasukuni-dori, walking away from Hakusan-dori.

The change in the economic status (and priorities) of students is evident here. Shops selling

Browsing in one of Jinbocho's bookshops

surf- or snowboards are everywhere. Music shops selling electric guitars seem as numerous as the bookshops.

Tsutenkyo bridge in Koishikawa Korakuen Garden

Koishikawa Korakuen Garden ⑮

小石川後楽園

Map 3 A3–4. **Tel** (03) 3811-3015. Ⓢ Korakuen stn, Marunouchi & Namboku lines. ◯ 9am–5pm daily. 📷

Korakuen, meaning "garden of pleasure last," is one of Tokyo's best traditional stroll gardens, a delightful place to spend a few restful hours. The name Korakuen comes from the Chinese poem *Yueyang Castle* by Fan Zhongyan: "Be the first to take the world's trouble to heart, be the last to enjoy the world's pleasure."

Construction of the garden started in 1629 and finished 30 years later. Once four times its present size of almost 8 hectares (20 acres), it belonged to the Mito branch of the Tokugawa family. An exiled Chinese Scholar, Zhu Shun Shui, helped design the garden including the **Engetsukyo** (full-moon) **bridge**, a stone arch with a reflection resembling a full moon. **Tsukenkyo bridge**, a copy of a bridge in Kyoto, is striking for the contrast between the vermilion of the bridge with the surrounding deep green forest.

The garden represents larger landscapes in miniature. Rozan, a famous Chinese sightseeing mountain, and Japan's Kiso River are two famous geographic features recreated here. In the middle of the large pond is **Horai island**, a beautiful composition of stone and pine trees.

Kanda Myojin Shrine ⑯

神田明神

Map 3 C4. **Tel** (03) 3254-0753. Ⓢ Ochanomizu stn, Marunouchi line. 🚉 Ochanomizu stn, Chuo & Sobu lines. ◯ 24 hours daily. **Museum** ◯ 10am–4pm Sat, Sun & public hols. 📷 🎏 Kanda Matsuri (mid-May in alternate, odd-numbered years).

Myojin is more than 1,200 years old, although the present structure is a reproduction built after the 1923 earthquake. The gate's guardian figures are two beautifully dressed, tight-lipped archers: Udaijin on the right and Sadaijin on the left. Just inside the compound on the left is a large stone statue of Daikoku, one of the *shichi-fuku-jin* (seven lucky gods). Here, as always, he is sitting on top of two huge rice bales.

Lions on the gate to Kanda Myojin Shrine

The vermilion shrine itself and its beautiful interior, all lacquer and gold and ornate Chinese-style decoration, are very impressive. Early morning is the best time to glimpse the Shinto priests performing rituals. The Kanda Matsuri *(see pp42–3)* is one of the greatest and grandest of Tokyo's festivals – come early and be prepared for crowds.

Behind the main shrine is a **museum** containing relics from the long history of Myojin. There are also several small shrines, hemmed in by the surrounding office blocks.

Akihabara Electronics District ⑰

秋葉原電気店街

Map 3 C4. Ⓢ Akihabara stn, Hibiya line. 🚉 Akihabara stn, Yamanote, Chuo & Sobu lines.

Akihabara electronics district surrounds Akihabara station. Directly under the station is a bazaar of tiny shops along narrow aisles selling any electronic device, simple or complex, from Christmas-tree lights to the latest chip. The market grew out of the ruins of World War II when the Japanese army had surplus equipment they wanted to dispose of. Students from the nearby universities, who desperately needed money, bought the surplus army parts and made radios – status symbols and much in demand – to sell on roadsides or in tiny shops here. Akihabara and electronics have been synonymous ever since. Later as the economy improved, the focus changed to televisions, washing machines, and refrigerators. You can still see these, dozens at a time, on display, but increasingly the emphasis is on computers, cell phones, and video games.

Brand-name goods are available at a three to ten percent discount – sometimes more. On Chuo-dori, **Laox** *(see p107)* is a famous source of tax-free goods for tourists.

Colorful shop fronts and advertisements in Akihabara district

Bustling electronics shops and stalls under the tracks at Akihabara ▷

NORTHERN TOKYO

The northern districts of Ueno and Asakusa contain what remains of Tokyo's old Shitamachi (low city). Once the heart and soul of Edo culture *(see p57)*, Shitamachi became the subject of countless *ukiyo-e* woodblock prints *(see p85)*. Merchants and artisans thrived here, as did Kabuki theater *(see p37)* and the Yoshiwara pleasure district near Asakusa. The last great battle in Japan took place in Ueno in 1868 when the Emperor Meiji's forces defeated the Tokugawa shogunate. Ueno and Asakusa are the best parts of Tokyo for just strolling and observing. Life in Asakusa still

In festival costume at Senso-ji Temple

revolves around the bustling Senso-ji Temple, its main approach packed with shops. Ueno is dominated by its huge park containing the National and Shitamachi Museums, among others. It is still possible to find pockets of narrow streets lined with tightly packed homes, especially in the Yanaka area, which escaped destruction by war and earthquake. Shopping is a pleasure in Northern Tokyo: as well as the traditional arts and crafts shops near Senso-ji Temple, there are specialists in plastic food in Kappabashi-dori, religious goods in neighboring Inaricho, and electronic items at Ameyoko Market.

SIGHTS AT A GLANCE

Temples
Senso-ji Temple pp86–7 **7**

Parks and Gardens
Ueno Park pp78–9 **1**

Notable Districts
Inaricho District and
  Kappabashi-dori **6**
Yanaka District **4**

Museums
Shitamachi Museum **3**
Tokyo National Museum
  pp80–83 **2**

Markets
Ameyoko
  Market **5**

KEY

S Subway station

R Train station

i Tourist information

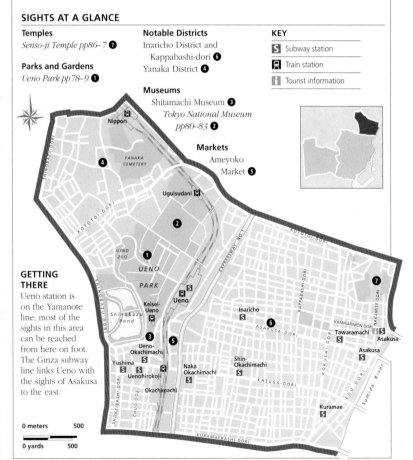

GETTING THERE
Ueno station is on the Yamanote line; most of the sights in this area can be reached from here on foot. The Ginza subway line links Ueno with the sights of Asakusa to the east.

0 meters   500
0 yards   500

◁ Detail of a kimono from a Noh play in the Tokyo National Museum

Ueno Park ❶

上野公園

Ieyasu, the first Tokugawa shogun, built the Kanei-ji temple and subtemples here in the 17th century to negate evil spirits that might threaten from the northeast. Judging by how long the Tokugawas lasted, it was a wise move. In 1873, five years after the Battle of Ueno, when the last supporters of the shogun were crushed by Imperial forces, the government designated Ueno a public park. A favorite since its earliest days, the park has figured in many popular woodblock prints and short stories. The Shinobazu pond (actually three ponds) is an annual stop for thousands of migrating birds. Several museums and temples are dotted around the park, and Japan's oldest and best zoo is here.

Boating on the Shinobazu pond

The Tokyo Metropolitan Art Museum, in a modern red-brick building, has a large collection of contemporary Japanese art, plus special exhibitions.

Ueno Zoo

★ Pagoda

This landmark five-story pagoda dates from the 17th century and is a survivor from the original Kanei-ji temple complex. Today it stands in the grounds of Ueno Zoo, a popular destination for Japanese schoolchildren, among others, due to its giant pandas.

★ Tosho-gu Shrine

This ornate complex of halls is one of Tokyo's few remaining Edo-era structures. Ieyasu was enshrined here and later reburied at Nikko (see pp264–71).

The Great Buddhist Pagoda was built in 1967. A Buddha statue formerly stood on the site; only its head remains.

The Gojo shrine is reached through a series of red *torii* (gates). Inside, red-bibbed Inari fox statues stand in an atmospheric grotto.

Benten Hall

Shinobazu pond

Shitamachi Museum (see p84)

KEY

ℹ️ Tourist information

STAR SIGHTS

★ Tokyo National Museum

★ Tosho-gu Shrine

★ Pagoda

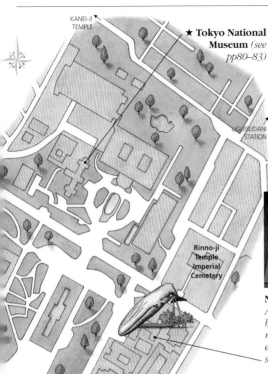

★ **Tokyo National Museum** *(see pp80–83)*

KANEI-JI TEMPLE

UGUISUDANI STATION

Rinno-ji Temple Imperial Cemetery

Baseball ground

Tokyo Metropolitan Festival Hall

UENO STATION

Japan Art Academy

Ueno Royal Museum

The main walkway is lined with hundreds of cherry trees. Boisterous *hanami* (blossom-viewing) parties are held here each spring.

The Tomb of the Shogi Tai is a small, leafy area containing two tombstones to the many samurai who died in the 1868 Battle of Ueno.

VISITORS' CHECKLIST

Map 3 C2–3, 4 D2. **S** *Ueno stn, Hibiya & Ginza lines.* Ueno & Uguisudani stns, many lines. **Ueno Zoo** 9:30am–5pm Tue–Sun. **Tokyo Metropolitan Art Museum** 9am–5pm Tue–Sun. **National Science Museum** 9am–4:30pm Tue–Sun. **National Museum of Western Art** 9:30am–5pm Tue–Sun.

National Science Museum
A steam engine and life-sized blue whale model mark this museum's entrance. Inside are exhibits on natural history, science, and technology.

National Museum of Western Art
Rodin's massive Gate of Hell *stands outside this building by Le Corbusier. On display are various Impressionist works, plus paintings by Rubens, Pollock, and others.*

Saigo Takamori Statue
The leader of the victorious Meiji forces, Saigo subsequently instigated the Satsuma rebellion against the emperor in 1877, but killed himself when it failed. He was posthumously pardoned, and this statue was erected in 1899.

0 meters 100

0 yards 100

Kiyo-mizu Hall
Part of the original Kanei-ji temple, this dates from 1631 and is dedicated to Senju (1,000-armed) Kannon. Kosodate Kannon, the bosatsu of conception, is also here, surrounded by numerous offerings of dolls.

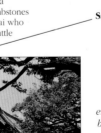

Tokyo National Museum ②

東京国立博物館

The group of buildings that makes up the Tokyo
National Museum is in a compound in the northeast corner of Ueno Park; tickets to all buildings are
available at the entrance gate. The Honkan is the
main building. To its east is the Toyokan (see p82).
The 1908 Beaux-Arts Hyokeikan is mainly used for
special exhibitions. Behind it is the Gallery of Horyu-ji
Treasures, containing stunning objects from Nara's
Horyu-ji temple, and the Heiseikan (see p83). More
than 110,000 items make up the collection – the best
assembly of Japanese art in the world – and the
displays change frequently.

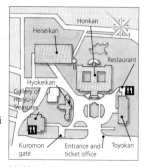

**MUSEUM COMPLEX
LOCATOR MAP**

Noh and Kabuki
*One of the exquisite
kimonos that forms
part of the textile
and mask collection,
this dates from the 16th
century when it was
used in a Noh play* (see p36).
*It depicts lilies and court
vehicles.*

Heiseikan

First floor

The museum shop
in the basement can
be reached via twin
staircases outside
and a central
one inside.

This building dates from
1938 and combines Japanese
and Western features.

GALLERY OF HORYU-JI TREASURES
When the estates of the Horyu-ji temple
(see p196) in Nara were seized as part of the
Meiji reforms, the impoverished temple
gave a number of its treasures to the
imperial family in exchange for money
to finance its repairs. Over 300 of those
priceless treasures are
housed in this modern
gallery, including rare
and early Buddhist
statues, masks used for
Gigaku dances, and
beautifully painted
screens.

Entrance

**Steps down to
museum shop**

**7th-century
gilt-bronze
Kannon statue**

**Rikishi mask, used for
Gigaku dances, 8th century**

★ Ukiyo-e and Costumes
Popular from the mid-17th through the 19th century, these wood block prints depicted everything from kabuki stars to famous landscapes, scenes of market life to scenes from the pleasure quarters, like this 18th-century print of "Beauty with Clock".

VISITORS' CHECKLIST

Map 3 C2, 4 D2. *Tel* (03) 3822-1111. **S** *Ueno stn, Hibiya & Ginza lines.* **R** *Ueno stn, many lines; Uguisudani stn, Yamanote line.* ◯ *9:30am–5pm Tue–Sun.* ♿ *www.tnm.jp*

Courtly Art
This collection includes scrolls, woodblock prints, and screens. This 16th-century gold screen is illustrated with a procession of noblemen, a scene from the Tale of Genji *(see p52).*

★ National Treasures
The themed exhibition in the National Treasures room changes about every five weeks. Exhibits may be of calligraphy, Buddhist statues, tea utensils, or even armor, like this 16th-century Muromachi period Domaru armor.

KEY TO FLOOR PLAN

- ☐ Donations Gallery
- ☐ Thematic Exhibition
- ☐ Sculpture
- ☐ Lacquerware and ceramics
- ☐ Ainu and Ryukyu materials
- ☐ Modern Art
- ☐ Ukiyo-e, costumes, Noh & Kabuki
- ☐ National Treasures
- ☐ Military Attire
- ☐ Decorative Arts
- ☐ Interior Furnishings and Painting
- ☐ Courtly Art
- ☐ Swords

Second floor

★ Sculpture
This serene, wooden 12th-century sculpture of the Juichimen Kannon Bosatsu (11-faced goddess of mercy) is about 3 m (10 ft) high. Mainly Buddhist, the pieces in the sculpture collection range from miniature to monumental.

GALLERY GUIDE: HONKAN
The collection is on two floors. The second floor is a counterclockwise, chronological arrangement of Japanese art as it develops from the Jomon era (from 10,000 BC) clay figures to 19th-century Ukiyo-e woodblock prints. In between is everything from calligraphy and tea utensils to armor, as well as textiles used in Noh and Kabuki. The first floor also works best when viewed counterclockwise. Its rooms are themed, with stunning exhibits of sculpture, lacquerware, swords, and Western-influenced modern art.

STAR COLLECTIONS

★ Sculpture

★ Ukiyo-e and Costumes

★ National Treasures

Tokyo National Museum: Toyokan

Opened in 1968, the Toyokan (Asian Gallery) has an excellent and eclectic collection of non-Japanese Eastern art, including textiles, sculpture, and ceramics. Many of the exhibits are from China and Korea – a result of their long ties with Japan. The layout of the three floors is in a rough spiral; a well-marked route takes visitors from the sculpture on the first floor up to the Korean collection at the top.

★ Korean Art
Dating from the Bronze Age (100 BC–AD 300), this dagger is one of the older pieces on display in the Korean collection.

★ Chinese Ceramics
Ceramics, such as this 8th-century Tang-dynasty camel, feature in the Chinese art section, along with bronzes, scrolls, jade, textiles, and glassware.

Chinese Buddha
One of a number of beautiful Buddhist statues on the first floor, this 11-faced Avalokitesvara from Xian in China dates from the 11th century.

Entrance

Third floor

Second floor

First floor

Vietnamese Ceramic Bowl
This delicately decorated 15th–16th-century bowl is part of the collection of Asian art on the first floor, which also includes fabrics and statuary.

KEY TO FLOOR PLAN

- ☐ Chinese and Indian sculpture
- ☐ Egyptian and West, Southeast, and South Asian art
- ☐ Chinese art and antiquities
- ☐ Korean and Central Asian art and antiquities
- ☐ Non-exhibition space

STAR COLLECTIONS

★ Chinese Ceramics

★ Korean Art

Indian Sculpture
This 2nd–3rd-century figure, from the borders of modern Afghanistan and Pakistan, is grouped with the Indian sculptures on the first floor.

Tokyo National Museum: Heiseikan

The Heiseikan opened in 1999 and was purpose-built to house major temporary exhibitions and a superb collection of Japanese archaeological artifacts. Its modern facilities do full justice to the fascinating displays. The first floor houses the Japanese archaeology gallery, with items from 10,000–7,000 BC onward. The temporary exhibitions on the second floor are of mainly – but not only – Japanese art. Captions are in English and Japanese.

KEY TO FLOOR PLAN

▨	Archaeological exhibits
▨	Temporary exhibitions
▢	Non-exhibition space

First floor

★ Haniwa Male Figure
This haniwa *is dressed as a warrior. Other human figures that have survived include singers, dancers, and farmers.*

★ Haniwa Horse
Haniwa *literally means "clay ring", and is used to describe earthenware sculptures that were made for 4th–7th-century tombs and were thought to protect the dead. Many forms have been found, including horses and other animals.*

Second floor

Entrance

STAR COLLECTIONS

★ Haniwa Sculptures

★ Jomon Figures

Honkan

Fukabachi Bowl
This large cooking pot is a fine example of Jomon pottery, which is among the oldest in the world. The curved, deep sides allowed the fire to be built up around it, while the flattened base ensured it could be balanced when in the hearth.

★ Jomon Figures
The prehistoric Jomon period (14,500–300BC) is thought to have produced Japan's first pottery, including dogu. This figurine is one of several female figures characterized by bulging eyes.

Shitamachi Museum ❸

下町風俗資料館

2-1 Ueno-koen, Taito-ku. **Map** 3 C3.
Tel (03) 3823-7451. **S** *Ueno stn,
Hibiya & Ginza lines.* **R** *Keisei-Ueno
stn, Keisei line; Ueno stn, many lines.*
⏱ *9:30am–4pm Tue–Sun.* 🖼

Dedicated to preserving the
spirit and artifacts of
Shitamachi *(see p77)*, this
museum is both
fascinating and fun. On
the first floor are re-
creations of Edo-era
shops such as a candy
store and a copper-
smith's. Second-
floor exhibits in-
clude traditional
toys, tools, and
photographs. All
50,000 exhibits were donated
by Shitamachi residents. The
nearby **Shitamachi Museum
Annex** (north of Ueno Park)
is in the traditional style of
shop-houses of the mid-Edo
period (late 17th century).

**Meiji-period doll,
Shitamachi Museum**

Yanaka District ❹

谷中地区

Map 3 C1. **R** *Nippori stn, many lines.*
Asakura Museum *Tel (03) 3821-4549.*
⏱ *9:30am–4:30pm Tue–Thu, Sat–Sun.*
🖼 **Daimyo Clock Museum** *Tel (03)
3821-6913.* ⏱ *Jan 15–Jun 30, Oct 1–
Dec 24: 10am–4pm Tue–Sun.* 🖼

This quiet area is rewarding
to wander through because
it survived the 1923 earthquake and bombing of World
War II. It preserves something
of the feel of old Shitamachi
with tightly packed houses
in narrow alleys, and
traditional food stalls
selling rice crackers and
old-fashioned candy.
The large **Yanaka
cemetery** is a must-see in
cherry-blossom season. Inside
is **Tenno-ji**, a temple with a
large bronze Buddha dating
from 1690. Nearby are tea
shops and florists. To the
west of Tenno-ji is the
Asakura Museum, home
of sculptor Asakura
Fumio (1883–1964). On
the second floor is a
delightful room full of
his small statues of
one of his favorite
subjects – cats – but
the garden is the real
highlight with a trad-
itional composition
of water and stone.
Sansaki-dori, the
area's main street, has some
traditional shops. The
understated **Daimyo Clock
Museum** has 100 Edo-era
clocks lovingly presented.

Ameyoko Market ❺

アメ横

Map 3 C3. **S** *Ueno stn, Hibiya &
Ginza lines; Ueno-Okachimachi stn,
Oedo line.* **R** *Okachimachi stn,
Yamanote line; Ueno stn, many lines.*

One of the great bazaars in
Asia, Ameyoko is a place
where anything is available,
almost always at a discount.
In Edo times this was the
place to come and buy *ame*
(candy). After World War II
black-market goods, such as
liquor, cigarettes, chocolates,
and nylons started appearing
here, and *ame* acquired its

**Shopping for a bargain at
Ameyoko Market**

second meaning as an
abbreviation for American
(*yoko* means alley). An area
of tiny shops packed under
the elevated train tracks,
Ameyoko is no longer a black
market but is still is the place
for bargain foreign brands,
including Chanel, Nike, and
Rolex. Clothes and accessories
are concentrated under the
tracks, while foods, including
a huge range of fish, line the
street that follows the tracks.

Inaricho District and Kappabashi-dori ❻

稲荷町地区とかっぱ橋通り

Map 4 D3, 4 E2–3. **S** *Inaricho &
Tawaramachi stns, Ginza line.*

Inaricho is the Tokyo headquarters for wholesale
religious goods. Small wooden
boxes to hold Buddhas and
family photos, paper lanterns,
bouquets of brass flowers
(*jouka*), Shinto household
shrines, and even prayer beads
can be found here. Most of
the shops lie on the south side
of Asakusa-dori, in the stretch
between between Inaricho
and Tawaramachi stations.
Kappabashi-dori, named after
the mythical water imps
(*kappa*) who supposedly
helped built a bridge (*bashi*)
here, is Tokyo's center for
kitchenware and the source of
the plastic food displayed in
almost every restaurant window.
Although the "food" is for sale,
prices are much higher than
for the real thing.

Some of the surviving old houses in Yanaka district

For hotels and restaurants in this region see p299 and p331

The Floating World of Ukiyo-e

In the Edo period, woodblock prints, called *ukiyo-e*, or pictures of the pleasure-seeking "floating world," became the most popular pictorial art of Japan. They had a profound influence on artists such as Matisse and Van Gogh. Although today they are credited to individual artists, they were in fact a cooperative effort between the publisher, responsible for financing and distributing the work; the artist, who produced a fine line drawing; the carver, who pasted the drawings onto blocks of wood and

Two Kabuki actors by Sharaku

carved away what was not to appear on the print, making one block for each color; and the printer, who inked the wooden blocks and pressed them onto the paper – one for each color, starting with the lightest. Editions were limited to 100–200 copies. The first artist known by name was Moronobu, who died in 1694. The golden age of *ukiyo-e* lasted from about 1790 to the 1850s. Beautiful women, Kabuki actors, scenes from Japan, including Shitamachi, and the supernatural were recurring themes.

A full-color *calendar of beautiful women published by Suzuki Harunobu in 1765 marked a transition from the earlier black-and-white techniques. Highly popular (and a moneymaker), the calendar's success attracted both financiers and artists to the medium.*

After *Harunobu's calendar, depictions of women were individualized and eroticized by artists such as Kitagawa Utamaro and Torii Kiyonaga. This print is by Utamaro.*

Landscape *prints were dominated by Hokusai (1760–1849) and his younger rival Hiroshige (1797–1858). This print is from the latter's Fifty-Three Stations of the Tokaido.*

This 1825 print *by Hokusai shows the carving and printing stages of woodblock print making. Printers relied on vegetable dyes, some of which were very expensive. The red dye* beni, *derived from safflowers, could be worth more than its weight in gold. Some prints required up to a dozen colors.*

Ghosts and goblins *were a favorite theme, especially in summer (to be scared was thought to be cooling). Utagawa Kuniyoshi (whose print is shown here), Taiso Yoshitoshi, and Kobayashi Kiyochika were masters of the genre, which marked the end of ukiyo-e 's golden age.*

Senso-ji Temple **❼**

浅草寺

Stroking the Nadi Botokesan Buddha

Popularly known as Asakusa Kannon, this is Tokyo's most sacred and spectacular temple. In AD 628, two fishermen fished a small gold statue of Kannon, the Buddhist goddess of mercy, from the Sumida River. Their master built a shrine to Kannon, then in 645, the holy man Shokai built a temple to her. Its fame, wealth, and size grew until Tokugawa Ieyasu bestowed upon it a large stipend of land. The Yoshiwara pleasure quarter moved nearby in 1657 only increasing its popularity. The temple survived the 1923 earthquake but not World War II bombing. Its main buildings are therefore relatively new, but follow the Edo-era layout. While these buildings are impressive, it is the people following their daily rituals that make this place so special.

Awashima Hall is dedicated to a deity who looks after women.

The garden of Dembo-in (abbot's residence) is a tranquil stroll garden used as a training center for monks. It is a masterly arrangement of woods, bamboo groves, lawns, and water.

Five-Story Pagoda
This replica of the original was constructed in 1973.

Nade Botokesan Buddha
This delicate statue has been polished smooth by the hands of those hoping for good luck and help with ailments.

★ Nakamise-dori
This street is a treasure trove of traditional wares, including specialists in obi sashes, haircombs, fans, dolls, and kimonos.

Kaminarimon Gate
"Thunder Gate" burned down in 1865 and was not rebuilt until 1960. The guardian statues of Fujin (right) and Raijin (left) have old heads and new bodies.

For more details about individual shops here, see pages 106–107

To Asakusa stations and tourist information office

This hexagonal temple is a rare survivor from the 15th or 16th century.

★ Main Hall
Inside the hall (1958) the gold-plated main shrine houses the original Kannon image. Worshipers come to pay their respects by throwing coins and lighting candles.

Yougoudo Hall houses eight recent Buddha statues.

Asakusa Jinja, built in 1649, is a shrine dedicated to the men who found the Kan

★ Main Hall
Several large paintings hang inside the main hall. The painting of angels with lotus flowers is a 20th-century work by Domoto Insho.

Niten-mon Gate was built in 1618 as the entrance to the original Tosho-gu shrine.

Statues donated by a wealthy Edo merchant

Benten-yama Shoro belfry stands amid a group of temple buildings. The bell used to ring on the hour in Edo.

Incense Burner
One of the temple's focal points, this incense burner (joukoro) is constantly surrounded by people wafting the smoke over them to keep them healthy.

Hozo-mon Gate
Built in 1964 of reinforced concrete, this two-story gate has a treasure house upstairs holding a number of 14th-century Chinese sutras.

STAR SIGHTS

★ Nakamise-dori

★ Main Hall

WESTERN TOKYO

S hinjuku and Shibuya, the dual centers of Western Tokyo, three stops apart on the Yamanote line, started to boom only after the 1923 earthquake. This part of the city is new Tokyo – all vitality and energy, fast-paced, constantly changing, and challenging the more traditional pleasures of Central and Northern Tokyo. Modern architectural landmarks are dotted around, from the Olympic Stadiums of Yoyogi Park to the magnificent twin-towered home for the city government

All dressed up in Harajuku

in West Shinjuku. Shibuya, along with neighboring Harajuku and Minami-Aoyama, is the epi-center of both young and haute-couture Japanese fashon. Nightlife is also in plentiful supply with Rop-pongi's cosmopolitan clubs, bars, and music venues, and the neon lights and *pachinko* par-lors of East Shinjuku. In these overwhelmingly modern sur-roundings, historical sights are few and far between but include the popular Meiji Shrine and the nearby Sword Museum.

SIGHTS AT A GLANCE

Notable Districts
Akasaka District ⑪
East Shinjuku pp90–91 ❶
Harajuku District ❼
Minami-Aoyama District ❾
Roppongi District ❿
Shibuya pp96–7 ❽
West Shinjuku pp92–3 ❷

Shrines
Meiji Shrine ❺

Museums
Sword Museum ❹

Stations
Shinjuku Station ❸

Parks
Yoyogi Park ❻

GETTING THERE
Shinjuku, Shibuya, Harajuku, and Yoyogi are all on the Yamanote line. The Ginza and Hanzomon subway lines stop in or near Harajuku, Minami-Aoyama, and Akasaka, and the Hibiya line serves Roppongi.

KEY

▨	Street-by-Street map pp90–91
▨	Street-by-Street map p92
▨	Street-by-Street map pp96–7
S	Subway station
R	Train station
▤	Long-distance bus station

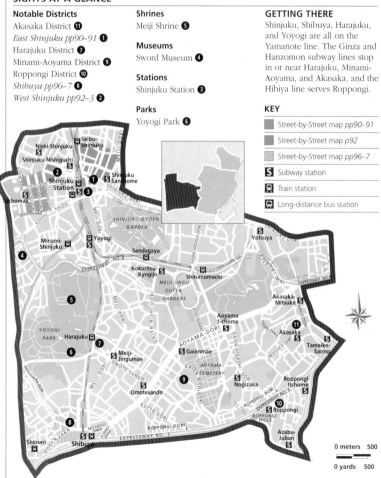

Street-by-Street: East Shinjuku ❶

東新宿

Façade of a café in Shinjuku

East Shinjuku is where Tokyo plays. The area has been a nightlife center from Edo times on, when it was the first night stop on the old Tokaido road to Kyoto. Since Shinjuku station opened in the 1880s, entertainments have been targeted at commuters (mainly men) en route back to the suburbs. Amusements are focused in the tiny bars of Golden Gai, and in the red-light district of Kabukicho. Daytime attractions include several art galleries, a tranquil shrine, and some of Tokyo's best department stores. A late-afternoon stroll as the neon starts to light up will take in both sides of this fascinating, bustling area.

The Koma Theater specializes in Japanese historical melodramas.

Seibu-Shinjuku station

Movie Houses
This corner of Kabukicho is dominated by cinemas, many showing the latest blockbusters.

West Shinjuku ←
(see pp92–3)

Kabukicho
Here hostess bars and pachinko parlors (see p97) flourish alongside cafés and restaurants. In this area of contrasts, prices range from ¥500 for a bowl of noodles to ¥10,000 for a drink.

YASUKUNI-DO

Panasonic

ALTA

Studio Alta
Instantly recognizable by its huge TV screen, Studio Alta stands opposite the crossing from Shinjuku station and is a favorite place for meeting up or just hanging out.

Shinjuku station
(see p93)

↓ Yoyogi

Kinokuniya bookstore has one of Tokyo's best selections of foreign books.

KEY

- - - Suggested walk route

▬▬ Train line

Golden Gai

Viewed in the day-time these scruffy alleys look anything but golden. Most of the bars here are just wide enough for a bar, a counter, and a row of stools. Each has a set of regulars – from writers to bikers – but few welcome strangers inside.

LOCATOR MAP
See Tokyo Street Finder Map 1

Hanazono Shrine

This Shinto shrine, founded in the mid-17th century, is a calm and surprising oasis among the concrete towers. In the tree-filled compound are a reconstructed traditional vermilion-and-white building and several Inari fox statues.

| 0 meters | | 100 |
| 0 yards | | 100 |

Imperial
Palace

Flags café is a convenient coffee stop opposite Mistsukoshi Department store.

Isetan Department Store

Top Japanese and Western designer boutiques make this stylish store a favorite with Tokyo's affluent young. The food hall in the basement is also worth a visit. On the 8th floor of the Shinkan annex building, the Isetan Art Museum has interesting special exhibitions.

West Shinjuku ❷

西新宿

Most of Tokyo's skyscraper office blocks (and some of its most expensive land) are clustered just to the west of Shinjuku station. About 250,000 people work here each day. Many of the hotels and some office blocks have top-floor restaurants with views of the city. In 1960 the government designated Shinjuku a *fukutoshin* ("secondary heart of the city"); in 1991, when the city government moved into architect Tange Kenzo's massive 48-story Metropolitan Government Offices, many started calling it *shin toshin* (the new capital). Tange's building was dubbed "tax tower" by some outraged at its US$1 billion cost.

West Shinjuku seen from Tokyo Metropolitan Government Offices

Island Tower

Mitsui Building

Hilton Tokyo

KITA-DORI

GIJIDO-DORI

CHUO-DORI

TOCHO

FUREAI-DORI

Sumitomo Building
Inside this block are a shopping center and, at the top, a free observatory.

Dai-Ichi Seimei Building

Century Hyatt Hotel

KOEN-DORI

Shinjuku Central Park

Tokyo Metropolitan Government Offices
This huge complex of two blocks and a semi-circular plaza is unified by the grid-detailing on its façades (see p88), recalling both traditional architecture and electronic circuitry. An observatory gives views from Mount Fuji to Tokyo Bay on a clear day.

The Washington Hotel has flowing curves (inside and out) and tiny windows in its white façade.

MINAMI-DORI

Keio Plaza Hotel

The NS Building is recognizable by its rainbow-hued elevator shafts. In the 30-story atrium is a 29-m (95-ft) high water-powered clock.

LOCATOR MAP
*See Tokyo Street
Finder Map 1*

Nomura
Building

**The Yasuda
Kasai Kaijo
Building**, with
its graceful
curving base, is
one of the
area's most
distinctive
buildings.

Shinjuku
Center Building

Shinjuku station and
East Shinjuku

**Monolith
Building**
*An imposing
building, as its
name suggests,
this block has a
pleasant courtyard
garden on the
north side.*

KDD
Building

0 meters   100

0 yards   100

Shinjuku Station ❸

新宿駅

Map 1 B1–2.

With over two million
people passing through
each day, this is the busiest
train station in the world. As
well as being a major stop on
both the JR and metropolitan
subway systems, Shinjuku
station is also the starting
point for trains and buses into
the suburbs. On the
Yamanote and Chuo line
platforms during the
morning rush hour (from
about 7:30 to 9am) staff
are employed to push
those last few commuters
on to the train, making sure
the odd body part isn't
slammed in one of the
closing doors.

The corridors
connecting all the lines
and train networks
together are edged with
hundreds of shops and
restaurants. It's easy to
lose your way in this
maze of seemingly
identical passages, and often
simpler to find your bearings
at ground level. For a time in
the 1980s and early 1990s a
substantial number of homeless (mostly men) built card-
board villages in the stations
corridors. In a controversial

**Ornate sword
handle**

move, the municipal government forcibly removed them;
they settled in new places,
including Ueno Park.

Sword Museum ❹

刀剣博物館

4-25-10 Yoyogi. **Map** 1 A3. *Tel* (03)
3379-1386. 🚉 Sangubashi stn, Odakyu line. ◯ 10am–4pm Tue–Sun. 📷

A little out of the way, this
museum is full of fine
Japanese swords dating back
to the 12th century. Like many
other artifacts in Japan, swords
combine art and ritual in the
pursuit of perfection.

On the first floor is an
interesting display of the
process by which a sword
is produced. The swords
themselves are exhib-
ited on the second
floor, every detail care-
fully refined, even
down to the pattern
of burnishing on the
blade's face. There is
also a display of deco-
rated hilts. English
explanations trace the history
of the sword, and the
processes of tempering and
sharpening, handling, and
maintenance. Old Japanese
texts, illustrated with beautiful
drawings, explain the finer
points of sword-making.

COMMUTER CULTURE

Commuters packed into trains are a common sight morning
and evening at Tokyo's major train stations. High urban
land prices force families to look farther out of the city for
affordable housing. A commute of at least an hour each way
is practically the standard. By far the majority of commuters
are men, as they are still the prime earners in most families.
The commute effectively removes them from family life:
they leave before children get up, come back after they are
in bed, and collapse on weekends with fatigue. The other
major group on the trains is unmarried young women (after
marriage women are generally expected to stay home and
raise the children).
An industry has
grown up around
these commuters:
dozens of maga-
zines are produced
for killing time,
and stand-up
restaurants offer
cheap meals to
those with a long
ride ahead.

Crowding onto a commuter train

One of the many stalls selling good-luck charms at the Meiji Shrine

Meiji Shrine ❺

明治神宮

Map 1 B3. **Tel** (03) 3379-5511.
🚋 Harajuku stn, Yamanote line.
Annex ⬭ 9am–4pm daily (to 4:30pm
Mar–Oct). **www**.meijijingu.or.jp/
english **Treasure House** 9am–4pm
Sat, Sun, and public hols. 🎫
Nai-en garden ⬭ daily (times vary).
🎫 🎏 Spring Festival (May 2–3), Fall
Festival (Nov 1–3).

The most important shinto
shrine in Tokyo, Meiji
Jingu (imperial shrine) dates
from 1920. The Emperor Meiji
(who reigned 1868–1912) and
his wife the Empress Shoken
are enshrined here. A focal
point for right-wing militarists
during Japan's colonial
expansion prior to World War
II, the shrine was destroyed
by Allied aerial bombardment
in 1945 but rebuilt with private
donations in 1958. During the
New Year holidays it is the
most heavily visited place in
Japan, with over three million
people worshiping here and
buying good-luck charms for
the year ahead.

A wide graveled road under
a huge *torii* (gate) and
shaded by cedars leads into
the shrine grounds. On the
right is an abandoned
entrance to the JR Harajuku
station. Just beyond is the
small entrance still used by
the emperor when he visits
by train for official functions.
Next on the right is a complex with a café and
restaurant, and the **Meiji
Treasure House Annex.** The
annex holds changing exhibitions of the royal couples'
artifacts, including clothes,
lacquerware, and furniture.
Tickets for the Treasure
House Annex are also valid
for the main Treasure House.

A left turn takes
you under the
massive **Otorii**
(gate), built in 1975
of huge logs that
came from a 1,500-
year-old Japanese
cypress on Mount
Tandai in Taiwan. A
short distance
beyond the gate, on
the left, is the
entrance to the **Nai-
en garden**, a
favorite of the Meiji imperial
couple. It is said that the
Emperor Meiji designed it himself for his Empress. Inside
there is a teahouse over-
looking a pond stocked with
water lilies and carp. To the
right of the pond, a path leads
to the beautiful **Minami-ike
Shobuda** (iris garden), at its
peak in June, and containing
over 150 species.

Past the entrance to Nai-en,
the road turns to the right and
enters the **main shrine** area,
set in the middle of a grove of
cedars. Another large wooden
torii leads to the outer gate
(Minami Shinmon) through
which is a spacious outer
courtyard. A second gate
(Gehaiden), straight ahead,
separates the public from the
inner courtyard and the shrine.
The simple shrine buildings
are made of unadorned aging
wood in deep hues of green;
the roof is copper, now oxi-
dized bright green. Gracefully
curving, the roof is in the
Shinto style of architecture
known as *shimmei*, used for
imperial shrines. Around the
other three sides of the outer
courtyard are booths selling
charms and prophecies for the

new year. Through a gateway
to the right is the **Kaguraden**,
a hall built in 1993 for sacred
music and dance.

To reach the **Meiji Treasure
House**, either return to the
Otorii and turn left, following
the signs, or walk through the
woods to the left of the shrine.
Lining the walls of the single
high-vaulted room of the
Treasure House are portraits
of every emperor going back
more than 1,000 years. The
objects on display change
regularly; watch for the
gorgeous kimonos worn by
the Emperor Meiji and the
Empress for court functions.

**Minami Shinmon gateway through
a wooden *torii*, Meiji Shrine**

Yoyogi Park ❻

代々木公園

Map 1 A4, 1 B4. 🚋 Harajuku stn,
Yamanote line.

Tange Kenzo's two **Olympic
Stadiums**, the landmark
structures in Yoyogi Park,
were completed in 1964 for
the Tokyo Olympics. They are
still used for national and
international sports competi-
tions. The impressive curves
of the shell-like structures are
achieved with the use of steel
suspension cables.

For almost three decades
the park filled with a fantastic
array of performers and
bands every Sunday.

The main Olympic Stadium in Yoyogi Park

These events were stopped by the authorities in the mid-1990s, supposedly due to worries about the rise in criminal activities and maintaining public order. Sundays are still a good time to visit, though, for the weekly flea market. At the entrance to the park you can still see members of the *zoku* (tribes) who used to perform here, from punks and goths to hippies and break-dancers.

Large advertising screens in Harajuku

Harajuku District ❼
原宿地区

Map 1 B4, 1 C4. **Ⓢ** *Meiji-jingumae stn, Chiyoda line.* **Ⓡ** *Harajuku stn, Yamanote line.* **Ota Memorial Museum of Art** *Tel* (03) 3403-0860. ◻ *10:30am–5:30pm Tue–Sun.* ◼ *27th–end of each month.* ▨

Harajuku station was the main station for the 1964 Tokyo Olympic village; that concentration of international culture had a great impact on the area, attracting the young and innovative of Tokyo. Today Harajuku remains a center for fashion from high-end international showcases to bargain boutiques.

Takeshita-dori, a narrow alley between Meiji-dori and Harajuku station, is the place to find what's hot in teen fashion and culture. Sundays bring the biggest crowds. Prices range from cheap to outrageous, as do the fashions. Starting from the Harajuku station end, about 200 m (220 yards) down, a left turn leads up some stairs to the **Togo Shrine,** founded for Admiral Togo, the commander who defeated the Russian fleet at the straits of Tsushima in the 1904–5 war. Known as Nihonkai Kaisen (the Battle of the Sea of Japan), it was a huge naval victory, the first of an Asian country over a Western one. Admiral Togo remains a hero in Japan, and his shrine has a beautiful garden and pond. An **antiques market** is held in the grounds of the shrine

Street performer in Harajuku

on the first, fourth, and fifth Sundays of the month. Back on Takeshita-dori, a short walk farther on is a right turn that leads about 30 m (33 yards) to a lifesized statue of Elvis Presley. It stands at the entrance to the **Rock and Roll Museum,** which is in fact a store filled with memorabilia for sale. The first floor is devoted to Elvis, the basement to rock 'n' roll items in general.

Running parallel to, and south of, Takeshita-dori is the more sophisticated **Omote-sando**. With its wide, tree-shaded sidewalks and dozens of boutiques showcasing top fashion designers and brands such as Celine, Fendi, and Dior, this is one of the best strolls in Tokyo.

Walking from Harajuku station, just before the intersection with Meiji-dori, a small street off to the left leads to the **Ota Memorial Museum of Art,** which houses one of the best collections of *ukiyo-e* prints *(see p85)* in Japan. A vivid image of a Kabuki actor portraying an *arogoto* (superhero) by Sharaku and a masterful program of a memorial Kabuki performance by Hiroshige are among many familiar works. There is a small restaurant and a shop selling prints and other *ukiyo-e* related souvenirs.

Just to the left down Meiji-dori is **LaForet,** a fashion mecca, with more than 150 boutiques. Leading off Omote-sando, just before the pedestrian bridge, a narrow lane to the left is lined with boutiques of up-and-coming designers and gives a good idea of residential life in this upscale area. Over the pedestrian bridge to the right is the landmark **Hanae Mori Building**. Designed by Tange Kenzo in 1974, it resembles a stack of glass blocks. Famous for incorporating butterflies in her designs, Hanae Mori's empire takes in everything from haute-couture clothing to place mats. Just before the Hanae Mori Building is the vermilion-and-white **Oriental Bazaar,** a collection of shops full of real and fake antiques and good handicrafts, ideal for souvenirs *(see p107).*

A group of teenagers, Harajuku

Street-by-Street: Shibuya ❽

渋谷

**Sign for a
pachinko parlor**

Shibuya is the *sakariba* (party town) for Tokyo's youth. It has been so since the 1930s, when façades featured rockets streaking across the sky. Today this is the place to see the latest in fashion, food, music, and gadgets. Shibuya really started to grow after the 1964 Tokyo Olympics, and its continuing expansion has been spurred by the affluent youth of the world's second-biggest economy. The area, which lies to the northwest of Shibuya station and south of Yoyogi Park, is a mix of trendy boutiques, fashionable department stores, and record shops, plus a couple of interesting museums, and the Bunkamura cultural center. Adjoining this area is Dogen-zaka, a jumble of sloping streets and alleyways lined with nightclubs, bars, and love hotels *(see p295)*.

VISITORS' CHECKLIST

🆂 *Shibuya stn, Hanzomon & Ginza lines.* 🚇 *Shibuya stn, Yamanote, Tokyu Toyoko, Denen-toshi & Keio Inokashira lines.* **TEPCO Electric Energy Museum** *Tel (03) 3477-1191.* ⬭ *10am–6pm Thu–Tue.* ⬤ *Thu if Wed is public hol.* **Tobacco and Salt Museum** *Tel (03) 3476-2041.* ⬭ *10am–5:30pm Tue–Sun.* ⬤ *Tue if Mon is public hol.* 🏷

Center Gai
The focus for youth entertainment in Tokyo, Center Gai is lined with shops, pachinko parlors, restaurants, and karaoke bars full of high-school and college-age kids.

Tokyu Hands is a huge store full of housewares and handicrafts.

Bunkamura
This cultural center is a popular site for rock and classical concerts, and has movies, an art gallery, and a theater.

Dogen-zaka
Named after a bandit who retired here as a monk, this nighttime destination includes old houses, now art galleries.

KEY

– – – Suggested walk route

▬▬▬ Train line

This purple clock tower stands in front of the Shibuya Ward Office and is overlooked by Yoyogi Park and the NHK Studios.

The Tobacco and Salt Museum has excellent, well-laid-out exhibits explaining the history of tobacco and salt (both former government monopolies) in Japan.

Yoyogi Park and Olympic stadiums

Tower Records has a good stock of Japanese and international music CDs at prices among the best in Tokyo.

Harajuku

LOCATOR MAP
See Tokyo Street Finder Map 1

TEPCO Electric Energy Museum
Housed in a modern building with a distinctive dome, this fun museum is packed with interactive exhibits illustrating the uses of electricity.

The Humax Pavilion Building is one of the more fanciful buildings in the area, resembling a cartoon rocket.

Marui Jam department store is a paradise for clothes – the place for fashionable under 25s.

Statue of Hachiko
A favorite meeting place, this 1936 statue depicts the dog who waited for his master at the station every night for more than a decade after his death. Another popular meeting point nearby is the Statue of Moyai.

PACHINKO

Japan's most popular form of recreation, *pachinko* is similar to pinball, but without the flippers and requiring little skill. Players buy some steel balls to feed into the *pachinko* machine, winning more steel balls; these are traded in for a prize (gambling for money is illegal). The prize in turn can be exchanged for money, usually in a small shop nearby. Shibuya and Shinjuku have hundreds of *pachinko* parlors, but they are found all over Japan.

A typical *pachinko* machine

Shibuya station

0 meters 100

0 yards 100

The Spiral Building, Minami-Aoyama

Minami-Aoyama District ⑨

南青山地区

Map 1 C4–5, 2 D4–5. **S** *Gaienmae stn, Ginza line.* **Museum of Contemporary Art Tel** (03) 3402-3001. ⬜ *11am–7pm Tue–Sun (9pm Wed).* 🖼 **Nezu Art Museum Tel** (03) 3400-2536. ⬤ *for renovation until 2009.* 🖼 **National Children's Castle Tel** (03) 3797-5666. ⬜ *12:30–5:30pm Tue–Fri, 10am–5:30pm Sat, Sun, public hols & school vacations.* 🖼 www.kodomono-shiro.or.jp

Favored by artists, writers, and young entrepreneurs, this district lies between the large Aoyama Cemetery and Shibuya. Aoyama-dori, the wide street at its heart, is a center for boutiques and up-scale life. Omote-sando crosses it just about in the middle.

On Gaien-Nishi-dori, a fashionable street nicknamed "Killer-dori", is the **Museum of Contemporary Art** (Watari-um). Exhibits are by international and Japanese artists, and change regularly. The bookstore stocks an excellent range of art books.

Back on Aoyama-dori, turn left at the Omote-sando junction for the **Nezu Art Museum**, which houses

Japanese, Chinese, and Korean art and is situated in landscaped gardens containing traditional tea houses. A short walk from here is Kotto-dori, another fashionable street which is full of antique shops selling scrolls, paintings, and porcelain, among many other items. This street is fast becoming one of the hottest in Tokyo, with some notable boutiques, cafés, and shops springing up. The area is a pleasant one in which to spend an afternoon shopping or just browsing. Returning to Aoyama-dori, near the Omote-sando junction toward Shibuya, the next landmark is the white, geometric **Spiral Building**, which owes its name to the large, spiral ramp inside. Designed by Maki Fumihiko in 1985, and one of the most popular places in Minami-Aoyama, this building is the figurative definition of cool. There is nothing in it that can't be described as hip and trendy (*torendi* in Japanese), and that includes most of the people seen here. Attractions inside comprise a first-floor exhibition and performance space, the Spiral Hall (on the third floor), also used for

exhibitions and performances, an Italian café, a French restaurant, a stationery and housewares boutique, and a beauty salon.

Farther along, the **National Children's Castle** is marked by a large, moon-faced sculpture by Okamoto Taro. There are many activities for kids here, open to Japanese and non-Japanese speakers alike, including areas for free play with toys, computers, music and art classes, and even a child-friendly hotel.

Roppongi District ⑩

六本木地区

Map 2 E5. **S** *Roppongi stn, Hibiya & Toei-Oedo lines.*

Roppongi is the music and club center of Tokyo. You can find just about any music you want here: jazz, blues, ska, hip-hop, classic disco, country and western, soul. This is also the place for big-name international restaurant chains such as the Hard Rock Café, Spago's, and Tony Roma's.

During the 1990s the district was rejuvenated by the construction of the Roppongi Hills development. Designed to be a "city within a city," it incorporates wide pedestrian squares, public walkways, and art gallery, as well as restaurants, shops, offices, and apartments.

Almond (*Amando* in Japanese), at the intersection of Roppongi-dori and Gaien-

Nighttime scene in the district of Roppongi

Flamboyant entrance to a nightclub in Roppongi

floor. It has an unrivaled collection of Edo-era screens, depicting scenes from the Edo court; one particularly fine example is *Namban* (Westerners in Japan). Traditional decorative arts are also well represented, with ceramics, lacquerware, and tea utensils.

About 200 m (220 yards) along Aoyama-dori from the Suntory Museum is the **Toyokawa Inari Shrine** (also called Myogon-ji). With its red lanterns and flags, and dozens of statues of foxes (the traditional messengers of Inari, a Shinto Rice deity), this is a pleasant place to linger for a while.

Back past the Suntory Museum and over the moat, you will see on the right the gleaming white **Akasaka Prince Hotel**, designed by Tange Kenzo. The open lobby has white marble floors

Ironware kettle in the Suntory Museum of Art

and interior walls, while the exterior wall is glass. Past this hotel on the left is the huge, luxurious **Hotel New Otani** (*see p300*). On the 17th floor is the revolving Blue Sky restaurant, which serves Chinese food and offers stunning views across central Tokyo and the Imperial Palace. In the grounds and open to all is the 400-year-old garden of Kato Kiyomasa, lord of Kyushu's Kumamoto area.

South of Akasaka-Mitsuke station is the shrine of **Hie Jinja**, with a history dating back to 830. Shogun Ietsuna moved it here in the 17th century to buffer his castle; the present-day buildings are all modern. Each year in mid-June the Sanno Matsuri is celebrated here with a grand procession of 50 *mikoshi* (portable shrines) and people in Heian-era costumes.

Higashi-dori, is the main rendezvous spot in Roppongi. The area to the south is where a great deal of the action is. Clubs come in all shapes and sizes, some just wide enough for a counter and stools. Most will welcome you warmly, but check the prices of drinks as they vary hugely. To the west of Almond, beyond the expressway, **Velfarre** is Japan's most famous nightclub and one of the largest in the world. West of Almond is the **Square Building**, full of more clubs, including Birdland jazz club (*see p113*).

Akasaka District ⓫
赤坂地区

Map 2 E3–4, 2 F3–4. **S** *Akasaka-Mitsuke stn, Ginza & Marunouchi lines; Nagatacho stn, Yurakucho, Namboku & Hanzomon lines.* **Suntory Museum of Art Tel** (03) 3470-1073. ☐ 10am–5pm Tue–Sun (to 7pm Fri). ☐ ☐ *Sanno Matsuri (Jun 16, Hie Jinja).*

With the Diet Building (*see p71*) and many government offices just to the east, Akasaka is a favorite place for politicians to socialize. Limousines carry dark-blue-suited men to the many exclusive establishments lining the streets here.

Opposite Akasaka-Mitsuke station is the **Suntory Museum of Art**, located in a single room on the 11th

A *shinowa* circle, erected for good luck, at Hie Jinja in Akasaka

YOUTH CULTURE

In Japan youth sells, although, ironically, the average age of the population is one of the highest in the world. Youth is seen by most Japanese as the time when life can be lived according to personal choice, before adult responsibilities – in the form of jobs or parenthood – take over. Products from beer and cars to CDs and fashions are aimed at the youth market, and are rapidly adopted and then shed as individuals are attracted by the new and the desire to keep up with their peers. A stream of teenage *idoru* (idols) become wildly famous when they are young; if they are girls they tend to drop out in their early twenties to marry and have children, while boys may become talk-show hosts or game-show contestants.

A Tokyo teenager on her cell phone

Farther Afield

A short distance from Tokyo city center are a number of interesting sights. The Japan Folk Craft Museum and Goto Art Museum are small gems in pleasant neighborhoods that give an idea of Tokyo life as well as its heritage; in contrast Ikebukuro, Daiba, and Ebisu are all modern urban centers in their own right. Ryogoku, the place for all things sumo, also has the Edo-Tokyo Museum. Rikugi-en, near Ikebukuro, is one of Edo's last great stroll gardens.

**Back carrier,
Japan Folk
Craft Museum**

SIGHTS AT A GLANCE

Arakawa Tram Line **4**
Daiba **8**
Ebisu District **10**
Goto Art Museum **1**
Ikebukuro District **5**
Japan Folk Craft
  Museum **2**
Rikugi-en Garden **6**
Ryogoku District **7**
Sengaku-ji Temple **9**
Tokyo Opera City **3**

0 kilometers   5

0 miles   5

KEY

Main sightseeing area

Expressway

Main road

Airport

Goto Art Museum **1**
五島美術館

3-9-25 Kaminoge, Setagaya-ku.
Tel (03) 3703-0662. Tokyu Denentoshi line from Shibuya stn to Futako-Tamagawaen, then Tokyu Oimachi line to Kaminoge.
10am–4:30pm Tue–Sun. when exhibitions change.

Set in a pleasant hillside garden, this museum show-cases the private collection of the late chairman of the Tokyu Corporation, Goto Keita. Avidly interested in Zen, he was originally attracted to Buddhist calligraphy, particularly that of 16th-century priests. His collection contains many examples of this work, called *bokuseki*. Also included are ceramics, calligraphy, paintings, and metalwork mirrors; items are changed several times a year. The museum's

most famous works, however, are scenes from 12th-century scrolls of the *Tale of Genji*, painted by Fujiwara Takayoshi, which have been designated National Treasures. They are shown once a year, usually in "Golden Week" *(see p368).*

Japan Folk Craft Museum **2**
日本民芸館

4-3-33 Komaba, Meguro-ku. **Tel** (03) 3467-4527. Komaba-Todaimae stn, Keio Inokashira line. 10am–5pm Tue–Sun.

Known to the Japanese as Mingeikan, this small but excellent museum was found-ed by art historian Yanagi Muneyoshi. The criteria for inclusion in the museum are that the object should be the work of an anonymous maker,

produced for daily use, and representative of the region from which it comes. The museum building, designed by Yanagi and completed in 1931, uses black tiles and white stucco outside.

On display are items ranging from woven baskets to ax sheaths, iron kettles, pottery, and kimonos; together they present a fascinating view of rural life. There are also special themed exhibits, such as 20th-century ceramics or Japanese textiles, and a room dedicated to Korean Yi-dynasty work. A small gift shop sells fine crafts and some books.

Tokyo Opera City **3**
東京オペラシティー

3-20-2 Nishi-Shinjuku, Shinjuku-ku.
Tel (03) 5353-0700. Hatsudai stn, Keio line.

Tokyo's newest music and theater complex has two main halls, one primarily for Japanese classical music and theater, and a larger opera hall with a soaring vaulted roof. Performances are fre-quent – phone for details or pick up a leaflet from the foyer information counter.

There are 54 floors, mostly offices. On the first three are an art gallery, shops, and res-taurants. The fourth has the **NTT Intercommunication Center**, with modern inter-active art. The 53rd and 54th floors hold a dozen restaurants and bars with great city views.

Exhibit at the NTT Intercommuni-cation Center, Tokyo Opera City

The aquarium at Sunshine City, Ikebukuro District

Arakawa Tram Line ❹

荒川都電

S *Edogawabashi stn, Yurakucho line.* **Sumida River trips** ℹ *(03) 5608-8869.*

As recently as 1955, 600,000 people a day were riding the dozens of tram lines that crisscrossed the city. Now the 13 km (8 miles) of the Arakawa line are all that is left. The others were eliminated as old-fashioned in the modernization for the 1964 Olympics.

The Arakawa tram line runs from Waseda in the west to Minowabashi in the east and costs ¥160 for each trip, short or long. Near the Waseda end of the line is the quiet stroll garden of **Shin Edogawa**. There are few outstanding sights en route, but the pleasure of this tram ride lies in seeing a quieter, residential side to Tokyo. A short walk from Arakawa Yuenchimae stop, past tightly packed, tiny houses, is a modest amusement park, **Arakawa Yuen Park**; Sumida River tourboat trips leave from here. Opposite the Arakawa Nanachome stop is **Arakawa Nature Park**.

Ikebukuro District ❺

池袋地区

S *Ikebukuro stn, Marunouchi & Yurachuko lines.* **R** *Ikebukuro stn, Yamanote & many other lines.*

With the second-busiest train station in Japan (after Shinjuku), Ikebukuro is a designated *fukutoshin* (sub-center) of Tokyo. By the station's south entrance is the flagship store of **Seibu**, perhaps the country's most innovative department store, with boutiques of up-and-coming designers and a large basement food market, where you can often try free samples. To the west of the station is the newer **Tobu** department store with a similar set-up.

The **Sunshine City** complex, including the **Sunshine 60** tower, is a short walk east of the station. It is built on top of what was Sugamo Prison, where seven Class-A World War II war criminals, including the prime minister, Tojo Hideki, were convicted and hung. The **Ancient Orient Museum**, on the 10th floor of the complex, has collections from Egypt, Iran, and Pakistan. A huge Sunshine City sign points down an escalator; just before here, investigate the **Tokyu Hands** store for home furnishings and kitchen gadgets. Down the escalator is **Amlux Toyota**, five stories packed with cars, where you can sit in any model. In Sunshine 60 there is also a planetarium, an aquarium, and a rooftop outdoor viewing platform.

Rikugi-en Garden ❻

六義園

S *Komagome stn, Namboku line.* **R** *Komagome stn, Yamanote line.* **Tel** *(03) 3941-2222.* ⏰ *9am–5pm daily.* 🖼

Yanagisawa Yoshiyasu, grand chamberlain of the fifth shogun, constructed this garden in seven years, starting in 1695. Yanagisawa had a well-earned reputation for debauchery, but he also managed to build this, one of the finest Edo-era stroll gardens. Iwasaki Yataro, Mitsubishi's founder, oversaw its Meiji-era renovation. The design recreates 88 landscapes in miniature from famous *waka* (31-syllable poems), so the view changes every few steps. Near the entrance is a weeping cherry that is beautiful all year. Numerous paths and seats offer opportunities to enjoy the views. Bush warblers and turtledoves are among the birds that can be seen here.

Manicured shrubs around the lake at Rikugi-en Garden

LIVING IN SMALL SPACES

Land, and therefore housing, is very expensive in Japan. The average home costs 7–8 times the family's yearly income, and space is at a premium. A traditional design has closets for storing rolled-up futons; in the morning the bedding is swapped for a low table at which the family sits cross-legged to eat meals. More and more families are opting for a semi-Western style with raised beds, table, and chairs, resulting in homes being even more cramped.

Ryogoku District ❼

両国地区

Map 4 E4–5. **S** *Ryogoku stn, Toei-Oedo line.* **R** *Ryogoku stn, JR Sobu line.* **Sumo Museum** 1-3-28 Yokoami, Sumida-ku. *Tel* (03) 3622-0366. ◯ 10am–4:30pm Mon–Fri. ● *public hols.* **www**.sumo.or.jp **Edo-Tokyo Museum** 1-4-1 Yokoami, Sumida-ku. *Tel* (03) 3626-9974. ◯ 9:30am–5:30pm Tue–Sun (7:30pm Sat). ◪ **www**.edo-tokyo-museum.or.jp

On the east bank of the Sumida River, Ryogoko was a great entertainment and commerce center in Edo's Shitamachi. These days it is a quiet place but it still has its most famous residents: sumo wrestlers. Many *beya* (sumo stables) are here, and it is not unusual to see huge young men walking the streets in *yukata* (light cotton kimonos) and *geta* (wooden sandals).

The **National Sumo Stadium** has been here since 1945; the current building dates from 1985. During a tournament *(see p111)* many of the wrestlers simply walk from their *beya* just down the street. Inside the stadium is a **Sumo Museum** lined with portraits of all the *yokozuna* (grand champions) dating back 200 years.

Beside the stadium is the huge **Edo-Tokyo Museum**, built to resemble an old style of elevated warehouse. One of Tokyo's most imaginative and interesting museums, its exhibition space is divided into two zones on two floors tracing life in Edo and

Image of a Kabuki actor, Edo-Tokyo Museum

then Tokyo, as Edo was renamed in 1868. The exhibits, some of which are interactive, appeal to both adults and children and have explanations in Japanese and English.

The route around the museum starts by crossing a traditional arched wooden bridge, a replica of Nihonbashi *(see p70)*. There are life-sized reconstructed buildings including the façade of a Kabuki theater. Marvelous scale-model dioramas, some of which are automated, show everything from the house of a *daimyo* (feudal lord) to a section of Shitamachi. Beside a scale model of Tokyo's first skyscraper is rubble

LIFE IN A SUMO STABLE

At the age of about 15 boys are accepted into a sumo *beya*. From that day they will probably not return home or see their parents for several years. Sumo society is supremely hierarchical, with newcomers serving senior wrestlers as well as cleaning and cooking for the entire *beya*. Their practices may start at 4am, with seniors starting about 6am. The day's single meal of *chanko-nabe*, a large stew, comes about noon with juniors getting what the seniors leave. That is followed by more work. The life is extremely grueling – it is a society and culture few foreigners have successfully entered.

Sumo wrestlers training in the early morning

from the 1923 earthquake that destroyed it. There is a rickshaw and Japan's first "light" automobile: a three-seater Subaru with a 360 cc engine. In the media section is a step-by-step example of how *ukiyo-e* woodblock prints *(see p85)* were produced. Models of the boats that once plied the Sumida River give some idea of just how important the river was to Edo life.

Daiba ❽

台場

R *Yurikamome monorail from Shinbashi stn; Rinkai Fukutoshin line to Tokyo Teleport.* **⛴** *from Hinode Pier 10:10am–7:10pm, every 20–25 mins.* **Museum of Maritime Sciences** *Tel* (03) 5500-1111. ◯ 10am–5pm daily (to 6pm Sat, Sun, public hols & in summer). ◪ **www**.funeno kagakukan.or.jp **National Museum of Emerging Science and Innovation** *Tel* (03) 3570-9151. ◯ 10am–4:30pm Wed–Mon. ◪

When the west started to force Japan to open up in the 1850s, the shogunate constructed a series of *daiba* (obstructions) across Tokyo harbor to keep the foreigners' powerful "black ships" out. Daiba (sometimes known as Odaiba), an island almost blocking the mouth of Tokyo

Reconstruction of a Kabuki theater in Ryogoku's Edo-Tokyo Museum

FARTHER AFIELD 103

Bay, takes its name from these.
The spectacular route to
Daiba is via the Yurikamome
monorail, which climbs a
loop before joining Rainbow
Bridge high over Tokyo
Harbor. On Daiba the monorail is a convenient way to
travel around, although most
places are within a short walk
of each other.

The first station, Odaiba-
Kaihin-Koen, leads to Tokyo's
only beach. Nearby is the
Daisan Daiba Historic Park,
with the remains of the original obstructions. A short walk
west is **Tokyo Decks** with five
floors of restaurants and shops
plus **Joypolis**, a huge Sega
center full of the latest electronic games. In front of Decks
is the station for water buses
from Hinode Pier. Behind it is
the headquarters of **Fuji TV**, a
new Tokyo landmark. Nearby
are a new cinema complex,
Mediage, and a shopping
mall, Aquacity. A pleasant,
tree-filled waterfront park
extends to the **Museum of
Maritime Sciences** (accessible
from Fune-no-Kagakukan
station), shaped like a boat.
Across from here, in Aomi, is
the **National Museum of
Emerging Science and
Innovation**, with interactive
robots, bio-technology, and
ecological exhibits.

At Aomi station is the **Palette
Town** development, including
Toyota's City Showcase with
state-of-the-art driving simula-
tors. In the History Garage are
cleverly displayed cars from
the 1950s on. Nearby is Future
World with a short virtual

Part of the Ebisu Garden Place complex, Ebisu

drive into the future. Right
beside all this is a large Ferris
wheel. **Wanza Ariake** building
has shops and restaurants and
is connected to Kokusai-
Tenjijo Seimon station, as is
Tokyo Big Sight (or Tokyo
International Exhibition Hall).

The gate of Sengaku-ji Temple

Sengaku-ji Temple ❾
泉岳寺

🚇 *Sengaku-ji stn, Toei Asakusa line.*
Museum ⏰ *9am–4pm daily.*

This temple is the site of the
climax of Japan's favorite
tale of loyalty and revenge, re-
told in the play *Chushingura*
and many movies *(see p55)*.
Lord Asano was sentenced to
death by *seppuku* (suicide by
disembowelment) for drawing
his sword when goaded by
Lord Kira. Denied the right to
seek revenge, 47 of Asano's
retainers, led by Oishi Kura-
nosuke, plotted in secret. In
1703, they attacked Kira's
house and beheaded him,
presenting the head to Asano's
grave at Sengaku-ji. They in
turn were sentenced to
seppuku, and are buried here.

Inside the temple gate and up
the steps on the right is the
well (now covered with wire)
where the retainers washed
Kira's head. Farther ahead on
the right are the retainers'
graves, still tended with
flowers. Back at the base of the
steps is an interesting **museum**
with artifacts from the incident
and statues of some of the 47.

Ebisu District ❿
恵比寿地区

🚇 *Ebisu stn, Hibiya line.* 🚉 *Ebisu stn,
Yamanote line.* **Tokyo Metropolitan
Museum of Photography** *Tel* (03)
3280-0099. ⏰ *10am–6pm Tue–
Sat (to 8pm Thu & Fri).* 💻 *www.
syabi.com* **Beer Museum Ebisu** *Tel*
(03) 5423-7255. ⏰ *10am–6pm Tue–
Sun. (Last adm 1 hr before closin g.)*

The completion in the mid-
1990s of **Ebisu Garden
Place**, a commercial and
residential center, brought this
area to life. The superb **Tokyo
Metropolitan Museum of
Photography**, to the right of
the entrance, has a permanent
collection of work by Japanese and foreign photographers,
and excellent special exhibitions. In the heart of Ebisu
Garden Place are a Mitsukoshi
store, boutiques, two cinemas,
a theater, and restaurants,
including Taillevent Robuchon,
a French restaurant that looks
like a 19th-century chateau.
The crowded central plaza is a
great spot for people-watching.
To the left of Mitsukoshi is
the small **Beer Museum
Ebisu** with exhibits and
videos about beer worldwide
and in Japan, and free samples.

The futuristic Fuji TV
headquarters, Daiba

SHOPPING IN TOKYO

You can buy almost anything you want in Tokyo, from a traditional *koneshiki* (cylindrical wooden doll) to a Chanel handbag or an up-to-the-minute computer game. Tokyo-ites love shopping and, budget permitting, the city is a paradise for browsing and buying, with its huge department stores, informal street markets, and fascinating one-of-a-kind shops. Although half the joy of shopping here is the amazing contrasts that can be found side-by-side, some areas do specialize in certain types of shops. Ginza is the place for traditional, upscale stores, while Shinjuku mixes huge arcades with electronics shops stacked high with the latest innovations. Harajuku and Minami-Aoyama are the areas for the funkiest fashions and designs; the older quarters around Ueno and Asakusa offer more traditional Japanese crafts. For general information on shopping in Japan, see pages 348–53.

Kanzashi hair-pin, Nakamise-dori, Asakusa

DEPARTMENT STORES

Department stores grew out of Edo-period mercantile houses. Customers would sit on *tatami* mats and describe what they wanted, then staff would bring out the goods for their perusal. After the 1923 earthquake, newly built stores allowed customers inside with shoes on for the first time, revolutionizing shopping. Since the collapse of the "bubble" economy in about 1990, the opulence of Tokyo's department stores has been more muted, and prices lower, but they continue to offer a huge variety and immaculate service. Basements are usually supermarkets, where free samples are handed out. Top floors are often filled with restaurants, both Western and Japanese, plus an art gallery and sometimes a museum, too. Ginza's

Mitsukoshi is perhaps Tokyo's most famous store; the main Mitsukoshi store is in Nihonbashi, with other branches in Ikebukuro, Shinjuku, and Ebisu. In Ginza **Matsuya** is more informal and aimed at a younger, yuppie crowd. Shinjuku has never been famous for department stores, but the new **Takashimaya** with an IMAX theater on the 12th floor has been a big success. For a heavy dose of youth culture, try **Marui Jam** in Shibuya.

If you have time for just one department store, visit the flagship **Seibu** store right over Ikebukuro station. Filled with hip designer boutiques as well as more established brand names, it elevates shopping to an art form. Also in Ikebukuro (and Shibuya, *see p96*) is **Tokyu Hands**, a cornucopia of housewares, which is always fun to browse through.

SHOPPING ARCADES

Labyrinths of corridors lined with shops occupy major subway and train stations. They are good for window-shopping and sometimes for bargains, but are notoriously disorienting. **Tokyo station** is packed with shops and kiosks. In **Shinjuku station** underground passages run for hundreds of meters to the "Subnade" (underground shopping street) below Yasukuni-dori. Tokyo's **Yaesu underground** is also huge, starting below the Daimaru department store side. Daiba's **Tokyo Decks** (*see p103*) is five floors of shops and a promenade

deck with restaurants. Nearby **Aquacity** and **Wanza Ariake** (*see p103*) are similar. The lower floors of **Tokyo Opera City** (*see p100*) also have restaurants and shops.

Crowds milling up and down Takeshita-dori in Harajuku

MARKETS

Street markets flourish outside many of the city's train stations. Tokyo's most famous station market is **Ameyoko** (*see p84*) under the tracks at Ueno station. **Takeshita-dori** in Harajuku (*see p95*) is full of shops for the young and fashion-conscious. The ultimate market experience is **Tsukiji Fish Market** (*see p68*); the area to the east is full of small restaurants where piles of dishes crowd the sidewalk, and shops with pungent crates of *wasabi* horseradish and dried fish hanging from storefronts.

Matsuya, one of Ginza's major department stores

One of West Shinjuku's huge camera stores

ELECTRONIC GOODS

The best place to buy electronic goods is Akihabara *(see p73)*. Computers, video games, and software fuel the economy here, but you can usually find just about anything. Prices in Japan are high, and even with the ten percent or so discount here, the cost is unlikely to be cheaper than elsewhere, though the selection is unmatched. Check that you are buying equipment that is compatible with voltage and systems back home *(see p371)*.

In Akihabara, **Laox** is a big favorite with tax-free shoppers, selling English-language computers and some English-language software. You will need to bring your passport for the tax-free price. **Ishimaru** and **Yamagiwa** are two more huge electronic department stores. **Akky** and **Takarada** are also duty free.

CAMERA EQUIPMENT

To be certain of buying genuine camera equipment, try **Yodobashi Camera** on the west side of Shinjuku, or **Bic Camera** in Yurakucho or Shibuya. Two of the biggest camera stores, each has several floors of every brand and every type of equipment. Prices are high, although the margin is not as much as it once was. The language of cameras is universal, and staff can usually help find anything. Ask for the duty-free price; you can even try and bargain a little, particularly if you are willing to pay cash.

JEWELRY AND ACCESSORIES

Pearls are the only form of jewelry native to Japan; all gem stones are either imported or synthetic. **Mikimoto** perfected the process and marketing of cultured pearls in 1893, and sells its jewelry in opulent surroundings. For a selection of silver and other types of jewelry, pay a visit to **Mori Silver** in the Oriental Bazaar *(see* "Clothing") and **Takane Jewelry**.

Japan's traditional jewelry for women was *kanzashi*, the hairpins worn in traditional hairstyles (with tortoise-shell combs). Nakamise-dori at Senso-ji Temple *(see pp86–7)* is the place to find these. **Matsuzakaya** sells *kanzashi*, plus other jewelry, and nearby **Ginkado** sells *kanzashi*, costume swords, and fans. Next door is **Bunsendo**, also selling fans. The last maker of handmade wooden combs is **Jusanya** in Ueno.

CLOTHING

A traditional japanese kimono can be incredibly expensive but makes a unique and beautiful souvenir; one supplier is **Kodaimaru** at the Imperial Hotel. Used kimonos are usually a much more reasonable price and are usually in excellent condition: try the **Oriental Bazaar**, a complex of several shops on Omotesando and **Hayashi Kimono**

in Yurakucho. *Yukata* (cotton kimonos suitable for men and women) or *hapi* (cotton kimono-style short jackets) are affordable alternatives.

Mainstream men's and women's clothes tend to be conservative, though immaculately designed and cut. Many international designers have their own outlets or are stocked by the major stores.

Designers aiming primarily at the young are doing very inventive things with bold colors and unusual materials and cuts. **Seibu** department store in Ikebukuro is full of boutiques of new, innovative designers. Gaien-Nishi-dori in Minami-Aoyama *(see p98)* is packed with trendy boutiques, as is Omote-sando *(see p95)* and its side streets.

Japan's internationally famous designers have outlets around the city. **Issey Miyake** has boutiques in several department stores and a shop in Minami-Aoyama. **Comme des Garçons** has two shops; go to the main store for directions to the second. **Hanae Mori** has a shop in her own building in Harajuku.

TEXTILES

Silk, cotton, linen, hemp, and wool all feature in Japan's long and rich textile

An *obi* sash on a kimono

history. While some traditional techniques are fading, most are alive and well. Department stores are often the best places to find a range of textiles. **Matsuzakaya** (in Ginza) grew from a Nagoya kimono merchant and stocks bolts of kimono cloth made in Kyoto and textured *furoshiki* (square wrapping cloths). The **Tokyo National Museum shop** *(see pp80–83)* has a good selection of *furoshiki* and scarves made using traditional techniques. Also good is **Bengara** *(see* "Traditional Arts and Crafts"). **Miyashita Obi** on Nakamise-dori at Senso-ji Temple *(see pp86–7)* has wonderful *obi* sashes, used to wrap the waist of a kimono.

Traditional umbrellas for sale in Nakamise-dori, near Senso-ji Temple

CONTEMPORARY ART AND DESIGN

Galleries and showrooms come and go in Tokyo; check local sources of information (see p108) for the latest shows. The **Spiral Garden** in Minami-Aoyama's Spiral Building (see p98) usually has something interesting by Japanese artists. The shop on the second floor has a selection of contemporary housewares.

In Ginza you can find works by Japanese artists at **Galleria Grafica**, **Plus Minus Gallery**, and **Yoseido Gallery**. **Ginza Graphic Gallery** exhibits both Japanese and foreign works. The **Karakuri Museum** in Shibuya displays and sells artworks based on optical illusions. In Shinjuku the **NTT Intercommunication Center** in Tokyo Opera City (see p100) features exhibits and installations using the latest technology. In the same building is the **Shinjuku Opera City Gallery** which displays Japanese painting, watercolors, and examples of graphic art of all types.

Excellent contemporary prints can be found at the **Tolman Collection** near the Tokyo Tower. For contemporary ceramics, try **Koransha** in Ginza. Good sources of modern housewares and kitchen gadgets are the department stores **Tokyu Hands** and **Matsuya**, which is also in Ginza.

TRADITIONAL ARTS AND CRAFTS

Crafts are thriving in Japan. Ceramics is by far the most active craft, and the average Japanese has a working knowledge of the distinct styles and techniques used in different areas of the country. The larger ceramic bowls used for *matcha* (a form of green tea) are striking in their simple, natural forms; good pieces will be firmly packed in a wooden box. Lacquerware plates, trays, chopsticks, and bowls make excellent souvenirs that are light and easy to transport. The various forms of Japan's beautiful paper, *washi*, also make lightweight gifts; it can be bought as writing paper or in packs of square sheets for origami.

Ironware kettle, Japan Traditional Crafts Center

Maruzen in Nihonbashi is an excellent source of many of these crafts, including ceramics, woodcraft, and lacquerware, as is **Takumi** in Ginza. **Itoya**, also in Ginza, is packed with crafts, especially *washi*; it also has brushes, ink, and inkstones for calligraphy. **Kurodaya**, at Senso-ji Temple (see pp86–7), has been selling *washi* for over 140 years and stocks everything from modern stationery to traditional kites, plus a wide selection of *chiyogami* (wrapping paper), and traditional masks and clay figurines. The **Japan Folk Craft Museum** (see p100) has a small, high-quality selection.

There is a whole tradition of dolls made for viewing in glass cases; these run into hundreds, even thousands, of dollars to buy. A good supplier is **Yoshitoku** in Asakusa. **Mataroningyou** in Ueno specializes in Edo *kimekomi* dolls. The small figurines in **Sukeroku**, at the end of Senso-ji's Nakamise-dori, are charming and easy to carry home.

Noren, the cloth curtains that hang over the entrances to many small shops, are unique mementos. **Bengara** specializes in *noren*, with beautiful cotton and silk designs.

Woodblock prints are rarely bargains, but are available at reasonable prices. In Jinbocho two famous shops are almost next to each other: **Oya Shobo** and **Hara Shobo**. For new prints of old woodblocks on *washi* **Isetatsu** is excellent; it also sells beautiful sheets of *chiyogami* from old designs.

SPECIALTY SHOPS

There are all kinds of small niche shops filled with uniquely Japanese items. The following are all in Nakamise-dori at Senso-ji: **Sanbido** sells religious statues and wooden dolls; **Nishijima Umbrellas** has traditional umbrellas; **Tokiwado** has been selling *kaminari okoshi* crackers – famous for crackling like a clap of thunder when bitten – for 200 years; **Nakatsuka** sells candies and sweet pastries.

Kappabashi-dori (see p84) is Tokyo's center for kitchenware and plastic food.

A traditional candy shop in Nakamise-dori, Senso-ji Temple

DIRECTORY

DEPARTMENT STORES

Marui Jam
1-22-6 Jinnan, Shibuya.
Map 1 B5.
Tel (03) 3464-0101.
⬤ *Wed.*

Matsuya
3-6-1 Ginza.
Map 5 C2.
Tel (03) 3567-1211.

Mitsukoshi
1-4-1 Nihonbashi.
Map 5 C1.
Tel (03) 3241-3311.

Seibu
1-28-1 Minami-Ikebukuro.
Tel (03) 3981-0111.

Takashimaya
5-24-2 Sendagaya.
Map 1 B2.
Tel (03) 5361-1111.

Tokyu Hands
1-28-10 Higashi-Ikebukuro.
Tel (03) 3980-6111.

ELECTRONIC GOODS

Akky
1-15-8 Soto-Kanda.
Map 3 C4.
Tel (03) 3253-4787.

Ishimaru
1-9-14 Soto-Kanda.
Map 3 C4.
Tel (03) 3255-1500.

Laox
1-2-9 Soto-Kanda.
Map 3 C4.
Tel (03) 3253-7111.

Takarada
1-14-7 Soto-Kanda.
Map 3 C4.
Tel (03) 3253-0101.

Yamagiwa
1-9-14 Soto-Kanda.
Map 3 C4.
Tel (03) 3255-3111.

CAMERA EQUIPMENT

Bic Camera
1-11-1 Yurakucho.
Map 5 B2.
Tel (03) 5221-1111.
1-24-12 Shibuya.
Tel (03) 5466-1111.

Yodobashi Camera
1-11-1 Nishi-Shinjuku.
Map 1 B2.
Tel (03) 3346-1010.

JEWELRY AND ACCESSORIES

Jusanya
2-12-21 Ueno.
Map 3 C3.
Tel (03) 3831-3238.
⬤ *Sun.*

Mikimoto
4-5-5 Ginza.
Map 5 B2.
Tel (03) 3535-4611.

Takane Jewelry
1-7-23 Uchisawaicho.
Map 5 B3.
Tel (03) 3591-2764.
⬤ *Sun.*

CLOTHING

Comme des Garçons
5-2-1 Minami-Aoyama.
Map 1 C5.
Tel (03) 3406-3951.

Hanae Mori
3-6-1 Kita-Aoyama.
Map 1 C4.
Tel (03) 3499-1601.

Hayashi Kimono
International Arcade,
2-1-1 Yurakucho.
Map 5 B2.
Tel (03) 3501-4012.

Issey Miyake
3-18-11 Minami-Aoyama.
Map 1 C5.
Tel (03) 3423-1408.

Kodaimaru
Imperial Hotel Arcade,
1-1-1 Uchisaiwaicho.
Map 5 B2.
Tel (03) 3508-7697.

Oriental Bazaar
5-9-13 Jingumae.
Map 1 C4.
Tel (03) 3400-3933.
⬤ *Thu.*

TEXTILES

Matsuzakaya
6-10-1 Ginza.
Map 5 B2.
Tel (03) 3572-1111.

CONTEMPORARY ART AND DESIGN

Galleria Grafica
1F and 2F Ginza S2 Bldg,
6-13-4 Ginza.
Map 5 B3.
Tel (03) 5550-1335.
⬤ *Sun & public hols.*

Ginza Graphic Gallery
DNP Ginza Bldg, 7-7-2
Ginza.
Map 5 B3.
Tel (03) 3571-5206.
⬤ *Sun & public hols.*

Karakuri Museum
2F King Bldg, 2-9-10
Shibuya.
Map 1 C5.
Tel (03) 5466-0711.

Koransha
6-14-20 Ginza.
Map 5 B3.
Tel (03) 3543-0951.
⬤ *Sun & public hols.*

Plus Minus Gallery
3F TEPCO Ginza-kan,
6-11-1 Ginza.
Map 5 B3.
Tel (03) 3575-0456.
⬤ *Wed.*

Tolman Collection
2-2-18 Shiba Daimon.
Map 5 A4.
Tel (03) 3434-1300.
⬤ *Tue.*

Yoseido Gallery
5-5-15 Ginza.
Map 5 B3.
Tel (03) 3571-1312.
⬤ *Sun & public hols.*

TRADITIONAL ARTS AND CRAFTS

Bengara
1-35-6 Asakusa.
Map 4 F2.
Tel (03) 3841-6613.
⬤ *3rd Thu of month.*

Hara Shobo
2-3 Kanda-Jinbocho.
Map 3 B5.
Tel (03) 3261-7444.
⬤ *Public hols.*

Isetatsu
2-18-9 Yanaka.
Map 3 B1.
Tel (03) 3823-1453.

Itoya
2-8-17 Ginza.
Map 5 C2.
Tel (03) 3561-8311.

Kurodaya
1-2-5 Asakusa.
Map 4 F3.
Tel (03) 3844-7511.
⬤ *Mon.*

Maruzen
2-3-10 Nihonbashi.
Map 5 C1.
Tel (03) 3272-7211.

Mataroningyou
5-15-13 Ueno.
Map 3 C3.
Tel (03) 3833-9662.
⬤ *Varies.*

Oya Shobo
1-1 Kanda-Jinbocho.
Map 3 B5.
Tel (03) 3291-0062.
⬤ *Sun.*

Takumi
8-4-2 Ginza.
Map 5 B3.
Tel (03) 3571-2017.
⬤ *Sun & public hols.*

Yoshitoku
1-9-14 Asakusabashi.
Map 4 D4.
Tel (03) 3863-4419.

ENTERTAINMENT IN TOKYO

Tokyo is one of the liveliest places on the planet. Contrary to the popular image, the Japanese are not simply a nation of workaholics – they play hard, too. The young in particular are demanding more "lifestyle" time. Traditionally Japanese gather with like-minded friends at small establishments catering to their interests; as a result, thousands of entertainment venues fill

National Theater poster

the city. There's a mind-boggling range of live music from jazz and blues to pop and techno, and the classical music scene is also very active. Tokyo is the best place to see traditional drama and is well served by touring local and international theater groups. Sports fans can head for packed baseball and soccer games, or sample traditional martial arts including sumo, the national sport.

INFORMATION SOURCES

Local guide *Metropolis* is a free weekly magazine (and website), published every Friday, with plenty of information on entertainment in Tokyo. The monthly magazine *Tokyo Journal* also has features, listings, restaurant reviews, and relevant maps. Saturday's *Japan Times* and Thursday's *Daily Yomiuri* also have good listings. All are available in stores selling English-language books, including **Kinokuniya**, **Tower Records**, and **Maruzen**. Information on current events in and around Tokyo can be accessed by visiting the **Japan National Tourist Organization (JNTO)** website.

Online magazines **TokyoQ**, **Outdoor Japan**, and **Japan Visitor** (a calendar of traditional festivals in and around the city) are other good sources of information.

BOOKING TICKETS

Tickets can go very quickly, so make decisions fast, be prepared for some disappointments, and have an alternative plan. For popular Japanese entertainment (such as Kabuki, Noh, sumo, or baseball) try to book ahead via a travel agent.

In Tokyo two of the main ticket agencies are **Ticket PIA** and **CN Playguide**. They can be hard to reach by phone, so it's often easier to book in person; a convenient office is **Ticket PIA** at Ginza's Sony Building *(see p66)*. Many department stores also have their own ticket offices. Alternatively, book direct by

phoning the venue; you pay when you pick up the tickets. Most agencies speak only Japanese, so try to have a Japanese-speaker help you. You can also book online through the weekly listings magazine **Metropolis**.

Staff ready to help at Daimaru department store ticket office

TRADITIONAL THEATER

Kabuki and Noh, the two main forms of traditional theater *(see pp36–7)*, are well represented in Tokyo. Many visitors find Noh heavy going due to the slow-paced action and dialogue in a foreign language. As a theatrical experience bordering on the mystical, however, Noh can be exceptionally powerful. The **Noh National Theater** near Sendagaya JR station usually has weekend performances. Tickets vary from ¥2,300 to ¥4,300. It is also possible to see plays at a Noh school, **Kanze Noh-gakudo**, for example. Noh can occasionally be seen as it was originally performed: on an outdoor stage

in front of a temple illuminated by torchlight.

Kabuki is an all-male flamboyant spectacle with rousing stories, elaborate sets, and amazing costumes. In 1986 Super Kabuki controversially combined avant-garde ideas and high-tech special effects (such as actors flying through the air) with traditional Kabuki. **Kabuki-za Theater** *(see p68)* is the main venue for Kabuki, with near daily performances starting mid-morning and lasting three or more hours. It is also possible to buy a ticket to see just one act as a taster or if short of time. Prices range from ¥2,400 to ¥16,000, or ¥900 for the one-act ticket. The National Theater has Kabuki performances in January, March, October, November, and December. Bunraku traditional puppet theater *(see p37)* is sometimes staged in the National Theater's Small Hall.

Kabuki in action at the Kabuki-za Theater

Movie poster in Shinjuku, one of Tokyo's centers for cinema

Kyogen is Japan's oldest form of drama, and includes acrobatics and juggling. Now played to comic effect, Kyogen is performed as part of Noh, or as individual plays between Noh plays. Another theatrical tradition is Rakugo, a form of storytelling which literally means "falling down". Dressed in a kimono and using a minimum of props, storytellers sit on *zabuton* cushions in small theaters such as **Suzumoto** in Ueno and pass on tales old and new. Manzai, or stand-up comedy, is a Kansai tradition that can be found in Tokyo, with Shinjuku's **Yoshimoto Lumine Shinjuku** a convenient venue.

INTERNATIONAL AND CONTEMPORARY THEATER AND DANCE

The theater scene encompasses everything from Shakespeare (at the **Tokyo Globe**) and Broadway musicals to comedy, classical ballet, and modern dance, with the main venues in Shinjuku, Shibuya, and Marunouchi. The level of performance is usually high.

The Tokyo Comedy Store offers non-Japanese and Japanese the chance to show off their comedy skills in English: two laughter-packed hours on the fourth Friday of the month at **Crocodile** in Harajuku.

A uniquely Japanese theater experience is Takaruza, a company divided into five

Poster advertising a Japanese theater production

troupes and composed entirely of women. With their own brand new, state-of-the-art **Takaruza Theater** in Yurakucho, they perform adaptations in Japanese of Western musicals and historic love stories, and are famed for their lavish productions.

Nihon Buyo Kyokai stages regular performances of traditional dance. Usually at the end of May, the Azuma Odori, an annual production of dance, drama, and music, brings Tokyo's geisha community on stage at the **Shinbashi Enbujo Theater**.

Buto – a unique and compelling art form – is contemporary dance combined with performance art. Developed in the 1960s, performances feature shaven-headed dancers, almost naked, painted with makeup. Slow, simplistic choreography seeks to create beauty out of the self-imposed grotesqueness.

CINEMA

Movie-going is not cheap in Japan, costing about ¥1,800 per person. However, on Cinema Day, usually the first day of each month, ticket prices are reduced. American and European films usually take at least six months to reach Japan. Non-Japanese films are usually shown in the original language with Japanese subtitles.

In Shibuya (*see pp96–7*), **Bunkamura** sometimes shows Japanese films with English subtitles and occasionally screens independent and European films. Also in Shibuya, the **Theater Image Forum**, designed by architect Takahashi Masaharu, uses the most advanced digital technology. The centrally located **Hibiya Chanter** cinema shows art-house and independent movies.

For mainstream movies, there are six cinemas around the square in which the **Koma** cinema is situated, in Shinjuku's Kabukicho (*see p90*). **Marunouchi Piccadilly** in the Mullion Building in Ginza (*see pp66–7*) has five screens, while **Ebisu Garden Place** (*see p103*) has two. The most recent arrival is **Toho Cinema Roppongi Hills** in the Roppongi Hills complex. Fans of Japanese cinema should visit the superb **National Film Center**.

The increasingly popular **Tokyo International Film Festival** is held every October/ November. A number of other worthwhile film festivals – homegrown and international – have also sprung up in recent years.

Live performance by the Tokyo Comedy Store

LIVE MUSIC

There is no shortage of venues to hear live music in Tokyo. Many big acts, Japanese and foreign, appear at Shibuya's **Club Quattro**. **O-West** and **O-East** are two other good venues in Shibuya for techno and J-pop. In Ebisu the **Liquid Room** is a trendy place to see a mix of bands. The **Akasaka Blitz** hosts J-pop groups and some foreign acts. Venues for live music and experimental performances range from the ever-exciting **Super Deluxe** in Nishi-Azabu, to expat-hangout **The Pink Cow** in Shibuya. The **Mandala Live House** has mostly Japanese bands.

For big-name jazz performers try the **Shinjuku Pit Inn**, the **Cotton Club** in Marunouchi, and the **Blue Note Tokyo**. **Birdland**, in Roppongi's Square Building, is one of Tokyo's longest-running jazz clubs. For a cozier, more intimate setting, try the **Blues Alley Japan**, a small club featuring blues, jazz, rock, world music, and other genres. In Roppongi, **STB139 Sweet Basil** offers a very eclectic mix of music.

The domestic and international classical music and opera scene in Tokyo is flourishing. **Tokyo Opera City** *(see p100)*, **Bunkamura** *(see p92)*, **New National Theater**, **Suntory Hall**, **NHK Hall**, and the **Tokyo International Forum** *(see p71)* are all popular spots.

Roppongi District, a focus for music and nightclubs in Tokyo

A popular karaoke club in downtown Tokyo

KARAOKE

Karaoke, which translates from the Japanese characters as "empty orchestra", dates from the 1960s. Today it is not only a prime pastime for most Japanese, irrespective of age, but a global phenomenon. Devotees sing favorite songs to pre-recorded tapes, CDs, and DVDs in bars, pubs, and even at home. Most popular are Western standards, current pop songs, and *enka*, the Japanese equivalent of French *chanson*.

In recent years it has become common for Japanese companies to build karaoke complexes consisting of small, cozy rooms for couples to much larger spaces for groups of friends and large parties. Food and drinks can be ordered. It is hard to escape karaoke – it is everywhere in the city.

Big Echo is the name of one major karaoke chain which operates in Tokyo, and the well known games company Sega operates another. Family restaurant chains such as Denny's, Jonathon's, and Royal Host are also strong supporters. Sometimes venues even star in movies: Karaoke-kan in Shibuya's Center Gai *(see p96)* is the famed location used in the 2003 movie *Lost in Translation* – the rooms used are 601 and 602 on the sixth floor.

GAMBLING

Pachinko *(see p97)* is a form of disguised gambling; it was devised in Nagoya just after World War II and is based on the American pinball machine. A good place to go if you want to experience pachinko firsthand is Maruhan Pachinko Tower in Shibuya. Here, each floor has a different theme, and there are love seats for couples.

Winnings from *pachinko* are generally exchanged for goods – brand-name goods in upscale areas – or for money, but the money exchange has to be done outside the premises to remain within the law, through a hole in the wall. This is because gambling for money is illegal in Japan, except for certain approved (and unsurprisingly highly popular) activities such as

Maruhan Pachinko Tower in Shibuya

horse-racing, powerboat racing, bicycle racing, and major lotteries.

More often than not, however, a blind eye is turned by the Japanese authorities to the ways in which people choose to indulge in gambling. Mahjong is played in private clubs and homes, for example. Some hostess clubs offer gambling in addition to their other services, as long as it is not for money.

NIGHTCLUBS

Tokyo's clubs are many and varied, and the club scene is very fluid; check current listings *(see p108)* for the latest information. There are several centers for nightclubs; Roppongi (see pp98–9), the city's upscale playground, is one of the most lively. The **Square Building** (see Birdland, under "Live Music") near Roppongi station is full of clubs from top to bottom. The Ni-chome area of Shinjuku is home to some 250 gay clubs, as well as numerous pubs and bars. Many famous DJs operate each night at **Oto**, in Shinjuku. **Atom**, in Shibuya, attracts a mainly young clientele and has two dance floors as well as a floor just for relaxation.

Other clubs currently drawing crowds for every type of dance music from salsa to techno and house disco are **Velfarre** (see p99), **Yellow**, **La Fabrique**, and **Club Core**.

Clubs with a show tend to get going early in the evening, around 7–8pm; the last show ends in time to catch the last trains out to the suburbs, about 11–11:30pm. Smaller clubs start and end later, while dance clubs won't warm up until around 11pm and often keep going all night. Expect a cover charge at most clubs of ¥2,000–4,000, usually including one drink.

SUMO

Sumo tournaments, each lasting 15 days, are held in Tokyo in January, May (when the emperor himself attends), and September, all at the impressive 10,000-seat **National Sumo Stadium** in Ryogoku (see p102).

Tournaments begin on a Sunday, with each fighter wrestling once a day. Bouts start each day at around 2:30pm with the lowest-ranking wrestlers and continue in ascending order, with the top ranks wrestling from 5–6pm, ending with a bout involving the highest-ranked wrestler, usually a *yokozuna* (grand champion). The stadium tends to fill up with spectators as the day goes on.

Sumo wrestlers stand for a ceremony at the Ryogoku stadium in Tokyo

The best views are on the north side of the stadium. It is advisable to book tickets in advance from **Playguide**, **Ticket PIA** at the Sony Building, or any **Lawson's** convenience store. Easiest to get are midweek tickets in the first week of a tournament. If you cannot buy tickets via an agency, try asking your hotel to check for returns, or lining up at the stadium itself at about 8am on the day.

If you are not in Tokyo during a tournament, you may be able to watch the daily practice at a sumo stable, or *beya* (see p102). Most are open to anyone who wants to watch, with a few basic rules: don't eat or use a camera flash, and be quiet. The closer a tournament is, the more likely you are to be politely turned away. The best time to view practice is 6–10am. Most of the *beya* are situated near Ryogoku station. Try **Kasugano Beya**, a tall new building with a green copper gable over the entrance, **Iztsu Beya**, or **Dewanoumi Beya**.

Banners outside the National Sumo Stadium, Ryogoku

In the last few years, sumo has been much enlivened by an influx of foreign wrestlers from Hawaii, Mongolia, and Europe, many of whom have become very successful. Some stables with an unusually open attitude have also made special trips abroad in order to raise awareness of sumo internationally; some of their stars even appear in television and other advertisements. While eyebrows may have been raised among purists, they cannot deny that such activities have been very good for business.

OTHER MARTIAL ARTS

Martial arts (see p35) are practiced in many places throughout Tokyo, but different establishments vary in their openness to non-Japanese as observers and participants. Contact **Tokyo TIC** for a list of *dojos* (practice halls) that allow spectators. To find out about participating in martial arts training, contact one of the national regulatory bodies (see pp 358–61).

BASEBALL AND SOCCER

Baseball's place as Japan's second national sport appears to be suffering in the face of soccer's rising popularity. Some young players are choosing to go abroad to escape samurai-like regimes of training but the game continues to stir fervor.

There are two professional baseball leagues in Japan: Central League and Pacific League. The winners face off at the end of the season for the final of the Japan Series. In 2006 the Pacific League's Hokkaido Nippon Ham Fighters, now based in Sapporo, won for the first time in over 40 years. However, the Central League's Yomiuri Giants remain Japan's most popular pro-baseball team (*see p359*). Their games in the **Tokyo Dome** are always sold out; book through an

Footballer, World Cup 2002

agent well in advance. The best place to enjoy a game in the capital is in the beautiful **Jingu Stadium**, home of the Tokyo Yakult Swallows (also Central League). Tickets are often available at **Ticket PIA**.

The J-League, Japan's professional soccer league, started in 1993. The World Cup, staged in Japan in 2002, sent interest soaring but Japan's failure to make the grade in Germany in 2006 changed attitudes. New teams continue to surface, however. **Ajinomoto Stadium** opened in 2001 with a capacity of 50,000. It is home to two J-League teams – FC Tokyo and Tokyo Verdi 1969. Tourist information centers have details of games, and tickets are available at **Ticket PIA** or from the stadium on the day of the match. Gangster-linked ticket touts are much in evidence in Tokyo so always use caution.

Baseball Hall of Fame, Tokyo Dome

OTHER SPORTS

For details on other sports check the Sports column in *Metropolis* magazine. Entries are mostly concerned with gathering together like-minded people wanting to play, but those people will also know where to watch their favorite sports, from tennis and rugby to basketball, cycling, and cricket. For mountaineering, skiing, and watersports see pp360–61.

DIRECTORY

INFORMATION SOURCES

Japan National Tourist Organization (JNTO)
Tel (03) 3201-3331.
www.jnto.go.jp

Kinokuniya
3-17-7 Shinjuku.
Map 1 B1.
Tel (03) 3354-0131.
www.kinokuniya.co.jp

Maruzen
1-6-4 Marunouchi.
Map 5 B1.
Tel (03) 5288-8881.
www.maruzen.co.jp

Metropolis
www.metropolis.co.jp

Tower Records
1-22-14 Jinnan.
Map 1 B5.
Tel (03) 3496-3661.

TokyoQ
www.tokyoq.com

Outdoor Japan
www.outdoorjapan.com

Japan Vistor
www.japanvisitor.com

BOOKING TICKETS

CN Playguide
Tel (03) 5802-9999.

Ticket PIA
Tel (0570) 02-9999.

Metropolis
www.metropolis.co.jp/tickets

TRADITIONAL THEATER

Kanze Nohgakudo
1-16-4 Shoto. **Map** 1 A5.
Tel (03) 3469-5241.

National Noh Theater
4-18-1 Sendagaya.
Map 1 C3.
Tel (03) 3423-1331.

National Theater
4-1 Hayabusa-cho.

Map 2 F3.
Tel (03) 3265-7411.
www.ntj.jac.go.jp/english/index.html

Suzumoto
2-7-12 Ueno.
Tel (03) 3834-5906.
www.rakugo.or.jp

Yoshimoto Lumine Shinjuku
7F (South Exit from station) 3-38-3 Shinjuku.
Tel (03) 5339-1112.

INTERNATIONAL AND CONTEMPORARY THEATER AND DANCE

Crocodile
6-18-8 B1 New Sekiguchi Building, Meiji-Jingumae, Shibuya.
www.tokyocomedy.com

Nihon Buyo Kyokai
2-18-1 Kachidoki.
Map 6 D4.
Tel (03) 3533-6455.

Shinbashi Enbujo Theater
6-18-2 Ginza.
Map 5 C3.
Tel (03) 3541-2600.

Takarazuka Theater
1-1-3 Yurakucho.
Map 5 B2.
Tel (03) 5251-2001.
www.kageki.hankyu.co.jp/english/index.html

Tokyo Globe
3-1-2 Hyakunin-cho, Shinjuku.
Tel (03) 3366-4020.
www.www.tglobe.net

CINEMA

Bunkamura
2-24-1 Dogen-zaka, Shibuya-ku.
Map 1 A5.
Tel (03) 3477 9111.
www.bunkamura.co.jp

Hibiya Chanter
Chanter Cine, 1-2-2 Yurakucho.
Map 5 B2.
Tel (03) 3591-1511.

For hotels and restaurants in this region see pp298–300 and pp330–34

DIRECTORY

Koma Theater
Kabukicho,
Shinjuku.
Map 1 B1.

Marunouchi Piccadilly
Mullion Building, 2-5-1
Yurakucho.
Map 5 B2.
Tel (03) 3201-2881.

National Film Center
3-7-6 Kyobashi.
Map 5 C2.
Tel (03) 3561-0823.

Theater Image Forum
2-10-2 Shibuya.
Map 1 C5.
Tel (03) 5766-0114.

Toho Cinema Roppongi Hills
6-10-2 Roppongi,
Minato-ku.
*Tel (03) 5775-6090
(press 9 for English).*

Tokyo International Film Festival
www.tiff-jp.net

LIVE MUSIC

Akasaka Blitz
TBS Square, 5-3-6
Akasaka.
Map 2 E4.
Tel (03) 3224-0567.

Birdland
B2 Square Building,
3-10-3 Roppongi.
Map 2 E5.
Tel (03) 3478-3456.

Blue Note Tokyo
Raika Building,
6-3-16 Minami-
Aoyama.
Map 2 D5.
Tel (03) 5485-0088.

Blues Alley Japan
Hotel Wing International
Megro,
1-3-14 Meguro.
Map 1 B1.
Tel (03) 5496-4381.

Bunkamura
2-24-1 Dogen-zaka,
Shibuya-ku.
Map 1 A5.
Tel (03) 3477 9111.
www.bunkamura.co.jp

Club Quattro
4F Quattro Parco, 32-13
Udagawa-cho.
Map 1 A5.
Tel (03) 3477-8750.

Cotton Club
2 F Tokia,
Tokyo Building,
2-7-3 Marunouchi,
Chiyoda-ku.
Map 5 B1.
Tel (03) 3215-1555.
www.cottonclubjapan.
co.jp

Liquid Room
3-16-6 Higashi,
Shibuya-ku.
Tel (03) 5464-0800.

Mandala Live House
B1 MR Building,
3-2-2 Minami-Aoyama
Map 1 C4.
Tel (03) 5474-0411.

New National Theater
1-1-1 Honmachi,
Shibuya-ku.
Tel (03) 5351-3011.

NHK Hall
2-2-1 Jinnan.
Map 1 B4.
Tel (03) 3465-1751.

O-East
2-14-8 Dogen-zaka.
Map 1 A5.
Tel (03) 5458-4681.

O-West
2-3 Maruyamacho.
Map 1 A5.
Tel (03) 5458-4646.

Shinjuku Pit Inn
B1 Accord Building,
2-12-4 Shinjuku.
Map 1 B1.
Tel (03) 3354-2024.

STB139 Sweet Basil
6-7-11 Roppongi.
Map 2 E5
Tel (03) 5474-0139.

Suntory Hall
1-13-1 Akasaka.
Map 2 E3.
Tel (03) 3584-9999.

Super Deluxe
B1F 3-1-25 Nishi-Azabu.
Map 2 E5.
Tel (03) 5412-0515.
www.super-deluxe.com

The Pink Cow
Villa Moderuna B1
1-3-18 Shibuya.
Map 2 E5.
Tel (03) 5412-0515.
www.thepinkcow.com

KARAOKE

Big Echo Karaoke
Ginza 4-2-14.
Map 5 C3.
Tel (03) 3563-5100.

7-4-12 Roppongi.
Tel (03) 3770-7700.

GAMBLING

Japan Association for International Horse Racing
(JAIR Keiba Kokusai Koryu
Kyokai)
Tel (03) 3503-8211.
www.jair.jrao.ne.jp

Maruhan Pachinko Tower
28-6 Udagawa-cho,
Shibuya.
Tel (03) 5458 3905.

Powerboat Racing (Kyotei)
www.kyotei.or.jp

Tokyo Racecourse
1-1 Hiyoshi-cho,
Fuchi-shi.
www.jair.jrao.ne.jp/
courses/jra.jra001.html

NIGHTCLUBS

Atom
4F-6F Dr Jeekahns
2-4 Maruyama-cho,
Shibuya
(along Rambling
Street).
Map 1 A5.
Tel (03) 5428-5195.

Club Core
TSC CCC Building B1,
b2 7-15-30
Roppongi.
Tel (03) 3470-5944.

La Fabrique
Gate B1F
16-9 Udagawa-cho,
Shibuya.
Tel (03) 5428-5100.

Oto
2F Wadahisa Building,
Kabukicho Ichibangai,
Shinjuku. **Map** 1 B1.
Tel (03) 5273-8264.

Velfarre
7-14-22 Roppongi.
Tel (03) 3402-8000.

Yellow
1-10-11 Nishi-Azabu.
Tel (03) 3479-0690.

SUMO

Dewanoumi Beya
2-3-15 Ryogoku.
Map 4 E5.

Iztsu Beya
2-2-7 Ryogoku.
Map 4 E5.

Kasugano Beya
1-7-11 Ryogoku.
Map 4 E5.

National Sumo Stadium
1-3-28 Yokoami.
Map 4 E4.
Tel (03) 3623-5111.
www.sumo.or.jp/eng/
index.html

BASEBALL AND SOCCER

Ajinomoto Stadium
376-3 Nishimachi, Chofu
City.
Tel (0424) 40-0555.

Jingu Stadium
3-1 Kasumigaoka.
Map 2 D4.
Tel (03) 3404-8999.

Tokyo Dome
1-3-61 Koraku.
Map 3 A3.
Tel (03) 5800-9999.
www.tokyo-dome.
co.jp/e

TOKYO STREET FINDER

Tokyo is notoriously hard for visitors to find their way around, due to the scarcity of street names and complex numbering system for buildings *(see pp384–5)*. The Tokyo sights covered in this guide, plus Tokyo hotels *(see pp298–300)*, restaurants *(see pp330–34)*, and many of the city's key landmarks are plotted on the maps on the following pages. Transportation points are also marked, and indicated by the symbols listed in the key below. When map references are given the first number tells you which Street Finder map to turn to, and the letter and number that follow refer to the grid reference. The map below shows the area of Tokyo covered by the six Street Finder maps. The Street Finder index opposite lists street names, buildings, and stations. For a map of the Tokyo subway, see the inside back cover.

KEY

Major sight		Police station	
Other sight		Temple	
Other building		Shrine	
Subway station		Church	
Train station		Post office	
Long-distance bus station		JR rail line	
Riverboat boarding point		Other rail line	
Tourist information		Expressway	
Hospital		Pedestrian street	

0 kilometers   2

0 miles   1

SCALE OF MAPS 1–6

0 meters   500

0 miles   500

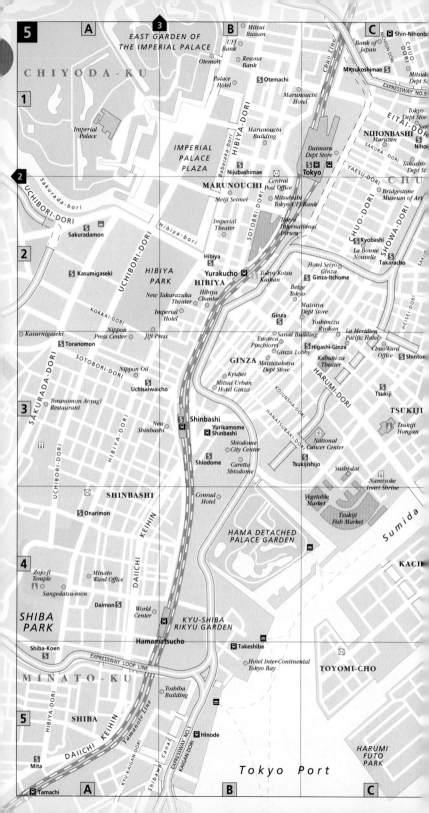

JAPAN REGION BY REGION

Japan at a Glance

Honshu, Japan's largest island, is characterized by its mountainous center and densely populated southern coastline. Most of Japan's ancient temples, shrines, and imperial cities are on Honshu, along with the vibrant capital, Tokyo. North of Honshu lies the island of Hokkaido, an unspoiled wilderness of national parks, snowbound for much of the year. The quiet, traditional island of Shikoku lies south of Honshu, as does Kyushu island, a varied mixture of modern cities, hot springs, and archaeological ruins. A string of subtropical islands with Okinawa at the center stretches away to the southwest.

The Inland Sea, separating Honshu and Shikoku islands

OKINAWA ARCHIPELAGO

Nakijin Castle Ruin (see p257) *on Okinawa's north coast dates from the 14th century. It is one of several historical and cultural sights that make this colorful, exotic island more than simply a beach resort destination.*

OKINAWA
(See pp250–59)

0 kilometers   100

0 miles   50

Konomine-ji *is Temple 27 on Shikoku's 88-temple pilgrimage (see pp228–9). The thousands of pilgrims who travel the route every year are following in the footsteps of Kukai, the 9th-century founder of Shingon sect Buddhism.*

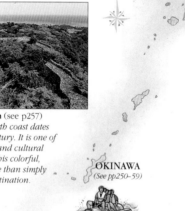

Miyajima *island's vermilion* torii *(gate) is one of Japan's most famous sights.*

WESTERN HONSHU
(See pp186–

SHIKOKU
(See pp220–29)

KYUSHU
(See pp230–49)

The Peace Park *in Nagasaki (see pp240–43) was the point of impact of the second atomic bomb, for which the city is now known worldwide. A cosmopolitan port for centuries, it has regenerated since the war to become a thriving urban center.*

↓ Okinawa

0 kilometers   100

0 miles   50

Shikotsu-Toya National Park (see pp284–5) *contains active and dormant volcanos, and hot springs. National parks are central to Hokkaido's appeal, encompassing coastal meadows, wetlands, and mountains.*

HOKKAIDO
(See pp280–91)

The Philosopher's Walk (see p170) *is a tranquil canalside walk famed for its cherry trees. The path links two of Kyoto's temples: Nanzen-ji and Ginkaku-ji.*

NORTHERN HONSHU
(See pp260–79)

Nikko (see pp264–71) *is a complex of shrines and temples in the mountains of Northern Honshu. The shrines are intricately carved with images of animals, birds, and flowers, painted in vivid colors.*

CENTRAL HONSHU
(See pp128–53)

TOKYO
(See pp60–123)

KYOTO CITY
(See pp154–85)

Hakone (see pp138–9) *is a hilly hot-spring town in Central Honshu on the old route between Edo (Tokyo) and Kyoto. Its many attractions include Lake Ashi, on which replicas of old ships sail; an open-air sculpture museum; and fine views of Mount Fuji, which dominates the plain to the west of Tokyo.*

Nara (see pp190–95) *was Japan's first capital and a center of Buddhism. It retains beautiful buildings in a traditional layout and is home to one of Japan's most spectacular festivals, Omizu-tori (see p42), each spring.*

CENTRAL HONSHU

*L*ying between Tokyo and Kyoto, Central Honshu epitomizes the contrasts of Japan today. Its densely populated coastal belt includes the country's second-and fourth-largest cities, while the interior contains its highest, wildest mountains. Between these extremes, much of the region is relatively accessible, yet remote enough to have kept traditional rural lifestyles, architecture, and festivals.

The mountains of Central Honshu incorporate not only Mount Fuji but also the North and South Japan Alps, with many peaks over 3,000 m (10,000 ft). They dictate the area's character, and offer hiking, skiing, and hot springs. During the Edo period (1603–1868) five post roads crossed the region, linking Edo (Tokyo) and Kyoto. Feudal lords were required to spend half their time in Edo, so long processions traveled the roads, and checkpoints and post towns grew up. Most heavily used were the Tokaido ("East Sea Way") via Yokohama, Hakone, and Shizuoka, and the Nakasendo ("Central Mountain Way") through the Kiso Valley. Remnants of both can be walked.

Postman from Tsumago in the Kiso Valley

Today there is a dramatic contrast between the modern, urban Pacific coast, including Yokohama and Nagoya, and underpopulated rural areas. Among the latter, the post towns of Kiso and thatched villages of Shokawa have found new life in tourism thanks to unspoiled architecture, while Takayama and Chichibu attract thousands to their festivals. The former regional capitals of Kamakura and Kanazawa maintain tradition in gardens, temples, culture, and crafts. Heavily forested, the region produces skilled woodwork: lacquerware in Takayama, Noto, and Kiso; carving in Kamakura; *yosegi-zaiku* in Hakone. Until the 1970s, silkworms were raised in Shokawa and Chichibu; silk was exported via Yokohama and is still dyed in Kanazawa. Central Honshu cuisine focuses on seafood coastally, while mountain fare comprises river fish, *sansai* (young ferns), tofu, and miso. Kanazawa's refined yet down-to-earth *Kaga ryori* uses fish and duck; Nagoya is known for eel, chicken, and stronger flavors.

The waterfront at Yokohama, Japan's second-largest city

◁ The snow-capped cone of Mount Fuji dominating the landscape

Exploring Central Honshu

The smooth cone of Mount Fuji – one of the great icons of Japan – rises from the Kanto Plain to the west of Tokyo, and is open to pilgrims and casual hikers in summer. Beyond this is the largely mountainous area known to the Japanese as Chubu. A cluster of cultural and scenic destinations, including Fuji, Hakone, Kamakura, and much of the industrialized Pacific coast, are an easy day-trip from Tokyo. Other areas, especially the more rural regions such as the Kiso and Shokawa valleys and the Noto peninsula, are harder to reach and require more time to explore.

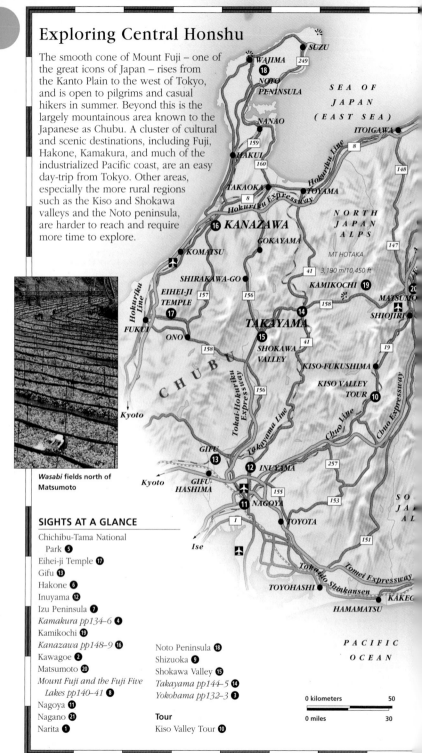

Wasabi fields north of Matsumoto

SIGHTS AT A GLANCE

Chichibu-Tama National
  Park ⑤
Eihei-ji Temple ⑰
Gifu ⑬
Hakone ⑥
Inuyama ⑫
Izu Peninsula ⑦
Kamakura pp134–6 ④
Kamikochi ⑲
Kanazawa pp148–9 ⑯
Kawagoe ②
Matsumoto ⑳
*Mount Fuji and the Fuji Five
  Lakes pp140–41* ⑧
Nagoya ⑪
Nagano ㉑
Narita ①

Noto Peninsula ⑱
Shizuoka ⑨
Shokawa Valley ⑮
Takayama pp144–5 ⑭
Yokohama pp132–3 ③

Tour
Kiso Valley Tour ⑩

0 kilometers   50

0 miles   30

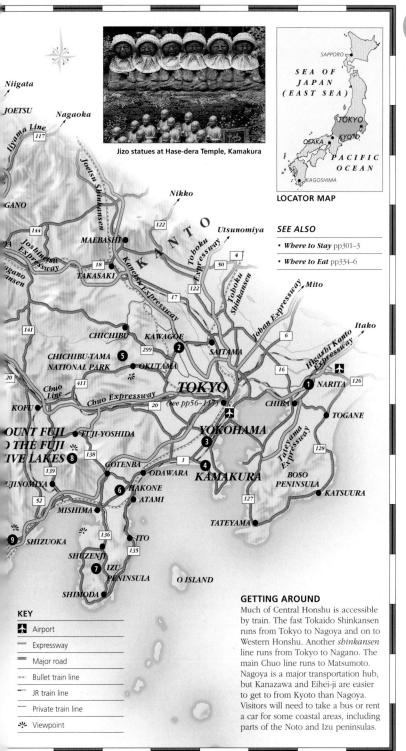

Jizo statues at Hase-dera Temple, Kamakura

LOCATOR MAP

SEA OF
JAPAN
(EAST SEA)

SAPPORO

TOKYO

OSAKA
KYOTO

PACIFIC
OCEAN

KAGOSHIMA

SEE ALSO

- **Where to Stay** pp301–3
- **Where to Eat** pp334–6

Niigata

JOETSU   Nagaoka

Iiyama Line   117

Joetsu Shinkansen

Nikko

GANO

144

Joshinetsu Expressway

MAEBASHI

TAKASAKI   18

Kanetsu Expressway

Nagano Shinkansen

Utsunomiya

122

Tohoku Expressway

50

4

Tohoku Shinkansen

Joban Expressway   Mito

141

CHICHIBU

CHICHIBU-TAMA **5**
NATIONAL PARK

KAWAGOE

299

OKUTAMA

17

122

SAITAMA

6

16

Higashi Kanto Expressway

Itako

20

Chuo Line

411

Chuo Expressway

20

KOFU

TOKYO
(see pp56–127)

CHIBA

1 NARITA   126

TOGANE

OUNT FUJI
) THE FUJI
IVE LAKES **8**   138

FUJI-YOSHIDA

139

JINOMIYA

52

GOTENBA

ODAWARA

6 HAKONE
ATAMI

MISHIMA

1

YOKOHAMA

3

4

KAMAKURA

Tateyama Expressway

128

BOSO
PENINSULA

KATSUURA

127

TATEYAMA

9 SHIZUOKA

136

135

ITO

SHUZENJI
7 IZU
PENINSULA

SHIMODA

O ISLAND

KEY

✈	Airport
▬	Expressway
▬	Major road
⋯	Bullet train line
▬	JR train line
—	Private train line
☼	Viewpoint

GETTING AROUND

Much of Central Honshu is accessible by train. The fast Tokaido Shinkansen runs from Tokyo to Nagoya and on to Western Honshu. Another *shinkansen* line runs from Tokyo to Nagano. The main Chuo line runs to Matsumoto. Nagoya is a major transportation hub, but Kanazawa and Eihei-ji are easier to get to from Kyoto than Nagoya. Visitors will need to take a bus or rent a car for some coastal areas, including parts of the Noto and Izu peninsulas.

Narita ❶
成田

Chiba prefecture. 🚶 120,000. ✈ 🚉 ℹ️ in front of JR stn (0476) 24-3198. **www**.city.narita.chiba.jp/english 🎎 Setsubun-e (Feb 3).

A quiet little town, worlds removed from nearby Narita Airport, Narita's main attraction is **Narita-san Shin-sho-ji**, an Esoteric-Shingon-sect temple founded in 940 and dedicated to Fudo Myo-o, Deity of Immovable Wisdom. Several times daily, the priests burn wooden sticks to symbolize extinguishing of earthly passions. The streets are full of traditional shops for the 12 million temple visitors a year.

Environs: Near Narita are over 1,000 ancient burial mounds (*kofun*); the best are in **Boso Historical Park**. The **National Museum of Japanese History** offers a good survey of Japan.

🌹 **Boso Historical Park**
15 mins by taxi from Narita stn.
Tel (0476) 95-3126. ⬜ Tue–Sun.

🏛 **National Museum of Japanese History**
15 mins walk from Sakura stn.
Tel (043) 486-0123. ⬜ Tue–Sun. 📷

Kawagoe ❷
川越

Saitama prefecture. 🚶 333,000. 🚉 ℹ️ at JR stn (049) 222-5556. **www**.city.kawagoe.saitama.jp 🎎 Ashi-odori (Leg-dancing, Apr 14), Kawagoe Festival (3rd weekend in Oct).

Nicknamed "Little Edo," Kawagoe preserves the atmosphere of 19th-century Edo (Tokyo) in its *kura*

Yokohama Bay Bridge

buildings. *Kura* structure, with thick clay walls, double doors, and heavy shutters, was used for warehouses and shops.

About 30 *kura* remain, and are a 10-minute walk north of Hon-Kawagoe station. The **Kura-Zukuri Shiryokan**, formerly a *kura* tobacconist, is a museum. Nearby, **Toki-no-kane** wooden bell tower was built in 1624 to tell the time and warn of fires. East of the *kura* streets is **Kita-in**, a Tendai-sect temple which includes the only extant rooms from Edo Castle.

Environs:
In Saitama, about 20 km (12 miles) east of Kawagoe, the **John Lennon Museum** celebrates the musician's life with photographs, videos, and music. There are also instruments, clothing, and hand-written lyric sheets donated by his wife, Yoko Ono.

🏠 **Kura-Zukuri Shiryokan**
Tel (049) 225-4287. ⬜ Tue–Sun.
🌙 4th Fri of month. 📷

🏛 **John Lennon Museum**
8 Shintoshin, Chuo-ku, Saitama.
Tel (048) 601-0009.
⬜ Wed–Mon. 📷

Yokohama ❸
横浜

Kanagawa prefecture. 🚶 3,600,000. ✈ 🚉 ℹ️ Sangyo Boeki Center Bldg (045) 641-4759. **www**.city.yokohama.jp 🎎 Chinese New Year (Feb), Yokohama Port Festival (May 3).

Japan's second-largest city, Yokohama has been a center for shipping, trade, foreign contact, and modern ideas since the mid-19th century. Formerly a small fishing village on the Tokaido road, it was made a treaty port in 1859; there followed an influx of foreign traders, especially Chinese and British, making it the biggest port in Asia by the early 1900s. The 1923 Kanto Earthquake wiped out 95 percent of the city, killing 40,000 people, then World War II bombing again destroyed half the city. After the war, Yokohama became a base for US soldiers. By the 1970s, it was once more Japan's largest port. The heart of the city is compact and walkable.

Minato Mirai 21, an area of redeveloped docks, has some creative architecture (with hi-tech earthquake-proofing) and on weekends comes alive with street performers. Its focal point is the **Landmark Tower**, built in 1993 under US architect Hugh Stubbins and, at 296 m (971 ft), Japan's tallest building. Reached by the world's fastest elevator (at 750 m (2,500 ft) per minute), the 69th-floor public lounge has a spectacular 360-degree view. To the north, Tange

A row of *kura* buildings in Kawagoe

For hotels and restaurants in this region see pp301–3 and pp334–6

Kenzo's **Yokohama Museum of Art** houses displays of modern art and photography.

In the older, more attractive part of town, the **NYK Maritime Museum** covers the history of shipping, with detailed models. Created on rubble from the 1923 Earthquake, **Yamashita Park** is a pleasant promenade overlooking ships, including the moored liner **Hikawa Maru**, which cruised between Yokohama and Seattle in 1930–60, and the 860-m (2,800-ft) long **Yokohama Bay Bridge** (1989).

Chinatown, the largest of Japan's few Chinatowns, has around 2,500 Chinese inhabitants, and a mass of restaurants, food shops, Chinese-medicine shops, and fortune-tellers. At its heart is the Chinese **Kantei-byo Temple** (1887), dedicated to ancient Chinese hero Kuan-yu, who was worshiped as a god of war but is now popular as a god of accountancy, business success, and prosperity.

Among the 4,500 tombs in the early 20th-century **Foreigners' Cemetery** is that of Edmund Morel, the English engineer who helped build Japan's first railroads, with a tombstone shaped like a railroad ticket. The lovely **Sankei-en Garden** belonged to silk-trader Hara Tomitaro (1868–1939). Among the ponds and flowers are 16 architectural treasures, including a three-story pagoda from Kyoto.

Landmark Tower
Tel (045) 222-5015. ☐ *daily.*

🏛 Yokohama Museum of Art
Tel (045) 221-0300. ☐ *Fri–Wed.* 📷

🏛 NYK Maritime Museum
Tel (045) 221-0280. ☐ *Tue–Sun.* 📷

Hikawa Maru
Tel (045) 641-4362. ☐ *daily.* 📷

⛩ Foreigners' Cemetery
Tel (045) 622-1311. ☐ *Apr–Nov: Sat, Sun, public hols.*

♣ Sankei-en Garden
10 mins by bus from Negishi stn (JR) to Honmoku Sankei-en Mae.
Tel (045) 621-0634. ☐ *daily.* 📷

Environs:
Outside the center are two entertaining venues: **Kirin Beer Village**, with tasting tours of the automated Kirin brewery; and **Shin Yokohama Ramen Museum** *(see p336).* On a more serious note, the **Hodogaya Common-wealth Cemetery** (a bus ride from Yokohama, Hodogaya, or Sakuragi-cho stations) contains Allied graves from World War II (including POWs).

Kirin Beer Village
🚉 *Namamugi stn, Keihin Kyuko line.*
Tel (045) 503-8250. ☐ *Tue–Sun.*

One of the colorful entrance gates to Yokohama's Chinatown

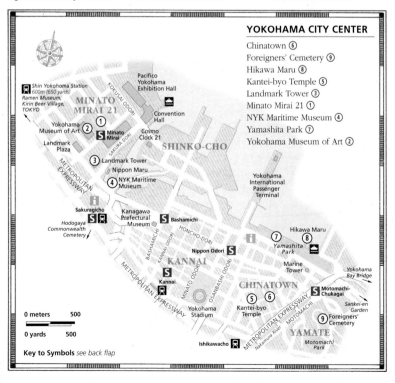

YOKOHAMA CITY CENTER

Chinatown ⑥
Foreigners' Cemetery ⑨
Hikawa Maru ⑧
Kantei-byo Temple ⑤
Landmark Tower ③
Minato Mirai 21 ①
NYK Maritime Museum ④
Yamashita Park ⑦
Yokohama Museum of Art ②

Shin Yokohama Station 600m (650 yards) Ramen Museum, Kirin Beer Village, TOKYO

MINATO MIRAI 21

KOKUSAI ODORI

Pacifico Yokohama Exhibition Hall

Convention Hall

Yokohama Museum of Art ②

① Minato Mirai

SAKURA DORI

Cosmo Clock 21

SHINKO-CHO

Landmark Plaza

③ Landmark Tower

Nippon Maru

④ NYK Maritime Museum

METROPOLITAN EXPRESSWAY

Sakuragicho

Hodogaya Commonwealth Cemetery

Kanagawa Prefectural Museum

Bashamichi

BASHAMICHI

KANNAI ODORI

HONCHO-DORI

Nippon Odori

KANNAI

Kannai

MINATO ODORI

OSANBASHI ODORI

Yokohama Stadium

Kantei-byo Temple

Ishikawacho

⑤ ⑥

CHINATOWN

Yokohama International Passenger Terminal

⑦ Yamashita Park

Marine Tower

Hikawa Maru ⑧

Yokohama Bay Bridge

Motomachi-Chukagai

METROPOLITAN EXPRESSWAY

MOTOMACHI

Nakamura River

YAMATE

Sankei-en Garden

⑨ Foreigners' Cemetery

Motomachi Park

0 meters 500
0 yards 500

Key to Symbols see back flap

Kamakura ❹

鎌倉

An Amida Buddha, Hase-dera temple

A seaside town of temples and wooded hills, Kamakura was Japan's capital from 1185 until 1333. As a legacy, today it has 19 Shinto shrines and 65 Buddhist temples, including two of Japan's oldest Zen monasteries (in Kita Kamakura, see p136). Many of the temples and gardens nestle against the hills ringing the town, and are linked by three hiking trails. Favored by artists and writers, Kamakura has numerous antique and crafts shops. In cherry-blossom season and on summer weekends it can be swamped by visitors. Some parts are best explored on foot, but there are one-day bus passes, and bicycles for rent at Kamakura station.

The path down the center of Wakamiya-oji, Kamakura's main street

🏯 Hase-dera Temple

🚉 Hase stn. 🚌 Tel (0467) 22-6300. ◯ daily. 📷 www.hasedera.jp

Simple and elegant, Hase-dera is home to a superb 11-faced Kannon, bosatsu of mercy. The Treasure House displays characterful Muromachi-era carvings of the 33 incarnations of Kannon and a 1421 image of Daikokuten, god of wealth. Beside it is the sutra repository; rotating the sutras is said to earn as much merit as reading them. The 1264 bell is the

town's oldest. Below it is a hall dedicated to Jizo, guardian of children, surrounded by countless statues to children who have died or been aborted.

🏯 Great Buddha

🚉 Hase stn. 🚌 Tel (0467) 22-0703. ◯ daily. 🚌

The Great Buddha (Daibutsu) is Kamakura's most famous sight. Cast in 1252, the bronze statue of the Amida Buddha is

13.5 m (44 ft) tall. Having survived tidal waves, fires, earthquakes, and typhoons, it now has shock-absorbers in its base. Its proportions are distorted so that it seems balanced to those in front of it – this use of perspective may show Greek influence (via the Silk Road). The interior is open to visitors.

🏛 Hachiman-gu Shrine

🚉 Kamakura stn. Tel (0467) 22-0315. ◯ daily. **Kamakura National Treasure House Museum** Tel (0467) 22-0753. ◯ Tue–Sun. 📷

Hachiman shrines are dedicated to the god of war; this one is also a guardian shrine of the Minamoto (or Genji) clan. Built in 1063 by the sea, it was moved here in 1191. The approach runs between two lotus ponds: the Genji Pond has three islands (in Japanese san means both three and life) while the Heike Pond, named for a rival clan, has four (shi means both four and death). The path leads to the Mai-den stage for dances and music. The main shrine above was

SIGHTS AT A GLANCE

Engaku-ji Temple ①
Great Buddha ⑫
Hachiman-gu Shrine ⑥
Hase-dera Temple ⑪
Hokoku-ji Temple ⑨
Kencho-ji Temple ④
Meigetsu-in Temple ③
Myohon-ji Temple ⑩
Sugimoto-dera Temple ⑧
Tokei-ji Temple ②
Zeni-arai Benten Shrine ⑤
Zuisen-ji Temple ⑦

YOKOHAM

Kita-Kamaku
Statio

Toke
Tem

Zeni-arai ⑤
Benten Shrine

Sasuke-no
Inari Shrine

SHIYAKUSH

Great Buddha
Hiking Trail

⑫
Great Buddha
(Daibutsu)

⑪ Hase-dera
Temple

Yuigahama
Station

Hase
Station

HIGHW

NATIONAL

Yuigahama
Beach

ENOSHIMA

0 meters   500

0 yards   500

Key to Symbols see back flap

The head of the Great Buddha, or Daibutsu

The Mai-den in front of the main shrine at Hachiman-gu shrine

reconstructed in 1828 in Edo style. To the east, the **Kamakura National Treasure House Museum** contains a wealth of temple treasures.

🔳 Myohon-ji Temple
Kamakura stn. **Tel** *(0467) 22-0777.* ⬜ *daily.*

On a hillside of soaring trees, this temple, with its unusually steep, extended roof, is Kamakura's largest of the Nichiren sect. It was established in 1260, in memory of a 1203 massacre.

🔳 Hokoku-ji Temple
Tel *(0467) 22-0762.* ⬜ *daily.* 🔲 *(for bamboo grove).*

A Rinzai Zen temple founded in 1334, Hokoku-ji's buildings are modern; its great attraction is its lovely bamboo grove. There is also a pleasant raked gravel and rock garden,

fed lake, rocks, and sand; a Zen meditation cave is cut into the cliff. Decorative narcissi also bloom here in January, and Japanese plum trees blossom in February.

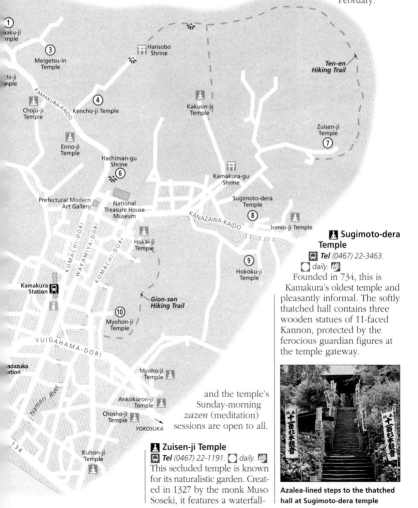

🔳 Sugimoto-dera Temple
Tel *(0467) 22-3463.* ⬜ *daily.* 🔲

Founded in 734, this is Kamakura's oldest temple and pleasantly informal. The softly thatched hall contains three wooden statues of 11-faced Kannon, protected by the ferocious guardian figures at the temple gateway.

Azalea-lined steps to the thatched hall at Sugimoto-dera temple

and the temple's Sunday-morning *zazen* (meditation) sessions are open to all.

🔳 Zuisen-ji Temple
Tel *(0467) 22-1191.* ⬜ *daily.* 🔲

This secluded temple is known for its naturalistic garden. Created in 1327 by the monk Muso Soseki, it features a waterfall-

Exploring Kita Kamakura

Zen Buddhism came to Japan from China at the end of the 12th century. Its simplicity and accessibility appealed to the ethos of Kamakura samurai warriors as well as to ordinary people. Kita (north) Kamakura, a tranquil area of wooded gullies, includes three of Kamakura's so-called "five great" Zen temples: Kencho-ji, Engaku-ji, and Jochi-ji (the others are

Statue above Kencho-ji

Jomyo-ji and Jufuku-ji). The area is served by its own train station, from which most sights can be reached on foot. Delicate vegetarian food *(see p326)*, which complies with Zen dietary rules, can be tried at several Kita Kamakura temples and restaurants.

Engaku-ji Temple

Kita Kamakura stn. **Tel** *(0467) 22-0478.* ◯ *daily.*

The largest of Kamakura's "five great" Zen temples, deep in trees, Engaku-ji was founded by the Hojo regent Tokimune in 1282. An influential *zazen* (meditation) center since the Meiji era, it now runs public courses.

Although much of Engaku-ji was destroyed by the 1923 Kanto Earthquake, 17 of its more than 40 subtemples remain, and careful rebuilding has made sure that it retains its characteristic Zen layout *(see opposite)*. One of its highlights, in Shozoku-in subtemple, is the Shariden. Japan's finest example of Chinese Sung-style Zen architecture, it is open only at New Year but can be seen through a gate at other times. Farther on, the Butsunichian, mausoleum of Engaku-ji's founder, serves *matcha* tea *(see p169)*. It was the setting for Kawabata Yasunari's 1949 novel *Senbazuru* (Thousand Cranes).

Bosatsu statue at Kencho-ji

Tokei-ji Temple

Kita Kamakura stn. **Tel** *(0467) 22-1663.* ◯ *daily.*

This quiet little temple was set up as a convent in 1285, at a time when only men were allowed to petition for divorce. However, if a woman spent three years here she could divorce her husband. Thus Tokei-ji was nicknamed the "divorce temple." In 1873 the law was changed to allow women to initiate divorce; in 1902 Tokei-ji became a monastery. It is still refuge-like, with gardens stretching back to the wooded hillside.

Meigetsu-in Temple

Kita Kamakura stn. **Tel** *(0467) 24-3437.* ◯ *daily.*

Known as the "hydrangea temple," Meigetsu-in is a small Zen temple with attractive gardens. As well as hydrangeas

Stone monuments in the peaceful cemetery at Tokei-ji temple

(at their peak in June), there are irises; these bloom in late May, when the rear garden, usually only tantalizingly glimpsed through a round window, is opened to the public.

Kencho-ji Temple

Kita Kamakura stn. **Tel** *(0467) 22-0981.* ◯ *daily.*

Kencho-ji is the foremost of Kamakura's "five great" Zen temples and the oldest Zen training monastery in Japan. Founded in 1253, the temple originally had seven main buildings and 49 subtemples; many were destroyed in fires, but ten subtemples remain. Beside the impressive Sanmon gate is the bell, cast in 1255, which has a Zen inscription by the temple's founder. The Buddha Hall contains a Jizo *bosatsu*, savior of souls of the dead, rather than the usual Buddha. Behind the hall is the Hatto, where public ceremonies are performed. The Karamon (Chinese gate) leads to the Hojo, used for services. Its rear garden is constructed around a pond supposedly in the shape of the kanji character for heart or mind. To the side of the temple a tree-lined lane leads to subtemples and up steps to Hanso-bo, the temple's shrine.

Zeni-Arai Benten Shrine

Kamakura stn. **Tel** *(0467) 25-1081.* ◯ *daily.*

This popular shrine is dedicated to Benten, goddess of music, eloquence, and the arts, and one of the "seven lucky gods" of folk religion. Hidden in a niche in the cliffs, it is approached through a small tunnel and a row of *torii* (gates). These lead to a pocket of wafting incense, lucky charms, and a cave spring where visitors wash money in the hope of doubling its value.

Washing money at Zeni-Arai Benten shrine

For hotels and restaurants in this region see pp301–3 and pp334–6

The Layout of a Zen Buddhist Temple

Japanese Zen temple layout is typically based on Chinese Sung-dynasty temples. Essentially rectilinear and symmetrical (in contrast to native Japanese asymmetry), Zen temples have the main buildings in a straight line one behind another, on a roughly north–south axis. The main buildings comprise the Sanmon (main gate), Butsuden (Buddha Hall), Hatto lecture hall, sometimes a meditation or study hall, and the abbot's and monks'

Bridge to Jochi-ji Temple

quarters. In practice, sub-temples often crowd around the main buildings and may obscure the basic layout. The temple compound is entered by a bridge over a pond or stream, symbolically crossing from the earthly world to that of Buddha. Buildings are beautiful but natural looking, often of unpainted wood; they are intended to be conducive to emptying the mind of worldly illusions, facilitating enlightenment. The example below is based on Engaku-ji.

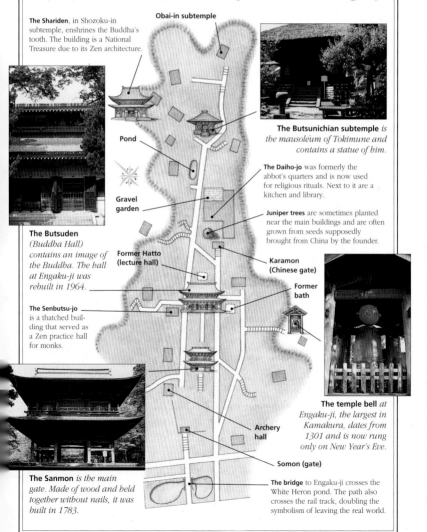

Obai-in subtemple

The Shariden, in Shozoku-in subtemple, enshrines the Buddha's tooth. The building is a National Treasure due to its Zen architecture.

Pond

Gravel garden

The Butsuden (Buddha Hall) contains an image of the Buddha. The hall at Engaku-ji was rebuilt in 1964.

Former Hatto (lecture hall)

The Senbutsu-jo is a thatched building that served as a Zen practice hall for monks.

The Butsunichian subtemple is the mausoleum of Tokimune and contains a statue of him.

The Daiho-jo was formerly the abbot's quarters and is now used for religious rituals. Next to it are a kitchen and library.

Juniper trees are sometimes planted near the main buildings and are often grown from seeds supposedly brought from China by the founder.

Karamon (Chinese gate)

Former bath

The temple bell at Engaku-ji, the largest in Kamakura, dates from 1301 and is now rung only on New Year's Eve.

Archery hall

Somon (gate)

The Sanmon is the main gate. Made of wood and held together without nails, it was built in 1783.

The bridge to Engaku-ji crosses the White Heron pond. The path also crosses the rail track, doubling the symbolism of leaving the real world.

Chichibu-Tama National Park ❺

秩父多摩国立公園

Tokyo, Saitama, Nagano, and Yamana-shi prefectures. 🏯 70,500 (Chichibu city). 🚇 Seibu-Chichibu stn, Seibu-Chichibu line; Chichibu stn, Chichibu line; Okutama or Mitake stns, JR line. ℹ️ Chichibu stn (0494) 25-3192. 🎎 Yo Matsuri (Dec 2–3, Chichibu city).

Chichibu-Tama National Park is a remote region of low mountains, rich in traditions and wildlife, stretching from the narrow valleys of Okutama in the south to the basin around Chichibu city in the north. The two parts of the park are separated by mountains, crossed only by a few hiking trails, and are reached by two separate rail networks. Within the park, railroads penetrate to a few spots, but travel is mostly by bus.

Chichibu was a prime silk-producing region until the early 20th century. Today it is known for its vibrant festivals and its pilgrim route linking 33 Kannon temples. To the north, at **Nagatoro**, the Arakawa River runs past rare crystalline schist rock formations.

In the Okutama area, **Mount Mitake** has good hiking, and an attractive mountaintop shrine village, easily reached by a funicular. Stalactite caves at **Nippara** are worth visiting.

🏞️ **Nippara Caves**
NW of Okutama. **Tel** (0428) 83-8491. 🕐 daily. 🎫

YOSEGI-ZAIKU WOODWORK

Originating in the 9th century, this woodcraft looks like in-laid mosaic but in fact employs a very different technique. It has been a Hakone specialty for over 200 years, and today there are about 100 *yosegi-zaiku* practitioners in the area.

Strips are cut from planks of up to 40 varieties of undyed woods and glued together to form blocks of pattern, which are in turn glued into larger blocks. These are then either shaped with a lathe into bowls and boxes, or shaved into cross-sectional sheets, used to coat items such as boxes and purses. The paper-thin sheets are flexible and can be laminated. Some of the most popular creations are "magic" boxes, opened in a sequence of moves to reveal a hidden drawer.

Craftsman making a yosegi-zaiku box

Environs:
South of Chichibu-Tama lies **Mount Takao,** (on the Keio train line to Takaosan-guchi.) Its slopes have pleasant walks with sweeping views of Tokyo and Mount Fuji.

Hakone ❻

箱根

Kanagawa prefecture. 🏯 14,000. 🚇 ℹ️ 698 Yumoto, Hakone (0460) 5-8911. **www**.hakone. or.jp/english/index.html 🎎 Toriiyaki (Aug 5, Lake Ashi), Daimyo Gyoretsu (Nov 3, Hakone-Yumoto).

Hakone is a hilly hot-spring town whose scattered attractions are both cultural and natural. Popular as a resort since the 9th century, it can be very crowded. The

Hakone area extends across the collapsed remains of a huge volcano, which was active until 3 to 4,000 years ago, leaving a legacy today of hot springs and steam vents.

Although Hakone can be visited as a long day trip from Tokyo, it is worth an overnight stay. Two- or three-day public-transportation passes are available on the Odakyu line from Shinjuku, Tokyo. A convenient circuit of the main sights starts from the *onsen* town of **Hakone-Yumoto**, taking the Tozan switchback train up the hillside to **Hakone Open-Air Museum**, with its modern sculptures. Continue via funicular to **Hakone Art Museum**, which has an excellent Japanese ceramic collection and garden. Via the funicular and then a ropeway

Crossing the rocky scree and steaming vents of Owaku-dani valley in Hakone

A statue of *The Izu Dancer* by a waterfall near Kawazu, Izu Peninsula

over the crest of the hill is the fascinating **Owaku-dani** ("valley of great boiling"), an area of sulfurous steam vents.

The ropeway continues to **Lake Ashi**, where replicas of historical Western-style boats run to **Hakone-machi** and **Moto-Hakone**. In clear weather there are stunning views of Mount Fuji. At Hakone-machi is an interesting reconstruction of the **Seki-sho Barrier Gate**, a checkpoint that used to control the passage of people and guns on the Edo-period Tokaido road between Edo (Tokyo) and Kyoto.

Yosegi-zaiku box, Hatajuku

From Hakone-machi it is a short walk to Moto-Hakone. In a prominent position on a hilltop overlooking Lake Ashi, **Narukawa Art Museum** exhibits 1,500 artworks by modern Japanese masters, and has spectacular views of the surrounding mountains. Over a pass beyond Moto-Hakone is the **Amazake-chaya** tea-house, and **Hatajuku** village, known for *yosegi-zaiku*, a form of decorative woodwork.

🏛 **Open-Air Museum**
Tel (0460) 2-1161. ⬜ *daily.* 🖋

🏛 **Hakone Art Museum**
Tel (0460) 2-2623. ⬜ *Fri–Wed.* 🖋

⛩ **Seki-sho Barrier Gate**
Tel (0460) 3-6635. ⬜ *daily.* 🖋

🏛 **Narukawa Art Museum**
Tel (0460) 3-6288. ⬜ *daily.* 🖋

Izu Peninsula ❼

伊豆半島

Shizuoka prefecture. 🚉 🛈 *Atami, Ito, and Shuzenji stns.* 🎏 *Daimonji Burning (Jul 22–3, Atagawa), Anjin Festival (Aug 8–10, Ito).*

A picturesque, hilly peninsula with a benign climate, Izu is popular for its numerous hot springs. It was a place of exile during the Middle Ages, and in the early 1600s was home to the shipwrecked Englishman Will Adams, whose story was the basis of the James Clavell novel *Shogun*. **Shimoda**, on the southern tip, became a coaling station for foreign ships in 1854, then opened to US traders. Today Shimoda has little of interest besides pretty gray-and-white walls, reinforced against typhoons with crisscross plasterwork.

Izu's east coast is quite developed, but the west has charming coves and fishing villages, such as **Toi** and **Heda**, offering delicious long-legged crabs and other seafood. The center is also relatively unspoiled, with wooded mountains and rustic hot springs, including **Shuzenji** *onsen* and a chain of villages from **Amagi Yugashima** to **Kawazu**. These latter were the setting for Kawabata Yasunari's short story *The Izu Dancer*, commemorated across Izu. Two-day transportation passes cover parts of the peninsula.

Mount Fuji and the Fuji Five Lakes ❽

See pp140–41.

Shizuoka ❾

静岡

Shizuoka & Yamanashi prefecture. 🏯 *713,000.* 🚉 🛈 *in JR stn (054) 252-4247.* **www**.pref.shizuoka.jp 🎏 *Shizuoka Festival (1st weekend Apr).*

Settlement in this area stretches back to AD 200–300. Later a stop on the old Tokaido road, and the retirement home of Tokugawa Ieyasu (*see p56*), Shizuoka is today a sprawling urban center, the city in Japan at greatest risk of a major earthquake. As a result it is probably the only place that is fully prepared.

The **Toro ruins** near the port have well-explained reconstructions of ancient buildings, and an excellent interactive **museum**. The view from **Nihondaira** plateau, in the east of the city, to Mount Fuji and Izu is superb. Nearby is **Kunozan Tosho-gu**, one of the three top Tosho-gu shrines.

🏛 **Toro Ruins**
Museum *Tel* (0542) 85-0476.
⬜ *Tue–Sun.* ⬛ *last day of month.* 🖋

Environs:
West of Shizuoka, **Kanaya** has one of Japan's largest tea plantations. Fields and processing plants can be visited, and the elegant **Ocha no Sato** museum portrays tea lore. Nearby, the **Oigawa steam railroad** takes you right into the untamed South Alps.

🏛 **Ocha no Sato**
Tel (0547) 46-5588. ⬜ *daily.*
⬛ *Tue.* 🖋

A reconstructed dwelling at the Toro site, Shizuoka

Mount Fuji and the Fuji Five Lakes ❽

富士山と富士五湖

Decorative drain cover in Fuji-Yoshida

At 3,776 m (12,390 ft), Mount Fuji (or Fuji-san) is Japan's highest peak by far, its near-perfect cone floating lilac-gray or snow-capped above hilltops and low cloud. Dormant since 1707, the volcano first erupted 8–10,000 years ago. Its upper slopes are loose volcanic ash, devoid of greenery or streams. Until 100 years ago, Mount Fuji was considered so sacred that it was climbed only by priests and pilgrims; women were not allowed until 1872. Today pilgrims are greatly out-numbered by recreational climbers. The Fuji Five Lakes area, at the foot of the mountain, is a playground for Tokyo-ites, with sports facilities and amusement parks.

Lake Sai
This is the least spoiled of the Fuji Five Lakes and offers beautiful views of Mount Fuji.

Lake Kawaguchi is the most accessible and commercialized lake.

KEY

🚉	Train station
🚌	Bus stop
ℹ️	Tourist information
⛩️	Shrine
▬▬	Expressway
══	Other road
▪▪	Trail

Lake Motosu, the deepest lake, is depicted on the 5,000-yen note.

Lake Shojin is the smallest lake, and good for fishing.

Kawaguchi-ko

Fugaku Wind Cave

Narusawa Ice Cave

Sea of Trees

The Sea of Trees (Aokigahara Jukai) is a primeval forest famed for being easy to get lost in.

Kawaguchi-ko trail is 5–6 hours up from the 5th stage, and 3 hours down. Another trail, the Yoshida, shares most of its route with this one.

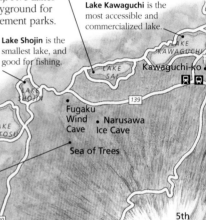

5th stage

5th stage

TIPS FOR WALKERS

Planning: The mountain is open for climbing only in July and August. Trails and huts can be very crowded on weekends.

Stages: The trails are divided into 10 stages. Climbers usually start at the 5th stage. To see the sunrise and avoid midday sun, it is usual to climb by night or start in the afternoon, sleep in a hut at the 7th or 8th stage, and rise very early to finish the climb.

Conditions: The climb is hard work as the steep volcanic cinder shifts underfoot like sand. Above the 8th stage, altitude sickness occasionally strikes: if you have a serious headache or nausea, descend at once. The summit is much colder than the base.

What to take: Sun-protection cream, hat, sweater, raincoat, hiking shoes, flashlight, and emergency drink supplies; a walking stick is useful.

The top is not a single summit, but a crater rim. A circuit of the rim takes about an hour.

Fujinomiya trail is 5 hours up from the 5th stage, and 3 hours 30 minutes down.

Approaching the Crater Rim

At the top, climbers and pilgrims can visit the Sengen shrine, 24-hour noodle stalls, a post office, an office for souvenir stamps, and a weather station.

Sengen Jinja

Many Sengen shrines, including this main one at Fuji-Yoshida, can be found around Fuji. The inner sanctum of Sengen shrines is on the crater rim at the summit. They are dedicated to the deity of the mountain.

VISITORS' CHECKLIST

Shizuoka & Yamanashi prefecture.
🚉 Fuji-Yoshida, Kawaguchi-ko, Gotenba, Mishima (Tokaido Shinkansen), or Fujinomiya.
🚌 summer only, from all stns to the nearest 5th stage, also direct from Tokyo (Shinjuku stn W side or Hamamatsu-cho) to Kawaguchi-ko, Gotenba, and Lake Yamanaka. 🛈 Fuji-Yoshida (0555) 22-7000. **www**.city.fujiyoshida. yamanashi.jp 🎴 Fuji-Yoshida Fire Festival (Aug 26 & 27).

OTSUKI AND TOKYO

Expressway

Fuji-Yoshida, the traditional pilgrim base, has old inns, and waterfalls for cleansing and praying before the climb.

• Oshino

Lake Yamanaka is popular for waterskiing and swimming.

Subashiri trail is 4 hours 30 minutes up from the 5th stage, and 3 hours down.

LAKE YAMANAKA

5th stage

h-stage

TOKYO

138

Gotenba

Gotenba trail is 8 hours up from the 5th stage, and 3 hours down.

Tomei Expressway

MISHIMA

| 0 kilometers | 5 |
| 0 miles | 5 |

MOUNT FUJI IN ART

Mount Fuji's graceful, almost symmetrical form, its changing appearance at different seasons and times of day, and its dominance over the landscape have made it both a symbol of Japan and a popular subject for artists. The mountain features in various series of 19th-century woodblock prints: Katsushika Hokusai (1790–1849) and Ando Hiroshige (1797–1858) both published series called *Thirty-Six Views of Mount Fuji*, and Hiroshige also depicted Fuji in his *Fifty-Three Stages of the Tokaido* published in 1833–4. It . often appears in the background of prints of downtown Edo (Tokyo), from where it is sometimes visible between high-rises even today. In other arts, Mount Fuji is echoed in decorative motifs, for instance on kimonos, in wood carvings, and even in the shape of window frames.

One of Hiroshige's *Thirty-Six Views of Mount Fuji*

Beneath the Wave off Kanagawa* from Hokusai's *Thirty-Six Views of Mount Fuji

Kiso Valley Tour ❿

木曽谷

The Kiso River runs through a picturesque mountain valley that was the route of the Nakasendo, one of the Edo-period post roads. Its 11 post towns, particularly Tsumago, Narai, and Magome, still retain much of that atmosphere, their narrow streets lined with wooden inns and stores. Parts of the old Nakasendo trail, especially between Tsumago and Magome, are as they were in the Edo days and can be followed past woods, farms, and milestones. More challenging hiking is found on nearby mountains such as Ontake.

TIPS FOR TRAVELERS

Tour length: 60 km (37 miles).
Travel: Car is the most flexible option. Most express trains stop only at Nakatsugawa and Kiso-Fukushima. Local trains run every hour. *Information:* Tsumago (0264) 57-3123; Magome (0264) 59-2336; Narai (0264) 34-2001. **www**.nagiso-town.ne.jp/english/engtop.htm

Narai ②
This well-preserved post town has streets lined with wooden buildings, plus a couple of interesting museums, giving an insight into how life was for travelers on the Nakasendo.

Kiso-Hirasawa ①
Lacquerware is a specialty here, perfected over the years to sell to travelers passing through.

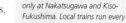

SHIOJIRI AND MATSUMOTO

Torii Pass ③
This pass has one of the main remaining sections of genuine, stone-paved Nakasendo road, with no modern road nearby to spoil it. It takes about 2 hours to walk over the pass.

Yabuhara

Miyanokoshi

Harano

MT ONTAKE

Kiso-Fukushima ④
This was the location of a major barrier gate on the Nakasendo road. Today it is the gateway to the sacred mountain of Ontake.

MT KISO-KOMAGATAKE

KEY
▬ Tour route
═ Other roads
🚉 Train station
-- Walk route
🔆 Viewpoint

0 kilometers   10
0 miles   5

Kiso River

Agematsu

Nezame-no-toko ⑤
This pretty gorge, about half-an-hour's walk from Agematsu, holds turquoise waters strewn with boulders.

Kuramoto

Suhara

Okuwa

Nojiri

Junikane

Nagiso

Tsumago ⑥
All signs of modernity have been hidden here – cables are buried and cars banned. A former high-class inn, the Okuya, is now an excellent museum of local and Nakasendo history.

NAKATSUGAWA

Magome ⑦
In the hills above the Kiso Valley, Magome is a good starting point for the 8.5-km (5-mile) Nakasendo walking trail to Tsumago.

Part of the *Tale of Genji* handscroll in Tokugawa Art Museum, Nagoya

Nagoya ⓫
名古屋

Aichi prefecture. 🏯 2,222,000. ✈
🚉 🛈 at Nagoya JR stn (052) 541-
4301.**www**.city.nagoya.jp/global/en
🎭 Atsuta Shrine Festival (Jun 5),
Nagoya Festival (mid-Oct).

A major transportation hub
for the region, Nagoya is
a pleasant and convenient, if
unexciting, base. It rose to
prominence in the 17th century
as a Tokaido castle town,
birthplace of Oda Nobunaga
and Toyotomi Hideyoshi *(see
pp54 and 56)*. Japan's fourth-
largest city and an industrial
center, it was heavily bombed
in World War II.

The city's one-day bus or
bus-and-subway passes are
good for exploring. **Nagoya
Castle**, built in 1610–12 and
one of the largest, most sophisticated of the Edo period,
was destroyed in a bombing
raid in 1945; today's concrete
reconstruction has a top-floor
observatory, and the modern
interior contains exhibits
about the castle.

A short bus ride east is the
Tokugawa Art Museum, with
superb Edo-period treasures, as
well as a 12th-century illustrated handscroll of the *Tale
of Genji*, part of which is exhibited each November. Photos
and reproductions of the scrolls
are on permanent display.

🏯 **Nagoya Castle**
Ⓢ Shiyakusho stn. 🚌 Nagoya-jo
Seimon-mae stop. **Tel** (052) 231-1700.
◯ daily. 🈶

🏛 **Tokugawa Art Museum**
🚌 Shindeki stop. **Tel** (052) 935-6262.
◯ Tue–Sun. 🈶

Environs:
Trips from Nagoya, all on the
Meitetsu rail line, include
Arimatsu, a Tokaido post
town, known for tie-dyeing
for centuries. Tours of the
Toyota Car Factory nearby
may be arranged.

Toyota Car Factory
Tel (0565) 29-3355. ◯ Mon–Fri.

**Meiji-era post office at Meiji Mura
near Inuyama**

Inuyama ⓬
犬山

Aichi prefecture. 🏯 74,900. ✈ 🚉
🛈 5 mins E of station (0568) 61-1000.
🎭 Tagata Honen-sai (Mar 15), Inuyama
Festival (1st weekend Apr).

Inuyama is a quiet, friendly
castle town on the Kiso River.
Its **castle**, built in 1537, is the
oldest in Japan. It places
more emphasis on de-
fense than show, but is
still small, simple, and
graceful, with panoramic
views across the river far
below. In nearby **Uraku-
en park** is Jo-an tea-
house, a classic example
of rustic simplicity.

🏯 **Inuyama Castle**
Tel (0568) 61-6000.
◯ daily. 🈶

Environs:
Outside Inuyama is **Meiji
Mura**, a park with over 60
Meiji-era (1868–1912) buildings,
including the lobby of Frank
Lloyd Wright's Imperial Hotel
from Tokyo. **Yaotsu**, where
Sugihara Chiune was born is a
train ride away. Japan's consul
in Lithuania in World War II,
Sugihara saved around 6,000
Jews using transit visas via
Japan. He is commemorated by
a monument and museum at
Yaotsu's **Hill of Humanity Park**.

🏯 **Meiji Mura**
15 min by bus from Inuyama.
Tel (0568) 67-0314. ◯ daily. ◯
Mon (Dec–Feb). 🈶

Gifu ⓭
岐阜

Gifu prefdature. 🏯 413,000. ✈ 🚉
🛈 at Gifu JR stn (058) 262-4415.
🎭 All-Japan Fireworks Contest (last
Sat in Jul). **www**.city.gifu.gifu.jp

A rather Garish spa town,
Gifu's main attraction is
ukai cormorant fishing *(see
p44)*. This tradition involves
using trained cormorants to
catch fish. Nightly from mid-
May to mid-October, except
at full moon or when stormy,
fishermen and their cormorants
go out on torchlit boats; the
birds dive for *ayu* (sweetfish)
and trout, which they are
prevented from swallowing
by a ring around their necks.

The town is also known for
its paper parasols and lanterns
and for the largest lacquer
Buddha in Japan, at **Shoho-ji
temple**. Dating from 1832, it
comprises a woven bamboo
frame covered with sutra-
inscribed paper, then coated in
clay and lacquered. **Gifu Castle**
is a modern reconstruction.

**The small, reconstructed castle at Gifu,
perched on a hilltop**

Street-by-Street: Takayama ⑭

高山

Takayama is a town of character surrounded by mountains. Agriculturally poor but rich in timber, it produced skilled carpenters; in the 8th century, when the region was unable to produce enough rice for its taxes (usually paid in the form of rice), it sent craftsmen instead. From 1692 to 1868 the area was under direct shogunate control as a source of timber. Its isolated mountain location has meant the survival of unspoiled Edo-period streets lined with tiny shops, museums, and eating places, while the pure water is ideal for sake brewing. The town also stages one of Japan's best-known festivals.

One of the floats at the Takayama Matsuri

Lion Mask Museum and Festival Float Hall *(see p146)*

Higashiyama temple district

SHIMO NINOMACHI

SHIMO SANNOMACHI

YAYOI BRIDGE

MIYA RIVER

Morning market

Yoshijima Heritage House
This beautifully maintained sake merchant's house retains its wooden beamed interior, lit by high windows.

| 0 meters | 50 |
| 0 yards | 50 |

STAR SIGHTS

★ Sannomachi Quarter

★ Kusakabe Heritage House

★ Kusakabe Heritage House
Rebuilt of Japanese cypress in 1879 after a fire, this house is a well-preserved money-lender's dwelling, and includes folk-craft items and a small garden.

★ Sannomachi Quarter
An unusually large, intact area of Edo-period merchants' shops and houses, this quarter includes specialty shops and sake brewers.

VISITORS' CHECKLIST

Gifu prefecture. 🚹 *66,000.*
🚆 *JR Takayama line.* ℹ *in front of JR stn (0577) 32-5328.*
www.hida.jp/e-taka.htm
Yoshijima Heritage House
Tel (0577) 32-0038. ◯ *daily; Dec–Feb: Wed–Mon.* 🏠 **Kusakabe Heritage House** *Tel (0577) 32-0072.* ◯ *daily.* 🏠 **Hirata Kinenkan Museum** *Tel (0577) 33-1354.* ◯ *daily.* 🏠 🎎 *Takayama Matsuri (Apr 14–15 & Oct 9–10).*

Hirata Kinenkan Museum
In a former candle and pomade shop, the Hirata family's collection includes Edo-period clothing and toys.

Kyodo Gallery of Traditional Toys is a small, quaint collection.

Shoren-ji temple

KAMI ICHINOMACHI

YASUGAWA-DORI

KAMI NINOMACHI

KAMI SANNOMACHI

SAN-MACHI-DORI

Station, tourist information

YANAGI BRIDGE

IKADA BRIDGE

Hida Archae-ology Museum displays local finds and crafts.

Takayama Jinya, Hida Folklore Village (*see p146*)

Miya River
Some of the old houses of the Sannomachi Quarter overlook the fast-flowing Miya River.

KEY

– – – Suggested route

Exploring Takayama

Takayama is best explored slowly on foot or by bicycle. Old merchant houses reveal high, skylighted ceilings, soot-painted beams, and fireproof storage rooms; the dirt-floor area at the front was the shop. The town's eight sake breweries can also be visited during the peak brewing week in January or February. To the east, the tranquil Higashiyama temple district has a 3.5-km (2-mile) walking course taking in 13 temples, five shrines, and a hilltop park.

Lion Mask Museum

Tel (0577) 32-0881. ◯ daily. 🕒
Lion dances, to drive away wild animals and evil spirits, are integral to festivals such as Takayama's. This museum contains over 800 lively lion masks from all over Japan, plus superb armor, screens, pottery, and coins. Included in the entry fee is a performance by *karakuri* marionettes, invented in Edo (Tokyo) in 1617.

One of the masks in the Lion Mask Museum

Festival Float Hall

Tel (0577) 32-5100. ◯ daily. 🕒
Takayama Matsuri dates from about 1690 and takes place twice a year, in spring, coinciding with planting, and in fall at harvest time. Both festivals involve processions of 11 tall, lavishly decorated floats, guided by townspeople in traditional costume. Four floats also feature *karakuri* marionettes. Between festivals, four of the magnificent floats are displayed in this museum

along with photographs of the others. Admission includes access to a gallery of exquisite scale models of Nikko Tosho-gu Shrine *(see pp266–9)*.

Takayama Jinya

Tel (0577) 32-0643. ◯ daily. 🕒
The Jinya was built in 1615 for Takayama's lord, but in 1692 the shogunate made it their provincial government office – the only one still in existence. The front of the building comprises rooms where people of various ranks waited or met officials; behind are kitchens and living quarters of the governor's family. To one side is a prison, with a small array of torture instruments. The storehouses contain items relating to the rice-tax system.

Environs:

Just outside Takayama is **Hida Folk Village**, over 30 houses from surrounding rural areas, including a *gassho-zukuri* house from the Shokawa Valley. There are also store-houses, a festival stage, and traditional crafts. The buildings, on a hillside with views of the Japan Alps, are interesting both architecturally and for what they reveal – such as the demands of a snowy climate or the life of a village headman.

Hida Folk Village

40 mins walk or 8 mins by bus from Takayama stn. *Tel* (0577) 34-4711. ◯ daily. 🕒

Gassho-zukuri houses in Shirakawa-go

Shokawa Valley ⑮
庄川渓谷

Gifu and Toyama prefectures. 🚌 *from Nagoya (summer only), Takayama, Gifu & Takaoka.* ℹ️ *(0576) 96-1013.* **http:**//shirakawa-go.org/english /index.html 🎎 *Doburoku Matsuri (Shirakawa-go, Oct 14–19).*

A remote mountain region with unique thatched houses, the Shokawa valley comprises two areas: **Shirakawa-go** (including Ogimachi) to the south and the five hamlets of **Gokayama** to the north. Under deep snow from December to March, the region was historically a refuge for the defeated and persecuted. Until the 1970s most families here produced silk, raising silkworms in *gassho-zukuri* thatched houses.

Of the original 1,800, less than 150 *gassho* houses remain. Three settlements – **Ogimachi**, **Suganuma**, and **Ainokura** – are World Heritage sites. Every April–May, a few houses are re-thatched, one roof taking 200 villagers and volunteers two days. Ogimachi is the largest village, with 59 *gassho* houses and an **Open-Air Museum**. Suganuma has nine *gassho* buildings. Ainokura is a hillside hamlet of 20 *gassho* houses (two open to visitors).

Open-Air Museum

Across the river from Ogimachi. *Tel* (05769) 6-1231. ◯ *Apr–Nov: daily; Dec–Mar: Fri–Tue.* 🕒

Inside Takayama's Festival Float Hall

Gassho-zukuri Houses

These houses are named for their steep thatched roofs, shaped like *gassho* ("praying hands"). The climate demands strong, steep roofs able to withstand heavy snow and shed rain quickly so that the straw does not rot. *Gassho* structures meet those requirements with a series of triangular frames on a rectangular base, creating a large interior space. Generally three or four stories, they traditionally accommodated extended families of 20–30 people on the ground floor, all

A gassho-style house behind a watermill

involved in silkworm cultivation; the upper floors housed the silkworms, permitting variations in light, heat, and air at different stages. To maximize ventilation and light, *gassho-zukuri* houses have no hipped gables, and windows at both ends are opened to allow the wind through – in Shirakawa-go, where winds always blow north–south along the valley floor, all houses are aligned on the same axis. Architectural details vary from village to village.

The straw used for thatching is miscanthus, a type of pampas grass. The thatch can be up to 1 m (3 ft) thick.

Horizontal poles near the top of the roof help to hold the thatch in place and are used for securing ropes when doing repairs.

No nails are used in the roofs – the timbers and braces are all bound together with straw rope. The lower part of the building is held together by wooden pins.

***Gassho* roofs** slope at about 60 degrees (most roofs in Japan are up to 45 degrees).

Slats in the ceiling allow smoke from hearth to penetrate the roof area, helping to protect the thatch against dampness and insects. If plenty of smoke reaches the thatch, it can last about 50 years.

A notched pole acts as a ladder.

Horizontal beams are often taken from trees that have been bent by snow; being slightly curved, they absorb stress better than straight beams.

The hearth *is a common feature of Japanese rural houses, and was used for heating, cooking, and drying. The exact style of hearth and way of hanging things over it varies between villages.*

Kanazawa ⑯

金沢

A city with a strong cultural identity, Kanazawa was historically shielded from outside influence by its location between alps and sea and supported by an ample rice yield. In 1583 the area, known as Kaga, passed from egalitarian government under the Ikko Buddhist sect to the firm rule of the Maeda lords; while much of Japan was still unstable, Kaga had three centuries of peace and became the richest domain in the land. Wealth encouraged cultural development, and artists from Kyoto came and developed new, more vibrant styles with less restraint. When Japan modernized, Kanazawa focused on culture; lack of industry meant the city escaped bombing in World War II and retains its heritage today.

Walled street in the Nagamachi Samurai quarter

Exploring Central Kanazawa

Most of Kanazawa's sights are located centrally. One-day bus passes are available, and bicycles can be rented at the station. **Kenroku-en Garden** is one of Japan's "great three" gardens, and is best seen un-crowded early or late in the day. Established in the mid-17th century, it was opened to the public in 1871. Kenroku-en means "garden of six qualities" (desirable in Chinese gardens): spaciousness, seclusion, air of antiquity, ingenuity, flowing water, and views.

At the edge of the lake is a two-legged stone lantern (see p31), known as Kotoji because it is shaped like the bridge of a *koto* (stringed instrument). The exquisite two-story **Seison-kaku Villa** adjoining Kenroku-en was built in 1863 by Maeda Nari-yasu, 13th lord, for his mother. Its lower floor has formal receiving rooms: walls are coated in gold dust, and *shoji* paper doors have rare Dutch stained-glass insets. Upstairs is more informal and colorful. The superb curved roof is made from *sawara* cypress shingles.

Kanazawa Castle, one of the largest in feudal Japan, was almost entirely destroyed by fire in 1881; only the armory and rear gate, Ishikawa-mon, survived. A section of the castle has been rebuilt and a park created. The nearby **Oyama Shrine** is dedicated to Maeda Toshiie.

The **Nagamachi Samurai Quarter** retains its earthenwalled streets. With its quality wood-work, costly windowpanes, and serene garden, **Nomura House** gives an idea of samurai

The unusual gate to the Oyama Shrine

life. In the **Nagamachi Kaga Yuzen Silk Center**, a former samurai house, an 18-step resist-dyeing process is used to produce Kaga *yuzen* silk, popular for formal kimonos.

Most of the city's museums are in the central area. The **21st Century Museum of Contemporary Art** opened in 2004 to explore emerging new work in visual arts, design, craft, fashion, architecture, and film, particularly in the areas of multiculturalism and transporta-tion, technology, gender issues, and the nature of identity. **Ishikawa Prefecture Traditional Pro-ducts and Crafts Museum** has sections on more than 30 Kanazawa crafts, such as silk, ceramics, gold leaf, and folk toys. Two-day "passport" tickets give access to this museum, the **Ishikawa Pre-fecture Art Museum** (the Maedas' collection), and the **Honda Museum** (Honda family possessions).

🌺 **Kenroku-en Garden**
Tel (076) 221-5850. ☐ *daily.* 🈺

🏯 **Seisonkaku Villa**
Tel (076) 221-0580. ☐ *Thu–Tue.* 🈺

🏯 **Nomura House**
Tel (076) 221-3553. ☐ *daily.* 🈺

🏯 **Nagamachi Kaga Yuzen Silk Center**
Tel (076) 264-2811. ☐ *daily.* 🈺

🎫 **21st Century Museum of Contemporary Art**
Tel (076) 220-2801. ☐ *daily.* 🈺

🎫 **Crafts Museum**
Tel (076) 262-2020. ☐ *daily.*
☐ *Apr–Nov: 3rd Thu in month; Dec–Mar: Thu.* 🈺

🎫 **Art Museum**
Tel (076) 822-9788. ☐ *daily.* 🈺

🎫 **Honda Museum**
Tel (076) 261-0500. ☐ *daily.*
☐ *Nov–Feb: Thu.* 🈺

Spring in Kenroku-en Garden

Exploring the Higashi (Eastern) Pleasure District

Established in 1820, this was the grandest pleasure district outside Kyoto and Edo (Tokyo). Full of atmosphere, the area has old-fashioned street lamps and wooden-lattice windows hiding elegant restaurants and crafts galleries. The evocative **Shima Geisha House** is as it was in the 19th century. On the upper floor are guest rooms with small stages where the geisha sang and danced. Downstairs are living quarters. Nearby, at **Fukushima Shamisen**, the Fukushima family have been hand-crafting musical instruments for 130 years. *Shamisen* are made from *karin* wood (a type of quince) and cat or dog skin; the three strings are silk. Visitors may play a finished instrument. The **Sakuda Gold-leaf Store** sells gold-leaf items and demonstrates production – it even has toilets tiled in gold. Kanazawa has produced gold leaf since 1593 and supplies 99 percent of Japan's needs.

Wall hanging of a geisha in the Shima Geisha House

🏠 **Shima Geisha House**
Tel (076) 252-5675. ◻ *daily.* 🎫

🎵 **Fukushima Shamisen**
Tel (076) 252-3703. ◻ *Mon–Fri.*

🏠 **Sakuda Gold-leaf Store**
Tel (076) 251-6777. ◻ *daily.*

Exploring Southern Kanazawa

Popularly known as the "ninja temple," **Myoryu-ji** is a Nichiren temple full of secret doors and passages. It was established in 1643 as both a place of worship for the Maedas and a watchtower on the edge of town. The architecture is highly complex, with 23 rooms linked by 29 staircases and a maze of corridors.

Nearby, **Kutani Kosen Kiln** is the only kiln in Kanazawa. Kutani porcelain originated in the village of Kutani, south of Kanazawa, in the mid-17th century. Old Kutani-ware uses deep, over-glazed blues, greens, and ochres; modern work has more delicate and varied designs. All pieces are handmade and fired two or three times.

🏛 **Myoryu-ji Temple**
Tel (076) 241-0888. ◻ *daily.* 🎫 🅿
(every 30 mins, reservation compulsory.)

🏠 **Kutani Kosen Kiln**
Tel (076) 241-0902. ◻ *daily.*

VISITORS' CHECKLIST

Ishikawa prefecture. 🚶 *454,900.*
✈ *Komatsu.* 🚉 *JR line.*
ℹ *(0762) 31-6311.*
www.city.Kanazawa.
ishikawa. jp
🎭 *Noh at Ono Minato Shrine (May 15), Hyakumangoku Matsuri (2nd Sat in Jun).*

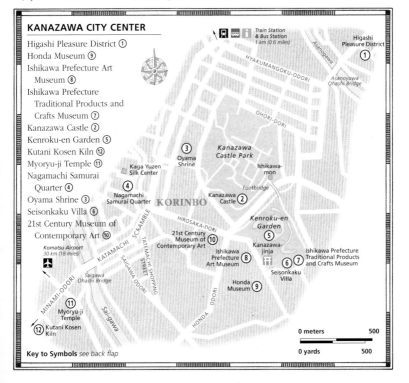

KANAZAWA CITY CENTER

Train Station & Bus Station
1 km (0.6 miles)
Higashi Pleasure District ①
Asanogawa
HYAKUMANGOKU-ODORI
Asanoyuwa Ohashi Bridge
OHORI-DORI
③ Oyama Shrine
Kaga Yuzen Silk Center
Kanazawa Castle Park
Ishikawa-mon
④ Nagamachi Samurai Quarter
KORINBO
Footbridge
Kanazawa Castle ②
KATAMACHI SCRAMBLE
TATEMACHI SHOPPING STREET
HIROSAKA-DORI
Kenroku-en Garden ⑤
Komatsu Airport 30 km (18 miles)
21st Century Museum of Contemporary Art ⑩
Kanazawa-jinja
SAIGAWA ODORI
Ishikawa Prefecture Art Museum ⑧
⑥ Seisonkaku Villa
⑦ Ishikawa Prefecture Traditional Products and Crafts Museum
MINAMI-ODORI
Saigawa Ohashi Bridge
Honda Museum ⑨
HONDA ODORI
⑪ Myoryu-ji Temple
Saigawa
⑫ Kutani Kosen Kiln

Key to Symbols *see back flap*

0 meters   500
0 yards   500

Chujakumon gate at the Zen temple of Eihei-ji

Eihei-ji Temple ⓱

永平寺

Fukui prefecture. 🚃 **Tel** (0776) 63-3102 (bookings and Zen training). 🎏 Lantern offering on the river (late Aug).

Established in 1244, Eihei-ji is one of the Soto Zen sect's two head temples and has been Japan's most active Zen meditation monastery since the late 16th century. In a classic rectilinear plan *(see p137)*, its halls and covered corridors climb up the wooded mountainside. Soto Zen pursues gradual enlightenment by practicing meditation away from the real world; the monastery has about 50 elders and 250 trainees. The atmosphere is cheerful, yet life is austere, with no heating and a simple diet. In the Sodo Hall (to the left), each trainee has just one *tatami* mat for eating, sleeping, and *zazen* (meditation). Silence is observed, as in the bath building and toilet. Laypeople wishing to experience the rigorous Soto Zen regime must book well ahead.

Noto Peninsula ⓲

能登半島

Ishikawa prefecture. 🚃 🚌 ℹ️ at Wajima stn (0768) 22-1503. 🎏 Seihakusai (May 3–5, Nanao); Abare Festival (Jul 7–8, Ushitsu); Toroyama Festival (Jul 20–21, Iida); Gojinjo Daiko (Jul 31–Aug 1, Nabune).

Projecting 70 km (45 miles) into the Japan Sea, Noto is a quiet region of fishing villages known for seafood and untouched traditions. The east

coast and the sandy west near Kanazawa are quite developed, but the north and northwest are rocky and picturesque. Public transportation around Noto is limited; bus and train are similar in time and cost, but the bus network is wider.

Wajima, a weathered fishing town, produces top-quality, durable lacquerware with at least 70 layers of lacquer. Nearby **Hegura** island is a stopping-off point for migratory birds. Just east of Wajima, **Senmaida** is famed for its "1,000" narrow rice terraces by the sea, while **Sosogi**'s coast has unusual rock formations. Many summer festivals feature demon-masked drummers and *kiriko* lanterns up to 15 m (50 ft) tall. Between events, drums are played at Wajima and Sosogi.

To the west, **Monzen** has the major **Soji-ji** Zen temple. In **Hakui** are the important shrine of **Keta Taisha** and a 2,000-year-old **sumo ring** – Japan's oldest, still used each September. Senmaida, Sosogi, and Monzen can be reached by bus from Wajima, Hakui by bus or train from Kanazawa.

Kamikochi ⓳

上高地

Nagano prefecture. 🚃 to Shin-Shima-shima, then bus. 🚌 from Hirayu Onsen. ℹ️ 3-min walk from Onota bus stop (0263) 94-2221. 🎏 Mountain-opening Festival (Apr 27).

An alpine valley with a handful of hotels and campsites, Kamikochi lies in the southern part of the Chubu Sangaku (North Japan Alps) National Park, at an altitude of 1,500 m (4,900 ft), and is a good hiking and climbing base. The valley is reached by a tunnel, open from late April to early November; in July, August, Golden Week *(see p44)*, and on some weekends, private cars are banned. Although Japan's highest (after Fuji) and wildest mountains are in the South Alps, the North Alps have more snow and more impressive scenery. Plentiful mountain refuges allow hikes of several days from hut to hut, often via a hot spring. Most huts open from early May to late October (no reservations needed); the main mountaineering season is July to September. Tents and climbing gear can be rented in Kamikochi.

The most spectacular climb is a three-day route from Kamikochi taking in angular **Mount Yari** and **Mount Hotaka** – at 3,190 m (10,470 ft), the highest peak in the North Alps – while short hikes include the rocky scree of **Mount Yake**, the only active volcano in the North Alps. In bad weather, walks are constrained to the valley floor, by the rushing river and through a half-submerged landscape shaped by eruptions from Mount Yake.

DOSOJIN STONES

A man and woman, each holding a bowl of sake, on a Dosojin stone

These pairs of jaunty stone figures, a male and a female, are guardian deities of travelers. They are found at many roadsides in northern Nagano prefecture, as well as at village boundaries. Typically rounded in shape, the pair are often depicted holding hands or with the female offering sake to the male.

Matsumoto ⑳

松本城

Nagano prefecture. 228,800. at Matsumoto JR stn (0263) 32-2814. www.city.matsumoto. nagano.jp/english/index.html firelit Noh at castle (Aug), Taimatsu (Oct 3).

Gateway to the Japan Alps, Matsumoto's main attraction is its **castle**, a 20-minute walk northeast of the station. It has the oldest five-tiered keep in Japan (1593) and walls and moat from 1504. Functional yet beautiful, it is well preserved. Devices for defense include niches for archers, guns, and dropping stones. The sixth floor, with superb mountain views, was the headquarters when under attack, and its ceiling contains a shrine to the goddess of the 26th night who was thought to protect against fire and invasion.

Beside the keep, reached by a covered passage, stands the **Moon-viewing Turret**, added in the 1630s for aesthetic purposes. The castle admission includes the **Japan Folklore Museum** in the grounds, featuring local geography, wildlife, history, dolls, and tools.

Also in Matsumoto are the **Japan Ukiyo-e Museum**, an excellent collection of woodblock prints, and **Matsumoto Folkcraft Museum**, with folk art from Japan and across Asia; on the edge of the city, a 20-minute bus ride away, **Asama** and **Utsukushigahara** have pleasant hot springs.

Matsumoto Castle
Tel (0263) 32-2902. daily.

Japan Ukiyo-e Museum
7 mins drive W of stn. Tel (0263) 47-4440. Tue–Sun.

Folkcraft Museum
15 mins by bus from stn, Mingeikan-mae stop. Tel (0263) 33-1569. Tue–Sun.

Environs:
North of Matsumoto, **Hotaka** has views over the fields of Japan's largest *wasabi* (horse-radish) farm, as well as *wasabi*-tasting. The fields are a 40-minute walk from Hotaka station.

Nagano ㉑

長野

Nagano prefecture. 383,000. at Nagano JR stn (026) 226-5626. www.city.nagano.nagano.jp Gokaicho (showing of statue, mid-Apr–mid-May, every six years – next showings 2009, 2015).

Surrounded by orchards and low mountains, Nagano is a skiing center and was the main venue for the 1998 Winter Olympics. In the town, the prime attraction is **Zenko-ji**, a non-sect temple that draws up to one million pilgrims a year. It has, unusually, always been open to women as well as men, and has male and female chief priests. Established in 670, it enshrines what is thought to be Japan's oldest Buddhist image, an Amida

An image of the physician Binzuru, follower of Buddha, in Zenko-ji, Nagano

triad brought from Korea in the 6th century. This is kept hidden, and a copy shown every six years. The temple also has a pitch-dark underground passage containing a "key to paradise": touching the key, positioned on the right-hand wall, is said to bring happiness in the afterlife.

Environs:
In nearby **Obuse**, the **Hokusai-kan** is a gallery devoted to artist Katsushika Hokusai (1760– 1849), who stayed in the town as an old man. Farther into the mountains **Jigokudani Onsen**, reached by bus from Yudan-aka, is famous for the 270 or so wild macaques living around its hot pools.

Hokusai-kan
10-min walk from Obuse stn. Tel (026) 247-5206. daily.

Bridge leading to the immaculately preserved Matsumoto castle

A row of *bosatsu* from the temple of Zenko-ji, Nagano ▷

KYOTO CITY

To truly understand Japan, the visitor must spend time in the backstreets and environs of its old imperial capital, where scores of the country's famous monuments are preserved within a lively modern city. Kyoto's citizens may grudgingly envy the economic vitality of Tokyo and nearby Osaka, but they take great pride in their refined cuisine, lilting dialect, and sensitivity to the seasons.

Founded in 794 as Heian-kyo (capital of peace and tranquility), the city was modeled on the Tang Chinese city of Chang-an. Bounded on three sides by mountains and bisected by a river flowing north to south, the site was considered ideal by Emperor Kanmu's geomancers. As the population grew, however, hygiene was a problem, especially when the Kamo River flooded. A series of rituals and festivals came into being to placate the spirits responsible for plagues and other catastrophes, resulting in a tightly knit fabric of ritual and custom, mostly still observed.

Kyoto women in traditional costume, a not uncommon sight

Kyoto culture became an amalgam of several influences, of which the imperial court and nobility were the first and most important. Later came the samurai, patrons of Zen Buddhism and the tea ceremony. Merchants were also influential, especially the silk weavers of Nishijin. The city was reduced to ashes at various times by earthquakes, fires, and the ten-year period of civil strife known as the Onin War (1467–77). During the Edo period (1600–1868), the balance of power shifted from Kyoto to Edo (Tokyo), and Kyoto eventually lost its status of capital in 1868.

At first glance, modern Kyoto may seem little different from other Japanese cities, but the pleasures of this repository of Japanese culture will soon reveal themselves. Life here is still largely tied to nature's rhythms, as can be gauged by visiting at different times of the year. *Kyo-ryori*, Kyoto's celebrated cuisine, for example, makes much of seasonality, and the city's exquisite gardens go through striking seasonal transitions.

Bridge on the northern edge of the Gion district, a remnant of old Kyoto

◁ Avenue of *torii* gates at Fushimi Shrine, southern Kyoto

Exploring Kyoto City

Kyoto is bounded by mountains to the west, north, and east. Many of the best monuments and gardens are found in the foothills, such as the Higashiyama (Eastern Mountains) district east of the Kamo River. Kyoto's treasures have to be sought out. Only by investigating side streets with their old shops and townhouses, exploring temples, and wandering through outlying districts will you begin to get a sense of the city's cultural riches.

SIGHTS AT A GLANCE

Temples and Shrines
Chion-in Temple ⑪
Daitoku-ji Temple ⑳
Ginkaku-ji: the Silver
 Pavilion ⑯
Kamo Shrines ⑲
Kinkaku-ji: the Golden
 Pavilion ㉒
Kitano Tenman-gu Shrine ㉑
Kiyomizu-dera Temple ⑩
Koryu-ji Temple ㉗
Myoshin-ji Temple ㉖
Nanzen-ji Temple ⑮
Ninna-ji Temple ㉕
Nishi and Higashi
 Hongan-ji Temples ⑤
Ryoan-ji Temple ㉔
Sanjusangen-do Temple ③
Shoren-in Temple ⑫
Toji Temple ①

Museums and Notable Buildings
Domoto Insho Museum ㉓
Kongo Nogakudo Theater ⑱
Kyoto National Museum ④
Kyoto Station ②
Nijo Castle pp160–61 ⑥

Districts
*Eastern Gion and the
 Higashiyama pp166–7* ⑨
Gion District ⑧
Imperial Park ⑰
Okazaki Area ⑬
Pontocho Alley ⑦

Walk
The Philosopher's Walk ⑭

SEE ALSO
• *Farther Afield* pp176–9

• *Where to Stay* pp303–4

• *Where to Eat* pp336–8

KYOTO ADDRESSES

Despite its gridlike layout, Kyoto has no more logical pattern to its address system than anywhere else in Japan. Residences and shops are organized into *cho*, or neighborhoods, many formed from the boundaries of medieval guilds. Locations are often given in relation to an intersection or well-known landmark. Because the city is built on an incline rising from south to north, south is indicated in an address by the word *sagaru* (go down) and north by *agaru* (go up).

VISITORS' CHECKLIST

Kyoto prefecture. 🏯 *1,473,000.*
🚄 *Sanyo Shinkansen and other
lines.* ℹ️ *(075) 344-3300.*
www.city.kyoto.jp/koho/eng/
index.html 🎏 *Aoi Matsuri
(Hollyhock Festival, May 15);
Gion Matsuri (Jul); Jidai Matsuri
(Festival of the Ages, Oct 22).*

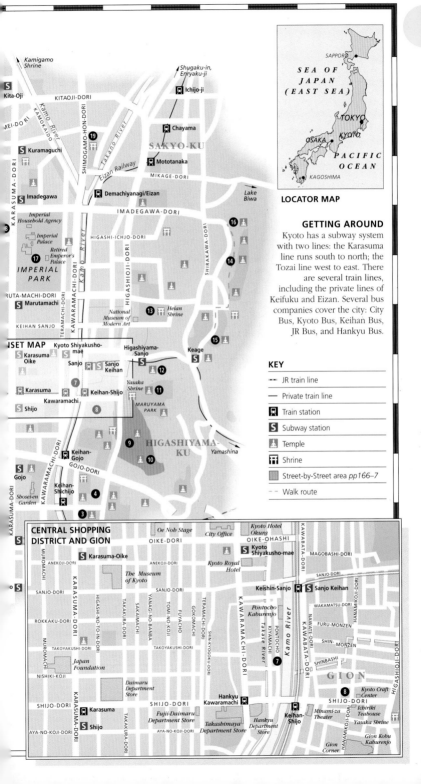

LOCATOR MAP

SEA OF JAPAN (EAST SEA)

SAPPORO
TOKYO
OSAKA
KYOTO
PACIFIC OCEAN
KAGOSHIMA

GETTING AROUND
Kyoto has a subway system with two lines: the Karasuma line runs south to north; the Tozai line west to east. There are several train lines, including the private lines of Keifuku and Eizan. Several bus companies cover the city: City Bus, Kyoto Bus, Keihan Bus, JR Bus, and Hankyu Bus.

KEY

⁃⁃	JR train line
—	Private train line
🚆	Train station
S	Subway station
卍	Temple
⛩	Shrine
▨	Street-by-Street area pp166–7
- -	Walk route

Kamigamo Shrine
Kita-Oji
KITAOJI-DORI
Shugaku-in, Enryaku-ji
Ichijo-ji
MEI-DORI
KAMOKAIDO
Kuramaguchi
SHIMOGAMO-HON-DORI
Kamo River
Takano River
Chayama
SAKYO-KU
19
KARASUMA-DORI
Imadegawa
Eizan Railway
Mototanaka
MIKAGE-DORI
Demachiyanagi/Eizan
Lake Biwa
Imperial Household Agency
IMADEGAWA-DORI
16
Imperial Palace
HIGASHI-ICHJO-DORI
Retired Emperor's Palace
17
IMPERIAL PARK
Kamo River
HIGASHIOJI-DORI
SHIRAKAWA-DORI
14
RUTA-MACHI-DORI
KAWARAMACHI-DORI
Marutamachi
National Museum of Modern Art
13
Heian Shrine
15
KEIHAN SANJO
TERAMACHI-DORI
HIGASHIOJI-DORI
Keage
NSET MAP
Kyoto Shiyakusho-mae
Higashiyama-Sanjo
Karasuma Oike
Sanjo
Sanjo Keihan
7
Karasuma
Keihan-Shijo
Yasaka Shrine
12
11
Kawaramachi
MARUYAMA PARK
Shijo
8
9
HIGASHIYAMA-KU
Yamashina
Keihan-Gojo
10
Gojo
GOJO-DORI
Keihan-Shichijo
4
KARASUMA-DORI
Shosei-en Garden
3

CENTRAL SHOPPING DISTRICT AND GION

MUROMACHI
Oe Noh Stage
City Office
Kyoto Hotel Okura
OIKE-DORI
OIKE-OHASHI
KAWABATA-DORI
S
Karasuma-Oike
ANEKOJI-DORI
Kyoto Shiyakusho-mae
MAGOBASHI-DORI
ANEKOJI-DORI
The Museum of Kyoto
Kyoto Royal Hotel
o S
KARASUMA-DORI
SANJO-DORI
HIGASHI-NO-TO-IN-DORI
TAKAKURA-DORI
SAKAIMACHI
YANAGI-NO-BANBA
TOMI-NO-KOJI
FUYACHO
GOKOMACHI
TERAMACHI-DORI
SHIN KYOGOKU-DORI
SANJO-DORI
Keishin-Sanjo
Sanjo Keihan
SANJO-DORI
WAKAMATSU-DORI
NAWATE-DORI
HANAMIKOJI-DORI
ROKKAKU-DORI
Pontocho Kaburenjo
KIYAMACHI
PONTOCHO
FURU-MONZEN
TAKOYAKUSHI-DORI
Japan Foundation
TAKOYAKUSHI-DORI
Takase River
SHIN-MONZEN
HIGASHIOJI-DORI
NISHIKI-KOJI
7
Kamo River
KAWARAMACHI-DORI
KAWABATA-DORI
SHINBASHI
GION
SHIJO-DORI
Karasuma
Daimaru Department Store
Hankyu Kawaramachi
SHIJO-DORI
8
Kyoto Craft Center
Ichibiki Teahouse
HIGASHIOJI-DORI
S
Shijo
Fuji-Daimaru Department Store
Takashimaya Department Store
Hankyu Department Store
Keihan-Shijo
Minami-za Theater
Yasaka Shrine
HANAMIKOJI-DORI
AYA-NO-KOJI-DORI
TAKAKURA-DORI
AYA-NO-KOJI-DORI
Gion Corner
Gion Kobu Kaburenjo

Toji Temple ❶
東寺

Toji stn, Kintetsu line. 42 to Toji Higashimon-mae. 8:30am–5:30pm daily (4:30pm winter).
Museum Tel (075) 691-3325. Mar 20–May 25; Sep 20–Nov 25.

Although it lacks the mossy beauty of many Kyoto temples, dusty, hoary Toji (actual name Kyo-o-gokoku-ji) impresses by the sheer weight of its history. Its Buddhas have been watching over the city ever since Kukai (see p229) founded the temple in 796. The city's religious foundations were laid here, and echoes of bygone rituals seem to linger in Toji's hallowed halls.

Kukai turned Toji into the main headquarters of Shingon Buddhism. The sect's esoteric rituals relied heavily on mandalas, and in the Kodo (lecture hall), 21 statues form a three-dimensional mandala, at the center of which is Dainichi Nyorai, the cosmic Buddha who first expounded the esoteric teachings. About 1,200 years old, these and other major images were carved from single blocks of wood.

Yakushi Nyorai, the Buddha of healing, and his attendants Gakko and Nikko, are enshrined in the two-story Kondo (main hall). First built in 796, the present structure dates from 1603 and is considered a masterpiece.

Rebuilt in 1644, Toji's magnificent five-story pagoda – at 55 m (180 ft) the tallest

Toji temple's five-story pagoda, the tallest in Japan

Soaring, light-filled main hall of Kyoto Station

wooden structure in Japan – has become a symbol of Kyoto. Inside are images of four Buddhas and their followers.

Northwest of the Kodo is the Miei-do or Taishi-do (great teacher's hall) where Kukai lived. It houses a Secret Buddha, a Fudo Myo-o image, shown on rare occasions, as well as an image of Kukai. A National Treasure, the graceful structure dates from 1380.

Kukai's death is commemorated on the 21st of each month, when a flea market, called Kobo-san by the locals, is held in the temple precincts. Many shoppers take time out for a brief pilgrimage to the Miei-do, where they offer money and incense, some rubbing the incense smoke onto whatever body part is troubling them.

Kyoto Station ❷
京都駅

Complex 2nd flr main concourse, left from escalator. **Tel** (075) 343-6655. 8:30am–7pm daily.
Kyoto Tourist Information 9th Floor, Kyoto station. **Tel** (075) 344-3300. 10am–6pm Mon–Sat.

A sleek complex of soaring spaces, glass surfaces, and bleacher-like staircases, Kyoto's new JR train station provides a futuristic entry to Japan's old imperial capital.

Completed in 1997, the structure is the work of architect Hara Koji, a Tokyo University professor whose design triumphed in an international competition. Although it has been criticized for its refusal to incorporate traditional Japanese motifs in its design, the station is undeniably eye-catching. Thanks to its open-air spaces it also ironically resembles a traditional wooden Kyoto house: pleasant in summer, but drafty and cold in winter.

Within the station is a shopping area called **The Cube**, which includes shops specializing in Kyoto craft items and food products.

Long hall and landscaped grounds of Sanjusangen-do

Sanjusangen-do Temple ❸
三十三間堂

Tel (075) 525-0033. Keihan Nanajo stn. 100, 206, 208 to Hakubutsukan Sanjusangen-do-mae. Apr–mid-Nov: 8am–5pm daily; mid-Nov–Mar: 9am–4pm daily.

Sanjusangen-do (popular name of Rengeo-in) induces an almost hallucinatory effect on its visitors who, once inside its elongated main hall, find themselves face to face with ranks of nearly identical Kannon (goddess of mercy) images – 1,001 of them, to be precise – all glimmering in the dark. The effect is magical, and a bit eerie.

Sanjusangen-do dates from 1164 and is the longest wooden structure in the world. Its name derives from the 33 *(sanjusan)* spaces between the building's pillars. The main, magnificent image of a 1,000-armed Kannon was carved in 1254 by Tankei at the age of 82. Upon its head are ten other heads, including a miniature image of the Amida Buddha. Stretching out on either side are 1,000 smaller images. Kannon was believed to have 33 manifestations, so the faithful would have invoked the mercy of 33,033 Kannons.

On the Sunday before Coming-of-Age Day *(see p47)* the temple hosts an archery contest for young women, who shoot arrows from one end of the veranda of the main hall to the other.

Kyoto National Museum ❹

京都国立博物館

Tel (075) 541-1151. **www**.kyohaku. go.jp ◯ 9:30am–5pm Tue–Sun (to 6pm or 8pm for special exhibitions).

The city's National Musem was established in 1895 by the Imperial Household Agency. It is noted for its pictorial works, including Buddhist and ink paintings, textiles and Heian-period sculptures. Special exhibitions are held in the Meiji-era brick building to the right of the entrance.

Nishi and Higashi Hongan-ji Temples ❺

西本願寺と東本願寺

Nishi Hongan-ji
Tel (075) 371-5181. 🚌 9, 28,75 to Nishi Honganji-mae.
◯ May–Aug: 5:30am–6pm daily; Sep, Oct, Mar, Apr: 5:30am–5:30pm daily; Nov–Feb 6am–5pm.
Higashi Hongan-ji *Tel* (075) 371-9181. 🚌 JR Kyoto Stn, then 5-min walk. ◯ Mar–Oct: 5:50am–5:30pm daily; Nov–Feb: 6:20am–4:30pm daily.

With their massive flower-decked altars, ornately carved transoms, and shimmering expanses of *tatami* matting worn smooth by millions of stockinged feet, the cavernous Hongan-ji temples testify to the power and popularity of the Jodo-Shinshu sect.

The two temples are almost identical in their layout, reflecting their common origin. Each has a huge Goei-do (founder's hall) and a smaller Amida-do housing an Amida Buddha image. **Nishi Hongan-ji** is rich in National Treasures, but not all are always on view. They include the Shoin (study hall), with its lavishly decorated Shiroshoin and Kuroshoin compartments; Kokei no Niwa, a garden featuring cycad palms; two Noh stages, one of which is thought to be the oldest Noh stage in existence; Hiunkaku, a large tea pavilion; and the Karamon, or Chinese gate. The

Mythical beast detail from Nishi Hongan-ji's gate

Shoin is open twice a month, but dates vary. (The Kuroshoin, however, is never shown.) Hiunkaku is open only once a year, on May 20 or 21. Entrance requires a large donation, which includes a bowl of tea and a Noh performance.

Higashi Hongan-ji's immense and lavish Goei-do gate is one of the first traditional structures visitors to Kyoto see as they head north out of Kyoto Station. The temple's Goei-do (founder's hall) dates from 1895 and claims to be the largest wooden structure in the world. The striking white plaster and gray tile walls on the temple's northern side belong to the temple kura, or storehouse.

Environs:
Two blocks east of Higashi Hongan-ji proper is **Shosei-en** (nicknamed Kikoku-tei), a spacious garden owned by the temple. Poet-scholar Ishikawa Jozan (1583–1672) and landscape architect Kobori Enshu (1579–1647) are said to have had a hand in its design. Herons, ducks, and other wildlife find refuge here.

Detail of the main gate fronting the street at Nishi Hongan-ji

Nijo Castle ⑥
二条城

With few of the grand fortifications of other castles in Japan, Nijo is instead best known for its unusually ornate interiors and so-called nightingale floors. The latter were designed to make bird-like squeaking sounds when walked upon, a warning of possible intruders. The complex was created by Shogun Tokugawa Ieyasu (1543–1616), and symbolized the power and riches of the newly established Edo-based shogunate. Ieyasu's grandson Iemitsu commissioned the best Kano School painters for the reception halls, in preparation for an imperial visit. Ironically, in 1867 the last Tokugawa shogun resigned at Nijo Castle, in the presence of Emperor Meiji.

Cherry Trees Painting
The painting of flowering cherry trees on the sliding door panels is attributed to Kano Naonobu (1607–50).

Shiroshoin (shogun's living chambers)

Kuroshoin (black study)

Garden
Nijo's garden is famous for the wealth and variety of its rocks.

NINOMARU COMPLEX
The focus of Nijo Castle is the Ninomaru reception rooms, a staggered group of buildings interconnected by covered wooden walkways.

★ **Ohiroma Ichi-no-ma**
(first grand chamber)
Dummies representing daimyo (feudal lords) are shown paying respects to the shogun on his dais.

STAR FEATURES

★ Karamon Gate

★ Ohiroma Ichi-no-ma

Large Cats Painting
This dynamic animal scene was painted at a time when Japanese artists mistook leopards for female tigers.

VISITORS' CHECKLIST

Entrance on Horikawa-dori. *Tel* (075) 841-0096. S *Nijojo-mae stn.* 9, 50, 101. 8:45am–5pm daily. Last admission 4pm. Dec 26–Jan 4 & Tue in Jan, Jul, Aug, Dec.

Shikidai (reception chamber)

The nightingale floors were carefully laid so that the cramps and nails below the floorboards would rub together and squeak gently when disturbed.

★ Karamon Gate
This Momoyama-period gate has a Chinese-style gable and gold-plated fixtures.

Entrance to Ninomaru compound

THE KANO SCHOOL PAINTERS

The Kano painters, originally from a low-ranking samurai family, grew to prominence in the 15th century for their Chinese-style landscapes, figures-in-landscape, and bird and flower scenes. The paintings at Nijo Castle are the largest Kano pieces executed. Among the motifs are life-size tigers and panthers crouching among bamboo groves, wild geese and herons in a winter landscape, pine trees, flitting swallows, and frolicking peacocks.

Huge pine trees in the Shikidai, by Kano Tanyu (1602–74)

Entrance to Palace
Above the carriage porch is an unusually ornate wood carving of flying birds, peacocks, and delicately twining flowers.

Pontocho Alley ❼

先斗町通り

🚉 *Kawaramachi stn, Hankyu Kyoto line.* 🚌 *5, 17, 205 to Shijo-Kawaramachi.*

This charming alleyway is best appreciated after dusk, when it is reminiscent of an *ukiyo-e* print *(see p85)*. Formerly a sandbar, the stretch of land began to be developed in 1670. The area flourished as an entertainment district and was licensed as a gay quarter, a role it continues to play. Although neon and concrete are encroaching, the street largely remains the preserve of the traditional wooden *ochaya* – the type of teahouse where geisha entertain clients.

Pontocho is also home to the tiny **Tanuki (Badger) Shrine**. In 1978 a fire broke out in Pontocho, taking the life of a geisha. Where it stopped, a ceramic *tanuki (see p317)* was found shattered by the heat. Believing that Mr. Tanuki had sacrificed himself on their behalf, the residents built this little shrine to house his remains. Throw in a coin and a recorded message imparts such pearls of wisdom as "beware of fire."

From the beginning of June to mid-September, many of Pontocho's riverside restaurants erect platforms, called *yuka*, over the canal running parallel to the Kamo River.

Two-story gateway to Yasaka Shrine, Gion district

The colorful Tanuki Shrine, dedicated to a badger in Japanese folklore

Gion District ❽

祇園地区

Several blocks north and south of Shijo-dori, bounded by the Kamo River to the west and the Higashiyama to the east. 🚉 *Shijo stn, Keihan line.* 🚌 *46, 201, 203, 207 to Gion.*

By turns tawdry and sublime, the Gion is Kyoto's best-known geisha quarter and symbol to the average Japanese male of all that's good in life: wine, women, and karaoke.

The Gion's history started in feudal times, with stalls catering to the needs of pilgrims and other visitors. These evolved into teahouses fulfilling a variety of appetites. In the late 16th century, Kabuki moved from the Kamo riverbank, where it had started, into several theaters just east of the river, furthering the Gion's reputation as a playboy's paradise. One of these, **Minami-za** *(see p184)*, still exists.

The **Yasaka Shrine**, whose striking two-story vermilion gate rises above the eastern end of Shijo-dori, was established around 656 and originally called Gion Shrine. Its deities protect from illness and, in 869, were paraded through the streets to stop an epidemic – the beginning of the famous Gion Matsuri *(see p184)*. On New Year's Day, thousands flock here to pray for health and prosperity, while in early April crowds stream through its gates on their way to **Maruyama Park**, a cherry-blossom viewing site.

Gion's main shopping area is the stretch of Shijo between Yasaka Shrine and Shijo Bridge, which includes shops with expensive kimono accessories. On the southeast corner of Shijo and Hanamikoji is the Gion's most famous *ochaya*, **Ichiriki**. Easily identified by its distinctive red walls, this teahouse is the setting of a scene in the Kabuki play *Chushingura*. **Hanamikoji** itself, a historically preserved zone, shows the Gion at its classic, and classy, best. The restaurants and *ochaya* here are the haunts of politicians and company presidents, and are likely to turn a cold shoulder to people without a proper introduction. More accessible to tourists are the nearby **Gion Corner** and the **Gion Kobu Kaburenjo** venues *(see p178)*.

Running east from Hanamikoji, north of Shijo, is **Shinbashi**, a street lined with *ochaya*, and nary a neon sign to be seen. At the eastern end of this beautifully preserved area is the tiny shrine of **Tatsumi Daimyo-jin**, its red surfaces plastered with name cards of Gion geisha, hostesses, and restaurant owners who have visited to pray for prosperity.

The average Gion-goer, however, is more likely to partake of drink and karaoke than engage in geisha play at a prestigious *ochaya*. His territory is the northeastern Gion, where the cluttered streets of neon and concrete are as gaudy as Shinbashi is refined.

Geisha, Geiko, and Maiko

Geisha are female professional entertainers whose knowledge of traditional arts, skill at verbal repartee, and ability to keep a secret win them the respect, and sometimes love, of their well-heeled and often influential male clients. The profession, dating from the 17th century, is in decline and blurred by the activities of so-called *onsen geisha* and others who offer more sexual than classical arts, or who are more glorified waitress than geisha. Kyoto's

A Kyoto maiko

proud geisha prefer the term *geiko* (child of the arts). Less polished than their *geiko* "sisters," *maiko*, apprentice geisha, are a Kyoto-only phenomenon. The city has four geisha enclaves: Gion-kobu, Pontocho, Miyagawa-cho, and Kamishichi-ken. Public dances are staged in each district in spring and fall. At other times, the only way to see geisha perform is at private functions, often held at *ryotei*, *ochaya*, and *ryokan* (upscale restaurants, teahouses, and inns).

The white face and delicately shaped red lips are classic ideals of beauty in Japan.

Under-kimono

Pontocho, one of Kyoto's historic geisha districts, has many ochaya, *where geisha are booked to entertain prestigious clients.*

Ornamental hairpins vary with the seasons.

A *maiko*'s hair is her own, not a wig.

The nape of the neck, accentuated by the unpainted part, is considered sensuous.

The *obi* (*sash*) of a maiko *hangs down at the back.*

Embroidered collar

THE MAIKO COSTUME

Only in Kyoto do young women training to be *geiko* wear their hair in a distinctive style and sport a unique costume featuring a long, hanging *obi*, tall *koppori* clogs, and an under-kimono with an embroidered collar. When becoming full-fledged *geiko*, they exchange the embroidered collar for a white one, a transition known as *eri-kae*, or collar change.

Tabi **socks**

The geisha world *moves to the rhythm of the* shamisen, *a three-stringed instrument that originated in Okinawa. Geisha who choose not to specialize in dance will instead master the* shamisen *or another instrument. The skills of older geisha are held in high regard.*

Poised and posture-perfect, *Umegiku, of the Kamishichi-ken district, performs classical dance with a fan as prop. For more formal occasions she will paint her face and wear a different kimono.*

Street-by-Street: Eastern Gion and the Higashiyama ❾

Sipping the sacred, cleansing water at Kiyomizu Temple

For most of Kyoto's history, the area comprising the Higashiyama (Eastern Mountains) district lay outside the official boundaries of the capital. As a result, it was always more rustic and secluded. Furthermore, being separated from the main city by the Kamo River, it was spared the fires that often ravaged Kyoto. Consequently, Higashiyama remains one of the city's most charming and unspoiled districts. The small area shown here includes the eastern side of the Gion, leading through some delightful stone-paved roads up to Kiyomizu Temple.

Maruyama Park
Kyoto's most famous cherry-blossom viewing site is mobbed until the petals fall.

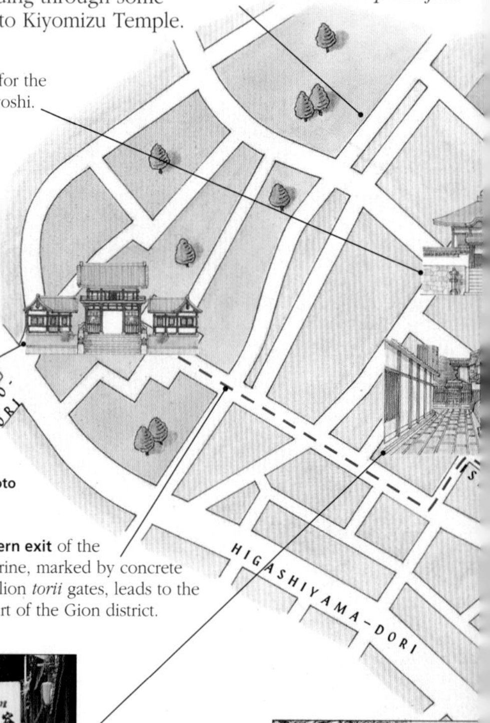
SHIJO-DORI
HIGASHIYAMA-DORI

Kodai-ji was built in 1605 for the widow of Toyotomi Hideyoshi.

★ Yasaka Shrine
On the edge of Kyoto's central shopping district, the Yasaka Shrine (see p162) *oversees the religious rites of the city's main festival, the Gion Matsuri, in July.*

Central Kyoto

The southern exit of the Yasaka Shrine, marked by concrete and vermilion *torii* gates, leads to the eastern part of the Gion district.

★ Ishibe-Koji Lane
This charming lane with discreet inns and teahouses is an extension of the Gion entertainment district (see p162). *The exquisite wooden buildings with tiny gardens reflect the peaceful atmosphere of old Kyoto.*

Ne-ne no Michi
Named after Hideyoshi's widow, "Ne-ne's road" is a wide flagstone-paved avenue, home to small, upscale shops and private galleries. Long, stone staircases lead up from the road to the temple of Kodai-ji and the Ryozen Kannon.

Yasaka Pagoda
*Not to be confused with
the Shinto shrine of the
same name to its north,
the elegant, five-story
Yasaka Pagoda is all
that remains of a
Buddhist temple that
once stood here.*

Ryozen Kannon
The 24-m (80-ft) high
concrete figure near
Kodai-ji Temple is
dedicated to the Japanese
soldiers who died in
World War II.

LOCATOR MAP
See Kyoto map page 157

Kiyomizu-yaki, a refined,
brightly colored porcelain,
is sold in numerous pottery
shops lining the roads
leading up to Kiyomizu.

★ Kiyomizu Temple
*This famous temple (see p168)
is over a thousand years old
and could almost be called an
institution of Kyoto life.*

KEY

－ － Suggested route

STAR SIGHTS

★ Stone-Paved Roads

★ Ishibe-Koji Lane

★ Kiyomizu Temple

★ Yasaka Shrine

★ Stone-Paved Roads
*Two flagstone-paved
streets called Sannen-
zaka ("three-year slope")
and Ninenzaka ("two-
year slope") are a pres-
ervation district. Take
care on the steps – local
lore maintains that a
slip here will bring two
or three years' bad luck.*

View from the veranda of the main hall at Kiyomizu-dera

Kiyomizu-dera Temple ⓾

清水寺

Tel (075) 551-1234. 🚌 *100, 206 to Kiyomizu-michi.* ⬚ *6am–6pm daily.* 📷

While many other famous temples are the preserves of certain sects, Kiyomizu-dera seems to belong to everyone. For over 1,000 years, pilgrims have climbed the slope to pray to the temple's 11-headed Kannon image and drink from its sacred spring (*kiyomizu* means pure water). The main hall's veranda, a nail-less miracle of Japanese joinery, offers wonderful views of Kyoto. To view the temple itself, walk to the pagoda across the ravine, and you'll see why the expression "to jump off Kiyomizu's stage" is the Japanese equivalent of "to take the plunge."

Statue of Kannon at t-dera

On the temple's north side is a small shrine where love charms can be purchased.

Chion-in Temple ⓫

知恩院

Tel (075) 531-2111. **S** *Higashiyama stn, Tozai line.* 🚌 *100 or 206 to Chion-in-mae.* ⬚ *Mar–Nov: 9am–4:10pm daily; Dec–Feb: 9am–3:40pm daily.* 📷

Chion-in's colossal Sanmon, the largest such gate in Japan, was built to proclaim the supremacy of Jodo-sect

Buddhism, of which Chion-in is the headquarters. It was also an emphatic statement of the authority of the Tokugawa shogunate, which funded the temple's restoration in 1633.

The well-endowed complex occupies the site where Honen, the founder of the Jodo sect, started to preach in 1175. It boasts a lavish founder's hall, a smaller hall enshrining an image of Amida Buddha, and elegant reception halls decorated with Kano School *(see p161)* paintings. The Gongendo mausoleum enshrines the spirits of Tokugawa Ieyasu, his son Hidetada, and grandson Iemitsu. The temple also possesses a huge bell that is solemnly rung 108 times (once for each sin Man is prone to commit) on New Year's Eve, an event broadcast on TV.

Shoren-in Temple ⓬

青蓮院

Tel (075) 561-2345. **S** *Higashiyama stn, Tozai line.* 🚌 *5 to Jingu-michi.* ⬚ *9am–5pm daily.* 📷

Oristocratic Shoren-in's symbol is its ancient camphor trees whose 700-year-old gnarled limbs spread majestically on either side of the front gate. The grounds are beautifully landscaped, with a bright pond garden on one side and a mysterious, camphor tree-shaded expanse of moss on the other. The teahouse in the garden has been newly rebuilt, the

original having been burned in April 1993 by left-wing radicals protesting the Emperor's visit to Okinawa.

Okazaki Area ⓭

岡崎公園一帯

🚌 *5 or 100 to Kyoto Kaikan Bijutsukan-mae.* 🎏 *Jidai Matsuri (Festival of the Ages, Oct 22, Heian Shrine).*

Okazaki is home to museums, galleries, sports grounds, the municipal zoo, and **Heian Shrine**, one of Kyoto's largest and newest shrines. Built in 1895, the shrine was intended to help boost the city's morale and economy – both at a low ebb after Tokyo was made capital in 1868. With its vermilion pillars and green tiles, the shrine harks back to Tang Dynasty China. Its pond garden is famous for irises and a Chinese-style covered bridge.

The **National Museum of Modern Art** houses an outstanding collection of paintings by a school of Kyoto artists active in the Meiji and Taisho eras. Across the street is the venerable **Kyoto City Museum of Fine Arts**, which hosts exhibitions of European and American works. The **Kyoto Exhibition Hall** (Mikako Messe), hosts a variety of shows, while its basement museum presents scores of Kyoto crafts, including Kiyomizu-*yaki* porcelain.

🏛 **Museum of Modern Art**
Tel (075) 761-4111. ⬚ *Tue–Sun.* 📷

🏛 **Museum of Fine Arts**
Tel (075) 771-4107. ⬚ *Tue–Sun.* 📷

🏛 **Exhibition Hall**
Tel (075) 762-2670. ⬚ *daily.*

Heian-jingu, the shrine built in 1895 in Okazaki

The Tea Ceremony

Valued for its medicinal qualities, tea was imported from China in the 8th century. The nobility took to drinking it at lavish parties, and Murato Shuko (1422–1502) later developed the custom's spiritual aspects, which appealed to the samurai. The point of the ritual *(chaji)*, in which a light meal and whipped powdered tea *(matcha)* are served by a host to a few invited guests, is summed up by the samurai notion "one lifetime, one meeting" *(ichigo, ichie)*. In other words, this is a unique moment to be treasured. In Kyoto, where the tea ceremony was developed, special rituals are put on for tourists *(see p185)*, with commentary about the complex etiquette and Zen ideals. Visitors can also enjoy *matcha* and a sweet *(wagashi)* without the ritual at many temples and specialty teashops.

Seasonal flowers in the *tokonoma*

Sen no Rikyu *(1522–91), a student of Shuko and adviser to warlord Hideyoshi, formalized the ritual, replacing Chinese utensils with native ones. His descendants continued the legacy, resulting in two main schools of tea: Omote Senke and Ura Senke.*

The ceremonial teahouse *is a small, hut-like building with a garden (see pp30–31), not to be confused with other types of teahouses, such as the geisha's ochaya, or those for wayfarers. The one shown here is at Daitoku-ji (see pp172–3), the spiritual home of the tea ceremony.*

The tea utensils *reflect Zen values of simplicity, refinement, and restraint.*

Whisk *(chasen)*

Tea jar *(natsume)*

Water jug *(mizusashi)*

Tea bowl *(chawan)*

Charcoal burner *(furo)*

Bamboo ladle *(hishaku)*

Kettle *(kama)*

To drink matcha, *even informally, hold the bowl with your right hand and place it in the palm of your left. Turn it clockwise about 90 degrees, raise it with both hands, then empty it in three gulps.*

THE WAY OF TEA

The tea ceremony is a well-orchestrated series of events. The ritual involves meeting your fellow guests, walking through the grounds of the teahouse, performing ablutions, entering a cell-like room, meeting your host, admiring the features of the room and tea utensils, watching the tea being prepared, bowing, and consuming the food and tea. Each part of the ritual is symbolic; ultimately it is your appreciation of the moment that counts.

The decorative alcove *(tokonoma)* has a hanging scroll *(kakemono)* and sometimes a flower arrangement or art object to be admired.

Guests sit *seiza*, kneeling on the *tatami* matting, an uncomfortable position for the uninitiated.

Guests bow when attendants offer individual bowls of the freshly prepared tea.

The Philosopher's Walk ⑭

哲学の道

One of Kyoto's best-loved spots, the Philosopher's Walk follows a cherry-tree-lined canal meandering along the base of the scenic Higashiyama (Eastern Mountains) between Ginkaku-ji south to Nyakuoji-jinja, and connects with roads leading to the precincts of Nanzen-ji. The route is so-named because a Kyoto University philosophy professor, Nishida Kitaro (1870–1945), used it for his daily constitutional. Coffee and craft shops, restaurants, and boutiques are scattered along the route. The path becomes a veritable promenade during the cherry and maple seasons, as couples from all over the Kansai region flock to enjoy its unspoiled natural beauty.

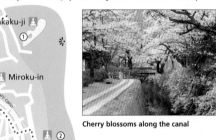

Cherry blossoms along the canal

NORTHERN KYOTO

Ginkaku-ji ①

Miroku-in

Shishigatani canal

SHISHIGATANI-DORI

Honen-in ②

Anraku-ji

Reigan-ji

Otoyo-jinja ③

Shishigatani canal

Koun-ji

Nyakuoji-jinja

Eikan-do ④

OKAZAKI PARK

Gate

Nanzen-ji ⑤

Sanmon

MURIN-AN AND KYOTO STATION

Ginkaku-ji ①
Often heaving with tour groups, Ginkaku-ji's so-called Silver Pavilion is set within a remarkable garden with ponds, raked gravel mounds, and pine trees.

Otoyo-jinja ③
Over a bridge to the east, Otoyo-jinja is one of a few small Shinto shrines among the great Buddhist foundations of the Higashiyama.

Honen-in ②
A short walk uphill, this small, Jodo-sect temple, with its rustic, thatched gate and mounds of raked sand, is well worth the detour from the canal path.

Eikan-do ④
This park-like temple complex of buildings connected by corridors houses an Amida Buddha. There are good views of Kyoto from the pagoda.

Nanzen-ji ⑤
Rebuilt after the disastrous Onin War (1467–77), most of Zen temple Nanzen-ji's structures date from the 17th century, apart from this celebrated, Western-style Meiji-period aqueduct.

KEY

• • • Walk route

🛕 Temple

⛩ Shrine

☀ Viewpoint

TIPS FOR WALKERS

Starting points: *Ginkaku-ji (to walk north to south) or Nanzen-ji (south to north).*
Length: *1.5 km (1 mile).*
Refreshments: *En-route, especially yudofu restaurants in precincts of Nanzen-ji.*

0 metres   200

0 yards   200

Colossal, free-standing Sanmon (gateway) at Nanzen-ji

Nanzen-ji Temple ⑮
南禅寺

Tel (075) 771-0365. **S** *Keage stn, Tozai line.* 🚌 *5 to Nanzen-ji-Eikan-do-michi.* ◯ *8:40am–5pm daily (Dec–Feb: to 4:30pm).* 📷

From its pine-studded outer precincts to the inner recesses of its subtemples, this quintessential Zen temple exudes an air of serenity. Nanzen-ji has been at the center of Japanese Zen history since 1386, when it was placed in control of Kyoto's Gozan, or "five great Zen temples."

The **Hojo** (abbot's quarters) includes a small but exquisite dry garden attributed to Kobori Enshu (1579–1647), and Momoyama-period paintings, including the Kano Tanyu masterpiece *Tiger Drinking Water*. Nearby is a room overlooking a waterfall and garden, where a bowl of *matcha* (ceremonial tea) and a sweet can be enjoyed for a small fee.

The temple's colossal **San-mon**, a two-story gate built in 1626 to console the souls of those killed in the Summer Siege of Osaka Castle, is said to have been the hideout of Ishikawa Goemon, a legendary outlaw hero who was later boiled alive in an iron cauldron.

Subtemples:
Three of Nanzen-ji's 12 subtemples are open to the public year-round. The most impressive, **Konchi-in**, boasts an authenticated work by Kobori Enshu, featuring pines and boulders arranged in a tortoise-and-crane motif.

Tenju-an has an elegant dry garden and a small, lush stroll garden. Secluded **Nanzen-in** occupies the original site of Emperor Kameyama's villa. Restored in 1703, it faces a pond-centered garden backed by a wooded mountainside.

The red-brick **aqueduct** in front of Nanzen-in may seem incongruous, but for Japanese tourists this "exotic" Western structure is one of Nanzen-ji's greatest attractions. Built in 1890, it formed part of an ambitious canal project to bring water and goods from neighboring Shiga prefecture into the city. It was one of Meiji Japan's first feats of engineering.

Nanzen-ji is synonymous with *yudofu*, boiled tofu, a delicacy best enjoyed during cold months. Specialty restaurants are located within the temple precincts (*see p337*).

Environs:
Gem-like **Murin-an** to the west of Nanzen-ji is the former villa of Meiji-era statesman Yamagata Aritomo. The garden's design makes good use of water from the aqueduct. North of Nanzen-ji, **Eikan-do** houses an image of Amida Buddha in the act of looking back over his shoulder, a very unusual pose.

Ginkaku-ji: the Silver Pavilion ⑯
銀閣寺

Tel (075) 771-5725. 🚌 *100 to Ginkaku-ji-mae.* ◯ *8:30am–5pm daily (Dec to mid-Mar: 9am–4:30pm).* 📷

Ginkaku-ji – actual name, Jisho-ji; English nickname, Silver Pavilion – is considered by some to be an unequaled masterpiece of garden design; others find it overrated. Not in dispute is the importance of Ginkaku-ji to Japanese culture, for within its walls the tea ceremony, Noh, flower arrangement, and ink painting found new levels of refinement.

The temple was originally the mountain retreat of shogun Yoshimasa (1358–1408), who is remembered for an artistic renaissance now referred to as Higashiyama culture. In tribute to his grandfather, who covered Kinkaku-ji in gold leaf (*see p174*), Yoshimasa intended to finish his pavilion in silver. However, the ruinous Onin War thwarted that ambition. Minus its final coating, the graceful Silver Pavilion now shines with the patina of age.

The Silver Pavilion, which never received its intended coating

The majestic Kenreimon gate within the Imperial Park

Imperial Park 🟡
京都御苑

🆂 *Imadegawa stn, Karasuma line.*
Imperial Household Agency
Tel *(075) 211-1215.* 🕐 *8:45am–noon,
1–4pm Mon–Fri. Apply here for
tickets to the imperial palaces and
gardens. (Passport required.)*
Imperial Palace 🎫 *tours in English
at 10am and 2pm Mon–Fri.*
Retired Emperor's Palace 🎫 *tours
in Japanese at 11am and 1:30pm.*
Both palaces 🕐 *Mon–Fri & 3rd Sat
of month (each Sat in Apr, May, Oct,
Nov).* 🌑 *Dec 28–Jan 4, public hols.*

With its stately pines and
vistas of the Higashiyama,
the Imperial Park (Kyoto
Gyoen) is a spacious
oasis in the heart of the
city. On its grounds are
the **Imperial Palace**
(Kyoto Gosho) and
**Retired Emperor's
Palace** (Sento Gosho),
whose impressive
stroll garden was
built by the Toku-
gawa for retired
emperor Go-Mizuno'o
in 1630. The **Imperial
Household Agency**
(Kunaicho), where
tickets are issued for
the imperial structures as well
as to Shugaku-in and Katsura
villas *(see pp176 and 178)*, is
in the northwest corner.

At the southern end of the
park is a delightful pond with
an arched bridge, all that remains of one of several noble
families' estates that occupied
much of what is now park-
land. From the bridge is an
unobstructed view all the way
north to the **Kenreimon**, the
majestic gate in the middle of
the south wall, which may be
used only by the emperor.

*Mannequin at the
Imperial Palace*

Kongo Nogakudo
Theater 🟡
金剛能楽堂

🆂 *Imadegawa stn, Karasuma line.*
Tel *(075) 441-7222.* 🕐 *daily.* 🎫 *for
performances.*

The new Kongo Noh theater
across from the Imperial
Palace grounds opened in
June 2003, following its
relocation from a site in Shijo
Muromachi. During the Edo
period (1603–1868) noh was
adopted as the official art of
the warrior class, and the
Kongo Theater has the longest history of regular use as a
noh stage in Japan; its
players are particularly
known for their agility
and acrobatic feats.
The new theater
incorporates sev-
eral features from
the earlier design,
including the out-
door stage, pillars,
and large acoustic
earthenware jars.
Regular perfor-
mances are held at
the theater, usually
on the last Sunday
of the month. Look
out for exhibitions of Noh costumes and masks in the lobby.

*Torii gates at Shimogamo, one of
the Kamo shrines*

Kamo Shrines 🟡
上賀茂・下賀茂神社

🚌 *46, 47 to Kamigamo-jinja-mae;
4, 205 to Shimogamo-jinja-mae.*
Nishimura House *Tel* *(075) 781-
0666.* 🕐 *Mar 15– Dec 8:
9:30am–4:30pm daily.* 🎫 🎎 *Aoi
Matsuri (Hollyhock Festival, May 15).*

At the northern reaches of
the Kamo River, the
Kamigamo Shrine has
probably existed since the 7th
century, while **Shimogamo**,
its southern counterpart, is a
century older. Both are dedicated to the thunder deity. Set
in sylvan Tadasu no Mori ("the
forest where lies are
revealed"), Shimogamo has
long played a role in ensuring
the success of the rice
harvest. The Aoi Festival
features a procession between
the shrines, horse races, and
archery. Kamigamo Shrine is
noted for its Haiden hall,
rebuilt in 1628, and mysterious cones of white sand. In
the vicinity are several *shake*,
priests' residences. One of
these, the **Nishimura House**,
is open to the public.

Daitoku-ji
Temple 🟡
大徳寺

Tel *(075) 491-0019.* 🆂 *Kita-Oji stn,
Karasuma line.* 🚌 *12, 204, 205, 206
to Daitoku-ji-mae.* 🕐 *9am–4:30pm
daily.* 🎫 *for most subtemples.*

An air of eloquent restraint
pervades the grounds of
Daitoku-ji, as befits a temple
intimately connected with the
world of the tea ceremony.
Founded in 1325, the temple
prospered in the latter half of

the 16th century, when it came under the patronage of warlords (and tea ceremony aficionados) Oda Nobunaga and Hideyoshi. Today, a host of subtemples, many with famous tearooms and jewel-like gardens, continue to promote the ways of Zen and Tea.

Daisen-in is famous for its Muromachi-period dry garden. Ink landscape paintings by Soami and Kano Motonobu grace its interior. The south garden of **Koto-in** features a grove of slender maples rising above an expanse of moss and a *roji*, or tea garden, to the west. **Zuiho-in**, built in 1535 as the memorial temple of a Christian *daimyo*, has a modern garden by Shigemori Mirei with rocks placed in the shape of a crucifix. **Ryogen-in**, founded 1502, has four gardens in different styles.

Interior at Ryogen-in, a subtemple of Daitoku-ji

Kitano Tenman-gu Shrine ㉑

北野天満宮

Tel (075) 461-0005. 📠 50, 101, 203 to Kitano Tenman-gu-mae.
🕐 5:30am–5:30pm daily (Apr–Sep: 5am–6pm).

Always thronged with students praying for success in exams, Kitano Tenman-gu enshrines Heian statesman Sugawara Michizane, or Tenjin-san, the deity of learning. Michizane's favorite tree, the plum *(ume)*, is found throughout the grounds. On the 25th of each month, the shrine is the site of a bustling flea-market, where everything from blue-and-white Imari porcelains to nylon stockings are for sale.

Kamishichi-ken, an *ochaya* (teahouse) and bar-lined street running from Kitano Tenman-gu to Imadegawa-dori, is Kyoto's smallest, but oldest *geiko* (geisha) district. On February 25 the *geiko* conduct a tea ceremony in the shrine's orchard, and perform dances for the public every spring and fall at the local theater.

THE SYMBOLISM OF DAISEN-IN ZEN GARDEN AT DAITOKU-JI

Daisen-in's garden is a three-dimensional version of the Chinese Sung monochrome landscape paintings that inspired its creation. Mankind's fate, relationship with nature, and place in the universe are all expressed in this masterpiece of dry-landscape garden design.

A "waterfall" of white gravel *flows from a rock representing mythical Mount Horai. Other rock groupings symbolize Earth and Heaven.*

Japan's Inland Sea (see p224) *is represented in this section.*

The wall *represents the point at which we are assailed by doubts.*

Hojo (abbot's quarters) with tatami mats

"The Great Ocean," *a white expanse of raked gravel, serves as an aid to meditation. The cone-shaped mounds are design accents, while the tree in the corner is said to be the same kind as that under which the Buddha achieved Enlightenment.*

The river of life *reemerges wider and deeper after being temporarily dammed. Takarabune ("treasure ship") Stone glides serenely down, but the nearby "turtle" tries vainly to swim upstream.*

The fabulous pavilion at Kinkaku-ji, its gold-leaf outer layer shining in the sun

Kinkaku-ji: the Golden Pavilion ㉒

金閣寺

Tel *(075) 461-0013.*
🚌 *12 or 59 to Kinkaku-ji-mae; 101, 204, 205 to Kinkaku-ji-michi.*
🕐 *9am–5pm daily.* 🈂

A glimmering legacy of medieval Japan, Kinkaku-ji (formal name Rokuon-ji) is more familiar to foreign tourists as the Golden Pavilion. It was built by the third Ashikaga shogun, Yoshimitsu (1358–1408), who, relinquishing his official duties (but not his hold on power), entered the priesthood at the age of 37. The temple originally served as his retirement villa. A fervent follower of the Zen priest Soseki, Yoshimitsu directed that the finished complex become a temple after his death, with Soseki as its superior.

The visitor approaches the temple along a tree-shaded path, then emerges into a bright garden, on the other side of which stands the fabled pavilion. An exact replica of the original, destroyed by arson in 1950 (an event dramatized in Mishima Yukio's novel *The Golden Pavilion*), the graceful three-story structure is totally covered in gold leaf and topped by a bronze phoenix.

Mount Kinugasa serves as a backdrop to the garden, a stroll-type, laid out around a central pond. The harmonious interplay of its various components makes it a superb example of Muromachi-period garden design. Both pavilion and garden are especially exquisite after a snowfall.

Domoto Insho Museum ㉓

堂本印象美術館

Tel *(075) 463-0007.*
🚌 *12, 15, 50, 59 to Ritsumeikan Univ.-mae.* 🕐 *9:30am–5pm Tue–Sun.* 🈂 *(free to disabled visitors and over 65s.)*

West of Kinkaku-ji, along the Kinukake-no-Michi, a stretch of road skirting the base of the Kitayama (Northern Mountains), lies the Domoto Insho Museum. It houses the impressive works of 20th-century *nihonga* master, Domoto Insho (1891–1975). Often translated as "Japanese-style painting," *nihonga* is a fresco-like painting technique that utilizes mineral pigments.

Ryoan-ji Temple ㉔

竜安寺

Tel *(075) 463-2216.* 🚃 *Ryoan-ji michi, Keifuku Kitano line (10-min walk).* 🚌 *59 to Ryoan-ji-mae.* 🕐 *8am–5pm daily (Dec–Feb: 8:30am–4:30pm).* 🈂

Founded in 1450, Ryoan-ji's claim to fame is grounded in its rock garden, a composition of white gravel and 15 stones that many consider to be the ultimate expression of Zen Buddhism.

Although various interpretations of the rocks' symbolism have been put forth, the significance of the garden, like that of Zen itself, defies definitions. Its riddles can be unraveled only by silent contemplation, something that the hordes of high-school students, not to mention the temple's recorded explanations, do little to facilitate. To avoid both, try to arrive just as the gates open.

Though overshadowed by the famous rock garden, the temple's lower pond-garden should not be overlooked. Created at a time when Zen had not yet arrived in Japan, its soft contours serve as an interesting foil to the spiritual rigors of the rock garden.

Ryoan-ji's Zen garden, the interpretation of which is up to the viewer

For hotels and restaurants in this region see pp303–4 and pp336–8

Ninna-ji Temple ㉕
仁和寺

Tel (075) 461-1155. 🚉 *Omuro stn, Keifuku Kitano line.* 🚌 *10, 26, 59 to Omuro Ninna-ji.* **Treasure House** ◯ *9am–4:30pm daily (4pm Oct, Nov).* 📷

Ninna-ji's colossal front gate, with formidable Nio (Deva King) guardians, serves as a reminder that this Shingon-sect temple used to be, until fires reduced it to its present size, a huge complex number-ing up to 60 subtemples.

Completed by Emperor Uda in 888, Ninna-ji was formerly known as the Omuro Palace. Until the Meiji Restoration (1868), it was always headed by an imperial prince. The Kondo (main hall) and its wooden Amida image are National Treasures. Other sights include a soaring five-story pagoda and a stand of dwarf cherry trees – the last of Kyoto's many *sakura* (cherry trees) to bloom.

Situated in the southwest of the precincts is the Omuro Gosho, a compound with a lovely Edo-period garden. On the mountain behind is the Omuro 88-Temple Pilgrim-age, which reproduces in miniature the temples on Shikoku's 88-Temple Pilgrimage (*see pp228–9*). It takes about two hours to complete the full circuit.

Nio guardian figure at the gate of Ninna-ji

Myoshin-ji Temple ㉖
妙心寺

Tel (075) 461-5226. 🚉 *Myoshin-ji stn, Keifuku Kitano line; Hanazono stn, JR Sagano line.* 🚌 *26 to Myoshin-ji Kitamon-mae.* ◯ *9:10am–3:40pm daily.* 📷

Founded at the behest of retired Emperor Hanazono in 1337, destroyed during the Onin War, and rebuilt on a grand scale, the spacious

Ninna-ji's soaring five-story pagoda, dating from the 1630s

Rinzai-sect Zen temple com-plex of Myoshin-ji boasts some 47 subtemples rich in Kano School paintings and other art objects. The main structures, aligned in a row in typically Zen fashion (*see p137*), include the Hatto (lecture hall), famous for a huge dragon painted by Kano Tanyu on its ceiling, and its bell, the oldest in Japan.

Subtemples normally open to the public include **Keishun-in**, noted for its four gardens and famous tea arbor, **Taizo-in**, which has both a dry garden by Kano Motonobu (1476–1559) and a modern

garden by Nakane Kinsaku (1917–95). Taizo-in's prize possession is one of the most famous examples of Zen ink painting, Josetsu's *Catching a Catfish with a Gourd* (1413). A copy is on display.

Daishin-in has three gar-dens. Subtemples **Reiun-in**, nicknamed the Motonobu Temple because of its many Kano Motonobu works, and **Tenkyu-in**, noted for paintings by Kano Sanraku, are open on special days in spring and fall.

Ajiro, a restaurant special-izing in *shojin ryori* (Zen vege-tarian cuisine) is near the temple's south gate (*see p337*).

Koryu-ji Temple ㉗
広隆寺

Tel (075) 861-1461. 🚉 *Uzumasa stn, Keifuku Arashiyama line.* 🚌 *11, 61, 62, 63, 71, 72, 73 to Ukyoku-Sogochosha-mae.* ◯ *9am–5pm daily (Dec–Feb: to 4:30).* 📷

A must-see for lovers of Buddhist art, Koryu-ji was founded in 622, by a clan of Korean immigrants who con-tributed greatly to the develop-ment of Kyoto. Among the impressive images in its Reihoden (treasure hall), is a Miroku Bosatsu (Buddha of the future) believed to have been brought to Japan from Korea in the 7th century. Kyoto's oldest image, the seat-ed figure is known throughout the nation for its beatific Mona Lisa-like smile. The temple's oldest structure, the Kodo, houses a 9th-century statue of the Amida Buddha.

Garden of subtemple Taizo-in, at the Myoshin-ji complex

Kyoto City: Farther Afield

Poets' hermitages, noblemen's villas, esoteric mountain temples, and unspoiled natural scenery are among the many attractions to be found in the outskirts of the old capital. Once remote regions boasting unique characteristics and customs, they are now easily accessible, and any itinerary of Kyoto should include at least two or three of these rewarding destinations.

SIGHTS AT A GLANCE

Arashiyama District ❷
Daigo District ⓬
Enryaku-ji Temple ❾
Fushimi Shrine ⓫
Katsura Imperial Villa ❶
Kurama District ❺
Manshu-in Temple ❼
Ohara District ❿
Sagano District ❸
Shisen-do Temple ❻
Shugaku-in Villa ❽
Takao District ❹
Uji City ⓭

0 km   5
0 miles 3

KEY

⬜ Central Kyoto (see pp156–7)

▭ Expressway

▬ Main road

Katsura Imperial Villa ❶

桂離宮

1-1 Misono, Katsura, Nishikyo-ku. **Tel** (075) 211-1215. 🚉 Katsura stn, Hankyu line. 🚌 33 to Katsura Rikyu-mae. ⬜ by appt only Mon–Fri: apply at Imperial Household Agency (see p166). 📷

With its flawless attention to detail, Katsura Imperial Villa is often cited as one of the finest examples of Japanese landscape design. Built in 1620 by Hachijo no Miya Toshihito, an imperial prince, it was later added to by his son, Toshitada. A sumptuous stroll garden (see pp30–31), Katsura is famous for the manner in which its paths and stepping stones control the visitor's line of sight, resulting in a series of ingeniously planned vistas. The view from the **Shokin-tei** (pine zither) tea arbor, replicates the scenery

of Amanohashidate (see p212). Many of the garden's scenic allusions are to places mentioned in the Chinese and Japanese classics. The somewhat hurried tour includes the **Shoka-tei** (flower-viewing teahouse) in the highest part of the garden, then down past the **Shoi-ken** (sense-of-humor teahouse), and on to the main villa, a set of halls poetically described as resembling a flock of geese in flight.

Arashiyama District ❷

嵐山地区

🚉 Arashiyama stn, Keifuku Arashi-yama line; Hankyu Arashiyama stn. 🚌 11, 28 or 93 to Arashiyama Tenryu-ji-mae.

With something to please the eye in any season, Arashiyama has long held a special place in the hearts of the Japanese. Even today, despite omnipresent shops specializing in items emblazoned with the likenesses of TV and movie celebrities, the area still offers a lot of unspoiled natural beauty. At its center is timeless **Togetsu-kyo**, the graceful "moon-crossing" bridge. North of the bridge, mountainsides thickly forested with cherries and pines drop steeply to the river, which in summer becomes the stage for *ukai*, fishing done by firelight with trained cormorants. *Hozugawa-kudari*, running the Hozu River rapids from Kameoka to Arashiyama, is another popular activity. The narrow-gauge **Torokko Train** provides a different way of viewing the same scenery.

Rinzai-sect temple **Tenryu-ji** was founded by the first Ashikaga shogun, Takauji, in 1339. The serene garden has survived intact and features a pond in the shape of the Chinese character, *kokoro*, or "enlightened heart."

Another Arashiyama treasure is **Okochi Sanso**, the private villa of silent-screen star Okochi Denjiro. The meticulously laid-out grounds offer wonderful vistas of Mount Hiei and the Hozu River gorge.

Togetsu-kyo, the wooden "moon-crossing" bridge in Arashiyama

Sagano District ❸

嵯峨野地区

🚃 JR Saga-Arashiyama stn, Sagano line. 🚌 28 or 91 to Daikaku-ji.

The home of rice fields, bamboo groves, temples, and cemeteries, Sagano's varied sights are by turn pastoral and poignant. The best point from which to launch an exploration is **Torii Moto**, where a vermilion shrine gateway *(torii)* marks the beginning of an ancient trail leading up to sacred Mount Atago, abode of the fire divinity. Two thatched teahouses near the *torii* have been offering refreshment to pilgrims for centuries.

From the *torii*, head south past traditional farmhouses to **Adashino Nenbutsu-ji**. From the Heian to Edo periods, Adashino was a remote place where corpses were often disposed of. Established to offer solace for the souls of these forgotten dead, the temple gathered together their grave markers – rocks on which a likeness of the Buddha had been carved. The sight of row after row of these silent stone figures is strangely moving. On the evenings of August 23 and 24, more than 1,000 candles are offered to them.

To the south is **Gio-ji**, a tiny thatched nunnery where Gio, a cast-off mistress of warlord Taira no Kiyomori (1118–81), took the tonsure. Known for the beauty of its fall foliage, the temple is bounded on one side by a magnificent stand of bamboo, while, to the front, slender maples rise from an emerald carpet of moss.

Located in central Sagano, Jodo-sect temple **Seiryo-ji** houses an image of the Shakamuni Buddha reportedly brought to Japan in 987. **Nison-in** has standing images of Amida and Shakamuni. The many maple trees on the temple's grounds attract large numbers of visitors in the fall. Charming **Rakushi-sha** (hut of the fallen persimmons) was the humble home of haiku poet Mukai Kyorai (1651–1704). Basho *(see p279)* composed his *Saga Diary* here in 1691.

Secluded Nichiren-sect temple **Jojakko-ji** is situated on Ogura-yama, a mountain whose beauty has been celebrated by poets since ancient times. A steep flight of stone steps leads to the temple from where there are great views of Kyoto and Mount Hiei. Halfway up the steps, a thatched gate houses two fierce-eyed Nio guards said to be the work of 13th-century sculptor Unkei. The temple's beautiful two-story pagoda is a symbol of the Lotus Sutra. The aristocratic temple complex of **Daikaku-ji**, in the northeast of Sagano, is the headquarters of one of Japan's most popular schools of ikebana (flower arranging). Next to it is **Osawa-no-Ike**, a pond built in imitation of Lake Tungting in China.

Rickshaw in the pastoral Sagano district

Takao District ❹

高雄地区

🚌 Takao bus or 8 to Takao.

Esoteric mountain temples and refreshingly pristine mountain scenery are Takao's main attractions. **Jingo-ji**, founded in the 8th century, houses a wealth of National Treasures including the Yakushi Nyorai (Buddha of healing). Set in an ancient cryptomeria forest, **Kozan-ji**, founded in 774, has the look of an elegant estate. Copies of the handscroll *Choju-giga* (frolicking birds and animals) are displayed in the **Sekisui-in**, a brilliant example of Kamakura residential architecture. Japan's first tea was cultivated nearby.

Traditional restaurant in the mountainous district of Takao

Kurama District ❺

鞍馬地区

🚃 Kurama stn, Eizan line. 🚌 95 from Ohara. 🎎 Kurama Matsuri (Oct 22).

Famous as the abode of gods, demons, and superheroes, Kurama was once an isolated village of foresters. Now a Kyoto suburb, it still retains an untamed feeling, a quality fully in evidence on the night of October 22, when the town celebrates its Fire Festival.

Kurama-dera was built in 770 to protect Kyoto from the evil forces that, according to Chinese geomancy, emanate from the north. A gate marks the beginning of a mountain trail to the main temple buildings; the main hall offers splendid views of the Kitayama mountains. From the Reihokan (treasure hall) a path winds beneath towering cryptomeria trees to the village of **Kibune**, a collection of inns and teahouses alongside a stream. Several Kurama shops sell pickled mountain herbs and vegetables. Watch for masks of *tengu*, a folkloric creature with a phallic-shaped nose.

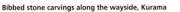

Bibbed stone carvings along the wayside, Kurama

The upper garden at Shisen-do, as viewed from the veranda

Shisen-do Temple ❻

詩仙堂

27 Monguchi-cho, Ichijo-ji, Sakyo-ku. **Tel** (075) 781-2954. 🚌 5 or 8 to Ichijo-ji Sagarimatsu-cho. ◯ 9am–5pm daily. 📷

A Samurai who had fallen out of favor with the shogun-ate, Ishikawa Jozan construct-ed this retirement villa in 1641. On a small plot below the Higashiyama mountains, this Confucian scholar and poet succeeded in creating a nearly perfect blend of building and garden. Although now a Soto-sect Zen temple, the hermitage retains the feel of a home.

The famous garden is divid-ed into two levels: the upper, best viewed from the main building's veranda, features a broad expanse of packed sand bordered by clipped azalea bushes. The lower level, which also makes use of areas of sand to add light and s pace, offers a fine view of the villa's tile-and-thatch roof and moon-viewing chamber.

Manshu-in Temple ❼

曼殊院

42 Takenouchi-cho, Ichijo-ji, Sakyo-ku. **Tel** (075) 781-5010. 🚌 5 to Shugaku-in Michi. ◯ 9am–4:30pm daily. 📷

Even in spring and fall when its cherries and maples draw the crowds, Manshu-in maintains an atmosphere of dignified repose. This Tendai-sect temple was restored in

1656 by the son of the prince who designed Katsura Villa *(see p176)*. Its elegant build-ings, with their cleverly crafted door pulls and other carefully planned details, call to mind those of the imperial villa. The beautiful garden is composed of islands of rock and vegetation amid swaths of raked gravel, with the Higashiyama mountains form-ing a harmonious backdrop.

Shugaku-in Imperial Villa ❽

修学院離宮

Yabuzoe, Shugaku-in. 🚉 Shugaku-in stn, Eizan line. 🚌 5 to Shugaku-in Michi. ◯ by appt only Mon–Fri: apply at Imperial Household Agency, (075) 211-1215 (see p172).

If Katsura Villa *(see p176)* could be said to be yin, then its counterpart imperial villa, Shugaku-in, could only be described as yang. While the former's garden, layered with literary and poetic allusions, is characterized by an inward-looking sensibility, spacious Shugaku-in might strike the viewer as extroverted.

Created by retired emperor Go-Mizuno'o (1596–1680), the garden was a lifetime labor of love. Divided into three levels, each with a teahouse, the com-plex is imbued with a spirit of understated simplicity. Yet, a surprise awaits: the approach to the uppermost teahouse is designed so that the visitor is

kept unaware until the last minute of the panorama from the top of the Kitayama mountains, spread out as if an extension of the garden.

Enryaku-ji Temple ❾

延暦寺

4220 Sakamoto Honmachi, Otsu, Shiga prefecture. **Tel** (077) 578-0001. 🚉 Yase stn, Eizan line, then cable car; or Hieizan Sakamoto stn, Kosei line, then cable car. 🚌 Enryaku-ji bus from Kyoto or Keihan Sanjo stns. ◯ summer: 8:30am–4:30 pm daily; winter: 9am–4pm daily. 📷

A once mighty monastery fortress with 3,000 sub-temples and thousands of *sohei*, or warrior monks, Enryaku-ji today is but a shadow of its former self. Still, the solemnity of its isolated mountain-top setting and grandeur of its remaining buildings make the trek to Mount Hiei worthwhile. Founded by the monk Saicho in 792, Enryaku-ji became the main temple of the Tendai sect *(see p275)*. Although initially entrusted to protect the city from evil forces, the temple itself became the bane of the capital. Emperor Go-Shirakawa (1127–92) once lamented that there were only three things beyond his control: the flooding of the Kamo River, the roll of the dice, and the warrior monks of Enryaku-ji. In 1571, however, warlord Oda

Konpon Chu-do, the inner sanctum of Enryaku-ji

Nobunaga, angered by the temple's resistance to his authority, sent his army to attack the mountain. The complex was burned to the ground, and every man, woman, and child massacred.

The temple is divided into three precincts, connected by shuttle bus. The **Kokuho-den**, a museum of treasures, is in the east precinct. Here, too, is the famous **Konpon Chu-do**, the inner sanctum, which enshrines a Healing Buddha image said to have been carved by Saicho. Nearby **Jodo-in** (Pure Land Hall) is the site of Saicho's tomb.

In the **Jogyo-do** hall in the west precinct monks circumambulate the altar, chanting an invocation called the *nembutsu*; in the **Hokke-do** hall they meditate upon the Lotus Sutra, a central tenet of Tendai belief. Beyond these two buildings is the **Shaka-do**, the main hall of the west precinct.

Ohara District ❿

大原地区

🚌 17 from Kyoto stn.

Known for thatched farmhouses, delicious pickles, and other rustic charms, Ohara is also home to two famous temples. Set in an incomparably beautiful setting, **Sanzen-in's** Amida Hall dates from 1148 and houses a meditating Amida Buddha. *Fusuma* (sliding door) paintings by Takeuchi Seiho (1864–1942) decorate the temple's Shinden. The approach to Sanzen-in is lined with shops selling such local products as *shiba-zuke*, a pickle dyed purple with the leaf of the beefsteak plant. Across the valley is tiny **Jakko-in**, a nunnery where Kenreimon-in (1155–1213) lived. The sole survivor of the Taira clan, she prayed here for the souls of her son and kin killed by the Genji.

Daigo-ji's Heian-era pagoda

Fushimi Shrine ⓫

伏見稲荷神社

68 Yabunouchi, Fukakusa, Fushimi-ku. 🚉 *Fushimi Inari stn, Keihan & Nara lines.* 🚌 *Minami 5 to Fushimi Inari Taisha mae.* **Tel** *(075) 641-7331.* 🕐 *24 hours.*

This most famous of the many thousands of shrines dedicated to Inari, the popular deity of rice and sake *(see p26)*, lies near the sake-making district of Fushimi. A much-photographed avenue formed out of hundreds of *torii* (gates) has been donated by businessmen *(see p154)*.

Daigo-ji Temple ⓬

醍醐寺

22 Higashioji-cho, Daigo, Fushimi-ku. 🚉 *Daigo stn, Tozai line.* **Sanpo-in Tel** *(075) 571-0002.* 🕐 *9am–4pm daily (to 5pm Mar–Oct).* 🈂️

Daigo-ji's main draw is subtemple **Sanpo-in**. Because Toyotomi Hideyoshi took a personal interest in restoring this after a visit in 1598, it contains some of the Momoyama period's most representative works of art. The lavish garden is noted for its many magnificent rocks, which were gifts to Hideyoshi from his *daimyo* (feudal lords). The rest of Daigo-ji is more ancient. The graceful five-story pagoda, built in 951, is one of only two Heian-era pagodas in existence. Those venturing to upper Daigo are mainly pilgrims. The white-clad ones are headed for **Juntei-do**, a hall housing a Kannon image – No. 11 of the 33 Kannon Temples pilgrimage route.

Uji City ⓭

宇治市

🚉 *Uji stn, Keihan-Uji or Nare lines.* **Temples** 🕐 *9am–4:30pm daily.* 🈂️ **Miho Museum** *300 Momodani, Shigaraki-cho, Shiga.* **Tel** *(074) 882-3411.* 🕐 *10am–5pm Tue–Sun.* 🈂️

In addition to some of the best green tea grown in Japan, the small city of Uji boasts **Byodo-in**, which is featured on the 10-yen coin. Built in 1053, the temple's Phoenix Hall *(see p30)* and Amida Nyorai image inside are marvelous remnants of one of Japan's greatest epochs.

While Byodo-in sought to imitate palaces depicted in Tang-dynasty mandalas, **Mampuku-ji** invoked the architectural traditions of Ming China. This most Chinese of Kyoto temples was established in 1661 by Ingen, a priest who fled China after the fall of the Ming dynasty. Ingen introduced the *sencha*, or leaf tea, ceremony.

Close by, in Shigaraki, the **Miho Museum** has some stunning examples of Japanese treasures such as Buddha statues, tea ustensils, and handscrolls, as well as Roman mosaics and treasures from Egypt and Persia.

Mampuku-ji, a Chinese-style temple in Uji city

SHOPPING IN KYOTO

Kyoto is famous throughout Japan for the quality of its crafts and food products, the result of many centuries of catering to the demanding tastes of its resident aristocrats, temple abbots, tea masters, and merchants. Venerable shops coexist with stores stocked with the latest fads, making shopping here a bizarre, but never boring, experience. As in other major Japanese cities, Kyoto has large

Kimono in shop window

branches of Japanese department store chains. Typically these offer a vast selection of goods, including foodstuffs in the basement. Specialty craft outlets are all over the city. ATM machines can be found in the basement of the Kyoto Tower building opposite Kyoto Station, as well as at the central post office. A map of the central shopping district is on page 157; details of opening hours are on page 348.

Modern storefronts along kawaramachi

SHOPPING DISTRICTS

The intersection of Shijo and Kawaramachi forms the heart of the downtown shopping district. During the day, the sidewalks of Kawaramachi, which serves as Kyoto's main street, are busy with shoppers, while at night *boso-zoku* (hot-rodders) cruise noisily along its store-lined length.

Smaller shopping districts include the area around JR Kyoto station and Kitayama-dori, where Kyoto's most upscale shops can be found.

DEPARTMENT STORES AND ARCADES

The **Hankyu** and **Takashimaya** department stores are located at the intersection of Kawaramachi and Shijo.

Takashimaya is the place to head for men's and women's fashions; inside are boutiques stocking Issey Miyake and other brand-name clothing. The city's other main department store, **Daimaru**, is six blocks further west on Shijo's north side. Many of Kyoto's famous old shops, such as the Ippodo tea store, have outlets in department store basements.

Just west of Takashimaya is **Fujii Daimaru**, a local department store which is unrelated to the larger Daimaru department store, and the **BAL Building**, a comprehensive, multistory collection of brand-name boutiques.

Shin-Kyogoku, a street situated within the network of arcades and roads between Shijo and Sanjo, caters to Japanese youngsters on school outings. Its varied offerings run the gamut from legitimate craft items to outrageous kitsch.

On the west end of Kyoto Station is **JR Kyoto Isetan**, the newest addition to Kyoto's department store line-up. Just to the north of the station is an old standby, the **Kyoto Kintetsu** department store. **Porta**, an underground shopping arcade, is located beneath the station's north

side, while to its south is **Avanti**, a building housing a variety of shops.

Within the station itself is a shopping area called **The Cube**, which contains a sizable number of souvenir shops specializing in Kyoto craft items and food products.

NISHIKI MARKET ALLEY

Nicknamed "Kyoto's Kitchen," Nishiki is a fascinating market alley north of, and running parallel to, Shijo, from Teramachi west to Takakura. This is where most of Kyoto's *kaiseki* chefs buy their ingredients. Many of the items sold, such as *fu* (wheat gluten) and *yuba* (soy milk skin), are unique to Kyoto cuisine. In particular, a wide selection of pickles, another local specialty, is available. **Aritsugu**, at Nishiki's eastern end, is known for Japanese knives and other kitchen utensils.

Nishiki market, the best place to shop for food items in Kyoto

ELECTRONIC GOODS

The city's main outlet for cheap electronic goods and appliances is the stretch of Teramachi running south of Shijo. This serves as Kyoto's version of Den Den Town in Osaka. **Duty Free Kyoto**, located in the center of this district, has English-speaking staff and stocks all kinds of electronic goods in most brands. Note that duty-free prices are only available on purchases over ¥10,001.

ANTIQUES

Having escaped the bombs of World War II, Kyoto's *kura* (family storehouses) continue to emit a small but steady stream of fascinating objects. The city's antiques fall into three main categories: Buddhist art, tea ceremony utensils, and everyday items. Some stores specialize in just one category, but most carry a range. Kyoto's most venerable antique shops are located between Nawate and Higashio-ji along Shinmonzen and Furumonzen streets. Especially reputable are **Kawasaki Bijutsu** (specializing in screens and chests), **Renkodo** (Imari-ware), and **Nakajima** (which sells a bit of everything). **Seikado** sells antique ceramics, tableware, and large items of furniture dating from the Edo and Meiji periods.

The city's up-and-coming antique district is the section of Teramachi from Oike to Marutamachi, where a host of new shops run by young but knowledgeable owners have suddenly sprouted. The **Kyoto Antiques Center** houses many shops under one roof. **Teramachi Club**, farther up Teramachi on the same side of the street, deals mainly in Meiji and Taisho period items. Across from it is

Handmade combs

Nagata, which buys not at auction but directly from family *kura*. Fans of old lacquerware should not miss **Uruwashi-ya**, on Maruta-machi, one and a half blocks west of Teramachi.

Antique lovers will also want to visit **Hirooka Antique**, which is just two minutes' walk east from Exit 2 of Kitayama station. The shop is a bit out of the way but worth the trip out of the city center – Hirooka's goods are first-rate and reasonably priced.

FLEA MARKETS

Antiques, household items, plants, food, and much more are on sale at Kobo-san, the market held on the 21st of every month at Toji Temple (*see p158*). Tenjin-san, a similar flea market, is held on the 25th at the shrine of Kitano Tenman-gu (*see p173*).

DIRECTORY

Specialty Souvenirs

Kyoto is one of the best places in Japan to buy crafts and souvenirs, many of them local specialties. Some outlets are actually outside the central shopping district. Among the best places to look are the roads leading up to major temples such as Kiyomizu-dera.

Craft shop on the canalside Philosopher's Walk

GENERAL CRAFTS

The Gion, or eastern, end of Shijo has a number of interesting craft shops, including the **Kyoto Craft Center**, which carries many contemporary craft items. The **Kyoto Handicraft Center**, north of Heian Shrine, gives regular handicraft demonstrations.

CERAMICS AND TABLEWARE

Kiyomizu-yaki is the city's refined porcelain ware. A fine selection of this and other porcelains can be found at **Tachikichi**. **Asahi-do** offers a comprehensive range, as does **Tojiki Kaikan**. **Asobe**, opposite Daimaru department store, is well known for lacquerware. **Ichihara**, south of Shijo, offers a good selection of chopsticks and bamboo utensils.

TEA

Tea in Kyoto means Uji-cha, for neighboring Uji is, with Shizuoka, one of Japan's most famous tea-producing regions. There are many fine tea shops in town, but **Ippodo Chaho** is the granddaddy of them all.

DOLLS

Kyoto dolls have been famous throughout Japan for centuries. **Oshido**, on the front approach to Kiyomizu Temple, has a fine selection of dolls, and all kinds of accessories such as *netsuke* and *kanzashi* (hair ornaments). They also stock a wide range of wooden sandals, Japanese swords, and textile goods. **Gallery K1** has an impressive collection of lifelike *Ichimatsu-ningyo*, which were once considered standard trousseau items. **Tanaka-ya** is known both for its dolls and its Noh masks.

INCENSE

Incense has been a Kyoto specialty since Heian times. **Kungyoku-do**, a shop with a 400-year-old history, has an aromatic selection in stick, chip, and pellet form. **Toyoda Aisan-do**, in the Gion, has a wide selection of incense and incense burners. **Lisn** is an intriguing boutique with some novel forms of incense.

PICKLES AND SWEETS

Kyoto's many vegetables are delicious; pickled (*tsukemono*), they become sublime. In addition to Nishiki Market (*see p174*), two stores are notable. **Narita**, east of Kamigamo Shrine, has preservative-free delicacies, including its famous *suguki-zuke* (turnip pickle). **Murakami-ju**, in the city center, has more than 20 types of pickles. Works of art, *wagashi* (sweets) come in a variety of styles. The exquisite *namagashi* are meant to be eaten the same day they are made, preferably accompanied by *matcha* (powdered tea). Those at **Tsukimochi-ya Naomasa** are traditional favorites.

FOOTWARE

On Nawate, **Minochu** has a stunning collection of traditional Japanese footwear, some in larger than standard sizes. The tall *koppori-geta* worn by Kyoto's apprentice geisha can be bought here.

BAMBOO PRODUCTS

An abundance of bamboo in neighboring Shiga prefecture and the development of the utensils used in the tea ceremony have helped make Kyoto a prime center for the production of this flexible natural material. **Kagoshin**, east of the Sanjo Bridge, makes wonderful bamboo craft items, including baskets for *ikebana* arrangements. **Tsujikura**, on Kawaramachi, north of Shijo, stocks a good selection of

One of Kyoto's famous dolls

handsome and sturdy bamboo umbrellas, as well as various types of paper lanterns.

Umbrella with a bamboo frame, a popular shade at restaurants

WASHI

Paper has been made in Japan since the 7th century. *Washi* (handmade paper) is made of tree and other plant fibers. Exquisite *washi* from all over Japan is available at **Morita Washi Wagami-no-mise**, on Higashi-no-Toin, a couple of blocks south of Shijo. **Kakimoto** also stocks an outstanding variety. **Kyukyo-do**, a shop famous for calligraphy supplies, paper, and incense, is located between Sanjo and Oike.

OTHER CRAFTS

Across from Takashimaya department store is **Terauchi**, a jewelry shop that carries a fine selection of pearls. At the corner of Rokkaku and Tomi-no-Koji is **Miyawaki Baisen-an**, an old shop that is famous for its elegant fans. **Kazurasei**, in the Gion, specializes in hair ornaments and makeup for apprentice geisha. For Japanese woodblock prints, probably the best gallery is **Nishiharu** in Teramachi.

Craftswoman making *washi*, Japanese handmade paper

DIRECTORY

GENERAL CRAFTS

Kyoto Craft Center
Gion, N side of Shijo.
Tel (075) 561-9660.
🌑 Wed.

Kyoto Handicraft Center
Kumanojinja higashi, Marutamachi-dori.
Tel (075) 761-5080.

CERAMICS AND TABLEWARE

Asahi-do
Kiyomizu, Higashiyama-ku.
Tel (075) 531-2181.

Asobe
Opposite Daimaru, Shimogyo-ku.
Tel (075) 211-0803.
🌑 Wed.

Ichihara
E side of Sakaimachi, S of Shijo, Shimogyo-ku.
Tel (075) 341-3831
🌑 phone to check.

Tachikichi
Corner of Shijo and Tomino-koji.
Tel (075) 211-3141.
🌑 Wed.

Tojiki Kaikan
Gojo-zaka, 100 m E of Higashi-oji intersection, Higashiyama-ku.
Tel (075) 541-1102.

TEA

Ippodo Chaho
E side of Teramachi, N of Nijo, Nakagyo-ku.
Tel (075) 211-3421.

DOLLS

Gallery K1
Muromachi-dori, S of Kita-oji.
Tel (075) 415-1477.
🌑 Thu.

Oshido
1-276 Kiyomizu, Higashima-ku.
Tel (075) 561-3361.

Tanaka-ya
N side of Shijo, E of Yanagi-no-Banba, Shimogyo-ku.
Tel (075) 221-1959.
🌑 Wed.

INCENSE

Kungyoku-do
E side of Horikawa, across from Nishi Hongan-ji, Shimogyo-ku.
Tel (075) 371-0162.
🌑 1st and 3rd Sun.

Lisn
2F Spiral Space 103 Bldg, Shimogamo-naka, N of Kitayama, Kita-ku.
Tel (075) 721-6006.
🌑 Wed.

Toyoda Aisan-do
Gion, N side of Shijo-dori.
Tel (075) 551-2221.
🌑 Wed.

PICKLES AND SWEETS

Murakami-ju
Nishi-Kiyamachi, S of Shijo, behind Hankyu dept store, Shimogyo-ku.
Tel 075-351-1737.

Narita
35 Yamamoto-cho, Kamigamo, Kita-ku (E of Kamigamo Shrine).
Tel (075) 721-1567.

Tsukimochi-ya Naomasa
E side Kiyamachi, N of Sanjo, Kiyamachi Sanjo-agaru, Nakagyo-ku.
Tel (075) 231-0175.
🌑 Thu.

FOOTWARE

Minochu
Yamato-oji (Nawate) at Shinmonzen, Higashiyama-ku.
Tel (075) 561-5189.
🌑 Wed.

BAMBOO PRODUCTS

Kagoshin
N side Sanjo, E of Sanjo Bridge, Higashiyama-ku.
Tel (075) 771-0209.
🌑 Mon.

Tsujikura
E side of Kawaramachi, N of Shijo, Nakagyo-ku.
Tel (075) 221-4396.
🌑 Wed.

WASHI

Kakimoto
E side of Teramachi, N of Nijo, Nakagyo-ku.
Tel (075) 211-3481.
🌑 Sun.

Kyukyo-do
W side of Teramachi, at Anekoji, Nakagyo-ku.
Tel (075) 231-0510.
🌑 Sun.

Morita Washi Wagami-no-mise
E side of Higashi-no-Toin, N of Bukkoji, Shimogyo-ku.
Tel (075) 341-0123
🌑 Sun & public hols.

OTHER CRAFTS

Kazurasei
Gion, N side of Shijo, nr Gion bus stop.
Tel (075) 561-0672.
🌑 Wed.

Miyawaki Baisen-an
N side Rokkaku, W of Tomi-no-Koji, Nakagyo-ku. *Tel (075) 221-0181.*

Nishiharu
Corner of Sanjo and Teramachi, Nakagyo-ku.
Tel (075) 211-2849.
🌑 2–7 daily.

Terauchi
Next to Takashimaya dept store, Kawaramachi, Shimogyo-ku.
Tel (075) 211-3511.
🌑 Wed.

ENTERTAINMENT IN KYOTO

Kyoto's entertainment scene is small but varied, catering to tastes both ancient and contemporary. In addition to performances of Kabuki and *buyo* (classical Japanese dance), the city offers bars and clubs where you can hear guest musicians playing anything from blues guitar to Latin rhythms. Thanks to its more than 1,200 years of history, a traditional

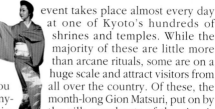

Geisha dancer

event takes place almost every day at one of Kyoto's hundreds of shrines and temples. While the majority of these are little more than arcane rituals, some are on a huge scale and attract visitors from all over the country. Of these, the month-long Gion Matsuri, put on by the silk merchants of the city, is probably the best-known festival. It culminates on July 14–17.

BUYING TICKETS

For help in obtaining tickets to events, check with the **Tourist Information Office** inside Kyoto Station. Tickets for most major events can be purchased at the **Ticket PIA** counter – also at Kyoto Station and at two other locations, in Takoyakushi and Kawaramachi-Oike. Some tickets can also be purchased at branches of the convenience stores **Lawson**, **Family Mart**, and **Seven Eleven**.

INFORMATION SOURCES

For an overview of what is happening, consult the *Kyoto Visitor's Guide*, a free monthly publication available at tourist information centers and major hotels, and on the internet. *Kansai Time Out*, a guide to events in the Kansai region (Kobe, Osaka, and Kyoto), is on sale at bookstores. The **Kyoto Prefecture** website has details of current events, and the website of **JNTO** (Japan National Tourist Organization, p371) has a section on Kyoto. The *Japan*

Times, and other newspapers in English also carry weekly listings of Kansai events.

FESTIVALS

Of Kyoto's many festivals, the big three are the Aoi Matsuri (Hollyhock Festival, May 15); Gion Matsuri (all of July, especially 14–17); and Jidai Matsuri (Festival of the Ages, October 22). The Aoi and Gion festivals both started as purification rites in the Heian period. The former involves a parade of costumed nobles, courtiers, horses, and ox-carts between the two Kamo shrines *(see p172)*. The latter centers around elaborately decorated floats belonging to various neighborhoods, which are pulled through the streets on the morning of July 17, then disassembled. The Jidai Matsuri was begun in 1895 to boost morale after the emperor abandoned Kyoto for Tokyo. Characters in costumes from every epoch of Kyoto's imperial past parade from the Imperial Palace to Heian Shrine.

An old teahouse in Gion, a long-established entertainment district

TRADITIONAL ARTS

For the tourist wanting a quick look at traditional arts, **Gion Corner** has a program from March to November that includes snippets of *kyomai* (classical Kyoto dance), *koto* music, Kyogen comic drama, and even *ikebana* (flower arranging). Performances take place at 7:40 and 8:40pm.

The geisha of Gion put on *Miyako Odori*, their gala dance spectacle, during April at the **Gion Kobu Kaburenjo** theater, while at Kamishichi-ken, the geisha district near Kitano Shrine, public dances, *Kitano Odori*, are staged from April 15 to 25 at the **Kamishichi-ken Kaburenjo**. Ponto-cho's géisha perform their *Kamogawa Odori* in May at the **Pontocho Kaburenjo**. Tickets for all can be bought at the theaters or at Takashimaya and Daimaru Playguide counters.

The **Minami-za** is the venue for *Kaomise Kabuki*, Kyoto's December Kabuki extravaganza. Performances of Noh and Kyogen are held at **Kyoto Kanze Kaikan** and **Kongo Nogakudo** on certain Sundays of every month. Check the *Visitor's Guide* for details.

Apprentice geisha performing at the Gion Kobu Kaburenjo theater

For hotels and restaurants in this region see pp303–4 and pp336–8

Anyone interested in experiencing the tea ceremony can do so at **Tondaya**. Located in Kyoto's famous Nishijin textile area, this architecturally exquisite town house is elegantly decorated with classical treasures.

NIGHTLIFE

Kyoto may not have as lively a nightlife as Osaka and Tokyo, but it still has plenty of bars, clubs, and live music spots, especially in the entertainment districts of Ponto-cho and Gion.

Takutaku, one of the most popular venues for rock and folk music, is in a former sake brewery near Shijo-Kawaramachi. Live music takes place most nights. Near Kyoto University, **Ringo** is a music café devoted to The Beatles. **Cafe David**, a sumptuous art-filled coffee house on the south side of Sanjo, between Takakura and Higashi-no-Toin, also has live music.

Pontocho district restaurants, with *yuka* platforms erected in summer

Kyoryukan, located a little north of the east gate of Shokoku-ji Temple, behind Doshisha University, hosts a varied schedule of performances, many of *butoh* and other dance forms. The **Pig & Whistle**, a British-style pub popular with the foreign community, offers reasonably priced food and drink in a comfortable atmosphere. Occasionally bands perform. **Café Indépendants**, in the basement of the old Mainichi Newspaper Building at the corner of Sanjo Street and Gokomachi Street, is a relaxed eating and drinking spot that also occasionally features live music. **Metro** hosts monthly events, including a drag show ("Diamond Night"), and a Latin music night.

Another watering hole popular with the city's foreign residents is **Bar Isn't It**, the Kyoto branch of an Osaka establishment. It plays varied music, with DJs and a disco, on Fridays, Staurdays, and the day before public holidays.

DIRECTORY

TICKETS AND INFORMATION

Kyoto Prefecture
www.pref.kyoto.jp/en/index.html

Kyoto Visitor's Guide
www.kyotoguide.com

Ticket PIA
Reservations:
Tel (0570) 02-9999.

1F Vivre 21 Fashion
Takoyakushi. ☐ 11am–8pm (10am–8pm Sat, Sun & public hols).

Zest Oike
Kawaramachi-Oike.
Tel (0570) 02-9111.

Kyoto Theater
Kyoto Station Bldg.
Tel (075) 341-2360.

Tourist Information Office
9th Fl Kyoto Station Bldg.
Tel (075) 344-3300.

JNTO
www.jnto.go.jp

TRADITIONAL ARTS

Gion Corner
Next to Gion Kobu Kaburenjo, E of Hanamikoji and S of Shijo, Higashiyama-ku.
Tel (075) 561-1119.
◉ Aug 16, Nov 30–Feb 28.

Gion Kobu Kaburenjo
Next to Gion Corner, Higashiyama-ku.
Tel (075) 561-1115.

Kamishichi-ken Kaburenjo
Kamishichi-ken, E of Kitano Tenman-gu Shrine, Kamigyo-ku.
Tel (075) 461-0148.

Kyoto Kanze Kaikan
Nio-mon, W of Jingu-michi, Higashiyama-ku.
Tel (075) 771-6114.

Kongo Nogakudo
S of Ichijo, Karasuma-dori, Kamigyo-ku.
Tel (075) 441-7222.

Minami-za Theater
Corner of Kawabata and Shijo, Higashiyama-ku.
Reservations:
Tel (0570) 000-489.
General inquiries:
Tel (075) 561-1155.

Pontocho Kaburenjo
On E side of Pontocho, S of Sanjo, Nakagyo-ku.
Tel (075) 221-2025.

Tondaya
W side of Omiya, N of Ichijo.
☐ 10am–4pm. ◉ Mon.
Tel (075) 432-6701.

NIGHTLIFE

Bar Isn't It
B1 Forum Nishi Kiyamachi (2nd street S of Sanjo).
Tel (075) 221-5399.

Cafe David
Sanjo, W of Takakura, Nakagyo-ku.
Tel (075) 212-8580.
◉ Wed.

Café Indépendants
1928 Bldg B1,
corner of Sanjo and Gokomachi, Nakagyo-ku.
Tel (075) 255-4312.

Kyoryukan
N of Shokoku-ji Temple's E gate,
Kamigyo-ku.
Tel (075) 213-0288.

Metro
Corner of Kawabata and Marutamachi (Keihan Marutamachi stn exit 2).
Tel (075) 752-4765.

Pig & Whistle
2F Shobi Bldg,
N side of Sanjo,
E of Sanjo Bridge.
Tel (075) 761-6022.

Ringo
23 Tanaka Monzen-cho, nr Kyoto University.
Tel (075) 721-3195.

Takutaku
Tomikoji, Shijo-Kawaramchi.
Tel (075) 351-1321.

WESTERN HONSHU

The cultural heartland of the country, Western Honshu is where Japan's first imperial courts held sway, in an area called Yamato. A rich fusion of literature, imagination, and religious mysticism permeates many tourist attractions, while Osaka and other teeming cities are vibrant places constantly reinventing themselves. Little wonder that this part of Japan sits high on the list of travelers.

The name Yamato refers to the Japanese mountains, where heaven and earth divide, and also to the land founded by the mythical son of the gods, emperor Jimmu. In the Japanese mind, Yamato is a holy place, a homeland "whose trees and rocks, streams and mountains," as legendary emperor Keiko expressed it in verse form almost two millennia ago, "house the gods."

Shinto priests, Miyajima Island

Legend solidified into fact in the 4th century AD when a clan called Yamato expanded its kingdom in the region. Japan's first emperors, the Yamato rulers set up court on the Yamato Plain, the site of present-day Nara prefecture.

Nature, religion, and architecture converge in the city of Nara, its antiquity evident in its aging wooden temples. Here, the rich pantheons of India and China, reinterpreted, are set against a city characterized by quiet stroll gardens, the smell of lingering incense, and the reflections of winged pagodas in green ponds.

Hiroshima, now a surprisingly pleasant city, the international port of Kobe, and Osaka are Western Honshu's great metropolitan centers. Osaka, an industrial dynamo best known for its business deals and copious appetite for good food, is being transformed by its restless inhabitants into a forum for the arts.

Elsewhere, a strong sense of regional character is apparent at such destinations as the exquisite ceramic town of Hagi, the sacred island of Miyajima, the willow-lined canals and storehouses of Kurashiki, and Ise Grand Shrine, whose inner precincts are solemnly dedicated to the Sun Goddess.

Meoto Iwa ("wedded rocks"), representing the gods Izanami and Izanagi, Ise Peninsula

◁ **Statue of Kokuzo Bosatsu, an Enlightened Being, at the temple of Todai-ji, Nara**

Exploring Western Honshu

Western Honshu includes the region called Kansai
(or sometimes Kinki), centered on the major
city of Osaka. Kyoto is also part of Kansai but has a
separate chapter in this book *(see pp154–85)*.
The area west of Osaka is called Chugoku, "Middle
Country," and, despite being the historic heartland of
Japan, it is now less densely
populated than Kansai and
Tokyo to the east. A spine of
mountains runs through the
middle of Western Honshu,
and the two coasts are quite
different in character, with
the San-in coast rugged and
more remote.

Hikone Castle garden, Lake Biwa

Kobe tower

SEE ALSO

• *Where to Stay* pp304–8

• *Where to Eat* pp338–41

MATSUE

IZUMO

SAN-IN COAST

CHUGOKU

HAMADA   *Hamada Expressway*

FUKIYA

MASUDA

Chugoku Expressway

TSUWANO

Sanyo Expressway

FUKU

HIROSHIMA

Sanyo Shinka

HAGI

Yamaguchi Line

MIYAJIMA ISLAND

AKIYOSHI-DAI
TABLELANDS

YAMAGUCHI

IWAKUNI

OGORI

SANYO COAST

INLAND
SEA

Kyushu

SIGHTS AT A GLANCE

| 0 kilometers | 50 |
| 0 miles | 30 |

KEY

✈ Airport

▬ Expressway

▬ Major road

✕✕ Bullet train line

— JR train line

— Private train line

☀ Viewpoint

Itsukushima shrine, Miyajima Island

LOCATOR MAP

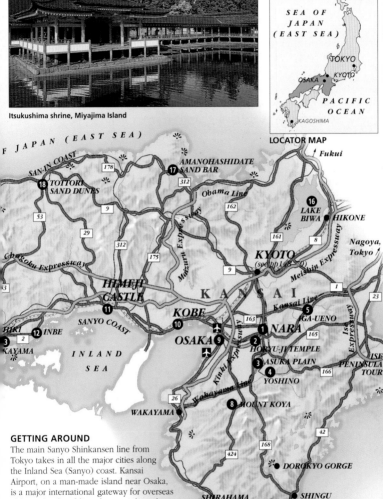

GETTING AROUND

The main Sanyo Shinkansen line from Tokyo takes in all the major cities along the Inland Sea (Sanyo) coast. Kansai Airport, on a man-made island near Osaka, is a major international gateway for overseas visitors. A railroad line also runs along the Sea of Japan (San-in) coast, but this is much slower than the Sanyo Shinkansen route.

Sanyo coast near Okayama

Nara ❶

奈良

Founded in 710 on the Yamato Plain, Nara, then known as Heijo-kyo (citadel of peace), became one of Asia's most splendid cities in its 74-year spell as Japan's first capital. Avidly absorbing ideas from mainland Asia, the city became the grand diocese of Buddhism and the far eastern destination of the Silk Road. Miraculously, many buildings have survived. With its wooded hills, temple parks, and some of the world's oldest wooden buildings, this ancient city remains a symbol of tranquillity.

The tree ensconced temple of Todai-ji, as seen from hills to the east

Deer – "messengers of the gods" – in Nara Park

Japan's foremost collections of Buddhist art, including an exquisite 8th-century statue of Ashura.

🏛 Nara National Museum
Tel (0742) 22-7771. ⬤ 9:30am–5pm Tue–Sun. ⬛
This important two-part museum consists of the original Beaux-arts building created in the 1870s,

Exploring Nara

Nara's rectangular design, a checkerboard of streets based on the ancient Chinese city of Ch'ang-an, is straightforward and clearly divided into zones. The downtown area around the two stations, JR Nara and Kintetsu Nara, is within walking distance of **Nara Park**, a 1,300-acre area where most of the temples are located. Over 1,000 tame deer *(shika)*, regarded as messengers of the gods, roam the park. South of the center is **Naramachi**, the old city. Other notable areas like **Nishino-kyo** and **Horyu-ji** *(see p196)* are to the west and southwest of Nara.

🏛 Kofuku-ji Temple
Tel (0742) 22-5370. ⬤ 9am–5pm daily. ⬛ for Treasure House and Eastern Golden Hall.
Kofuku-ji, approached up a wide staircase from Sarusawa Pond, was founded in 669. Of the 175 buildings in the original complex only a precious

few remain. In Nara, however, even reconstructions can lay claim to antiquity. The current five-story pagoda, burned to the ground no less than five times, dates from 1426. The temple's Eastern Golden Hall, containing several priceless statues, is of similar vintage. In the Treasure House is one of

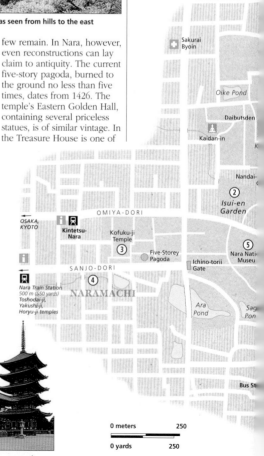

Sakurai Byoin

Oike Pond

Daibutsden

Kaidan-in

Nandai-

② Isui-en Garden

⑤ Nara Nati Museu

OSAKA, KYOTO

Kintetsu-Nara

Kofuku-ji Temple ③

OMIYA-DORI

Five-Storey Pagoda

Ichino-torii Gate

SANJO-DORI

Nara Train Station 500 m ($50 yards) Toshodai-ji, Yakushi-ji, Horyu-ji temples

④ NARAMACHI

Ara Pond

Sag Pon

Bus St

| 0 meters | | 250 |
| 0 yards | | 250 |

The temple of Kofuku-ji, with its five-story pagoda

now housing the permanent collection, and a modern annex serving as a site for special exhibitions. Most of the exhibits, including Buddhist sculptures, paintings, objects found in sutra mounds, and calligraphy, date from the Nara and Heian periods. The museum holds an annual exhibition in October and early November of rarely seen treasures from the Shoso-in, a storehouse in the Todai-ji complex that was built to preserve Emperor Shomu's private collection. The Shoso-in itself houses over 9,000 precious objects, some of which are of Central Asian and Persian extraction, evidence of Nara's interaction with these regions through its position at the end of the Silk Road.

Some of the 3,000 lanterns at Kasuga Shrine

🌿 Isui-en Garden
Tel (0742) 25-0781. 🕐 9:30am–4:30pm Wed–Mon. 🈂️
The powerful shapes of Mount Wakakusa and Kasuga, and the megalithic roof of Todai-ji form a backdrop to this essentially Meiji-era garden, which is popular in spring for its plum, cherry, and azalea blooms, and in autumn for red maples. Stone lanterns, a meandering stream, and teahouses with thatched and cryptomeria-bark roofs complete the picture. In the teahouses, visitors can eat *mugitoro*, a potato, wheat, and rice mixture esteemed by health-food advocates.

🛕 Todai-ji Temple
See pp186–7.

⛩️ Kasuga Grand Shrine
Tel (0742) 22-7788.
🕐 9am–4pm daily. 🈂️ for museum.
Originally built as the tutelary shrine of the Fujiwaras, one of the families who helped to establish Nara, Kasuga is one of the best known and most photographed Shinto sites. The original building was completed in 710 but, according to the strictures of purity and renewal governing Shinto beliefs, the structure, like the Great Shrine at Ise (see p198), was demolished and rebuilt in identical fashion every 20 years. This was repeated around 50 times over the centuries, but the

SIGHTS AT A GLANCE

VISITORS' CHECKLIST
Nara prefecture. 🏯 364,000.
🚉 JR line from Kyoto, Kintetsu line from Kyoto. ℹ️ at Kintetsu Nara stn (0742) 24-4858.
www.pref.nara.jp/nara_e/
🎎 Omizu-tori (Mar 1–14).

current structure has been preserved since 1863.

Surrounded by a wood, the approach road and walkways around this vermilion-colored shrine boast an astonishing 3,000 or so stone and bronze lanterns. Donated by ordinary people as tokens of faith and thankfulness, the lanterns are an impressive spectacle when they are lit for several days during festivals in early February and mid-August.

🛕 Shin-Yakushi-ji Temple
Tel (0742) 22-3736. 🕐 9am–5pm daily.
This temple was built by Empress Komyo (701–60) as an offering to the gods whose intercession she sought in the recovery of her husband from an eye disease. Some structures were rebuilt in the 13th century, but the main hall, with 12 striking clay figures of Yakushi (Amida's incarnation as the Healing Buddha), is original.

House in the residential and crafts quarter of Naramachi

🏠 Naramachi District
The old quarter of **Naramachi** includes traditional *machiya* (merchant homes), mostly from the mid-18th–19th centuries, converted into galleries and craft shops. The buildings are distinguished by narrow frontages and surprising depth, a design that developed due to taxes that were assessed by the width of a building's frontage. The tourist office has free maps of the area.

Nigatsu-do

Sangatsu-do

Nara Park

Kasuga Grand Shrine ⑦

Deer Enclosure

Shin-Yakushi-ji Temple ⑥

Exploring Nara: Todai-ji Temple

The Todai-ji complex consists of a vast Buddha hall (Daibutsuden), subtemples, halls, pagodas, and gates of exceptional historical and architectural interest. The construction of Todai-ji, completed in 752, was ordered by Emperor Shomyo, ostensibly to house Nara's Great Buddha image but also to consolidate the position of the city as the capital and a powerful center of Buddhism. Natural

Stone lantern at Todai-ji Temple

disasters have not diminished the scale of the 16-m (53-ft) high statue. From time to time, when the figure is given a dusting, visitors may be startled to see four or five monks standing in the Buddha's upturned palm.

The 19-m (62-ft) high Nandaimon (great southern gate) of Todai-ji

Koumokuten, a heavenly guardian, dates from the mid-Edo period.

Kokuzo Bosatsu
This bosatsu, *or* bodhisattva – *meaning an Enlightened Being – was completed in 1709.*

Entrance

★ Great Buddha Vairocana
The casting of this vast statue in 752 deployed hundreds of tons of molten bronze, mercury, and vegetable wax. Fires and earthquakes dislodged the head several times; the current head dates from 1692.

GREAT BUDDHA HALL
The main hall of Todai-ji was rebuilt several times. The current structure, completed in 1709, is only two-thirds of the original size but is still the largest wooden building in the world. The seated figure inside is the world's largest bronze image of the Buddha.

VISITORS' CHECKLIST

Nara Park. **Tel** (0742) 22-5511. Daibutsuden Kasuga-Taisha-mae stop. Apr–Sept: 7:30am–5:30pm daily; Oct: 7:30am–5pm daily; Nov–Feb: 8am–4:30pm daily; Mar: 8am–5pm daily.

★ **Wooden Hall**
The unusual bracketing and beam-frame construction of this vast wooden hall, built in 1688–1709, were possibly the work of craftsmen from southern China.

Roofline
The striking roofline, with its golden "horns" and curved lintel, was an 18th-century embellishment.

Tamonten, another heavenly guardian, dates from the same period as Koumokuten on the other side of the hall.

Niyorin Kannon Bosatsu, like the Kokuzo Bosatsu to the left of the Great Buddha, is an Enlightened Being and dates from 1709.

Covered walkway in compound

Behind the Buddha is a small hole bored into a large wooden pillar. A popular belief holds that if you can squeeze through the hole you will attain Nirvana.

STAR FEATURES

★ Great Buddha Vairocana

★ Wooden Hall

The beguiling "three-story" pagoda at Yakushi-ji

Beyond Nara Park: Nishinokyo District

Time permitting, two more temples in the Nara vicinity should not be missed.

Founded in 759 by the blind Chinese sage and priest Ganjin, **Toshodai-ji's** original main hall and lecture hall, designated National Treasures, are still standing. Be sure to visit the temple's stunning 5.5-m (18-ft) high Senju Kannon statue.

A little south of Toshodai-ji, more Buddhist statuary can be found at **Yakushi-ji**. Emperor Tenmu had the temple built in the hope of effecting a recovery for his wife, a gesture that seems to have worked as she outlived him by several years. Dedicated to the Buddha of healing, the temple's masterpiece is its famous three-story east pagoda, the only original structure remaining.

The pagoda, built in 730, appears to have six levels, but three are intermediary roofs placed between the main floors, creating an appealing optical effect. The 19th-century American scholar Ernest Fenollosa, on a visit to Yakushi-ji, compared the striking geometry of the pagoda to "frozen music."

Toshodai-ji, where its founder, Ganjin, is entombed

Horyu-ji Temple ❷

法隆寺

Regarded as the cradle of Japanese Buddhism, the Horyu-ji complex is also thought to contain some of the world's oldest surviving wooden structures, dating from the early 7th century. The temple was erected by Prince Shotoku (573–621) in his effort to entrench Buddhism alongside Shinto as a pillar of the Japanese belief system. Some exceptional works of art, including ancient images of the Buddha, are housed here.

VISITORS' CHECKLIST

10 km (6 miles) SW of Nara.
🚃 JR Kansai Honsen line from Nara, then 15-min walk. 🚌 from Kintetsu Nara stn to Horyu-ji-mae stop. ◯ daily: Nov–Feb 8am–4:30pm; Feb–Nov 8am–5pm. 📷

The nine rings *(kurin)* of the finial are made of bronze.

Gate at the Horyu-ji compound

Four scythes, a feature unique to Horyu-ji's pagoda, are said to stop it from being destroyed by lightning.

Yakushi Nyorai images *dating from the 10th century are among the treasures of Horyu-ji.*

Wind chime

FIVE-STORY PAGODA

The pagoda is one of Horyu-ji's oldest buildings and the oldest one of its kind in Japan. The pagoda style was brought from China, which in turn had been developed from the Buddhist stupa in ancient India. The symbolism of such buildings is subject to debate. Some say that a five-story pagoda represents the elements, as shown; others disagree.

Level 5: Sky

Level 4: Air/Wind

Ornamental roof crays are made of bronze.

Level 3: Wood

The central column is fashioned from a single cypress tree. The bowed shape of pillars at Horyu-ji are reminiscent of classical Greek style, a legacy of the Silk Route.

Level 2: Water

Level 1: Earth

Four sculpted scenes *from the life of the Buddha face north, south, east, and west. Here, on the north side, the Buddha passes into Nirvana.*

A fragment of the Buddha's bone is enshrined at the base of the central pillar.

Asuka Plain ❸

飛鳥地方

Nara prefecture. 🚉 *Asuka.*
ℹ️ *(0744) 54-3624.*

The Asuka Plain is scattered with excavation sites from the proto-capital Asukakyo, which flourished in the 5th to 7th centuries. The best way to explore the burial tombs, temples, and early Buddhist statuary is by bicycle.

One of the best-known sites, **Takamatsuzuka Kofun**, is similar in design to Korean tombs of the same period and contains vivid murals of stars and mythological animals. Notable images elsewhere include **Sakabune Ishi**, a concentric stone that may have been used to make sake, **Kame and Saru Ishi**, turtle and monkey-shaped statues, and **Nimen Seki**, a stone with faces carved on each side.

Asuka-dera dates from the late 6th century. It was the country's first Buddhist temple but was overshadowed in fame by Prince Shotoku's Horyu-ji.

Takamatsuzuka Kofun, a tomb site on the Asuka Plain

Yoshino ❹

吉野

Nara prefecture. 🚉 ℹ️ *(07463) 2-3081.* 🎎 *Setsubune (Feb 3); Sakura Festival (Apr 11–12).*

The attractive, elevated village of Yoshino, its multistoried houses built on graduated levels on the side of a remote mountain, is one of Japan's most popular cherry blossom viewing spots. Mount Yoshino boasts

Cherry trees blossoming at altitude in Yoshino

100,000 trees planted in four groves at different altitudes. Each level blooms in succession, extending the viewing period to almost three weeks.

Environs:
Uphill from the main road, **Chikurin-in** is a temple renowned for its stroll garden designed by the tea master Sen no Rikyu *(see p169)*. The two temples at the summit of **Sanjo-san**, regarded by pilgrims as the most sacred mountain here, afford superb views of the area. Another pilgrimage site, to the peak of **Omine-san**, is off-limits to women climbers. **Yoshino Mikumari Shrine**, an hour's trek from the village, is a popular spot for couples who come to pray for fertility. Children's clothes and small cotton circles representing women's breasts are hung in the shrine precincts as offerings.

Iga-Ueno ❺

伊賀上野

Mie prefecture. 🚉 🎎 *Ueno Tenjin Matsuri (October 23–25).* ℹ️ *at stn (0595) 24-0270.*

A provincial castle town, Iga-Ueno was home to the ninja, the most inventive and feared spies of Japan's feudal era, and the birthplace of Japan's most revered haiku poet, Matsuo Basho *(see p279)*. Several sites in town, including Basho's house, a museum, and the odd **Haeseiden**, an octagonal building said to replicate Basho's standing figure, are dedicated to the poet.

The main attraction for most people, though, is the extraordinary **Iga Ninja Museum**, a clan farmhouse that served as the secret headquarters of the Iga sect of professional spies and assassins. The well-restored building retains hidden panels, spy holes, secret escape routes and trapdoors intended to repel night attacks from enemy warlords and rival ninja groups. Ninja methods are enthusiastically demonstrated by local guides dressed in pink day-glo ninja outfits.

🏯 **Iga Ninja Museum**
Tel (0595) 23-0311. ⏰ *daily.* 📷

THE NINJA

Ninjutsu, the "art of stealth," was developed during the bloody clan warfare of Japan's feudal era. The ninja elevated their profession of spying and assassination into a sophisticated discipline by practicing mountain asceticism and studying such subjects as astronomy, herbalism, medicine, and nutrition. They developed ingenious devices to outwit enemies, including lock picks, collapsible floats for crossing water, clothing designed to conceal swords and knives, and over 30 different kinds of *shuriken*, which are deadly throwing stars made of metal.

Ninja sword exhibit at Iga Ninja Museum

Local guide demonstrating ninja methods

Ise Peninsula Tour ⑥

伊勢志摩国立公園

The city of Ise, its Grand Shrine – the most sacred in Japan – and the Ise-Shima National Park are the main tourist attractions of this peninsula. Its jagged, indented coast, the center of cultured oyster pearl production in Japan, is in striking contrast to the undulating evergreen-clad hills inland, which are the habitat of monkeys, wild boars, and flying squirrels.

Mikimoto Pearl Island ③
Just offshore from the tourist town of Toba, this island has a memorial hall to Mikimoto Kokichi who created the original cultured pearl in 1893. Women divers can be seen collecting seaweed and sea urchins.

Futamigaura Beach ②
Two rocks called the Meoto Iwa (wedded rocks), representing the parent gods of Japan, Izanami and Izanagi, are connected by a sacred rope *(see p187).*

Ise Shrines ①
Reconstructed every 20 years in accordance with Shinto principles of purity and renewal, Ise's shrines are in two main groups: the Ge-ku (outer shrine) and Nai-ku (inner shrine, *see pp26–7.*)

Ise-Shima Skyline ⑥
A good route back on a clear day, this road goes over the summit of Mount Asama, with views of the peninsula and, occasionally, even to Mount Fuji in Central Honshu.

Goza Beach ⑤
The most popular stretch of sand on the peninsula, Goza Beach can be reached by road or by boat from Kashikojima.

KEY

▬	Tour route
▬	Expressway
⋯	Other road
⚡	Viewpoint

ISE BAY
Toshi Island
Toba
Suga Island
TOBA BAY
HISAI
42
2
3
1
6
167
Pearl Road
Isobe
KUMANO
MATOYA BAY
Ago
60
260
AGO BAY
5
Shima

0 kilometers 5
0 miles 3

TIPS FOR TRAVELERS

Tour length: *110 km (70 miles).*
Alternative transportation:
The area has excellent bus and train services. Trains run to Ise, Futamigaura, Toba, and Kashikojima, while buses run to many destinations from Toba, and between the Ise shrines.

Kashikojima ④
This is one of the peninsula's best resort areas, with fine views of Ago Bay. You can take a boat trip past scenic islets, fishing boats, and hundreds of oyster rafts.

Kii Peninsula ❼

紀伊半島

Wakayama, Mie, and Nara prefectures. ✈ *Shirahama.* 🚃 *JR Kinokuni line.* 🛈 *Shingu City Tourist Office (0735) 22-2840.* 🎎 *Nachi no Hi-Matsuri (Jul 14).*

The Kii Peninsula, with densely forested mountains at its center and craggy headlands, pine-covered islands, and coves along its shoreline, has largely avoided the industrial development that scars much of Japan's Pacific coastline.

A good starting point is the small port town of **Shingu**, on the east coast. From here you can take a bus to Shiko, then a 50-minute boat trip takes you along the Kumano River to **Dorokyo**, one of Japan's most spectacular gorges. From May to June rhododendrons and azaleas bloom on the river's banks.

A 20-minute bus ride inland from Shingu lies **Nachi-no-taki**, Japan's highest waterfall. A stone path ascending parallel to the falls leads to **Nachi Taisha** shrine, its origins reaching back over 1,400 years. The next port south of Shingu is **Katsuura**, a pleasant pine-studded bay with several picturesque islets. Visitors interested in the Japanese perspective on whaling should go to nearby **Taiji**, a whaling community since the 17th century. For insight into a complex subject, visit the **Taiji Whale Museum.**

Farther south, the resort of **Kushimoto** is known for a chain of 30 rocks, **Hashi-gui-iwa**, that seem to march out to sea, connecting the town to

Typically forested hillsides on the Kii Peninsula

the island of Oshima. The peninsula's southernmost point is marked by **Shio-no-misaki**, a headland with a white lighthouse dating from 1873. One of the three best hot springs in Japan, **Shirahama Onsen**, on the west coast, also has one of the area's finest beaches.

🐋 **Taiji Whale Museum**
Tel (0735) 59-2400. ⬜ *daily.* 🈪

Mount Koya ❽

高野山

Wakayama prefecture. 🚡 *4,600.* 🚃 *Nankai line from Osaka, then cable car from Gokurakubashi stn.* 🛈 *nr Senjuinbashi bus stop (0736) 56-2616.* **www.shukubo.jp/eng/index.html** ⬜ *daily.* 🈪 *some buildings.* 🎎 *Aoba Matsuri (Jun 15), Rosoku Matsuri (Candle Festival, Aug 13).*

Set amid clumps of black cedar at an altitude of 900 m (3,000 ft) in the heart of the Kii Peninsula, Mount Koya, or Koya-san, is Japan's most venerated Shingon-Buddhist site. It is host to over one million pilgrims a year. Saint Kukai (774–835), also known by his posthumous name, Kobo Daishi, established a monastic retreat here in 816. There were almost a thousand temples on the mountain by the Edo period, but typhoons and fire have since reduced the number to 123. The mountain's unique atmosphere is best experienced with an overnight stay. Traditional vegetarian cuisine is served in Koya-san's 53 temple lodgings.

The western part of Koya-san contains the grandest and most revered structures.

Kano-school screens inside Kongobu-ji, Mount Koya

Kongobu-ji, built in 1592 by Toyotomi Hideyoshi *(see p56)*, is Koya-san's chief temple. Its rhododendrons and the sliding doors of its inner chambers, painted in the 16th century by artists of the Kano school, are among its special attractions. The magnificent **Danjogaran** complex, a short walk away, includes the oldest building on the mountain, the **Fudo-do** (Fudo Hall), built in 1197, and the **Konpon Dai-to**, an impressive two-story vermilion-and-white pagoda. Rebuilt in 1937, the pagoda is regarded as the symbol of Koya-san.

The aptly named **Reihokan** (Treasure House) stands opposite the complex, a cornucopia of over 5,000 paintings, statues, and mandalas displayed in two separate buildings. The gigantic **Daimon** (great gate), the traditional main entrance to Koya-san, lies a little west of here on the edge of the plateau. It affords a matchless view of mountains, valleys and, on clear days, distant Shikoku and Awaji islands.

In the eastern half of Koya-san is a necropolis of over 200,000 tombs, and the **Okuno-in** (inner sanctum), Kukai's mausoleum. Great status is attached to burial on Koya-san. The stone-paved approach to Okuno-in is flanked with statues, monuments, and tombs housing the remains of Japan's most powerful and illustrious families. In front of Kukai's mausoleum is the **Toro-do** (Lantern Hall). Day and night 11,000 lanterns burn here, including two that are said to have remained lit since the 11th century.

A burial stone at Okuno-in, Mount Koya

Osaka 9

大阪

Theater poster in Osaka

Osaka's prominence as a merchant city dates from Toyotomi Hideyoshi's building of Osaka Castle in 1586. He also encouraged traders from other parts of Japan to settle in the city. In the 1920s and '30s it became an industrial powerhouse. Nowadays, though, the nondescript skyline is being replaced with galleries, international hotels, futuristic living spaces, and exciting postmodernist architecture. The city's extravagant nightlife and culinary predilections are famous. A Japanese saying, "*Kyoto kidaore; Osaka kuidaore,*" suggests that Kyoto-ites are apt to go bankrupt from buying kimonos, Osakans from eating out too much.

Exploring Osaka

Central Osaka is split into two main districts, which meet at Chuo-odori. **Kita-ku**, the northern ward around the main Osaka and Umeda stations, is where many of the city's big hotels, restaurants, and underground shopping precincts are found. It also includes the small island of Nakanoshima, between the Dojima and Tosabori rivers. **Minami**, the southern district, includes the lively downtown area called **Namba**, the core of the old merchant city where you will find Osaka's best eating and drinking options, including **Dotonbori**. This lane, running alongside the canal of the same name and crammed with pink salons, karaoke bars, and pachinko parlors, is also a mecca of cheap restaurants and bars. Namba's many pedestrian shopping zones include **America Mura** and **Europe-dori**, with their imported goods, both north of, and parallel to, Dotonbori, and **Den Den Town**, Osaka's premier electronics district which is south of Sennichimae-dori. **Chuo-ku**, the old central ward and historic center of the city is to the east; this is where Osaka Castle stands. **Osaka Port** is west of the city center.

Plenty of information and signs in English make Osaka a relatively easy place to negotiate in comparison with other major

Young Osakans at leisure in the Dotonbori canal district

Japanese cities. The city center is served by a user-friendly loop system called the JR Kanjo Line. Its color-coded subway system is also easy to ride. Visitors who intend to cover a lot of sightseeing in a limited period will benefit from buying a one-day pass *(ichi nichi joshaken)* that offers a day's unlimited travel on subways, trams, and local train lines.

🏛 Osaka Museum of History

1–32 Otemae Yon-Chome. **Tel** (06) 6946-5728. **S** *Tanimachi-Yon-Chome stn, Chuo or Tanimachi lines.* **◻** *Wed–Mon* **www.mus-his.city.osaka.jp**

This modern museum uses life-size reconstructions, miniature models, and video presentations to bring alive the history of Osaka from ancient times to the modern day. Its most notable exhibits are objects excavated from the 7th-century Naniwa Palace. On the 10th floor there is a reconstruction of the Daikokuden, the main building of the palace, including replicas of the vermillion-painted pillars.

The present-day museum is built partly on the site of the Naniwa Palace. Excavations in the museum basement and on the adjacent archaeological site reveal the remains of warehouses and palace walls.

Other floors explore the "Water City" of the Edo Period and a panorama of Osaka in more modern times. There are good views of Osaka Castle from various points in the museum. Of special interest to children is the Resource Center on the 8th floor. Children can complete a jigsaw puzzle using ancient pottery pieces or play with Banraku puppets.

🏯 Osaka Castle

R *Osakajo-koen stn, JR Kanjo line.* **S** *Tanimachi-Yonchome stn, Chuo or Tanimachi lines.* **◻** *daily.* **www.osakacastle.net**

The present reconstruction of the main donjon, dating from 1931, is smaller than the castle completed by Hideyoshi in

Sweeping view of downtown Osaka

For hotels and restaurants in this region see pp304–8 and pp338–41

The imposing keep of Osaka Castle

modernized lower floors of the main keep display a collection of armor and memorabilia connected with Hideyoshi, including letters. An elevator whisks you up to the 8th floor for excellent views of the city.

1586 but still gives some idea of the power and majesty of the original. The largest castle in the country at the time, Osaka-jo's turbulent history began when it was besieged and destroyed by the Tokugawa shogunate in 1615. The castle was rebuilt but struck by lightning a few years later. The remains were burned down in a fire in 1868, just before the Meiji Restoration.

Some ancillary buildings, including the Tamon tower and the impressive Otemon gate, have survived from the Tokugawa period. The

🏛 National Museum of Art

4-2-55 Nakanoshima. *Tel* (06) 6447-4680. 🚃 Keihan Yodoyabashi stn. Ⓢ Yodoyabashi stn, Midosuji line. ◯ Tue–Sun. 📷

The stunning entrance of the National Museum of Art, made from curved steel and extending high above the building itself, was designed to invoke both the strength and the flexibility of bamboo. The collection inside is equally impressive, with works by Picasso, Cézanne, Miró, and Warhol, as well as ancient Chinese treasures and modern Japanese art.

🏛 Museum of Oriental Ceramics

Nakanoshima Island. *Tel* (06) 6223-0055. 🚃 Keihan Yodoyabashi stn. Ⓢ Yodoyabashi stn, Midosuji line. ◯ Tue–Sun. www.moco.or.jp/en

With over 1,000 items of mostly Chinese and Korean origin, this museum houses one of the world's finest collections of Oriental ceramics. The display comes from the Ataka Collection, once owned by a wealthy Osaka industrialist. Computer-regulated, light-sensitive rooms highlight the surfaces of the items. A few of the Japanese pieces are National Treasures.

OSAKA CITY CENTER

Floating Garden Observatory ①
Japan Folk Art Museum ⑦
Museum of Oriental Ceramics ③
National Bunraku Theater ⑥
National Museum of Art ②
Osaka Castle ⑤
Osaka Museum of History ④
Shitenno-ji Temple ⑧
Spa World ⑨

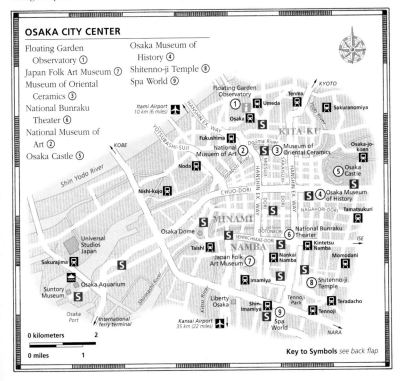

Exploring Osaka

Today, Osaka is Japan's third largest city after Tokyo and Yokohama. It also joins Tokyo and Kyoto as the top three culinary centres of Japan, with a local cuisine known for its practicality rather than finesse – instant noodles were invented here in 1958. Working Osakans eat out about six times a week. Favorite local dishes include *oshizushi*, in which sushi is placed in stainless steel molds and sliced; *udon suki*, buckwheat noodles and meat in a rich broth served in a ceramic stew pot; and *okonimiyaki*, a batter and vegetable pancake-type dish developed in 1700 as a Buddhist ritual food. For recommended restaurants see pages 340–41.

Crab restaurant and motif in downtown Osaka

Osaka's Umeda Sky Building, topped by the Floating Garden Observatory

🔲 National Bunraku Theater

🚉 *Nipponbashi stn, Kintetsu line.* Ⓢ *Nipponbashi stn, Sennichi-mae & Sakaisuji lines.* **Tel** *(06) 6212-2531.*

Japan's main venue for Bunraku puppet dramas *(see p37)* can be spotted from the colorful banners hanging outside the theater. Bunraku performances take place every January, April, June, July, August, and November, programs running normally for about 20 days at a time with shows at 11am and 4pm. The acoustics in this specially designed theater are excellent; headsets are available for foreign tourists, with English translations for some performances.

☀ Floating Garden Observatory

Umeda Sky Bldg. 🚉 *JR Osaka or Umeda stns.* ◯ *10am–10pm daily.*

This futuristic structure, reached by taking an exposed glass escalator to the 39th floor, is not for those who suffer from vertigo or fear of being caught in high places in earthquake-prone regions.

The observatory, 173 m (576 ft) above ground, straddles the twin towers of Hara Hiroshi's Umeda Sky Building. Views of Osaka and the port area from the top are well worth the palpitations. High-tech displays and a virtual-reality game center also occupy the observatory, but neither can really compete with the panoramas.

🎬 Universal Studios Japan

🚉 *Universal Studio City stn, JR Yumesaki line.* **Tel** *(06) 6465-3000.* ◯ *daily.* 🎟 *(for individual rides and activities).* **www**.usj.co.jp/e_top.html

Opened in 2001, this theme park aims to attract people of all ages and nationalities, and is fast becoming a major landmark of Osaka. There are nine themed areas, as well as live entertainment throughout the site. Among the attractions are the Hollywood Premiere Parade, Hollywood Magic, and, in the "New York" area, a St. Patrick's Day Celebration. Children will especially love the Animal Actors Stage and Snoopy's Playland.

♨ Spa World

🚉 *Shin-imamiya stn, JR Kanjo line.* Ⓢ *Dobutsuenmae stn, Midosuji line.* **Tel** *(06) 6631-0001.* ◯ *10am–8:45am.* 🎟

Built to cater for up to 5,000 people at any time, Spa World offers an amazing bathing experience. Piping hot water comes from springs almost 900 m (3,000 ft) underground. The main part of the complex is divided into zones representing bathing characteristics of such parts of the world as the Middle East, Europe, India, Japan, and Asia. The Chinese section concentrates on traditional Chinese medicine, while the Turkish section has mosaic-tile flooring.

🏛 Japan Folk Art Museum

🚉 *Koen-Higashi-Guchi monorail.* 🚇 *Nihon-teien-mae.* **Tel** *(06) 6877-1971.* ◯ *Thu–Tue.* 🎟

This modest building contains an outstanding collection of traditional folk arts and crafts, one of the best of its type in Japan. It offers a superb introduction to regional handicrafts centering on textiles and fabrics, ceramic ware, bamboo, furniture, toys, and more. There are examples of modern crafts by living masters.

Ceramic bowl, Folk Art Museum

🏯 Shitenno-ji Temple

Ⓢ *Shitenno-ji stn, Tanimachi line.* ◯ *daily.* 🎟

Prince Shotoku ordered the construction of the original temple here in 593. The complex is considered the birthplace of Japanese Buddhism. Destroyed many times by fire, the current concrete buildings, dating from 1965, are of no intrinsic value. As exact replicas of the originals, however, they are of interest to visitors wishing to know more about early Buddhist architecture. An excellent flea market is held on the 21st of every month.

Tempozan Harbor Village
S *Osaka-ko stn, Chuo line.* **Suntory Museum** ◯ *Tue–Sun.* 🖼 www. suntory.com/culture-sports/smt **Aquarium** ◯ *daily.* 🖼 www. kaiyukan.com

Begun as a reclamation program in the 1830s, this waterfront project in Osaka Port is the new face of an older, Edo-period landfill. The **Suntory Museum**, a supermodern structure by world-famous architect Ando Tadao, has a formidable collection of posters by artists such as Mucha and Toulouse-Lautrec, and also rare glass art objects.

Nearby **Osaka Aquarium** is set apart by its innovative and challenging design. Built around the concept of the Pacific "Ring of Fire," the aquarium holds almost 13.5 million liters (3 million gallons) of water. Visitors descend through 14 levels representing fish and mammal habitats found within the Pacific Ocean belt. Over 35,000 creatures inhabit the aquarium, including manta rays and whale sharks.

The Harbor Village complex also has a theater and what is claimed to be the world's largest IMAX screen. **Tempozan Marketplace** is a large center for restaurants and shopping.

Curved glass façade of the Suntory Museum, Tempozan Harbor Village

Across the bay, and linked by an underwater tunnel, is **Cosmo Square**, with an observatory, the Osaka Wine Museum, and the Nanko Bird Sanctuary.

Liberty Osaka Museum
📷 *Ashiharabashi or Imamiya stns, JR loop line.* ◯ *10am–5pm Tue–Sun.* 🖼

The Liberty is also known as the Osaka Human Rights Museum and provides a sobering insight into the dark side of Japan. Exhibits take a critical look at subjects rarely discussed by Japanese. Topics include the Burakumin section of society – descendants of leather-workers, who disposed of the dead and did other jobs considered polluted. Discrimination against ethnic minorities and foreigners, and environmental issues are also covered.

Environs:
Situated 35 km (22 miles) south of Osaka, **Kansai International Airport** (KIX) sits on a man-made island 2 km (1 mile) offshore in Osaka Bay.

Connected to the mainland by a bridge, the airport is a long, thin, futuristic compression of glass and steel.

Osaka is also at the cutting edge of research into high-speed train technology in the form of magnetic-levitated trains (Maglevs). A prototype runs between Kadoma-minami and Taisho stations. Experiments with more advanced Maglevs have reached speeds of 550 kph (340 mph).

Takarazuka lies northwest of Osaka, in Hyogo prefecture. The town is closely associated with the enormously popular all-female Takarazuka Troupe, which was founded in 1914. Their revues can be classified as adaptations of heroic romances. Performances at the **Takarazuka Grand Theater** are held once or twice a day except Wednesday.

Takarazuka Grand Theater
🚉 *Hankyu & JR lines.* **Tel** (0570) 00-5100.

A large tattoo, often the sign of a *yakuza* member

THE YAKUZA

The word *yakuza* was originally used to describe the classless groups of thieves, gamblers, and outlaws who floated around large cities and ports during the Edo period. Osaka is the center of the modern *yakuza* and many of the country's largest and most influential crime syndicates. *Yakuza* are involved in a wide range of illegal activities that run from prostitution, drug- and light-arms-smuggling to loan-sharking. Gangs are also adept at corporate extortion, preventing, for

Yakuza **member with the trademark missing finger**

a suitable fee, embarrassing questions being asked at stockholder meetings. *Irezumi* (tattoos), though traditionally an art form, are considered anti-social in Japan and are strongly associated with the *yakuza*. If you see a tattooed person with a missing finger or two – the result of a self-mutilation equated in the *yakuza* world with machismo – the chances are that the person will be a gang member.

Kobe ⑩

神戸

Gateway detail, Chinatown

Kobe enjoyed a brisk trade with China and Korea from the 8th century on and was one of the first ports to benefit when Japan reopened to Western trade in 1868. Today, there is a large expatriate community, notably Chinese and Koreans, but also Europeans, Americans, and Indians. The city became famous overnight in 1995 when a massive earthquake struck. However, there is little evidence of the disaster now, so effectively has this lively, cosmopolitan city been rebuilt. The downtown area is famous for its nightlife. Kobe beef, meanwhile, is the world's most expensive meat.

One of the elegant European residences in Kitano-cho

Exploring Kobe

Kobe's central business, shopping, and nightlife districts, Kitano-cho, nearby Chinatown, and the narrow north-south axis of Flower Road are easily negotiated on foot. With little room left to expand beyond these urban parameters, Kobe has turned to the sea for extra space. Reclamation projects include Rokko and Port Islands.

The excellent subway system has lines running east-west. An unmanned monorail, the Port Liner, runs from Sannomiya station in a circle around Port Island. The City Loop bus offers a day pass that includes most of the city's key sights.

🏠 Kitano-cho

12-min walk from Sannomiya stn along Kitano-zaka. 🏠 *some houses.*

Wealthy foreign traders and diplomats built homes in this area after Kobe was chosen to serve as one of Japan's major international ports at the start of the Meiji period. Over 20 of these beautifully preserved homes are open to the public. The stone and clapboard buildings, many in the Gothic Victorian style, are called *ijinkan*. The area, which suggests fin de siècle European elegance to many Japanese people, enjoys a reputation as one of Kobe's more fashionable districts.

🏠 Chinatown

5-min walk S of Motomachi stn.

The city's 40,000 or more Chinese residents have turned this quarter (Nankin-machi) into a lively and colorful slice of Kobe life. Approached through four large gateways, the central plaza, Nankin Park, is surrounded by Chinese restaurants, souvenir and trinket shops, and is filled with street vendors. The park has statues representing the 12 animals of the Chinese astrological calendar. Chinatown is a popular dining spot for Kobe residents.

🏛 Kobe City Museum

10-min walk S of Motomachi stn. ◻ *Tue–Sun.* 🖼

This museum is an excellent introduction to the history of the city from the earliest times until its reconstruction after the 1995 earthquake. There is an intriguing display of objects retrieved from the old foreign concession in Kitano-cho and a scale model of the area. The museum also has the world's premier collection of 16th-century Nanban art. The word Nanban ("Southern Barbarian") was at first applied to all foreigners who arrived from the south, mainly the Portuguese. Later it was applied to Europeans in general.

🌸 Meriken Park

🚃 *Port Liner monorail.* **Museum and Port Tower** ◻ *daily.* 🖼

A little west of the monorail bridge that takes you across to Port Island lies Meriken Park. Meriken was the Meiji-

THE GREAT HANSHIN EARTHQUAKE

Shoehorned into a narrow strip of land between hills to the north and the Inland Sea to the south, Kobe paid a high price for its location on the morning of January 17, 1995. At 5:46am the Great Hanshin Earthquake struck, its

epicenter 10 miles beneath the Akashi Strait near Kobe. The tremor lasted almost a minute and measured 6.9 on the moment magnitude scale. The initial quake, hundreds of aftershocks, and ensuing fires together destroyed over 100,000 buildings and killed over 5,000 inhabitants.

The center of Kobe in ruins following the January 1995 earthquake

Sake brewery in Kobe, open to visitors

era rendition of "American." From the park you will see the distinctive outline of the **Kobe Maritime Museum**, a glass structure with a roof designed like a ship. The displays inside it focus on the city's role as a port. For a good overview of the area climb the **Port Tower** on Naka Tottei Pier.

🏯 Sake Breweries

Although most of the best breweries were razed during the earthquake, reconstruction and preservation of the few that were left has been going on at a furious pace, and it is now possible once again to visit some the best-known brand-name producers. Reservations are required to visit

Kikumasamune Shuzo Kinenkan, a brewery located within three minutes' walk of Rokko Liner Minami Uozaki station. Although its storehouses perished in the quake, the watermill cottage survived and now houses a small but interesting display of brewing utensils. At **Hamafukutsuru Ginjo Kobo**, a five-minute stroll from Hanshin Uozaki station, visitors can watch the fermenting process. Sake tasting takes place at both breweries.

Environs:
Behind Shin-Kobe station, the **Nunobiki Falls**, with four picturesque cascades, have been celebrated in Japanese literature since the 10th century. **Mount Rokko**, the highest peak of the chain of the same name, can be reached by cable car. The view of the Inland Sea and city below is sensational. On the north slope is **Arima Onsen**, a spa that has been

VISITORS' CHECKLIST

Hyogo prefecture. 🏛 *1,528,000*. ✈ *Kansai airport, 25 mins by high-speed boat; Kobe City Air Terminal (K-CAT), Port Island.* 🚃 *JR Shin-Kobe stn, Sanyo Shinkansen line; Sannomiya stn, JR Tokkaido, Hankyu, & Hanshin lines.* 🛈 *in front of stn (078) 322-0220.* **http**://feel-kobe.jp/index-e.html 🎏 *Kobe Matsuri (3rd weekend in May); Torchlight Noh (Aug 1).*

operating since the 7th century. The waters were a favorite of the 16th-century shogun Toyotomi Hideyoshi and his wife, who sometimes came with the tea ceremony master, Sen no Rikyu.

The cable car ride up Mount Rokko

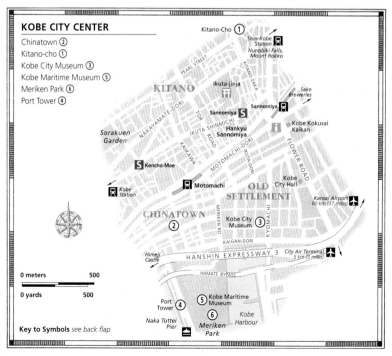

KOBE CITY CENTER

Chinatown ②
Kitano-cho ①
Kobe City Museum ③
Kobe Maritime Museum ⑤
Meriken Park ⑥
Port Tower ④

Kitano-Cho ①
Shin-Kobe Station
Nunobiki Falls, Mount Rokko
PEARL STREET
KITANO
Ikuta-jinja
KITANO ZAKA
Sake Breweries
NAKAYAMATE-DORI
TOR ROAD
IKUTA SHINMICHI
KAKAWA
Sannomiya
Sannomiya
Hankyu Sannomiya
Kobe Kokusai Kaikan
Sorakuen Garden
FLOWER ROAD
MOTOMACHI-DORI
IKUTA-DORI
Kencho-Mae
Motomachi
Kobe City Hall
OLD SETTLEMENT
Kobe Station
Kansai Airport 60 km (37 miles)
CHINATOWN ②
MERIKEN RD
Kobe City Museum ③
KYOMACHI
Himeji Castle
KAIGAN-DORI
City Air Terminal 5 km (3 miles)
HANSHIN EXPRESSWAY 3
HAMATE BYPASS

0 meters 500
0 yards 500

Port Tower ④
Naka Tottei Pier
⑤ Kobe Maritime Museum
⑥ Meriken Park
Kobe Harbour

Key to Symbols *see back flap*

Himeji Castle ⑪

姫路城

Built on a high bluff, Himeji-jo, the grandest of
Japan's 12 remaining feudal castles, dominates the
city of Himeji. The building is better known among the
Japanese as Shirasagi-jo, the "white egret castle," because
of the supposed resemblance of its plastered walls,
stretched either side of the main donjon, to the image
of a bird taking flight. For many people its military
architecture, ameliorated by graceful aesthetic lines,
qualifies Himeji-jo as the ultimate samurai castle. Its
cinematic potential was exploited by Akira Kurosawa
who used the castle's stunning exterior for his 1985 film
Ran. The castle is now designated a
UNESCO World Heritage Site.

**View from lower floor of donjon
to the modern city of Himeji**

West bailey
(nishi-nomaru)

Vanity Tower
*The abode of Princess
Sen (1597–1667)
and other women
was locked
each night
under guard.*

**Gates and
Passageways**
*Though never put to the test,
the castle's labyrinth of
passageways and gateways in
the outer zones were designed
to confuse enemies.*

Entrance

Sangoku moat

TIMELINE OF HIMEJI CASTLE

1333 Norimura Akamatsu builds a fort in a strategic location on top of a hillock at Himeji	**1600** Battle of Sekigahara *(see pp54–5)*, after which Ikeda Terumasa, son-in-law of Tokugawa Ieyasu, is rewarded with Himeji Castle	**1609** Five-story donjon completed **1618** Buildings in west bailey added by Tadamasa Honda	**1749** Sakai Tadasumi and descendants live in castle until Meiji Restoration of 1867

1400	1500	1600	1700

1467 Two baileys added by Akamatsu Masanori	**1581** Toyotomi Hideyoshi adds a three-story donjon to the fort	**1601** Ikeda Terumasa begins digging three moats around castle	*17th-century crest tile from gable of castle*

★ Main Tower

The current five-story donjon was developed by Ikeda Terumasa in 1609, transforming a modest military stronghold into a symbol of the Tokugawa shogunate's newly consolidated power. For more details about the main tower see pages 208–209.

VISITORS' CHECKLIST

1 km N of Himeji stn, Himeji city, Hyogo prefecture. **ℹ** (0792) 85-3792. **www**.city.himeji.hyogo.jp/english/himeji/index.html 🚉 Himeji stn, Shinkansen line. ◯ 9am–4pm daily (to 5pm Jun–Aug). 📷 🎎 Matsubara Festival (Oct 14, 15).

Main bailey *(honmaru)*

Second bailey *(ninomaru)*

The waist quarter *(koshi-kurawa)*, behind the main tower, is the weakest point of the stronghold.

The suicide quarter may have been intended as a place for ritual suicide when it was built. However, it was probably used only for its water supply.

| 0 meters | 50 |
| 0 yards | 50 |

STAR FEATURES

★ Fan Walls

★ Main Tower (see pp208–209)

★ Fan Walls

Samurai castles are notable for their graceful fan-shaped stone walls, which were very difficult for enemies to scale.

Exploring Himeji Castle: the Main Tower

The stronghold of Himeji Castle, the main tower was used by the feudal lords in the event of a seige or during drills. From the exterior, the tower appears to have five floors. In fact, it has six floors and a basement – the second and third floors from the top appear to be one floor from the outside. Visitors today enter the keep through its door in the basement and climb to the top.

Fish Motifs
Dolphin-like shachi-gawara *motifs on the roof are of a mythical beast believed to protect the main tower from fire.*

The uppermost chamber offers panoramas on four sides.

The division between these two floors is not obvious from the exterior.

Slippery wooden stairs ascend through rooms of diminishing size.

Interior of Keep
Originally an armaments store, the interior remains largely unadorned and houses exhibits relating to castle life.

Entrance through basement

Portholes in the shape of circles, triangles, and rectangles were for musketeers and archers.

Basement level

Rock Chutes
Angled chutes set at numerous points in the walls enabled stones, boiling oil, and water to be dropped on the heads of any invaders.

Museum of Weaponry
Displays of samurai arms and armor are complemented by guns and pouches of gun powder, introduced to Japan by the Portuguese in the 16th century.

View of Himeji Castle in April, when the cherry trees are blossoming

Modern facade of Hyogo
Prefectural Museum of History

Gables
*Dormer gables
combined with
Chinese arched
gables create an
undulating
effect.*

Storehouses
for grain

Latticed
Windows
*Latticed bay windows,
called* degoshimado,
*are on first level above
the basement.*

Castle Environs:
The grounds at Himeji are
particularly attractive during
April, when the cherry trees
are in bloom. **Koko-en**, an
elegant composite of nine
separate Edo-style gardens,
merits attention. It was built
in 1992 on the site of former
samurai homes. The **Hyogo
Prefectural Museum of History**
provides excellent exhibits,
including models of Japanese
castles and a section on
Bunraku puppet drama, with
models that can be operated
by the public.

Just beyond the castle
grounds, the **Himeji City
Museum of Literature** pays
tribute to nine influential local
writers, but it is more notable
for its architecture, designed
by one of Japan's most respected contemporary architects,
Ando Tadao *(see p25)*.

On the nearby hill called
Shoshazan, **Shoshazan
Enkyo-ji** is a well-known
Buddhist training center and
pilgrimage sight. Priceless
sculptures include the Kongo
Satta, a Buddha image carved
in 1395. The Yakushido is the
oldest building here, dating
from the 14th-century Kamakura period. At the foot of the
hill is **Shosha Art and Craft
Museum**, with traditional
crafts and toys from all over
Japan, and craft demonstrations by artisans on Sundays
and public holidays.

♣ Koko-en Garden
Castle grounds, W of main entrance.
Tel (0792) 89-4120. ◯ *daily.* 📷

**⊞ Hyogo Prefectural
Museum of History**
Just behind castle. 📷

**⊞ Himeji Museum of
Literature**
84 Yamanoi-cho, NW of castle.
Tel (0792) 93-8228. ◯ *Tue–Sun.* 📷

**⊞ Shosha Art and Craft
Museum**
Tel (0792) 67-0301. ◯ *Tue–Sun.* 📷

Koraku-en Garden in Okayama, with carefully landscaped mounds and an artificial lake

Inbe ⑫

伊部

Okayama prefecture. 🚶 41,900. 🚉 ⓘ in Inbe JR stn (0869) 64-1100. 🎏 Bizen-yaki Matsuri (Pottery Festival, 3rd weekend in Oct).

The home of Bizen pottery, Inbe has a huge range of shops, galleries, and kilns. Originating in the Kamakura period, Bizen-ware is earthy, unglazed, and prized by tea-ceremony enthusiasts. The **Bizen Pottery Traditional and Contemporary Art Museum**, near the station, has modern pieces and superb examples from the Muromachi, Momoyama, and Edo periods.

🏛 **Bizen Pottery Museum**
Tel (0869) 64-1400. ⬤ daily. ⬤ Mon in Dec–Mar & Jun–Sep. 🈂

Okayama ⑬

岡山

Okayama prefecture. 🚶 674,700. ✈ 🚉 ⓘ in JR stn (086) 222-2912. **www**.city.okayama.okayama. jp/index-e.htm 🎏 Saidai-ji Eyo (3rd weekend in Feb).

The former center of a domain ruled by the feudal Ikeda family, Okayama today is a vibrant modern city, much visited by Japanese tourists who come to marvel at the 9-km (6-mile) long **Seto Ohashi Bridge** (see 189), connecting Oka-

yama with Shikoku. Trains now reduce the crossing time, which used to take an hour by ferry, to 15 minutes. The main sights are just over 1 km (half a mile) east of the station.

A highlight is the **Koraku-en Garden**, one of Japan's "famous three" gardens. Commissioned by Lord Ikeda, it was completed in 1700. Though a classic stroll garden, it was the first in Japan to use large expanses of lawn in the overall design. The garden is divided into three sections and features bamboo, pine, plum, and cherry trees, along with tea bushes. The nearby castle is incorporated into the composition as "borrowed scenery," a classic device in Japanese gardens. Also included are streams and a pond crossed by an elegant red bridge.

Okayama Castle is nicknamed the "Crow's Castle" due to its black walls. Destroyed in World War II, the exterior of the 16th-century castle was faithfully reconstructed in 1966. The interior has an authentic period collection of palanquins, samurai helmets, swords, and the like.

The reconstructed keep of Okayama castle, with its striking black walls

Visitor facilities include an elevator to the top of the four-story keep, and in the river below the castle, rental paddle-boats shaped like swans and teacups. More items owned by the Ikeda clan, notably armor, swords, pottery, lacquerware, and an excellent collection of Noh costumes, are on view at the **Hayashibara Museum of Art**, just south of the castle.

To the northeast is the **Orient Museum**, tracing how Near-Eastern art reached and influenced Japan via the Silk Route. The nearby **Okayama Prefectural Museum of Art** has an interesting collection of mostly 20th-century Japanese paintings and a few works by older artists including the 15th-century master Sesshu.

🌷 **Koraku-en Garden**
🚋 Koraku-en-mae stop. ⬤ daily. 🈂

🏯 **Okayama Castle**
⬤ daily. 🈂

🏛 **Hayashibara Art Museum**
Tel (086) 223-1733. ⬤ Tue–Sun. 🈂

🏛 **Orient Museum**
Tel (086) 232-3636. ⬤ Tue–Sun. 🈂

🏛 **Okayama Prefectural Museum of Art**
Tel (086) 225-4800. ⬤ Tue–Sun. 🈂

Kurashiki ⑭

倉敷

Okayama prefecture. 🚶 476,000. 🚉 ⓘ next to stn (086) 424-1220. **www**.city.kurashiki.okayama.jp/ index_e.html

Civic pride and a strong preservation ethic have saved the Edo-period mercantile town of Kurashiki from the development that has swept away so much of Japan's architectural heritage. Kurashiki means "storehouse village," a reference to the dozens of granaries (*kura*), characterized by mortar and black-tiled walls, that are the main feature of the town.

In the heart of the old city, the **Bikan Historical Area** just south of the station, 200-year-old *kura* flank a tranquil canal lined with willows. Many of the kura have been converted into galleries, restaurants, Japanese inns, and tasteful shops and boutiques. The largest commercial conversion, a short walk from the canal, is **Kurashiki Ivy Square**, a complex of shops, restaurants, hotels, museums, and an orchid center housed in the former Kurabo Textile Mill.

In the old district the finest museum is the **Ohara Museum of Art**. The collection was commissioned by industrialist Ohara Magosaburo in 1930 on the premise that great art should be accessible – even to the people of a relative backwater such as Kurashiki. It includes some rare works by the likes of Matisse, Renoir, Picasso, Degas, and Gauguin. Some genuine masterpieces, like El Greco's *The Annunciation*, are here. The **Kogeikan** annex, converted from a traditional storehouse, houses an outstanding collection of works from Japan's *mingei* (or folk-craft) movement, among them ceramic objects crafted by

Asian exhibits at the Japan Rural Toy Museum, Kurashiki

Hamada Shoji, Kawai Kanjiro, and Bernard Leach, founders of the movement in the early 20th century.

The **Kurashiki Archaeological Museum** occupies an old *kura* by the canal and includes items excavated in the region along with comparative objects from elsewhere in the world. In the **Kurashiki Folk Art Museum** are folk crafts housed in connecting *kura*. The **Japan Rural Toy Museum** has a delightful and extensive display of traditional old toys, both international and Japanese. Several of the latter are painted red, a defense, it was believed, against smallpox. A charming shop near the entrance sells

Woven rush shoes from Kurashiki

traditional toys. **Kurashiki Tivoli Park**, by the north exit of the staion, is an immensely popular Danish theme park.

🏛 **Ohara Museum of Art**
Tel (086) 422-0005. ◯ Tue–Sun. 📷

🏛 **Archaeological Museum**
Tel (086) 422-1542. ◯ Tue–Sun. 📷

🏛 **Folk Art Museum**
Tel (086) 422-1637. ◯ Tue–Sun. 📷

🏛 **Japan Rural Toy Museum**
Tel (086) 422-8028. ◯ daily. 📷

🎡 **Kurashiki Tivoli Park**
Tel (086) 434-1111. ◯ variable. 📷

Fukiya ⑮
吹屋

Okayama prefecture. 👥 200. 🚌 from Bitchu Takahashi.

A prosperous boom town at the center of a local copper and red-ochre mining industry in the 19th century, Fukiya is now a rustic hamlet tucked into some of the area's most beautiful mountain countryside. Well-to-do mine owners and merchants put much of their wealth into building grand houses. Characterized by white plaster walls and red-ochre colored latticework windows and doors, these distinctive buildings, the work of master carpenters, are the village's main cultural asset.

Several are open to the public, including the former house of the ochre-rich Katayama family, now Fukiya's **Local History Museum**, several renovated stores, and an old plaster-and-tile schoolhouse. One of the prefecture's six International Villas, an inn based on the design of a traditional soy sauce warehouse, is in Fukiya *(see p304)*.

Just outside the village is a copper and ochre mine, which can be visited. An unusual Edo-period home called the **Hirokane-tei**, about 4 km (2 miles) outside, resembles a fortified chateau.

🏛 **Local History Museum**
Tel (0866) 29-2222. ◯ daily. 📷

🏠 **Hirokane-tei**
Tel (0866) 29-3182. ◯ daily. 📷

One of Kurashiki's storehouses, now a shop

View of boats and hotels at Lake Biwa

Lake Biwa ⑯
琵琶湖

Shiga prefecture. 🚉 🛈 *at Otsu stn (077) 522-3830.* 🎏 *Sanno Matsuri (Apr 12–15, Otsu).*

With a total mass of 674 sq km (263 sq miles), and a depth at some points of 105 m (340 ft) Biwa-ko, Japan's largest lake, covers an area greater than any Japanese city, including Tokyo. A calm expanse of water dotted with islets, the lake is named after the *biwa*, a Japanese musical instrument whose outline it is said to resemble. In the 15th century the highlights of Lake Biwa were named Omi Hakkei, "the eight views of Omi." Although development has changed some of these views radically, Lake Biwa is still one of Western Honshu's most beautiful places, its shore fringed with shrines, temples, hotels, and modest pensions.

Otsu, on the southwest edge, is the lake shore's largest city with a population of nearly 290,000. Visitors come here to see **Onjo-ji** temple complex of over 20 buildings, about 15 minutes' walk from the station. One of its huge gates, the Todaimon, leads to **Ishiyama-dera** temple, which has some 8th-century buildings. Murasaki Shikibu, author of the *Tale of Genji*, is believed to have used one of the chambers of the Main Hall in which to write her early 11th-century masterpiece.

Hikone, on the lake's eastern shore, has the 17th-century **Hikone Castle**, remarkable for retaining its original structure virtually intact. From the top floor of the keep is a superb view of Lake Biwa.

> 🏯 **Hikone Castle**
> **Tel** *(0749) 22-2742.* ◯ *daily.* 💲

Amanohashidate Sand Bar ⑰
天橋立

Kyoto prefecture. 🚉 *Amanohashidate.* 🛈 *at Amanohashidate stn (0772) 22-8030.*

One of the highlights of Miyatsu Bay, along the San-in coast, is Amanohashidate, the "bridge of heaven." The 4-km (2-mile) pine-studded sand bar separates the bay from Asoumi lagoon. According to Japanese mythology, Amanohashidate is the spot where the gods conceived the Japanese islands. Many writers have used the setting for novels and poetry. Visitors usually take the boat across the lagoon from the pier near the station, then the cable car from the base of Kasamatsu Park to its hilltop summit, which is the best viewing point of the

Windsurfing on Lake Biwa

sand bar. It is said that if you look at Amanohashidate upside down through your legs it seems to be floating in mid-air.

Tottori Sand Dunes ⑱
鳥取砂丘

Tottori prefecture. 🚉 *Tottori.* 🚌 *from stn to entrance to dunes.* 🛈 *at Tottori stn (0857) 22-3318.*

A huge expanse of wavy, sahara-brown and yellow undulations, the Tottori sand dunes stretch for 16 km (10 miles) along the San-in coast. To the Japanese, the towering dunes, some rising to 90 m (300 ft), and the shifting patterns and shadows formed across the sand, are lyrical reminders of the human condition. Abe Kobo's powerful existential novel, *The Woman in the Dunes* (1962), made into a classic Japanese film, is set here. Commercialization has inevitably hit the area – head east acrosss the dunes or rent a bike for a quieter experience.

Matsue ⑲
松江

Shimane prefecture. 🏘 *194,000.* ✈ *Yonago and Izumo.* 🚉 🛈 *at Matsue JR stn (0852) 21-4034.* **www**.city.matsue.shimane.jp/ 🎏 *Matsue Castle Festival (Apr 1–15), Doh Matsuri (Nov 3).*

Situated at the intersection of Lake Shinji with Miho bay and Nakaumi lagoon, Matsue is, not surprisingly, also known as the "water city."

The towering keep of Matsue Castle

Lafcadio Hearn's residence with its well-tended garden, in Matsue

Rarely included in the itineraries of foreign visitors, the area has several worthwhile cultural features. Matsue is referred to at length in *Glimpses of Unfamiliar Japan* (1894), by Lafcadio Hearn, a journalist of Irish-Greek descent who spent 15 months in the town.

Hearn described **Matsue Castle** in the colorful superlatives that mark his style as "a veritable architectural dragon, made up of magnificent monstrosities." One of the few in Japan to remain intact, the castle was built in 1611 of pine and stone, then partially reconstructed 31 years later. Its five-story keep is Japan's tallest.

Within five minutes of the castle are two more modest architectural gems. The **Buke Yashiki** is an interesting mansion built in 1730 by the Shiomi family, who were chief retainers at the castle. Furniture and household items provide an insight into their life. Above Shiome Nawate street is the **Meimei-an Teahouse** (1779), one of Japan's oldest and best preserved. Along the same street is the **Tanabe Art Museum**, with a refined collection of tea bowls and other tea-related objects.

Just north of the castle, the **Lafcadio Hearn Residence** is beautifully preserved. Its immaculate garden inspired one of Hearn's most engaging essays, *In A Japanese Garden*. Beside the house, the **Lafcadio Hearn Memorial Hall** has a good collection of his memorabilia, including such items as manuscripts, photos, and his desk and smoking pipes.

⌂ Matsue Castle
Kencho-mae stop. **Tel** (0852) 21-4030. ⬜ *daily.* 📷

⌂ Buke Yashiki
Tel (0852) 22-2243. 📷

⌂ Meimei-an Teahouse
Tel (0852) 21-9863. ⬜ *daily.* 📷

♨ Tanabe Art Museum
Tel (0852) 26-2211. ⬜ *Tue–Sun.* 📷

⌂ Lafcadio Hearn Residence
Tel (0852) 23-0714. ⬜ *daily.* 📷

⌂ Lafcadio Hearn Memorial Hall
Tel (0852) 21-2147. ⬜ *daily.* 📷

Izumo ⓴
出雲

Shimane prefecture. 👥 *146,900.* ✈ 🚉 ℹ *at Taisha-mae stn; (0853) 53-2298.* 🎎 *Daisairei (May 14–16), Kamiari Festival (11–17th days of 10th lunar month).*

Alive with myths, legends, and tales of the supernatural, Izumo, known until the 3rd century as the "eightfold-towering-thunder-head land," has an enthralling heritage. The town is well known throughout Japan for the **Izumo-Taisha**, one of the most revered and oldest Shinto shrines in the country. It is dedicated to Okuninushi-no-Mikoto, a deity who is closely associated with agriculture and medicine, as well as marriage – the latter explaining the popularity of the shrine for wedding ceremonies.

The entrance to the shrine, through 11 *torii* (gates), is impressive. Unusually tall, the **Honden** (Main Hall) is not open to the public, although the **Treasure House** can be visited. The shrine's environs are sacred and therefore ecologically pristine, with towering cryptomeria trees surrounding the main compound. Just east of the shrine are a number of old houses occupied by priests who serve here. Note the traditional clay and stone walls.

Just past Izumo-Taisha, on Route 431 to Okuni, there is a **monument** to a nun who is said to have danced on the banks of the Kamo River in Kyoto to raise money for the shrine. The dance was developed into the Kabuki theatrical form *(see pp36–7)*.

Izumo-Taisha
Tel (0853) 53-3100. ⬜ *daily.* 📷 *(Treasure Hall).*

Izumo shrine, dominated by the distinctive rafters of the Honden

---

LAFCADIO HEARN

Lafcadio Hearn (1850–1904) arrived in Japan in 1890. He published several books, many of which are still in print and widely read, such as *In Ghostly Japan*, *Japan: An Interpretation*, and *Glimpses of Unfamiliar Japan*. The Japanese continue to be fascinated by Hearn, whose books allowed them for the first time to view their culture through the eyes of a foreigner. He was also one of the foremost interpreters of Japan for the West. A bold and unconventional thinker in his time, he was interested in the folklore and superstitions of Japan. Hearn's first Japanese home was Matsue, where he took up a teaching post, but quickly fell ill. The woman who nursed him back to health – the daughter of a local samurai family – eventually became Hearn's wife. He later acquired Japanese citizenship, changing his name to Koizumi Yakumo.

Writer and journalist Lafcadio Hearn

Hiroshima ㉑

広島

For the worst of reasons, Hiroshima needs no introduction. Each year millions of visitors are drawn to the city where so many people were wiped out in one instant of apocalyptic destruction. An unusual tourist attraction, the sober monuments of Hiroshima can induce an unexpected sense of listlessness and enervation in many visitors. However, there is more to the reconstructed city than its sorrowful atomic legacy.

The Peace Memorial Museum, with exhibits on the bomb's effects

Hiroshima's Peace Memorial Park and the A-Bomb Dome

Exploring Hiroshima

Rather than resurrect the tortuous pre-war streets, the modern city was rebuilt on a grid system, making it easy to negotiate. Trams are the most convenient form of transportation. Downtown Hiroshima lies to the east of the Peace Park. The lively nightlife area of Nagarekawa is not far away.

The A-Bomb Dome, all that remains of the old bombed city

⚜ Peace Memorial Park

🚋 Genbaku-Domu-mae. **Museum Tel** (082) 241-4004. ⬜ daily. 🈸

Located at the confluence of the Ota and Motoyasu rivers, just outside the park proper, the **A-Bomb Dome** is a haunting reminder of the

destructive forces that were unleashed on the city. The former Industrial Promotion Hall stood close to the hypocenter, or ground zero, the point at which the bomb exploded. The occupants of the building were killed instantly. Its twisted girders, gaping holes, and piles of rubble have been preserved as a UNESCO World Heritage Site.

By the northern entrance to the park is the **Peace Bell**, which visitors can ring themselves. Nearby is the **Memorial Mound** containing the ashes of tens of thousands of people cremated on this spot. Farther into the park is the **Children's**

Peace Monument, depicting a girl with outstretched hands. A crane, the Japanese symbol of longevity and happiness, passes above her. The work refers to the story of a child victim of the bomb who believed that if she could make 1,000 paper cranes she would recover from her illness. The girl did not survive, but her story is known throughout Japan, and fresh paper cranes sent by school children from all over Japan always adorn the memorial.

Across the road is the **Flame of Peace**, which will be extinguished only when all nuclear weapons have been eliminated from the earth. Adjacent to it is the **Cenotaph**, designed by Tange Kenzo, for the victims of the bomb. It contains the names of all those who died, together with an inscription that reads "Rest in peace. We will never repeat the error."

The centerpiece of the park is the **Peace Memorial Museum**. This graphically explains the consequences of

THE BOMBING OF HIROSHIMA

As World War II dragged on into the summer of 1945, the US decided to deploy an entirely new, untested weapon to force Japan to surrender. On August 6 a B29 bomber dropped the first atomic bomb on Hiroshima, a city that had seen little conventional bombing. It exploded at 8:15am, 580 m (1,900 ft) above the city center. Tens of thousands of people were killed instantly by the blast, and the death toll rose to 180–200,000 over the following years as after-effects took hold. Nagasaki (*see pp240–41*) suffered a similar fate three days later.

The ruins of Hiroshima in 1945, all but flattened by the atomic blast

the bomb on the city by means of photos, videos, and the personal effects of victims. Poignant exhibits inclued a half-melted bronze Buddha, a mangled tricycle, and the imprint of a dark shadow on the granite steps of the Sumitomo Bank building – the sole remains of someone who was sitting there at the time.

Outside the museum are the so-called **Phoenix trees** which were growing 1.5 km (1 mile) from the hypocenter. Transplanted here since, they still show scorch marks on one side of their crowns.

Other Sights in Hiroshima

A look at the city's other attractions helps to dispel the gloom that descends on some visitors to the Peace Memorial Park. A relaxing spot is the **Shukkei-en** stroll garden. Its pond, islets, streams, miniature bridges,

The Flame of Peace, fringed by sculpted bushes

and pine-studded banks carefully replicate scenes from a legendary lake in China.

Hiroshima Castle was destroyed in the bomb, but a faithful reconstruction was completed in 1958. The **Museum of Contemporary Art** was designed by world-renowned Japanese architect Kurokawa Kisho and houses a collection of modern, post-war art. An outdoor sculpture garden is attached to the museum. The fascinating

Hiroshima Children's Museum has lots of hands-on equipment and displays.

♣ **Shukkei-en Garden**
Nr Shukkei-en-mae stop. ◯ daily. 📷
🏯 **Hiroshima Castle**
🚃 Kamiya-cho. ◯ daily. 📷
🏛 **Museum of Contemporary Art**
🚃 Hijiyama-shita. ◯ Tue–Sun. 📷
🏛 **Hiroshima Children's Museum**
10-min walk from Genbaku-dome mae. ◯ Tue–Sun.

PEACE MEMORIAL PARK

The park was built in the 1960s, covering an area close to the hypocenter of the blast. The half-melted wreckage of the Industrial Promotion Hall (A-Bomb Dome) is the only remnant from the destruction. Scores of monuments have been erected on behalf of different groups of victims. The main memorials of interest to foreign visitors are shown here.

The Cenotaph, erected in memory of the victims of the bombing

SIGHTS AT A GLANCE

A-Bomb Dome ①
Cenotaph ⑥
Children's Peace
   Monument ④
Flame of Peace ⑤
Memorial Mound ③
Peace Bell ②
Peace Memorial
   Museum ⑧
Phoenix Trees ⑦

Children's Peace Monument, surrounded by paper cranes

Ota River
AIOI BRIDGE
MOTOYASU BRIDGE
HONKAWA BRIDGE
Motoyasu River
Ota River
WEST PEACE BRIDGE
PEACE BRIDGE

0 meters   250
0 yards   250

Miyajima Island ㉒

A jewel of the Sanyo coast, Miyajima is symbolized by a looming vermilion *torii* (Shinto gate) set in the sea, which denotes that the whole island is sacred. There are no maternity wards or cemeteries because no one is permitted to give birth or die on Miyajima. Felling trees is also forbidden – the island is covered in virgin forest, which provides a habitat for scores of bird species. Tame deer are allowed to roam at will.

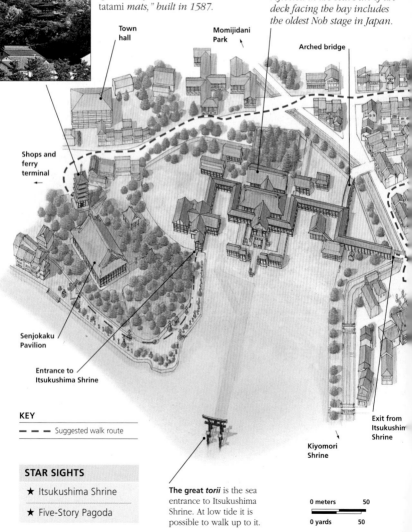

★ Five-Story Pagoda
On a bluff overlooking the shrine is the Goju-no-to, a five-story pagoda built in 1407. Next to it is the Senjokaku, or "pavilion of the thousand tatami mats," built in 1587.

★ Itsukushima Shrine
This famous shrine, founded in 593, is built on stilts over a cove. It is best viewed at high tide when the buildings are reflected in the sea. Part of the deck facing the bay includes the oldest Noh stage in Japan.

Town hall

Momijidani Park

Arched bridge

Shops and ferry terminal ←

Senjokaku Pavilion

Entrance to Itsukushima Shrine

Exit from Itsukushima Shrine

Kiyomori Shrine

KEY

— — — Suggested walk route

STAR SIGHTS

★ Itsukushima Shrine

★ Five-Story Pagoda

The great *torii* is the sea entrance to Itsukushima Shrine. At low tide it is possible to walk up to it.

0 meters	50
0 yards	50

VISITORS' CHECKLIST

Hiroshima prefecture. ⬛ *from Hiroshima to Miyajima-guchi, then ferry.* ⬛ *from Hiroshima port or Miyajima-guchi stn.* ⬛ *at ferry terminal (0829) 44-2011.* www.hiroshima-cdas.or.jp/ miyajima/english/top2.htm 🎏 *Kangensai Music Festival (Jul, or Aug – varies).* **All sights** ◯ *daily.*

Mount Misen

On the slopes behind the shrine is Momijidani ("maple leaf valley") Park. A cable car station in the park goes to the summit of Mount Misen, where there is a monkey sanctuary and superb views of the Inland Sea (see p224). There are also several nature trails on the mountainside.

Mount Misen nature trails and monkey sanctuary

Daisho-in Temple is a delightful complex with an eclectic mix of Buddhist statuary. It is blissfully peaceful, away from the crowds of the waterfront and Itsukushima Shrine.

Treasure House
This building, completed in 1934, houses a valuable collection of gifts presented to the shrine by the Taira clan and other patrons over the centuries.

Two-story Tahoto Pagoda

Miyajima Aquarium

THE FAMOUS FLOATING TORII

Acclaimed by the Japanese as one of the country's three most scenic views (Nihon Sankei), the *torii* of Itsukushima Shrine appears to float in the water. (The sand bar Amanohashidate, *see p212*, and Matsushima Bay, *see p276*, are the two other famous sights.) The warlord Taira no Kiyomori, who provided funds for the shrine, built the first *torii* in the bay in the 12th century. The present structure dates from 1875 and is about 16 m (50 ft) high. Its four-legged (*yo-tsuashi*) style provides stability.

The *torii* at dusk

Municipal History and Folklore Museum
Housed in a beautiful mid-19th century mansion is a collection of artworks, household utensils, and furniture.

Iwakuni ㉓

岩国

Yamaguchi prefecture. 153,000. Sanyo Shinkansen line to Shin-Iwakuni, JR Sanyo line to Iwakuni. at 2F bus terminal near Iwakuni stn (0827) 21-6050. www.city.iwakuni.yamaguchi.jp

The town of Iwakuni's main draw is the elegant **Kintai-kyo**, or "brocade sash" bridge. It earns its name from the rippling effect created by its five linked arches. The original structure, built in 1673, was destroyed by a typhoon in 1953. Rebuilt in an almost exact replica of the original, the bridge depends on first-rate joinery and an invisible quantity of reinforced steel.

Beyond the bridge in **Kikko Park** are a number of samurai houses, including the beautiful **Mekata House**. A short stroll west of the park lies **Iwakuni Historical Museum**, housing an impressive display of armor and weapons. A cable car takes you to **Iwakuni Castle**, a faithful 1962 reconstruction of the original 1608 donjon. There is a good view from here of the town and surrounding countryside and, on fine days, the islands of the Inland Sea.

Mekata House
Tue–Sun.

Iwakuni Historical Museum
Tel (0827) 41-0506. Fri–Wed.

Yamaguchi ㉔

山口

Yamaguchi prefecture. 191,600. (083) 933-0090. www.city.yamaguchi.lg.jp/kanko/org/eng/index.html Gion Matsuri (Jul 20–27).

Laid out in the 14th century, Yamaguchi was modeled on Kyoto. When the Jesuit Francis Xavier visited here in 1550 he found a city of incredible wealth and sophistication. The **Xavier Memorial Chapel**, built in 1952, marks the 400th anniversary of the priest's two-month stay. The painter Sesshu (1420–1506) designed a masterly garden for the temple of **Joei-ji** on the outskirts of town. To the north of Yamaguchi, the temple of **Ruriko-ji** has a Japanese cypress-wood, five-story pagoda. Nearby is a set of tombs belonging to the Mori family, another influential local clan.

Akiyoshi-dai Tablelands ㉕

秋吉台

Yamaguchi prefecture from Yamaguchi. at bus station (0837) 62-0304.

Akiyoshi-dai is a massive limestone plateau of grassland and rocky outcrops, which tour buses pass on their way to **Akiyoshido Cave**, one of the largest limestone grottos in Asia. The

In the limestone Akiyoshido Cave in the Akiyoshi-dai Tablelands

cave is 10 km (6 miles) deep, not all of it open to the public. Passageways are well lit, and a clear map is provided.

Akiyoshido Cave
Tel (0837) 62-0304. daily.

Hagi ㉖

萩

Yamaguchi prefecture. 60,400. by stn (0838) 25-1750. Hagi-yaki Festival (May 1–5).

An intensely cultural town, Hagi was a minor fishing port until Mori Terumoto fortified it in 1604. Mori samurai helped spark off the anti-Tokugawa revolt in the mid-19th century, and many of Meiji Japan's founding fathers

Five-arched "brocade sash" bridge at Iwakuni

came from Hagi. Today it is best known for its 400-year-old pottery-making tradition. Hagi's charm is in the details: its tea-houses, mossy cemeteries, and the tiny, purple bloom of bush clover (*hagi*), the town's namesake.

The central **Teramachi** district contains old temples and shrines, each with its own special features. **Jonen-ji** is noted for its finely carved gate, **Hofuku-ji** its bibbed Jizo statues, **Kyotoku-ji** for its immaculate garden, and **Choju-ji** for an atmospheric cemetery. Camellias and *natsu mikan* (summer oranges) hanging over long, whitewashed mud walls typify the **samurai quarters** to the west of Teramachi. Several residences are located here, including the homes of the Kido and Taka-sugi families, and **Kikuya House**, a merchant villa with a small museum and beautiful garden attached. The **Ishii Tea Bowl Museum** has a superb ceramics collection.

Yoshida Shoin monument, outside Hagi

Wealthy merchants appointed by the Mori clan once owned the fine collection in the **Kumaya Art Museum** to the north of here. It includes tea-ceremony utensils, literati paintings, and screens.

Little remains of the original **Hagi Castle** – about 4 km (2 miles) west of Higashi-Hagi station – except its stone walls and broad moat. The picnic grounds include **Hagijo Kiln**, a good place to watch potters at work. Beside the castle walls **Hananoe Tea House** is a lovely thatched-roof building, where green tea is served in local ware.

🏠 **Kikuya House**
Tel (0838) 25-8282. ◯ *daily.* 💳

🏛 **Ishii Tea Bowl Museum**
Tel (0838) 22-1211. ◯ *Thu–Tue.* 💳

🏛 **Kumaya Art Museum**
Tel (0838) 22-7547. ◯ *Tue–Sun.* 💳

Cemetery of Toko-ji temple near Hagi

Environs:
East of the river is the house of Yoshida Shoin, an influential late-Edo educator, philosopher, and revolutionary. **Shoin shrine** and **memorial** are dedicated to him. The nearby temple of **Toko-ji**, with its impressive three-story gate, was founded in 1691 by the third Mori lord. The Mori tombs are at the end of a path flanked by almost 500 stone lanterns.

The natural salt-water **Myojin Lagoon** is 5 km (3 miles) from town. A volcano, **Mount Kasayama**, stands beside the far end of the lake.

Tsuwano ㉗

津和野

Shimane prefecture. 👥 9,500. 🚉
🚌 ℹ️ *next to Tsuwano stn* (0856) 72-1771. 🎭 *Sagimai (Heron Dance Festival, Jul 20, 24, 27).*

This tiny 700-year old former castle town, tucked into a river valley deep in the mountains, has a large number of well-preserved samurai houses. Thousands of colorful carp inhabit the town's brooks, outnumbering the residents, it is said, by ten to one.

Tsuwano's **Catholic Church** (1931) commemorates 36 Japanese Christians who were martyred here in 1868.

On the other side of town, the hillside **Taikodani Inari Shrine** is one of the most important Inari (fox) shrines in Japan. It is reached through a tunnel of vermilion *torii* (gates), 1,174 in all. A cable car goes up the other side of the slope to the scant remains of **Tsuwano Castle** with a stunning view from the top.

Nishi Amane (1829–97), a Meiji-period statesman and philosopher, was born here. **Nishi House**, now a museum, is on a quiet street in the south of town. Opposite is **Mori House**, a museum to the army surgeon, writer, and translator Mori Ogai (1862–1922), known for novels such as *The Wild Geese* and *Vita Sexualis*, and also a Tsuwano native.

🏠 **Nishi House**
◯ *Mon.* ⬤ *Dec–mid-Mar.*

🏠 **Mori House**
Tel (0856) 72-3210. ◯ *daily.*
💳

Taikodani Inari Shrine in the town of Tsuwano

HAGI'S CERAMIC ARTS

Hagi's first kilns date from the Heian period, but the town's reputation for refined tea vessels and other wares began in the 16th century with the introduction of apprentice potters from Korea. A distinguishing mark of *hagi-yaki* (Hagi-ware) is its translucent glaze. *Hagi-yaki* improves with age, the muted pinks and pastels of the stoneware softening to beiges and umbers as tannin from the tea soaks through the porous glaze. Members of some of Hagi's oldest families, like the Sakas and Miwas, have been designated Living National Treasures.

Hagi's pink stonewear

SHIKOKU

The Inland Sea formed a natural barrier for centuries, isolating Japan's fourth largest island from much of the forces of population growth and Westernization. Still relatively off the tourist track, despite the construction of three bridge systems across the Inland Sea, Shikoku offers a nostalgic glimpse of fishing and farming villages, of rice paddies set against a backdrop of forested hills, castles, and temples.

Late Paleolithic sites and *kofun* (tumuli) dating from the 3rd century AD are evidence of early human activity on Shikoku. The Dogo Onsen (spa) in Matsuyama is referred to in the *Kojiki*, Japan's oldest chronicle, written in 712. Despite such ancient sites, however, Shikoku has mainly been on the margin of Japanese history. The island's most famous figure is Kukai, who was born into a poor aristrocratic Shikoku family in 774. This Buddhist priest, who has been called the Father of Japanese Culture, visited 88 of the island's temples in a pilgrimage that has been imitated by others for more than a thousand years.

Statue of Jizo on the 88-Temple Pilgrimage

In 1183, as chronicled in the *Tale of the Heike*, the war between the Taira and Minamoto clans for dominance of Japan spilled over into the Inland Sea and Shikoku. Some of the defeated Taira went into hiding in a gorge in central Shikoku, where many of their descendants still live.

Farmland and mountains continue to dominate Shikoku's landscape, although agriculture employs only three percent of the island's four million residents. Assembly of autos and manufacture of electronic goods, particularly in the ports along the Inland Sea, are the most important industries and are expected to be enhanced by the three new bridge links with Honshu. Other industries include fruit farming (mandarin oranges in particular), seaweed and pearl cultivation, food and chemical processing, and papermaking.

Whereas construction has altered most of Japan's coastal areas, Shikoku's coastline remains relatively unspoiled. The capes that jut into the Pacific, Muroto to the east and Ashizuri to the west, offer panoramic vistas such as are rarely seen in Japan.

Matsuyama Castle, first built in 1603 and reconstructed in 1835 after a lightning strike

◁ Pilgrims on the steps of Konomine-ji, number 27 on the 88-Temple Pilgrimage

Exploring Shikoku

Shikoku's north coast facing the Inland Sea is much more industrialized than its south coast, but not as much so as Western Honshu's Sanyo coast. The interior of the island is mountainous and rugged and not conducive to rice cultivation. Shikoku's main cities and historical sights, including most temples on the pilgrimage circuit, are thus on or near the Inland Sea coast. Takamatsu is a popular entry point. Kochi is the main city on the Pacific coast.

Vine suspension bridge at Shikoku Mura village, near Takamatsu

Reclining image of the Buddha at Uchiko

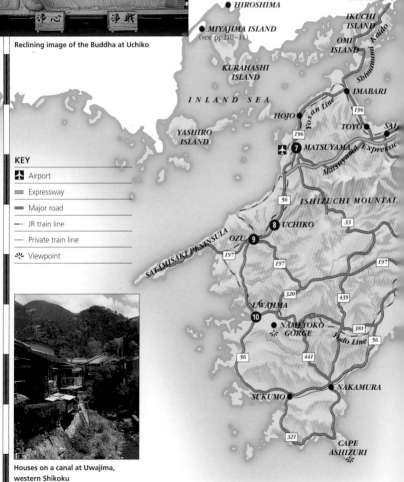

● HIROSHIMA

● MIYAJIMA ISLAND
(see pp210–11)

Onomichi

IKUCHI ISLAND

OMI ISLAND

Shimanami Kaido

KURAHASHI ISLAND

INLAND SEA

IMABARI

HOJO

Yosan Line

196

TOYO

SAI

196

MATSUYAMA

Matsuyama Expressw

YASHIRO ISLAND

KEY

✈ Airport

▬ Expressway

▬ Major road

┄ JR train line

— Private train line

❀ Viewpoint

ISHIZUCHI MOUNTAI

56

8 UCHIKO

33

OZU

9

SATAMISAKI PENINSULA

197

197

197

320

439

UWAJIMA

10

NAMETOKO GORGE

381

Yodo Line   56

56

441

NAKAMURA

56

SUKUMO

321

CAPE ASHIZURI

Houses on a canal at Uwajima, western Shikoku

GETTING AROUND

Taking a direct train from Okayama to Takamatsu, via the Seto-Ohashi Bridge, is the most popular gateway for tourists traveling from Honshu to Shikoku. Matsuyama, the island's main city, has an airport with good links to other parts of Japan. There is no *shinkansen* line, but the other types of train lines are efficient and connect all the main towns. However, unless you plan to emulate walkers on the 88-Temple Pilgrimage, it is best to rent a car to explore the mountainous interior and visit the rugged southern capes.

LOCATOR MAP

INLAND SEA
SHODO ISLAND
Okayama
Seto-Ohashi Bridge
TAKAMATSU
YASHIMA
SAKAIDE
Kotoku Line
KOTOHIRA
193
Takamatsu Expressway
KAN-ONJI
Tokushima Expressway
192
KAWANOE
USHIMA
Kochi Expressway
32
TSURUGI MOUNTAINS
193
Dosan Line
195
193
55
Mugi Line
ANAN COAST
KOCHI
OSA
55
493
CAPE MUROTO

Akashi Kaikyo Bridge, Kobe
28
AWAJI ISLAND
11
Naruto Bridge
NARUTO
NARUTO WHIRLOOLS
TOKUSHIMA

0 kilometers 50
0 miles 30

SEE ALSO

SIGHTS AT A GLANCE

Seto-Ohashi Bridge near Takamatsu, joining Shikoku to Honshu

Typical view of islands in the so-called Inland Sea, which separates Shikoku from Honshu and Kyushu

The Inland Sea ❶
瀬戸内海

Setonaikai-kisen (Inland Sea cruises) (082) 253-1212.

The Inland Sea, Japan's most beautiful body of water, is not landlocked, as its name suggests, but seems almost so with its serene waters and over 3,000 pine-studded islands. Donald Richie, in his classic travelogue *The Inland Sea* (1971), sets the scene of a boat journey westward through the narrow defiles of water: "On the left are first the sharp and Chinese-looking mountains of the island of Shikoku, so different that it appears another land, and then the flat coasts of Kyushu. This shallow sea is a valley among these mountainous islands."

You can cycle along a path that stretches from Onomichi to Imabari. Bridges, local ferries, and cruise boats provide access to the 750 or so inhabited islands. The remote fishing villages on these islands, with their salt-weathered wooden houses and black ceramic-tiled roofs, seem to hail from a different era. Among the most visited are **Awaji**, the largest island, **Setoda**, **Omi**, and **Shodo**, a beautiful island that, with its olive and orange groves, seems to belong more to the Mediterranean than the Orient.

Takamatsu ❷
高松

Kagawa prefecture. 🏠 426,500. ✈ 🚆 🛈 *at JR stn* (087) 851-2009. **www**.city.takamatsu.kagawa.jp 🎎 *Takamatsu Matsuri (Aug 12–14).*

The capital of Kagawa prefecture on the Inland Sea, Takamatsu is the main hub between Shikoku and the outside world. Nonetheless, it maintains a local charm with its neighborhood shops and historic landmarks. The town expanded after Ikoma Chikamasa erected **Takamatsu Castle** in 1588, the remains of which can still be seen. When the Tokugawa shoguns assumed power in 1600, they granted the town, castle, and surrounding fiefdom to their relatives, the Matsudaira clan. The family devoted nearly a century to landscaping the six ponds and 13 artificial hillocks that make **Ritsurin Park** the city's most famous landmark.

Takamatsu's location as an entry port for Shikoku made it the setting for such historic battles as the one between the Minamoto and the Taira clans in 1185. The **Wax Museum of the Tale of the Heike** offers a surprisingly effective recreation of the story's high points, which are also the subject matter of the classic Noh play *Yashima*.

🏛 **Wax Museum**
Tel (087) 823-8400. ⬜ *daily.* ⬜

Environs:
At Yashima volcanic plateau, **Shikoku Mura Museum** is a village where immaculately preserved buildings and other artifacts of rural life display Shikoku craftsmanship.

🏠 **Shikoku Mura**
Tel (087) 843-3111. 🚆 *Kotoden Yashima stn.* ⬜ *daily.* ⬜

Kotohira ❸
琴平

Kagawa prefecture. 🏠 10,000. 🚆 🛈 *booth 2 mins from stn* (0877) 75-3500. 🎎 *Kotohira-gu Reitaisai (Grand Festival, Oct 9–11).* **www**.town.kotohira.kagawa.jp/ english/index.html

Kotohira, which can be reached by train via either the charming, old-fashioned Kotoden or the JR line from Takamatsu, is the home of famous shrine

Bridge within the landscaped grounds of Ritsurin Park, Takamatsu

Palanquin on the steps leading up to Kompira-san

complex **Kotohira-gu**, also affectionately known as **Kompira-san**, the spiritual guardian of seafarers. The target of pilgrimages for centuries, the shrine now attracts four million visitors per year and is believed to bestow good luck upon fishermen and sailors.

A 785-stair climb (or ride in one of the palanquins available) takes visitors up the rugged mountainside to the shrine, set in beautiful grounds. Within the complex, the Asahi shrine is built of zelkova, a rock-hard wood that forms an excellent medium for carved relief work. The nearby Omote Shoin and Oku Shoin have celebrated screen paintings by Maruyama Okyo. The first presents burly tigers bristling with Zen energy, the second includes a waterfall flowing acrosss a corner of the room.

An old wooden Kabuki theater, the **Kanamaru-za**, can also be found in the town.

Votive hall at Kompira-san, near Kotohira

AWA-ODORI DANCING

Tokushima's celebrations for O-Bon, the festival of the dead on August 12–15, are the liveliest in Japan. Special dances, called Awa-Odori, are meant to welcome ancestral spirits on their yearly visit to the land of the living. Nicknamed "the fool's dance" because the refrain "you're a fool whether you dance or not, so you might as well dance" is sung, the Awa-Odori allegedly originated when rice wine was passed out to the townspeople of Tokushima to celebrate completion of a castle.

Awa-Odori dancers, Tokushima

Naruto Whirlpools ❹

鳴門の渦潮

Tokushima prefecture. 🚉 *Naruto stn, then bus to Naruto Park.* ⛴ *Uzushio line ferry (088) 687-0613; Aqua Eddy (088) 687-2288.*

Where the tip of Awaji Island nearly touches Shikoku – a wedge between Osaka Bay, the Inland Sea, Honshu, Shikoku, and the Pacific Ocean – the tidal pull on these distinct bodies of water creates large disparities spawning powerful currents and whirlpools. Navigating the churning waters of this 1.6 km (1-mile) strait has been a part of Shikoku lore for over a millennium.

Sightseeing boats now ply the 20-kmph (13-mph) currents and whirlpools, and provide startling views of the Naruto suspension bridge, part of a bridge system linking Shikoku and Honshu via Awaji Island. When the northern end of the system was completed in 1998, it had stretched 1 m (3 ft) as a result of ground shifts caused by the Kobe earthquake.

At the Awaji end of the bridge, the **Onarutokyo Memorial Hall** includes exhibits of

Awaji ningyo joruri, a variant of Bunraku puppet theater.

🏛 **Memorial Hall**
Tel (079) 952-2888. ⭕ *daily.* 🗺

Tokushima ❺

徳島

Tokushima prefecture. 🏯 267,800. ✈ 🚉 ⬛ ℹ *6F Clement Plaza (088) 656-3303.* 🎎 *Awa-Odori (Awa dancing festival, Aug 12–15).* **www**.city.tokushima.tokushima.jp

Tokushima forms the gateway into Shikoku from the Kansai region of Honshu and is the traditional point of entry for those who set out to duplicate Kukai's pilgrimage *(see pp228–9)*. The old name of the province, Awa, gives its name to the town's Awa-Odori celebration in August, which is broadcast nationwide.

Environs:
South of Tokushima, the **Anan Coast** is known for fishing villages, beaches, and the sea turtles that lay and hatch eggs from June to August.

The suspension bridge at Naruto, completed in 1985

Flooded rice fields near Kochi

Kochi ❻

高地

Kochi prefecture. 🚶 333,400. ✈
🚉 ℹ at JR stn (088) 882-7777.
www.city.kochi.kochi.jp/
🎏 Yosakoi Matsuri (Aug 9–12).

Kochi city offers a rare blend of sandy beaches, mountain views, and well-preserved historic sites.

The Kochi region, formerly called Tosa, is known for its forging of cutlery, and shops selling knives line the street in front of **Kochi Castle**, built in 1603. A startlingly long sword, over 1.5 m (5 ft) in length, is among the weapons on display in the castle. Breathtaking views can be seen from the top floors.

At Katsurahama, a white-sand beach area in the southern part of the city, the **Sakamoto Ryoma Museum** is devoted to the Tosa patriot admired for his part in the overthrow of the shogunate and restoration of the emperor in the 1860s. He was assassinated in 1867. Most Japanese visitors make a point of viewing and paying homage at a bronze statue of the man looming over the beach. Also at Katsurahama is the **Tosa Token Center**, the venue for the Tosa Fighting Dogs. Dogfights are staged here in a caged enclosure rather like a miniature Sumo wrestling stadium. The animals are also paraded in Sumo-like garments. To create the Tosa fighting dog of today, breeders matched its local ancestors with mastiffs and other powerful Western dogs. A photo exhibition documents major events in the history of this sport, including visits by the emperor. The gambling that helped make the fights popular is now illegal, and increasing numbers of people are repulsed by the dogfights.

Statue of patriotic figure Sakamoto Ryoma, Kochi

🏯 **Kochi Castle**
Tel (088) 872-2776. 🔲 daily. 📷

🏛 **Sakamoto Ryoma Museum**
Tel (088) 841-0001. 🔲 daily. 📷

ℹ **Tosa Token Center**
Tel (088) 842-3315. 🔲 daily. 📷

Environs:
Kochi is a good starting point for day trips to **Cape Muroto** at the southeast tip of Shikoku or **Cape Ashizuri** to the southwest. Both have panoramic views of the Pacific Ocean and some unusual rock formations.

Matsuyama ❼

松山

Ehime prefecture. 🚶 470,000. ✈
🚉 ℹ at JR stn (089) 917-5678.
www.city.matsuyama.ehime.jp

The capital of Ehime prefecture and a castle town since 1603, Matsuyama has many powerful associations for the Japanese.

The **Dogo Onsen**, a famous hot-spring spa, has been in use for over a millennium, and has a fine 19th-century bathhouse. Deeper into the mountains behind the historic bathhouse, **Oku-Dogo Onsen** is a much newer resort area. Natsume Soseki, an author whose portrait appears on the ¥1,000 bill, moved to Matsuyama in 1895 and later wrote about the town in his autobiographical novel *Botchan* (1906).

The **Shiki Masaoka Museum** is devoted to Soseki's friend Shiki (1867–1902), a Matsuyama native held by many to be Japan's finest modern haiku poet. Shiki was also a fine painter, and the museum's highly visual presentation includes manuscripts, paintings, and photographs of Shiki and Soseki in the city.

Matsuyama Castle is an extensive complex on a bluff overlooking the city and Inland Sea. Plaques offer intelligent commentary on the castle's strategic features.

🏛 **Dogo Onsen**
🚋 from stn. *Tel* (089) 921-5141.
🔲 daily. 📷

🏛 **Shiki Masaoka Museum**
3-min walk from Dogo Onsen.
Tel (089) 931-5566. 🔲 Tue–Sun. 📷

🏯 **Matsuyama Castle**
🚋 Kencho-mae stop, then steep walk, or Shinonome-guchi stop, then cable car or lift. *Tel* (089) 921-4873.
🔲 daily. 📷

Exterior of the bathhouse of Dogo Onsen, Matsuyama

Stage of the historic Kabuki Theater in Uchiko

Uchiko ❽
内子

Ehime prefecture. 🚶 20,000. 🚉 ℹ️
Uchiko Preservation (0893) 44-2111.
www.islands.ne.jp/uchiko/e1.html

Located in a small valley where the Oda River splits into three branches, the town of Uchiko is famous for its historic Kabuki theater, the **Uchiko-za**, and its sloping street of two-story wooden buildings with whitewashed walls, tiled roofs, and broad fronts. In 1982 the government moved to ensure the preservation of these structures, which date from the mid-19th century. Several are open to the public, and others function as craft shops and restaurants. The area is often used for location shooting of historical dramas for film and television. A quaint touch is the steam locomotive preserved in front of the station.

Hand-made umbrellas, Uchiko

🎭 **Uchiko-za**
Tel (0893) 44-2840. ◯ *daily.* 📷

Ozu ❾
大洲

Ehime prefecture. 🚶 51,000. 🚉
ℹ️ *at JR stn (0893) 24-2111.*
📷 *Kawa Matsuri Hanabi Taikai (River Festival Fireworks, Aug 3–4).*

A castle town built where the Hiji River snakes in an S-curve through a valley rimmed by picturesque bluffs, Ozu is known to insiders as the "little Kyoto" of Ehime prefecture. However, whereas it could be argued that Kyoto offers well-preserved relics of Japan's past, Ozu offers a past that is still alive. The riverfront is lined by quaint, narrow streets of tile-roofed bars and restaurants with sliding wood shutters. A riverside villa called **Garyu Sanso**, built in 1907, is one of the most spectacular buildings. On the river itself, shallow-bottomed skiffs shunt cormorant fishermen back and forth through the river breezes. Traditional culture is still the norm in Ozu, where raw silk, dairy products, and vegetables form the basis for the local economy. The town's restaurants serve fish and eel caught in nearby rivers.

The panorama of seasonal change is especially vivid in the wooded hillsides of Ozu.

August is marked with a festival of fireworks launched from an islet in the river.

🏯 **Garyu Sanso**
Tel (0893) 24-3759. ◯ *daily.* 📷

Uwajima ❿
宇和島

Ehime prefecture. 🚶 91,000. 🚉
ℹ️ *1 min from stn (0895) 22-3934.*

Uwajima, a harbor town with a castle, old temple district, and mountain setting, is probably best known for its bullfighting, conducted on a system with ranks modeled on Sumo wrestling. The bullfights are held on six days each year, but a video presentation is available year-round at the **Shiei Togyu-jo**.

The **Taga-jinja** shrine has famously sexually explicit statues and other objects associated with fertility.

🏛 **Shiei Togyu-jo**
Tel (0895) 25-3511. ◯ *Mon–Fri for video; bullfights Jan 2, 1st Sun Apr, Jul 24, Aug 14, 2nd Sun Nov.* 📷

Environs:
Uwajima is best appreciated as a hopping-off spot for trips by car, bus, or boat to the nearby islands and beautiful coastal areas. In the mountains northwest of Uwajima, just off Route 320, the **Nametoko Gorge** is noted for its waterfall and fine views.

🎋 **Nametoko Gorge**
ℹ️ *Matsuno tourism dept (0895) 42-2004.*

Grave markers in the old temple district of Uwajima

The 88-Temple Pilgrimage

四国八十八箇所巡礼

When pilgrims retrace the route of Kukai, the
founder of Shingon Buddhism *(see p275)* who
made a pilgrimage of 88 of the island's minor temples
in the 9th century, they are honoring a cultural icon
and hoping some of the magic rubs off. Those who
hope to atone for a grave error complete the
pilgrimage in reverse order; it is believed they will
encounter the saint as they
walk or in their dreams.
In Shingon, 88 represents
the number of evils that can
beset us. About 100,000
pilgrims complete the
circuit each year; countless
others follow part of it.

Popular with tour groups,
Temple 51: Ishite-ji, in Matsu-
yama, is associated with the
legend of a rich man breaking
Kukai's begging bowl.

The birthplace of Kukai *is*
marked by Temple 75:
Zentsu-ji, one stop
from Kotohira.

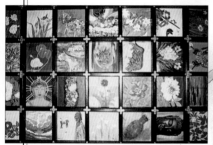

These unusually colorful ceiling paintings
are found at Temple 37: Iwamoto-ji. The 90-
km (55-mile) stretch between this temple and
number 38 is the longest on the circuit.

TIPS FOR PILGRIMS

Length: *About 1,100 km (700 miles).*
Walking time: *average six to eight weeks for*
the whole circuit.
Alternative transportation: *bus tours*
organized by numerous operators take about
a week. Helicopter tours are another option.
Accommodations: *many temples offer*
lodgings and meals to pilgrims for around
¥4,000, and there are numerous inns and
restaurants all along the route.
Official stamps: *pilgrims can collect a series of*
rubber stamps as they visit each temple in turn.
Waymarkers: *signs on rocks and posts are*
mostly in Japanese.
Information: *Tokushima (088) 656-3303.*
Guides for foreign visitors *: Oliver Statler's*
book Japanese Pilgrimage (Tuttle, 1984) has
extensive background. Personal accounts in
English, French, and other languages can be
found on the World Wide Web.

Matsuyama

Yawatahama

Uwajima

Sukumo　　Nakamura

White-robed
pilgrims *are*
called benro,
seen here at
Temple 31,
Chikurin-ji.

Temple 1: Ryozen-ji, *near Naruto, is the start and end of the pilgrimage on Shikoku, though devout pilgrims will extend the start and end to Koya-san (see p199) on Honshu, the headquarters of the Shingon sect. Temple stalls sell the traditional garments for pilgrims: straw hats, white cotton coats, colored sashes, and staves. Visitors sign the book of completion here.*

The Gokuraku *in the name of Temple 2: Gokuraku-ji, refers to the Pure Land, or Western Paradise, of the Amida Buddha, a fundamental concept in Shingon Buddhism.*

Between temples 11 and 12 is an uphill trek notorious as the "pilgrim crusher."

TO KURASHIKI OKAYAMA

Takamatsu

Naruto

Toku-shima

Kochi

Muroto

Incense urn at Temple 24, Hotsumisaki-ji

KEY

▨▨▨ Expressway

═══ Other roads

0 kilometers 25
0 miles 15

Shingon deities *come in both benign and, as this Fudo figure at Temple 27, Kounomine-ji, demonstrates, fierce guises.*

KUKAI (774–835)

Kukai, who was also known as Kobo Daishi (Great Saint) after his death, helped to integrate Buddhism into Japanese life. Sailing to China as a student monk, he returned to found Japan's esoteric Shingon sect. Spending most of his time in the Kansai region of Honshu, he later returned to his native Shikoku to visit some of its temples. His accomplishments were legion: he invented the *kana* syllabary, wrote influential religious treatises, achieved lasting distinction as a poet, calligrapher, and sculptor, wrote Japan's oldest extant dictionary, and founded a school.

Statue of Kukai

KYUSHU

L ong regarded as a backwater by the rest of Japan, the island of Kyushu's history of interaction with China, Southeast Asia, and Europe has, in fact, made it one of Japan's most cosmopolitan and culturally progressive regions. Such diversity creates the sensation, as you journey from prehistoric sites to urban centers like the main city of Fukuoka, of traveling through a microcosm of Japan.

Organized communities settled in Kyushu in the Jomon period (14,500–300 BC). According to legend, it was from Kyushu that the first emperor of Japan, Jimmu, set out on his campaign to unify the country in the 6th century BC. And it was through Kyushu in the 4th century AD that Chinese and Korean culture, including Buddhism and the Chinese writing system, first infiltrated Japan. Not all foreign incursions were welcomed, however. The natives of the island repelled several Mongolian invasions, the last and most formidable in 1274 only by the intervention of a powerful storm, the *kamikaze* (divine wind), which scuttled the Mongolian fleet.

In the 16th century, Christianity, firearms, and medicine were introduced through the port cities of Nagasaki and Kumamoto by the merchants and emissaries of Portugal, Spain, and Holland. Later, during the two centuries of Japan's self-imposed isolation, the tiny island of Dejima off the coast of Nagasaki was the country's sole entrepôt for Western trade and learning.

Taroemon pot from Karatsu

The island landscape is characterized by volcanic activity. Kagoshima lies in the shadow of Sakurajima, which daily belches ash; Mount Aso is the world's largest caldera; and steaming fissures and fumeroles are found at Beppu, Unzen, and other spa towns.

Kyushu is one of the world's foremost ceramic centers. Pottery and porcelain techniques, learned from craftsmen brought from Korea, were perfected at the workshops and kilns of Arita, Imari, and Karatsu.

The island offers the visitor a rich concentration of sights, ranging from feudal castle towns and Shinto mountain shrines to hi-tech museums.

Buddhist figures carved into the cliffs at Usuki

◁ **Boatmen navigating one of the many canals in the town of Yanagawa**

Exploring Kyushu

The northern tip of Kyushu is separated from Honshu only by the narrow Kanmon Straits, less than one kilometer (half a mile) wide in parts. The island's mild climate and geothermal character has created a land of undulating green countryside, ancient volcanic cones, lava spills, hot-spring resorts, and lush, subtropical vegetation.

SEE ALSO

View over the rooftops of the historic port of Nagasaki

SIGHTS AT A GLANCE

Korea Straits

IKI ISLAND

FUKUOKA
202

KARATSU

HIRADO ISLAND

SAGA POTTERY TOWNS TOUR ⑫

204

IMARI

Nagasaki Expressway

YOSHINOGA

34

ARITA

YANAG

Nagasaki Line

NAKADORI ISLAND

206

34

SHIMA PENIN
⑭
MT UNZE
700 m/2,80

NAGASAKI

251

FUKUE ISLAND

AMAKUSA ISLA
324

USHIBUKA

AKUNE   Kago

3

KOSHIKI ISLANDS

KUSHI

CHIK

MAKU

KEY

✈	Airport
═	Expressway
━	Major road
━	Minor road
┅	Bullet train line
━	JR train line
─	Private train line
☼	Viewpoint

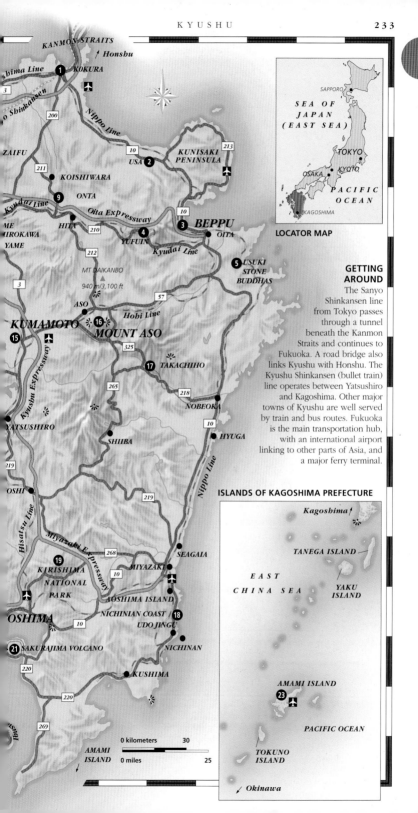

KANMON STRAITS

↗ Honshu

KOKURA

1

3

200

Nippo Line

Shima Line

to Shinkansen

ZAIFU

USA

2

KUNISAKI PENINSULA

213

211

KOISHIWARA

ONTA

9

Kyudai Line

ME
IROKAWA
YAME

HITA

210

Oita Expressway

BEPPU

3

OITA

4

YUFUIN

Kyudai Line

212

USUKI STONE BUDDHAS

5

MT DAIKANBO
940 m/3,100 ft

ASO

Hobi Line

57

KUMAMOTO

15

MOUNT ASO

16

325

TAKACHIHO

17

265

218

NOBEOKA

Kyushu Expressway

YATSUSHIRO

SHIIBA

10

HYUGA

219

Nippo Line

OSHI

219

Hisatsu Line

Miyazaki Expressway

268

SEAGAIA

19

10

MIYAZAKI

KIRISHIMA
NATIONAL
PARK

AOSHIMA ISLAND

NICHINIAN COAST

18

OSHIMA

10

UDO JINGU

SAKURAJIMA VOLCANO

21

NICHINAN

220

KUSHIMA

220

269

AMAMI
ISLAND

0 kilometers   30

0 miles   25

LOCATOR MAP

SEA OF JAPAN (EAST SEA)

SAPPORO

TOKYO

KYOTO

OSAKA

PACIFIC OCEAN

KAGOSHIMA

GETTING AROUND

The Sanyo Shinkansen line from Tokyo passes through a tunnel beneath the Kanmon Straits and continues to Fukuoka. A road bridge also links Kyushu with Honshu. The Kyushu Shinkansen (bullet train) line operates between Yatsushiro and Kagoshima. Other major towns of Kyushu are well served by train and bus routes. Fukuoka is the main transportation hub, with an international airport linking to other parts of Asia, and a major ferry terminal.

ISLANDS OF KAGOSHIMA PREFECTURE

Kagoshima

TANEGA ISLAND

EAST
CHINA SEA

YAKU
ISLAND

AMAMI ISLAND

23

PACIFIC OCEAN

TOKUNO
ISLAND

↗ Okinawa

Gardens surrounding Umi Jigoku, or Ocean Hell, in Beppu

Kokura ❶

小倉

Fukuoka prefecture. 🏠 395,000. 🚆
🛈 Kitakyushu Tourist Information
(093) 541-4151. 🎏 Mekari Shinji
(Shinto ceremony, early Feb); Kokura
Gion Daiko (3rd weekend in Jul).

The gateway to northern
Kyushu, Kokura is also
known as Kita Kyushu. Its
image as a modern city is
embodied in the designs of
architect Arata Isozaki, especially **Chuo Toshokan** (Central
Library, 1974). The city and its
environs – including **Dan no
Ura** battlefield, where the
Taira clan were defeated, and
the straits of **Shimonoseki** –
can be seen in one sweep
from **Kokura Castle** . Next to
the castle, the beautifully laid
out **Kokura Garden**
surrounds a samurai house.

🏛 **Chuo Toshokan**
Nr Kokura Castle. **Tel** (093) 571-1481.
☐ Tue–Sun.

🌿 **Kokura Garden**
Tel (093) 582-2747. ☐ daily. 📷

Usa ❷

宇佐

Oita prefecture. 🏠 62,600. 🚆 🚌
Teiki Kanko bus tour recommended.
🎏 Usa Furusato Matsuri (mid Nov).

The center of Tendai-sect
sanctuaries and shrines
dedicated to Hachiman, the
god of war, the area including
Usa and the Kunisaki Peninsula

is believed to have been the
nucleus of ancient Buddhist
sites of Korean inspiration
and origin. The most famous
site, **Usa Jingu**, a shrine to
the ancient Japanese deities, is
also identified with the influential figure of Hachiman.
   On the peninsula, to the
east of Usa, are stone tombs,
Heian-period statues, and, at
Kumano Magaibutsu, the
largest carved rock-face reliefs
in Japan. The ancient ambience
of the peninsula can be sensed
near the summit of Mount
Futago, where stone guardians
mark the approach to **Futago-
ji**. Twin avatars of the mountain are enshrined at the
temple hall here, built into the
side of a cliff. The oldest religious structure on Kyushu, the
main hall of the **Fuki-ji**, dating
from the Heian period, has
faint, eerily beautiful frescoes
of the Buddhist paradise.

Doorway at the vermilion hall of
Usa Jingu

Beppu ❸

別府

Oita prefecture. 🏠 125,000. ✈ Oita.
🚆 ⛴ from Osaka, Kobe, and
Hiroshima. 🛈 Beppu stn (0977) 24-
2838; also Foreign Tourist Information
Service at stn (0977) 23-1119.
www.city.beppu.oita.jp

If you can accept its brazen
commercialism, Beppu, a
glitzy, neon-strung hot-spring
resort, situated in a wide bay
and visited by over 12 million
tourists a year, constitutes an
amazing thermal and entertainment roller coaster. The
city's porous skin is punctured
by an infinite number of vents
from which steam continuous-
ly rises, making it feel at times
like a huge, malfunctioning
boiler room.
   Scalding water not only surfaces at the 3,750 hot springs
and 168 public baths but is
also piped into private homes
to heat rooms and fuel ovens.
   Beppu offers some interesting variations on the theme of
a hot bath. Visitors can soak
in a series of tubs of graded
temperatures, plunge into
thermal whirlpools, be buried
in hot black sand, or sit up to
the neck in steaming mud.
   The most famous sights are
the **Boiling Hells** (Jigoku) –
pools of mineral-colored water
and bubbling mud. A circuit
of the Nine Hells is recommended; seven of them are
within walking distance of
each other in the Kannawa
district in the north of Beppu.

Each has a different function, color, and mineral property. For example, the waters of Ocean Hell (Umi Jigoku) are the color of a tropical sea, while Blood Pond Hell (Chi-no-Ike Jigoku) takes its color from dissolved red clay. Visitors are shown and sold baskets of eggs that have been lowered into pools for hard-boiling.

Waterwheel at Yufuin Folk Art Village

Many of the baths are attached to hotels but also open to the public. For high kitsch and hilarity, the hugely popular **Suginoi Palace**, on the western fringes of town, is an irresistible hot-spring fantasy. Built in 1879 just inland from Beppu Bay, **Takegawara Bathhouse** is one of Beppu's oldest public baths, in which visitors are buried in black-sand baths before plunging into adjacent hot pools. Up in the hills north of Kannawa, **Myoban Hot Spring** is a quieter place to which Japanese have been coming for well over a thousand years for curative baths. For an overview of Beppu, climb the 125-m (410-ft) **Global Tower**, between the station and Suginoi Palace.

🛁 **Boiling Hells**
Tel (0977) 66-1577. ⭕ *daily.* 🈪

🛁 **Suginoi Palace**
Tel (0977) 24-1160. ⭕ *daily.* 🈪

🛁 **Takegawara Bathhouse**
Tel (0977) 23-1585. ⭕ *daily.* 🈪

🛁 **Myoban Hot Spring**
Tel (0977) 24-2828. ⭕ *daily.* 🈪

Eggs cooking at one of Beppu's Boiling Hells

Yufuin ❹
由布院

Oita prefecture. 🚶 *11,400.* 🚉 🛈 *at JR stn* (0977) 84-2446. 🎬 *Film Festival (late Aug); Music Festival (late Jul).*

Yufuin spa town, known throughout Japan for picturesque wisps of morning mist rising from its thermally warm lake, is located at the foot of Mount Yufudake. In contrast to Beppu, it aspires to be a more refined hot spring, priding itself on elegant country inns, boutiques, summer concerts, and a host of museums and galleries.

Yufuin's more highbrow pretensions are evident from the moment you arrive at **JR Yufuin Station**, a cedarwood construction with a sooty, black exterior intended to suggest the boiler of a locomotive. The station, which was built in 1990 by Arata Isozaki, has art displays in its exhibition hall, and the floors are heated from an underground hot spring.

Serene **Lake Kinrin** is the centerpiece of Yufuin. A walking and cycling path follows the shore, passing through lakeside woods. **Shitan-yu** is an old outdoor bath with a thatched roof beside the lake. The bathing here is mixed, as baths often were before the arrival, during the Meiji period, of Americans and Europeans who shamed the Japanese into segregating their baths.

The **Sueda Art Museum** and the **Yufuin Museum** are both worth visiting for their original postmodernist architecture. A cluster of traditional samurai and thatched-roofed houses, located beside a warm stream, have been carefully converted into a collection of folk-craft galleries at the **Kyushu Yufuin Folk Art Village**. It contains a museum of crafts, and local artisans can be seen at work making ceramics, toys, and glassware, among other items. There is also an indigo dyeing house and a miso factory.

🏛 **Sueda Art Museum**
Tel (0977) 85-3572. ⭕ *daily.* 🈪

🏛 **Yufuin Museum**
Tel (0977) 85-3525. ⭕ *Wed–Mon.* 🈪

🏯 **Yufuin Folk Art Village**
Tel (0977) 85-2288. ⭕ *daily.* 🈪 ·

Usuki Stone Buddhas ❺
臼杵石仏

Oita prefecture. 🚉 *Usuki stn, then JR bus to Usuki-Sekibutsu.* 🛈 *(0972) 63-1111.* 🈪

Despite the wide dissemination of images of Oita's Seki Butsu (stone Buddhas) throughout Japan, the site itself is, fortunately, only a minor tourist area. Although some realignment and fissuring has been caused by centuries of earth tremors in the area, the 60 or more consummately carved Buddhas at Usuki remain remarkably intact.

Though it is probable that the work was begun during the late

One of the Usuki stone Buddhas

Heian period and completed in the early Kamakura era, there appears to be no consensus regarding the origin of the site, who commissioned or executed the carvings, or why such a large, relatively remote area was dedicated for the images.

All of this adds a great deal of mystery and charm to the place. Late afternoon is very atmospheric, when sculptured sunlight draws out the earth hues from the faces and torsos of these mysterious and peaceful Buddhas.

Riverside view of the Nakasu district, Fukuoka

Fukuoka ❻

福岡

Fukuoka prefecture. 🏯 *1,367,000.* ✈
🚆 ℹ *Hakata stn (092) 431-3003;*
Rainbow Plaza, IMZ Bldg, Tenjin (092)
733-2220. **www.***city.fukuoka.jp/*
index-e.html 📅 *Hakata Dontaku Matsuri*
(May 3–4); Yamagasa Matsuri (Jul 1–15).

Strikingly modern, Fukuoka
bills itself as the gateway
to southern Japan. Divided in
two by the Naka River, the
city is also known as Hakata,
a name deriving from its first
mercantile district. Eschewing
the heavy manufacturing industries of nearby Kokura in favor
of administration, wholesaling,
and distribution, Japan's closest
city to mainland Asia has, for at
least a millennium, been the
country's main port of entry for
Chinese and Korean culture.
This has lent it an attractive
foreign Asian flavor that the
local government is eager to
exploit. **Tenjin**, to the west of
the river, is the city's commercial and shopping district,
while **Nakasu**, just to
the east of the river, is
an entertainment
district with over 3,000
nightclubs, restaurants,
and bars. **Fukuoka
Yahoo Dome** is a large
baseball stadium with a
12,000-ton retractable
roof. The stadium is also
used for rock concerts.

A newer feature of
the city is **Momochi**,
a waterfront develop-
ment, dominated by
the **Fukuoka Tower**
and the massive resort
of **Hawks Town**. The nearby
Fukuoka City Museum has
exhibits tracing the relationship
between the city and its Asian
neighbors, including a gold 3rd
century Chinese seal Chinese.

Despite its modernity,
Fukuoka also has religious
sights of impressive antiquity.
Shofuku-ji, northwest of
Hakata station, is said to be
the oldest Zen Buddhist temple
in Japan. It was founded in
the late 12th century by the
priest Eisai, who introduced
both Zen and tea to Japan.

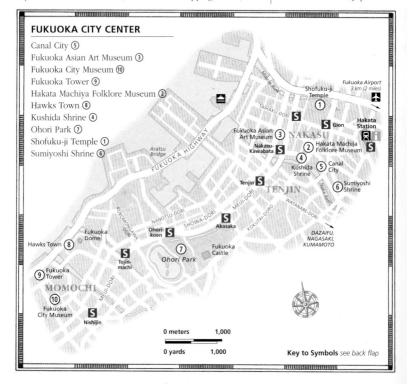

FUKUOKA CITY CENTER

Canal City ⑤
Fukuoka Asian Art Museum ③
Fukuoka City Museum ⑩
Fukuoka Tower ⑨
Hakata Machiya Folklore Museum ②
Hawks Town ⑧
Kushida Shrine ④
Ohori Park ⑦
Shofuku-ji Temple ①
Sumiyoshi Shrine ⑥

Fukuoka Airport
3 km (2 miles)

Shofuku-ji
Temple ①

Hakata
Station

Gion

Fukuoka Asian ③
Art Museum NAKASU

Nakasu-
Kawabata ② Hakata Machiya
Folklore Museum

④ ⑤ Canal
Kushida City
Shrine

Tenjin ⑥ Sumiyoshi
Shrine
TENJIN

Aratsu
Bridge

FUKUOKA HIGHWAY

TAIHAKU-DORI

MEIJI-DORI

WATANABE-DORI

Akasaka

Ohori-
koen

NANOTSU-DORI

SHOWA-DORI

KOKUTAI-DORI

DAZAIFU,
NAGASAKI,
KUMAMOTO

Fukuoka
Dome

Hawks Town ⑧

Fukuoka ⑦
Castle

⑨ Fukuoka
Tower

Tojin-
machi

Ohori Park

MOMOCHI

⑩
Fukuoka
City Museum

Nishijin

| 0 meters | 1,000 |
| 0 yards | 1,000 |

Key to Symbols *see back flap*

The **Kushida Shrine**, just to the west, dates from the 8th century and displays one of the Yamagasa festival floats. Almost opposite is the **Hakata Machiya Folklore Museum**, its exhibits and dioramas within this traditional building celebrating the heritage of the area. It is also possible to watch local artisans at work here, including demonstrations of Hakata silk weaving.

A huge and vibrant shopping mall in the center of town, **Canal City**, features sleek shops in a setting of hanging gardens and exploding fountains, a variety theater, and a 13-screen cinema complex. The **Asian Art Museum** holds an interesting collection of contemporary Asian art.

On a hillside southwest of Hakata station, **Sumiyoshi Shrine**, dotted with cedar and camphor trees, contains a working Noh theater. The city hosts a sumo tournament here in mid-November. In the southwest, **Ohori Park** is the city's most popular green space, with delightful pathways, lakes, pavilions, and islets connected by traditional bridges.

Fukuoka is regarded as one of the best places to eat in Japan and is celebrated for its *yatai*. These sit-down food stalls are legendary, with their colorful, lamp-lit stalls serving steaming bowls of buckwheat noodles and open-pot stews.

A Shinto priest inside the shrine of Dazaifu Tenman-gu

🏛 **Fukuoka City Museum**
Tel (092) 845-5011. ⬜ Tue–Sun. 📷

🏛 **Hakata Machiya Folklore Museum**
Tel (092) 281-7761. **S** Gion stn. ⬜ daily. 📷

🏛 **Asian Art Museum**
Tel (092) 263-1100. **S** Nakasu-Kawabata stn. ⬜ Thu–Tue. 📷

Dazaifu ❼

太宰府

Fukuoka prefecture. 🏠 67,000. 🚉 🛈 at Nishitetsu-Dazaifu stn (092) 925-1880. 🎎 Usokae (Bullfinch Exchange, Jan 7); Sentomyo Festival (Jul 25 and Sep 25).

Dazaifu was of military importance under the Yamato government *(see p187)* and an administrative center in the later Nara period. Most visitors come here today to visit the shrine of **Dazaifu Tenman-gu**. Located in a tranquil district close to the station, the shrine is dedicated to the calligrapher, scholar, and poet Sugawara Michizane. The guardian of learning, Michizane, who died in AD 903, is also known by his divine name of Tenjin. The shrine is a site of pilgrimage for students who pray for success in their exams, writing their wishes on small, votive wooden boards *(ema)*. The Treasure House can be visited, and just behind it a hall displays curious tableaux of Hakata clay dolls representing scenes in Michizane's life.

The nearby **Kyushu National Museum** opened in 2005 and focuses on the interaction of Japan with other Asian countries. Exhibits include 75 hand-drawn Edo period *Um sum* cards depicting Japanese and Chinese customs.

Visitors can also enjoy a stroll around the stone, sand, and moss garden of the nearby temple, **Komyo Zen-ji**. Ten minute's walk away, **Kyushu History Museum** has some good displays of Jomon-, Yayoi-, and Kofun-period items excavated at Dazaifu.

Kanzeon-ji, a temple to the southwest of the station, contains a great bell and a number of highly prized statues, including an unusual horse-headed Kannon.

⛩ **Dazaifu Tenman-gu Shrine**
Tel (092) 922-8225. ⬜ Tue–Sun. 📷 (for Treasure House).

🏛 **Kyushu National Museum**
Tel (092) 918-2807. ⬜ Tue–Sun. 📷

🏛 **Kyushu History Museum**
Tel (092) 923-0404. ⬜ Tue–Sun.

Statue of a bull near the shrine of Dazaifu Tenman-gu

A detail from the festival float at Kushida Shrine, Fukuoka

Kurume ❽
久留米

Fukuoka prefecture. 🚹 305,600. 🚉
🛈 (0942) 30-9137. 🎋 Suiten-gu
Spring Festival (May 5–7); Mizu-no-
Saiten (water festival, Aug 3–5).

The unattractive, sprawling
city of Kurume is the
center of *kasuri* textiles. These
employ a distinctive ikat weaving style, in which the threads
have been tie-dyed before
weaving; unlike Southeast
Asian forms of ikat, both the
warp and weft are patterned.
The **Kurume Regional
Industry Promotion Center**
has a superb display and sells
kasuri textiles.
Rantai-shikki is a
local basket-
weaving style
whereby layers
of lacquer are
applied to bam-
boo to produce
attractive, durable
basketware.
Examples can be
bought at **Inoue
Rantai-Shikki**,
opposite the
Honmachi-yon-
chome bus stop.
The **Ishibashi
Bunka Center**, a
five-minute bus ride from the
station, has an art museum and
Japanese garden. By the river
is the **Suiten-gu**, the head
shrine of a popular sect.

Kasuri cloth from
Kurume

🏭 **Kurume Regional
Industry Promotion Center**
2nd flr, Jibasan Kurume Center.
Tel (0942) 44-3700. ○ daily.

🏛 **Ishibashi Bunka Center**
Tel (0942) 33-2271. ○ Tue–Sun.

Environs:
Many artisans work in the
villages of **Hirokawa** and
Yame, a 40-minute bus ride
from Kurume. In Hirokawa,
the **Workshop of Moriyama
Torao** is well worth a visit.
Paper-making, using mulberry-
tree fibers, dates from the 16th
century. Traditional cauldrons
can still be seen in use at
Yamaguchi Seishijo paper
workshop in Yame.

🏭 **Workshop of Moriyama
Torao** **Tel** (0943) 32-0023 (reservation
required). ○ Mon–Sat. 📷

A boatman plying one of Yanagawa's canals

Onta ❾
小鹿田

Oita prefecture. 🚹 60. 🚉 Hita, then
bus. 🛈 (0973) 23-3111. 🎋 Onta
Pottery Festival (2nd weekend in Oct).

Tucked into a wooded
mountain valley, this tiny
village has been producing
Onta-ware since a group of
Korean potters set up their
kilns here in 1705. Later lumi-
naries of the *mingei* (folk craft)
movement, such as Yanagi
Soetsu and Bernard Leach,
praised Onta-ware for its unpretentious rustic quality. The
kilns, dug into the hillside
and water-powered, are still
used. Ten families have converted their homes into open
galleries. The simple, functional
objects are characterized by
marked, dribbled glazes in
earth colors.

Potter at work in Onta

Yanagawa ❿
柳川

Fukuoka prefecture. 🚹 75,300. 🚉
🛈 Inari-machi (0944) 73-2145.
🎋 Dorotsukudon Matsuri (early Oct).

The Stone Quays of Yana-
gawa are not as busy as
they used to be, but the canals
and old moats that run through
this former castle town are

still vital to its economy.
Visitors can board gondolas
to glide past old samurai villas
and storehouses. The canals
are at their best in spring.
Other Yanagawa sights in-
clude **Suiten-gu**, a pretty shrine
used by the same sect as the
shrine in Kurume; **Toshi-
mashi-tei**, an Edo-period tea
garden; and a house-museum,
Hakushu Seika, the birthplace
of Kitahara Hakushu (1885–
1942), a prolific writer best
known for children's poems.

🏠 **Hakushu Seika**
Tel (0944) 72-6773. ○ daily. 📷

Yoshinogari
Archaeological
Site ⓫
吉野ヶ里遺跡

Saga prefecture. 🚉 Yoshinogari-koen,
then 15-min walk or take taxi.
🛈 (0952) 55-9333. ○ daily.

Pit dwellings and hundreds
of burial urns excavated at
Yoshinogari point to the existence of a sophisticated Yayoi-
period society (300 BC–AD
300) in the region. Irrigation
systems and rice cultivation
were begun in this
period, laying the
pattern for later
Japanese society.
The area is
believed by
some to be the
home of Queen
Himiko, men-
tioned in 3rd-
century Chinese
annals. Watch-
towers and Yayoi-
period homes
have been re-
constructed.

Urn in the mus
at Yoshinoga

For hotels and restaurants in this region see pp309–11 and pp342–4

Saga Pottery Towns Tour ⑫

佐賀県陶器生産地

Ceramics enthusiasts will have a field day in Saga prefecture, where pottery towns have been producing high-quality wares for at least 500 years. Korean potters were brought to Kyushu in the 1590s and given sovereign control over the kilns they set up. The three main pottery towns – Arita, Imari, and Karatsu – are all within convenient distances of each other, and provide access to other interesting destinations nearby.

Imari ④
Imari porcelain was exported in the 17th century via the Dutch East India Company to Europe where it was highly prized. Today much Imari-ware is produced in the kilns of Okawachi-yama, a nearby village.

Yobuko ⑥
In this fishing town, the daily produce market includes stalls devoted to good-quality ceramics that are reasonably priced.

Karatsu ⑤
Karatsu-ware resembles Korean pottery and is much sought after by tea ceremony practitioners. The Nakazato Taroemon Kiln is run by descendants of the first Korean potters who lived here.

Arita ③
This small town has ceramic-decorated bridges, a shrine to potters, and dozens of kilns. The Kyushu Ceramic Museum gives an overview of the range of the region's pottery.

0 kilometer ——— 10

0 miles ——— 5

Sea caverns

Chinzei ⑥

KARATSU BAY

204

MAEBARU AND FUKUOKA

Furuyu Onsen

Kuahata-mura

Matsuura River

Arita River

202

TAKU

Nagasaki Expressway

Ushizu ②

34

OGORI

④

Nishiarita ③

35

Rokkaku River

Takeo

SASEBO

Saga City ②
The 170,000-strong prefecture capital hosts a major annual balloon competition in November.

KEY

▬ Tour route by car

═ Other roads

☼ Viewpoint

Yoshinogari ①
This site, with its 2,500-year-old ceramics and reconstructed buildings, is a good starting point for the tour.

Nagasaki ⑬

長崎

Statue in Sofuku-ji Temple

A history of contact and interaction with Europe, its tragic fate as victim of the second atomic bomb, and miraculous resurgence since the war have made Nagasaki one of the most cosmopolitan and eclectic cities in Japan. After the Portuguese were expelled from the country in 1638, the Dutch, confined to the tiny island of Dejima, were the only foreign power permitted to remain throughout Japan's long period of self-imposed isolation. When Japan opened its doors to foreigners in 1854, Nagasaki thrived once more as a center of Western trade and culture.

Figures carved on the façade of the shrine to the 26 Martyrs

Ornate red gateway leading into Nagasaki's Chinatown

Getting Around Nagasaki

Despite the encroachments of modern industry, Nagasaki – with its magnificent harbor setting, meandering streets, and beautiful terraced slopes – is a city of which its inhabitants are roundly proud. Although the main sights are fairly scattered, signs in English and well-marked walking routes make Nagasaki an easily navigable city. Surprisingly inexpensive streetcars are the easiest means of transportation with four main lines running through the center of the city. Organized bus tours provide another perspective on the city. The main concentration of shops, restaurants, and nightspots is to the southeast of Nagasaki Station in the Hamanmachi arcade district, while the Peace Park, an essential place of pilgrimage for any visitor to Nagasaki, lies to the north of the station. Chinatown, once an artificial island but now attached to the mainland, is located in the district of Shinchi. Shrines, temples, and churches are scattered between.

🔼 Shrine to the 26 Martyrs

5-min walk N of stn.

Christianity was officially banned in 1587 by the shogun Toyotomi Hideyoshi who feared that conversions would lead to political intrigues and the undermining of the state by foreign powers. In that year, to emphasize the point, 26 defiant, Christians were rounded up and crucified on Nishizaka Hill, the first of over 600 documented martyrdoms in the Nagasaki area alone.

A short walk from the station leads to the shrine built on the site of the martyrdom. A stone relief, a small chapel, and a museum honor the martyrs who, in 1862, were declared saints by the pope. The museum's treasures include letters by Saint Francis Xavier. Without a clergy or a single chapel to worship in, Christianity, astonishingly, managed to survive covertly for 200 years after the martyrdoms until the end of Japan's isolationism.

NAGASAKI CITY CENTER

🏠 Dejima

🔲 Dejima. **Dejima Museum & Dutch Factory Historic Site**
Tel (0958) 21-7200.
⬜ daily. 📷
The old Dutch enclave of Dejima was once surrounded by mud walls, and the only people allowed to enter were traders, prostitutes, and monks collecting alms. **Dejima Museum**, which is housed in Japan's first Protestant seminary, and **Dejima Dutch**

Inner gate detail at the temple of Sofuku-ji

① Suwa Shrine

Suwa-jinja-mae

Nagasaki Museum of History and Culture
⑫

Nakashima River

Kofuku-ji Temple
②

Spectacles Bridge

J-DORI
TERAMACHI-DORI

MOMACHI
Daion-ji Temple

Shianbashi

ANBASHI

Sofuku-ji Temple
③

Shokaku-ji-shita

0 meters 250

0 yards 250

Key to Symbols *see back flap*

Factory Historic Site next door contain historical artifacts from excavations on the site. Nearby is the **Nagasaki Art Museum**, featuring the Suma collection of Spanish art.

🏠 Spectacles Bridge

🔲 Nigiwaibashi, Kokaidomae.
One of the most photographed sights of Nagasaki is the modest but curious Spectacles Bridge (Megane-bashi), a Chinese bequest to the city. Built by the Chinese Zen priest Mozi in 1634, it remains the oldest stone bridge in Japan. The curve of the bridge reflected in the Nakashima River resembles a pair of spectacles.

About 10 minutes' walk north from here is the **Nagasaki Museum of History and Culture**, featuring exhibits such as crime notebooks from the city's magistrate's office and "trample tablets" used in Christian persecution.

🏯 Sofuku-ji Temple

Sofuku-ji-dori. 🔲 Shokakuji-shita. 📷
The Chinese provenance of this temple is proclaimed in the entrance gate. This depicts the gateway that, according to legend, is to be seen in the Chinese undersea paradise. A second, more illustrious gate known as First Peak Gate farther into the temple precinct has been designated a National Treasure of the late Ming period. Also worth seeing is the Treasure Hall.

Sofuku-ji is one of the three largest Chinese places of worship in Nagasaki. The temple was founded, with the help of local Chinese residents, by a monk from Fukien province in 1629. The gigantic cooking pot that stands enigmatically in the temple grounds was

used to make gruel to feed over 3,000 people each day during one of Nagasaki's worst famines in 1682. A fascinating 20-minute walk north from here along narrow streets leads to Kofuku-ji

🏯 Kofuku-ji Temple

Teramachi-dori. 🔲 Kokaidomae. 📷
Kofuku-ji, located at the heart of the Teramachi district, was Japan's first Obaku Zen Buddhist temple. Founded by a Chinese priest in 1623, the building is also known as the Nanking Temple and is often visited by residents from that city. The main buildings, including the Buddha hall, are constructed in Chinese style.

⛩ Suwa Shrine

Kaminishiyama-dori. 🔲 Suwa Jinjamae.
Located in a wooded hilltop precinct at the top of 227 stone steps, Suwa Shrine affords fine harbor views. The original buildings were destroyed by fire in 1857 but later beautifully restored. The purpose of this popular shrine, home to the city's pantheon of Shinto gods, was to promote Shintoism and eradicate the last vestiges of Christianity from the area. The autumn festival, Kunchi Matsuri, is celebrated here, with blazing floats and dragon dances.

The Chinese-style Buddha hall in the temple of Kofuku-ji

Exploring Nagasaki

To the north and south of the city center there are many sights of interest, most of them reflecting the diverse foreign influences that have shaped Nagasaki. For a view of the city take a boat trip from Ohato Pier, or, better still, cross the harbor and take the ropeway to the lookout tower on the summit of Mount Isa.

View over Glover Park, with its 19th-century colonial-style residences

⚏ Confucian Shrine

🎌 Oura Tenshudo. 🖼

Vibrant yellow roof tiles and vermilion walls instantly announce this building as a shrine dedicated to the scholar Confucius. Built by the Chinese community in 1893, the repairs and extensions accorded the shrine after it was damaged in the atomic bombing included the addition in 1982 of a National Museum of Chinese History. The antiquities on display are on loan from the Chinese National Museum and the prestigious Palace Museum in Beijing.

♣ Glover Park

🎌 Oura Tenshudo Shita.
◯ daily. 🖼

With the reopening of the port to Westerners in the latter half of the 19th century, Nagasaki flowered as a prosperous and sophisticated international city. Suitable housing was required for the sudden influx of foreigners who made their homes here. Many of the comfortable stone and clapboard residencies that were built during this period survive today, preserved in Glover Park, overlooking Nagasaki harbor. The best-known European-style residence here is **Glover House**. Built in 1863, it was the setting for Puccini's opera *Madame Butterfly*. Thomas Glover, who was responsible for bringing the first steam locomotive to Japan, was an extraordinary British entrepreneur whose ventures included coal mining, a tea import house, ship repair yards, and the founding of a beer company, the forerunner of today's Kirin Beer.

Statue of Petitjean, Oura church

Other notable buildings in the park include **Ringer House**, standing on foundation stones brought from Vladivostok, and **Walker House**, with a private garden and hall displaying the colorful floats used in the annual Kunchi festival. The **Old Hong Kong and Shanghai Bank Building** is a restored stone structure that now houses displays tracing Nagasaki's contact with Western ideas.

✝ Oura Catholic Church

🎌 Oura Tenshudo Shita. 🖼

This white church was built in 1864 under the direction of Bernard Petitjean, a French priest who became the first Bishop of Nagasaki. The church, which boasts some impressive stained-glass windows, was erected in order to serve the foreign community that settled in Nagasaki after the new trade treaties were signed. It was also intended to honor the city's 26 martyred saints. Shortly after its foundation, Father Petitjean was approached by members of a group of Japanese Christians who had practiced their faith in secret and at risk for over 200 years.

Classed as a National Treasure, Oura is one of the oldest churches in Japan and the country's earliest Gothic wooden structure. A wooden building beside the church contains items connected with the persecution of Nagasaki's early Christians.

⛩ Hollander Slope

🎌 Shimin-Byoin-mae.

A pleasant cobblestone street built by the Dutch, the Slope was once the center for the city's expatriate community. For a time, all Westerners, irrespective of nationality, were called "Hollanders" by the Japanese. Some of the wooden houses along the Slope are open to the public. One of the most imposing, the 1868 **Junibankan**, was once the Prussian Legation building.

Interior of the Atomic Bomb Museum

Tulips by the canal in Huis Ten

♣ Peace Park
Matsuyama-machi.
A black stone pillar marks the spot where the US detonated its second atom bomb at 11:02 on August 9, 1945, three days after Hiroshima. The intended target was the nearby ship-yards. The blast killed an estimated 75,000, while 75,000 more were injured in its wake. Small wonder that the citizens of Nagasaki have become staunch advocates of world peace, erecting several monuments in the park, including a 9-m (30-ft) tall Peace Statue. A 1959 reconstruction of the **Urakami Catholic Church**, which stood at the epicenter, stands near the park.

✿ Atomic Bomb Museum
Tel (095) 844-1231. ◯ *daily.*
This museum is a must for anybody visiting the city. Displays depict Nagasaki before and after the explosion and also the reconstruction. It traces with great objectivity and

fairness the events leading up to the bombing, the history of nuclear weapons, and the evolution of the peace movement. Photographs, artifacts, videos, and dioramas vividly re-create the event. A clock, frozen at the moment the bomb exploded, is one of the most poignant items.

⬛ Huis ten Bosch
Near Sasebo. ◻ *Huis ten Bosch.* **Tel** (0956) 27-0001. ◯ *daily.*
Built in 1992 at the staggering cost of US$1.75 billion, Huis ten Bosch is a reproduction of a traditional Dutch village. Replete with churches, houses, shops, windmills, a farmhouse, and canals, it is one of the largest theme parks in Japan. Replicas of Queen Beatrix's palace and of Holland's tallest church tower are highlights. Horse-drawn carriages, old-fashioned taxis, and canal boats complete the picture.

➤ Penguin Aquarium
◻ *From Nagasaki stn to Suizokukan-mae.* **Tel** (095) 838-3131. ◯ *daily.*
Children and adults will enjoy this aquarium, which has a huge 4-m (13-ft) deep pool for the penguins to frolic in. There are seven different types of penguin here.

The scenic Nita Pass in the Shimabara peninsula

Shimabara Peninsula ⓮
島原半島

Nagasaki prefecture. ◻ *Shimabara city.* 🚢 *from Kumamoto.* ℹ *Unzen Spa (0957) 73-3434; Shimabara City Hall (0957) 63-1111.*

Ruled until 1616 by the Christian Lord Arima, Shimabara peninsula is known as the site of anti-Christian pogroms ordered by the Tokugawa shogunate. However, in the 1880s, **Unzen Spa** became a resort for Westerners. At an altitude of 700 m (2,300 ft) and surrounded by pine forests, it was an ideal retreat from the summer heat. Thousands of azaleas bloom in the peninsula in spring, and in autumn the maple leaves turn brilliant shades of red. In 1934 the **Unzen-Amakusa National Park**, Japan's first such protected area, was created.

Most hotels in Unzen Spa have their own hot-spring baths. Visitors in a more somber mood can see the notorious **Hells** (Jigoku): scalding sulfurous cauldrons in which 30 Christians were boiled alive after the outlawing of Christianity in Japan. As a demonstration of the ferocity of the waters in the Hells, elderly ladies in bonnets and smocks lower eggs placed in baskets into the pools and sell them hard-boiled to tourists.

Mount Unzen, thought to be dormant until one of its peaks erupted in 1991, can be climbed from the Nita Pass, reached by bus from Unzen.

FOREIGNERS IN NAGASAKI
The Portuguese and Dutch were the first to arrive when the harbor opened to international trade in 1571, followed by Chinese merchants who established their own community. Portuguese cargos of guns and Catholicism, however, foreshadowed Kyushu's troubled history of rebellion and persecution. Only the Dutch were allowed to trade between 1638 and 1854. After the port reopened, British, American, French, German, and Prussian trade missions came to the city. The legacy of this extraordinary foreign contact survives in some of the local festivals and cuisine, like the Portuguese *castella*, an egg and flour mixture, and the Chinese *champon* noodles, invented in 1899.

Replica of the 17th-century Dutch cargo ship *Prince Willem*

The eaves and roofs of Kumamoto Castle, one of the great fortresses of Japan

Kumamoto ⑮

熊本

Kumamoto prefecture. 🏠 *669,600.* ✈ 🚉 ℹ *(096) 352-3743.* www.city.kumamoto.kumamoto.jp/ 🎎 *Hinokuni Matsuri (Fire Festival, Aug 11–13); Fujisaki Hachiman-gu Shuki Reitaisai (Sep 11–15); Kumamoto Oshiro Matsuri (Kumamoto Castle Festival, mid-Oct–Nov 3).*

A city with a small-town atmosphere, a mild climate, and semitropical flora, Kumamoto was an important seat of power during the Tokugawa shogunate (1603–1868). Its star attraction, one of the largest castles in Japan, dates from this period. The city's main shopping precinct and sights are compressed into an area south of Kumamoto castle, the original location of merchants' and artisans' quarters attached to the castle.

The longevity of Kumamoto's feisty residents (the city has numerous centenarians) is ascribed to a passion for living and a healthy diet. The latter includes *karashi renkon* (deep-fried lotus root stuffed with mustard miso) and various brands of sake made from water supposedly purified by the area's rich volcanic soil.

Dominating the center of the city from an imposing hill, **Kumamoto Castle** was constructed on the orders of Kato Kiyomasa, a warrior who

fought alongside Tokugawa Ieyasu at the decisive Battle of Sekigahara in 1600. He was rewarded for his loyalty with lands encompassing most of present-day Kumamoto. The castle was completed in 1607 – a hard seven-year undertaking. Unlike more decorative castles such as Himeji *(see pp206–209),* Kumamoto's citadel is stridently martial in appearance with steep, almost impregnable walls. The original structure had 49 towers and 29 gates, but it was almost completely destroyed during the Seinan War in 1877. Although the main keep was reconstructed on a smaller scale using ferroconcrete in 1960, it is a highly effective replica, successfully evoking the fearsome magnificence of the original.

Gyobu-tei, a 300-year-old residence owned by Lord Gyobu, is located a little northwest of the castle grounds. It presents insights into the way the feudal elite lived during the Edo period.

The family possessions of the powerful Kato and Hosokawa clans can be found near the castle in the **Kumamoto Prefectural Art Museum,** a distinctive modern building with a pleasant tea room. The museum also has interesting replicas of ancient burial mounds and archaeological finds from the region.

Suizen-ji Garden, Kumamoto's other main attraction, was laid out by the Hosokawa family in 1632 as the grounds for a detached villa. With a central spring-fed lake, it is a classic stroll garden *(see pp30–31).* Its representational designs are not labeled and not always apparent. They include scenes in miniature from the 53 stages of the old Tokaido Highway and outlines of Lake Biwa and Mount Fuji.

Kumamoto is renowned for its crafts, especially damascene inlay designs, Amakusa pearls, and Yamage lanterns. These lanterns, made from gold paper, are a feature of the city's festival in August. The **Kumamoto Traditional Crafts Center** has a good selection of these local crafts.

🏯 **Kumamoto Castle**
Tel (096) 352-5900.
◯ daily. 🎫

🏯 **Gyobu-tei**
Tel (096) 352-6522.
◯ daily. 🎫

🏛 **Kumamoto Prefectural Art Museum**
Tel (096) 352-2111.
◯ Tue–Sun. 🎫

🌸 **Suizen-ji Garden**
Tel (096) 383-0074.
◯ daily. 🎫

🏮 **Kumamoto Traditional Crafts Center**
Tel (096) 324-4930. ◯ Tue–Sun. 🎫 for 2nd flr

Guard on duty outside the castle

Mount Aso ⑯

阿蘇山

Kumamoto prefecture. 🚉 *Aso, then bus.* 🚌 *Kyushu Kokusai Kanko sightseeing bus from Beppu or Kumamoto.* 🎎 *Aso-no-hi Matsuri (Aso Fire Festival), Kuginomura (mid-Mar).*

Actually a series of five volcanic cones, Mount Aso is the world's largest caldera, with a circumference of 130 km (80 miles). Of the five peaks, **Mount Daikanbo,** at about 940 m (3,100 ft), is the highest. **Mount Nakadake** is still active, emitting sulfurous fumes and hot gases, earning

Blocks of sulfuric rock on sale at the top of the Nakadake cable car

The fuming crater of Nakadake, one of the five volcanic cones in the Mount Aso caldera

Kumamoto the epithet *hi-no-kuni* ("the land of fire").

Below these peaks, the caldera is dotted with towns set among forests, grasslands, bamboo groves, and hot springs. Arriving tour buses pass a curious, grass-covered mountain resembling an inverted rice bowl, aptly named **Komezuka** (Rice Mound), and often stop at the pretty **Kusasenri Meadow**.

A cable car runs to the top of Nakadake, providing, on clear days, awesome views into the depths of the crater and its malodorous green lake. Hikers can follow a path to the summit for a closer look. A popular hiking route starts at the top of the ropeway, proceeds to **Mount Takadake** around the crater rim, and descends to **Sensuikyo Gorge**.

Mount Aso Volcanic Museum, at the base of Nakadake, offers a fascinating preview of the mountain even when the crater is closed due to a high level of dangerous, sulfuric fumes. Two cameras on the crater wall relay continuous images of the cone's volcanic activity.

🎦 **Mount Aso Volcanic Museum**
Tel (0967) 34-2111. ⬜ *daily.* ⬛

Takachiho ⓱

高千穂

Miyazaki prefecture. 🚶 15,038. 🚉
ℹ️ (0982) 73-1212. 🎎 Amano Iwato Shrine Festival (May 2–3, Sep 22–23); Yo-Kagura Kokai Festival (Nov 22–23).

The Takachiho mountain region, a place of homage for those with an affection for Japan's ancient pantheon of gods and goddesses, is alive with the resonances of legend.

Most of the sights on or around the 1,575-m (5,150-ft) mountain, sanctified by Shintoism, are connected with Japan's rich mythology. Kagura, a mime-dance said to have been first performed by the Sun Goddess Amaterasu Omikami, is thought to have originated here.

Shrine in the Mount Aso caldera

The cave into which Amaterasu vanished, casting the world into a temporary gloom until she could be lured out, faces **Ama no Iwato Jingu**, a pavilion-style shrine noted for a sacred tree that stands in its grounds. A short walk from here, **Ama no Yasugawara** is the grotto where the gods are supposed to have convened in order to devise a way to entice the Sun Goddess from her lair. The entrance to the cavern is next to a clear, pebble-strewn river. Many visitors have placed miniature cairns there in the hope that, by association, some of the wisdom and power of the gods will rub off on them.

The area's main shrine, **Takachiho Jinja** is famous for its ancient cryptomeria trees, a common feature of Japanese shrines and temple grounds. The shrine stages nightly extracts of Kagura lasting half an hour and giving a rare opportunity to witness a performance in such atmospheric surroundings. Visitors usually try to factor into their itinerary a rowboat trip along **Takachiho Gorge**, with its scenic rock formations and waterfalls.

Waterfall in the picturesque Takachiho Gorge

Horse and sightseers dwarfed by a large eruption of smoke and ash at Mount Aso ▷

Udo Jingu, a cave shrine on the Nichinan Coast dedicated to fertility

Nichinan Coast ⑱

日南海岸

Miyazaki prefecture. 🚉 Nichinan line from Miyazaki.

The Nichinan coastal landscape is known in Japanese as Onino Sentakuita, the "devil's washboard," an apt description for the eroded, rippled effect presented by the rock shelves.

The gateway to the coast is **Aoshima Island**, barely a mile in circumference and connected to the mainland by a walkway. An attractive vermilion shrine stands at the center of this densely forested islet, which can get crowded in summertime. **Miyazaki** city, to the north, is known for its year-round flowers.

Udo Jingu, another vermilion-colored shrine about 30 km (20 miles) south of Aoshima, stands in a cave beside the ocean. The shrine is dedicated to Emperor Jimmu's father, who is believed to have been washed there at birth, and serves as a catalyst for propitious marriages and fertility. The water dripping from breast-shaped rocks is compared to mother's milk, and milk candies are sold at the shrine shop. North of Udo Jingu is **Sun-Messe Nichinan**, where perfectly reproduced statues of Moai, officially approved by Easter Island, are displayed. One stop farther on the Nichinan line lies **Obi**, an old castle town, where the ruins of the castle and samurai houses may be visited. Farther south, **Ishinami Beach** is a stretch of fine white sand.

Kirishima National Park ⑲

霧島国立公園

Miyazaki and Kagoshima prefectures. 🚉 Kobayashi or Ebino Iino stn (JR Nippo line), then Miyazaki Kotsu bus.

This region, identified with Japanese foundation myths, centers on the volcanic plateau of **Ebino-Kogen** (Shrimp Meadow), which is surrounded by volcanoes, crater lakes, and hot springs. The Ebino-Kogen Nature Trail is the best of several hiking routes, going past three ponds, two of which are cobalt blue. The climb up to the peak of Mount Karakunidake is popular in summer. Two hot springs, **Ebino-Kogen Rotenburo** (in a beautiful location) and **Hayashida Onsen**, are the main tourist centers of the region.

Kagoshima ⑳

鹿児島

Kagoshima prefecture. 👥 604,396. ✈️ 🚉 🚌 from Osaka and Nagasaki. 🛈 at stn (099) 253-2500. www. city.kagoshima.lg.jp 🎏 Soga-don no Kasayaki (4th Sat in Jul).

With one of the most stunning settings of any city in Japan, Kagoshima looks out across the broad sweep of a bay to the brooding silhouette of Sakurajima, an active volcano that sometimes showers the city in a gray blanket of volcanic ash.

Historically, this semitropical city, far from the old capital of Edo, enjoyed an unusual degree of independence. Center of the feudal domain of Satsuma, Kagoshima's Shimazu clan ruled Okinawa for eight centuries, absorbing much of the culture of China and Southeast Asia transmitted through the islands. The legacy of that contact is evident today in a cuisine that relies on sweet potatoes rather than rice, and in its typically Okinawan preference for pork dishes.

Shochu, Kagoshima's favorite liquor made from sweet potatoes, is believed to have passed through Okinawa from China or Korea. There are over 120 *shochu* distilleries in Kagoshima alone. Local craft traditions, particularly Satsuma ceramics and fine silk brocades, reflect an aesthetic of Asian provenance. Kagoshima's sultry climate is apparent at **Iso Garden**, where semitropical plants grow alongside plum trees and bamboo groves. The garden's centerpiece is a pond and miniature waterfall.

On an artificial island in the harbor is the **City Aquarium**, with species from local waters and the coral reefs around the Nansei islands, southwest of Kyushu. Also worth seeing is the **Art Museum**, with its displays of Satsuma ceramics.

Japan first came into contact with Christianity at Kagoshima, in 1549, in the person of the Spanish missionary Francis Xavier. The 20th-century **St. Xavier's Church** commemorates this event. The city is also associated with Saigo Takamori (1827–77), who led

Roof detail from Iso Garden, Kagoshima

Fish in one of the tanks of Kagoshima's City Aquarium

Sakurajima volcano across the strait from Kagoshima

the ill-fated Seinan Rebellion. Japanese visitors pay their respects to him in a cave on Shiroyama Hill where he committed ritual suicide.

🍁 **Iso Garden**
Tel (099) 247-1551. ⬜ daily. 🏞️

✈️ **City Aquarium**
Tel (099) 226-2233. ⬜ daily 🏞️

🏛️ **Art Museum**
Tel (099) 224-3400. ⬜ Tue–Sun. 🏞️

Sakurajima Volcano ㉑

桜島

 *every 15 mins from the pier near Kagoshima stn.*

A dramatic eruption of Sakurajima in 1914 deposited three billion tons of lava in the narrow strait separating the peninsula, thus joining the island to the mainland. The rich volcanic soil produces the world's largest white radishes, giant specimens growing to a diameter of 1.5 m (5 ft). Such is the fascination of the cone that one of Japan's foremost writers, Endo Shusaku, is said to have had himself lowered by helicopter into the smoking crater of Sakurajima, the model for his 1959 novel *Kazan (Volcano)*. One

particular sight is the **Kurokami Buried Torii Gate**, the protruding lintel of a stone Shinto gate, a casualty of the 1914 eruption.

Chiran ㉒

知覧

Kagoshima prefecture. 🚶 13,800. ⬜ from Kagoshima. ℹ️ (0993) 83-2511. **www**.town.chiran.kagoshima.jp

Tucked into the green folds of neatly manicured tea plantations and wooded hills, exquisite Chiran was one of 102 castle-towns built to protect the feudal lords of Satsuma. Seven preserved samurai houses and gardens on **Samurai Lane** can be visited with a single entrance ticket. **Sata** combines a dry-

landscape garden, an expanse of white raked sand, and mountains used as "borrowed scenery." **Morishige** is a stroll garden with a pond representing the sea with islands. **Hirayama** is composed almost entirely of hedges, clipped with precision into the illusion of undulating hills blending seamlessly with a backdrop of mountains. A hill above the village was the site of a World War II training ground for kamikaze pilots. Cherry trees are dedicated to 1,026 young men who flew their fatal missions from Chiran.

Amami Island ㉓

奄美大島

Kagoshima prefecture. 🚶 68,500. ✈️ ⬜ from Kagoshima to Naze. ℹ️ at airport (0997) 63-2295. **www**.amamikankou.jp

Subtropical Amami is home to a wealth of flora and fauna. The coral reefs and offshore islets of **Setouchi**, in the south, are part of a protected marine park offering excellent diving, snorkeling, fishing, and boat trips.

The **Amami Oshima Tsumugi Mura** is an artisan village set aside for the production of *tsumugi* (also known as Oshima pongee), a delicate handwoven silk fabric used to make kimonos. It can take up to one year to produce sufficient silk to make a single kimono. Halfway down the east coast, two rivers form a salt-water delta, which supports the world's most northerly mangrove forest.

One of the six perfectly maintained samurai gardens in Chiran

OKINAWA

*A*n exotic coral bar slicing through the Pacific Ocean and East China Sea, the Okinawa archipelago was a vassal of China from the 15th century; its masters named it Liu-chiu (Ryukyu in Japanese). Under the Chinese, then later suzerainty of the Satsuma domain, the islands assimilated diverse influences, creating a unique, exotic culture that still sets them apart from mainland Japan.

Present day Okinawans, a people with a reputation for warmth and native good manners, are the heirs of a diverse racial intermingling, the result of maritime migrations from Southeast Asia, the Philippines, Mongolia, China, and the peninsula of Korea. The geography of the islands matches this rich ethnographic map. Encircled by stunning coral reefs and transparent waters, Okinawa has a richly varied topography and subtropical flora and fauna. This is one source of inspiration for the exquisite handiwork of the islanders, particularly their textiles. Created using light, natural fabrics and innovative dyeing methods, they vary from island to island.

Okinawa, the largest and busiest island in the group, gives its name to the prefecture, which was established in 1879. In the closing stages of World War II, this was the scene of fierce fighting, in the Battle of Okinawa, and the mass suicide of thousands of civilians. Naha, the main city, was damaged in the battle but has since become a heady mix of refined civilization and neon glitz. Art galleries and teahouses stand alongside red-light bars, snake restaurants, and karaoke cabins. Ceramic *shisa* lions, topping the red-tiled roofs of traditional Okinawan houses, add to the eclectic mix of war memorials, sacred groves, flower-covered coral walls, craft shops, luxury hotels, and discos.

Those who venture to the more remote islands southwest of Okinawa itself will encounter idyllic beaches, tropical rainforests, and superb diving – the nearest thing to terra incognita it is possible to find in the Japanese archipelago.

A kimono of traditional Okinawan fabric

Part of the Nakamura House on Okinawa, a fine example of traditional architecture

◁ **A sweep of coast, ending at the cape of Higashi Henna, on Miyako Island**

Exploring Okinawa

The archipelago, also known as the Ryukyu islands, consists of 65 subtropical islands stretching for 685 km (425 miles) from the southwest coast of Kyushu to within television-reception distance of Taiwan. About 45 islands are inhabited. Just 135 km (80 miles) long, narrow Okinawa island is the most accessible part for tourists, with its vibrant capital Naha, beach resorts, and historical monuments. The more remote islands to the southwest are part of Okinawa prefecture; ones to the northeast are actually part of Kyushu's Kagoshima prefecture.

Battle of Okinawa war memorial at Cape Kyan

The massive remaining wall at Nakijin Castle, Okinawa

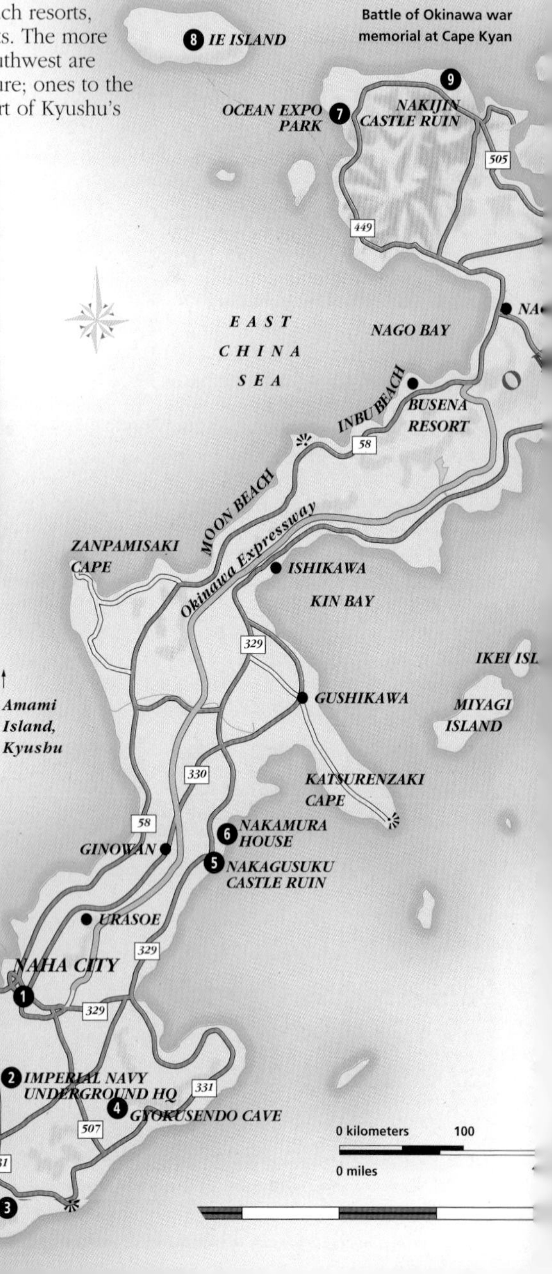
8 IE ISLAND
9 NAKIJIN CASTLE RUIN
OCEAN EXPO PARK 7
505
449
EAST CHINA SEA
NAGO BAY
INBU BEACH
BUSENA RESORT
58
MOON BEACH
Okinawa Expressway
ZANPAMISAKI CAPE
ISHIKAWA
KIN BAY
329
IKEI ISL
GUSHIKAWA
MIYAGI ISLAND
330
KATSURENZAKI CAPE
58
6 NAKAMURA HOUSE
GINOWAN
5 NAKAGUSUKU CASTLE RUIN
URASOE
329
NAHA CITY
1
329
2 IMPERIAL NAVY UNDERGROUND HQ
331
4 GYOKUSENDO CAVE
507
331
OKINAWA BATTLE SITES 3
KEY
Airport
Expressway
Major road
Minor road
Ferry route
Viewpoint
Amami Island, Kyushu
Kume Island
Miyako & Yaeyama Islands
0 kilometers 100
0 miles

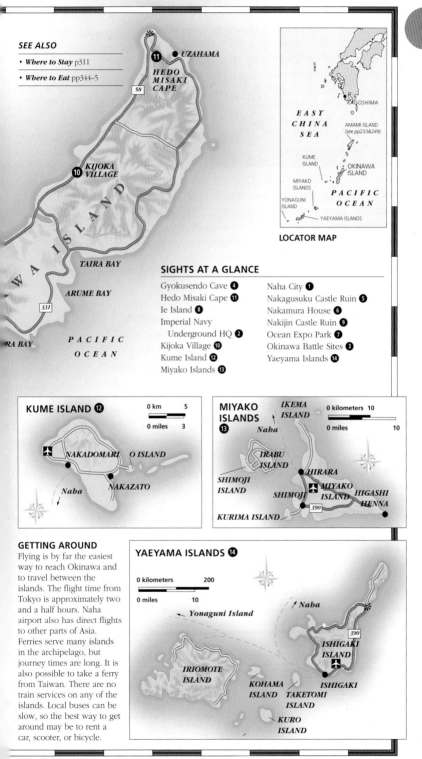

SEE ALSO

- *Where to Stay* p311
- *Where to Eat* pp344–5

LOCATOR MAP

SIGHTS AT A GLANCE

Gyokusendo Cave **4**
Hedo Misaki Cape **11**
Ie Island **8**
Imperial Navy
  Underground HQ **2**
Kijoka Village **10**
Kume Island **12**
Miyako Islands **13**

Naha City **1**
Nakagusuku Castle Ruin **5**
Nakamura House **6**
Nakijin Castle Ruin **9**
Ocean Expo Park **7**
Okinawa Battle Sites **3**
Yaeyama Islands **14**

KUME ISLAND 12

MIYAKO ISLANDS 13

GETTING AROUND

Flying is by far the easiest way to reach Okinawa and to travel between the islands. The flight time from Tokyo is approximately two and a half hours. Naha airport also has direct flights to other parts of Asia. Ferries serve many islands in the archipelago, but journey times are long. It is also possible to take a ferry from Taiwan. There are no train services on any of the islands. Local buses can be slow, so the best way to get around may be to rent a car, scooter, or bicycle.

YAEYAMA ISLANDS 14

Kokusai-dori, Naha's vibrant main shopping street

Naha City ❶

那覇市

Okinawa Island. 🚶 315,000. ✈
🚢 Naha. 🚌 🛈 Airport 1F (098)
857-6884. **www**.city.naha. okinawa.
jp 🎏 Naha Matsuri (around Oct 10).

Shuri, the most historical
settlement in Okinawa, was
its capital until the islands
became part of Japan in 1879,
after which Naha was declared
the capital. The two cities have
since expanded and merged.
Naha prospered through its
seaborne trade with other parts
of Asia and, eventually, the
West. The city that emerged
from the ruins of World War II
is a bustling center, with the
archipelago's best restaurants,
nightlife, and shopping.

Exploring Central Naha
A long shopping and entertainment thoroughfare in the heart
of Naha, **Kokusai-dori** (International Street) typifies the new
city, with its boutiques and
craft shops selling Okinawan
crafts. The atmosphere along
Heiwa-dori market street (to
the south, off Kokusai-dori)
harks back to an older Naha.
Started by widows who
had lost their husbands
in the Battle of

Okinawa, the market is full of
Asian aromas, crowded alleys,
and stalls selling Okinawan
art, crafts, bric-a-brac, and
exotic foods.

To the east, along Himeyuri-
dori, the pottery quarter of
Tsuboya dates from the late
17th century. Over 20 workshops still produce wine flasks,
tea bowls, and *shisa* (statues
of a legendary lion,
used all around the
island as propitious
roof ornaments).
The **Tsuboya
Pottery Museum**
has displays.

Also of interest in
central Naha are
the **Sogen-ji Ishi-
mon Gates**. The
temple itself, origin-
ally a 16th-century memorial
to the Ryukyu kings, was
destroyed in the war, three of
the original arched stone
gates have been restored.

The **Commodore Perry
Memorial** by Tomari port
marks the point where the
commander of the American
"black ships" landed on June
6, 1853, leading to the end of
Japan's 250-year isolation.

🏺 **Tsuboya Pottery Museum**
Tel (098) 862-3761. ⬤ *Tue–Sun.* 🈲

Tsuboya pottery
from Naha

Exploring Shuri
The 500-year-old former
capital, 6 km (4 miles) east of
central Naha, contains various
shrines, temples, ceremonial
gates, and fortifications – a
reminder of the sophistication
of the Ryukyu kingdom.
Ryusen and *bingata* fabrics
are made, exhibited, and sold
at the **Shuri Ryusen Traditional Crafts Museum**. With
over 4,000 exhibits, the **Okinawa Prefectural Museum**
is a good introduction to the
area's culture, and has the
original bells from Shuri Castle
and the temple Engaku-ji.

Shuri Castle was the headquarters of the Japanese High
command during the war,
resulting in its total destruction.
Shurei-mon, the castle's ceremonial entrance gate, was rebuilt in 1958; as the symbol of
Okinawa, it is popular with
tour groups. The grand
Seiden (hall) has also
been well restored.
Natural disasters
and war have led
to the constant re-
building of the
16th-century **Ben-
zaiten-do** temple,
north of the castle
park. Now it is sur-
rounded by a lotus
pond spanned by stone bridges.

The **Kinjocho Stone-Paved
Road**, from the reign of King
Shin in the 15th century, is a
vestige of old Naha, meandering past old red-roofed homes
with small tropical gardens
enclosed by sturdy coral walls.

🏛 **Okinawa Prefectural
Museum**
Tel (098) 834-2243. ⬤ *Tue–Sun.* 🈲
🏺 **Shuri Ryusen Traditional
Crafts Museum**
Tel (098) 886-1131. ⬤ *daily.*

The splendid restored Seiden state hall at Shuri Castle

Cliffs at Cape Kyan, also called Cape of Tragedy

Imperial Navy Underground HQ ❷

旧海軍司令部壕

5 km (3 miles) S of Naha. 🚌 from Naha bus terminal to Tomigusuku Koen-mae. **Tel** (098) 850-4055. ◯ 8:30am–5pm daily. 🈂

Parts of the subterranean rooms and tunnels where the Japanese Navy conducted the closing stages of World War II have been restored and opened to the public. The Imperial Navy Admiral was one of over 4,000 men who committed suicide here on June 13, 1945. Many of the officers dispatched themselves by *seppuku* (ritual disembowelment); others used hand grenades – scorch marks can still be seen on tunnel walls.

Okinawa Battle Sites ❸

沖縄戦跡国定公園

15 km (9 miles) S of Naha. 🚌 bus tour from Naha recommended.

At the southern end of Okinawa, the scene of the heaviest fighting at the close of World War II, are various battle sites and memorials to victims and those who committed suicide rather than surrender to advancing American forces. **Cape Kyan** saw some of the fiercest exchanges. Many locals jumped to their deaths here. To the northeast, **Himeyuri no To** is a much-visited memorial to a group of schoolgirls and teachers who died while working as volunteer nurses during the Battle of Okinawa. A total of 210 people died inside a cave while trying to escape. Others perished from the effects of a gas bomb fired into the cavern, or by suicide. **Konpaku no To**, 2 km (1 mile) south, is a cliffside memorial where 35,000 unknown soldiers and civilians were interred.

The single heaviest loss of life was on **Mabuni Hill**. Now a memorial park, it is dotted with monuments dedicated to both military and civilian dead. A comprehensive display, with photos, memorabilia, and personal accounts of the battle can be seen at the nearby **Peace Memorial Museum**.

🏛 **Peace Memorial Museum**
Tel (098) 997-3844. ◯ Tue–Sun. 🈂

Gyokusendo Cave ❹

玉泉洞

30 km (19 miles) SW of Naha.

Japan's largest stalactite grottoes were discovered in 1967 by students from Ehime University. With over 460,000 stalactites, this natural fantasia is negotiated with the help of rather slippery pathways and wooden walkways. The stalactites have been likened to giant bamboo, wine glasses, organ pipes, and statues by Rodin. At the center is a pond known as Golden Cup.

The cave lies near the **Gyokusendo Okokumura**, a park and museum with a large snake collection, including the *habu*, Okinawa's most poisonous reptile.

🏛 **Gyokusendo Okokumura**
Tel (098) 949-7421. ◯ daily. 🈂

Densely packed stalactites in Gyokusendo Cave

THE BATTLE OF OKINAWA

Kamakazi attack on an American battle ship

Few conflicts in modern history have been fought with such ferocity on both sides as the Battle of Okinawa. The final phase in the Pacific War began when five American divisions, supported by a massive aerial and naval bombardment, landed on Easter Sunday, April 1, 1945. Although logistically outnumbered, the Japanese were well prepared for the attack with a maze of tunnels and shelters. The horrors of these engagements, utilizing flame-throwers, grenades, bayonets, and kamikaze pilots (Japanese suicide bombers), almost defies imagination. By the end of the battle, which lasted 82 days, 13,000 American soldiers and 250,000 Japanese soldiers and civilians had died.

Guest room in the Nakamura House

Nakagusuku Castle Ruin 5

中城城跡

13 km (9 miles) NE of Naha City, 5-min walk E of Nakamura House. **Tel** *(098) 935-5719.* 8:30am–5pm daily (6pm Jun–Sep).

Built by Lord Gosamaru in about 1450, Nakagusuku, the first stone castle to be built in Japan, is said to have strongly impressed Commodore Perry when he visited the site. The views from here along the east coast of central Okinawa are excellent. Lord Gosamaru was betrayed by the northern noble Amawari, who convinced the Shuri king, falsely, that Gosamaru was raising troops against him. The king sent forces to attack, and Gosamaru committed suicide at his castle rather than oppose a ruler he loyally supported. The only structures to survive the ravages of time, and the 1458 Amawari Rebellion, are its walls. Passages link three main compounds, each enclosed by high, fortified walls.

Shisa ornament, Nakamura House

Nakamura House 6

中村家

13 km (9 miles) NE of Naha City. Ryukyu bus 21 to Ishihara. **Tel** *(098) 935-3500.* 9am–5pm daily.

A visit to this well-to-do 18th-century farmhouse, now a museum with exhibits about Okinawan daily life, offers rare insights into a more refined style of rural architecture. It consists of five buildings around a stone courtyard. Okinawan masons were renowned, and even the pig pens here, with their finely cut stones, are remarkably well made. A stone enclosure, with a barrier to repel evil spirits – a typical Okinawan feature – faces the entrance. Descendants of the Nakamura family continue to live in the private inner quarters of the house.

Ocean Expo Park 7

海洋博記念公園

20 km (12 miles) NW of Nago. Kinenkoen-mae. 9:30am–5pm (7pm in summer) daily. for some attractions. **www**.oki-park.jp/ocean_park/index_e.html

The Okinawa International Ocean Exposition was held here in 1975; since then several new attractions have been added to this coastal park, which is also known as the Ocean EXPO Park and the Commemorative National Government Park. The **Dolphin Theater** is popular with families who come to see the regular shows. The adjacent **Aquarium** has recently been renovated and houses almost 300 species of fish in three sections: tropical, ocean, and deep sea. The **Oceanic Culture Museum** relates the development of the Okinawan people to the maritime culture of Oceania through fishing and navigation exhibits.

The **Native Okinawan Village** is a faithful reconstruction of traditional 17th- and 18th-century dwellings, incorporating sacred springs and forest, places of worship, store houses, and an arboretum with native plants. On the coast close by is the **Tropical Dream Center**, a complex of high-tech greenhouses and botanical gardens.

Environs:
There are beaches about 30 km (19 miles) to the south of the park, along the coast of **Nago Bay**. Between Cape Busena and Inbu Beach is one of the world's finest underwater observatories, at **Busena Resort**. Don't miss the excellent undersea aquarium.

Busena Resort
Tel *(0980) 52-3379.* daily.

Ie Island 8

伊江島

5,190. from Motobu port. (0980) 49-2906.

Ie is a picturesque little island ideal for bicycling. Bike rentals are plentiful, and the whole island can be explored in under eight hours. The north terminates in steep cliffs, while the interior is an expanse of sugarcane, tobacco, and pineapple fields, and old houses with kitchen gardens. **Gusukuyama**, Ie's only hill, provides a first-rate view.

Sea turtle at Ocean Expo Park

View of Ie Island from the entrance to Ocean Expo Park

OKINAWAN ARTS AND CRAFTS

Okinawan artists and craftsmen are honored as masters or, in a few rare cases, Living National Treasures. The island's textiles are among the finest in Japan, particularly the linen-dyed *bingata* and *ryusen* fabrics, *bashofu*, and *kasuri*, a high-quality cloth made from the finest natural fibers. Equally, the glossy, black Okinawan lacquerware has been made for over 500 years, using the wood of the indigenous *deigo* tree as a base. New crafts have appeared since the war, most notably Okinawan glassware, its vibrant colors reflecting the island's sparkling coral seas.

Dyeing fabric in a *ryusen* workshop

The island saw considerable action in World War II. **Nya-teiya-gama**, a cave in the southwest, was used as a shelter by locals during the fighting. The **Ernie Pyle Monument** is dedicated to the US war correspondent who died when his jeep was blown up on the island only a few weeks before the end of the conflict.

Visitors are welcome at the friendly cooperative where locals process the day's catch of fish and seaweed.

Nakijin Castle Ruin ❾

今帰仁城跡

🚌 *66 from Nago to Nakijin Joseki* **Tel** *(0980) 56-4400.* ⏰ *8:30am–5:30pm daily (to 6pm Apr–Oct).* 📷

The foundations, gate, and 1,100-m (3,600-ft) stretch of remaining wall give some indication of the original size of Nakijin Castle. It was built in the 14th century by King Hokuzan, founder of the North Mountain Kingdom, an esoteric and short-lived domain.

The entrance, with its flat stone ceiling, is still intact. Because the castle faced the sacred island of **Iheya**, three wooden shrines were built here to allow the local priestesses to conduct rituals, but none has survived. There are stunning views across the East China Sea toward several other offshore islands including the Amami and Yoron groups.

Kijoka Village ❿

喜如嘉村

🚶 *25 km (16 miles) N of Nago.* 👥 *400.* 🚌 *from Nago.* ℹ️ *(0980) 44-3232.*

The main reason for a visit to Kijoka village is to watch the making of *bashofu*, a rare textile made of plantain fiber, closely associated with Okinawa. The village is famous for the cloth, which is exported to mainland Japan and sold at prices far above those here. Unlike traditional Japanese kimonos, Okinawan apparel was made from plain woven cotton, ramie, and lightweight fabrics such as *bashofu*. The stages involved in producing this increasingly scarce linen can be seen at the **Bashofu Kaikan**, a workshop with a high reputation.

Stone lion from Kijoka village

🏠 Bashofu Kaikan

Tel *(0980) 44-3033.* ⏰ *Mon–Fri & every 1st & 3rd Sat of month.*

Hedo Misaki Cape ⓫

辺戸岬

🚶 *50 km (31 miles) N of Nago.* 🚌 *67 from Nago to Hentona.*

The remote, northernmost point of the island is a wild and breathtaking area of great natural beauty and, mercifully, few tour buses. A grassy plateau runs to the edge of a steep, 100-m (330-ft) high cliff, beyond which are coral reefs. The views of distant Yoron, Iheya, and Izena islands are magnificent.

The road to Hedo Point passes through traditional villages. One of the most interesting is **Ogimi Mura**, renowned for pale yellow *bashofu* cloth. A short distance east of Hedo Point is the village of **Uzahama** and the remains of a prehistoric settlement.

Hedo Misaki, the northernmost cape of Okinawa

Tatami-ishi pentagonal stones on O Island, just off Kume

Kume Island ⑫
久米島

100 km (60 miles) W of Okinawa Island.
✈ from Naha. 🚌 9,400. ⛴ from
Naha Tomari port. 🛈 (098) 985-3431.

Regarded by many as the most beautiful island in the prefecture, volcanic Kume is famous for its sugarcane and pineapple plantations, and Kumejima-*tsumugi*, an exquisite silk pongee. Buses serve many of the island's sights.

The village of **Nakadomari**, in the southwest, boasts the the oldest house in Okinawa. **Uezu-ke** was built in 1726 in the Okinawan samurai style. An extraordinary tree, the **Goeda no Matsu**, which has five separate trunks spanning out, is just a short walk from the house. Rice-planting rituals and prayers for rain are still conducted at **Chinbei-donchi**, the island's foremost shrine, north of Nakadomari. Nearby, the sacred **Yajiya-gama Cave** was used for burials 2,000 years ago.

To the north, the 200-m (650-ft) high **Hijayo Banta** cliff affords good views toward the Aguni and Tonaki islands and the barrier reef below, one of Kume's outstanding natural sights. The Teida-ishi (sun stone), in a beautiful grove not far from the cliff, was used as a sundial.

Nakazato village, in the east of the island, is one of its most traditional settlements, with several well-preserved buildings. You can see women weaving and dyeing Kume-jima-*tsumugi* here. Nearby **Eef Beach** is Kume's largest resort.

Tiny **O Island** is well worth the 20-minute walk across a connecting bridge from Naka-zato's Tomari port. In the southwest is a mosaic of over 1,000 pentagonal stones, called Tatami-ishi, which resemble flattened tortoise shells.

Miyako Islands ⑬
宮古諸島

330 km (200 miles) SW of Okinawa
Island.

Set amid coral reefs in a transparent emerald sea, Miyako consists of eight almost perfectly flat islands. Unique customs and a distinct dialect set the inhabitants of Miyako apart from Okinawan mainlanders. Spared the devastation of World War II, traditional houses are squat, one-story buildings with red-tiled roofs and surrounding coral walls that serve as shelters against typhoons.

Miyako Island
🚌 53,000. ✈ from Naha and
Ishigaki Island. ⛴ from Naha. 🛈 at
airport (09807) 2-0899.

Hirara, with a population of over 30,000, is the island's main business and cultural center and its principal port. North of the port is **Harimizu Utaki** shrine, dedicated to the two gods who created the island. The fascinating **mausoleum** of the 15th-century chieftain Nakasone Toimiya has graves and tombs that combine local styles with the more elaborate Okinawan style. Northeast of Hirara, the **Hirara Tropical Botanical Gardens** contain over 40,000 tree and almost 2,000 plant species from around the world.

In the backstreets of Hirara you can see women drying strips of Miyako-*jofu* indigo cloth, used as a tributary payment when the islands were under nominal Chinese rule. Just north of Hirara is the 1.4-m (55-in) stone, called the **Nintozeiseki**, used to access tax eligibility when the

Sweep of sand at Yonaha Maehama Beach, Miyako Island

islands fell under the suzerainty of the Satsuma domain in the 17th century. When someone grew to the height of the stone they were deemed old enough to start paying taxes.

At the tip of **Higashi Henna** cape on the east coast you can look out over the Pacific Ocean to the left and the East China Sea to the right.

On the southwest coast, facing Kurima island, **Yonaha Maehama Beach**, a 4-km (2-mile) stretch of pristine white sand, offers the island's best swimming, fishing, and diving.

🌺 **Hirara Tropical Botanical Gardens**
Tel (0980) 72-3751. 🕐 *daily.*

Other Islands

🚢 *from Miyako Island; or by road bridge to Kurima and Ikema.*
Mostly set aside for sugarcane plantations, **Kurima** is of interest to ornithologists as sea hawks rest here for a few days in October on their way to the Philippines. The main sight on **Ikema**, off the far north of Miyako, is the Yaebishi reef, which emerges in all its splendor during low spring tides.

Off the west coast is **Irabu**, linked by six bridges to neighboring Shimoji. On **Shimoji**, two deep green lakes called Tori-ike are connected to the sea by an underground river and tunnel. Locals believe that the lakes are haunted; for those brave enough, the area is a superb diving locale.

Yaeyama Islands ⑭

八重山諸島

430 km (270 miles) SW of Okinawa Island.

The Yaeyamas are Japan's most southerly islands, its last frontier of tourism. Some of the finest scuba diving in Asia is found here.

Ishigaki Island

🚶 *47,000.* ✈ *from Naha and Miyako.* 🚢 *from Naha and Hirara port, Miyako Island.* ℹ *(0980) 82-2809.* 🎎 *Angama Festival (late Aug).*
Ishigaki's airport and harbor serve the outlying islands in the group. Glimpses of the unique Yaeyama culture can

Shiritsu Yaeyama History Museum, Ishigaki Island

be seen at the **Shiritsu Yaeyama Museum**, near the harbor, which contains ancient ceramics, old Yaeyama-*jofu* textiles, and Polynesian-style canoes. Not far away is **Miyara Donchi**, a superb 19th-century nobleman's home. **Shiraho Reef**, off the southeastern tip of the island, is the world's largest expanse of blue coral. **Kabira Bay** on the north shore, is full of small islets and supports a cultured black pearl industry.

🏛 **Shiritsu Yaeyama Museum**
Tel (0980) 82-4712. 🕐 *Tue–Sun.* 🎫
🏛 **Miyara Donchi**
Tel (0980) 82-2767. 🕐 *Wed–Mon.* 🎫

Taketomi Island

🚶 *340.* 🚢 *from Ishigaki.* ℹ *(0980) 82-5445.*
Meaning "prosperous bamboo," Taketomi is a quiet, unspoiled island. Its neatness stems from an old custom by which it was, and still is, the responsibility

The orderly, sandy lanes of Taketomi Island village

A dancer in traditional costume, Ishigaki Island

of all householders to sweep the street in front of their own property. The island can easily be explored on foot or by bike. Taketomi is famous as the source of *minsa*, an indigo fabric used for kimono belts, which can be seen in the main village. It also has some of Okinawa's best-preserved houses.

To the west, **Kondoi Misaki**, the island's finest beach, has star-shaped sand – the fossilized skeletons of tiny sea animals. The stunning aquamarine waters here support bountiful tropical sealife, and brilliantly colored butterflies swarm around the beach.

Iriomote Island

🚶 *2,000.* 🚢 *from Ishigaki.* ℹ *(09808) 2-5445.*
Possibly the wildest landmass in Japan, nine-tenths of Iriomote is forest and jungle. Visitors can take cruises along its three rivers, the **Nakama**, **Urauchi**, and **Kuira**, where black oyster beds, mangroves, and tropical trees, including the rare Yaeyama coconut palm, can be seen. The three-stage **Maryudo Falls** end the Urauchi River trip. The island is famous as the last habitat of the Iriomote wild cat.

Yonaguni Island

🚶 *1,700.* 🚢 *from Ishigaki.* ✈ *from Naha.* ℹ *(09808) 7-2402.*
Yonaguni is the ultimate retreat – the last island in the archipelago. Excellent swordfish and bonito fishing provide interest along with Japan's strongest sake – *awamori*.

NORTHERN HONSHU

When haiku poet Matsuo Basho set out in 1689 on his five-month trek in northern Japan, he likened it to going to the back of beyond. Three centuries later, shinkansen lines and expressways provide easy access, and the north is as much a part of the information age as the rest of Japan. The region nevertheless retains its quiet, rural image, a place where life is lived at a more congenial pace.

The backcountry reputation of Northern Honshu belies its rich history. Long ago it was home to indigenous people, who may have been Ainu *(see p287)*. In the 11th century, Hiraizumi was the capital of the Northern Fujiwara clan, rivaling Kyoto in splendor. During feudal times, Morioka, Tsuruoka, Hirosaki, and Aizu-Wakamatsu were thriving castle towns. Foremost, though, was Sendai, ruled by the north's most powerful clan, and now the region's largest city. These and other north-country wonders, such as the shrines and temples of Nikko and Dewa Sanzan, are now tourist attractions. Despite rapid development in recent decades, the region still has much unspoiled natural beauty: rugged mountains, virgin forests, deep lakes, *onsen* (hot-spring resorts), and dramatic coastlines.

Kokeshi doll from Sendai

Towada-Hachimantai, Bandai-Asahi, and Nikko national parks are accessible and exciting destinations for hikers, climbers, campers, and skiers.

Known for its excellent rice and fine sake, northern Japan is the country's main rice-producer. Agriculture is now mechanized, but farmers still work hard for a living. Mushrooms in autumn, wild edible vegetables in spring, oysters in winter, and good seafood all year are other reasons to visit the north, while its cool summers provide relief from the heat and humidity farther south. The wealth of crafts and folk arts, such as Nanbu *testsubin* (iron kettles) in Morioka, wooden *kokeshi* dolls, Aizu and Tsugaru lacquerware, *kabazaiku* (cherry-bark craft), and Mashiko pottery, are renowned in Japan and internationally.

One of the extravagant carvings by the Yomeimon gate at Nikko's Tosho-gu Shrine

◁ The five-story Buddhist pagoda at the start of the climb up Mount Haguro, Dewa Sanzan

Exploring Northern Honshu

Northern Honshu is much more rural than Central
and Western Honshu. Snow-covered mountains,
thick forests, and rice paddies characterize most of
the region, with towns and ski resorts fairly evenly
scattered. North of the major city of Sendai, tiny
pine-covered islands lie in calm bays facing the
Pacific Ocean, forming some of the most beautiful
coastal scenery in Japan. The six northeastern
prefectures of Aomori, Akita, Iwate, Yamagata, Miyagi,
and Fukushima make up the area known as Tohoku.
This chapter also includes parts of Niigata, Tochigi,
Gunma, and Ibaraki prefectures.

A *kabuto-zukuri*-style farmhouse in the grounds of
Chido Museum, Tsuruoka

SIGHTS AT A GLANCE

SEE ALSO

- *Where to Stay* pp311–13
- *Where to Eat* pp345–6

Clear waters and the rugged
coastline of Sado Island

LOCATOR MAP

GETTING AROUND

Two main *shinkansen* lines penetrate this region: one
from Tokyo to Niigata, the other from Tokyo to Hachinohe
via Sendai. Branch *shinkansen* lines run to Yamagata and
Akita. From Hachinohe, a main line continues north and
on to Hokkaido via the Seikan Tunnel. Much slower
branch lines – some private – serve towns along both
coasts and in the interior. Nikko is an easy day trip from
Tokyo; elsewhere allow plenty of time for travel. A rental
car is a good option for getting off the beaten track.

PACIFIC
OCEAN

| 0 kilometers | 50 |
| 0 miles | 30 |

KEY

✈	Airport
▬	Expressway
▬	Major road
▪▪▪	Bullet train line
▪▪	JR train line
—	Private train line
– –	Tunnel
❀	Viewpoint

Map labels:
21 SHIMOKITA PENINSULA
4
ORI
TOWADA 102
18 TOWADA HACHIMANTAI NATIONAL PARK
104
HACHINOHE
Tohoku Line
Tohoku Shinkansen
Hachinohe Shinkansen
Hachinohe Expressway
Hachinohe Line
46
15 MORIOKA
MIYAKO 106
13 HANAMAKI
283
14 TONO
45
HIRAIZUMI
12
284 45
11 MATSUSHIMA
SHIOGAMA
SENDAI
Tohoku Shinkansen
6
Joban Line
IWAKI

Locator map labels:
SAPPORO
SEA OF JAPAN (EAST SEA)
TOKYO
KYOTO
OSAKA
PACIFIC OCEAN
KAGOSHIMA

Weeping cherry trees in Hirosaki

Nikko ❶

日光

Over 1,200 years ago, the formidable Buddhist priest Shodo Shonin, on his way to Mount Nantai, crossed the Daiya River and founded the first temple at Nikko. Centuries later, Nikko was a renowned Buddhist-Shinto religious center, and the warlord Tokugawa Ieyasu *(see p267)* chose it for the site of his mausoleum. When his grandson Iemitsu had Ieyasu's shrine-mausoleum Tosho-gu built in 1634, he wanted to impress upon any rivals the wealth and might of the Tokugawa clan. Since then, Nikko, written with characters that mean sunlight, has become a Japanese byword for splendor.

Bato Kannon, with a horse on the headdress, at Rinno-ji Temple

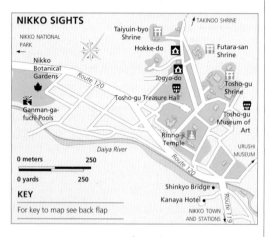

NIKKO SIGHTS

- Taiyuin-byo Shrine
- NIKKO NATIONAL PARK
- Hokke-do
- TAKINOO SHRINE
- Futara-san Shrine
- Nikko Botanical Gardens
- Route 120
- Jogyo-do
- Tosho-gu Treasure Hall
- Ganman-ga-fuchi Pools
- Tosho-gu Shrine
- Rinno-ji Temple
- Tosho-gu Museum of Art
- Daiya River
- URUSHI MUSEUM
- Route 120

0 meters 250
0 yards 250

KEY

For key to map see back flap

- Shinkyo Bridge
- Kanaya Hotel
- NIKKO TOWN AND STATIONS
- Route 119

Exploring Nikko Town

Of the two stations in Nikko, the JR station, the oldest in eastern Japan, is a classic. The graceful wooden edifice, built in 1915, was designed by American architect Frank Lloyd Wright. Buses to many of Nikko's sights run from

here. The 1-km (about half-a-mile) long avenue from the train stations to the Tosho-gu precincts is lined with shops, restaurants, and inns. A good shop for Nikko wood carvings and *geta* (wooden sandals) is Tezuka, on the left halfway up the street. An

architectural treat is the venerable 19th-century Kanaya Hotel *(see p312)*, situated on a rise to the left, just before the Daiya River.

Shinkyo Bridge

⬜ *daily.*
This red-lacquered wooden bridge, just to the left of the road bridge, arches over the Daiya River where, legend has it, Shodo Shonin crossed the river on the backs of two huge serpents. The original, built in 1636 for the exclusive use of the shogun and imperial messengers, was destroyed by flood. The current bridge dates from 1907.

🛕 Rinno-ji Temple

⬜ *daily.*🈂
The first temple founded at Nikko, by Shodo Shonin in 766, was originally called Shihonryu-ji. When it became a Tendai-sect temple in the 17th century, it was renamed Rinno-ji. Its **Sanbutsu-do** (Three Buddha Hall) is the largest hall at Nikko. The three gilt images, of Amida Buddha, Senju (thousand-armed) Kannon, and Bato (horse-headed) Kannon, enshrined in the hall correspond to the three mountain deities enshrined at Futara-san Shrine. Beyond the hall, the nine-ringed bronze pillar, **Sorinto**, contains

The Shinkyo Bridge spanning the Daiya River

1,000 volumes of sutras (Buddhist scriptures) and is a symbol of world peace. The **Treasure Hall** (Homotsuden) has a large and fascinating array of temple treasures, mainly dating from the Edo period. Behind it is the **Shoyoen**, a lovely Edo-style 19th-century stroll garden carefully landscaped for

The Sanbutsu-do hall at Rinno-ji

interest in all seasons. Its path meanders around a large pond, over stone bridges, and past mossy stone lanterns.

⛩ Tosho-gu Shrine
See pp266–7.

⛩ Tosho-gu Treasure Hall and Museum of Art
Tel (0288) 54-2558 (Treasure Hall); (0288) 54-0560 (Museum of Art).
☐ daily. 🈺
In the Treasure Hall are shrine treasures along with armor and swords used by the Tokugawa shoguns. In the Museum of Art is an outstanding collection of early 20th-century painted doors and panels by Yokoyama Taikan and others.

🏯 Hokke-do and Jogyo-do
These two halls belong to Rinno-ji and house Buddhist relics. Linked by a corridor, they are often referred to as the twin halls.

⛩ Futara-san Shrine
☐ daily. 🈺
Founded by Shodo Shonin in 782, this shrine is dedicated to the gods of Mounts Nantai

(male), Nyotai (female), and Taro, their child. It is actually the main shrine of three; the other two are at Lake Chuzenji and on Mount Nantai. The bronze *torii* (gate) here is an Important Cultural Property. More interesting is the tall bronze lantern, which was said to take the shape of a monster at night. The gashes in the lantern are from the sword of a terrified samurai.

⛩ Takinoo Shrine
Tel (0288) 21-0765.
☐ daily.
A quiet 30-minute uphill walk through the woods via a stone path to the left of Futara-san Shrine, this peaceful, rustic shrine, thought to be dedicated to a female deity, draws women and those looking for love. Toss a stone through the hole in the top of the *torii* (gate) and into the shrine grounds and your wish, they say, will come true.

Shrine interior at Futara-san

VISITORS' CHECKLIST

Tochigi prefecture. 🏘 94,200.
🚉 JR and Tobu-Nikko lines.
ℹ at Tobu Nikko stn (0288) 54-2496. 🎎 Tosho-gu Grand Festival May 17–18); Tosho-gu Fall Festival (Oct 17).
www.city.nikko.lg.jp/fl/index.html

⛩ Taiyuin-byo Shrine
See pp270–71.

🏞 Ganman-ga-fuchi Pools
🚌 to Nishisando bus stop.
Lava flows from an old eruption of Mount Nantai combine with the limpid waters of the Daiya River to make these unusual scenic pools, which are a spot sacred to Buddhism. About 70 stone statues of Jizo, the *bodhisattva* of children, line the path by the river. They are known as phantom statues because their numbers always appear to change.

🌸 Nikko Botanical Gardens
🚌 to Rengeishi bus stop.
Tel (0288) 54-0206.
☐ Tue.–Sun. ● Dec 1–Apr 14. 🈺
Some 3,000 varieties of plants and flowers from Japan and around the world are at these gardens, a branch of the Koishikawa Botanical Gardens of the University of Tokyo. Flora from Nikko National Park are showcased. April to July, when skunk cabbages and irises bloom, is a lovely time to visit.

⛩ Urushi Museum
🚌 to Marumi bus stop. **Tel** (0288) 53-6807. ☐ Mar 20–Nov 20: Sat, Sun, Mon. 🈺
This small museum, which opened in 1998 in wooded Ogurayama Park, showcases the lacquer arts of Nikko and Japan – *urushi* is Japanese for lacquer. Used in Japan for over 5,000 years, lacquer has reached the height of refinement only in the past 1,000 years. The museum collection also includes examples of lacquerware from China, India, and Egypt.

Painted sliding doors at the Tosho-gu Museum of Art

Nikko: Tosho-gu Shrine

Tokugawa Iemitsu set out to dazzle with this mausoleum-shrine for his grandfather Ieyasu. For two years some 15,000 artisans from all over Japan worked, building, carving, gilting, painting, and lacquering, to create this flowery, gorgeous Momoyama-style complex. Almost anything that can be decorated is. Although designated a shrine in the Meiji period, it retains many of its Buddhist elements, including its unusual pagoda, sutra library, and Niomon gate. The famed *sugi-namiki* (Japanese cedar avenue) leading to the shrine was planted by a 17th-century lord, in lieu of a more opulent offering.

Sleeping Cat Carving
Over an entrance in the east corridor, this tiny, exquisite carving of a sleeping cat is attributed to Hidari Jingoro (Hidari the Left-handed).

Bell tower

Honden *(inner sanctuary)*

Haiden *(sanctuary)*

The Karamon gate is the smallest at Tosho-gu.

The Honji-do's ceiling is painted with the "crying dragon," which echoes resoundingly if you clap your hands beneath it.

Drum tower

The Rinzo contains a sutra library of Buddhist scriptures in a revolving structure.

★ **Yomeimon Gate**
Lavishly decorated with beasts and flowers, this gate has one of its 12 columns carved upside-down, a deliberate imperfection to avoid angering jealous spirits. Statues of imperial ministers occupy the niches.

STAR SIGHTS

★ Yomeimon Gate

★ Sacred Stable

★ Pagoda

Sacred Fountain
The granite basin (1618), for ritual purification, is covered with an ornate Chinese-style roof.

TOKUGAWA IEYASU

Ieyasu (1543–1616) was a wily strategist and master politician who founded the dynasty that would rule Japan for over 250 years. Born the son of a minor lord, he spent his life accumulating power, not becoming shogun until 1603, when he was 60. He built his capital at the swampy village of Edo (now Tokyo), and his rule saw the start of the flowering of Edo culture. He ensured that, after his death, he would be enshrined as a god and *gongen* (incarnation of the Buddha). His posthumous name was Tosho-Daigongen (the great incarnation illuminating the East).

Ieyasu's treasure tower, containing his ashes

↖ To Ieyasu's tomb and treasure tower

The three sacred store-houses are built according to a traditional design.

The Niomon (or Omotemon) gate is guarded by two fearsome Nio figures, one with an open mouth to pronounce the first letter of the Sanskrit alphabet (ah), the other with a closed mouth for the last letter (un).

★ Pagoda

Donated by a daimyo (feudal lord) in 1650, this five-story pagoda was rebuilt in 1818 after a fire. Each story represents an element – earth, water, fire, wind, and heaven – in ascending order.

Ticket office

Granite *torii* (gate)

Entrance

★ Sacred Stable

A carving of the three wise monkeys decorates this unpainted wooden building. A horse given by the New Zealand government is stabled here for several hours a day.

The highly ornate Yomeimon gate at the shrine of Tosho-gu ▷

Nikko: Taiyuin-byo Shrine

Finished in 1653, Taiyuin-byo is the mausoleum of Tokugawa Iemitsu (1603–51), the
grandson of Ieyasu and powerful third
shogun, who closed Japan to foreign commerce and isolated it from the world for
over 200 years. Tayuin is his posthumous
Buddhist name. If Tosho-gu is splendid,
Taiyuin-byo is sublime. Set in a grove of
Japanese cedars, it has a number of ornate
gates ascending to the Haiden (sanctuary)
and Honden (inner sanctuary). The shogun's
ashes are entombed
beyond the sixth
and final gate.

The Honden (usually
closed to the public) holds
a gilded Buddhist altar with
a wooden statue of Iemitsu.

Kokamon Gate
*This unusual
Ming-dynasty
Chinese-style gate is
beside the path to
Iemitsu's tomb.*

**The Ai No
Ma** is a richly
decorated
connecting
chamber.

★ Haiden
*Decorated with carvings
of dragons, the Haiden
also has some famous
17th-century lion paint-
ings by Kano School
painters. Its exterior is
decorated with black
and gold lacquer.*

The Karamon
gate is adorned
with delicate
carvings, such
as a pair of
cranes.

**Drum
tower**

Yashamon Gate
*The third gate is beautifully
gilded and contains four statues
of Yasha, a fierce guardian
spirit. It is also known as
Botanmon, or peony gate, after
its detailed peony carvings.*

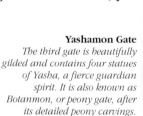

Niomon Gate
*This marks the
main entrance to
the shrine. One
Nio warrior god
stands guard on
each side.*

Entrance

VISITORS' CHECKLIST

Tel *(0288) 53-1567.* 🏢 🕐 *8am–4:30pm daily (3:30pm Nov–Mar).*

Bell Tower

This structure forms a pair with the drum tower. They are no longer used, but the drum signifies positive/birth, while the bell is negative/death.

★ Nitenmon Gate

Four guardian statues occupy the niches here. At the front are the gods Komoku and Jikoku, while at the back are the green god of wind and the red god of thunder.

Granite Fountain

On the ceiling above the basin is a dragon painting by Kano Yasunobu, which is sometimes reflected in the water below.

Stone lanterns were donated over the years by *daimyo* (feudal lords).

STAR SIGHTS

★ Nitenmon Gate

★ Haiden

A monkey by the roadside, Nikko National Park

Nikko National Park ❷

日光国立公園

Tochigi, Fukushima, and Gunma prefectures. 🚌 *from Nikko stations.* 🛈 *(0288) 54-2496.*

The magnificent national park that includes Tosho-gu and its environs is largely a mountainous volcanic plateau, studded with lakes, waterfalls, hot springs, and swamplands. For a taste of Oku-Nikko, the mountainous interior, take the bus west from Nikko to **Lake Chuzen-ji**. The hairpin curves of Irohazaka, along the old ascent to the sacred **Mount Nantai**, start at Umagaeshi (horse return), where pilgrims had to give up their horses and walk. Halfway up, at Akechidaira, there is an excellent view of Mount Nantai, which dominates the lake. At the east end of the lake, the **Kegon Falls**, named for the Buddhist principle of universal unity, cascade 96 m (315 ft) to the Daiya River below. An elevator through the cliff runs to an observation deck at the base of the falls.

At the nearby temple of **Chuzen-ji**, the main image is the Tachiki Kannon, a 1,000-armed Kannon said to have been carved from a live tree by Shodo Shoin, Nikko's founder. On July 31 hundreds of pilgrims make an overnight climb of Mount Nantai, reaching the top by sunrise. **Yumoto**, a lakeside *onsen* town, linked by bus to Nikko station and Lake Chuzen-ji, is one of several spas in the park.

Mashiko ❸

益子

Tochigi prefecture. 🚶 25,000.
🚊 (local trains only). 🚊 from Tobu-
Utsunomiya stn. 🛈 next to Mashiko
stn (0285-70-1120). 🎭 Pottery
Festivals (end Apr to early May; end
Oct to early Nov).

Known for its folk pottery,
Mashiko was home to the
world-famous potter Hamada
Shoji (1894–1978), a founder of
the *mingei* (folk art) movement. A long stretch of a town,
Mashiko has hundreds of
pottery shops and workshops.
Bicycles are easy to rent and
are the best way to explore.

The excellent **Mashiko Reference Collection Museum**
contains Hamada's studio and
kiln, and his eclectic
collection of ceramics and
other crafts, housed in
beautifully restored local
buildings. Moegi and Toko
galleries, on the main street,
showcase local potters. On
the corner, by Toko, is the
eighth-generation **Higeta
Dyeworks** and its indigo dye
vats, sunk in the floor of a
thatched workshop.

🏛 **Mashiko Museum**
Tel (0285) 72-5300. ⃝ Tue–Sun. 🏷

🏺 **Higeta Dyeworks**
Tel (0285) 72-3162. ⃝ daily.

Aizu-Wakamatsu ❹

会津若松

Fukushima prefecture. 🚶 131,000.
🚊 🛈 in View Plaza at JR stn.
www.city.aizuwakamatsu.
fukushima.jp/e/index.htm 🎭 Aizu Aki
Matsuri (Fall Festival, Sep 22–24).

Once home to the north's
second most powerful
clan, Aizu-Wakamatsu takes
pride in its samurai past. With
ties to the Tokugawas, the
Matsudaira clan bitterly resisted
the 19th-century movement to
reinstate the emperor.
In the 1868 Boshin
War, the Byak-
kotai (White
Tigers), a band of
teenage samurai
fighters against
imperial forces,
mistakenly thought
the castle had fallen
and committed

**Lacquerware bowl
from Aizu-Wakamatsu**

Shimenawa (straw rope) at the entrance to Kumano Jinja near Kitakata

mass suicide on **Iimoriyama**,
the hill (east of the station)
where they are now buried.
On the hill is a Pompeian
marble column topped by a
bronze eagle, sent by Rome in
1928 as a salute from the
Fascist party to the Byakkotai.

The main sights are fairly
spread out: all-day bus passes
are available at the station bus
office. **Tsuruga Castle** has
been the heart of the city for
over 600 years. It was last
rebuilt in 1965 as a museum.
To the east, the **Samurai
Residence** (Buke-yashiki), a
good reproduction of a 38-
room samurai manor, shows
feudal life, down to a 160-
year-old rice mill. Nearby, the
Oyakuen (medicinal herb
garden) of a 17th-century villa
contains over 200 herbs.

For shopping,
Nanukamachi-
dori is lined with
old shops selling
traditional crafts,
including painted
candles, kites, striped
Aizu cotton, and the
famed Aizu
lacquerware.

🏯 **Tsuruga Castle**
🚌 to Tsurugajo. *Tel* (0242) 27-
4005. ⃝ daily. ● 1st Mon–Thu in
July & 1st Tue–Thu in Dec.
🏷

🏯 **Samurai Residence**
🚌 Aizu bus to Bukeyashiki-mae.
Tel (0242) 28-2525. ⃝ daily. 🏷

🌿 **Oyakuen**
🚌 Haikarasan bus to Oyakuen.
Tel (0242) 27-2472. ⃝ daily. 🏷

Kitakata ❺

喜多方

Fukushima prefecture. 🚶 56,000. 🚊
🛈 next to JR stn (0241-24-2633).
www.city.kitakata.fukushima.jp 🎭
Suwa Jinja Matsuri (Aug 2–3).

Mud-walled *kura* (ware-
houses) were long used
to keep sake, miso, rice, and
other provisions from fire, theft,
and vermin. Kitakata has more
than 2,600, including a *kura*-
style temple. Most are tucked
away on back streets. South
of the **Kai Honke**, a handsome sake-merchant's house
with a coffee-shop inside, is a
kura-lined walking lane. Along
the way, the **Sake-Brewing**

Museum offers informative tours, with tastings of Yamatogawa sake. Kitakata is also known for its *ramen* noodles and *oki-agari* dolls, which roll upright when knocked over.

🏯 **Kai Honke**
Tel (0241) 22-0001. ◯ variable. 📷

🏛 **Sake-Brewing Museum**
Tel (0241) 22-2233. ◯ variable.

Environs: Seven km (5 miles) south of the station is the remarkable open-air **Kumano Jinja**, an 11th-century shrine restored in the 1970s with natural wood columns supporting a heavy thatched roof.

Souvenir dolls from Kitakata

Bandai-Asahi National Park ❻
磐梯朝日国立公園

Yamagata, Niigata, and Fukushima prefectures. 🚉 to Fukushima, Koriyama, or Inawashiro. 🛈 at Yamagata and Aizu-Wakamatsu stns. 🎎 Bandai Matsuri (last weekend in Jul, Inawashiro).

On July 15, 1888, Mount Bandai erupted, killing 477 people. Dammed streams formed hundreds of lakes and marshes, creating the lush natural beauty of the Bandai-Asahi National Park. Crisscrossed by five scenic toll roads, including the Bandai-Azuma Skyline (open April 22–November 5), the park is studded with hot springs and camping grounds. The best way to explore is by car or bus.
  Goshikinuma (five-colored marshes) is a popular 4-km (2-mile) trail starting at the Bandai-kogen or Goshikinuma bus stops. In Inawashiro the **Aizu Minzokukan** folk museum has over 24,000 items, and a garden of phallic rocks associated with fertility.

🏛 **Aizu Minzokukan**
🚉 from JR Inawashiro stn. *Tel* (0242) 65-2600. ◯ Apr 1–Nov 15: daily; Nov 16–Mar 31: Fri–Wed. 📷

Lake on the Bandai-Asahi plateau

Sado Island ❼
佐渡島

Niigata prefecture. 👥 69,000. 🚢 ferry or hydrofoil from Niigata (city) to Ryotsu. 🛈 Niigata port (025) 245-1234. 🎎 frequently, spring to fall.

Though it receives more than a million visitors a year, Sado Island still feels remote. This mellow little island, 60 km (37 miles) off Honshu's northwest coast, offers a chance to enjoy fresh seafood and meet friendly people. For centuries, Sado was home to political exiles, including the emperor Juntoku in 1221, the priest Nichiren in 1271, and Zeami, the Noh actor and playwright, in 1433. Of the 88 Noh theaters once here, about 35 are left. In 1601 the discovery of gold in Aikawa brought an influx of convicts to work as slaves in the mines.
  Buses connect the island's small towns, and tour buses stop at major attractions. In the main port of **Ryotsu** in the east, outdoor Noh performances are held at the **Honma Noh Stage**. In **Aikawa**, on the west coast, the touristy **Gold Mine** has mechanical dolls recreating the harsh mining conditions. **Aikawa**

Museum has exhibits on gold mining, ragweaving, and the local red-clay pottery.
  Recently, the **Kodo** drummers have put Sado on the international map. The group, based in **Ogi**, in the southwest, should be contacted directly for further information. Nearby **Shukunegi**, with outlying rice paddies, is one of the island's loveliest villages.

🛈 **Gold Mine**
🚌 to Aikawa Eigayosho. *Tel* (0259) 74-2389. ◯ daily. 📷

🏛 **Aikawa Museum**
🚌 to Aikawa Hakubutsukan-Mae. *Tel* (0259) 74-4312. ◯ daily. 🌙 Jan, Feb: Sat, Sun & public hols. 📷

🏛 **Kodo**
148-1 Kaneta Shinden, Sado City, Niigata 952-0611. *Tel* (0259) 86-3630. www.kodo.or.jp

Clear seas and jagged rocks off the coast of Sado Island

THE KODO DRUMMING GROUP

A Kodo drummer beating a huge *o-daiko* drum

Kodo, one of the most famous and dynamic *taiko* drumming groups, formed in 1981, is known for performances of drum, flute, song, and dance. Kodo means both "children of the drum" and "heartbeat". The throbbing heart of Kodo is the *o-daiko*, a convex wooden drum used in Japanese folk festivals. Kodo spends much of the year performing in Japan and worldwide, and hosts an annual three-day Earth Celebration, when international musicians come to Sado to perform.

Tsuruoka ❽

鶴岡

Yamagata prefecture. 142,000. ☐ outside JR stn (0235) 25-2111. Tenjin Matsuri (May 25), Shounai Taisai (Feudal Lord's Procession Aug 15).

Gateway to Dewa Sanzan, Tsuruoka was the Sakai clan's castle seat. Best of this friendly town's attractions is the **Chido Museum**, west of the former castle grounds. It includes a *kabuto-zukuri* (helmet-style) farmhouse, and marvelous folk objects such as lacquered sake caskets, bamboo fishing poles, and decorative straw *bandori* (backpacks). Southeast of the castle is the 1806 **Chidokan**, a school for young samurai. For the famous local painted candles, visit the 300-year-old Togashi Candle Shop.

Bandori backpack, Chido Museum

🏯 **Chido Museum**
Tel (0235) 22-1199. ☐ daily. 📷

🏯 **Chidokan**
Tel (0235) 23-4672. ☐ Tue–Sun.

Dewa Sanzan ❾

出羽三山

Yamagata prefecture. 🚌 from Shoko Mall near JR Tsuruoka stn. 🛈 at Tsuruoka stn (0235) 25-7678. **Mt Haguro** ☐ daily. Hassaku Matsuri (Aug 31), Shoreisai Matsuri (Dec 31). **Mt Gassan** ☐ Jul 1–fall. **Mt Yudono** ☐ late Apr–early Nov.

Dewa is the old name for this region and Sanzan are its three mountains – Haguro-san (Mount Black Wing), Gassan (Mount Moon), and Yudono-san (Mount Bath) – opened for religious purposes 1,400 years ago by Hachiko, an imperial prince turned wandering priest. The three are sacred to *yamabushi*, followers of the Shugendo sect.

Millions of pilgrims and sightseers visit Dewa Sanzan on foot or by toll road. The route to the peak of **Mount Haguro** is a climb up the 2,446 stone steps of the Japanese cedar-lined path. Take the bus to Haguro Center to start the climb. At the second stage is a teahouse with a grand view of the Mogami River valley. A side path goes to the ruins of a temple where Basho stayed. At the top is the **Dewa Sanzan Shrine**, an impressive lacquered building with the largest thatched roof in Japan, and Prince Hachiko's tomb. After the 1868 Meiji Restoration, all Shugendo temples were turned into Shinto shrines. The only true Buddhist structure left is the graceful five-story **pagoda** (*see p260*) at the foot of the stone steps.

Mount Gassan, also topped by a shrine, offers alpine flowers and summer skiing. It is a two-hour hike to the top from the Hachigome bus stop. The shrine on **Mount Yudono**, a 2.5-km (2-mile) hike from the Yudonosan Hotel bus stop, has a sacred hot-water spring in which pilgrims bathe their feet. Mummified priests, examples of *sokushin jobutsu* (living Buddhas), can be seen at the temples of **Dainichi-bo** and **Churen-ji**, on the way to Mount Yudono.

Statue of Masamune, Sendai

Sendai ❿

仙台

Miyagi prefecture. 🚄 1,024,000. ✈ 🚉 🛈 at Tohoku Shinkansen stn. **www**.city.sendai.jp/index-e.html Sendai Aoba Matsuri (3rd weekend in May), Sendai Tanabata (Weavers' Festival, Aug 6–8).

Laid out in a grid pattern in the 1600s by the dynamic lord Date Masamune, Sendai is the north's largest city. The few historic sights to survive World War II bombing lie outside the town center. **Osaki Hachiman Shrine** is a black lacquer architectural beauty in the northwest of the city. Overlooking the ruins of **Aoba Castle** from 1602 is a statue of the warrior Masamune, nicknamed the "one-eyed dragon." The ruins are set in a park a bus ride to the west of the station. Nearby, the ornately carved Date mausoleums at **Zuihoden**, rebuilt after the war, are remarkable replicas of Momoyama-period architecture. With tree-lined avenues and a dense, lively downtown, modern Sendai is fun. Intriguing shops and restaurants line the shopping arcades Ichibancho and Chuodori. Shimanuki, in Ichi-bancho, on the left as you come from the station, has *kokeshi* dolls and other crafts from all over Miyagi. Gourmets will want to try *hoya* (sea squirt), a regional specialty, at the city's many good seafood eateries.

Cedar-lined stone steps up to Mount Haguro

Buddhist Sects

In the course of 1,500 years or so, since the time that priests from mainland Asia first brought Buddhism *(see pp28–9)* to the archipelago, hundreds of separate Buddhist movements, sects, and subsects developed in Japan. Contrasting beliefs appealed to different groups of nobility, samurai, and commoners, who each adapted practices to their own

Priest, Nara

ends. In the eyes of many foreigners today, Zen, one-time favorite of the samurai, is the quintessential religion of Japan, but it is just one of several major movements originating in China, and is itself subdivided into various sects. Of other movements flowering in Japan, the Tendai and Shingon sects of esoteric Buddhism still have millions of devotees.

ZEN BUDDHISM

The Taoist-inspired Chan school from China first gained popularity in Japan during the Kamakura period (1185–1333). There are three main Zen sects: Soto, Rinzai, and Obaku. All place emphasis on *zazen* (sitting meditation) and self-help. As developed in the great Zen temples of Kyoto during the feudal era, the rigorous mindset and uncluttered aesthetics of Zen have had a profound influence on Japanese culture at large.

Zen gardens *express a sublime harmony between humanity and nature.*

The large gong is used when the ceremony begins.

Small gong

The *mokugyo* (wooden fish) is struck to keep the rhythmn during sutra chanting.

At Zuiho-in, *a subtemple of the great Zen temple Daitoku-ji (see p173) in Kyoto, priests use percussion instruments while chanting the sutras as part of their daily training.*

The cushion is used to sit on while listening to lectures.

SHINGON

This branch of esoteric Mahayana Buddhism was founded in Japan in the 9th century by Kukai *(see p229)*. It incorporates such Hindu elements as mandalas and multi-armed deities, and places emphasis on hand gestures *(mudra)* and the chanting of mantras. The headquarters are at Mount Koya *(see p199)*, and there are 50 or so subsects today.

Shingon deity from Mount Koya *displaying the* yogan semui-in *mudra with the hands.*

Shingon sect follower

TENDAI

Brought to Japan in the 9th century by Saicho, Tendai is another branch of esoteric Buddhism and places emphasis on selfless devotion. From its base at Mount Hiei, Tendai helped spawn the Jodo (Pure Land), Jodo Shin, and Nichiren sects.

The Amida Buddha *(Amida Nyorai) of the Tendai sect leads the way to the Pure Land.*

SHUGENDO

Dewa Sanzan in Northern Honshu is the most sacred site for the Shugendo sect. This offshoot of Shingon combines Buddhism and Shinto, and promotes ascetic practices on mountain retreats.

Yamabushi (ascetic) at **Shugendo-sect Dewa Sanzan**

Irregularly shaped pine-covered islands in Matsushima bay

Matsushima ⓫
松島

Miyagi prefecture. 🚶 16,000. 🚆 to Matsumisha and Matsushima-Kaigan. 🚢 from Shiogama. ℹ️ outside JR Matsushima-Kaigan stn (022) 354-2263. 🎎 Toronagashi Hanabi Taikai (floating lanterns, Aug 15), Osegakie (Consolation Festival, Aug 16, Zuigan-ji).

Take a hint from Matsuo Basho's 1689 visit to the bay of Matsushima and make Shiogama your starting point. The fishing grounds off Miyagi are among the world's richest, and the busy **Shiogama Wholesale Fish Market**, active from early morning until about 1pm, is known for its huge tuna auctions. Dedicated to both mariners and mothers-to-be is the beautiful hilltop **Shiogama Shrine**. Make time to lunch at one of Shiogama's superb sushi restaurants before taking the ferry to Matsushima.

Dotted with hundreds of islets, Matsushima bay has been known for centuries as one of Japan's "three famous views." Now, however, it is clogged with sediment and marred by forgettable tourist venues. In Matsushima itself is **Zuigan-ji**, a handsome Zen training temple; its carved kitchen and corridors are National Treasures. One side of its wooded grounds is lined with meditation caves.

Hiraizumi ⓬
平泉

Iwate prefecture. 🚶 9,050. 🚆 ℹ️ next to JR stn (0191) 46-2110. 🎎 Fujiwara Matsuri (May 1–5 & Nov 1–3).

Nine hundred years ago, the Northern Fujiwara clan, under Fujiwara Kiyohira, made this small town into a cultural and economic capital, second only to Kyoto. Three generations later, Hiraizumi was in ruins. Yoshitsune, Japan's archetypal tragic hero, sought refuge here from Yoritomo, his jealous brother and Japan's first shogun, but was betrayed by Yasuhira, the last Fujiwara leader, and killed. Yoritomo then turned against Yasuhira and had the clan wiped out.

At its peak, Hiraizumi had a population of 100,000. Wishing to create a Buddhist paradise on earth, Kiyohira enriched the 9th-century temples Chuson-ji and Motsu-ji. **Chuson-ji** is 5 minutes by bus from the station, followed by a long climb lined with towering Japanese cedars. Only two of its many original buildings remain: the small **Golden Hall**, splendid with gold leaf, lacquer, and mother of pearl, where the first three Fujiwara leaders are buried; and the **Sutra Hall**. In the **Treasure Hall** are remarkable treasures from the Fujiwara coffins and the temple.

All that remains of the original **Motsu-ji** (a 10-minute walk from the station) are its foundations and beautiful Heian-period paradise garden, the best in Japan.

Hanamaki ⓭
花巻

Iwate prefecture. 🚶 105,000. ✈️ 🚆 ℹ️ at JR Shin-Hanamaki and JR Hanamaki stns. www.city.hanamaki.iwate.jp 🎎 Hanamaki Matsuri (Fri-Sun, 2nd weekend in Sep); Kenji Sai (Kenji Festival, Sep 21).

Miyazawa Kenji (1896–1933), one of Japan's best-loved writers, was born in Hanamaki, a thriving *onsen* town. He wrote more than 1,200 poems and 90 children's stories, and worked to improve conditions for poor farmers in Iwate. Each year

Steps up to Hiraizumi's Golden Hall at Chuson-ji, Hiraizumi

For hotels and restaurants in this region see pp311–13 and pp345–6

some 250,000 people visit the **Miyazawa Memorial Museum**. Exhibits reflect Kenji's lifelong interests in minerals, astronomy, wildlife, agriculture, Esperanto, and Buddhism. There is also a quirky garden and the Ihatov, a free arts and research center. Ihatov was Kenji's Esperanto name for Iwate.

🏛 Miyazawa Memorial Museum
Tel (0198) 31-2319. ⬜ *daily.* 📷

A wooden *torii* (gate) to Mount Hayachine

Tono ⑭
遠野

Iwate prefecture. 👥 *31,000* 🚃
ℹ️ *by JR stn* (0198) 62-1333.
🎌 *Tono Matsuri (mid-Sep).*

In Tono people still live in rhythm with nature, and observe old ways and traditions. Much has changed, though, since folklorist Yanagita Kunio compiled the *Legends of Tono* in 1910. Few of the *magariya*

(L-shaped houses, shared by people and horses) are left, but the mountains ringing the Tono basin are still beautiful. Storytellers tell the age-old story of *oshirasama*, about a young woman falling in love with a horse.

Tono is divided into the town center and seven outlying districts. Attractions are best reached by car or bicycle, both of which can be rented at the station. At the private **Nakayama House**, in Kamigo district, you can see wonderful 350-year-old *oshirasama* dolls. The **Municipal Museum** in the town center introduces local folkways. At **Denshoen**, a mellow tourist venue in Tsuchibuchi district, local experts teach traditional crafts. A short walk away are **Kappabuchi** stream and the temple of **Joken-ji**, both traditionally the home of *kappa* (water imps). Northwest of the railroad station **Tono Furusato Village** has six *magariya*, where you can see traditional craftwork being made. **Hayachine Shrine**, a 30-minute drive from the station, is known for its Kagura (sacred dances), and **Mount Hayachine** is popular with climbers. Most evocative is the **Ravine of the 500 Rakan** (Buddha's disciples), a

Morioka's "stone-splitting" tree

10-minute drive west of town, with natural boulders carved centuries ago to appease the souls of famine victims.

🏠 Nakayama House
Tel (0198) 65-2609. ⬜ *by appt only.*

🏛 Municipal Museum
Tel (0198) 62-2340. ⬜ *Apr–Oct: daily; Nov–Mar: Tue–Sun.* ● *last day of month in May–Oct, Mar 1–4, Nov 24–30, public hols.* 📷

Morioka ⑮
盛岡

Iwate prefecture. 👥 *300,000.* 🚃
🚌 *2nd flr, JR stn* (019) 625-2090. 🎌
Chagu-chagu Umakko (Horse Festival, 2nd Sat in Jun). **www**.city.
morioka.iwate.jp

An old castle town, once the center of the Nanbu domain, Morioka is now Iwate's capital and a transportation hub for the north, known for

Nanbu iron kettle

its Nanbu *tetsubin* (iron kettles) and Mount Iwate, the majestic volcano overlooking it. In October salmon run up the Nakatsu River, one of three rivers that bisect the city.

All that remains of **Morioka Castle**, in Iwate Park, are its stone walls and moats. Nearby is the "stone-splitting" cherry tree.

Over Nakatsu River is the **Morihisa Iron Studio**, which has superb iron pieces on display. If you want to buy folk crafts, head for **Konya-cho** (dyers' street), to the north, and **Zaimoku-cho** (lumber street), to the left across Asahi bridge.

🏛 Morihisa Iron Studio
Tel (019) 622-3809. ⬜ *daily.*

JAPANESE DOLLS

More than a thousand years ago, simple cloth dolls called *sarukko* were attached to babies' clothing as charms against harm. The thousands of clay dolls unearthed at Jomon-period sites are also believed to have had symbolic functions. These dolls remind some scholars of *oshirasama* dolls – stick figures, usually of a horse and a girl, made of mulberry or bamboo and draped in layers of cloth – still found, and venerated, in parts of northern Japan. Other favorites include: the limbless painted *kokeshi* dolls, made by woodturners at *onsen* towns around northern Japan; *ohinasama*, the elaborate tiered arrays of silk court dolls displayed each Girls' Day (March 3); and *anesan ningyo* (big sister dolls), ingenious figures folded from paper.

Oshirasama dolls in Tono's Nakayama House

Kakunodate 16

男鹿半島

Akita prefecture. 🏯 31,000. 🚉
📍 outside JR stn (0187) 54-2700.
🎎 Aki Matsuri (Fall Festival, Sep 7–9).

Famed for its samurai quarter and weeping cherry trees, Kakunodate has only a sprinkling of its original samurai houses remaining on Uchimachi, to the northwest of the station. However, the broad avenue, faced with the gated houses, wonderfully evokes the past. More than 150 of the weeping cherries on Uchimachi, brought from Kyoto almost 300 years ago, have been designated National Natural Treasures.

Among the samurai houses that are open to the public, the large **Aoyagi-ke** has three small museums in its grounds. Look for the ceilings painted with waves as protection from fire. At the classic **Ishiguro-ke**, known for its beautiful garden, note the transoms between rooms, carved to project shadows by candle-light. Also on Uchimachi, the red-brick **Denshokan Museum** has exhibits of historical and craft items and demonstrations of outstanding local crafts, including *kabazaiku* (objects of polished cherry bark) and *itayazaiku* (baskets and folk objects woven of split maple).

🏯 **Aoyagi-ke**
Tel (0187) 54-3257. ⬜ daily. 🎫
🏯 **Ishiguro-ke**
Tel (0187) 55-1496. ⬜ daily. 🎫
🏛 **Denshokan Museum**
Tel (0187) 54-1700. ⬜ daily. 🎫

Looking into the garden from Ishiguro-ke samurai house, Kakunodate

Oga Peninsula 17

男鹿半島

Akita prefecture. 🚉 JR Oga stn. 📍 next to JR Oga stn (0185) 23-2111. 🎎 Namahage Sedo Matsuri (2nd Fri–Sun in Feb); Namahage (Dec 31).

Kicking 20 km (12 miles) into the Sea of Japan (East Sea), this foot-shaped peninsula has a scenic rocky coastline, pleasant little fishing villages, good seafood, and hills covered with Akita cedar. The lookout on **Mount Kanpu**, at the neck of the peninsula, offers a panoramic view of mountains, sea, and spreading rice fields. The peninsula is best known for its Namahage Festival, held on New Year's Eve, when men dressed in horned demon masks and bulky straw coats go from house to house, scaring children into being good and idlers into working. A tourist version of the festival, the Namahage Sedo Matsuri, is held at **Shinzan Shrine**, in the city of Oga.

Towada-Hachimantai National Park 18

十和田八幡平国立公園

Akita, Aomori, and Iwate prefectures. 🚉 JR Morioka & JR Aomori stns. 🚌 from stns to Lake Towada. 📍 at Lake Towada (0176) 75-2425.

Touching three prefectures, the Towada-Hachimantai National Park is in two sections with the mountainous Hachimantai section 60 km (37 miles) south of the Towada section. Car is the best way to get around: trains are limited and buses not available in winter. **Hachimantai** offers hiking and ski trails, frozen lava flows, alpine flora, and mountain views. A favorite with Japanese tourists, it has scenic toll roads, hot-spring and ski resorts, and a variety of tourist facilities. Good stopping places include **Goshogake** *onsen*, **Hachimantai Resort** ski complex, and the tourist village of **Putaro**.

In the **Towada** section highlights include **Lake Towada**, a lovely caldera lake. Its symbol, a statue of two maidens (1953) by Takamura Kotaro, is on the southern shore. More dramatic is the 9 km (6-mile) **Oirase Gorge** to the east of the lake. While it is possible to travel the gorge by bus, car, or bike, it is best to get off the busy highway and walk. Also impressive are Towada's virgin beech forests, rightly dubbed an ocean of trees. North of the lake are some atmospheric spa inns, such as the excellent Tsuta Onsen.

Beech forest in the Towada section of Towada-Hachimantai National Park

Hirosaki ⑲

弘前

Aomori prefecture. 👥 187,000. 🚉
ℹ️ Kankokan, Otemon Square (0172)
37-5501. www.city.hirosaki.aomori.
jp 🎭 Neputa Matsuri (Aug 1–7).

Long the cultural and educational center of Aomori, Hirosaki is a delight to explore, its main attraction being its castle, a pocket of feudal history in a thriving modern city. Most streets lead, more or less, to **Hirosaki Park**, the old castle grounds of the Tsugaru lords. The castle was destroyed by lightning but its picturesque 1810 keep, some smaller towers, several gates, and three moats remain. **Kamenoko-mon**, the imposing main gate, is on the north, where historic samurai houses still stand. Nearby is the **Tsugaruhan Neputa Mura**, displaying the Neputa floats used in Hirosaki's more refined version of Aomori's Nebuta festival.

The wooded castle park is famous for its cherry blossoms, at their best in late April. The **Municipal Museum**, inside the park, has exhibitions of local history, including old photographs of the Neputa Festival.

One of the temples en route to Chosho-ji, Hirosaki

Twenty-two temples line the approach to **Chosho-ji**, the family temple of the Tsugaru, about a 15-minute walk southwest of the park, built on a bluff overlooking the Hirosaki plain and Mount Iwaki. Its handsome two-story gate has extra-deep eaves because of the heavy snows common in the area. A side hall contains interesting polychrome statues of the Buddha's 500 disciples. The naturally mummified body of the 12th Tsugaru lord is displayed in the main hall.

Like most feudal towns, the streets around the castle were designed to twist and turn to confuse enemy forces. The large **Kankokan** (municipal information center) just south of the park is a good place to get oriented. It also has displays of local crafts. Other good craft outlets include Tanakaya, on the corner of Ichiban-cho, which has a fine selection of traditional and contemporary Tsugaru lacquerware. Miyamoto Kogei, on Minami Sakura-cho, handles baskets of *akebi*, a vine that grows wild in the mountains. Not to be missed is the bar-restaurant Yamauta *(see p345)*.

🎪 **Tsugaruhan Neputa Mura**
NE corner outside castle park.
Tel (0172) 39-1511. ⭕ daily. 🎟️
🏛️ **Municipal Museum**
Tel (0172) 35-0700. ⭕ Tue–Sun. 🎟️
⛩️ **Chosho-ji**
Tel (0172) 32-0813. **Main hall**
⭕ Mar–Nov: daily (at other times by appointment). 🎟️

Reconstructed dwellings at Sannai-Maruyama

Aomori ⑳

青森

Aomori prefecture. 👥 313,000. 🚉
ℹ️ JR Bus stn bldg (017) 723-4670.
www.city.aomori.aomori.jp
🎭 Nebuta Matsuri (Aug 2–7).

Rebuilt after World War II, Aomori is a nondescript city with two outstanding attractions. One is the Nebuta Matsuri *(see p46)*; the other **Sannai-Maruyama**, a Jomon-period (10,000–300 BC) site. Since its discovery in 1993, the site has yielded relics and ruins from 4,000–5,500 years ago, including a woven pouch, red lacquerware, and clay figures. Most impressive are the reconstructed pit dwellings and a standing-pillar building.

🎪 **Sannai-Maruyama**
🚌 from JR stn to Sannai-Maruyama Iseki. *Tel* (017) 734-9924. ⭕ daily.

Shimokita Peninsula ㉑

下北半島

Aomori prefecture. 🚉 JR Ominato stn. ℹ️ at JR Ominato stn.

This ax-shaped peninsula offers unspoiled beauty. In the interior is the desolate **Osorezan** (Mount Dread), one of three Japanese mountains sacred to spirits of the dead, with a crater lake and sulfur hot springs. It is open from May to October. Blind mediums communicate with the spirits from July 20–24. Take the ferry from Sai along the west coast to **Hotoke-ga-ura** (Buddha Coast) with sea-worn cliffs and rock formations. In the southwest the port of **Wakinosawa** is home to sassy snow monkeys. A ferry runs from here to Aomori.

MATSUO BASHO AND HAIKU

Matsuo Basho (1644–94), a master of style and a thinker to whom life and art were one, perfected the haiku form. Originating in Japan, haiku is now practiced internationally. A classical haiku is 17 syllables (written 5-7-5), includes a seasonal word, and refers to an objective image in the present. Basho spent most of his life traveling and writing haiku. His most famous travel journal, a superb guide to northern Japan, is *The Narrow Road to the Deep North*, about his five-month pilgrimage in 1689; the northernmost point of his journey was Akita prefecture.

Statue of Basho

HOKKAIDO

J apan's northernmost island is on the Pacific "ring of fire" at the southern edge of the Okhotsk Sea. Russia lies to the north, west, and east, while the deep Tsugaru Strait to the south separates Hokkaido from Honshu. With both sea-ice and active volcanoes, it is truly a land of fire and ice. Dramatic peaks, gorges, and lakes all contribute to making Hokkaido the part of Japan where nature is at its most vivid.

First settled 20,000 years ago, this remote northern island became the only homeland of the indigenous Ainu people after the 12th century. The Japanese made early forays to Yezo, as the island was called, from 659, but it was perceived as remote, inhospitable, and cold. For centuries only the persecuted Ainu, refugee warriors, and banished criminals lived here. In the late 1860s, however, the new Meiji government decided officially to settle the island. Thereafter it became known as Hokkaido, or "north sea road."

Skiing in central Hokkiado

Since then, the population has risen to just under 6 million. The few Ainu left number somewhere between 24,000 and 60,000. Fishing, farming, forestry, and mining are the main industries, but tourism draws several million people north each year.

Sapporo, the capital, is a lively, fast-growing city, home to spectacular festivals. Outside Sapporo, the lifestyle of the Ainu is about the only point of cultural and historical interest for the visitor. By contrast, numerous national parks offer boundless opportunities for outdoor enthusiasts, including camping, hiking, and hotspring bathing. Extensive forests, broad mountain ranges, numerous lakes and wetlands, and a long coastline support a wealth of plant, animal, and birdlife.

The prevailing winter winds blow in from Siberia, resulting in a sub-arctic winter climate, with temperatures sometimes dropping to -30°C (-22°F). This means a guaranteed snow season with perfect powder snow for skiers. Between May and September temperatures rise into the 20s (70s Fahrenheit).

Nighttime scene in Susukino, the entertainment district of Hokkaido's modern capital, Sapporo

◁ Dramatic view of Sounkyo gorge, in Daisetsu-zan, Japan's largest national park

Exploring Hokkaido

Just five percent of the Japanese population has settled on Japan's second-largest island, mainly in the capital, Sapporo, and the port of Hakodate. Volcanic mountains, caldera lakes, and rocks stained by yellow sulfur characterize the wild interior, while forests and wetlands provide breeding grounds for wildlife. Wildflowers are bountiful on coasts and mountains in spring and summer. Information in English is scarce outside Sapporo and Hakodate, and distances between sights are great, so planning ahead is essential if time is limited. Allow at least a week to explore the island.

Hakodate harbor and city from Mount Hakodate

WAKKANAI

RISHIRI-REBUN
REBUN
ISLAND
NATIONAL PARK

RISHIRI
ISLAND

40

HAMATONBETSU

238

HORONOBE

Soya Line

OTOINEPPU

232

NAYORO

TOMAMAE

239

SHIBETSU

ASAHIKAWA
MT ASAH
2,290 m/7

FUKAGAWA

DAISETSU-ZA
NATIONAL PAR

TAKIKAWA

Nemuro Line

38

231

12

OTARU

SAPPORO

IWAMIZAWA

234

Sekisho Line

SEA OF
JAPAN
(EAST SEA)

5

NISEKO SKI
RESORT
MT YOTEI
1,900 m/6,230 ft

230

Lake
Shikotsu

HIDAKA

237

SHIKOTSU-TOYA
NATIONAL PARK
Lake
Toya

229

Doo Expressway

37

TOMAKOMAI

228

MURORAN

MT
KOMAGATAKE
1,330 m/4,360 ft

ONUMA QUASI-
NATIONAL PARK

HAKODATE

↓ Honshu

GETTING AROUND

Sapporo international airport is the main gateway to Hokkaido and also offers internal flights to many parts of the island. Hokkaido is connected by rail to Honshu via a 25-km (16-mile) tunnel; it is possible to take an overnight train all the way from Tokyo to Sapporo. Several JR rail lines cover the island, offering relatively fast links. Buses run to many destinations, although a car or bicycle provides more flexibility. Numerous hiking routes crisscross the national parks.

KEY

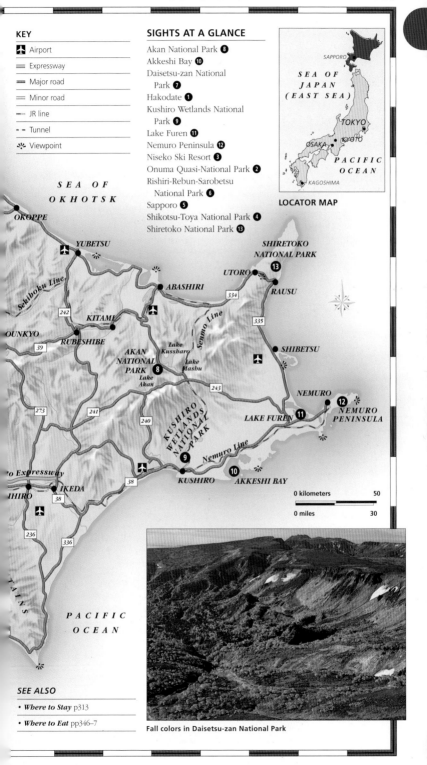

✈ Airport

▬ Expressway

▬ Major road

═ Minor road

╌╌ JR line

- - Tunnel

✲ Viewpoint

SIGHTS AT A GLANCE

Akan National Park ⑧

Akkeshi Bay ⑩

Daisetsu-zan National
Park ⑦

Hakodate ①

Kushiro Wetlands National
Park ⑨

Lake Furen ⑪

Nemuro Peninsula ⑫

Niseko Ski Resort ③

Onuma Quasi-National Park ②

Rishiri-Rebun-Sarobetsu
National Park ⑥

Sapporo ⑤

Shikotsu-Toya National Park ④

Shiretoko National Park ⑬

LOCATOR MAP

SEA OF JAPAN (EAST SEA)

SAPPORO

TOKYO

ŌSAKA KYOTO

PACIFIC OCEAN

KAGOSHIMA

SEA OF OKHOTSK

OKOPPE

YUBETSU

Sekihoku Line

SHIRETOKO NATIONAL PARK

UTORO ⑬

RAUSU

ABASHIRI

334

Senmo Line

242

KITAMI

335

OUNKYO

39

RUBESHIBE

Lake
Kussharo

AKAN NATIONAL PARK ⑧

Lake
Mashu

SHIBETSU

243

NEMURO

273

241

240

NEMURO PENINSULA ⑫

LAKE FUREN ⑪

KUSHIRO WETLANDS NATIONAL PARK ⑨

Nemuro Line

o Expressway

38

236 IKEDA

IHIRO 38

KUSHIRO ⑨

AKKESHI BAY ⑩

0 kilometers   50

0 miles   30

236 336

PACIFIC OCEAN

SEE ALSO

• *Where to Stay* p313

• *Where to Eat* pp346–7

Fall colors in Daisetsu-zan National Park

Blossom-viewing in Hakodate's Goryokaku Park

springtime spectacle. The pentagon-shaped **Goryo-kaku Fort** was built in 1865 to defend against the Russians, but it fell to imperial forces in 1869.

Environs:
Hot-spring enthusiasts will want to stay at the *onsen* resort of **Yunokawa** 15 minutes from the center. An hour's drive to the east of the city is the active **Mount Esan** volcano with nearby azalea gardens and forested slopes.

Hakodate ❶

函館

🚶 294,000. ✈ Hakodate. 🚉 from Sapporo. ⛴ from Aomori.
🛈 next to stn (0138) 23-5440.
www.city.hakodate.hokkaido.jp
🎏 Hakodate Port Festival (Aug 1–5).

Once an island, the fan-shaped city of Hakodate now straddles a low sandbar that links it to the mainland. In 1854, Hakodate was designated one of the first treaty ports in Japan. Fifteen years later the city was the scene of one of the last battles heralding the Meiji Restoration.

Within easy reach of the center is **Mount Hakodate**, the peak of which can be reached by cable car, road, or on foot. There are pleasant country walks and spectacular panoramas – at night the shimmering city lights can be seen fanning out between two dark arms of the sea.

The quiet **Motomachi** district, nestling beneath Mount Hakodate in the south of the city, is the most attractive area. Western-style buildings are a feature here, a legacy of the treaty-port status. They include the **Old Public Hall**, with its stately blue-and-yellow clapboarding; the **Russian Orthodox Church** with its spire and onion domes; and, nearby, the **Old British Consulate**.

In the north, **Goryokaku Park** provides a peaceful haven for strolling, and its more than 1,500 cherry trees create a popular

Onuma Quasi-National Park ❷

大沼国定公園

🚉 Onuma-Koen stn. 🚌 from Hakodate. 🛈 next to stn (0138) 67-2170.

Three large, islet-studded lakes – Onuma, Konuma, and Junsainuma – are surrounded by forest and form the Onuma Quasi-National Park. Deer and foxes inhabit the forests, and the lakes support several kinds of waterfowl, particularly during the spring and fall migrations. Wildflowers are abundant in summer, while overhead Latham's snipe perform the bizarre zigzag display flights that earn them the local name of "lightning bird." The graceful form of **Mount Komagatake** provides a stunning backdrop to the north.

An easily followed hiking trail from the north side of Lake Onuma to the upper mountain provides a fabulous view of southwestern Hokkaido.

Niseko Ski Resort ❸

ニセコスキーリゾート

🚉 Niseko stn. 🚌 from Sapporo.

Some of Japan's best skiing can be found in the Niseko Mountains. Snowboarders and skiers alike favor this area for its long, cold winter season, numerous slopes, and quality off-piste powder. In summer it offers adventure-sports vacations. At **Hirafu**, the main ski runs are linked physically but run by competing companies – you need to buy a separate pass for each. The beauty of the slopes is not matched by the resort – its cluster of hotels and pensions lacks style, and few facilities are available outside the package accommodations.

Shikotsu-Toya National Park ❹

支笏洞爺国立公園

🚉 Toya stn. 🚌 from Sapporo. 🛈 at Toya stn (0142) 75-2446.

The disjointed Shikotsu-Toya National Park is like an open-air museum to vulcanology. It contains the 1,900-m (6,230-ft) high **Mount Yotei** (also known as Ezo-Fuji, due to its conical shape), two large crater lakes, and the

Mount Komagatake across Lake Onuma

spa towns of **Jozankei** in the north and **Noboribetsu** in the south. Summer weekends and fall tend to be busy with visitors from nearby Sapporo.

By **Lake Shikotsu** is the popular hot-spring resort of **Shikotsu Kohan**, as well as the remarkable moss-covered **Kokenodomon** gorge. The lake is dominated to the north by the rugged peak of **Mount Eniwa**, and to the south by the recumbent forms of **Mount Fuppushi** and **Mount Tarumae**, with its cinder cone.

Lake Toya, 40 km (25 miles) farther southwest, contains the picturesque central island of Oshima and three smaller satellite islands. Nearby stands Japan's youngest volcano, the bare-sloped **Showa Shinzan** (formed 1943–5), beside the extremely active **Mount Usu**.

The mountains in the park make for rewarding day hiking; trails are well defined, and the views from the tops of Eniwa and Tarumae are superb.

Sapporo ❺

札幌

🏯 1,888,000. ✈ Shin-Chitose, Okadama. 🚉 🛈 Sapporo International Communication Plaza (011) 211-3678; booth in stn (011) 213-5062. www.welcome.city. sapporo.jp/english/index/html
🎏 Snow Festival (1st week in Feb); Hokkaido Shrine Festival (Jun 14–16); Summer Festival (Jul 21–Aug 20); Bon Odori (mid-Aug).

Capital of Hokkaido, the modern city of Sapporo lies on the Ishikari plain, straddling the Toyohira River. Four subway lines, street cars, and a well laid-out grid structure make getting around fairly straightforward. At Sapporo's heart lies the long **Odori Park**, dominated at the east end by the metal television tower and at the west by a view to the mountains. One block north, opposite the historic wooden **Tokei-dai** clocktower, is the **Sapporo International Communication Plaza**, an essential stop for information on travel all over Hokkaido, with friendly staff to help with planning and booking.

Neon lights in Sapporo's busy Susukino district

The city gives its name to the famous local beer; its brewing is shown at the **Sapporo Beer Garden and Museum** south of the station. Nightlife is focused in the **Susukino** area, two stops south of the station on the Nanboku subway line, with thousands of restaurants and bars. Local specialties include "Genghis Khan" – mutton and vegetables barbecue-grilled in a cast-iron pan.

A huge collection of Ainu artifacts is displayed at the **Ainu Museum** in the **Botanical Gardens**. The gardens themselves are a refreshingly quiet spot, with a representative collection of Hokkaido's flora. The large-scale outdoor sculptures at the **Sapporo Art Park**, set amid wooded hills, make for an interesting hands-on excursion.

🍺 **Sapporo Beer Museum**
Tel (011) 731-4368. ⭕ daily.

🍺 **Botanical Gardens and Ainu Museum**
10-min walk SW of stn. *Tel* (011) 221-0066. ⭕ end Apr–early Nov daily. 🎫

🍺 **Sapporo Art Park**
Tel (011) 592-5111. ⭕ daily. ⬤ Nov 4–Apr 28: Mon.

Environs:
Lying 14 km (9 miles) east of the city, **Historical Village of Hokkaido** commemorates the official settlement of the island in the 1860s. This cluster of evocatively restored late 19th-century buildings has been gathered from around Hokkaido. Some have displays of traditional life.

🏛 **Historical Village of Hokkaido**
Tel (011) 898-2692. ⭕ Tue–Sun. 🎫

SAPPORO SNOW FESTIVAL

The annual Snow Festival (Yuki Matsuri) transforms Sapporo's Odori Park and the nearby Susukino area and Makomanai Park into a fairytale land of snow sculptures and ice carvings, drawing up to two million visitors. Watching the making of these imaginative and complex forms (from about a week before the start of the festival) can be even more interesting than seeing the finished objects. The festival overlaps with the Sapporo White Illumination: (mid-November to mid-February) strings of white lights adorn Odori Park and Ekimae-dori. A night visit is magical.

One of the elaborate snow carvings at Sapporo's Snow Festival

Rishiri-Rebun-Sarobetsu National Park ❻

利尻礼文サロベツ国立公園

🚹 Wakkanai. 🚉 Wakkanai stn.
🚢 from Wakkanai to both islands.

Consisting of the Sarobetsu coast of north Hokkaido and the two islands of Rishiri and Rebun, this park is within sight of the Russian island of Sakhalin. Although remote – at least a 6-hour drive north of Sapporo – the park is easily accessible by plane or train. The coastal meadows in the **Sarobetsu** area and the shores of the shallow lagoons in the coastal plain, are carpeted with flowers in summer, including yellow-orange lilies, white cotton grass, white rhododendrons, and purple irises.

About 20 km (12 miles) offshore, the startling 1,720-m (5,650-ft) high conical peak of **Mount Rishiri** (Rishiri-Fuji) appears to rise straight from the sea. A road runs around its coastline, making for scenic cycling and linking the various settlements including **Oshidomari**, the main port, and **Kutsugata**, the second port on the west side. Trails to the top of Mount Rishiri thread through a host of alpine summer flowers. Those less inclined to hike may choose to fish or simply relax and enjoy the excellent fresh fish at local restaurants.

Rebun, Rishiri's partner and Japan's northernmost island, is lowly in comparison but is renowned as the "isle of flowers." **Kabuka** is its main port; the fishing village of **Funadomari** is at the opposite, north end of the island. There's great hiking (sometimes hard-going), especially on the west coast; the island's youth hostel organizes guided walking groups.

Women cutting dried kelp at Kutsugata on Rishiri Island

Daisetsu-zan National Park ❼

大雪山国立公園

🚹 Okadama and Asahikawa. 🚉 Asahikawa and Obihiro stns.

At 2,310 sq km (890 sq miles), Daisetsu-zan is Japan's largest national park. A huge raised plateau ringed with peaks, right in the center of Hokkaido, the park was established in 1934. **Asahikawa** to the northwest or **Obihiro** to the south make the best starting points for visiting the park, with easy car access by routes 39 and 273. Buses connect the major *onsen* resorts of **Sounkyo**, **Asahi-dake**, and **Tenninkyo**. The plunging **Sounkyo gorge**, with the cascading Ryusei and Ginga waterfalls, is best explored by bicycle or on foot. The ropeway at Sounkyo and the cable car at Asahi-dake tend to be packed but offer quick access; away from the top stations people become scarcer and the views more spectacular.

In Ainu legend the peaks of the Daisetsu mountains are the dwelling places of benevolent but powerful god-spirits who, in human form, helped in times of need. To hike among these mountains is certainly to feel among the gods. A network of trails provides everything from day hikes to week-long tramps, and it is worth taking the time to hike or take the cable car up from the low access roads to the higher levels for the breathtaking views. The dramatic, conical, steam-venting peak of **Mount Asahi** (or Asahi-dake), Hokkaido's highest at 2,290 m (7,500 ft), offers an uplifting panorama across the high plateau. June and July bring alpine flowers, while fall colors are at their best in late August and September. En route, you may see bears and pika, rubythroats and nutcrackers among other species.

An excellent route for the fit day-hiker starts from Sounkyo *onsen*. From there take the ropeway and cable car, then hike southwest over Mount Kurodake, continuing along well-marked trails to Mount Asahi. From the top, descend via the cablecar to Asahi-dake *onsen*. It should take around 7 hours in total.

Snow-capped peaks in Daisetsu-zan National Park

Lake Mashu, one of Hokkaido's most beautiful sights, in Akan National Park

Akan National Park ⑧

阿寒国立公園

🚉 *Memanbetsu (Abashiri), Nakashi-betsu, and Kushiro.* 🚉 *Teshikaga and Kawayu stns.* 🚌 *from Kushiro stn.* ℹ️ *near Akan Kohan bus terminal (0154) 67-3200.* 🎏 *Marimo Festival (Oct 8–10).*

This enormous National Park of 905 sq km (350 sq miles) in east-central Hokkaido is possibly the most beautiful in Japan. Travel around the park is limited; there are tour buses, but cycling, hitching, or rental-car are all better options.

The western portion, around **Lake Akan** (famed for its bizarre green spherical algae known as *marimo*) is dominated by a pair of volcanic peaks: in the southeast is the 1,370-m (4,500-ft) **Mount O-Akan** while in the southwest is the still-active **Mount Me-Akan**, at 1,500 m (4,920 ft). The day hike up Me-Akan from **Akan Kohan** *onsen* and down the other side on a well-trodden trail to attractive **Lake Onetto** affords marvelous views in any season, but especially in fall. O-Akan is a more serious hike but also possible in a day.

East of Akan, over the pass toward **Teshikaga** (a spectacular drive in itself), are splendid views back to the two volcanoes. Farther east lies **Lake Kussharo**, in a huge caldera with a 57-km (35-mile) perimeter. Beautiful all year, this enormous lake freezes over almost entirely in winter

when the harmonics created by pressure in the ice make the lake sound as if it is singing. Thermal vents keep tiny portions ice-free; here flocks of whooper swans remain throughout the winter.

Farther east again lies **Lake Mashu**, prized as one of the greatest scenic spots in all Hokkaido, especially when the weather is kind. The crater's steep internal cliffs rise 200 m (650 ft), the water of the lake is astonishingly clear, and the lake has no inlets or outlets. The panoramic view from the crater rim takes in Mount Shari to the north, the Shiretoko Peninsula to the northeast, and Lake Kussharo and beyond to the Akan volcanoes in the west.

The park's forests are home to many woodpeckers, including the black woodpecker, other forest birds, red foxes, sika deer, red squirrels, and Siberian chipmunks.

For those interested in geothermal activity, in addition to active Me-Akan, there are simple outdoor hot-spring pools at **Akan Kohan** and **Wakoto**, both on Lake Kussharo's south shore, steaming sulfuroles on **Mount Iou** (between Kussharo and Mashu lakes), and "bokke" (small areas of bubbling mud) beside Lake Akan. The larger and more tourist-oriented spa resorts of **Kawayu** and **Akan** are crowded with souvenir shops selling Ainu carvings.

AINU CULTURE

Ainu culture in Japan is believed to have developed its distinctive characteristics between the 8th and 14th centuries. Physically large, typically bearded, and often with wavy hair, the Ainu more closely resemble Caucasians than do Japanese. Their relationship with nature was a powerful one, linked to their dependence on it for food, clothing, and building materials. Animals they hunted or encountered were often revered as *kamui* (gods), and killing for food was a necessity that invoked rituals to thank the god-spirits. The lives of many animal and bird species were intimately known. Ainu dances, including a crane dance, mimic nature, and their crafts include implements and clothing made from locally available materials such as salmon skin and deer antlers.

After the Japanese settled Hokkaido in the 1860s, Ainu land was confiscated and hunting and fishing rights suppressed. Much of the traditional orally transferred wisdom disappeared as the Ainu were encouraged to "assimilate." Only recently have many of the old oral epics or *yukars* been transcribed. Few people now use the language, even though there has been something of a revival since 1990.

A traditionally dressed Ainu man and woman

Whooper swans on Lake Kussharo in Akan National Park ▷

Kushiro Wetlands National Park ❾

釧路湿原

🚶 *Kushiro.* 🚋 *Kushiro stn.* 🚌 *from Kushiro.* ℹ️ *JR Kushiro stn (0154) 22-8294.*

If any creature represents japan, it is the beautiful *tancho*, or red-crowned crane, regarded as a symbol of happiness and long life (myth has it that it lives a thousand years). To the Ainu, the crane is a god of the marshes – *sarurun kamui*. The Kushiro Wetlands National Park is typical of its natural environment. This enormous peat swamp, an expanse of undulating reed beds bisected by streams, north of the coastal port city of Kushiro is one of the main homes of these enormous, graceful birds that stand 1.4 m (4 ft 6 in) high. The cranes are also found in other wetlands of southeast Hokkaido, albeit in smaller numbers.

In the early 20th century, the cranes were pushed to the verge of extinction in Japan by a combination of hunting and loss of habitat, but now protection and provision of food for them during the winter months has helped the young cranes survive, boosting the population to around 700 birds.

During the winter nights (December to March) the cranes roost in the safety of flowing rivers. By day, they forage along streams and marsh edges, or fly to one of three major feeding sites north of Kushiro: two in **Tsurui** village and one in **Akan** village. These sites offer the best opportunities for viewing the cranes year round. On late winter days, the birds display, calling and dancing to one another in the snow as they prepare for the breeding season ahead. In summer (May to September), the cranes are territorial, occupying large, traditional nesting grounds where they usually raise just one chick, or occasionally two. In the lush green summer reed beds, even these tall birds are well hidden, but may be spotted at the marsh fringes.

A red-crowned crane

Akkeshi Bay ❿

厚岸湾

🚶 *Kushiro.* 🚋 *Akkeshi stn.*

Akkeshi's sheltered tidal lagoon is renowned for the quality of its oysters. The bay is extensively farmed, and there is a shrine to the oysters on a rocky islet. Throughout the winter, and especially during spring and fall migration, hundreds of whooper swans gather in the inner bay, while in summer red-crowned cranes breed upriver and at the nearby **Kiritappu wetland**. The coastal road from Akkeshi

Whooper swans congregating at Akkeshi Bay

around to Kiritappu is well worth driving – both for the scenery and for an insight into the fishing and seaweed-harvesting lifestyles of some of the people in this region. Walking at the cape beyond Kiritappu is exhilarating, but early summer mornings are best avoided because this is when a sea mist is most likely to conceal the view.

Lake Furen ⓫

風蓮湖

🚶 *Kushiro.* 🚋 *Nemuro stn.*

A far cry from Japan's crowded cityscapes, the huge 52 sq-km (20 sq-mile) lagoon of Lake Furen is surrounded by expansive, eye-relaxing landscape. Situated on Hokkaido's east coast, this lake is the seasonal haunt of hordes of birds: migrating waterfowl in spring and fall, sea eagles in winter, and breeding red-crowned cranes during summer.

Nearly 20 km (12 miles) long and up to 4 km (2 miles) wide, the lagoon is only 2 m (6 ft) deep or less in places. It is fringed by forests of fir and spruce, with alder and birch scrub in wetter areas. Some easy forest walks start from the south end of the lake, at **Hakkuchodai** and **Shunkunitai**, offering a wealth of birdwatching opportunities and plenty of wildflowers en route. In winter, the frozen lagoon and adjacent areas are good for cross-country skiing.

Kushiro Wetlands, Japan's largest peat swamp

Nemuro Peninsula ⑫

知床半島

🛫 Nemuro-Nakashibetsu.
🚃 Nemuro stn.

In contrast to the rugged, mountainous Shiretoko Peninsula of northeast Hokkaido, the Nemuro Peninsula in the southeast is low-lying, essentially a coastal plateau carved by streams into steep-sided gullies, and well loved by naturalists. The best way to explore the area is by car.

The red fox is common here and, in forests around the base of the peninsula, particularly in the Onetto area, there are also many sika deer. In summer, lilies, fritillaries, and other wildflowers are abundant, while in winter, although the cape appears bleak and inhospitable, both white-tailed and Steller's sea eagles can be seen. Offshore and in the many sheltered harbors and bays, there are flocks of sea duck, particularly scoter and harlequin, and many other seabirds can be spotted in the coastal waters.

At the base of the peninsula, the quiet town of **Nemuro** has little to offer the visitor, apart from being a practical base. At **Cape Nosappu** the viewing tower overlooks the Russian-occupied islands across the narrow Nemuro Channel.

A red fox, often seen on the Nemuro Peninsula

supports one of the healthiest remaining populations of brown bears left in Hokkaido. Sightings are few and far between, although the boat ride from **Utoro** (on the northwest coast) north to the cape during the summer is one possible way of seeing them as they forage along the coastal strip.

Minke whales, dolphins, and porpoises may be seen in summer, too, along with seabirds such as spectacled guillemots, Japanese cormorants, and migratory short-tailed shearwaters. Several pairs of white-tailed sea eagles nest along the peninsula. In winter their numbers are swollen by hundreds more arriving from Russia, but then they are overshadowed by the world's

Steller's sea eagle

largest and most magnificent eagle: Steller's sea eagle. Both types of eagles are best seen in winter north of **Rausu** on the southeast coast.

North of Utoro lie the pretty **Shiretoko Five Lakes**, reflecting Mount Rausu. There is an easy 2-km (1-mile) trail starting beyond the Visitor Center, and *onsen*-enthusiasts will not want to miss the hot waterfall known as **Kamui-wakka**, northeast of here. From June to October the high pass from Utoro to Rausu (Route 334) is open, and the view east from here to Kunashiri island is dramatic. This road passes through the subalpine zone, which is dominated by dwarf stone pine trees. From near the pass, a hiking trail strikes off south for Lake Rausu and Mount Onnebetsu, while another heads north for Mounts Rausu, Io, and Shiretoko and the cape beyond. For most levels of fitness, Mount Rausu is a manageable day hike along a good trail. The journey to the cape, however, requires several days and careful planning. The long, cold winters and short summers here make hiking possible only from June to September.

Shiretoko National Park ⑬

根室半島

🛫 Memanbetsu (Abashiri) or Nakashibetsu. 🚃 Shiretoko-Shari stn.
ℹ️ Shiretoko Shizen center (01522) 4-2114.

This rugged finger of land, jutting 65 km (40 miles) northeast into the Okhotsk Sea, was named Shiretoko ("the end of the earth") by the Ainu. Japan's wildest national park, its 386 sq km (150 sq miles) consist of a well-forested mountainous ridge of volcanic peaks dominated by the 1,660-m (5,450-ft) **Mount Rausu**. The peninsula

Utoro lighthouse on the northwest coast of Shiretoko National Park

TRAVELERS' NEEDS

WHERE TO STAY

The tradition of hosting travelers is so deep-rooted in Japan that every town is well endowed with welcoming places to stay. There are two basic classifications of accommodations: Western-style and traditional. No visit to Japan is complete without staying at least one night in a traditional Japanese inn, called a *ryokan (see pp296–7)*. These tend to be multi-generational enterprises, offering a glimpse into a more traditional way of life. The

Sign for the Palace Hotel, Central Tokyo *(see p292)*

range of hospitality is diverse in every sense – style, price, the size and quality of rooms, and facilities provided. There is also a certain amount of cultural crossover. Only the quality of service is a non-variable: friendly and eager to please. Indeed, staff who lack communication skills in languages other than their own, willing to provide nothing but the best, have been known to turn foreigners away rather than compromise their renowned quality of service.

HELPFUL ORGANIZATIONS

Designed for overseas visitors, the **Welcome Inn Reservation Center** (WIRC) arranges free bookings through their website for approved traditional inns (*ryokan*), government-run lodges, business hotels, and pensions. JNTO offices *(see p371)* stock the *Directory of Welcome Inns*. In Japan, there are WIRC counters in the arrivals lobbies of Tokyo's Narita airport, Osaka's Kansai airport, and at Tokyo's TIC *(see p387)*; in Kyoto, go to the tourist information office in Kyoto Station *(see p158)*.

Many of the traditional inns approved by the WIRC also belong to the **Japanese Inn Group**, which covers about 80 moderately rated *ryokan* that are geared to receiving mainly foreign visitors.

The **Japan Hotel Association** has online information

Western-style façade of the Japanese airline-owned ANA hotel, Nagasaki

about member hotels and advance bookings. The **Japan Economy Hotel** (JEH) **Group** offers clean, modern rooms at reasonable rates in convenient locations.

BOOKING AND PAYING

Booking accommodations in advance is advisable, especially at times of major public holidays *(see p47)*. Reservations made directly need to be confirmed by letter, fax, or e-mail. Rates quoted are often per person, not per room.

Most hotels accept the best-known international credit cards. The bill is usually payable on departure, but business hotels and some others request advance payment. A 10–20 percent service charge (on top of the 5 percent consumption tax) is often added, depending on the style and quality of the hotel. A small hotel tax is also added in Tokyo hotels for rooms priced above 10,000 yen per person.

DELUXE HOTELS

Top American chains such as the Hilton, Sheraton, Hyatt, Westin, and Four Seasons are well established in Japan.

Among Japanese-owned hotels, there is a vast range: staid conservatism; over-the-top opulence; discreet exclusivity; chic minimalism; quaint eccentricity. Increasingly common are "intelligent" hotels, which monitor temperature, have electronic cards in place of room keys, computerized toilets, a voice-mail message system, and broad-band telecommunication networks.

MID-RANGE HOTELS

Many hotels in Japan offer an appealing combination of Western-style rooms with their own bathrooms, and Japanese-style flourishes such as an optional communal bath. Often there is a choice of Western-style or *tatami*-matted, Japanese-style rooms.

Sleek curves of the Portopia Hotel in the port area of Kobe

◁ Okinawan fabrics for sale at an indoor market in Naha

PENSIONS

Western-style pensions have become popular in recent years. Located mostly in resort areas, they are rustic and relaxed in style and offer good hearty meals. Generally managed by married couples, they fall somewhere between a *minshuku (see p297)* and the more service-oriented pamperings of a small hotel.

BUSINESS HOTELS

As the name suggests, business hotels *(bijinesu hoteru)* cater to budget-concious business travelers. Anyone can stay, and being generally located in city centers around train stations, they are very convenient. Do not expect English to be spoken.

Rooms are Western-style, small, and clean. Slippers and a cotton robe are generally supplied. There is no room service, but vending machines offer the ubiquitous "health drinks," beer, and sake. There is usually at least one restaurant with a choice of Japanese or Western-style breakfasts.

Sign showing rates for a Tokyo love hotel

CAPSULE HOTELS

Unique to Japan, these custom-built hotels feature encapsulated beds in and out of which guests must slide, since there is no room to sit up, let alone stand up. Rattan blinds or curtains can be pulled across for a degree of privacy. Usually constructed in two tiers, they cater mainly to *"salarymen"* who are too tired or inebriated to make the last train home. Most are clustered around major train stations or nightlife areas. Facilities include a personal TV, radio, alarm call system, and air-conditioning. Smoking is not allowed. Vending machines may be nearby. Baths and sometimes saunas are included in the price.

The size of such hotels varies widely, ranging from 50 capsules to over 600. Some still cater only to men, but women are increasingly being accepted and encouraged to stay.

LOVE HOTELS

Love Hotels are designed especially for dating couples and married partners living in extended families, who may feel that they need some privacy. They are mainly found in entertainment areas and along expressways and highways, much like motels. Prices are twofold: "rest" (for a quickie) and "stay" (up to an overnight stay). The most entertaining offer thematic decor as an additional turn-on.

YOUTH HOSTELS

Some 360 youth hostels are scattered across Japan, mostly in out-of-the-way places or on the edges of built-up areas. The quality is

Lobby of a youth hostel in Sendai, a mix of traditional and modern

variable, and house-parents range from the welcoming to dictatorial. A membership card is required for the cheapest rates, but anyone can stay for an additional charge, and there is no upper age limit.

CAMPING

There are about 2,800 official campsites, where tents, lodges, and bungalows can be rented. A minimum charge applies for setting up independently. Facilities include running water, toilets, baths and showers, stoves for cooking, restaurants, and vending machines. The JNTO leaflet *Camping in Japan* gives details. Overcrowding is common in holiday seasons.

DIRECTORY

Japan Economy Hotel Group
www.kid97.co.jp/~jeh-group/jeh-group.html

Japan Hotel Association
Tel (03) 3279-2706.
Fax (03) 3274-5375.
www.j-hotel.or.jp/welcome-e.html

Japanese Inn Group
Tel (03) 3843-2345.
Fax (03) 3843-2348.
www.members.aol.com/jinngroup

Welcome Inn Reservation Center
www.itcj.or.jp

For JNTO offices and website see p371.

Typical capsule hotel, with two tiers of encapsulated beds

Traditional Accommodations

A *ryokan* is a unique fusion of private and communal styles of living. Such Japanese traditions as removing shoes at the right point are important, no matter what the cost of the room, and the most expensive of these traditional inns may demand a high level of etiquette. A family-run *minshuku* – a type of guesthouse – is an even more intimate way to experience the Japanese lifestyle. There are also options that are *ryokan* at heart, but with Western-style touches such as private bathrooms.

Bamboo fencing at a guesthouse on Miyajima Island

WHAT IS A RYOKAN?

A *ryokan* is a traditional inn, as likely to be found in a city area as a mountain hamlet. Some are set in Edo-period buildings – confections of wood, glass, bamboo, paper screens, and *tatami* matting. Others have a more contemporary setting. Of the 80,000 *ryokan* scattered nationwide, most cater only to Japanese tourists, but they will usually welcome foreigners. About 1,500 *ryokan* are registered as well-suited to providing for foreign visitors.

Certain important Japanese customs apply: the biggest difference and surprise for many foreigners is that bathing facilities are traditionally communal, not private. The bathing facilities may be quite elaborate, and when part of a hot spring resort the establishment is called an *onsen (see pp354–5)*.

Most *ryokan* place emphasis on the quality of their meals, and the room price often includes breakfast and dinner (as specified in the listings). This can be ideal in quiet towns where few restaurants are open in the evening, but a constraint elsewhere. Another possible problem, mainly for elderly foreigners, is the Japanese tradition of living at floor level, using legless chairs and beds.

Note that many *ryokan* impose a curfew around 11pm, so make special arrangements about keys in advance if you plan to stay out late.

ARRIVING AT A RYOKAN

Guests generally check into a *ryokan* in the mid- to late afternoon, to allow plenty of time for bathing and dinner. At larger *ryokan*, there may be a doorman to smooth the way, but in smaller establishments, guests should slide open the front door and politely call *"gomen kudasai"* to announce arrival.

Do not step up into the lobby proper until the *okamisan* (female owner or manager) appears. This is the signal to remove outdoor shoes and step up into a pair of waiting house slippers *(see p373)*. Then, before entering the guestroom, remove the house slippers and leave them outside the door.

TYPICAL ROOMS

Guestrooms are floored in *tatami* mats *(see p33)*. In one corner of the room is an alcove, called *tokonoma*, which may contain a hanging scroll, flowers, or other artifacts. The *tokonoma* is to be respected: no suitcases, ashtrays, or drinks. There will also be a low table surrounded by cushions *(zabuton)*, or folding chairs. On the table top will be a tray, bearing a tea set and possibly traditional sweets *(wagashi)*.

Your futon mattress and bedding will be stowed in cupboards when you first enter the room. These will usually be laid out discreetly for you in the evening while you are out of the room.

Ordinarily a room will be further supplied with a TV and air conditioner and/or heater. There is usually a telephone, although it may not have an international connection. You should also find a small towel in a box or basket, which you can take to the communal bathroom to use as a washcloth. A personal outdoor bath *(rotenburo)* counts as luxury. A screened-off veranda, with Western-style table and armchairs, is more commonplace. There may be other Western-style touches.

Handle everything in the room with care, and walk only in bare feet or socks on the fragile *tatami*.

Room with *tatami* mats, low table, and *zabuton*, and additional Western-style daybed

Small communal bath and separate low shower for actual cleansing

WEARING YUKATA

Somewhere in the room will be traditional robes for you to wear, called *yukata*. Most people change into *yukata* for the duration of their stay, since the loose cotton kimonos symbolize relaxation and leisure time. In resort towns and hot springs, they are even worn outside on the streets, together with the high wooden sandals called *geta*. A loose jacket may also be provided. It is best to follow the example of others as to exactly where and when to wear the robes.

Fold *yukata* left-side over right. Right-side over left symbolizes death in Buddhism and can cause upset. Use the *obi* sash provided to secure the gown.

BATHING ARRANGEMENTS

Within the *ryokan* will be at least one communal bath and a toilet block with either Western-style cubicles or Japanese squat toilets or a choice of the two styles.

In smaller *ryokan* with only one bath, bathing times may differ for men and women. In larger establishments bathing is segregated, with one entrance for men, another for women *(for symbols see page 379)*. Mixed-sex bathing used to be the norm but is very rare these days. The size of the bath and bathroom naturally dictate how many people can bathe at any one time. Check with the *okamisan* if you are unsure about the house rules, which vary between establishments.

In the bathroom there will be an area for undressing; a low shower or tap area; and the large bath itself. The golden rule to observe is that you must perform ablutions with the shower first and not enter the hot bath until you are clean. The bath itself is intended only for therapeutic relaxation. The same bathwater is used by other guests, thus it is considered extremely bad manners to contaminate the water either with an unwashed body or soap and shampoo.

People wearing *yukata*, the design of which is specific to each *ryokan*

EATING ARRANGEMENTS

Meals are sometimes served in a dining room, but more often in the room by a maid or the *okamisan*. The more exclusive the establishment, the more likely meals will be served in private.

Meal times are usually set quite early in the evening. Depending on the situation, the *okamisan* may stay for a while, explaining the dishes, demonstrating how they should be eaten, and to chat. Or she may leave discreetly, returning only to clear the table.

STAYING IN A MINSHUKU

These family-run enterprises open the family home to travelers as and when demand requires. With rates from ¥4,000–¥10,000, this is an economical option as well as a good opportunity to see how regular working people live. The atmosphere is more homey than professional; guests are treated as part of the family at mealtimes and bathtime, and should fold up and stow away their own bedding.

STAYING IN A TEMPLE

Some temples, for example Mount Koya *(see p306)*, are geared to accepting overnight visitors. Food is vegetarian in the Buddhist tradition *(see p326)*. Gates to the compound may close early in the evening. You should follow rituals, including morning prayers, with due reverence even if you are not Buddhist. Fees start from around ¥3,000.

STAYING IN LODGES

People's lodges, or **Kokumin-Shukusha**, are moderate-rated accommodations within the national parks. Rooms, baths, and toilets are Japanese style. Meals based on local produce are often very good. Mountain lodges, Yamagoya, are aimed at hikers and range from the relatively comfortable to spartan.

DIRECTORY

Japan Ryokan Association
Tel (03) 3231-5310.
Fax (03) 3548-8080.
www.ryokan.or.jp

Japan Minshuku Center
Tel (03) 3683-3396.
www.minshuku.jp
@ abc@minshuku.jp

Kokumin-Shukusha Association
Tel (03) 3581-5310.
Fax (03) 3581-5315.

Choosing a Hotel

The hotels in this guide have been selected across a wide price range for their locations, character, and good value. Hotels are listed by region, starting with Tokyo and its environs. It is a good idea to request a map showing a hotel's location when booking, as Japanese addresses can be difficult to find *(see pp384–5)*.

PRICE GUIDE
Price categories per night for two people sharing a room, including tax and service charges.

Ⓨ Under ¥8,000
ⓎⓎ ¥8,000–¥15,000
ⓎⓎⓎ ¥15,000–¥25,000
ⓎⓎⓎⓎ ¥25,000–¥35,000
ⓎⓎⓎⓎⓎ over ¥35,000

TOKYO

CENTRAL TOKYO Capsule Inn Akihabara Ⓨ
6-8 Akihabara Taito-ku, 110-0006 **Tel** *(03) 3251-0841* **Fax** *(03) 3251-0844* **Rooms** *169*   **Map** *3 C/D4*

Right in the middle of Akihabara, this is great value, and certainly more of an experience than your normal night in a hotel. Rooms are 1m (3ft 3in) x 1m (3f 3in) x 2m (6ft 6in), but have a TV and radio, and there's a business lounge. There are also rooms big enough for four. For women only. **www.capsuleinn.com**

CENTRAL TOKYO Mitsui Urban Hotel Ginza ⓎⓎⓎ
8-6-15 Ginza, 104-0061 **Tel** *(03) 3572-4131* **Fax** *(03) 3572-4254* **Rooms** *265*   **Map** *5 B3*

Well located, this is a good business hotel with the full range of facilities, but tourists might well be swayed by its price and location – within walking distance of the Imperial Palace. The rooms are a good size and very clean but don't expect much by way of atmosphere. **www.mitsuikanko.co.jp**

CENTRAL TOKYO Yamanoue Hilltop Hotel ⓎⓎⓎ
1-1 Surugadai, Kanda Chiyoda-ku, 101-0062 **Tel** *(03) 3293-2311* **Fax** *(03) 3233-4567* **Rooms** *75*   **Map** *3 B4*

With plenty of personality and charm, the Yamanoue prides itself on its green surroundings. The rooms are unexcitingly decorated, but clean and well equipped, and there are a number of restaurants, from traditional Japanese to modern Italian and French, and a wine bar. **www.yamanoue-hotel.co.jpl**

CENTRAL TOKYO Yoshimizu Ryokan ⓎⓎⓎ
3-11-3 Ginza, 104-0061 **Tel** *(03) 3248-4432* **Fax** *(03) 3248-4431* **Rooms** *11*   **Map** *5 B3*

Just 11 *tatami* rooms, so book ahead. Pared down and simple, with no TV, radio, or CD in the rooms, which makes a lovely change in Tokyo. But it's the small touches that make this such a great place to stay – artfully placed flowers and thoughtfully put together food. Communal Japanese bath. **www.yoshimizu.com**

CENTRAL TOKYO Capitol Tokyu ⓎⓎⓎⓎ
2-10-3, Nagata-cho, Chiyoda-ku, 100-0014 **Tel** *(03) 3581 4511* **Fax** *(03) 3581-5822* **Rooms** *444*   **Map** *2 F3*

The bedrooms here are particularly large and well equipped. It's most definitely a business hotel, but there are still personal touches, and it's well located within walking distance of the Imperial Palace. There are seven restaurants and bars, and a small outside swimming pool in season. **www.capitoltokyu.com**

CENTRAL TOKYO Conrad Hotel ⓎⓎⓎⓎ
1-9-1, Higashi-Shinbashi, Minato-ku, 108-8567 **Tel** *(03) 6388-8000* **Fax** *(03) 6388-8001* **Rooms** *290*   **Map** *1 B1*

Opened in July 2006, and overlooking Tokyo Shiodome and Tokyo Bay, this is pure glamour, with dark wood, polished marble surfaces, and enormous floor-to-ceiling windows. In addition to gorgeous bedrooms, they have upped the stakes by calling on the services of British chef Gordon Ramsay for their restaurants. **www.conradtokyo.co.jp**

CENTRAL TOKYO Le Meridien Pacific Hotel ⓎⓎⓎⓎ
3-13-3 Takanawa, Minato-ku, 108-8567 **Tel** *(03) 3445-6711* **Fax** *(03) 3445-5137* **Rooms** *884*   **Map** *5 B3*

Just 15 minutes from Ginza and Rippongi, in the newly-developed Odaiba Town waterfront (a conference and hotel area that is surprisingly green and pleasant), this well-equipped business hotel has six international restaurants and large bedrooms. **www.starwoodhotels.com/lemeridien**

CENTRAL TOKYO Palace Hotel ⓎⓎⓎⓎ
1-1-1 Marunouchi, Chiyoda-ku, 100-0005 **Tel** *(03) 3211-5211* **Fax** *(03) 3211-6987* **Rooms** *389*   **Map** *5 B1*

Overlooking the Imperial Palace grounds, this high-rise hotel is hardly attractive but is well located. It has a pool, gym, and squash courts, and there are good views of the city. Bedrooms are spacious and there are 10 restaurants and bars, from traditional Japanese to a British-style pub serving curries. **www.palacehotel.co.jp**

CENTRAL TOKYO Hotel Seiyo Ginza ⓎⓎⓎⓎⓎ
1-11-2 Ginza, 104-0061 **Tel** *(03) 3535-1111* **Fax** *(03) 3535-1110* **Rooms** *77*   **Map** *5 B3*

This is a very elegant hotel, with a sweeping staircase, polished floors, and heaps of fresh flowers everywhere. There's a perfectly presented bar, lounge, restaurant, and delicious bakery/patisserie. No pool, but a reasonable fitness center, and the bedrooms have intimate touches like books and cushions. Good-sized bathrooms. **www.seiyo-ginza.com**

Key to Symbols *see back cover flap*

CENTRAL TOKYO Imperial Hotel

1-1-1 Uchisaiwai-cho, Chiyoda-ku, 100-8558 **Tel** *(03) 3504-1111* **Fax** *(03) 3581-9146* **Rooms** *1057* **Map** *5 B2*

Designed by Frank Lloyd Wright and open for over a century, this is truly a Tokyo institution and counts among its former guests royalty, presidents, and half of Hollywood. There are 17 eating and drinking options, and a full-sized swimming pool. Glamorous it is, intimate it definitely is not. **www.imperialhotel.co.jp**

CENTRAL TOKYO Tokyo Four Seasons

2-10-8, Sekiguchi, Bunkyo-ku, 112-8667 **Tel** *(03) 3943-2222* **Fax** *(03) 3943-2300* **Rooms** *57* **Map** *3 C2*

The relatively small number of rooms gives you a clue to the kind of welcome you are going to get, and the kind of check you will receive on departure. In a word – exclusive. The sumptuous rooms are the largest in the city, and all come with flat-screen TV. **www.fourseasons.com/tokyo**

NORTHERN TOKYO Homeikan

5-10-5 Hongo, Bunkyo-ku, Tokyo-to, 113-0033 **Tel** *(03) 3811-1181* **Fax** *(03) 3811-1764* **Rooms** *54* **Map** *3 A3*

A popular *ryokan* in a leafy part of town, and all the rooms have traditional *tatami*-mats. It has a lovely entrance, three communal baths, and beautiful downstairs rooms with sliding screen doors. Unlike most *ryokans*, there's no curfew, so you can still enjoy Tokyo's nightlife. **www.japaneseguesthouses.com**

NORTHERN TOKYO Sawanoya Ryokan

2-3-11 Yanaka, Taito-ku, 110-0001 **Tel** *(03) 3822-2251* **Fax** *(03) 3822-2252* **Rooms** *12* **Map** *3 C1*

In a quiet residential area near Ueno Park, this is uninspiring outside but pretty within, and all rooms come with thoughtful touches like a summer kimono (*yukata*) and slippers – and free tea and coffee. Family-run and really friendly, but there is a curfew, so don't stay here if you want late nights. **www.sawanoya.com**

NORTHERN TOKYO Ryokan Asakusa Shigetsu

1-31-11, Asakusa, Taito-ku, 111-0032 **Tel** *(03) 3843-2345* **Fax** *(03) 3843-2348* **Rooms** *23* **Map** *4 E2*

Located by the Sumida River and Tobu Asakusa station, this is in a quiet residential area and feels very much like a retreat from the noise of Tokyo. There are Japanese-style baths on the 5th floor, and some Western-style rooms, although the Japanese style are much nicer. Excellent restaurant, friendly service. **www.shigetsu.com**

NORTHERN TOKYO Asakusa View Hotel

3-17-1 Nishiasakusa, Taito-ku, 111-8765 **Tel** *(03) 3847-1111* **Fax** *(03) 3842-2117* **Rooms** *337* **Map** *4 E2*

Right next to the Sumida river, you have the choice of Japanese and Western rooms – it doesn't matter which, just ask for a river view. The hotel has nine restaurants, but you're going to want to wander outside, because this is the heart of Old Tokyo, and a great area for exploring. **www.viewhotels.co.jp**

NORTHERN TOKYO Sofitel Tokyo Hotel

2-1-48 Ikenohata, Taito-ku **Tel** *(03) 5685-7111* **Fax** *(03) 5685-6171* **Rooms** *83* **Map** *4 E2*

Come here for a taste of upscale Paris, in the heart of Old Tokyo, and easy walking distance from Ueno Park. There is a very chic interior, and excellent outside architecture by Kikutake Kiyonori. The rooms are luxurious down to the last detail, and the French accent goes right through the excellent restaurant. **www.sofiteltokyo.com**

WESTERN TOKYO Arca Torre

6-1-23 Roppongi, 106-0032 **Tel** *(03) 3404-5111* **Rooms** *77* **Map** *2 E5*

You might want to take ear plugs along, as this is very close to the nighttime attractions of Roppongi-dori, but it's excellently priced for the location, and has very friendly staff. There's a really good choice of free cable TV in the nicely decorated bedrooms as well, for nursing hangovers! Good café also. **www.arktower.co.jp**

WESTERN TOKYO Asia Center of Japan

8-10-32, Akasaka, Minato-ku, 107-0052 **Tel** *(03) 3402-6111* **Fax** *(03) 3402-0738* **Rooms** *173* **Map** *2 E5*

This friendly budget hotel is a popular option, so you need to book months in advance. It looks and feels a bit like a college dorm but it's very clean, the staff speak English, and you can always find someone to give you the latest tips about where to go in the city. **www.asiacenter.or.jp**

WESTERN TOKYO Children's Castle Hotel

5-53-1 Aoyama, Shibuya-ku, 150-0001 **Tel** *(03) 3797-5666 / 5677* **Fax** *(03) 3797-5676* **Rooms** *209* **Map** *1 B5*

An unusual choice, a few floors above the National Children's Castle recreational center, but good value and well located in the heart of Shibuya. You may be brave staying here if you don't have a young family in tow, but you get simple rooms at affordable rates, and there's a gym and roof terrace. **www.kodomo-shiro.or.jp**

WESTERN TOKYO Hotel Tateshina

5-8-6 Shinjuku, Shinjuku-ku, 160-0022 **Tel** *(03) 3350-5271* **Fax** *(03) 3350-5275* **Rooms** *67* **Map** *1 A1*

You'll find this is a good budget option, with mainly Western-style rooms, but a few Japanese-style if you book early enough; the latter are a lot more charming than the Western rooms, where the bedspreads should be in a museum! There is WiFi (for a fee) in every room, and a restaurant – for breakfast only. **www.tateshina.co.jp**

WESTERN TOKYO Vintage Shinjuku Hotel

2-40-3 Kabuki-cho, Shinjuku, 160-0021 **Tel** *(03) 3205-6300* **Fax** *(03) 3205-6311* **Rooms** *194* **Map** *1 A1*

It's great fun, if slightly unnerving, to stay right in the heart of the red light Kabuki-cho district, but rest assured this is very definitely a "legitimate" business hotel! It's slightly kitsch, and the bedrooms could do with an update, but it has plenty of atmosphere and very friendly staff. Excellent value. **www.hotel-vintage.co.jp**

WESTERN TOKYO Hotel B Roppongi

3-9-8 Roppongi, Minato-ku **Tel** *(03) 5412-0451* **Fax** *(03) 5412-9353* **Rooms** *65*   **Map** *2 E5*

Recently rebranded, refurbished, and immeasurably improved, this is now a stylish boutique hotel, offering great value and well located within easy walking distance of Roppongi's many bars and restaurants. The rooms are slightly small but have good linen, real hairdryers, and lots of bathroom goodies. **www.ishinhotels.com**

WESTERN TOKYO Roppongi Prince Hotel

3-2-7 Roppongi, Minato-ku, 106-0032 **Tel** *(03) 3587-1111* **Fax** *(03) 3587-0770* **Rooms** *216*   **Map** *2 E5*

Very close to Roppongi-dori, the hotel building has a futuristic look outside, and some fun touches inside to make it a good choice for the money. There's an open-air inner courtyard with a small outdoor heated swimming pool. The rooms are minimalist, verging on uninteresting. **www.princehotelsjapan.com**

WESTERN TOKYO Shinjuku Washington

3-2-9 Nishi-Shinjuku, Shinjuku-ku **Tel** *(03) 3343-3111* **Fax** *(03) 3342-2575* **Rooms** *1296*   **Map** *1 A1*

A standard, fairly unattractive hotel with a number of bonuses – it is within easy walking distance of Shinjuku station, has clean and well-equipped rooms, is more intimate than many business hotels and, best of all, it has a *shabu-shabu* restaurant in a Japanese garden. **www.wh-rsv.com**

WESTERN TOKYO Keio Plaza

2-2-1 Nishi Shinjuku, Shinjuku-ku, 160-8330 **Tel** *(03) 3344-0111* **Fax** *(03) 3345-8269* **Rooms** *1451*   **Map** *1 A1*

This is a big hotel, but somehow that feels okay in the heart of Shinjuku, and the view from the top floors is quite amazing. Other benefits include a sky pool on the 7th floor of the building, a mind-bogglingly wide range of restaurants and, to top it all, a karaoke bar. **www.keioplaza.com**

WESTERN TOKYO Grand Hyatt at Roppongi Hills

6-10-3 Roppongi, Minato-ku **Tel** *(03) 4333-1234* **Fax** *(03) 4333-8123* **Rooms** *389*   **Map** *2 E5*

This sought-after hotel in Roppongi Hills uses polished reds and blacks set against exposed stone walls and warm wood – it's all about textures, and is quite beautiful. Great bedrooms, and a large spa. One of the many excellent food places has an outside terrace overlooking fashionable Keyakizaka Street. **www.grandhyatttokyo.com**

WESTERN TOKYO Hotel New Otani

4-1 Kioi-cho, Chiyoda-ku, 102-8578 **Tel** *(03) 3265-1111* **Fax** *(03) 3221-2619* **Rooms** *1533*   **Map** *2 E3*

Often winning awards as a great business hotel, this is well located with friendly staff and reliable service. All rooms and facilities are spread over three buildings, with plenty of greenery in between. Rooms are stylish with far-reaching views. The Tokyo outpost of famous Parisian restaurant, La Tour d'Argent, is here. **www.newotani.co.jp**

WESTERN TOKYO Park Hyatt

3-7-1 Nishi Shinjuku, Shinjuku-ku, 163-1055 **Tel** *(03) 5322-1234* **Fax** *(03) 5322-1288* **Rooms** *178*   **Map** *1 A2*

This already iconic hotel has grown even more in stature since being featured in the movie *Lost in Translation*. Just to show they're not resting on their laurels, the New York Bar has recently reopened after a face lift – and the views really are amazing. Even the smallest rooms are huge. **http://tokyo.park.hyatt.com**

FARTHER AFIELD Kimi Ryokan

36-8, 2chome, Ikebukuro, Toshima-ku, 171-0014 **Tel** *(03) 3971-3766* **Fax** *(03) 3987-1326* **Rooms** *38*

Anyone who has been to Tokyo on a budget will have heard of this place – it's a very popular *ryokan*, so book well in advance. The English-speaking staff will always be happy to give you advice for travel in Tokyo or farther afield. There's a choice of Western or *tatami*-mat bedrooms. **www.kimi-ryokan.jp**

FARTHER AFIELD Andon Ryokan

2-34-10 Nihonzutsumi Taito, 111-0021 **Tel** *(03) 3873-8611* **Fax** *(03) 3873-8612* **Rooms** *24*

Billed as Japan's first "designer *ryokan*", this is slightly out of the way, but worth traveling for. It has a gorgeous mix of traditional Japanese and Western antiques, plus 21st-century touches – free internet access and DVDs in each room, a jacuzzi, and clean, modernist lines everywhere. Friendly, English-speaking staff. **www.andon.co.jp**

FARTHER AFIELD Hotel Excellent Ebisu

1-9-5 Ebisunishi, Shibuya-ku, 150-0021 **Tel** *(05) 5458-0087* **Fax** *(05) 5458-8787* **Rooms** *127*

You'll get very good value at this cheap, cheerful hotel. The rooms are slightly slanted, but they are kept in pristine condition and the bathrooms are well stocked for a budget option. There's a chintzy marble entrance and lots of flowers. The area around the hotel is full of interesting restaurants and shops. **www.soeikikaku.co.jp**

FARTHER AFIELD Radisson Hotel Narita Airport

650-35 Nanae, Tomisato-shi, Chiba, 286-0221 **Tel** *(04) 7693-1234* **Fax** *(04) 7693-4834* **Rooms** *493*

A very large outside swimming pool gives this hotel an extra draw, but the convenience of its location by Narita airport means it's heavily accented toward the business customer. This means high-speed internet access, plenty of conference services, and a few good international-styled restaurants. **www.radisson.com**

FARTHER AFIELD The Westin Tokyo

1-4-1 Mita, Meguro-ku, 153-8580 **Tel** *(03) 5423-7000 (switchboard)* **Fax** *(03) 05423-7600* **Rooms** *438*

One of the granddaddys of Tokyo hotels, this is aimed at the business audience, and stuffed full of amenities. There are some lovely outside dining spaces among its eight restaurants, good jogging routes from the hotel, and very large bathrooms in all guest rooms. There are botanical gardens very close to the hotel. **www.westin.com**

Key to Price Guide *see p298* **Key to Symbols** *see back cover flap*

CENTRAL HONSHU

FUJI 5 LAKES Sunnide Village

2549-1 Ohishi Yamanashi, 401-0305 **Tel** *(0555) 76-7140* **Fax** *(0555) 76-7299* **Rooms** *20*

The Sunnide is on a former noble's estate on the north side of the lake. The rooms are small but comfortable, and you can soak in the outdoor hot spring bath while viewing Mount Fuji. The staff are friendly, try hard at English, and will pick you up at the station if you arrange this in advance. A local bus from the station takes 15 minutes.

FUJI 5 LAKES Hotel Konanso

4020-20 Kawaguchiko Yamanashi, 401-0301 **Tel** *(0555) 72-2166* **Fax** *(0555) 73-1844* **Rooms** *54*

A great place to experience a Japanese *ryokan*. There are great views of Mount Fuji from the upper floor indoor and outdoor baths. A private family bath can be reserved. The food is great, with a choice of "mountain" or "sea" (two meals included in the price). Pick-up at the station can be arranged. Expect comfort and great service.

HAKONE Fuji-Hakone Guest House

912 Sengokuhara Kanagawa, 250-0631 **Tel** *(0460) 4-6577* **Fax** *(0460) 4-6578* **Rooms** *14*

Run by the friendly, helpful, English-speaking Takahashi family and staff, this is a good choice even if you're not on a budget. There's a comfortable lounge and use of a refrigerator, microwave, toaster, and coin laundry. There's also free internet access, plus indoor and outdoor hot spring baths. Breakfast available. **www.fujihakone.com**

HAKONE Fujiya Hotel

300 Miyanoshita Kanagawa, 250-0404 **Tel** *(0460) 2-2211* **Fax** *(0460) 2-2210* **Rooms** *146*

A classic hotel which has been welcoming foreigners since 1878 (see *p334*). Some of the buildings are listed as National Cultural Assets for their combination of Japanese and Western elements. There are beautiful gardens, a golf course, and a greenhouse using the hot spring waters to maintain a tropical environment. **www.fujiyahotel.co.jp**

HAKONE Ichinoyu

90 Tonosawa Kanagawa, 250-0315 **Tel** *(0460) 5-5331* **Fax** *(0460) 5-5335* **Rooms** *24*

Around 375 years old, this wonderful *ryokan* stands beside a rushing river. Antique paintings and furnishings are everywhere. The top rooms face the river and some even have a private outdoor hot spring bath. Rates go up on the weekend. A six-minute walk from Tonosawa station.

IZU Hotel Marseille

1-1-15 Higashihongo Shizuoka, 415-0035 **Tel** *(0558) 23-8000* **Fax** *(0558) 23-8001* **Rooms** *24*

This business hotel has a French theme that extends from the lobby into the rooms. The single rooms are cramped, the twins and doubles are much better and good value. The location is unbeatable: right next to the station and convenient for all the sights. **www.izu-is.com**

IZU Ryokan Inaba

12-13 Higashimatsubara-cho Shizuoka, 414-0022 **Tel** *(0557) 37-3178* **Rooms** *15*

This 85-year-old registered national treasure sits beside the Matsukawa River. Every room has a balcony overlooking the river. Enjoy a *ryokan* experience guided by English-speaking Mrs Inaba. Breakfast and an elaborate Japanese dinner are included. The hot spring baths here are gorgeous. A short walk from Ito station. **www.inaba-r.co.jp**

IZU Taikanso

7-1 Hayashigaoka-cho Shizuoka, 413-0031 **Tel** *(0557) 81-8137* **Fax** *(0557) 83-5308* **Rooms** *44*

Set in the hills above Atami and built in 16th-century Kyoto style, this was originally a steel tycoon's mansion. Now a classic *ryokan*, each luxurious room has a private hot spring bath, plus there are a total of six indoor/outdoor public baths. The food is outstanding. There is even karaoke and mah-jong, too. **www.heartonhotel.com**

KAMIKOCHI Nishi-Itoya Mountain Lodge

Azumikamikochi Nagano, 390-1516 **Tel** *(0263) 95-2206* **Fax** *(263) 95-2206* **Rooms** *30*

Only a 10-minute walk from Kamikochi station, this looks, feels, and even smells like a mountain lodge. The owner takes pride in the hotel his ancestor started in 1865. Rooms are clean and pleasant. You get a 10 percent discount on the second night, and 20 percent every night after that. Friendly staff. **www.nishiitoya.com**

KAMIKOCHI Kamikochi Imperial Hotel

4468 Azumikamikochi Nagano, 390-1516 **Tel** *(0263) 95-2001 / 2006* **Fax** *(026)395-2412* **Rooms** *75*

The most luxurious accommodations in Kamikochi, this sister of Tokyo's Imperial Hotel has a pseudo-Swiss chalet design with massive log beams and posts. The lobby is impressive, and the large fireplace and rustic tables and chairs inviting after a day out hiking. The rooms and service are first rate. Continental cuisine. **www.imperialhotel.co.jp**

KANAZAWA Ryokan Murataya

1-5-2 Katamachishikawa, 920-0981 **Tel** *(076) 263-0455* **Fax** *(076) 263-0456* **Rooms** *11*

It's not the newest hotel, but everything is spotless and well maintained. The staff are anxious to help you, and you can't beat the location: about 3 km (2 miles) from the station, but less than 1 km (half a mile) from Kenrokoen, the castle, and the museums. Breakfast is available and there's a coin laundry. **www.spacelan.ne.jp**

KANAZAWA Kanazawa Miyako Hotel

6-10 Konohanacho, Ishikawa, 920-0852 **Tel** *(076) 261-2111* **Fax** *(076) 261-2113* **Rooms** *193*

The Miyako is a business hotel and has one floor reserved entirely for women, with special decor and amenities in the rooms and a 20 percent discount for women, too. All rooms are pleasant and have refrigerators. It's connected by underground arcade to the station. Japanese and continental restaurants. **www.miyakohotels.ne.jp**

KISO VALLEY Tajimaya Minshuku

4266 Magome Nagano, 399-5102 **Tel** *(264) 59-2048* **Fax** *(264) 59-2466* **Rooms** *12*

Tajimaya sits about a third of the way up Magome's main street – look for the wooden wagon wheels outside the building. The family that runs this *minshuku* serve good food based around local produce. The rooms are spotless, and there's an *irori* to sit around in the cold months. **www.japaneseguesthouses.com**

KISO VALLEY Ryokan Fujioto

Tsumago Nagano, 399-5302 **Tel** *(0264) 57-3009* **Fax** *(0264) 57-2239* **Rooms** *9*

This Edo-style building is set back from the road and there is a wonderful Japanese garden behind the hotel. The owner's daughter is happy to give you a tour (in English) if you let her know in advance. The owner also speaks English. Lots of fresh mountain vegetables and excellent trout served. **www.japaneseguesthouses.com**

MASHIKO Mashiko Clock

Mashiko-cho Tochigi, 321-4217 **Tel** *(0285) 72-7201* **Fax** *(0285) 72-7201* **Rooms** *7*

A classic Japanese *pension*, Mashiko Clock isn't luxurious, but very nice. There is a gallery with Mashiko pottery for sale and an attached café/restaurant with mostly Western cuisine made from local organic produce. Try the big hot tub on the outdoor deck. Not far from Mashiko's main street. **www.mashiko-dokei.com**

MATSUMOTO Marumo Ryokan

3-3-10 Chuo Nagano, 390-0811 **Tel** *(026) 332-0115* **Fax** *(026) 335-2251* **Rooms** *8*

This has been a *ryokan* since Edo times. It's about 15 minutes' walk from the station to this well-maintained, attractive whitewashed *kura*-style building close to the castle and other attractions. It's quiet and comfortable, and the friendly staff are used to foreigners. Breakfast is available. **www.avis.ne.jp**

MATSUMOTO Yado Ichiyama

2-1-12 Chuo Nagano, 390-0811 **Tel** *(0263) 32-0122* **Fax** *(0263) 32-3968* **Rooms** *13*

This is a modern building built in the homely style of a *kura*. The whitewashed walls, dark wooden beams, and local architectural features give a comfortable, homey feel but it has modern conveniences. It's down a side street just far enough to make this centrally-located hotel very quiet. Breakfast is available.

NAGOYA Sofitel The Cypress Nagoya

2-43-6 Meieki Nagoya, 450-0002 **Tel** *(052) 571-0111* **Fax** *(052) 569-1717* **Rooms** *115*

Just a one-minute walk from the bullet train station and Sakae subway, this hotel has a boutique feel. The rooms are a little small but well furnished, including high-speed internet port, satellite TV, and a minibar. Upper rooms have good city views, with shopping and restaurants (besides two in the hotel) nearby. **www.accorhotels-asia.com**

NARITA Ohgiya Ryokan

474 Saiwai-cho Chiba, 286-0028 **Tel** *(0476) 22-1161* **Fax** *(0476) 24-1663* **Rooms** *15*

Relax in the comfortable armchair of your room's alcove looking at the hotel's beautiful Japanese garden. Just 10 minutes' walk from the station, and five minutes from Narita-san Temple complex, this is a great location and a very comfortable hotel. Dinner and breakfast are available if reserved ahead. **www.naritakanko.jp**

NOTO PENINSULA Seto

2-81 Uedo-Machilshikawa, 927-1216 **Tel** *(0768) 82-0544* **Fax** *(0768) 82-0544* **Rooms** *11*

This modern-style *ryokan* is noted for its delicious fresh seafood. Small wonder, since it's right by the ocean, an easy 10-minute walk from Uedo train station. The guest rooms aren't fancy but all rooms have views of the bay, and there is a Japanese garden in front of the hotel.

SHIRAKAWA Minshuku Koemon

457 Ogimachi Gifu, 501-5627 **Tel** *(05769) 6-1446* **Fax** *(05769) 6-1748* **Rooms** *4*

The friendly, English-speaking owner, Mr Otani, has completely modernized his 200-year-old farmhouse (including heated floor) without sacrificing the old-time character. Try to get a room facing the pond. Relax around the *irori* fireplace and after dinner enjoy a video on the area. It's best to book ahead through the tourist office in Takayama.

TAKAYAMA Rickshaw Inn

54 Suehiro-cho Gifu, 506-0016 **Tel** *(0577) 32-2890* **Fax** *(0577) 32-2469* **Rooms** *10*

Spotless rooms and a comfortable lounge, complete with satellite TV and a common kitchen, make this a great budget choice. The friendly staff all speak English. There is a coin laundry and internet access for a fee, and it's close to the station and the sights. Breakfast is available for an extra charge. **www.rickshawinn.com**

TAKAYAMA Ryokan Sumiyoshi

Honmachi 4-21Gifu, 506-0011 **Tel** *(0577) 32-0228* **Fax** *(0577) 33-8916* **Rooms** *10*

With the Miyagawa River on one side and the town's famous morning market on the other, this is a great location. This 100-year-old one-time silkworm factory is now an eclectic *ryokan* with antiques everywhere, including a prized antique doll collection. The rooms are pleasant and overlook the river. **www.sumiyoshi-ryokan.com**

Key to Price Guide *see p298* **Key to Symbols** *see back cover flap*

YOKOHAMA Toyoko Inn Yokohama

6-55 Sakuraragi-cho Kanagawa, 231-005 **Tel** *(045) 671-1045* **Fax** *(045) 671-1046* **Rooms** *216*

The rooms in this business hotel aren't very big but they are spotless. Rooms have satellite TV, a refrigerator, coffee maker, free high-speed internet access, and even a trouser press. It's only five minutes from Sakuragi-cho station. Some of the rooms are non-smoking, and a Japanese breakfast is included. **www.toyoko-inn.com**

YOKOHAMA Navios Yokohama

2-1-1 Sinko-cho Kanagawa, 231-0001 **Tel** *(045) 633-6000* **Fax** *(045) 633-6001* **Rooms** *135*

The rooms are spacious and have every amenity: LAN, satellite TV, refrigerator, even a bidet. There's a restaurant, coffee shop, and the International Seaman's Club Bar. Try the breakfast buffet and ask for an upper room facing Landmark Tower for gorgeous nighttime views. A short walk to Sakuragi-cho station. **www.navios-yokohama.com**

KYOTO

CITY CENTER Hearton Hotel Kyoto

Higashi-no-Toin Dori, Oike Agaru, Nakagyo Ku, 604-0836 **Tel** *(075) 222-1300* **Fax** *(075) 222-1313* **Rooms** *294*

A big but welcoming hotel, with very comfortable rooms, car parking, and 24-hour access. The entrance is non-descript, but the hotel is very smart and good value, as there are a number of more upscale touches (all the single rooms have semi-double beds, for example), and two good restaurants. **www.heartonhotel.com/hearton_hotel_kyoto.htm**

CITY CENTER Hotel Gimmond

Takakura-Oike-dori, Nakagyo-ku, 604-8105 **Tel** *(075) 221-4111* **Fax** *(075) 221-8250* **Rooms** *140*

A Western-style hotel that is very well located on the main shopping street and just round the corner from the Kyoto Museum. The rooms are light and airy, and there's a great Japanese restaurant in the basement that is very relaxed. Home-style dining and a smart Italian eating spot upstairs. **www.gimmond.co.jp**

CITY CENTER Karasuma Kyoto Hotel

Karasaumura Shiijyo, Shimogyu Ku, 604-0861 **Tel** *(075) 371-0111* **Fax** *(075) 371-2424* **Rooms** *255*

Great location in the heart of the business district, with clean, spacious, and simple Western-style rooms (there are a few Japanese-style rooms, but not many). The decoration isn't exactly worth a postcard home, but the welcome is genuine and there is free high-speed internet access. **www.kyotohotel.co.jp**

CITY CENTER Mitsui Garden Hotel

707-1 Myoudennji-cho, Nishidoin-dori, Shijyo-sagaru, 600-8472 **Tel** *07 5361 5531* **Fax** *07 5361 5100* **Rooms** *221*

Located downtown, in central Kyoto, the same hotel group has another Garden Hotel by the station. This one has a Japanese restaurant and a tea room as well as a traditional bath house in the Japanese-style garden. The bedrooms are uninspiring but clean and well equipped. **www.gardenhotels.co.jp**

CITY CENTER Kyoto Hotel Okura

Kawaramachi-Oike, Nakagyo-ku, 604-8558 **Tel** *(075) 211-5111* **Fax** *(075) 254-2529* **Rooms** *322*

Centrally located, the hotel is close to the shopping district of Shijo-Kawaramachi, but still has pretty views of the mountains beyond the city from many of the bedroom windows. Lavishly decorated, with warm wood paneling everywhere. There are seven restaurants. Best of all are the huge armchairs in the lobby. **www.kyoto.okura.com**

EASTERN KYOTO Watazen Ryokan

Rokkaku-Sagaru, Yanaginobaba, Nakagyo-ku, 604-8113 **Tel** *(075) 223-0111* **Fax** *(075) 223-0112* **Rooms** *24*

This is a beautiful but rather modest inn, dating back to 1830. One of the many distinctive features of the Watazen Ryokan is its restaurant, which offers *nabe*, or hot-pot dishes, prepared in a hot pot, usually at the table. **www.watazen.com**

EASTERN KYOTO Yoshimizu Hotel

Bentendoue, Maruyama Koen, Higashiyama-ku, 605-0071 **Tel** *(075) 551-3995* **Fax** *(075) 551-3996* **Rooms** *14*

In the hills of Maruyama Park, this is a lovely quiet hotel but still very close to Gion district. Breakfast and light meals are served on wooden tables outside in summer months, and inside it has traditional *tatami*-mat floors. It has recently opened a sister *ryokan* in Ginza, Tokyo. **www.yoshimizu.com**

EASTERN KYOTO Kinmata Ryokan

407 Gokomachi Shijo-agaru, Nakagyo-ku, 604-8094 **Tel** *(075) 221-1039* **Fax** *(075) 231-7632* **Rooms** *6*

Experience the upper-end of luxury at this exquisite, traditional *ryokan*, first opened in the early 1800s. Only six rooms means you feel like you're being welcomed into the home of a (very wealthy and formal) Japanese family, and the *kaiseki* cuisine is almost impossibly artistically presented. Communal Japanese bath also. **www.kinmata.com**

EASTERN KYOTO Westin Miyako Hotel

Keage, Sanjo, Higashiyama-ku, 605-0052 **Tel** *(075) 771-7111* **Fax** *(075) 751-2490* **Rooms** *516*

An elegant and luxurious hotel, with an annex styled as a Japanese tea room for those wanting *ryokan*-style accommodation (the traditional rooms are far more expensive, and the Western rooms are gorgeous). Outdoor pool, and even a wild bird sanctuary and walking trail. **www.westinmiyako-kyoto.com**

IMPERIAL PALACE Hotel Harvest Kyoto

Karasuma-dori / Marutamachi Sagaru, 563-0043 **Tel** *(075) 251-1092* **Fax** *(075) 251-1239* **Rooms** *81*

A large, modern red-brick building, this is well located right by the Imperial Palace. The good-sized, Western-style doubles are reasonably priced. The hotel prides itself on a traditionally hospitable welcome, and guest rooms, although not large, are well equipped. Nijo Castle is within easy walking distance. **www.hotel-harvest.com**

IMPERIAL PALACE Ana Hotel

Nijo-jo-mae, horikawa-dori nakagyo-ku, 604-0055 **Tel** *(075) 231-1155* **Fax** *(075) 231-5333* **Rooms** *303*

The Ana overlooks Nijo Castle and does its best to enter into the spirit of Kyoto – gentle music in the lobby, Japanese gardens, and traditional *kaiseki* food in the restaurant (there is also an excellent counter-style *teppanyaki* restaurant). The rooms continue the calming atmosphere, with muted color schemes. **www.anahotels.com**

KYOTO STATION Budget Inn

295 Aburanokohi-cho, Shimogyo-ku, 600-8231 **Tel** *(075) 344-1510* **Fax** *(075) 344-1510* **Rooms** *6*

Opened in 2003, after the owner had been traveling and wanted to create something similar to the fun of friendly backpacking hostels, this *ryokan*-style hotel has reasonably priced rooms and is within five minutes' walk of the station. A choice of both dormitory and private rooms (private rooms are from ¥9,500). **www.budgetinnjp.com**

KYOTO STATION Tour Club

362 Momiji-cho, Higashinakasuji, Shimogyo-ku, 600-8231 **Tel** *(075) 353-6968* **Fax** *(075) 353-6968* **Rooms** *11*

With the same owner as Budget Inn (this was the first one that he opened), it's worth knowing about both. An easy walk from Kyoto station. The price is for your first four nights in a dorm room, but goes down for longer stays. The price goes up to ¥6,650 for a Western-style private room. **www.kyotojp.com**

KYOTO STATION Matsubaya Ryokan

Nishi-iru, Kamijuzuyamachi-dori, Shimogyo-ku, 600-8150 **Tel** *(075) 351-3727* **Fax** *(075) 351-3505* **Rooms** *11*

Mrs Hayashi is always happy to welcome you in to her *ryokan*, which has been receiving guests since 1885. You'll find a very pretty inner courtyard (it's tiny, but is a lovely focal point and a spot of greenery), and traditional *tatami*-mat rooms with sliding screen doors. Shared bathroom. **www.matsubayainn.com**

KYOTO STATION Granvia

901 Higashi-Shiokoji-cho, Shimogyo-ku, 600-8216 **Tel** *(075) 344-8888* **Fax** *(075) 344-4400* **Rooms** *539*

The Granvia is expensive but lovely, with a good indoor pool and sauna, and is very close to the station (it is, in fact, part of the stylish station building). The best part is the Sky Bar on the 15th floor, which serves great cocktails (no need to be a guest) and has views over the city. **www.granvia-kyoto.co.jp**

KYOTO STATION Kyoto Tokyu Hotel

Gojo-sagaru, Horikawa-dori, Shimogyo-ku, 600-8519 **Tel** *(075) 341-2411* **Fax** *(075) 341-2488* **Rooms** *432*

A modern, clean, and well-located business hotel with internet access (WiFi in the lobby), and non-smoking rooms available. Five minutes by car from Kyoto station and Nijo Castle. There are Chinese and Western-style restaurants, but the best food is at Tankuma Kitamise restaurant. **www.tokyuhotels.co.jp**

NORTHERN KYOTO Green Peace Kyoto

14-1 Matsugasaki / Shibamoto-cho, 606-0913 **Tel** *(075) 791-9890* **Fax** *(075) 791-9890* **Rooms** *11*

Very popular with backpackers, a minimum of three nights' stay is required here, but for that you get great prices and an excellent source of inside information about Kyoto. The rooms are very definitely basic but they are clean and there is a communal kitchen. **www.greenpeacekyoto.com**

NORTHERN KYOTO Tani House

8 Daitokuji-cho, Murasakino, 603-8231 **Tel** *(075) 492-5489* **Fax** *(075) 493-6419* **Rooms** *10*

Located right by the Daitoku-ji monastery, this is a reliable, slightly careworn but friendly guesthouse. There's a kitchen to cook your own meals, and traditional *tatami*-mat rooms (you pay per number of *tatami* mats, exactly as you would if you were renting an apartment). **www.kansaiconnect.com**

WESTERN HONSHU

AMANOHASHIDATE Genmyoan

Amanohashidate, Miyazu-shi, Kyoto-ken, 626-0001 **Tel** *(0772) 22-2171* **Fax** *(0772) 25-1641* **Rooms** *20*

Genmyoan is a small, traditional inn built in the *sukiya* style and established in the Tempo-era (latter 19th century). It is well positioned on a hill to provide breathtaking views. The rooms are spacious and comfortable, and the lobby features a collection of antique figurines, calligraphy, and lacquerware. **www.genmyoan.com**

FUKIYA Fukiya International Villa

836 Fukiya Nariwa-cho, Takahashi-shi, Okayama, 719-2341 **Tel** *(086) 256-2535* **Fax** *(086) 256-2576* **Rooms** *5*

Modeled after a traditional Okayama soy sauce warehouse, this villa is run by the non-profit Okayama International Villa Group. It is for the exclusive use of non-Japanese and their Japanese guests, aiming to encourage international exchange. Clean and basic accommodation, akin to a youth hostel. **www.harenet.ne.jp**

Key to Price Guide *see p298* **Key to Symbols** *see back cover flap*

HIMEJI Himeji Castle Hotel

210 Sanzaemonbori Nishino-machi, Himeji-shi, 670-0940 **Tel** *(079) 284-3311* **Fax** *(0792) 84-3729* **Rooms** *257*

Conveniently located close to Himeji station, Himeji Castle Hotel provides good service at an affordable price. Knowledgeable staff make it one of the most stress-free hotels in town. Cheap-end twin rooms are available, as are several package deals. Seven restaurants to choose from. **www.himejicastlehotel.co.jp**

HIROSHIMA World Friendship Center

8-10 Higashi Kan-on, Nishi-ku Hiroshima-shi, 733-0032 **Tel** *(082) 503-3179* **Fax** *(082) 503-3191* **Rooms** *3*

Cozy bed-and-breakfast place run by a welcoming American couple working for the non-profit WFC, an organization promoting international friendship and peace. Rooms are Japanese-style with a Western-style buffet breakfast. Regular activities are organized, and volunteer guides lead tours around the Peace Park. **http://wfchiroshima.net**

HIROSHIMA Rijyo Kaikan

1-5-3 Oote-machi, Chuo-ku, Hiroshima-shi, 730-0051 **Tel** *(082) 245-2322* **Fax** *(082) 245-2315* **Rooms** *50*

From its entrance mosaic entitled "the Sound of Waves," by ceramic artist Tokuro Kato, to its clean and comfortable rooms, Rijyo Kaikan is a sanctuary amid the bustle of downtown Hiroshima. This public facility offers basic accommodation at a budget price. Perfect location, adjacent to the Peace Park. **www.chikyosai.or.jp/rijyo-kaikan/**

HIROSHIMA Hiroshima Prince Hotel

23-1 Motoujina-machi, Minami-ku, Hiroshima-shi, 734-8543 **Tel** *(082) 256-1111* **Fax** *(082) 256-1134* **Rooms** *550*

This large, deluxe hotel is an unusual 23-story prism-shaped tower with spectacular views of the Seto Inland Sea, Hiroshima Port, and Miyajima Island. Tours of the nearby islands depart from the hotel's private wharf. Excellent facilities include internet access, child care, and a doctor on call. **www.princehotels.co.jp**

HIROSHIMA Sun Route Hotel

3-3-1 Ote-machi, Naka-ku, Hiroshima-shi, 730-0051 **Tel** *(082) 249-3600* **Fax** *(082) 249-3677* **Rooms** *234*

Situated on the banks of the Motoyasugawa river near the Peace Park, this hotel is part of a nationwide chain of business hotels. It is well run and has good extra facilities such as non-smoking rooms and free high-speed Internet access in all rooms. There are two restaurants, one Italian and one Japanese. **www.sunroute.jp**

ISE Hoshidekan

2-15-2 Kawasaki, Ise City, Mie Prefecture, 516-0009 **Tel** *(0596) 28-2377* **Fax** *(0596) 27-2830* **Rooms** *5*

A traditional Japanese *ryokan* in business since 1926, Hoshidekan provides good-value accommodation and is conveniently located for sightseeing. Internet access and washing machines are available. Organic vegetables are used in the cooking; macrobiotic meals are available. Small extra charge for meals. **www.hoshidekan.jp**

IWAKUNI Weekly Hotel Urban Wing Marifu

1-6-16 Marifu-machi, Iwakuni-shi, Yamaguchi-ken, 740-0018 **Tel** *(0827)21-6888* **Fax** *(0827) 21-6875* **Rooms** *47*

Part of a chain of "weekly hotels" favored by people on business, Urban Wing Marifu also welcomes tourists, and offers accommodation at a budget price. The rooms are basic but comfortable, with Internet access in some rooms. Convenient location three minutes from Iwakuni station. **www.ub-hotel.co.jp**

IZUMO Takenoya

857 Kidzukiminami, Taisha-cho, Izumo-shi, 699-0711 **Tel** *(0853) 53-3131* **Fax** *(0853) 53-3134* **Rooms** *44*

Located directly opposite Izumo Shrine, this traditional Japanese inn has been catering to visitors since the late-19th century. With its well-tended pine trees at the entrance, Takenoya has a distinct character; it is steeped in history and its wooden corridors and *tatami* rooms have a nicely weathered feel. **www.takenoya-ryokan.jp**

KOBE Green Hill Hotel Urban

2-5-16 Kano-cho, Kobe-city, Hyogo, 650-0011 **Tel** *(078) 222-1221* **Fax** *(078) 242-1194* **Rooms** *102*

Green Hill Hotel Urban is centrally located, within walking distance of both Shin-Kobe station and Sannomiya station. It has a comfortable, if slightly dated, interior and offers clean and compact accommodation for a reasonable price, with Japanese-style and non-smoking rooms available. All the usual amenities. **www.ghu.jp**

KOBE The B Kobe

2-11-5 Yamate-dori, Chuo-ku, Kobe-shi, 650-0011 **Tel** *(078) 333-4880* **Fax** *(078) 333-4876* **Rooms** *158*

Opened in 2006 as part of a successful nationwide chain, The B Kobe is decorated in a chic, modern style, and its rooms are comfortable and well equipped. Four minutes' drive from Shin-Kobe station and three minutes' walk from Sannomiya station. A good value option. **www.ishinhotels.com/theb-kobe/jp**

KOBE Hotel Okura Kobe

2-1 Hatoba-cho, Chuo-ku, Kobe-shi, 650-8560 **Tel** *(078) 333-0111* **Fax** *(078) 333-6673* **Rooms** *489*

Part of the prestigious Okura flagship, this 35-story luxury hotel is perfectly located next to Kobe's Meriken Park and the Port Tower. A wide range of comfortable rooms is available from Standard through "Hollywood Twin" to Presidential. A business center, gym, indoor and outdoor pool are among the facilities. **http://kobe.okura.com**

KOBE Portopia

10-1,6 Chome, Minatojima Nakamachi, Chuo-ku, 650-0046 **Tel** *(078) 302 -1111* **Fax** *(078) 302- 6877* **Rooms** *745*

With a magnificent night view of Kobe to the north and a panorama of Osaka Bay to the south, the elegantly designed Portopia Hotel is a well-situated luxury hotel. A full range of facilities is available, from indoor and outdoor swimming pools, gyms, and saunas to a boutique. Twelve restaurants and bistros. **www.portopia.co.jp**

KURASHIKI Kurashiki Ishiyama Kadan

1-25-23 Chuo-ku, Kurashiki-shi, 710-0046 **Tel** *(086) 422-2222* **Fax** *(086) 422-7449* **Rooms** *75*

This eight-story building looks like a functionally-designed hotel from the outside, but it is actually a large-scale *ryokan*. All its rooms are Japanese-style *tatami* rooms. Seasonal, locally-grown ingredients are used in its popular *kaiseki* cuisine. Free shuttle service to and from JR Kurashiki station. **www.kurasiki.co.jp**

KURASHIKI Kurashiki Sakura Stay

1-9-4 Chuo-ku, Kuruashiki-shi, 710-0046 **Tel** *(086) 435-7001*   **Rooms** *29*

The simple, pleasing design of this fashionable hotel features a charming patio area with smooth white walls sweeping around a central atrium. After dark, candles create a soothing atmosphere. Well located, it offers all the usual facilities, including free computer and Internet usage. **www.sakurastay.jp**

KURASHIKI Ryokan Kurashiki

4-1 Honmachi Kurashiki City, 710-0054 **Tel** *(086) 422-0730* **Fax** *(086) 422-0990* **Rooms** *5*

Ryokan Kurashiki is a converted warehouse from the Edo period and each of its immaculate rooms is adapted to respect the original layout. Among its assorted rooms there is a 250-year-old converted rice store, once the favorite room of one of Japan's most popular postwar writers, Shiba Ryotaro. **www.ryokan-kurashiki.jp**

LAKE BIWA Biwako Hotel

2-40 Hamamachi, Ootsu-shi, Shiga-ken, 520-0041 **Tel** *(077) 524-7111* **Fax** *(077) 524-1384* **Rooms** *171*

Just a two-minute walk from the lake shore, this hotel is perfectly located for lakeside strolls and sightseeing around Ozumi bay. Numerous recreational facilities are available, which include pleasure cruises of the bay. A natural hot spring and outdoor bath are among the other assets of this comfortable hotel. **www.biwakohotel.co.jp**

MATSUE Hotel Ichibata

30 Chidori-machi, Matsue-shi, Shimane-ken, 690-0852 **Tel** *(0852) 22-0188* **Fax** *(0852) 22-0230* **Rooms** *142*

Hotel Ichibata is located in the hot spring section of town, on the shore of the picturesque Lake Shinji. Natural spring water is pumped from 1,250 m (4,125 ft) underground to the bathing area on the top floor, which affords wonderful views of the city. High-speed internet access is available in all rooms. **www.ichibata.co.jp**

MATSUE Terazuya

60 Tenjin-Machi Matsue-City Shimane, 690-0064 **Tel** *(0852) 21-3480* **Fax** *(0852) 21-3422* **Rooms** *8*

This small, intimate inn near Shirakata Tenmangu Shrine has been run by the same family since 1893. The Japanese-style rooms are comfortable, although they do not have en-suite bathrooms or toilets. Dinner and breakfast are available as optional extras. Internet access is available. **www.mable.ne.jp**

MIYAJIMA ISLAND Guesthouse Kikugawa

796 Miyajima-cho, Hatsukaichi City, 739-0500 **Tel** *(0829) 44-0039* **Fax** *(0829) 44-2773* **Rooms** *8*

Just a five-minute walk from Miyajima Port, this friendly, family-run *pension* has its own tiny garden and simple, comfortable rooms. The owner speaks English. Food is nourishing, made with fresh local produce, and the needs of vegetarian guests can be met if sufficient notice is given. **www.itcj.jp**

MIYAJIMA ISLAND Iwaso

Momiji-tani, Miyajima-cho, Saekigun, 739-0500 **Tel** *(0829) 44-2233* **Fax** *(0829) 44-2230* **Rooms** *38*

The longest-running *ryokan* in Miyajima, Iwaso has been in business since 1893. With a picturesque location in Momijidani Park, the *miya-daiku*-style wooden structure is flanked by maple trees. Traditional Kyoto-style meals are served, with vegetarian meals available on request. **www.iwaso.com**

MOUNT KOYA Tentoku-in

370 Koya-san, Koya-cho, Ito-gun, 648-0211 **Tel** *(0736) 56-2714* **Fax** *(0736) 56-3618* **Rooms** *45*

Located roughly halfway up the mountain, near Kongoubuji, the Shingon sect head temple, Tentoku-in has a Japanese garden which is designated as an important cultural property. A tranquil space surrounded by great scenic beauty. The hospitality here includes authentic Buddhist vegetarian cooking. **www.h3.dion.ne.jp**

NARA Ryokan Seikan-so

29 Higashi-Kitsuji-cho, Nara City. **Tel** *(0742) 22-2670* **Fax** *(0742) 22-2670* **Rooms** *9*

Conveniently positioned in the center of Nara, Ryokan Seikan-so is close to major tourist attractions such as Kasuga Shrine, Todai-ji Temple and Kofuku-ji Temple. The worn old building, which was formerly a *geisha* house dating from the 17th century, has a charming little garden. Helpful, English-speaking staff. **seikanso@chive.ocn.ne.jp**

NARA Nara Hotel

1096 Takabatake-machi, Nara-shi, 630-8301 **Tel** *0742) 26-3300* **Fax** *(0742) 23-5252* **Rooms** *129*

Reminiscent of the grand old hotels of the Orient, this hotel has views of Wakakusayama Mountain and the temples Todai-ji and Kofuku-ji. Try to stay in the old wing with its high ceilings, period fixtures and fittings, cypress paneling, and eaves. The garden is a designated cultural treasure. **www.narahotel.co.jp**

NARA Asuka-sou

1113-3 Takabatake-machi, Nara-shi, 630-8301 **Tel** *(0742) 26-2538* **Fax** *(0742) 26-0658* **Rooms** *31*

This small but comfortable *ryokan* in the center of town is just 10 minutes' walk from Kintetsu-Nara station. Deer can be seen strolling in the quiet surroundings, and beautiful views of the Kofukuji pagoda and Nan'endo can be enjoyed from the rooftop outdoor bath. Its delightful garden is illuminated at night. **www.asukasou.com**

Key to Price Guide *see p298* **Key to Symbols** *see back cover flap*

OKAYAMA Matsunoki ¥

19-1 Ekimoto-cho, Okayama-City, 700-0024 **Tel** *(086) 253-4111* **Fax** *(086) 253-4110* **Rooms** *59*

Matsunoki is a family-owned *ryokan* located just a two-minute walk from JR Okayama station. The clean and comfortable rooms are mostly Japanese-style. Meals are served in a shared dining hall, although you might try their nearby restaurant Matsunoki-tei *(see p340)*. Midnight curfew. **http://ww3.tiki.ne.jp/~matunoki/english.htm**

OSAKA Flexstay Shinsaibashi Inn ¥¥

1-9-30 Nishi Shinsaibashi, Chuo-ku, 542-0086 **Tel** *(06) 6282-9021* **Fax** *(06) 6282-9017* **Rooms** *54*

Just a two-minute walk from Shinsaibashi subway station, this "weekly mansion" (short term rental apartments) also accommodates one-night stays. Its basic but comfortable rooms are well equipped, with microwave ovens, refrigerators, and TVs. Good location for sightseeing. **www.wmt-osaka.jp/shinsaibashi/index.html**

OSAKA Hotel Sunroute Kanku ¥¥

5-1 Nagisa-machi, Izumiootsu-shi, 595-0055 **Tel** *(0725) 20-1111* **Fax** *(0725) 31-1313* **Rooms** *150*

Hotel Sunroute Kanku has a bright, spacious interior and comfortable rooms. There are good facilities, including a massage service, and a choice between Japanese and Italian restaurants. There are impressive night views of the city and a free shuttle service from Kansai Airport. **www.ishinhotels.com/sunroute-kanku/en/index.html**

OSAKA Apa Villa Hotel ¥¥¥

1-27-1 Noninbashi, Chuo-ku, 540-0011 **Tel** *(06) 4790-2111* **Fax** *(06) 4790-0411* **Rooms** *339*

Apa Villa Hotel is a one-minute walk from Tanimachi Yon-chome subway station. Simple, pleasingly-designed rooms make this a good option for the price. Facilities include a bathing area and sauna. High-speed Internet access is available on request. **www.apahotel.com/hotel/avh_osakatanimachi/index.html**

OSAKA Il Monte ¥¥¥

7-13 Doyama-cho, Kita-ku, 530-0027 **Tel** *(06) 6361-2828* **Fax** *(06) 6361-3525* **Rooms** *122*

Hotel Il Monte was designed by the acclaimed Italian architect Aldo Rossi and it has cozy and stylish rooms. Tea and coffee are provided free of charge in the salon, as are printers and computers with Internet access. Conveniently located in central Osaka, within walking distance of JR Osaka station. **www.ilmonte.co.jp/index.html**

OSAKA Rihga Grand Hotel ¥¥¥

2-3-18 Nakanoshima, Kita-ku, 530-0005 **Tel** *(06) 6202-1212* **Fax** *(06) 6227-5054* **Rooms** *310*

First opened in 1958, the Grand underwent extensive refurbishment in 2000 and combines conventional European decor with modern facilities such as plasma screen TVs and high-speed Internet access in each room. There are seven restaurants and bars in total. Located by Higobashi subway station. **www.rihga.com/osgrand/index.html**

OSAKA Rihga Royal Hotel Osaka ¥¥¥

5-3-68 Nakanoshima, Kita-ku, 530-0005 **Tel** *(06) 6448-1121* **Fax** *(06) 6448-4414* **Rooms** *974*

This luxury hotel, originally opened in 1935, is one of Osaka's oldest, although the sleek modern landmark now towering between the Tosabori and Dojima rivers does not give that impression. A total of 20 restaurants cater to every taste, plus a jacuzzi, great swimming pool, and shopping arcade. **www.rihga.com/osaka/index.html**

OSAKA Hotel Hankyu International ¥¥¥¥¥

19-19 Chayamachi, Kita-ku, 530-0013 **Tel** *(06) 6377-2100* **Fax** *(06) 6377-3622* **Rooms** *168*

There are splendid night views of Osaka and excellent service at this elaborately-decorated luxury hotel 10 minutes by taxi from Shin Osaka station. The spacious guest rooms come in a range of decors from classic European to traditional Japanese, and have marble bathrooms. **www.hankyu-hotel.com/hotels/18hhinternational/**

SHIRAHAMA Hotel Kawakyu ¥¥¥¥¥

3745 Shirohama-cho, Nishimuro-gun, 649-2211 **Tel** *(0739) 42-3322* **Fax** *(0739) 42-2666* **Rooms** *88*

The fantastical, dreamlike architectural design of this unusual deluxe hotel conjures up images of a fairytale castle. The rooms are spacious and comfortable and are consistent with the exterior in the originality of their design; no two rooms have the same interior. Ask for one of the rooms overlooking the Pacific. **www.hotel-kawakyu.jp/**

TSUWANO Ryokan Meigetsu ¥¥

Uomachi, Tsuwano-cho, Kanoashi-gun, 699-5605 **Tel** *(0856) 72-0685* **Fax** *(0856) 72-0637* **Rooms** *13*

Ryokan Meigetsu has picturesque views and wonderful cypress bathtubs. An old-fashioned *ryokan* in business for over a century, it is steeped in tradition; the kitchen knife of the first generation owner is still used to prepare the food, which is based on local specialties. **http://gambo-ad.com/tsuwano/hotel/meigetsu/index.htm**

TSUWANO Wakasagi-no Yado ¥¥

93-6 Morimura, Tsuwano-cho, Kanoashi-gun, 699-5604 **Tel** *(08567) 2-1146* **Fax** *(08567) 2-1146* **Rooms** *8*

This cozy little *minshuku* is close to the center of town. The food, mainly fresh fish and mountain vegetables, is home cooked, with homemade sesame tofu prepared each day. The friendly staff provide a free pick-up and send-off service on request. Bicycles are available for rent. **www.iwami.or.jp/tsuwanok/genki/wakasagi/sagi.htm**

YAMAGUCHI Matsudaya Hotel ¥¥¥¥¥

3-6-7 Yudaonsen, Yamaguchi-shi, 753-0056 **Tel** *(083) 922-0125* **Fax** *(083) 925-6111* **Rooms** *33*

Matsudaya Hotel has a colorful past stretching over 300 years, and hosted some key figures of the Meiji Restoration, among them the heroic visionary Sakamoto Ryouma. The Meiji-era bath which these samurai used dates from 1860 and is designated as a cultural treasure. **www.matsudayahotel.co.jp/index.html**

YOSHINO Keisho-no-yado Ho-un Kan

 ⓨⓨⓨⓨ

2340 Yoshino-yama, Yoshino-cho, Yoshino-gun, 639-3115 **Tel** *(07463) 2-3001* **Fax** *(07463) 2-8633* **Rooms** *25*

This *ryokan* first opened for business in 1754 and has captivating views of the national park forests that surround it. There are two shared bathing areas and some of the guest rooms have private outdoor baths attached. The cherry and Yoshino cedar wood interiors create a warm ambience throughout. **www.hounkan.co.jp/e/**

SHIKOKU

ANAN COASTAL AREA Shiroi Todai Hotel

ⓨⓨⓨⓨ

455 Hiwasa-ura, Hiwasa-cho, Kaihu, 779-2304 **Tel** *(0884) 77-1170* **Fax** *(0884) 77-1174* **Rooms** *27*

Perched on a cliff-top in the Anan coastal region, this is a great base for exploring the area's natural treasures. There's a wonderful hot spring overlooking the ocean, and also a small swimming pool which shares the same stunning view. Staff are extremely welcoming and two meals are included. **www.shiroitodai.burari.biz**

CAPE ASHIZURI AREA Ashizuri Thermae

ⓨⓨ

Higashibata 1433-3, Ashizuri Misaki, Tosa Shimizu City, 787-0315 **Tel** *(0880) 88-0301* **Fax** *(0880) 88-0304* **Rooms** *60*

Traditional Japanese rooms and also simple, modern Western-style rooms are available at this scenically-located hotel in the hills of Cape Ashizuri. There is an ocean-view hot spring and a large indoor pool. Not all floors are served by the elevator, so let them know if you have a problem with stairs when booking. **www.terume.com/**

KOCHI Comfort Hotel Kochi

ⓨ

2-2-12 Kitahonmachi, 780-0056 **Tel** *(088) 883-1441* **Fax** *(088) 884-3692* **Rooms** *66*

This functional hotel may not look like much from the outside, but it offers outstanding value for money and a good location, not too far from Kochi station. The rooms are simple, large, and comfortable, and the staff are efficient. Breakfast is even included in the affordable overnight fee. **www.daiichi-hotel.co.j**

KOCHI Jyoseikan Ryokan

ⓨⓨⓨⓨⓨ

5-34-2 Chome, Kamimachi **Tel** *(088) 875-0111* **Fax** *(088) 824-0557* **Rooms** *72*

This luxurious hotel in Kochi city is housed in a beautiful old traditional Japanese building, and prices include a selection of mouthwatering meals. Most of the rooms are spacious, opulent, and Japanese in style, although there are some Western-style ones available too. The hotel's hot spring is out of this world. **www.jyoseikan.co.jp**

KOTOHIRA Kotobuki Ryokan

ⓨⓨ

245-5 Shinmachi, Kotohiracho, Nakatado-gun, Kagawa, 766-0002 **Tel** *(0877) 73 3872* **Fax** *(0877) 73-3872* **Rooms** *7*

This charming little picturesque family-run inn is housed in a quaint old building in Kotohira city. Intimate and beautifully decorated, rooms are Japanese in style, and two delicious meals are included. Staff speak only Japanese, but are helpful and welcoming. **www.town.kotohira.kagawa.jp/onsen/kotobuki/kotobuki.html**

MATSUYAMA Hotel Patio Dogo

ⓨⓨ

20-12 Dogo Yunomachi, 790-0842 **Tel** *(089) 941-4128* **Fax** *(089) 941-4129* **Rooms** *101*

Right in the middle of Matsuyama's Dogo hot spring district (one of Japan's oldest, at 1,000 years), Hotel Patio Dogo offers clean, functional rooms that are great value. Staff are super friendly, speak a little English, and are happy to share their local knowledge. Visit their website for discount offers. **www.patio-dogo.co.jp**

MATSUYAMA Dogokan Ryokan

ⓨⓨⓨⓨⓨ

7-26 Dogo Takou-cho, 790-0841 **Tel** *(089) 941-7777* **Fax** *(089) 941-7777* **Rooms** *90*

While the architecture of this large concrete building leaves a little to be desired, the interior is elegant and stylish. The large, Japanese-style rooms are exquisite, and an overnight stay means you will be served two excellent Japanese meals. The hot spring is deservedly one of the most famous in Shikoku. **www.dogokan.co.jp**

NARUTO Sanukiya Ryokan

ⓨⓨ

39 Aza, Mitsuicho, Benzaiten, Muya-cho, 772-0014 **Tel** *(088) 686-3301* **Fax** *(088) 686-3347* **Rooms** *12*

Conveniently located in the centre of Naruto city, this small, family-run inn is traditionally decorated and housed in a cute old Japanese building. Rooms are small but cozy, and lovingly-prepared meals are available if desired – the seafood is as fresh and delicious as it comes. Nightly curfew at 11pm. **www12.ocn.ne.jp/~sanukiya**

NARUTO Renaissance Naruto Resort

ⓨⓨⓨⓨ

16-45 Oge-Tosadomoariura, 772-0053 **Tel** *(0886) 872-2580* **Fax** *(087) 687-2211* **Rooms** *208*

This luxury resort hotel with generously-sized rooms (Western and Japanese) is the perfect place for relaxation. With dramatic views, amazing hot springs, putter golf, tennis courts, a pool, and a host of other activities, you certainly won't have time to get bored. Two sumptuous meals are included. **www.renaissance-naruto.com**

TAKAMATSU Rihga Hotel Zest

ⓨⓨⓨ

9-1 Furujinmachi, 760-0025 **Tel** *(087) 822-3555* **Fax** *(087) 822-3555* **Rooms** *122*

Situated in downtown Takamatsu, this smart hotel is modern and Western-style in design. Service here is impeccable, and rooms are warm and inviting. There are a number of good restaurants to choose from, and even an open-air one to enjoy in the warmer months. **www.rihga.com**

Key to Price Guide *see p298* **Key to Symbols** *see back cover flap*

TAKAMATSU Takamatsu Tokyu Inn Hotel

9-9 Hyogomachi, Takamatsu-shi, Kagawa, 760-0024 **Tel** *(087) 821-0106* **Fax** *(087) 821-0109* **Rooms** *188*

Part of the highly-successful Tokyu hotel chain and a short walk from Takamatsu station, this large, contemporary hotel is new and efficient. The tastefully-designed rooms are bright, comfortable, and well equipped. Staff speak a little English. Their website makes reservations easy. **www.tokyuhotels.co.jp/en/TI/TI_TAKAM/index.html**

UWAJIMA Tsukigase Ryokan

1-5-6 Miyuki-machi, 798-0013 **Tel** *(0895) 22-4788* **Fax** *(0895) 22-4787* **Rooms** *5*

This small Japanese inn is in a gorgeous old building with a particularly charming garden, reminiscent of those found in the Zen temples of Kyoto. Rooms are quaint and Japanese in style, and the staff are extremely welcoming. The restaurant is of particularly high quality. Meals are included. **http://www18.ocn.ne.jp/~tsukigase/**

KYUSHU

AMAMI ISLAND Resort Hotel Marine Station Amami

970 Sokaru, Setouchi-cho, Ooshima-gun, 894-1523 **Tel** *(0997) 72-1001* **Fax** *(0997) 72-3932* **Rooms** *45*

Beautifully located on a quiet white beach at the southern tip of Amami Island, this hotel has excellent diving, sea kayaking, and boating facilities. Trained guides are on hand to assist first-timers, while a wide range of equipment from masks, snorkels, and fishing tackle to bicycles is available for hire. **www.marinestation.jp/**

BEPPU Sakaeya

2 Ita, Kannawa, Beppu-shi, Oita, 874-0043 **Tel** *(0977) 66-6234* **Fax** *(0977) 66-6235* **Rooms** *7*

Beppu's oldest *minshuku* is one of its most charming, with Meiji-period fixtures and fittings in some rooms. A stone oven in the courtyard is powered by steam from a hot spring, as is the *kotatsu* (a covered table heated from below). Outdoor bath; separate indoor bathing areas for men and women. **www.coara.or.jp/kannawa/sakaeya/**

BEPPU Yukemuri no Sato Azumaya

1029-1 Kannawa, Beppu-shi, Oita, 874-0024 **Tel** *(0977) 27-7547* **Fax** *(0977) 27-7548* **Rooms** *8*

This recently remodeled traditional building exudes calm and the service is attentive. One of its greatest assets is the dazzling night view of Beppu, with the sea and mountains beyond, seen from a partially-roofed bath on the top floor, or through large windows in each room. Private cypress wood baths. **www.gloria-g.com/azumaya/**

FUKUOKA Kashima Honkan

3-11 Reisen-cho, Hakata-ku , 812-0039 **Tel** *(092) 291 0746* **Fax** *(092) 271-7995* **Rooms** *27*

A Taisho-period house built in the *sukiya* style and ideally located near Fukuoka's famed Kushida Shrine, this tranquil *ryokan* has a long history; the cozy interior and Japanese garden make it an oasis within the city. Free internet access and refreshments are available in the lobby. Basic but adequate accommodation.

FUKUOKA Il Palazzo

3-13-1 Haruyoshi, Chuo-ku , 810-0003 **Tel** *(092) 716-3333* **Fax** *(092) 724-3330* **Rooms** *62*

The creation of Italian architect Aldo Rossi and leading Japanese designers, Il Palazzo has comfortable, spacious rooms with marble baths and is conveniently located between Nakasu and Tenjin. Enjoy excellent French food in the restaurant or sip a cocktail in the labyrinthine bar, conceived by Italian artist Gaetano Pesce. **www.ilpalazzo.jp/**

FUKUOKA Tokyo Daiichi Hotel Fukuoka

5-2-18 Nakasu, Hakata-ku, 810-0801 **Tel** *(092) 281-3311* **Fax** *(092) 281-3938* **Rooms** *217*

Conveniently located in Nakasu, and a short walk from Tenjin, this hotel offers efficient service at an affordable price. Try the stone spa, where you can lie on heated bedrock to dissolve stress and fatigue, easing shoulder tension or back pain. Massages are also available. **www.daiichihotel-fukuoka.co.jp/index.shtml**

FUKUOKA Hotel With The Style Fukuoka

1-9-18 Hakataminami, Hakata-ku, 812-0016 **Tel** *(092) 433-3900* **Fax** *(092) 433-3903* **Rooms** *16*

This hotel, created by acclaimed designer Ryu Kosaka, is a triumph of sleek minimalism. Luxurious warmth pervades the rooms, which have private terraces, while a rooftop spa and penthouse are available. The ground floor has a sushi bar, restaurant and a bar, and a courtyard pool. Advance reservation advised. **www.withthestyle.com/**

KAGOSHIMA Nakazono Ryokan

1-18 Yasui-cho Kagoshima-shi, 892-0815 **Tel** *(099) 226-5125* **Fax** *(099) 226-5126* **Rooms** *10*

Nakazono Ryokan offers basic accommodation in a convenient location, with public baths nearby. The simple, Japanese-style *tatami* rooms do not have en-suite facilities and meals are not available, but the friendly owner speaks English and provides sightseeing information. **www.satsuma.ne.jp/myhome/shindon/**

KAGOSHIMA Kagoshima Tokyu Hotel

22-1 Kamoikeshinmachi, Kagoshima-shi, 890-0064 **Tel** *(099) 257-2411* **Fax** *(099) 257-6083* **Rooms** *206*

Located on the waterfront within walking distance of town, this hotel's balcony rooms afford a good view of Kagoshima's volcano, Sakurajima, rising up out of Kinko bay, especially at sunset. Natural hot-spring jacuzzis and two outdoor swimming pools are among the hotel's other assets. **www.kg-tokyu-hotel.co.jp/**

KAGOSHIMA Hakusuikan

12126-12,Higashikata, Ibusuki-shi, Kagoshima-ken, 891-0404 **Tel** *(0993) 22-3131* **Fax** *(0993) 23-3860* **Rooms** *205*

Flanked by pine trees, this well-known *ryokan* has a spectacular view of Kinko bay. As well as its spacious rooms, Hakusuikan features a courtyard Japanese garden and an outdoor bath and pool overlooking the sea. It also offers a chance to experience Ibusuki's unique steaming sand bath. **www.hakusuikan.co.jp**

KUMAMOTO Romanesque Resort Kikunan

659 Tsuruhadamachi, Kumamoto-shi, 861-5513 **Tel** *(096) 344-5600* **Fax** *(096) 344-5554* **Rooms** *86*

This hotel's stated aim is to combine Japanese hospitality and attention to detail with the relaxed ambience of a Western resort. From the lobby's Cassina seats and moon-like ceiling light to the pleasing simplicity of the rooms, its contemporary decor evokes a feeling of spaciousness throughout. **www.rresort-kikunan.com**

KUMAMOTO Wasuki Tsukasa Kan

7-35 Kamitoori-cho, Kumamoto-shi, 860-0845 **Tel** *(096) 352-5101* **Fax** *(096) 354-8105* **Rooms** *44*

There is a choice between rooms with beds or futons at this centrally-located Japanese-style hotel, which was remodeled in 2006. Its stately black-and-white exterior has a refined grandeur reminiscent of a feudal castle. A stone spa and massage facilities are among the hotel's other assets. **www.tsukasahotel.co.jp**

MIYAZAKI Jizoan

1-6-4 Aoshima, Miyazaki-shi, 889-2162 **Tel** *(0985) 65-0039* **Fax** *(0985) 65-1916* **Rooms** *6*

Private baths of Japanese cedar are attached to the rooms at this intimate *ryokan*, with miniature gardens planted between the mud walls of the buildings and its annexes; everything was hand-built by the owner with the aid of a carpenter. There is hearty food, based mainly around seafood from Aoshima. **www.jizoan.jp**

MOUNT ASO Pension Okanoie

4732-10 Kawayo, Minamiaso-mura, Kumamoto-ken, 869-1404 **Tel** *(0967) 67-1818* **Fax** *(0967) 67-2156* **Rooms** *9*

This quaint lodge, complete with sociable dog and a beautiful flower garden, is ideally located to combine tranquillity with convenient access to the surrounding sightseeing spots. The elegant, wood-furnished dining hall affords a spectacular view of the southern rim of the crater. **http://asopension.com**

MOUNT ASO Ikoi Ryokan

Kawabata-dori, Kurokawa Onsen, Minamioguni-machi, 869-2400 **Tel** *(0967) 44-0552* **Fax** *(0967) 44-0807* **Rooms** *12*

Popular for its hot spring water, which is said to have beautifying properties, this well-reputed *ryokan* has an outdoor mixed bathing area with a view of a backlit waterfall. An unusual 1.5-m (5-ft) indoor bath features hanging bamboo poles for bathers to hold on to while bathing standing up. **www.ikoi-ryokan.com**

NAGASAKI Hotel Belle View

1-20 Edomachi, Nagasaki-shi, 850-0861 **Tel** *(095) 826-5030* **Fax** *(095) 826-5051* **Rooms** *201*

Conveniently located two minutes by car from Dejima, or 10 minutes' walk from Nagasaki station, this business hotel offers surprisingly good service for its budget price. The rooms are plain but comfortable, with good sound insulation. Free high-speed Internet access, plus wireless LAN in the lobby. **www.hotel-belleview.com**

NAGASAKI The Hamilton Nagasaki

7-9 Maruyama-cho, Nagasaki-shi, 850-0902 **Tel** *(095) 824-1000* **Fax** *(095) 827-8111* **Rooms** *62*

The Hamilton Nagasaki provides friendly and efficient service, achieving a scaled-up version of the relaxed hospitality of an English B & B with its deliberately nostalgic decor and buffet-style Western breakfast. The guest lounge has free internet access and there are displays outlining Nagasaki's history. **www.hamilton-gr.jp**

NAGASAKI ANA Hotel Glover Hill

1-18 Minami-yamate-cho, Nagasaki-shi, Nagasaki-ken, 850-0931 **Tel** *(095) 818-6601* **Fax** *(095) 818-6110* **Rooms** *217*

Perfectly situated two minutes' walk from the important tourist attractions of Glover Garden and Oura Catholic Church, this well-established hotel provides attentive service. The decor varies from the elaborately plush lobby to more conventionally-designed rooms, but is bright and comfortable throughout. **www.ana-gloverhill.co.jp**

NAGASAKI Sakamoto-ya

2-13 Kanaya-cho, Nagasaki-shi, 850-0037 **Tel** *(095) 826-8211*   **Rooms** *17*

Established in the early Meiji-era (1894), this small inn is a bastion of historical Nagasaki, having hosted numerous distinguished guests in the past, including artists Tougou Seiji and Yamashita Kiyoshi. Most rooms have private Japanese-style wooden tubs for bathing; one has a small private garden attached. **www.sakamotoya.co.jp**

SAGA Karatsu Seaside Hotel

4-182 Higashi Karatsu, Karatsu-shi, 847-0017 **Tel** *(0955) 75-3200*   **Rooms** *114*

Wonderful views of the sea can be enjoyed throughout Karatsu Seaside Hotel, which explains the repeated stays by Jacques Mayol, the Frenchman famous for making the first recorded dive deeper than 100m (330ft) without oxygen. A beachside pool and spa are among the hotel's assets. **www.seaside.karatsu.saga.jp**

UNZEN Kyushu Hotel

320 Unzen, Ohama-cho, Unzen-shi, 854-0697 **Tel** *(0957) 73-3234* **Fax** *(0957) 73-3733* **Rooms** *85*

Kyushu Hotel dates from 1917, although it underwent complete refurbishment in 2006. Behind its modest façade is a charming, spacious interior with chic rooms of contemporary Japanese design, and a dining room which faces on to steaming hot springs. There are four spas and massage is available. **www.kyushuhtl.co.jp**

Key to Price Guide *see p298* **Key to Symbols** *see back cover flap*

YUFUIN Wa No Yado Sagiritei

811-1 Kawakami, Yufuin-cho, Yugu-shi, Oita-ken, 879-5102 **Tel** *(0911) 85-4292* **Rooms** *10*

Secluded in a leafy grove, this enchanting *ryokan* holds time at a standstill. The guest rooms are little bungalows among the trees, while the thatched main building is where dinners are served. The food includes charcoal-grilled meat. At night, torches burn in iron baskets to create a magical atmosphere. **www.gloria-g.com/sagiritei/**

OKINAWA

ISHIGAKI-JIMA Pension Kohamoto

441-1 Tonoshiro, Ishigaki City, 907-0004 **Tel** *(098) 082-2369* **Fax** *(098) 088-0592* **Rooms** *8*

This guesthouse in Ishigaki, run by a music teacher, has been open for around 30 years now. As well as running a cozy establishment, he will also teach the *sanshin* to anyone who is interested. A convenient location between the airport and city center makes this excellent budget accommodation. **www.kohamoto.com**

KUME-JIMA Hotel Nikko Kume Island

411 Magari, Kume-jima Town, 901-3112 **Tel** *(098) 985-8001* **Fax** *(098) 985-8009* **Rooms** *201*

This beautiful resort sits right on Eef Beach, a 2-km (1-mile) white-sand beach which is perfect for relaxing and swimming. A variety of marine sports are offered, from jet-skiing to scuba diving. The atmosphere is calm and serene, and fits in with the surroundings perfectly. Recommended for a relaxing holiday.

NAGO Nago Guest House

497-2 Miyasato, Nago City, 905-0011 **Tel** *(0980) 54-2823* **Fax** *(0980) 54-2823* **Rooms** *7*

This hostel is located just outside Nago and right on top of a beach naturally made from coral. Although the facilities are relatively basic, there is a friendly atmosphere and the owner will arrange water sports and hiking tours for you. A good place to stay if your budget is tight. **www.nago-mp.com**

NAGO Busena Terrace

1808 Kise, Nago City, 905-0026 **Tel** *(0980) 51-1333* **Fax** *(0980) 51-1331* **Rooms** *401*

This luxurious resort was the setting for the 2000 G8 Summit, and those members couldn't have wished for better surroundings. The Busena Terrace offers everything you could wish to find in a resort, from watersports to a butler service. Ideal if you have a little extra money to spend. **www.terrace.co.jp**

NAHA Minami Kaze

2-4-6 Tomari, Naha City, 900-0012 **Tel** *(098) 863-1183* **Rooms** *8*

Minami Kaze has recently been renovated and looks much better in its new state. Reminiscent of a Mediterranean villa, this hostel offers clean rooms or dormitory beds at an excellent price. You can also rent bicycles or scooters from here. Centrally located and very convenient. **www.minamikaze-cg.com**

NAHA Okinawa Rainbow Hotel

1-19-17 Matsuo, Naha City, 900-0014 **Tel** *(098) 866-5401* **Fax** *(098) 863-4163* **Rooms** *123*

An especially environmentally-friendly hotel, each room in the Okinawa Rainbow Hotel emits negative ions for your comfort. Conveniently located a few minutes' walk from Kokusai-dori, this hotel is always busy and has an excellent restaurant and in-house bakery. **www.rainbowhotel.co.jp**

NAHA Toyoko Inn Asahibashi

2-1-20 Kume, Naha City, 900-0033 **Tel** *(098) 951-1045* **Fax** *(098) 951-1047* **Rooms** *145*

Toyoko Inn is a huge chain of hotels throughout Japan. Usually frequented by businessmen on work-related trips, the hotel offers in-room internet access, a fax machine service, and conference rooms. If you need to be located close to the Naha's business district, this is the place to go. **www.toyoko-inn.com/e_hotel/00076/index.html**

OKINAWA CITY Grand Mer Hotel

1205-2 Yogi, Okinawa City, 904-2174 **Tel** *(098) 931-1500* **Fax** *(098) 931-1509* **Rooms** *300*

This hotel is very popular with both domestic Japanese tourists and military personnel. A free shuttle bus runs to and from Naha airport to this centrally-located resort. In many rooms the views down the hillside and over the Pacific Ocean are breathtaking. The two restaurants here cater for every taste. **www.daiichihotel-okinawa.com**

NORTHERN HONSHU

AIZU-WAKAMATSU Hotel Keizan

984-3 Ashinomaki, Oto-Machi **Tel** *(0242) 92-2031* **Fax** *(0242) 92-3075* **Rooms** *11*

This small, friendly hotel lies right beside the Okawa River. There are indoor baths, or you can enjoy the sound of the river and wind in the trees soaking outside. You can reserve a private family bath. The food is noted for using locally-grown organic rice and vegetables. There's easy access from Ashinomaki Onsen train station.

AIZU-WAKAMATSU Shibakawa-Don

3-28 Nanoka-Machi, Fukushima **Tel** *(0242) 28-4000* **Fax** *(0242) 26-6464* **Rooms** *21*

Once the home and shop of a wealthy dried fish wholesaler, this is now a great place to experience the architecture and atmosphere of early Taisho, with most of the modern amenities. There's a lush garden, gleaming wood floors in the halls, and even a hearth to sit around. Famed writer Yukio Mishima once stayed here.

HANAMAKI Sansuikaku

181 Osawa Aza Yuguchi, Iwate, 025-0244 **Tel** *(0198) 25-2021* **Fax** *(098) 25-2551* **Rooms** *57*

This is a modern *ryokan* with good-sized rooms overlooking a river and forest. There are indoor and outdoor hot springs looking on to the river's rock cliffs and overhanging greenery, or reserve a private family bath. A shuttle bus from Hanamaki station takes about 30 minutes. A great place to relax and be pampered.

KAKUNODATE Folkloro Kakunodate

14 Nakasudazawa, Akita, 014-0368 **Tel** *(0187) 53-2070* **Fax** *(0187) 53-2118* **Rooms** *26*

Like all the hotels in this popular JR East chain, this is good value. Right next to the station and convenient for all the sights. Expect friendly, good service. Rooms can be reserved with credit card at any JR East Plaza, and there's a 10 percent discount for rail pass holders. The price includes breakfast.

KAKUNODATE Tamachi Bukeyashiki Hotel

23 Tamachi Shimocho, Akita, 014-0312 **Tel** *(0187) 52-1700* **Fax** *(0187) 52-1701* **Rooms** *12*

A very modern hotel cleverly created with a tasteful Edo-era feel, all dark, gleaming wood floors and cream *shoji* screens, with great attention to detail. Breakfast is included, while dinner is an option and the restaurant is good. A five-minute walk from a hot spring. There are discounts available in winter. **www.bukeyashiki.jp**

KAMIKITA Himemasu Sanso

16 Aza Towada, Aomori, 018-5501 **Tel** *(0176) 75-2717* **Fax** *(0176) 75-2717* **Rooms** *8*

This is a good budget choice, only five-minutes' walk from the JR bus station and right by the lake. Don't be surprised to find fresh trout from the lake for dinner, and expect fresh mountain vegetables. The rooms aren't luxurious, but there is a hot spring bath and great mountain views.

KAMIKITA Towada Hotel

Kosaka-machi, Aomori, 018-5511 **Tel** *(0176) 75-1122* **Fax** *(0176) 75-1313* **Rooms** *50*

Originally built in 1938 by temple carpenters, this old building has beautiful wood craft, and the newer annex has spacious, Western-style rooms. The top-floor Japanese rooms have great atmosphere and lake views. There is no true hot spring, but try the jacuzzi and sauna. Both Japanese and Western cuisine is available. **www.towada-hotel.com**

MATSUSHIMA Folkloro Matsushima

17 Shanjukari, Miyagi, 981-0213 **Tel** *(022) 353-3535* **Fax** *(022) 353-3588* **Rooms** *29*

Another good value option from this JR East hotel chain, which is a 10-minute walk from Matsushima Kaigan station. The hotel, on a steep hill above the station, has a lovely terrace for enjoying your breakfast (included in the price). The rooms have a small refrigerator and a coffee pot as well as a TV. Rail pass holders get a 10 percent discount.

MORIOKA Hotel Ace Morioka

11-35 2-chome Chuo-dori, 020-0000 **Tel** *(019) 654-3811* **Fax** *(019) 654-3815* **Rooms** *270*

Don't expect spacious rooms in this business hotel. But for a reasonable price you do get satellite TV, a hot pot, and a Western buffet breakfast. Ask for a room in the new wing. Some rooms have free internet access. Staff are friendly and speak some English. You get a ¥400 discount if you reserve online. **www.hotel-ace.co.jp**

NIKKO Hotori-An Turtle Annex

2-16 Takumi-cho Tochigi, 321-1433 **Tel** *(0288) 53-3663* **Fax** *(0288) 53-3883* **Rooms** *11*

Down a quiet residential street, beside the Daiyamagawa River and lush green forest, and only a short walk to Tosho-gu Shrine. Pleasant, clean, non-smoking rooms with a refrigerator and microwave are available next to the comfortable living/dining room. There's also a coin laundry and free internet access. **www.turtle-nikko.com**

NIKKO Nikko Kanaya Hotel

1300 Kamihatsuishi, Tochigi, 321-1401 **Tel** *(0288) 54-0001* **Fax** *(0288) 53-2487* **Rooms** *70*

The Kanaya has been welcoming guests with style and excellent service since 1873. "Classic" describes just about every aspect of this hotel. Charles Lindbergh, Shirley MacLaine, and Indira Gandhi are just a few of the celebrities who have stayed here. Tosho-gu Shrine is a five-minute walk. Excellent French and Japanese cuisine. **www.kanayahotel.co.jp**

SADOGASHIMA Minshuku Hananoki

78-1 Jukuneki, Niigata, 852-0612 **Tel** *(0259) 86-2331* **Fax** *(0259) 86-2339* **Rooms** *7*

Set in the countryside a short way from the town of Ogi, this *minshuku* is converted from a pleasant, traditional home with a garden. Rooms share a common toilet and bath. The owners are glad to drive you to a ¥500 public hot spring about five minutes away. Dinner can be arranged for ¥3,500 per person. **www2.ocn.ne.jp/~hananoki**

SENDAI Hotel Central Sendai

4-2-6 Chuo, 980-0021 **Tel** *(022) 711-4111* **Fax** *(022) 711-4110* **Rooms** *97*

Right in the middle of everything, minutes from the bus and train stations, this business hotel especially welcomes single travelers and women. The friendly staff know some English. Most rooms are non-smoking, and all have internet connections . The rooms aren't big, but are bright and nicely furnished. **www.hotel-central.co.jp**

Key to Price Guide *see p298* **Key to Symbols** *see back cover flap*

TONO Minshuku Magariya

30-58-3 Niisato **Tel** *(0198) 62-4564* **Fax** *(0198) 62-4564* **Rooms** *10*

The owners here are friendly and full of good advice and local lore. Surrounded by an apple orchard, this family-run *minshuku* is a converted *magariya*, a traditional L-shaped building shared by people and horses. Settle by the *irori* (hearth) in winter, enjoy the cherry blossoms in spring, and apples, too. **www.tonotv.com/members/magariya/T1**

HOKKAIDO

HAKODATE Niceday Inn

9-11 Otemachi, 040-0064 **Tel** *(0138) 22-5919*   **Rooms** *3*

An affable, helpful lady (who can speak English), runs this inviting, inexpensive and homely inn, and she is happy to give tips on the best places to visit in the city. Clean, basic, warm, and not far from Hakodate JR station, this place offers a personal, authentic Japanese experience.

HAKODATE Wakamatsu Ryokan

1-2-27 Yunokawa-cho, 042-0932 **Tel** *(0138) 59-2171* **Fax** *(0138) 59-3316* **Rooms** *24*

This historic, traditional Japanese inn is patronized by the Japanese imperial family, and although rather expensive, some sublime Japanese cuisine is included in the price. The impressive hot springs are particularly delightful and have an amazing view of the ocean. A little English is spoken by the staff. **www.wakamatsuryokan.com**

KUSHIRO Kushiro Tokyu Inn

13-1-14 Kita-odori, 085-0015 **Tel** *(0154) 22-0109* **Fax** *(0154) 24-5498* **Rooms** *150*

Comfortable and well-located directly opposite Kushiro station, this large, inexpensive hotel chain is particularly popular with young people. Rooms are warm and tastefully decorated, and staff are friendly and efficient. Good transport links to the most popular attractions. **www.tokyuhotels.co.jp**

NISEKO Niseko, Higashiyama Prince Hotel

Higashiyama-onsen, Niseko-machi, Abuta-gun, 048-1592 **Tel** *(0136) 44-1111* **Fax** *(0136) 44-3224* **Rooms** *506*

Enjoy a breathtaking view of Mt Yotei and enchanting hot springs at this large hotel, particularly popular during the winter months due to its prime location next to a world-class ski area. In summer it is a popular destination for golfers and rafters. Traditonal decor and comfortable rooms. **www.princehotels.co.jp**

RISHIRI AND REBUN Kitakuni Grand Hotel

Omodomari Sakae Cho 93, Rishiri Fuji Cho, Rishiri Gun, 097-0101 **Tel** *(0163) 82-1362* **Fax** *(0163) 82-2556* **Rooms** *75*

A great base from which to explore one of the most remote islands in Japan. This hotel is modern in design, and the rooms are light, spacious, and comfortable. The hot spring here is particularly inviting, and a great way to relax tired muscles after a long day's hiking. **www.rishiri-yado.com/kitakuni**

SAPPORO Safro Spa Capsule Hotel Sapporo

Minami 6 jo, Nishi 5 chome, Chuo-ku, 064-0805 **Tel** *(011) 531-2233*   **Rooms** *86*

This surprisingly comfortable capsule hotel in the heart of Sapporo has separate floors for men and women, and entrance to their rather luxurious rooftop spa and hot spring is included in the inexpensive overnight fee. But be warned – people with tattoos will be refused admission to the bathing areas. **www.safro.co.jp**

SAPPORO Keio Plaza

2-1 North5 West 7, Chuou-ku, 060 0005 **Tel** *(011) 271 0111* **Fax** *(011) 271-7943* **Rooms** *510*

In a great location opposite the beautiful botanical gardens, this large Japanese-style hotel is highly recommended for families. Staff are affable and helpful, and rooms are pristine if not spacious. The hotel also offers a number of bars, a swimming pool, and hot spring facilities. **www.keioplaza-sapporo.co.jp**

SAPPORO Sapporo Grand Hotel

North 1, West 4, Chuo-ku, 060-0001 **Tel** *(011) 261-3311* **Fax** *(011) 231-0388* **Rooms** *565*

This elegant hotel, a stone's throw from the central station, was established in 1934 as the first Western-style hotel in Sapporo city. It still retains all of its original European elegance, and guests can expect a warm welcome, efficient service, and spacious, luxurious rooms. **www.grand1934.com**

SAPPORO Monterey

Kita 4 Jo Higashi 1-3, Chuo Ku, 060-0034 **Tel** *(011) 232-7111* **Fax** *(011) 242-2424* **Rooms** *181*

Grandeur was obviously on the minds of the architects of this imposing building in downtown Sapporo. The English-style interior is classically lavish. Despite the opulent theme, inexpensive rooms are available, although you may find them a little on the small side. **www.hotelmonterey.co.jp**

SOUNKYOU Hotel Taisetsu

Sounkyo-onsen, Kamikawa-cho, Kamikawa-gun, 078-1701 **Tel** *(01658) 5-3211* **Fax** *(01658) 5-3420* **Rooms** *229*

This hotel is situated high above the rest of the village and offers guests a haven for relaxation and pampering. The hot springs offer spectacular views of Sounkyou Gorge and Hokkaido's highest mountain, Daisetsu-zan. Rooms are spacious, uncluttered, and Japanese in style. Staff are friendly. **www.taisetsu-g.com**

WHERE TO EAT

Considering the country's present profusion of restaurants (about 80,000 in Tokyo alone) and its wealth of regional and foreign cuisines, it is hard to believe that for centuries the average Japanese diet consisted of little more than rice, miso soup, and pickles. In a land of limited resources austerity was the rule, but it taught the Japanese to make the most of seasonal foods, and to serve them artfully so that a little looked appetizing.

Typical *bento* box

Tokyo, Osaka, and Kyoto are the celebrated culinary centers, but each town takes pride in its specialties. Budget and mid-range restaurants can often be found clustered around train stations, in malls, and taking up whole floors of department stores. Many eateries can be identified by the half-curtains *(noren)* above the door, with the name of the restaurant written on them in Japanese. Some may have small mounds of salt near the entrance.

Multistory building entirely full of restaurants, Ginza, Tokyo

MEALS AND MEAL TIMES

Most *ryokan (see pp296–97)* and some hotels serve traditional breakfasts *(see p324)* from 7–9am. When Japanese eat breakfast out, they usually do so in coffee shops called *moningu* (morning), consisting of coffee, toast, a hard-boiled egg, and a small salad.

Lunch runs from about 11:30am to 1:30 or 2pm. Many restaurants then re-open for dinner around 6. Upscale restaurants generally stop serving around 9 or 10, while establishments catering to the after-hours office crowd stay open to around 11 or midnight.

Soba (noodle) shops generally open around 11:30am and continue to serve until early evening. In major cities, street stalls selling *ramen* (Chinese noodles) and other

snacks might open for business late in the evening and serve beyond midnight. In smaller towns and rural areas, few restaurants may be open after 7pm in the evening, because most visitors will be dining at their *ryokan*.

RESERVATIONS AND DRESS CODE

Reservations are essential at many *kaiseki* restaurants *(see p322)* – occasionally months in advance – but it is quite normal to turn up at others, even good places, without a reservation. Hotel concierges are usually willing to help with bookings, and to draw a map of a restaurant's location *(see p384–5)* for you.

Jeans and casual shirts are acceptable in most places, provided they are not torn or dirty. Women may find long, loose clothing advantageous when dining at a place with *zashiki* seating *(see p318)*. Also be sure to wear clean socks or stockings without holes if traditional seating on *tatami* mats is involved, as you will have to take off your shoes. Avoid wearing strong perfumes or colognes if dining at a *kaiseki* restaurant or participating in a tea ceremony.

SET DISHES AND TEISHOKU

Budget restaurants often have wonderfully realistic-looking plastic "dishes" in their windows, or photographs on the menu or wall. Simply

point to the item you want if you don't know its name. At some canteens, you may need to use a ticket machine with buttons corresponding to certain dishes, before you eat.

Many restaurants offer *teishoku* (set menus), especially at lunch, allowing you to choose *teishoku* A or B. You may be met with bewilderment if you request any variations within a set menu. In upscale restaurants *(see p316)*, you will probably need to choose among various elaborate set menus ("courses") for each diner. For advice about ordering à la carte, including communal dishes, see page 318.

PRICES AND PAYING

The price range between restaurants in Japan is vast. While you can eat a satisfying bowl of noodles for

Realistic-looking plastic "food" display in restaurant window

just ¥500, a single dish with the famous Kobe steak – with beer-fed, hand-massaged beef – may cost up to ¥20,000.

Many upscale restaurants, whose dinner courses may start at ¥10,000 or ¥20,000, might offer excellent value at lunchtime in the ¥3,000– 5,000 range.

The consumption tax of 5% is included in the quoted price (if not, this should be clearly stated on the menu). At coffee shops and lunch places, the bill is usually automatically placed on your table, and you should take it to the cashier to pay. Even if you have exact change, do not leave it on the table and walk out.

At bars and certain restaurants you have to ask for the bill. The amount, written on a slip of paper, will generally be presented to you on a small tray. You place the money on this tray, and your change will be returned on the same tray.

Tipping is not expected, even when the tray is used, and may even be refused. Rounding the bill up rather than taking the change ("*Otsuri wa ii dess*" means "I don't need change") is sometimes welcomed, but many places will still insist that you take the change.

The Japanese usually divide the bill equally among diners, or one person pays for all. Asking for an itemized breakdown for groups of three or more is rarely done and is most unpopular.

VEGETARIAN FOOD

Japanese cuisine is rich in vegetables and non-animal high-protein foods such as tofu, *natto* (fermented soybeans), and other soy products. Unfortunately, it is not quite a vegetarian's paradise, because almost every dish relies to some degree for its flavoring on the *bonito*-based fish stock called *dashi*. The exception to this rule is *shojin ryori (see p316)*, which uses kelp- and mushroom-based stocks.

Lunchbox counter in shopping mall

FAST FOOD AND CONVENIENCE STORES

Western chains such as McDonald's are everywhere. Japan has its own fast-food chains, too, including one called Mosburger, which has come up with some innovative twists on the hamburger theme.

Convenience stores offer a good selection of *bento* boxes *(see p325)* and snack foods such as *onigiri (see p320)*.

FOOD HALLS AND MARKET STALLS

Cavernous food halls are found in the basements of many department stores. The colorful delicatessen-type stalls might include uncut sushi rolls, *bento* boxes, and imported foodstuffs. About an hour before closing time, stores lower the prices of many food items by ¥100–300. You may also be offered free samples, with no obligation to buy.

Food markets have artful displays and stalls offering snacks and presentation boxes of sweets, tea, rice crackers, and fruit.

BAKERIES

Bakeries abound but much of what is sold tends to be of the sweet-bun variety; bread for the Japanese is still more snack than staple. Do not be surprised if that innocent-looking French croissant turns out to be filled with red-bean paste.

In large cities almost every kind of bread, including most recently bagels, can be found. In rural areas the plain white loaf bread called *shokupan* (meal bread) is still predominant.

VENDING MACHINES

You won't travel far in Japan without passing a public vending machine, one of the bonuses of Japan's almost vandal-free society. These dispense all kinds of snacks, soft drinks, chilled or hot coffee, green tea, and even cans of beer. The machines are easy to use, prices (written in Arabic numerals) are reasonable, and change is automatically dispensed with the item.

Types of Restaurants and Bars

Japan has a restaurant to suit every taste and budget, from hole-in-the-wall noodle stands to havens of haute cuisine called *ryotei*. If you have difficulty distinguishing between different types, stick to restaurants with a menu and prices posted outside near the door. Lanterns mark out restaurants by name or description, though in some places they may bear the name of a district or event.

Restaurant with white lantern and *noren* (half curtains) in Takayama

RYOTEI AND KAISEKI RESTAURANTS

Sanctums of manicured courtyard gardens and spare but elegant private rooms, *ryotei* are the ultimate in Japanese dining. These are where the politicians and business elite entertain their customers with *kaiseki (see p322)*, the haute end of Japanese cuisine, and also maybe *geisha (see p163)* hired for the evening. Used to catering to an established clientele, many *ryotei* will not accept new customers without introductions.

More accessible to tourists are what are termed *kaiseki* restaurants, which serve the same food as *ryotei*, but in a less exclusive setting.

KYO-RYORIYA

Akyo-ryoriya (Kyoto-style restaurant) is usually another name for a *kaiseki* restaurant, Kyoto being the place where *kaiseki* achieved its apotheosis. Outside Kyoto, the name will emphasize that flavors conform to Kyoto standards, being delicate and light, and that typical Kyoto ingredients (*fu*, wheat gluten, and *yuba*, soy-milk skin, for example) will be featured.

SHOJIN RYORIYA

Shojin ryori also developed in Kyoto, in the kitchens of the city's Zen monasteries. The vegetarian cuisine is served on lacquered utensils in private rooms. Most *shojin ryoriya* are located near large monastery complexes.

KAPPO, IPPIN-RYORIYA, KORYORIYA, AND IZAKAYA

Akin to French bistros or Spanish tapas restaurants, these are places where one goes to drink and eat, rather than eat and drink. Most dishes are à la carte. *Kappo* tend to be pricey; the quality and seasonality of food is closer to that of *kaiseki* restaurants. *Ippin-ryoriya* and *izakaya* (the two are almost synonymous) feature fancier versions of Japanese home-cooking. Many will have large platters of pre-cooked items on their counter tops. *Koryoriya* means a "small dish" restaurant. Without reading Japanese, visitors may find such places hard to distinguish from one another.

NOMIYA AND AKA-CHOCHIN

Tavern-like *nomiya* (literally "drink shop") and *aka-chochin* are proletariat versions of the restaurants described above. The *aka-chochin*, or "red-lantern restaurant," is named after the gaudy lantern often hanging over the door (but note that not all red lanterns denote a "red-lantern restaurant"). They rarely have menus, the shop's offerings being written on strips of paper pasted on the wall or handwritten on a blackboard. They tend to be frequented almost entirely by locals.

SUSHI RESTAURANTS

Restaurants specializing in sushi *(see pp326–7)* vary in style from low-priced *kaiten-zushi* shops, where the sushi comes to you on a conveyor belt, to astronomically expensive places where

Restaurants in Kyoto decorated with lanterns naming a local festival

everything, from the fish to the ginger, is of optimum freshness and quality. As a general rule, if there are no prices listed anywhere, you are in for an expensive dinner.

If you sit at the counter, it is customary to order *nigiri-zushi* (hand-pressed sushi) a serving at a time. A serving consists of two "fingers," which are placed on the counter in front of you. If you sit at a table or on a *zashiki* (see p318) then it is customary to order a combo of *nigiri-zushi*. It will be brought all at once on a platter or slab of polished wood.

NOODLE BARS

Noodles in Japan come in two main forms: the domestic variety and the Chinese version known as *ramen (see p320)*. The former is found at *sobaya*, which in spite of the name, sell not only *soba* (brown buckwheat) noodles, a staple of Edo cuisine (*see p322-3*) but also white wheat *udon* noodles. *Ramen* are served in cheap Chinese restaurants called *chuka-ryoriya*, in specialty shops called *ramenya*, and at night street stalls called *yatai*.

SPECIALTY RESTAURANTS

Many restaurants in Japan specialize in one dish, such as tempura or *tonkatsu* (*see p321*) Restaurants featuring *kani-nabe* (crab hot pot) are popular during the cold months. *Odenya* serve *oden*, a simmered dish. *Unagiya* specialize in eel, grilled to

perfection over charcoal. *Yakitoriya* accomplish the same thing with chicken. *Fugu* restaurants serve up that delight of the adventurous gourmet, the poisonous globefish, raw and cooked.

FOREIGN ASIAN RESTAURANTS

Yakinikuya are Korean-style barbecue restaurants with plenty of red meat, as well as the more esoteric parts of the cow, plus the standard spicy *kimchi* pickles. *Chuka-ryoriya* are cheap Chinese restaurants. So-called *esunikku* (ethnic) restaurants, found only in urban centers, serve a mixed bag of Southeast Asian-inspired dishes.

French-style restaurant and bar in the Akasaka district, Tokyo

WESTERN RESTAURANTS

Yoshoku (Western meal) restaurants are modest places that serve such things as *ebi-furai* (fried shrimp) and *korokke* (croquettes). These items became immensely popular among Japanese during the Meiji and Taisho periods. The Japanese still think of these dishes as Western although outside of Japan they would hardly be recognized as such. Rice is served on a plate, not in a bowl, and eaten with a fork. *Famiri resutoran* (family restaurants) are American-style chains (Royal Host is a typical example), whose extensive picture menus, late hours, and parking lots have won them a devoted following in Japan.

Specialty *dengaku* restaurant (see p337)

In the major cities, French and Italian restaurants are abundant. Servings, especially of wine, however, tend to be skimpy, and bread comes by the piece, not the basket.

KISSATEN, COFFEE SHOPS, AND BARS

For decades the Japanese have taken their breaks at tea rooms called *kissaten*, where, over an unrefillable cup of painstakingly brewed *kohi* (coffee), served either *hotto* (hot) or *aisu* (iced), they can spend hours leafing through magazines and chain smoking. *Kissaten* also offer such standbys as *kare raisu* (see p320), *pirafu* (rice pilaf), and *sando* (sandwiches, of the pale English variety).

The neighborhood *kissaten* still exists but is increasingly being challenged by international coffee shop chains such as Douter and Starbucks, which offer the novel items espresso and cappuccino.

Any fair-sized Japanese town will have a bar quarter, a warren of hole-in-the-wall places each presided over by a *"mastaa"* (master) or *"mama."* In large cities, entire buildings will be filled with such places, each its own little universe. Customers come as much for the atmosphere as the drinks. Karaoke is the main form of entertainment in "hostess bars." Note that some are little more than rip-off joints.

THE TANUKI

In Japanese folklore badgers are celebrated as lovable buffoons or drunken rascals. This is one of the reasons why the ceramic likeness of the *tanuki* is often found at the entrance of *nomiya* and other drinking places.

Food Customs and Etiquette

Eating food in Japan is markedly different from eating in Western countries. Seating arrangements, tableware, and much of the etiquette surrounding the social eating of food differ even from those in nearby countries such as Korea and China. The main point of etiquette is to remove your shoes for traditional seating. The Japanese assume that you will not be able to use chopsticks properly and will be impressed if you show any finesse at all.

Sitting *seiza*-style on

SEATING ARRANGEMENTS

Many Japanese restaurants have a few Western-style tables and chairs, and/or a counter, as well as traditional *zashiki* seating.

The *zashiki* is a low wooden platform covered with *tatami* mats and low tables. Diners sit here on cushions (*zabuton*), feet tucked behind. Remove your shoes before you step up onto the *zashiki*.

Women wearing skirts sit *seiza* (on their knees with their buttocks on their heels) or mermaid-style. Men usually sit cross-legged, although if there is a formal toast they will adopt the more uncomfortable *seiza* pose until it is over.

Some *zashiki* actually have sunken areas for the diners' legs, a definite plus for long-legged customers and foreigners who find sitting on the floor uncomfortable. Alternatively, chairs may be used that have backs but not legs.

In restaurants with a choice of seating, the counter is by no means regarded as a second-rate option. In sushi places, particularly, it is the preferred seat of the gastronome who wants to watch the food being skillfully prepared by chefs with years of training.

HOW TO ORDER

If a set menu (*see p314*) is not available, then follow these guidelines for ordering à la carte.

Specify drinks (*see pp328–9*) first, usually from a choice of sake, beer, *sho-chu* liquor, perhaps wine, and whiskey.

If you are in an area frequented by foreigners, the menu may have some English translations. Menus are often divided into the main categories of Japanese cuisine: grilled, simmered, and so on (*see p321*). Sashimi is ordered first. If you can't decide on one fish, ask for a *moriawase*, or combination.

The custom is to have about three or four dishes to start and more later as you deem fit. Calling *"sumimasen!"* (excuse me!) is the standard method of attracting attention.

Alternatively, tell the chef behind the counter how much you want to spend (between ¥3,000 and ¥5,000 per person is reasonable), and let him make the decisions for you.

POLITE PHRASES AND TOASTS

Japanese people say *"Itadaki-mass"* ("I humbly receive") before eating, and *"gochiso-sama desh'ta"* ("I have been treated") at the end.

Japanese drinking etiquette requires that you pour for the other person and vice versa. When on the receiving end, you should pick up your glass, supporting the bottom with the fingers of the other hand. When a toast (*kanpai*) is made, beer and whisky glasses should be clinked, while sake cups are generally raised in a salute.

WHAT TO DO WITH THE OSHIBORI

Most restaurants offer customers an *oshibori* at the beginning of a meal. This small damp cotton or paper towel is used first to wipe your hands (in strict etiquette, not the face and neck). You then leave it on the table top and use it discreetly to dab fingers and spills, rather than placing it on your lap. It is fine to use your own hand-kerchief as a napkin on your lap. However, remember never to blow your nose into the *oshibori* or any handker-chief in public.

USING CHOPSTICKS

Chopsticks (*hashi*) are shorter and more delicate than Chinese chopsticks, with a pointed lower end. The use of disposable wooden

Sitting on stools at the counter of a *yatai* noodle stall in Fukuoka

chopsticks in restaurants is widespread. Knives and forks are rarely seen except in staunchly Western restaurants and for certain dishes still regarded as foreign such as *kare raisu (see p320).*

Spearing food with your chopsticks is considered bad form, as is pushing food straight from the bowl into the mouth (entirely acceptable in China). Passing food from your chopsticks to those of another and sticking them upright in a bowl of rice are both associated with funerary customs and are therefore strictly taboo at the dinner table. Gesturing and pointing with your chopsticks are also definite no-nos, as is using them as levers to pull or push things around the table.

If some morsel proves difficult to cut on the plate, you can take a chopstick in each hand and make a sawing motion to cut it. This may not be the most elegant of moves but is unavoidable in some situations.

When they are not in use, lay the chopsticks on your chopstick rest *(hashi-oki),* or if a rest is not provided then across the lowest dish. Lay them neatly and uncrossed, and parallel with your side of the table.

USING TABLEWARE

Japanese tableware is wonderfully eclectic and can run to over a dozen vessels per person, of wildly differing shapes and materials such as porcelain, lacquer, wood, and even leaves. When several dishes are served at once, feel free to take morsels from them in whatever order you please, including from lidded pots containing soups.

Many small bowls and plates are designed to be picked up and brought to about chest level, easing the path of each morsel to the mouth. Do this rather than bending your head down to get to the food. It is perfectly good manners to sip directly from small bowls of soup.

HOW TO HOLD CHOPSTICKS (HASHI)

A common mistake by foreigners is to hold chopsticks too close to the ends instead of a third of the way down, thus losing leverage. They also often hold them too tightly, leading to hand cramps and dropped food.

Thumb and first finger doing most of the leverage with the top stick

Third finger acting as a rest for the lower stick

The lower stick should rest in the crook of the thumb and on the third finger, while the thumb, first, and second fingers control the movement of the top stick. Note that the *hashi* and technique are slightly different from those used in China.

However, do not eat directly from any communal serving platters and bowls. Instead, put one or two bite-sized portions first onto the *kozara,* which is a small saucer-like plate provided for each diner. Use the separate chopsticks and spoons, if provided, for communal dishes. Note that it is fine to bite off part of a piece of food and return the uneaten part to your *kozara* until ready for the next bite.

Ceramic teapot

EATING RICE

Japanese rice has a slightly glutinous, heavy texture. Japanese people treat it with respect, and do not feel they have truly eaten until they have consumed rice in some form.

In a meal with several dishes, rice is always served in a separate bowl. If alcohol is drunk, then the bowl of rice is saved till the end of the meal, when it is eaten with miso and pickles *(see p324).* Since sake is a rice derivative, the two are often considered too similar to consume together.

No matter how tempted, do not take rice from the bowl and put it on your plate to soak up any juices or sauces or pour juices (even soy sauce) onto it. As

Kamameshi, a one-pot rice dish

acceptable as this is elsewhere, it will be an unappetizing sight in Japan. The exception to this rule is one-pot rice dishes, in which vegetables and meat are placed on the rice in a deep bowl, almost hiding the rice.

SEASONAL EATING PATTERNS

The seasons have a major influence on Japanese eating habits. The temperature of food is seen as an important way of regulating body temperature. Hence, tea and sake are drunk hot in winter and cold in summer. Similarly, *nabemono* (hot pot) dishes are consumed during cold months, while cold noodles are welcomed in warm ones. Tempura is normally a cold weather dish, and the desire of tourists to eat it on a hot summer day is baffling to some Japanese. Some restaurants famous for seasonal fish such as *fugu (see p327)* may serve an entirely different menu at other times.

SLURPING

The Japanese slurp with gusto when eating noodles or soupy rice dishes. Indeed, an audible intake of air is necessary to eat piping hot noodles without scorching the mouth. Many foreigners are loathe to make this noise, with the result that it takes them three times as long to eat *soba.*

Reading the Menu

General vocabulary likely to be useful when eating out is given in the *Phrase Book* on pages 415–16. Individual ingredients are also listed there. A selection of some of the most popular dishes and styles of cooking are listed in this glossary, including Japanese script to help you read menus in Japanese. Further details about some of the dishes follow on pages 322–27.

DONBURI: RICE-BOWL DISHES

Katsudon
カツどん
Rice bowl topped with a breaded, deep-fried pork cutlet and semi-cooked egg.

Nikudon
肉どん
Rice bowl with beef, tofu, and gelatinous noodles.

Oyakodon
親子どん
Rice bowl with chicken, onions, and runny, semi-cooked egg.

Tamagodon
卵どん
Rice bowl topped with a semi-cooked egg.

Tendon
天どん
Rice bowl that has one or two shrimp tempura and sauce.

Unadon
鰻どん
Rice bowl with grilled eel.

OTHER RICE DISHES

Kamameshi
釜飯／かまめし
Rice and tidbits steamed in a clay or metal pot with a wooden lid. Served in the container it was steamed in.

Kare raisu
カレーライス
"Curry rice". Can be *ebi-kare* (shrimp curry), *katsu-kare* (with deep-fried pork cutlet), etc.

Makunouchi bento
幕の内弁当
Classic *bento (see p325)*.

Ocha-zuke
お茶漬け
Rice in a bowl with a piece of grilled salmon, pickled plum, etc., over which tea is poured.

Omu-raisu
オムライス
Thin omelet wrapped around rice mixed with tomato sauce and chicken or pork bits.

Onigiri
おにぎり
Two or three triangular chunks of rice wrapped with strips of dried seaweed *(nori)*.

Unaju
鰻重
Grilled eel served over rice in a lacquered, lidded box.

Yaki-onigiri
焼おにぎり
Variation of *onigiri*, without seaweed, grilled over a flame.

Onigiri and yaki-onigiri

Zosui
雑炊
Rice soup made with the leftover stock of a one-pot *(nabemono)* meal.

NOODLE DISHES

Kitsune soba/udon
きつねそば／うどん
Soba or *udon* noodles in flavored *dashi* broth with pieces of fried tofu.

Nabe yaki udon
鍋焼うどん
Udon noodles simmered in a lidded ceramic pot *(donabe)* with a flavored *dashi* broth, perhaps with shrimp tempura, shiitake mushroom, and egg. Popular in winter.

Ramen
ラーメン
Chinese noodles in pork broth. Usually there are some thin slices of roast pork on top, along with sliced leeks, spinach, and a slice of fish-paste roll.

Reimen (Hiyashi chuka)
冷麺（冷やし中華）
Chinese noodles topped with strips of ham or roast pork, cucumbers, and cabbage. Dressed with a vinegar and sesame oil sauce. Popular summer dish.

Somen
そうめん
Very thin white noodles, usually served in ice water. A summer dish.

Tamago-toji soba/udon
卵とじそば／うどん
Soba or *udon* in a flavored *dashi* broth into which an egg has been dropped and stirred to cook gently.

Tempura soba/udon
天ぷらそば／うどん
Soba or *udon* in a flavored *dashi* broth with one or two pieces of shrimp tempura.

Yakisoba
焼そば
Soft Chinese noodles sautéed on a griddle with vegetables and some form of meat or fish.

Zarusoba
ざるそば
Soba noodles served cold on a bamboo rack. Variation: *ten-zarusoba* has shrimp and vegetable tempura next to noodles.

RICE CRACKERS AND NIBBLES

Crackers *(senbei* or *osenbe)* are sold in supermarkets all over Japan. Beautifully made and presented, they are also sold at station gift counters and stalls at the popular tourist attractions.

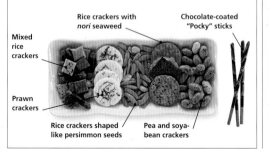

Rice crackers with *nori* seaweed

Chocolate-coated "Pocky" sticks

Mixed rice crackers

Prawn crackers

Rice crackers shaped like persimmon seeds

Pea and soya-bean crackers

DISHES PREPARED AT THE TABLE

Mizutaki/Chirinabe
水焚き／ちり鍋
Nabemono (one-pot meal) of vegetables, tofu, and chicken (*mizutaki*) or fish (*chirinabe*).

Okonomiyaki
お好み焼
Thick pancake-shaped mix of cabbage, egg, shrimp, squid, or pork cooked on a griddle.

Shabu-shabu
しゃぶしゃぶ
Nabemono (hot pot) with thinly sliced beef and vegetables cooked in a brass pan.

Table condiments: seven-spice *shichimi* powder, jar of soy sauce, and *ichimi* ground chili pepper

Sukiyaki
すき焼き
High-quality pan-cooked beef and vegetables.

Teppanyaki
鉄板焼
Meat and/or shrimp or squid and vegetables grilled on a griddle in front of the diner.

Udon-suki
うどんすき
Udon noodles, chicken, and sometimes clams or shrimp simmered in a soup.

SUSHI

Chirashi-zushi
ちらし寿司／鮨
"Scattered" sushi (see p326).

Nigiri-zushi
握り寿司／鮨
"Fingers" of sushi (see p326).

Maki-zushi
巻寿司／鮨
"Rolled" sushi (see p327).

SET MEAL

Teishoku
定食
A set meal (see p314), with rice, soup, some vegetables, salad, a main meat dish, pickles.

MENU CATEGORIES

Aemono
和え物
Dressed salad dishes.

Agemono
揚げ物
Deep-fried foods.

Nimono
煮物
Simmered foods.

Sashimi (Otsukuri)
刺身（お造り）
Raw fish (see p327).

Sunomono
酢の物
Vinegared dishes.

Yakimono
焼き物
Grilled foods.

À LA CARTE

Agedashi-dofu
揚げだし豆腐
Deep-fried tofu (bean curd) in a stock.

Chikuzen-ni
筑前煮
Vegetables and bits of chicken simmered together.

Eda mame
枝豆
Soybean steamed in the pod. Popular summer snack.

Hiya-yakko/Yudofu
冷やっこ／湯豆腐
Cold/simmered tofu.

Kinpira
きんぴら
Sautéed burdock and carrot strips seasoned with sauces.

Natto
納豆
Fermented soybeans.

Niku-jaga
肉じゃが
Beef or pork simmered with potatoes and other ingredients.

Oden
おでん
Hot pot with fried fish cakes and various vegetables.

Ohitashi
おひたし
Boiled spinach or other green leafy vegetable with sauce.

Shio-yaki
塩焼
Fish sprinkled with salt and grilled over a flame or charcoal.

Tamago-yaki
卵焼
Rolled omelet.

Tonkatsu
豚カツ／トンカツ
Breaded, fried pork cutlet with shredded cabbage.

Grilled eel (*unagi*) basted in a sweet sauce, a *yakimono* dish

Tori no kara-age
鶏の空揚げ
Fried chicken pieces.

Tsukemono no moriawase
漬物の盛り合わせ
Combination of pickles.

Yakitori
焼鶏／やきとり
Chicken grilled on skewers.

Yakiniku
焼肉
Korean-style beef barbecue.

CHINESE-STYLE DISHES

Gyoza
餃子／ギョウザ
Fried dumplings.

Harumaki
春巻
Spring roll.

Shumai
焼売／シュウマイ
Small, pork dumplings crimped at the top and steamed.

Yakimeishi
焼めし／チャーハン
Fried rice.

IZAKAYA SNACKS

Cucumber and sea-weed

Dried squid

Onion and bonito

At *izakaya* and *ippin-ryoriya* establishments (see p316), which are tavern-like places serving food rather than restaurants, dishes such as dried strips of squid and pickles complement the beer, *shochu* and other drinks (see pp328–9).

The Flavors of Japan

More so than in most developed countries, where the produce of the entire world is available in supermarkets all year round, Japan is a country in which local and seasonal produce is still highly valued. The Japanese often use a region's speciality as a reason for travel, going out of their way to find a restaurant famed for local cuisine. The food cultures of Tokyo and the Kansai region were in competition for hundreds of years. The eventual dominance of Tokyo's Edo cuisine mirrors the historical trend whereby Kyoto and the Kansai region gradually lost their cultural supremacy.

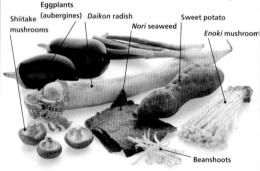

Ramen noodles

Chef at work, using chopsticks to arrange exquisite dishes

EDO CUISINE

In the early 16th century Tokyo, then known as Edo, became the capital of Japan when the powerful Tokugawa family moved there. With them arrived thousands of rich landowning samurai and wealthy merchants. This led to the development of Edo cuisine, a fusion of dishes from diverse parts of the

country, that is today the most commonly recognized form of Japanese food.

The story of the ascendancy of Edo cuisine is also that of the decline in dominance of typical Kansai flavors. Soba has been a popular food among Edo residents since the late seventeeth century and is renowned as one of the true tastes of Edo cuisine. As more people from the north of Japan moved to

Edo, udon noodles, which were popular in the south, were replaced by soba noodles. Soba is most commonly eaten in the same simple way that it was eaten all that time ago: in a *zaru* (a small bamboo sieve). The weaker soy sauce of the Kansai region also became less favored when people in Edo adopted a stronger tasting sauce. Even grilled eel, which is thought

Eggplants
Shiitake (aubergines) *Daikon* radish
mushrooms *Nori* seaweed
Sweet potato
Enoki mushroom

Beanshoots

Selection of vegetables that feature in Japanese cuisine

TRADITIONAL JAPANESE SPECIALITIES

A typical banquet, such as might be served at a *ryotei (see p316)*, may have up to 20 courses. Much is made of seasonal ingredients, with decorative flourishes also chosen to reflect the time of year. *Kaiseki* is a traditional style of cuisine in which a dozen or more dishes are served to each person, categorized on the menu according to cooking method, not ingredients. Sake *(see p329)* is the usual accompaniment.

Bonito tuna flakes

Vegetarian cusine, called *shojin ryori*, uses protein-rich tofu rather than meat or fish. It was developed by Zen Buddhists and is now found in many restaurants located in or near the precincts of Zen temples. The Japanese have also elevated tea snacks to an art form – delicate and pretty *wagashi* are usually made from sweet bean paste.

Unadon, *featuring grilled eel over a bed of rice, is popular as it is thought to have great health benefits.*

Tuna being laid out for sale at Tokyo's Tsukiji Fish Market *(see p68)*

internationally sought-after beef. Certain dishes from Osaka have also made their mark on the rest of Japan. One of the most popular snacks in the Kansai region is *takoyaki*, which is deep-fried in octopus in batter. *Takoyaki* stalls have sprung up in most Japanese cities. Another famous dish from Osaka is *okonomiyake*, which is often likened to a pancake or pizza. The name means "as you like it" and, as the phrase suggests, it is made with any ingredients the customer wants.

to be a typical part of Edo cuisine, was originally a dish from Kyoto, but it is the Edo method of cooking the eel and preparing the sauce that we know today. Other foods which feature strongly in Edo cuisine are sushi, tempura, and oden, a hotpot of fishcake, boiled eggs, and other ingredients.

KANSAI CUISINE

Although in many respects the Kansai region has lost its position as the most important area in Japan's culinary landscape, it should not be seen as a spent force: food from the Kansai region is still one of the strongest regional cuisines in Japan. Top quality local produce can be found in the area. In this inland region, seafood has not been as central to

the cooking of Kyoto as in the rest of Japan. Instead, Kyoto's superb chefs have developed a vast range of dishes using their top-quality tofu, which is famous all over Japan. In nearby Kobe, many dishes celebrate the area's

Omoide Yokacho, a lane of restaurants in Shinjuku, Tokyo

KOBE BEEF

One significant contribution that the Japanese have given to meat connoisseurs across the world is Kobe beef. The black *wagyu* cows of Hyogo prefecture, of which Kobe is the capital, are bred and reared using strictly guarded and time-honoured traditions to make some of the highest quality beef in the world. Although similar cows are raised in America and Australia, the meat is not considered to be genuine if it's not from Hyogo, which makes authentic Kobe beef an expensive delicacy. Kobe beef is an extremely tender meat, and it is identifiable by the striations of fat that run through it. It is used in a range Japanese dishes – it can be eaten raw as *sashimi*, cooked as *teppanyaki* or, as is popular nowadays, served simply as a big hearty steak or even a luxurious burger.

Tempura, *originally a Portuguese dish, is lightly battered deep-fried vegetables or fish.*

Okonomiyake *is a thick, pancake-shaped mix of egg and other ingredients, cooked on a griddle.*

Yakiudon *are thick noodles fried with seafood, seaweed, shiitake mushrooms, tuna flakes, and beansprouts.*

The Japanese Meal

Along with the indispensable rice and miso soup (made from fermented soy bean paste), a Japanese meal always consists of a variety of smaller dishes which are designed to complement each other. Plain ingredients are often given strong flavors, such as a bowl of rice topped off with an *omeboshi* (sour plum) or pickled ginger, or tofu that has been marinated in a strong, vinegary sauce. Two liquid ingredients central to most Japanese dishes are *dashi*, a light stock made from giant kelp *(konbu)* and dried bonito shavings, and Japanese soy sauce *(shoyu)*.

Firm tofu

Japanese family enjoying breakfast together

THE JAPANESE BREAKFAST

One of the many attractions of staying in the home of a Japanese family, or in a traditional Japanese hotel, is sampling the Japanese breakfast. Like most other Japanese meals, it consists of different dishes served separately. At its heart is a bowl of rice and some miso soup. It is polite for the rice to be placed to the left and the soup to the right of the sitter. Not only is it common for there to be variations in miso soup from region to region, individual families tend to have their own idiosyncratic method of producing this most Japanese of soups. The basic rice and soup are accompanied by a range of side dishes, of which the most common is a portion of grilled fish, usually salted salmon or mackerel. Other dishes may include dried seaweed, omelette, and a small portion of pickles.

Natto is a dish made out of fermented soy beans and it is a much-loved breakfast dish among health-conscious Japanese. Usually eaten with rice, it is famous not only for being extremely healthy, but also for the noxious smell that it gives off.

Pickled eggplant (aubergine) · Miso soup · Shiso ume pickled plums · Rice · Nori seaweed · Pickled radish · Tofu · Grilled salmon

Some of the ingredients for a typical Japanese breakfast

PREPARATION AND PORTIONS

A fastidiousness about detail characterizes both the preparation and presentation of Japanese food. Good presentation is vital to a Japanese restaurant's success, but it is not only the highly expensive, multi-course *kaiseki* meals that display this quality; even the cheapest food has a touch of the meticulous about it. This attention to culinary aesthetics naturally favors portions that are small and served individually to maximize the impact that they have on both taste and sight. Vegetables are cooked to remain crisp and retain their colors and, even when fried, food is is not allowed to become greasy – the oil is heated high enough to seal the food instantly. The serving of small portions also has health benefits, and it should come as no surprise that obesity is much less of a problem here than in Western developed countries. Nowhere else in the world is healthy eating so attractive, varied or delicious.

Small portions of a number of complementary dishes

The Bento Box

A *bento* is a take-home meal in a compartmentalized box: office workers buy them for lunch, schoolchildren eat from them at their desk, and business travelers have them with a beer on the bullet train. In its neat, individual compartments there will invariably be a large portion of rice, a main serving of meat or fish, pieces of omelette, some vegetables, and a selection of pickles. But part of the charm of the *bento* is that anything goes. It is not uncommon to open a bento and find a small octopus or a tiny whole fish gazing up at you, or even something that completely defies identification.

Slivers of pickled ginger

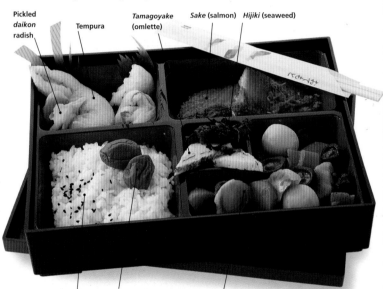

Pickled *daikon* radish   Tempura   *Tamagoyake* (omlette)   *Sake* (salmon)   *Hijiki* (seaweed)

Rice with black sesame   *Shiso ume* (pickled plums)   *Onishime* (pickled vegetables)

Typical selection of food to be found in a bento box

IN THE BENTO BOX

Agedofu Fried tofu.

Chikuwa Tubular steamed fishcakes.

Furikake Variety of condiments to add extra flavor, including nori (seaweed) flakes and toasted sesame seeds.

Jako Miniature whole dried fish.

Kabocha Squash, often served simmered.

Konnyaku Gelatinous paste made from Devil's Tongue (similar to sweet potato).

Korokke Croquettes filed with potato and meat.

Kurage Jellyfish.

Magura sashimi Tuna sashimi.

Negi Salad onion, used for flavoring and garnish.

Onigiri Triangles of rice with various fillings.

Saba sashimi Mackerel sashimi.

Takenoko Bamboo shoots.

Tonkatsu Deep-fried breaded pork.

Tsukemono Pickled vegetables.

Umeboshi Pickled apricot.

Unagi Grilled eel in black bean sauce.

Yakiniku Miniature meatballs.

Japanese student eating lunch from a *bento* box

Sushi and Sashimi

Newcomers to Japan are often both fascinated and intimidated by these native dishes. The term "sushi" applies to a variety of dishes (usually written with the suffix "-*zushi*") in which cold, lightly sweetened and vinegared sushi rice is topped or wrapped up with raw fish or other items such as pickles, cooked fish, and meat. Sliced fillets of raw fish served without rice are called sashimi.

Shiso leaf garnish for sashimi

Even those visitors used to Japanese restaurants abroad may be surprised at how ubiquitous such foods are in Japan. There is no need to worry unduly about hygiene: Japan's highly trained chefs always use fresh fish, and the vinegar in sushi rice is a preservative.

Sushi bar counter and sushi chefs with years of training

Nigiri-Zushi
Here, thin slices of raw fish are laid over molded fingers of sushi rice with a thin layer of wasabi *(green horseradish) in between. Using chopsticks or fingers, pick up a piece, dip the fish lightly in soy sauce, and consume in one mouthful.*

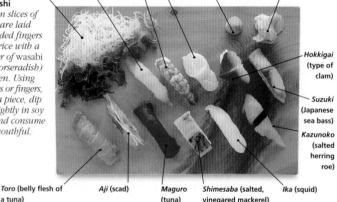

Shredded *daikon* — *Hirame* (turbot) — *Ebi* (shrimp) — *Hotategai* (scallop) — *Wasabi* (Japanese horseradish) — *Gari* (ginger), eaten separately

Hokkigai (type of clam)

Suzuki (Japanese sea bass)

Kazunoko (salted herring roe)

Toro (belly flesh of a tuna) — *Aji* (scad) — *Maguro* (tuna) — *Shimesaba* (salted, vinegared mackerel) — *Ika* (squid)

Tamagoyaki (sweetened egg omelet), a popular non-fish item often accompanying sushi and sashimi

Kazunoko (prepared herring roe)

Aji (scad)

Uni (the ovaries of a sea urchin), a highly prized delicacy in Japan

Ikura (salmon roe)

Slice of *kamaboko*, a type of steamed fish-paste roll with pink-dyed rim

Denbu, flakes of shrimp and whitefish that have been boiled, then dried and seasoned

Ebi (shrimp)

Thin slice of *ika* (squid)

Gari (ginger)

Chirashi-Zushi
The "scattered" style of sushi involves a colorful combination of toppings arranged artfully with a deep bed of cold sushi rice. There are two main regional variations. In Tokyo, slices of raw fish, fish roe, chunks of omelet, and other raw or cooked vegetables are placed on top of the rice (as shown). In Osaka, the fish and vegetable toppings are cooked, then mixed with the rice and overlaid with strips of omelet.

Maki-Zushi

"Rolled" sushi is becoming increasingly familiar outside Japan – the California roll, for instance, is a version using avocado and other non-Japanese ingredients. For maki-zushi the sushi rice is combined with slivers of fish, pickles, or other morsels, and rolled up in a sheet of toasted seaweed (nori).

Temaki-zushi
is rolled by hand into a large cone shape.

Kappa (cucumber)

Takuan (pickled daikon)

Tamago (egg)

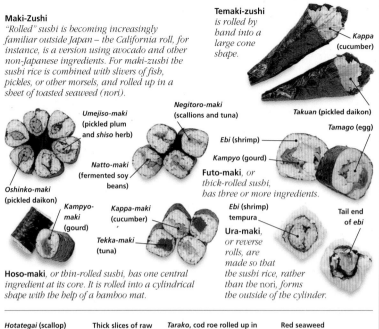

Umejiso-maki (pickled plum and *shiso* herb)

Negitoro-maki (scallions and tuna)

Ebi (shrimp)

Kampyo (gourd)

Futo-maki, *or thick-rolled sushi, has three or more ingredients.*

Natto-maki (fermented soy beans)

Oshinko-maki (pickled daikon)

Kampyo-maki (gourd)

Kappa-maki (cucumber)

Tekka-maki (tuna)

Ebi (shrimp) tempura

Ura-maki, *or reverse rolls, are made so that the sushi rice, rather than the* nori, *forms the outside of the cylinder.*

Tail end of *ebi*

Hoso-maki, *or thin-rolled sushi, has one central ingredient at its core. It is rolled into a cylindrical shape with the help of a bamboo mat.*

Hotategai (scallop) arranged in the shell

Thick slices of raw *maguro* (tuna)

Tarako, cod roe rolled up in squid and strips of seaweed

Red seaweed garnish

Sashimi
Sliced fillets of the freshest uncooked fish may be served as a single course. Sashimi is delicate and creamy, and the only accompaniments should be soy sauce, wasabi, daikon, and maybe a shiso leaf.

Hotate (scallop) arranged with thin strips of nori (seaweed)

Hokkigai, out of its shell

Tako (octopus)

Aji (scad), topped with finely sliced scallions

Wasabi (green horseradish) molded into the shape of a shiso leaf

---

Fish display at Kochi street market

POPULAR FISH IN JAPAN

Of the 3,000 or so varieties of fish eaten in Japan, the most common, available year-round, are *maguro* (tuna), *tai* (sea bream), *haze* (gobies), *buri* (yellowtail), *saba* (mackerel), crustaceans such as *ebi* (shrimp) and *kani* (crab), and fish that are usually salted such as *sake* (salmon) and *tara* (cod). Spring is the start of the season for the river fish *ayu* (sweetfish), traditionally caught by trained cormorants *(see p44). Bonito* is available in spring and summer, *unagi* (eel) in midsummer, *sanma* (saury) in the fall. Winter is the time for *dojo* (loach), *ankou* (monkfish), and the famous *fugu* (globefish), prized for its delicate flavor but also feared for deadly toxins in its liver and ovaries.

What to Drink in Japan

Green tea and sake are the traditional drinks of Japan. Both have ancient histories, and the appreciation of each has been elevated to connoisseur-ship. The tea ceremony *(see p169)* is the ultimate expression of tea appreciation, a social ritual imbued with Buddhist ideals. Sake (rice wine) has

Tea ceremony

long associations with Shinto – the fox god Inari presides over sake *(see p26)* – and some Shinto festivals still involve the drink as a central theme. Other Japan-ese drinks include *shochu* spirit and "health" drinks.

Picking green tea in May, when leaves are at their most tender

TYPES OF TEA

Green tea leaves are divided into three main grades – *gyokuro*, which are the most tender, protected leaves that come out in May; *sencha*, which are tender leaves picked in May or June; and *bancha*, which are large leaves left until August. Leaves are sterilized with steam and then dried. *Bancha* is often roasted or mixed with other ingredients such as brown rice to form robust teas. Other teas are available; of foreign ones the Japanese especially enjoy imported fine English teas.

Basic green tea *is sold loose or in tea bags.*

Mugicha *is a tea brewed from roasted barley.*

Hojicha *is roasted* bancha, *a coarse tea.*

Genmaicha *is brown rice (gen-mai and* bancha.

Sencha *is a pop-ular medium-to-high grade of tea.*

Gyokuro *is a delicate, high grade of tea.*

Powdered *mat-cha is used at the tea ceremony.*

SOFT DRINKS

With names that conjure up disturb-ing images for English-speaking foreigners, Calpis and Pocari Sweat are among the most popular Japanese brands of canned soft drinks. Some are marketed as quick energy and vitamin boosters. Vending machines *(see p315)* stock them alongside canned green tea and coffee, and a wide range of fruit juices in cartons.

Chawan, a wide-brimmed cup without handles

Kyusu (teapot)

Wagashi (see p326)

Tea leaves, *usually loose, are placed in a teapot.* Bancha *is brewed with boiling water, but* sencha *and* gyokuro *should be brewed with boiled water that has been allowed to cool slightly first. The brewing tea should then stand for about a minute.*

SAKE (RICE WINE)

Sake is made from rice and water, which are fermented together then pasteurized to create a superb alcoholic "wine." Many connoisseurs judge sake on the five qualities of sweetness, sourness, pungency, bitterness, and astringency. Sake can be drunk warm, but the finer types should be lightly chilled to retain the subtle flavors. Unlike grape wine, sake is rarely expected to improve in the bottle. Store it in a cool, dry place for no more than a few months.

Everyday *hon-jozo* type by Gekkeikan

Fine *ginjo* type by Nihonsakari

Finer *dai-ginjo* by Tsukasa Botan

Taruzake (cask sake) *is matured in wooden casks made of cypress. Casks are often presented to Shinto shrines as offerings. The brewer's logo is displayed prominently.*

The finest grade of sake, *dai-ginjo, is made from the hardest core of the rice – more than 50 percent of each grain is shaved away. For the* ginjo *type about 40 percent is shaved; for hon-jozo, the average sake, about 30 percent. Some are brewed with added alcohol; those without are called* junmai, *"pure rice."*

A classic serving set *consists of a ceramic bottle* (tokkuri) *and matching cups* (sakazuki). *The bottle can be placed in hot water to warm the sake to about 50°C (122°F).*

Sake breweries *traditionally hang a ball of cedar leaves* (sakabayashi) *and sometimes a sacred rope* (shimenawa) *over their entrance.*

OTHER ALCOHOLIC DRINKS

Japan has several beers that have become well known around the world. Suntory whisky is also sold abroad, popular with those who prefer a milder whisky. Less well known abroad, *shochu* is a name for a group of Japanese spirits made from barley or other grains, or potatoes.

The alcohol content of *shochu* varies from 40 to 90 proof. The distilled spirit is often mixed with hot water or used as a base for cocktails, but it is also drunk neat, either heated or on the rocks. It is also used to make bottled fruit liqueurs such as *umeshu*, which uses whole Japanese apricots.

Suntory whisky　　**Sapporo beer**　　**Asahi beer**　　**Barley *shochu***　　**Rice *shochu***

Choosing a Restaurant

The restaurants in this guide have been selected across a wide price range for their exceptional food and good value. Restaurants are listed by region, starting with Tokyo and its environs. As with hotels, check the location before trying to find a restaurant. See pp314–29 for more detailed information about types of cuisine and particular dishes.

PRICE CATEGORIES
Price categories for an average-size dinner for one. Lunchtime special menus are often cheaper.

Ⓨ Under ¥1,500
ⓎⓎ ¥1,500–¥3,000
ⓎⓎⓎ ¥3,000–¥6,000
ⓎⓎⓎⓎ ¥6,000–¥10,000
ⓎⓎⓎⓎⓎ Over ¥10,000

TOKYO

CENTRAL TOKYO Decks Tokyo Beach
🚻 ♿ 📷 Ⓥ　　　　　Ⓨ

1-6-1, Daiba, Minato-ku, 135-0091 **Tel** *(03) 3599-6500*　　　　**Map** 5 A4

You'll get cheap and cheerful food here, and lots of possibilities from this collection of small stands, cafés, and restaurants built around a shopping and entertainment center. Possibly best is the Little Hong Kong section, with its crispy noodles and duck dishes, but there is plenty of good Japanese food also.

CENTRAL TOKYO Hantei
🚻 Ⓥ　　　　　Ⓨ

Nezu 2-12-15, Bunkyo-ku, 112-0005 **Tel** *(03) 3828-1440*　　　　**Map** 3 B2

This is a good choice for traditional food. The restaurant is over three floors in a traditional wooden building – one of the few spared by the 1922 Tokyo Earthquake and the fire that followed, and now declared a National Treasure. The food is elegantly presented, with everything coming on wooden skewers.

CENTRAL TOKYO Sushi-dai
📋 🚻　　　　　Ⓨ

Tsukiji Fish Market, 4-5-1-Tsukiji, Chuo-ku, 105-7337 **Tel** *(03) 3452-1111*　　　　**Map** 5 C4

The infamous Tokyo fish market still holds its daily auctions, but they are no longer open to the public. However, there's still plenty to see – and lots of great sushi bars around the outside of the market. This one is very fresh, and good value for those on a budget.

CENTRAL TOKYO Ginza Lobby
ⓎⓎ

2-7-7 Ginza, 104-0061 **Tel** *(05) 3538-5322*　　　　**Map** 5 B3

This is a sleek restaurant and late-night venue with a bar (where the emphasis, unusually, is on sherry), and a downstairs bar/café that stays open until 5am. The downstairs café specializes in *shiokara* –a type of seafood that is often downed in shot glasses, and usually followed by a straight whisky.

CENTRAL TOKYO Champ de Soleil
🚻 🍴　　　　Ⓨ Ⓨ Ⓨ

1-10-6 Uchi-Kanda, 101-0047 **Tel** *(03) 5281-0333.*　　　　**Map** 3 B4

There's a wide selection of Belgian beers and a good wine list featuring mainly French wines (although these can get expensive) at this relaxed and friendly French/Belgian beer bar, best known for its mussels and *frites* (the thin and crispy kind), as well as a number of other fish dishes and salads.

CENTRAL TOKYO Columbus
🍴 Ⓥ　　　　Ⓨ Ⓨ Ⓨ

2-12-2 Uchi Kanda, 101-0047 **Tel** *(03) 3254-3638*　　　　**Map** 3 B4

Reasonably-priced *izakaya*-style restaurant (this is a similar idea to tapas, where you are encouraged to share food) in Kanda with a good selection of wines and beer. The menu is mainly Italian, so expect some good pasta dishes, but they often mix and match with other Western styles. Good cocktails as well.

CENTRAL TOKYO Ferrara
♿ 🚻 📷 🍴 Ⓥ　　　Ⓨ Ⓨ Ⓨ

3-11 Kanda Surugadai, 101-0047 **Tel** *(03) 3293-5855*　　　　**Map** 3 B4

Hidden away among the Kanda office blocks is this seriously upscale Italian restaurant (the name comes from a small town in northern Italy). Its decor is very modern, and big windows make it light and airy inside. The extensive menu changes daily. There's also a good range of pizzas from a very reasonable ¥1,000.

CENTRAL TOKYO La Bonne Nouvelle
🚻 📷　　　　Ⓨ Ⓨ Ⓨ

1F Nishimura Building, 2-5-3 Kyobashi 1-Chome, Chuo-ku, 104-8340 **Tel** *(03) 3567-0877*　　　　**Map** 5 C2

This newish French restaurant is from renowned chef Taka. It offers well-priced bistro fare, from steak and *frites* to more elaborate fish and meat dishes. It is popular with ex-pat French people living out in Tokyo, which has got to be a good recommendation. Good wine list and attractively-decorated, Western-style room.

CENTRAL TOKYO Myojinshita Kandagawa Honten
🚻　　　　Ⓨ Ⓨ Ⓨ

2-5-11 Soto-kanda, Chiyoda-ku, 101-0021 **Tel** *(03) 3251-5031*　　　　**Map** 3 A5

This restaurant is a specialist in broiled eel *kabayaki*, where the sauce is made from a 200-year-old recipe – in fact, they recently celebrated their bicentennial, as the restaurant opened in 1805! During the eel season, from June to October, there are often unusual varieties of wild eel on the menu. Traditional *tatami*-mat floors.

Key to Symbols *see back cover flap*

CENTRAL TOKYO Asian Table

Intercontinental Hotel, 1-16-2, Kaigan, Minatu-ku, Tokyo Bay, 105-7337 **Tel** *(03) 5404-2222* **Map** *5 B5*

The fairly new and very smart Hotel Intercontinental, which overlooks Tokyo Bay, has an excellent restaurant on the 3rd floor that offers an array of Asian, not just Japanese, food – there's a mix of Chinese, Vietnamese, and Thai dishes. There are also great views over Rainbow Bridge and the Bay.

CENTRAL TOKYO Dynasty

Hilton Tokyo Bay, 1-8 Maihama, Urayasu-shi, Chiba, 279-0031 **Tel** *(04) 7355-5000* **Map** *1 A1*

On the other side of the bay, looking back toward Tokyo itself, Dynasty is another very famous hotel restaurant with an excellent chef – in this case Sohzoh Miyamoto, who has become one of the country's most famous chefs for Chinese food (he's actually Japanese, but trained in top Chinese kitchens).

CENTRAL TOKYO Gordon Ramsay at Conrad Tokyo

Conrad Hotel, 1-9-1 Higashi-Shinbashi, Minato-ku, 105-7337 **Tel** *(03) 6388-8000* **Map** *5 B5*

This is a gorgeous restaurant, and British celebrity chef Gordon Ramsay's first outing to Tokyo. The food is international, with an accent on fresh flavors of whatever is in season. There's a great three-course lunch at ¥5,000. Evening gets a little more expensive – but you're paying for the glamor, as well as the great food.

CENTRAL TOKYO Kyubei

8-7-6 Ginza, 104-0061 **Tel** *(03) 3571-6523* **Map** *5 B3*

You'll find sushi here, and lots of it. This popular restaurant is housed in a charming traditional building with a discreet entrance, and *tatami*-mat floors. If you're feeling up for it, there is a blow-out *kaiseki* menu (Kyoto style, with endless small courses laid out like conceptual art) at ¥30,000.

CENTRAL TOKYO Beige Tokyo

Chanel Ginza Building, 3-5-3 Ginza, 104-0061 **Tel** *(03) 5159-5500* **Map** *5 B3*

Alain Ducasse's latest venture in Tokyo is on the 10th floor of the Chanel building in Ginza – expect very serious prices for international (mainly French, of course) cuisine. The menu changes monthly, with specials every day. The wine list has a different emphasis for lunch and dinner. Try their eight-dessert special!

CENTRAL TOKYO Enoteca Pinchiorri

5-8-20, Ginza Core Building, 104-0061 **Tel** *(03) 3289-8081* **Map** *5 B3*

One of Italy's most exclusive restaurants has had an outpost in Ginza since 1992. Expect eye-watering prices, but excellent food. You're not going to find hearty pasta and pizza – this is high-end Italian dining, straight from the court of Katerina de' Medici; presented beautifully, with delicate flavors and the freshest produce.

CENTRAL TOKYO La Tour d'Argent

New Otani Hotel, 4-1 Kioi-cho, Chiyoda-ku, 102-8578 **Tel** *(03) 3239-3111* **Map** *5 B5*

Considered by many to offer the very finest French dining in Japan (the mother restaurant even jostles for this title in Paris), the Akasaka branch of this celebrated Parisian dining hall serves classic cuisine in a dramatically opulent setting. The menu is very definitely classic, and perfectly presented.

CENTRAL TOKYO Les Saisons

Imperial Hotel, 1-1-1 Uchisaiwaicho, Chiyoda-ku, 100-8558 **Tel** *(03) 3539-8087* **Map** *5 B5*

The dining room is very formal (even with the recent redecoration, they have reined in any modernist influences) and you just know this is going to be expensive. But the food isn't at all stuffy – instead, Thierry Voisin, fresh from Reims' multi-Michelin-starred Les Crayères, puts fresh twists on classic dishes.

NORTHERN TOKYO Kamiya Bar

1-1-1 Asakusa, Taito-ku, Tokyo, 111-0032 **Tel** *(03) 3841 5400* **Map** *4 E2*

This place has a beer hall on the first floor, a traditional restaurant on the second, and a hot-pot palace on the third floor. There is a mix of *tatami*-mat floors and Western-style wooden floors with long bench tables – and all three floors are very fun and friendly, with good prices. Hilariously kitsch bar also.

NORTHERN TOKYO Hatsuogawa

2-8-4 Kaminarimon, Taito-ku, Asakusa, 111-0034 **Tel** *(03) 3844 2723* **Map** *4 E2*

Family-run, dating back to the Edo period, and famous for its delicious *unagi* (fresh water eel) grilled over hot coals and served with a top-secret sauce, this restaurant is small (there is room for only 12 diners) and very sought after, so you will need to book ahead.

WESTERN TOKYO Dexee Diner

2-26-16 Higashi Shibuya, 150-0011 **Tel** *03 5778 3236* **Map** *1 B5*

The Dexee Diner is very cool and extremely popular; good value international food and cocktails, and a big selection of magazines to flick though while you're waiting for your friends. Open from 11:30am to 4:30am seven days a week, this is quickly going to become a favorite spot – especially for the terrace on sunny days.

WESTERN TOKYO Maisen

Jingumae 4-8-16, Omotesando, 150-0011 **Tel** *(03) 3470-0071* **Map** *1 B5*

Another pork restaurant, like Tonki *(see p333)*, but in a very interesting building that was previously a bath house, and has now been transformed into an airy eating spot. They've even got the original bathing instructions on the wall. Good value, and plenty of options – but you really want to go for their *tonkatsu*.

WESTERN TOKYO Standard Deli

4-1-7 Shinjuku, Journal Standard 3F, 160 - 0011 **Tel** *(03) 5367-0185*   **Map** *1 A1*

As you walk from Shinjuku station to Takashimaya Times Square, this has a small terrace, a bright yellow sign, and a retro 50's-style trailer home that's been converted into a café. Fantastically unpretentious, which can make a nice change in Tokyo, so come here for the burgers, the ginger ale, and the atmosphere.

WESTERN TOKYO Toritake

Star Building, 1st floor, 5-14 Maruyama-cho, Shibuya, 150-0011 **Tel** *(03) 3461-5475*   **Map** *1 B5*

A good range of Japanese dishes, including noodles and rice dishes, plus good cheap *yakitori* from ¥600. You can watch it all being prepared in front of you, and although the staff don't speak much English, they are more than happy to let you sample the different sakes from their extensive selection.

WESTERN TOKYO Chinese Café Eight

Court Annex 2F, Nishi-Azabu 3-2-13, Roppongi, 106-0032 **Tel** *(03) 5414-5708*   **Map** *2 E5*

Deep in Roppongi Hills, this is all-night Chinese food (and it really is all night – it's a 24-hour restaurant). The dining room is huge, and is best enjoyed from one of the big communal tables. Like any Chinese restaurant, you're going to be presented with a huge array of small dishes, but their Beijing Duck is legendary.

WESTERN TOKYO Christon Café

Shintaiso Building 2 B1, 2-10-7, Dogenzaka, Sibuya, 150-0043 **Tel** *(03) 5728-2225*   **Map** *1 A5*

This café-bar is decorated like a church, right down to the stained-glass windows and statue of Jesus. The original is in Osaka, and it has proved equally popular in Tokyo. It is open from 5pm until 5am. There is also a prison-themed restaurant in the same building!

WESTERN TOKYO Fujimamas

Jingumae 6-3-2, Harajuku, 150-0001 **Tel** *(03) 5485-2262*   **Map** *1 B4*

The best thing is the weekend brunch at this friendly Japanese restaurant, between Harajuku and Omotesando, with an international feel. The two-story wooden building was originally built as a family home, and keeps that feel, despite its popularity. There's a special children's menu and fun drinks like home-brewed lemonade.

WESTERN TOKYO Immigrant's Café

Kyodo Building B1, 5-9-15 Minami-Aoyama, Minato-ku., 113-034 **Tel** *(03) 5766-8995*   **Map** *2 D4*

The original Immigrant's Café is in Niigata province, but they seem to have settled into Tokyo nicely. It's a lively and young-feeling café bar, with DJ booth and eclectic menu. The food is Thai-style, with plenty of chicken and vegetable curries. They also have happy hours in the early evening.

WESTERN TOKYO Moti

Roppongi Hama Building 3F, 6-2-35 Roppongi, Minato-ku, 106-0032 **Tel** *(03) 3479-1939*   **Map** *2 E5*

This Indian restaurant first opened in Aoyama in 1978, and now has six locations around Tokyo. You get the full-on kitsch interior – gold vases, red carpets, cheesy folk art on the walls ... and great, genuine Indian cuisine. Don't leave without trying the *saag aloo*.

WESTERN TOKYO The Pink Cow

Villa Moderuna B1, 1-3-18 Shibuya, 150-0011 **Tel** *(03) 3406-5597*   **Map** *1 B5*

Harajuku's highly-popular café bar, restaurant, gallery, and general entertainment space. Close to both Shibuya and Omotesando stations, this lively spot serves plenty of international dishes and has a good range of wine and beers. DJs play weekend evenings, and there's an-all-you-can-eat buffet on Friday and Saturday nights.

WESTERN TOKYO Civetta

Omotesando, 2-1-8 Shibuya., 150-0011 **Tel** *(03) 6418-8007*   **Map** *1 B4*

This late-night spot serves excellent pastas at good prices – mixing sauces and pasta shapes, from ¥500 for small dishes. There is also a range of good fixed-price menus, and thin-crust pizzas in a range of toppings. But really you come here for the people-watching, particularly as the night draws on.

WESTERN TOKYO Jap Cho Ok

Alteka Belte Plaza B1F , Minami-Aoyama 4-1-15, Gaienmae, 107-0062 **Tel** *(03) 5410-3408*   **Map** *2 D4*

As Korean food becomes more and more trendy in Tokyo, Jap Cho Ok is leading the field. This is not exactly traditional Korean food (although you still get the hot, spicy flavors), but more of an Asian-fusion with the emphasis on Korea. Particularly good are the soups, grills, and inevitably the *kimchi*.

WESTERN TOKYO Kakiden

Yasuyo Building, 3-27-11 Shinjuku, 160 - 0011 **Tel** *(03) 3352-5121*   **Map** *1 A1*

Serving authentic Japanese food for more than 25 years, this is a good place to try a ritualized dining experience where you can sit on *tatami* mats and have the full banquet, tea-ceremony style. There are also less expensive options available. Guests usually sit on traditional *tatami* mats, but tables are available.

WESTERN TOKYO Marché aux Puces

2-5-8 Ebisu, Sibuya, 150-0013 **Tel** *(03) 5485-2262*   **Map** *1 B5*

A simple and unpretentious French restaurant offering great value for money in airy surroundings. Perhaps not surprisingly, it's extremely popular and you're more than likely to find plenty of French expats dining here, a ringing endorsement in itself.

Key to Price Guide *see p330* **Key to Symbols** *see back cover flap*

WESTERN TOKYO Soba Giro

*Prudential Plaza 1F, Nagatacho 2-13-10, Chiyoda-Ku, Akasaka, 100-0014 **Tel** (03) 3500-5720* **Map** 2 E4

This is from Italian restaurateur Panzetta Girolamo, and features bamboo walls contrasted against dark wood, sleek *tatami*-mat floors, and beautifully-presented food from a focused but inventive menu. It's easy to forget just how good simple noodles can be, and this place is certainly expensive, but very good.

WESTERN TOKYO Sweet Basil 139

*6-7-11 Roppongi, Minato-ku, 106-0032 **Tel** (03) 5474-0139* **Map** 2 E5

There's live music every night and a very loyal crowd at this Roppongi institution, enjoying a mix of jazz, classical, world music, and modern rock – often big-name international stars. Long tables make the atmosphere sociable and relaxed, and the Italian food is always fresh, quick, and tasty. You might also hear it referred to as STB139.

WESTERN TOKYO L'Atelier de Joël Robuchon

*Hillside 220, Roppongi Hills, 106-0032 **Tel** (03)5772-7500* **Map** 2 E5

No reservations are possible here, which is just as well, or you'd never get a table. It's very cool – all the staff are dressed in black, and the emphasis is on dramatically-presented food. There's a long bar where you can sit and eat tapas-style, or tables for more formal dining – and all in a glass-fronted, hangar-like space.

WESTERN TOKYO Gesshinkyo

*Jingumae 4-24-12, Harajuku, 150-0001 **Tel** (03) 3796-6575* **Map** 1 B4

This is a rare vegetarian restaurant in Tokyo, using ingredients from all over Japan in a Tokyo twist on *shojin ryori* (traditional Buddhist food). There's only one choice of menu, and you'll get over a dozen courses of beautifully-presented food, full of clean flavors and contrasting textures. Simple *tatami*-mat rooms and dinner only.

WESTERN TOKYO Hotel de Mikuni

*1-18 Wakaba, Shinjuku, 160 - 0011 **Tel** (03) 3351-3810* **Map** 1 A1

A renowned and very classy restaurant in Shinjuku district (actually in an old church in the quiet residential suburb of Yotsuya). Kiyomi Mikuni is one of Tokyo's best chefs, and this is a classic Tokyo dining spot serving French food that would be cooed over in Paris. There are just 20 tables, so book well ahead.

WESTERN TOKYO New York Grill

*3-7-1-2 Nishi Shinjuku, Shinjuku-ku, 163-1055 **Tel** (03) 5323-3458* **Map** 1 A1

Probably Tokyo's most famous restaurant, this is the hotel from *Lost in Translation* (they have recently opened a fantastic Japanese restaurant, too), but was famous way before Bill Murray ever stepped over the threshold. No terrace – but one of the best views in the city. Very good beef and seafood, all cooked in an open kitchen.

WESTERN TOKYO Nobu

*6-10-17 Minami-aoyama, Minato-ku, 107-0062 **Tel** (03) 5467-0022* **Map** 2 D4

Sample the iconic Japanese restaurant on its home turf. Exposed brick walls showcase artwork from Robert de Niro's father (he's a shareholder in the restaurant). The menu is extensive and very, very good. If you don't want to scorch your credit card, stick to lunch, when they do a very reasonable tasting menu at ¥6,000.

WESTERN TOKYO Oak Door

*Grand Hyatt 6F, Roppongi, Roppongi Hills, 106-0032 **Tel** (03) 4333-8784* **Map** 2 E5

This excellent steak restaurant (you can get Kobe beef here), cooks everything to perfection in wood-burning ovens that are open for viewing in the dramatically-lit kitchen. There's a lovely terrace in summer, and a range of international wines. A romantic spot, as nighttime sees well-heeled couples gazing at each other over candlelit tables.

WESTERN TOKYO Sant Pau

*Coredo Nihonbashi Annex 1/2F, Nihonbashi 1-6-1, 106-0032 **Tel** (03) 3517-5700* **Map** 5 C1

Excellent Spanish food from this outpost of a two-starred Michelin restaurant in Catalonia. The tasting menu is expensive, but it's a great introduction to this creative, inventive, and really delicious food. There's a wine list of over 500 references. Closed on Mondays.

FARTHER AFIELD Ippudo

*Hiroo 1-3-12, Ebisu, 150-0021 **Tel** (03) 5420-2225*

A *ramen* bar, part of a well-known group, which stays open until 4am and prices are reasonable. This is the same *ramen* place that has a branch in the *ramen* museum in Shin-Yokohama (see p336), so you know you're in the hands of experts. Wooden tables give a friendly atmosphere. Highly recommended!

FARTHER AFIELD Tonki

*1-1-2 Shimo Meguro , Meguro-ku, 153-8573 **Tel** (03) 3491-9928*

A Tokyo classic, serving up the best pork in town. You'll very likely have to stand in line before trying their famous fried cutlets (served with the traditional accompaniments of shredded cabbage, pickles, and rice) but it'll be worth it. And everything is prepared right before your eyes.

FARTHER AFIELD Trocadero Bistro

*3-30-3 Kitazawa, Setagaya-ku, Shimokitazawa, 155-0031 **Tel** (03) 3467-1991*

A very relaxed café bar with good French food (tarte tartin and boeuf bourguignon have both been on the menu). Expect plenty of Edith Piaf as well – it's very kitsch, in true Shimokitazawa fashion. Their Sunday brunch is one of the most popular attractions in the area, so book ahead. And if that's not enough, there's also a roof terrace.

FARTHER AFIELD Zetton

1F SPC Japan Bldg 1-1-33 Hiroo Shibuya, 150-0021 **Tel** *(03) 5774-1917*

Very popular tapas-style (but Japanese food) restaurant that has become popular very quickly, so make sure you book ahead because there always seem to be queues outside. If you do make it through the door, it's very stylish, but cozy and carefully laid out to maintain a feeling of intimacy.

FARTHER AFIELD Café le Bretagne

1st floor, Comfort Kagurazaka 4-2, Kagurazaka, Shinjuku, 162-0825 **Tel** *(03) 3235-3001*

Looking on to the Kagurazaka river, this restaurant is run by the charmingly Gallic Bertrand Lacher and provides possibly the best crêpes this side of Brittany. There are buckwheat *galettes* with a variety of fillings, both sweet and savory. There's another branch in Omotesando.

CENTRAL HONSHU

FUJI FIVE LAKES Mama-no-mori

N side of Yamanaka, Lake Yamanashi, 401-0305 **Tel** *(0555) 62-0346*

Dine on *kaiseki ryori* in a classic old thatched-roof restaurant, sitting on the north side of Yamanaka Lake. You'll get good food and gorgeous views of Mount Fuji (when the weather co-operates). The restaurant is named after the popular area mother who started this restaurant.

GIFU Kawaraya

Near Jozai-ji Temple Gifu, 500-8023 **Tel** *(058) 262-1530*

In season, *ayu* (sweetfish or river smelt) are served fresh from the river as sashimi or grilled. The main menu here is classic *kaiseki ryori*, so the menu and the ingredients change with the seasons. There are various courses, and dinner here can get pretty steep, but with dozens of dishes it's a unique experience. Served in *tatami* rooms.

HAKONE Bella Foresta

Hakone Open-Air Museum, 1121 Ninotaira, Kanagawa, 250-0493 **Tel** *(0460) 2-1141*

Hakone's top atraction, the Open-Air Museum, features a great lunch buffet at the Bella Foresta restaurant. The bright and airy room overlooks the lovely scenery of the museum park, and there is something for everyone at the large buffet. Open for lunch only.

HAKONE Shikajaya

Ebisu Ryokan, 250-0404 **Tel** *(0460) 5-5751*

Located in the first floor of Ebisu Ryokan, Shikajaya is convenient, just five minutes from the station. The tables are grouped around a large open-hearth fire, which is just the thing after a cool evening walk. The menu is based around tofu, prepared in various ways with a wide variety of ingredients.

HAKONE Fujiya Hotel

359 Miyanoshita, 250-0404 **Tel** *(0460) 2-2211*

Good Western food is served in Hakone's oldest and grandest hotel (*see p301*). The bright dining room is from "an age gone by", complete with crisp, white tablecloths and attentive, bow-tied staff. There are good views and great food: everything from spaghetti to rainbow trout to sirloin steak. Reservations required for dinner.

IZU Fujiichi

Ito 7-6 Shizumi-cho Shizuoka, 414-0002 **Tel** *(0557) 37-4705*

Fujiichi is right on the Ito waterfront, next to the fish market, and don't be put off by the rundown building. Well-loved by locals, this simple, second-story restaurant serves great fresh food at very reasonable prices. There are fantastic views of the harbor. Choose either the excellent *teishoku* or a more expansive (and expensive) set.

KAMAKURA Hachinoki

Near Kencho-ji Kanagawa, 247-0062 **Tel** *(0120) 22-8719 (free dial) (0467) 22-8719*

Artfully-presented *shojin ryori* (Buddhist vegetarian cuisine). Dine in an old, thatched-roof building at tables or on *tatami* mats. The staff are used to foreigners and happy to help with any questions. There are a total of three Hachinoki in Kamakura, all under the same management. Try this one by Kencho-ji Temple first.

KAMAKURA Miyokawa

1-16-17 Hase Kanagawa, 248-0016 **Tel** *(0467) 25-5556*

Just across the street from the Great Buddha Statue, this is a great place to introduce yourself to *kaiseki ryori*. It also has cheaper set meals, *bento* (boxed lunches), and even children's meals. Menus change with the seasons to use the freshest ingredients. Seating is casual, but the food is excellent.

KANAZAWA Kitamaro

2-3-3 Katamachi, Ishikawa, 920-0981 **Tel** *(076) 261-7176*

This restaurant has 140 years of history and experience backing up its wonderful food. Most famous are the *kojitsu obento* (sashimi, pork, chicken, and seasonal vegetables in a box) and the *jibuni teishoku* featuring duck stew, a regional specialty. There are courses to fit most budgets at lunch. *Kaiseki* dinner (¥5,000) must be reserved.

Key to Price Guide *see p330* **Key to Symbols** *see back cover flap*

KANAZAWA Miyoshian

1-1 1 Kenrokumachi, Ishikawa, 920-0936 **Tel** *(076) 221-0127*

Right in Kenrokuen Garden, Miyoshian consists of three wooden buildings; try to get into the one extending over the pond. Only set meals of the local *kaga* cuisine are served. All sets include *jibuni*, a local duck and vegetable stew. You can also just opt for sweets and green tea for about ¥650. Open for lunch only.

KANAZAWA Kotobukiya

Near Owari-cho bus stop, Ishikawa, 920-0902 **Tel** *(076) 231-6245*

Everything has an elegance here, from the *shojin ryori* (Buddhist vegetarian cuisine) and the beautiful dishes it's served in, to the serving staff and the beautiful 160-year-old one-time merchant's house you dine in. The lunch course is half that of dinner, and there is a boxed lunch for half of that again. Reservations required for dinner.

KAWAGOE Ichinoya

1-18-10 Matsue-cho Saitama, 350-0056 **Tel** *(0492) 22-0354*

This is the place to come in Kawagoe for eel *(unagi)*, said to increase your stamina, particularly in hot weather. Ichinoya has been serving food since 1832 and the restaurant today skillfully blends traditional and modern style. *Kaiseki ryori* is also available. The use of stone lanterns in the decor is very effective. Western and Japanese seating.

KAWAGOE Unton

Kawashima-cho, Saitama, 350-0152 **Tel** *(049) 297-0041*

Outside, this is a beautiful old-style *kura* building, inside it is a relaxing blend of old and new. It's specialty is *udon* noodles, but it also serves rice blended with *kuromai* (black rice) and organic vegetables. Both Western and *tatami* seating, and a variety of sets for various budgets. You can also get a snack of sweets and thick, frothy *matcha*.

MASHIKO Yamani

On main street, Tochigi, 321-1404 **Tel** *(0285) 72-7111*

Behind the showroom of the Yamani Otsuka Gallery, this bright, airy restaurant serves very good *soba* and *udon* noodle sets. It also has sweets and *matcha*. With stone floors and walls and wood-slab tables, it's a pleasant place. Across the street is it's coffee shop sister Keyaki, serving pasta and pilaf, at similar prices.

MATSUMOTO Kiso-ya

4-6-26 Ote, Nagano, 390-0874 **Tel** *(0263) 32-0528*

Established in 1887, this restaurant in an old *kura* specializes in *dengaku*, food on a skewer coated with a miso paste and grilled on a charcoal fire. Kiso-ya's *dengaku* is known for the mild, slightly sweet taste of its paste. It is just 10 minutes' walk east of the castle and furnished with Matsumoto-style furniture.

MATSUMOTO Kura

1-10-22 Chuo, Nagano, 390-0811 **Tel** *(0263) 33-6444*

Built 100 years ago by the Watanabe family to store seaweed and dried seafood (*kura* means storeroom), about 40 years ago it was converted into a restaurant. Today, this Nakamachi restaurant with massive whitewashed walls is popular for its tasty *soba*, but also known for *basashi* (raw horse meat). Other courses include *kaiseki* (order ahead).

NAGANO Kosugetei

367 Niomon-cho, Nagano, 380-0852 **Tel** *(026) 232-2439*

Established in 1895, this shop makes its *soba* noodles from scratch each day and also takes great pride in its *tsuyu* (noodle dipping broth). The specialty is delicious *soba*, but it also serves some *teishoku* rice meals – check the menu. There's a huge display of lucky cat statues, friendly staff, and all-*tatami* seating.

NAGOYA Kappa

12th floor Towers Plaza, Nagoya Station **Tel** *(052) 541-7888*

Kappa is actually two restaurants. The dining room has Western seating with a screen giving added privacy. Check the display case full of plastic food to decide what you want. The other half is *kaitenzushi*. A conveyor belt carries tiny, color-coded plates of sushi past you. Pick what you want; your pile of plates determines your bill. Great fun.

NAGOYA Yamamoto-ya Honten

25-9 Meieki, Nagoya –ku, 450-0002 **Tel** *(052) 565-0278*

This is the flagship of the Yamamoto chain. It's not fancy, but it is famous for delicious Nagoya-style miso *nikomi udon* – handmade thick, chewy wheat noodles in a big bowl of miso soup, topped with meat and vegetables. There's an English menu listing this and a variety of other choices

NAGOYA Toriei

3-8-3 Sakae, Nagoya, 8 min from Sakae subway station, 460-0008 **Tel** *(052) 241-5552*

Nagoya has been famous for its chicken cuisine for over 200 years. At Toriei you can have it grilled, raw, fried, or in a *nabe* hot pot. There is generous Western seating and elegant private *tatami* rooms, too. The lunch menu is considerably cheaper, and this is also a good place for drinks and snacks.

NARITA Kikuya

385 Naka-cho, Chiba, 286-0027 **Tel** *(0476) 22-0236*

Kikuya is now into the 11th generation of the Ishibashi family. You'll often find Mrs Ishibashi greeting guests at the entrance of Kikuya, right across from the tourist pavilion. Both she and her husband speak English. Kikuya is famous for *unagi*, but the (English) menu also has sashimi, *tempura*, and tasty *yakitori*. Very understanding of foreigners.

NOTO Shoya-no Yakata

Suzu-shi, Noto, 927-1326 **Tel** *(0768) 32-0372*

Try this small, thatched-roof restaurant on Route 249 north of the beach, outside Wajima. Seafood, as you'd expect, is the specialty here. Perhaps best is the *kamameshi*, rice steamed in a clay pot with a heavy wooden lid. What makes it great is all the fresh seafood and vegetables mixed with the rice before cooking.

SHIMODA Gorosaya

5-25 1-chome, Shimoda, 415-0021 **Tel** *(0558) 23-5638*

Well-loved by locals for its *teishoku* meals, Gorosaya is a great place to get the freshest seafood at reasonable prices. Try the *Iso no mai* course, which includes baked fish, shellfish, and sashimi. For a side dish try seafood *shyumai* (like dim sum). There's an English menu highlighting the wide range of prices and the staff are very friendly.

TAKAO Ukai Toriyama

3426 Minami, Asakawa Tokyo, 193-0846 **Tel** *(0426) 61-0739*

At the foot of Mt Takao, a group of thatched-roof cottages surround a garden with rushing streams and moss-covered waterwheels. Each party gets their own cottage, served by kimonoed staff. The menu is standard (chicken, beef, and fish) but well prepared, and it's a gorgeous setting. A great way to finish a day of hiking on the mountain.

TAKAYAMA Agura

4-7 Shinmeicho, Gifu, 506-0015 **Tel** *(0577) 37-2666*

This is a quirky place set in an old rice *kura*. Pizzas cooked in a wood stove, a variety of salads, Vietnamese spring rolls, and steaks feature on the English menu. High ceilings, wood floors, wooden-slab tables, and bentwood chairs add to a comfy atmosphere. Waiters grooving to the jazz on the sound system add to this enjoyable restaurant.

TAKAYAMA Suzuya

24 Hanakawa-cho, Gifu, 506-0015 **Tel** *(0577) 32-2484*

Look for the cedar ball under the eaves. Regional specialties on the English menu include famous Hida beef, *sansai* miso *nabe* (vegetables and mountain ferns, and chicken simmered in miso soup), and *hoba* miso (tofu, vegetables, and miso roasted on a magnolia leaf). Locally brewed sake is ready and the owners are noted for their friendliness.

TAKAYAMA Susaki

N4-14 Shinmeicho, Gifu, 506-0821 **Tel** *(0577) 32-0023*

Just off San-machi dori, near Nakabishi bridge, the same family has been serving Honzen cuisine here since 1794. This is sure to be an unforgettable highlight of your trip to Japan, with beautiful meals served with gentle smiles in a classic building. Reservations are recommended. Less expensive lunches are available.

YOKOHAMA Chinatown

Ten minute walk from Ishikawa-cho Station

There are over 150 Chinese restaurants crammed into a few square blocks here. Eat on the cheap or go as high as you want. Walk, snack, or sit down and take your time. Heichiro is famous (prepare to wait) for dim sum. Edosei serves great steamed buns (filled with meat or sweet bean). Suro Saikan Honkan features Shainghai cuisine.

YOKOHAMA Enokitei

89-6 Yamate-cho, Nakaku, 7-minute walk from Ishikawa-cho Station **Tel** *(045) 623-2288*

Take high tea in Yokohama. Housed in a 1927 Western-style mansion, you can sit inside or out in the Rose garden and people-watch as you sip black tea, herb tea, or coffee (espresso, too) and nibble a variety of homemade cakes and cookies. Right beside Minato-mieruoka Park, 10 minutes' walk east of Chinatown.

YOKOHAMA Shin Yokohama Ramen Museum

2-14-21 Shin Yokohama, near Shin-Yokohama station **Tel** *(045) 471-0503*

There actually are some exhibits on *ramen* noodles in Japan, particularly the development of instant noodles. You win one video game by eating the most virtual noodles. Best are the eight real noodle shops in a recreated 1958 *shitamachi* neighborhood. It's nostalgic with good food: regional dishes feature the squiggly noodles.

KYOTO

CENTRAL KYOTO Mughal

Teramachi Oike-agaru, Nakagyo-ku, 604-0923 **Tel** *(075) 241-3777*

For something a little different, try this popular spot for its renowned Indian cooking from tandoori chicken to lamb *masala*. Best of all is the all-you-can-eat weekend buffet – the price is rather unfairly cheaper for women than men! They also do a good take-home "party set" to cook at home.

CENTRAL KYOTO Shizuka

Shinkyogyoku Ryuko-dori, Nakagyo-ku, 604-8042 **Tel** *(075) 221-5148*

Hidden away and not easy to find, but great fun for a night out when you want a break from the beauty of Kyoto's history. What you get here is definitely no frills. It's popular with local journalists and artists (half of whom seem to have written or drawn on the walls), all enjoying cheap finger food, sake, and beer.

CENTRAL KYOTO Le Bouchon

71-1 Enokicho, Nijo-Teramachi, Nakagyo-ku **Tel** *(075) 211-5220*

As soon as you see the outside of this place, you want to push open the door and go on in. It serves old-fashioned French cuisine, complete with checkered table cloths, and a wooden bar to sit at if you just want a quick bite or a glass of wine. Well located in central Kyoto, just near the City Hall.

CENTRAL KYOTO Al Matsuo

55 Tokobankicho-Teramachi, Nijo-agaru, 604-0915 **Tel** *(075) 212-1988*

Elegant, modern Italian dining found just off the Teramachi shopping street. The menu includes plenty of pasta and fish dishes (but no pizzas), and some very interesting additions like slow roast lamb with seasonal vegetables. The decor is low-key and sophisticated, and there's a good wine list concentrating on northern Italy.

CENTRAL KYOTO Tagoto Meigetsuan

Yanagi-banba-dori, Shijo-agaru, 604-8122 **Tel** *(075) 212-8811*

An inexpensive way of trying some traditional *kaiseki* food, this plain and simple restaurant aims to give a taste of *kaiseki* without breaking the bank. Evening meals can be quite expensive, but you can try a mini menu that is just ¥2,700, and there are take-out *bento* boxes too, as well as a good buffet option.

EASTERN KYOTO Menami

Kiyamachi, Sanjo-agaru, Nakagyo-ku, 606-8004 **Tel** *(075) 231-1095*

This is a busy but relaxing restaurant serving high-quality Japanese home cuisine, *obanzai*-style. This means you'll get dishes such as egg rolls stuffed with rice noodles, and warming pork and rice dishes. Good finger food, too, to be washed down with a few beers. Always book ahead, as it's very small – and try to get a place at the counter.

EASTERN KYOTO Misoka-An Kawamichi-Ya

Sanjo-agaru, Fuya-cho-dori, Nakagyo-ku, 606-8085 **Tel** *(075) 221-2525*

A 300-year-old famed noodle destination, right in the center of Old Kyoto, attracting clients from all over Japan. There's a lovely central courtyard (but not for eating in). The main dishes are plain buckwheat noodles, but you can get an array of broths and toppings to accompany them. *Tatami*-mat rooms of varying sizes going over two floors.

EASTERN KYOTO Takocho

1-237 Miyagawasuji, 605-0000 **Tel** *(075) 525-0170*

Fantastic and varied, quality broths (*oden*, over 18 varieties, from octopus to miso) are served over-the-counter in a simple shop in Gion, found right by Donguri-dori and Kawabata-dori. The shop has been on this site for over 100 years, and some of the clientele look like they've been coming since opening night!

EASTERN KYOTO Kyoto Nama Chocolat Organic Tea House

76-15 Tenno-cho, Ozakaki, 606-8435 **Tel** *(075) 751-2678*

With a name like that, you just know this is going to be good. You can choose betweeen gorgeous handmade chocolates or slices of cake, and there's an array of herbal and green teas. Traditional *tatami*-mat rooms, a communal table, and a pretty garden at the back make this one of Kyoto's more relaxed dining experiences.

EASTERN KYOTO Matsuno

Minamiza-higashi 4-ken-me, Shijo-dori, Higashiyama-ku, 605-0000 **Tel** *(075) 561-2786*

The menu at this family-run restaurant is centered on gourmet eel dishes, but also some lovely delicate broths (the house specialty contains liver), *udon* noodles, and other local favorites. The restaurant is housed in a traditional building, and cherry blossoms spill over the entrance during March and April. The set meal is very good value.

EASTERN KYOTO Okutan

86-30 Fukuji-cho, Nanzen-ji, Sakyo-ku, 606-8435 **Tel** *(075) 771-8709*

Located in a beautiful house opposite the Nanzen-ji Temple, Okutan serves classic Buddhist cuisine. This means tofu in a range of guises, from grilled tofu skewers, to deep-fried tofu, and elaborate tofu broths. The set meals are excellent value. There's also a lovely garden with a pond full of carp, and a small area for eating outside.

EASTERN KYOTO Sfera Bar Satonaka

17 Benzaiten-cho, Higashiyama-ku, 605-0086 **Tel** *(075) 532-1139*

This is a fantastic bar in the Gion quarter, with an Italian restaurant, Sfera Salon, that opened in 2006. The sleekly-modern building also houses a more informal Italian-style café and wine bar, a Japanese restaurant, a book and CD shop, and gallery space. Expensive but very much the place to be seen.

EASTERN KYOTO The River Oriental

180 Minoya-cho, Kiyamachi-dori, Matsubara-agaru, Shimogyo-ku, 605-0086 **Tel** *(075) 351-8541*

Good restaurant, very stylish, and well positioned by the Kamagawa River, with a terrace and "Sky Bar" during the summer months and a candle-lit interior over winter. The food is modern Japanese, mixed with plenty of international ingredients – so you might get a Thai green curry, or char-grilled snapper. All perfectly presented.

EASTERN KYOTO Hyotei

35 Nanzenji, Kusagawa-machi, 606-8437 **Tel** *(075) 771-4116*

This is one of the finest restaurants in Kyoto, serving classic *kaiseki* feasts, presented like tiny plates of modern art, using all seasonal ingredients. Remortgage-your-house expensive, but a real experience. *Tatami*-mat floors (don't expect chairs) and no outside tables, but the sliding screens can be drawn back to open the room to the garden.

IMPERIAL PALACE Kyo-tofu Fujino

90-4 Onmae-dori Ichijo, Kamigyo-ku, 602-8384 **Tel** *(075) 463-7035*

Traditional, simple shop-house serving renowned tofu that you can watch being made at the factory just a few doors away. *Tatami*-mat rooms, but you do have the option of sitting on benches here rather than the floor. Part of a very well-regarded chain. Open at lunchtime only, and closed Mondays.

IMPERIAL PALACE Mankamero

Inokuma-dori, Demizu Agaru, 602-8118 **Tel** *(075) 441-5020*

The nearby Imperial Court is said to have been the inspiration for the Imperial take on Kyoto food *(yusoku ryori)* served at this exclusive 270-year-old restaurant in a beautiful, traditional building. Expect to pay heavily for the *yusoku* food, although the rest of the menu is more reasonable, and there are cheaper lunch *bento* boxes from noon–3pm.

KYOTO STATION Edogawa

11 F The Cube Kyoto Station Bldg, Higashi Shiokoji-cho, Shiokoji-sagaru, Karasuma **Tel** *(075) 365-8733*

Modern Japanese food is served at Edogawa, which specializes in eel dishes (the charcoal-grilled eel is delicious). Located in Kyoto station, so perfect for a quick, easy lunch – and very good value for what is excellent, if simple, food. Recreations of all the dishes are laid out in plastic across the counter top, so it's also very easy to order.

NORTHERN KYOTO Azekura

30 Okamoto-cho, Kamigamo Kita-ku, 603-8081 **Tel** *(075) 701-0161*

This is a renowned homemade-noodle destination on the northern outskirts of the city, in the Skake-machi district that has remained unchanged for centuries. Many of the *tatami* seating spots overlook the lovely garden. Good value, hearty food with a small but excellent choice of noodles and accompaniments. Lunch only, closed Mondays.

NORTHERN KYOTO Tawaraya

Bakucho Onmae-dori, Imakoji sagaru, Kamigyo-ku, 602-8386 **Tel** *(075) 463-4974*

A 400-year-old noodle establishment, just south of Kitano Shrine, which should not to be confused with Tawaraya Ryokan, one of the oldest and most expensive places to stay in Kyoto. They serve the full array of hot and cold noodles – from the wide *udon* noodles to thinner buckwheat noodles, with a variety of toppings, or clear broths.

NORTHERN KYOTO Izusen

Murasakino, Daitokuji-cho, 603-8231 **Tel** *(075) 341-4201*

Fresh Buddhist vegetarian cuisine is served here, and there is a wider variety of beers and sakes than at some of the temple restaurants. The main branch is found here at Daitoku-ji Temple, but there is also one at Kyoto station. The broths are incredibly delicate, and served so hot that you need to sip them slowly, promoting quiet contemplation.

NORTHERN KYOTO Konohana

Bakurocho Onmae, Imakoji-agaru, Kamigyo-ku, 602-8386 **Tel** *(075) 461-6687*

This traditional stone-floored restaurant, built in the late 19th century, serves classic hot and cold noodle dishes, washed down with eye-watering homemade sake (the building used to be a sake warehouse, giving a pleasing sense of continuity). It's located by the entrance to Kitano Shrine. Excellent value lunch, no evening service.

NORTHERN KYOTO Tenryu-ji Shigetsu

66 Susukinobanba-cho, Sagatenryuji, Ukyo-ku, 616-8385 **Tel** *(075) 822-9725*

A Zen temple serving only at lunchtime, with fantastic views over the gardens of Tenryu-ji Temple. You'll get simple vegetarian food, served in *bento* boxes, in a very traditional setting – the menu concentrates on six flavors which each have their own religious significance, and are presented cleanly and simply. You need to book in advance.

NORTHERN KYOTO Daitokuji Ikkyu

20 Daitokujimae, Murasakino, Kita-ku, 603-8215 **Tel** *(075) 493-0019*

They've been serving Zen Buddhist cuisine here since the 1400s. Try their innovative tofu and vegetable-based dishes in a traditional setting, with beautiful presentation on red laquerware dishes, in large *tatami*-mat rooms with Japanese scrolls on the walls. The walls are also painted with pastoral scenes, and there's a Zen garden.

NORTHERN KYOTO Kitcho

58 Susukinobaba, Saga Tenryuji, Ukyo, 616-8385 **Tel** *(075) 881-1101*

Kitcho is one of Kyoto's most exclusive restaurants, in a pretty district on the outskirts of the city, right by Tenryu-ji Temple. There is *kaiseki* food, served on laquerware plates, in *tatami*-mat rooms, plus gorgeous views of cherry blossoms in the right season. Open in the evening, but last orders are at 7pm, so get there early.

WESTERN HONSHU

HIMEJI Wi Japone

Will E Building 1F, 1-21 Nakanoda, Shikama, Himeji City, Hyogo Prefecture, 670-0000 **Tel** *(079) 235-9990*

Serving creative Japanese cuisine from fresh, seasonal ingredients, Wi Japone is a trendy *izakaya* with a cozy white-walled interior accented in black bamboo. Try the sashimi, made with fish delivered fresh from the market, or the sweet prawn and vegetable *carpaccio*. Private rooms on the second floor require reservations.

HIROSHIMA Okonomimura

5-13 Shintenchi, Chuo-ku, Hiroshima City, Hiroshima Prefecture, 730-0034 Tel (082) 241-2210

An *okonomiyaki* "village", with three floors of shops to choose from, each offering its own take on Hiroshima's famous specialty. Variations range from the basic meat and egg form to more deluxe versions whose ingredients range from squid, prawn, and cheese to *kimchee*. If the choice is daunting, just follow your nose.

HIROSHIMA Suishin ¥¥¥

6-7 Tatemachi, Chuo-ku, 730-0032 Tel (082) 247-4411

Suishin is a successful chain in Hiroshima, established in 1951. The large main restaurant offers *kamameshi*, a dish of rice and vegetables with meat or seafood, served in a small pot. *Kaiseki* and *fugu* (blowfish) courses are also available. For something simpler, try their small but well-known "sushi dojo" just around the corner.

HIROSHIMA Kanawa ¥¥¥¥¥

3-1-4, Ootemachi, Chuo-ku, Hiroshima City, Hiroshima City, 730-0051 Tel (082) 241-7416

Hiroshima is famous for its oysters, which are cultivated on rafts in the Seto Inland Sea. Kanawa has an immaculate Japanese-style interior, making it easy to forget that it is a boat (moored near Heiwa Oohashi bridge). Oysters are served in various ways: baked, fried, steamed, marinated, and in soups.

KOBE Puja ¥¥

4-1-18 Motomachi, Chuo-ku, 650-0022 Tel (078) 382-2728

More than 20 different curries are served at this authentic Indian restaurant. All dishes are cooked to order. The service is timely and the food is good value for the price. Try the light and nourishing vegetable curry. An after-dinner *chai* is recommended, and for smokers Indian cigarettes are on sale at the cash register.

KOBE La Cucina Italian Mi-na ¥¥¥

Kobe Center Building 1F, 3-3-7 Tamondoori, Chuo-ku, 650-0015 Tel (078) 371-3143

With its simple, tastefully-lit interior and relaxing ambience, La Cucina Italian Mi-na is a good choice for reasonably-priced Italian cuisine. The menu makes the most of fresh local produce, so it changes with the season. Vegetarian dishes are also available on request, and there is no non-smoking section.

KOBE Recette ¥¥¥

Silk Heights B1F, 2-2-13 Yamamoto-dori, Chuo-ku, 650-0003 Tel (078) 221-0211

Recette combines seafood fresh from the Seto Inland Sea with game meat imported from France to provide a menu that changes with the seasons. Comprehensive wine list, with a choice of 15 labels available to drink by the glass, and relaxing ambience in an interior that is carefully styled, down to its designer tableware from Limoges and Christofle.

KOBE Kitano Club ¥¥¥¥

1-5-7 Kitanomachi, Chuo-ku, 650-0002 Tel (078) 222-5123

Reopened after extensive refurbishment just in time for its 50th anniversary in 2007, this stylish French restaurant and bar has enduring popularity for its lunch specials and views of the city. The dinner menu is mainly based around Kobe beef and also features foie gras and sweet prawn. Organic vegetables are used throughout the cooking.

KOBE Mouriya ¥¥¥¥

Kitano Phoenix 401, 1-17-6 Chuo-ku, 650-0004 Tel (078) 327-2355

Established in 1885, this popular restaurant serves thick slices of the finest quality Kobe beef deliciously seasoned with natural salt, hand-ground sesame seeds, and homemade miso sauce or *ponzu* (tangy sauce made from citrus fruit and vinegar). Sit at the counter to savor the aroma as the chef cooks the meat on a hot plate in front of you.

KURASHIKI 9494 (Kushukushu) ¥¥

2-16-41 Achi, Kurashiki-shi, 710-0055 Tel (086) 421-0949

This fashionable *izakaya* uses fresh seasonal vegetables to combine nourishing international food with Japanese food based on local delicacies. Try the crispy Vietnamese egg rolls or the specialty, potato and cheese croquettes. The light, healthy food and stylish ambience at Kushukushu have earned it a loyal following among the younger set.

KURASHIKI Hisago Shikitei ¥¥¥

3-6-14 Achi, Kurashiki, 710-0055 Tel (086) 422-2525

This delightful traditional Japanese restaurant is located just two minutes' walk west of Kurashiki station and serves seasonal Okayama specialties and *kaiseki* cuisine, making excellent use of fresh seafood from the Inland Sea. The first floor has low tables and a counter, while upstairs are partitioned, Japanese-style dining rooms with sliding doors.

KURASHIKI Luxe as a Dining Bar ¥¥¥

Achi Building 2F, 2-6-24 Achi, Kurashiki, 710-0055 Tel (086) 427-8882

This spacious and comfortable *izakaya* is popular with its mainly female clientele for its tasty food and trendy interior. The "Luxe Original Course" is good value, including seven food items and two hours of all-you-can-drink, and the pork and *kimchee* spring rolls are worth trying. Relaxing atmosphere, with jazz music and low lighting.

MATSUE Yakumo-an ¥

308 Shiominawate, 690-0000 Tel (0852) 22-2400

An excellent lunch spot located in an old samurai house with a beautiful garden and carp pond. Yakumo-an's main dish is handmade Yakumo *soba* in a wild duck broth. For dessert, try the *fumaiko* – a mix of green tea jelly and ice cream, which is a delicious and unusual blend of bitter and sweet tastes.

MATSUE Yakitori Bankichi

491-1 Asahi-machi, 690-0003 **Tel** *(0852) 31-8308*

Formerly known as Daikichi, this friendly *yakitori* joint is affiliated to a successful chain of restaurants of the same name. It is easily identified by two large red lanterns hanging outside. Popular with young locals, Yakitori Bankichi usually has a lively atmosphere at the weekends. The owner speaks good English.

MIYAJIMA ISLAND Tonokajaya

Omachi, near five-storied pagoda, 739-0521 **Tel** *(0829) 44-2455*

Catering to visitors to Miyajima Island since 1949, this small teahouse is a good option for a light snack, serving *zenzai* (sweet adzuki bean soup with rice cakes) and *matcha* (green tea). Different types of *udon* and rice cakes are also served. All of the seats are non-smoking.

MIYAJIMA ISLAND Tachibana

Kitano-cho, Miyajima (on the path connecting Itsukushima Shrine & ferry terminal), 738-0000 **Tel** *(0829) 44-0240*

Tachibana is a small restaurant which has been in business since the early 1950s and is well located for a rest from sightseeing. Fresh seafood from the Inland Sea features throughout the cooking, including Hiroshima oyster and the house specialty of *anago donburi*, a flavorsome dish with eels. Usually crowded at lunchtime on weekends.

NARA Harishin

15 Nakanoshin'ya-cho, 630-8333 **Tel** *(0742) 22-2669*

This 200-year-old building was used as a money-exchange business during the Edo period but now houses a lovely traditional restaurant which serves only one set lunch and one dinner *bento* (lacquered box of food), the contents of which vary and are meant to be a surprise. Expect liberal amounts of soup, rice, meat, fish, and fresh vegetables.

NARA Tsuzumian

2-488 Sanjo-cho, 630-8244 **Tel** *(0742) 20-5800*

Tsuzumian serves healthy *kaiseki* cuisine using seasonal vegetables and fresh fish. The simply-designed interior of cream panels and wooden framing includes soft lighting from lamps placed on the floor. Private dining booths are partitioned by sliding doors. Try the Sanrin set, which includes a total of 10 dishes, along with coffee and dessert.

NARA Washokuya Happo

22 Nakamachi Higashimuki, 630-8215 **Tel** *(0742)26-4834*

Just a minute's walk from Nara station, Washokuya Happo serves authentic Japanese food in a relaxed, cheerful environment. Choice of seating at *horikotatsu* (low tables with leg-room space), at counters, or in partitioned booths. The wooden interior has a deep fragrance of cedar. English-speaking staff, and non-smoking seats available.

NARA Yanagi Chaya

4-48 Noborio-ji-cho, next to Kofukui-ji main hall, 630-8312 **Tel** *(0742) 22-7560*

Monks from the temples of Kofuku and Todai prepare vegetarian dishes here, including Nara *chameshi*, a rice porridge with tofu cooked in green tea, a dish that was previously in decline. *Chagayu*, a tea-flavored rice gruel, is also served. Non-vegetarian set lunches available, and evening dinner possible by special reservation.

OKAYAMA Matsunoki-tei

20-1 Ekimoto-machi, 700-0024 **Tel** *(086) 253-5410*

This well-known restaurant has a graceful interior decorated with hanging scrolls and *ikebana* (a traditional Japanese flower arrangement). Reasonably-priced *kaiseki* menu and good *shabu-shabu* options. Free use of a karaoke room available during lunchtime. Matsunoki tends do be crowded at weekends, so reservations are recommended.

OKAYAMA Maganedo

1-8-2 Uchisange, Okayama-shi, 700-0824 **Tel** *(086) 222-6116*

Opened in the 1920s and still run by the same family, this small restaurant serves *udon*, *soba*, and *donburi* and recommends the *inaka soba* (country *soba*) to visitors; *soba kaiseki* is served in the evenings. The owner is a sake connoisseur and will make recommendations to customers for labels to try.

OKAYAMA Kappo Fuji

6-11 Tamachi, 700-0825 **Tel** *(086) 233-3434*

The ethos at Kappo Fuji is to provide delicious food which is not limited to the local dishes of Okayama; this is seen in the variety of Japanese food served here. Options include beef steak and even whale fried in ginger. *Kaiseki* courses are also available. There is a choice of seating in partitioned booths or at the counter.

OSAKA Chigusayaki

4-11-18 Tenjinbashi, 530-0041 **Tel** *(06) 6351-4072*

This much-loved establishment in Tenjinbashisuji shopping arcade, in business for over 50 years, remains faithful to the original concept of *okonomiyaki*, which literally translates as "cook what you like." Chigusa offers you the chance to cook your own Osaka-style *okonomiyaki* on a hot plate; friendly staff will show you how it's done.

OSAKA Hermanos

2-3-23 Dotonbori, 542-0071 **Tel** *(06) 6213-9612*

Hermanos offers a good variety of Mexican dishes such as *burritos*, *tacos*, avocado salads, and Spanish *enchiladas*. The garlic *chorizo* sausages are delicious and, like all the food here, are handmade using natural ingredients. There are good options for vegetarians. Friendly service, cheerful atmosphere, and good value.

OSAKA Malaysia Boleh

1-4-20 Oyodominami, 531-0075 **Tel** *(06) 6450-1128*

This authentic restaurant has Malaysian decor and specially-imported furniture. The seasonal menu uses fresh ingredients, with rice-based options such as *nashi goren* (spicy fried rice), coconut rice, and a range of curries. *Kangkung belacan*, wok-fried water spinach in a pungent sauce of shrimp paste and hot chilli peppers, is a popular choice.

OSAKA Namaste

3-7-46 Jusou Honmachi, Yodogawa-ku, 534-0000 **Tel** *(06) 6886-6609*

Authentic Indian food prepared and served by friendly Indian staff, with 23 varieties of curry to choose from, including vegetarian options. The chef recommends the chicken hyderabadi and eggplant tomato curry, as well as the tandoori *murgh* and *reshmi* kebab. Tell the waiter how spicy you would like the food to be.

OSAKA Yancha Gontaro

6F Umeshinkai-kan, 2-7-2 Sonezaki, 530-0057 **Tel** *(06) 6364-6868*

Yancha Gontaro is a stylish *izakaya* of modern Japanese design which combines nourishing, homely food with a relaxed, cheerful atmosphere. The house specialty, *torichan-yaki*, a stir-fry of chicken and cabbage, is a must. Separate dining booths are available. Friendly, young staff, and good value food.

OSAKA Bull Blanc J's

2-6-19 Minamihorie, 550-0015 **Tel** *(06) 6533-8400*

Bull Blanc J's tasteful interior and mellow lighting make it a good choice for an intimate dinner. The "Japonisme" cuisine melds Japanese and French influences. An extensive menu combines local seasonal vegetables with the finest imported ingredients, including Norwegian salmon, Iberian ham, and Hungarian chicken.

OSAKA Mimiu Honten

4-6-18 Hirano-cho, 541-0046 **Tel** *(06) 6231-5770*

This high-class *udon* restaurant was first opened over 200 years ago and the well-known Osaka dish called *udon-suki* was first made here. Mimiu Honten is uncompromising in choosing only the best ingredients, and the flour and noodles are handmade. Dishes, including chicken, shrimp, clams, and seasonal vegetables, are made at your table.

OSAKA Umenohana

2F Snow Crystal Building, 2-6-20 Umeda, 530-0001 **Tel** *(06) 6343-6320*

Umenohana is famous for its *kaiseki* courses consisting of a range of *yuba* (sheets of dried soy milk), tofu (bean curd), and vegetable dishes. Great attention to detail goes into every aspect, from the efficient service to the look of the food and the harmonious Japanese interior. A healthy, inexpensive choice for vegetarians and non-vegetarians.

TSUWANO Shouintei

Ro 70, Ushiroda, Tsuwano-cho, 699-5605 **Tel** *(0856) 72-1661*

This charming restaurant in an old samurai house uses only natural ingredients from the Tsuwano area to make local *kaiseki* cuisine. A beautiful view of the garden can be enjoyed while dining. For those not requiring a meal, there is also the option of drinking freshly-prepared *matcha* (high-grade green tea) in a traditional tea-ceremony room.

TSUWANO Yuki

Ro 271-4 Hon-machi, Tsuwano-cho, 699-5605 **Tel** *(0856) 72-0162*

Carp sashimi and carp miso soup are specialties at Yuki, whose menu also incorporates fresh mountain vegetables. Try the *yamafugu* ("mountain blowfish") which is not fish at all, but a jelly made from pressed vegetables and is so named because it resembles the light gelatinous texture of *fugu*.

YAMAGUCHI Karatachi no Hana

2F Chimakiya, 3-3 Nakaichi-machi, 753-0086 **Tel** *(083) 921-5803*

This buffet-style restaurant is ideal for vegetarians and health-conscious people in general. At dinnertime there is an array of as many as 45 different dishes to choose from. The mainly vegetable ingredients come from carefully-selected natural produce of the Chugoku region. The homemade tofu soft cream is a popular choice for dessert.

SHIKOKU

KOCHI Tsukasa

Hariyama Cho 1-2-15, 780-0822 **Tel** *(088) 873-4351*

This handsome sashimi restaurant, in a charming old building just a one-minute walk from Harimayabashi, serves a selection of local specialty sashimi and delicately-flavored Japanese dishes. This restaurant has an extremely good reputation and deservedly so, because the food is light and delicious, and the portions are generous.

KOCHI Tokugetsuro

Hariyama Cho 1-17-3, 780-0822 **Tel** *(088) 882-0101*

Like something out of a picture book, this sashimi restaurant is so pretty – the building is old and handsome, the koi carp water garden is utterly peaceful, and the interior is meticulously detailed. There are even some beautiful plum bonsai. A sophisticated dining experience like this doesn't come cheap, but the food is utterly sumptuous.

KOTOHIRA Soba Restaurants

Street at foot of stairs outside Kotohira-gu shrine

Shikoku is best known for its 88-shrine pilgrimage, the most popular in Japan and a trip which dedicated Buddhists have been making for hundreds of years. These restaurants have an equally long history, and hungry visitors to the Kotohira-gu shrine can stop off here to partake in some delicious handmade *soba* and delicate green tea.

MATSUYAMA Marco

Nibancho 2-7-17, 790-0002 Tel (089) 932-2882

An extremely popular meat and seafood restaurant with stylish, modern-Japanese interior, where you can watch the chefs preparing the Asian-fusion dishes in the open-plan kitchen. Food presentation is impeccable, and prices are well below what you might expect to pay. It can get busy on weekends so booking is advisable.

MATSUYAMA Sukekaku

Sanban Cho 2 Chome 5-4, 790-0003 Tel (089) 932-8118

There's an elegant, ambiently-lit interior at this restaurant in Matsuyama city, which serves up a host of local delicacies, including sashimi, cooked fish, and meat. The *shima aji* dishes (horse mackerel) are a recommended local specialty, and the *hirame* (plaice) dishes are also delicious. Tasty barbequed vegetables are also on offer for vegetarians.

OZU Aburaya

Ozu-Honmachi 2 Chome, 795-0012 Tel (089) 323-1139

Aburaya is a beautiful, traditionally-decorated restaurant in the historic town of Ozu serving a selection of tasty Japanese and Western-fusion dishes. The dessert menu is particularly mouthwatering. Popular with locals and tourists alike, the *kaiseki* options are great value for money. Open for both lunch and dinner; closed on Wednesday.

TAKAMATSU Kanaizumi Udon

Konya Machi 9-3, 760-0044 Tel (087) 868-0123

Shikoku is renowned throughout Japan for its delicious *udon* noodles and you can sample some of the region's best right here. Hot, tasty, and freshly made right before your eyes, with prices this cheap there's little room for complaint. Tempura, *oden*, and soup are available for those not in the mood for slurping.

TAKAMATSU Nakamura Kome Takamatsu

Sunport 2-1 Symbol Tower, 29th floor, 760-0019 Tel (087) 825-5656

This elegant sushi and seafood restaurant has tasteful, Western-style decoration and a stunning view of the ocean – come in the early evening to enjoy an unforgettable sunset with your meal. Food is fresh and exquisitely presented and the waiting staff are charming and attentive. Set meals offer great value.

TOKUSHIMA Takashima Kohiten

Yaoya Machi 2-20-1, 770-0841 Tel (088) 652-1071

This mall but sleek coffee shop in Tokushima city emanates pre-war charm. It is massively popular with the locals and offers a selection of delicious, freshly-brewed coffees, tasty fruit juices, a huge selection of to-die-for grilled sandwiches, and other café-style snacks. Open every morning at 6.30am, with last orders at 7.30pm.

UWAJIMA Kadoya

Nishiki Machi 8-1, 798-0034 Tel (0895) 22-1543

You'll find this reasonably-priced restaurant in the quaint, historic town of Uwajima. It serves a selection of Japanese food and a number of local specialties – the seafood dishes are of a particularly high quality. There are also a number of beef dishes to choose from. The interior is clean and inviting. Open daily but last orders are taken at 9pm.

KYUSHU

BEPPU Kogetsu

8-1-26 Ishigakihigashi, Beppu-shi, 874-0919 Tel (0977) 25-2735

At this restaurant every measure is taken to produce natural and healthy food: the noodles and *chashu* pork are handmade; the Chinese cabbage in the *kimchee* is home-grown; and the water is drawn from a private well. The soup, made with a soy and salt base to the same secret recipe for years, is rich and flavorsome.

BEPPU Fugumatsu

3-6-14 Kitahama, Beppu-shi, 874-0920 Tel (0977) 21-1717

An opportunity to sample *fugu*, or blowfish, even out of season, is provided by this well-established restaurant, which has this potentially-deadly delicacy delivered fresh from the nearby Bungo Straits, year-round. The tangy citrus fruit *kabosu*, a specialty of Oita prefecture, complements the light flavor of the *fugu* wonderfully.

CHIRAN Takian

6239 Chiran-cho, Kawanabe-gun, 897-0300 Tel (0993) 83-3186

Local dishes here are served in the drawing room of an Edo Period samurai house, with a lovely view of the *karensui*–style garden. Try the popular Takian set which comes with its own low table, or if a sweet snack is all that is needed, opt for the *zenzai* (sweet adzuki bean soup with pieces of rice cake).

Key to Price Guide *see p330* **Key to Symbols** *see back cover flap*

FUKUOKA Isshin Furan

2-6-5 Daimyo, Chuo-ku, 810-0041 Tel (092) 733-3768

If eager to taste Fukuoka's famous *tonkotsu* (pork) *ramen* but shy of the outdoor stalls, try the increasingly-popular Isshin Furan, which offers authenticity with a minimum of fuss. Order your *ramen* from photograph-labeled buttons on a coin-operated machine, with the main options color-coded according to the broth recipe used.

FUKUOKA Jamin Kah
¥¥

BF Nanpu Building, 1-1-20 Daimyo, Chuo-ku, Fukuoka-shi, 810-0041 Tel (092) 771-3108

Serving excellent Thai food at a reasonable price since 1983, Jamin Kah is Fukuoka's longest-running ethnic restaurant. With fish fresh from the Genkai Strait, native Thai chefs prepare delicious seafood such as the Phuket-style charcoal grill. The "Asian plate" set is great value and, for dessert, don't miss the superb banana egg rolls.

FUKUOKA Jan Jan
¥¥

1F Ogawa Building, 1-1-15 Maizuru, Chuo-ku, 810-0073 Tel (092) 762-8080

Run by a friendly young couple, the menu at this cozy restaurant spans Indian, Nepalese, and Sri Lankan cuisines to include tandoori chicken, shish kebabs, and a wide range of curries, made with homemade curry powder and complemented by delicious, homebaked nan bread. The lentil curry and chicken tikka are highly recommended.

FUKUOKA Bassin
¥¥¥

1-9-63 Daimyo, Chuo-ku, Fukuoka-shi, 810-0041 Tel (092) 739-3210

An interior of elegant minimalist design creates the perfect ambience for this sophisticated Japanese-European fusion restaurant. The Parma ham with bamboo shoot is excellent, as are the succulent beef steaks and grilled chicken, both the produce of Saga Prefecture. The manager is friendly and speaks good English.

KAGOSHIMA Tenmonkan Mujaki

5-8 Sennichi-cho, Kagoshima-shi, 892-0843 Tel (099) 222-6904

Throughout its five floors this building offers affordable food ranging fromh Japanese fare such as *okonomiyaki* and *donburi* to Western and Chinese dishes. But Tenmonkan Mujaki is most popular for its shaved ice invention known as *shirokuma* ("polar bear"), a specialty since 1949. Don't miss the chance to try this dessert in any of 18 flavors.

KAGOSHIMA Yudofu Gonbee
¥¥

8-12 Higashisengoku-cho, Kagoshima-shi, 890-0000 Tel (099) 222-3867

This restaurant, specializing in homemade tofu, has been in business since 1918 and the warm, nostalgic atmosphere attests to this. Only the best *konbu* (kelp) is used to make the stock, and the food includes up to 12 seasonal vegetables at any time. The dipping sauce, made with the citrus fruit *yuzu*, is wonderful.

KAGOSHIMA Karen
¥¥¥

JA Food Plaza 3F-4F, 3-12 Yamanokuchi, Kagoshima-shi, 892-0844 Tel (099) 223-8877

Run by the Japan Agricultural Cooperatives' Kagoshima branch, Karen has access to Kagoshima's finest black cattle beef and black pork. The Kagoshima black pork *shabu-shabu* (simmered meat), black pork loin, and first-rate Kagoshima black cattle beef are of unsurpassed tenderness and succulence. Sets include rice, vegetables, soup, and dessert.

KUMAMOTO Fudokoro Koba

5-8 Minami Tsuboimachi, Kumamoto-shi, 860-0848 Tel (096) 353-5497

Near Kumamoto castle, this restaurant's history extends over 17 generations back to the Edo period. For over 200 years, the family has specialized in *namafu* (wheat starch), which is used in one of the menu's main features, *shojin ryori* (Zen vegetarian cooking). The Shokado Bento includes fish and seasonal vegetables.

KUMAMOTO Teshio Ryouri Kogyan
¥¥¥

7-13 Minami Tsuboimachi, Kumamoto-shi, 860-0848 Tel (096) 352-8820

The owner has traveled the country to research the finest seasonal ingredients, which he has delivered fresh every morning. The menu is changed daily to bring out the best of these. As well as the variety of seafoods, numerous *basashi* (horsemeat) dishes are also available to try in this restaurant, which has an intimate and relaxed atmosphere.

MOUNT ASO Nouka Restaurant Tangoyama
¥¥¥

285 Mikubo, Aso-shi, 869-2302 Tel (0967) 32-5070

Raising red cattle on its own farm, this farmhouse restaurant serves deliciously tender beef of the highest standard, along with organic rice and vegetables in a charming setting of wooden beams and hanging paper lanterns. The beef is lightly fried and served with salt and pepper or *ponzu* (citrus fruit and vinegar sauce), which bring out its rich flavor.

NAGASAKI Harbin
¥¥¥

2F Hamacho Bldg, Yorozuya-machi, Nagasaki-shi, 850-0852 Tel (095) 824-6650

Harbin has a record dating back to 1959 and an intimate ambience, with an elegant interior illuminated by soft lamplight. The first floor has a café and bar, while the upstairs restaurant offers a choice of Russian and French dishes. The bortsch soup, a perfect blend of sweetness and tartness complemented by homemade rye bread, is a must.

NAGASAKI Kouzan Rou

13-13 Shinchi-machi, Nagasaki-shi, 850-0842 Tel (095) 820-3735

This restaurant, located by the East Gate of Chinatown, serves Chinese food in the Nagasaki tradition. It is a great place to sample *champon*, a Nagasaki invention of partially Chinese origin. The wealth of ingredients mixed to make this dish includes vegetables, noodles, and seafood such as shark fin, prawn, squid, and oyster.

NAGASAKI Nagasaki Shippoku Hamakatsu

Kajiya-machi 6-50, Nagasaki-shi, 850-0831 **Tel** *(095) 826-8321*

Shippoku cuisine, Nagasaki's unique blend of Portuguese, Dutch, and Chinese influences, can be enjoyed here at the original branch of Hamakatsu which, before developing its successful nationwide franchise of *tonkatsu* (pork cutlet) restaurants, was a sophisticated restaurant dating back to the Meiji Period. Free refills of rice, miso soup, and cabbage.

NAGASAKI Ichiriki

8-20 Suwa-cho, Nagasaki-shi, 380-0873 **Tel** *(095) 824-0226*

Established in 1813, this is Nagaski's oldest restaurant and was frequented by key samurai in the Meiji Restoration, although the building was remodeled in the 1920s. An excellent place to try Nagasaki's specialty of *shipppoku*; courses in this style combine sashimi, soup, and tender stewed pork and are served on low red-lacquered tables.

SAGA Steak Sho

1780 Oozatokou, Niri-cho, Imari-shi, 848-0032 **Tel** *(0955) 22-6661*

Imari beef is classed among the highest ranks of Japanese beef, with cattle raised on only the highest quality feed to produce a deliciously tender and flavorsome beef. The steak set is good value, as is the Imari beef "healthy course," which includes appetizer, soup, salad, steak, rice, dessert, and coffee.

YUFUIN Yamaga Ryouri Yu no Takean

Kame no Ii Besso, 2633-1 Kawakami, Yufuin-machi, Yufu-shi, 879-5102 **Tel** *(0977) 84-2970*

The quaint cottage of Kame no Ii Besso ("Well of the Turtle" Villa) was rebuilt in 1999, complete with thatched roof, and is home to the restaurant Yu no Takean. A perfect, cozy setting in which to enjoy nourishing, healthy food such as carp, homade sesame tofu, steamed Bungo beef, and seasonal vegetables. The Yamaga Bento is recommended.

OKINAWA

CHATAN Transit Café

2-220-2F Miyagi, 904-0113 **Tel** *(098) 936-5076*

This stylish restaurant is on the Sunabe sea wall, with one of the most fashionable bathrooms you'll find! You can sit inside or find a table on the balcony, looking on to the sea. Popular with domestic Japanese tourists as well as residents. Excellent food and service, and a relaxed atmosphere makes this a must-visit on any trip to Okinawa.

ISHIGAKI-JIMA Go! Go! Café

1F 198 Okawa, Ishigaki, 907-0311 **Tel** *(098) 083-5126*

This café has a huge menu, featuring Western (particularly Hawaiian) cuisine, as well as Japanese food. They serve an excellent Camembert and bacon sandwich, and arguably the best and only genuine hamburger is available here. Most dishes are served with potatoes, salad, and tea, coffee, or espresso (the latter is not for the meek!).

ISHIGAKI-JIMA Club Med Kabira

1 Kabira Ishizaki, Ishigaki, 907-0453 **Tel** *(098) 084-4600*

Although part of the huge Club Med Kabira resort, the restaurant also welcomes non-guests. Both Japanese and Western tastes are catered for, with the pizzas here being particularly good. The atmosphere is always quite lively, with many hotel guests chatting with other visitors. A little expensive but definitely worth it.

NAHA Food Colosseum

3rd floor, DFS Galleria Okinawa, 4-1 Omoromachi, 900-0006 **Tel** *(098) 860-1441*

A mainstay for any traveler in Japan, this excellent restaurant and food court is well worth a visit. It features Western, Japanese, Chinese, and numerous other styles of food, so there's something for everyone. You can also just pop in to enjoy one of their delicious fresh fruit smoothies.

NAHA Nanak

1-3-1 Esprit Court B1, Kokusai Dori, Naha, 900-0014 **Tel** *(098) 861-2579*

For the best Indian food in Okinawa, you just have to walk on to Kokusai Dori in Naha. A Nepalese chef cooks an exquisite range of curries, from mild to very spicy, washed down with a refreshing *lassi*. Slightly higher prices than the norm, but a firm favorite for an evening meal in Naha.

NAHA Thai Thai

Okinawa Suntory Building 2F, 2-1-15 Route 58, Naha, 900-0032 **Tel** *(098) 941-0232*

A visit to Thai Thai is certainly an experience. You can't miss the place as you're driving on the main road through Naha – there are flaming torches and vines covering the outside of the building, and an eclectic decor inside, plus (of course) a good selection of Thai food. Make sure you take your camera and a healthy appetite.

NAHA Ryukyu Cuisine Mie

1-8-8 Kumoji, Naha, 900-0015 **Tel** *(098) 867-1356*

For those people wanting something a little special during their trip to Okinawa, this wooden restaurant on two floors in the center of Naha serves traditional Okinawan food in excellent surroundings. Each restaurant booth is separated from the others by sliding doors. Reservations are highly recommended.

Key to Price Guide *see p330* **Key to Symbols** *see back cover flap*

TAMAGUSUKU Hamabe no Chaya

Tamagusuku 2-1, Tamagusuku, Nanjo-shi, 901-0604 **Tel** *(098) 948-2073*

This café couldn't be closer to the sea, with most of the seating facing the window across the ocean. A famous Okinawan artist/designer's favorite haunt, this café is now always full of domestic and international tourists. Snacks, light meals, and a range of teas and coffees can be enjoyed in a laid-back atmosphere.

TOMIGUSUKU Yoshinoya

3-25-12 Gushi, Naha-shi, 901-0146 **Tel** *(098) 852-1381*

One of 12 branches in Okinawa, Yoshinoya is a mainstay in Japan. The clientele is very mixed, from businessmen getting some lunch on the run, to families grabbing food on a day out. Noodles, soups, and a variety of broths are the staple diet in this 24-hour chain of restaurants.

URASOE Applemint Café

5-5-1 Maki Port, Urasoe, 901-2131 **Tel** *(098) 878-4452*

This organic café, which is a very rare thing in Okinawa, has a variety of excellent dishes. Lunch or dinner sets will provide you with between three and eight types of food. The restaurant has a very homely feel to it, and it even has its own garden (a rarity in Okinawa, where land is so scarce).

URASOE Café y te Soluna

4-34-2 Gusukuma, Urasoe, 901-0233 **Tel** *(098) 879-6495*

A Mexican restaurant, offering a wide range of meat, seafood, and vegetarian dishes. There is also a huge variety of teas, coffees, and *chai*. This is a great place to come for a meal, or simply a quiet coffee and some escapism from the hustle and bustle of Okinawa.

NORTHERN HONSHU

AIZU-WAKAMATSU Kiriya

2-34 Uwamachi Fukushima, 965-0041 **Tel** *(0242) 25-3851*

This area is well known for its *soba* (buckwheat noodles), and Kiriya is famous here. Kiriya uses the best grade *soba* for specialties like *Iide gongen soba*, made with paulownia powder and *aizu ganko*, 100 percent *soba*. Regular *soba*, both hot and cold, is also available. This friendly restaurant is downtown near the Century Hotel.

AIZU-WAKAMATSU Mitsutaya

1-1-25 Omachi, 965-0000 **Tel** *(0242) 27-1345*

Housed in an old miso factory and about 150 years old, this popular restaurant specializes in *dengaku*. Vegetables, deep-fried cubes of tofu, fish, and *konnyaku* (jellied devil's tongue starch) are put on a skewer, dipped in miso paste, and grilled over charcoal right before your eyes – if you're sitting at the counter.

DEWA-SAN Sanko-in

Haguro-machi, Yamagata **Tel** *(0235) 62-2302*

If you make it to Dewa-san you really should try the Buddhist *shojin ryori*. Strictly vegetarian, it doesn't even permit onions and garlic. The *yamabushi* who favor this cuisine are tough customers, and the food is delicious. If you get to the top try the *shojin ryori* at Sanrojo, near Yudono Shrine, with similar prices to Sanko-in.

HIROSAKI Kenta

3 Okeya-cho Aomori, 036-8004 **Tel** *(0172) 35-9514*

Sitting on the edge of Hirosaki's entertainment district, this inexpensive restaurant is very popular because of its excellent *robatayaki* – you point to what you want and it's grilled before your eyes then served, all using a wooden paddle. This place can fill quickly, especially on weekends. There is another branch around the corner.

HIROSAKI Live House Yamauta

1-2-4 Omachi Aomori, 036-8004 **Tel** *(0172) 36-1835*

Since 1964 Yamauta has been home to great music, when Yamda Chisato started to have a place to play his *tsugaru-jamisen*, the northern style of *shamisen* (sort of Japanese bluegrass and blues). The *izakaya*-style food is very good, and don't be surprised if your waiter or waitress jumps up on the stage and starts pounding on a *shamisen*.

KAKUNODATE Aoyagi Samurai Manor

Higashi Katuraku-cho, Akita, 014-0325 **Tel** *(0187) 55-5241*

After seeing the samurai homes and buildings in Kakunodate, try the satisfying and reasonably-priced *udon* here. The specialty is *inaniwa udon*, a regional blend of mushroom, onion, and bamboo shoots. Vegetarians should enjoy *sansai udon*, made with mountain vegetables. Open for lunch only. Closed weekdays in winter.

KAKUNODATE Sakura-tei

Yokomachi 18 Akita, 014-0323 **Tel** *(0187) 53-2970*

A classic old building with *tatami*-mat dining rooms looking over a Japanese garden and a pond stocked with koi. Good food, including free-range chicken. Try the *oyakodon* (chicken and egg atop a bowl of rice) or *kiritampo nabe* (stew cooked in clay pot with everything thrown in). There are also sets with homemade noodles.

KAKUNODATE Ryotei Inaho

Tamachi Kami-cho Akita, 014-0311 **Tel** *(0187) 54-3311*

This 50-year-old *ryotei* offers delicious meals based on classic northern cuisine. The building is classic, too, with tasteful flower arrangements and decor. The menu can include wild vegetables and duck. Choose from a variety of set menus. There is a beautiful Japanese garden to enjoy as you eat.

MATSUSHIMA Donjiki Chaya

Entsuin-mae Miyagi, 981-0213 **Tel** *(022) 354-5855*

Have an inexpensive lunch in a 400-year-old thatched-roof building. It's close to the Entsuin Temple, a five-minute walk from the station. It serves various *soba* meals and *odango*: pounded rice (golf-ball size) balls on a skewer, covered with sweetened sauce of seasame, soy, or red bean. Great for a snack. There is an English menu.

MATSUSHIMA Ungai

67 Aza-chonai Miyagi, 981-0213 **Tel** *(022) 353-2626*

On the grounds of Entsuin Temple, this restaurant serves classic Buddhist vegetarian cuisine: many small dishes with various vegetables and tofu. Dine seated in a *tatami* room, looking out to a temple garden. There are three set meals to choose from. None are cheap, but eating here gets you free admission to the temple. Reservations required.

MORIOKA Chokurian

Odori, 5 minutes east of the castle, 020-0034 **Tel** *(019) 624-0441*

One of the most famous places for Morioka's specialty: *wanko-soba*. One tiny bowl of *soba* after another is placed before you. Choose from a variety of ingredients to add, slurp it up, and reach for the next bowl. Delicious fun, but bring a good appetite because it's all-you-can-eat. There are also standard size (and cheaper) selections.

NIKKO Gyoshin-Tei

2339-1 Sannai Tochigi, 321-1433 **Tel** *(0288) 53-3751*

A little difficult to find, but well worth it, this is a four-minute walk northeast of Rinnoji Temple, next to Meiji-no Yakata (another good restaurant). Gyoshin-Tei specializes in *kaiseki* and Buddhist vegetarian cuisine. You're sure to have *yuba* (to tofu as cream is to milk). Served in a *tatami* room beside a beautiful garden of pines, moss, and bonsai.

SADO ISLAND Shichiuemon

643 Saiwai-cho Niigata, 952-0604 **Tel** *(0259) 86-2046*

Shichiuemon is famous for its *soba* noodles, made from buckwheat flour which is ground fresh each day. The noodles are served both hot and cold. Ask anyone in town and they'll direct you to this local favorite in a handsome old building. It's not fancy, just very good.

SENDAI Tachibana

3-3-25 Ichiban-cho 5F Miyagi, 980-8477 **Tel** *(022) 223-3706*

In a good location right on Ichiban-cho, Sendai's main shopping and amusement area, this 5th-floor modern sushi restaurant is comfortable and welcoming. Lunch is less expensive than dinner, and good if you are squeamish about traditional raw fish sushi because they also serve *aburi-zushi*, lightly-fried seafood sushi. Reservations recommended.

TONO Ichiriki

5-27 Chuo-dori, Iwate, 028-0522 **Tel** *(0198) 62-2008*

Just a five-minute walk from Tono station, you can expect good, well-prepared food. Ichiriki uses local freshwater fish (the catch of the day) and locally-harvested wild vegetables. Especially good is *kamameshi*, a steaming pot of rice in a clay pot covered with a heavy wooden lid, mixed with scallops, chestnuts, and other fresh ingredients.

TSURUOKA Kanazawaya

Haguro-machi, Yamagatai, 997-0166 **Tel** *(0235) 62-4564*

The north is famous for its *soba*, and this restaurant is famous for its *soba* in the north, so enjoy! There's a variety of hot and cold *soba* dishes on the menu – all of them excellent. The restaurant is about 15 minutes by car from the JR station, just over the river in Haguro.

TSURUOKA Hyakkenbori

Town Square, opposite Chido Museum Yamagata, 997-0035 **Tel** *(0235) 29-0888*

This pleasant, modern concrete and wood restaurant sits beside a pond. The interior is bright but comfortable. In good weather you can sit outside on a deck beside the pond. The menu features fresh fish dishes and locally-produced chicken in dishes the region is known for. The lunch menu is particularly good value.

HOKKAIDO

HAKODATE Hakodate Beer

5-22 Ohtemachi, Meijikan Ave, 040-0064 **Tel** *(0138) 23-8000*

This charming brick building was the first place serving the locally-brewed Hakodate beer, among an extensive selection of beers and ales. Enjoy some delicious fresh seafood dishes or more Western-style fare, in a cozy environment. The smiling staff make customers feel at home. Stained-glass windows contribute to a European vibe.

Key to Price Guide *see p330* **Key to Symbols** *see back cover flap*

HAKODATE Kihara Sushi
Yukawa, 2-1-2 (Yu no Kawa Hotsprings), 046-0011 **Tel** *(0138) 57-8825*

If it's good sushi you're after, then the port town of Hakodate offers Japan's most delicious fare. This cozy and welcoming Japanese-style sushi restaurant offers a comprehensive selection of exquisite sashimi, and the squid is as fresh as it comes – direct from the restaurant's tank! The menu features 52 types of sake. Closed Wednesdays.

HAKODATE Gotoken
4-5 Suehiro-cho **Tel** *(0138) 23-1106*

Authentic French and Russian dishes are included on the very varied menu at this restaurant, which was established in 1879 and is housed in a period building. You can eat in the restaurant or in the more casual lounge – the latter is famous for its good-value curry.

KUSHIRO Tototo
1-2-7 Ashino, Kushiro, 085-0014 **Tel** *(0154) 39-2288*

Close to Kushiro river, this unpretentious eaterie offers excellent and affordable meat, fish, and tofu dishes. Unusually for Japan, vegetarians are well catered for. Minimally decorated in elegant Japanese style, the soft lighting lends a romantic ambience. Open until 3am on weekends; be prepared to wait a little longer for service during busy periods.

NISEKO Café Jojo's, NAC (Niseko Adventure Centre)
53-179 Aza Yamada, Kutchan-cho Abuta-gun Hokkaido, 044-0081 **Tel** *(0136) 23-2093*

This perennially popular, Australian-run café-style restaurant has a funky, modern interior and a stunning view of dramatic Mt Yotei. Choose from a wide range of health-conscious Western and Asian-fusian dishes made with the freshest local ingredients, and complement it with an in-house specialty smoothie or imported beer or wine.

RISHIRI/REBUN ISLANDS Kanoutei
Rishiri-fuji-cho, Oshidomari, Azaminato Machi, Rishiri Island, 097-0101 **Tel** *(0163) 82-1064*

Rishiri and Rebun islands are nothing short of a fisherman's paradise and the quality of the seafood restaurants on these far-flung shores reflects the abundance of sealife in this area. This simple and very cheaply-priced restaurant serves a seafood menu rich in seasonal specialties, and the generously portioned seafood *ramen* is not to be missed.

SAPPORO Voyage
1st Floor Matui Building, West 5 chome, North 22, Kita-ku, 001-0022 **Tel** *(011) 758-2500*

Soup curry is a phenomenon which has exploded in Hokkaido in recent years, and it all started with the Indian-inspired Voyage. Hugely popular with Sapporo's city dwellers, a visit to this soup curry store is now the quintessential Hokkaido dining experience. Sample a bowl of this spicy local specialty, bursting with vegetables, meat, or seafood.

SAPPORO La Piazza
1-35 West 11 chome, South 23, Chuo-ku, 064-0923 **Tel** *(011) 563-7717*

Simply the best Italian in Hokkaido, this friendly restaurant serves over 30 handmade pasta dishes, pizza worth your first-born, scrumptious olive paste *bruschetta*, and a wealth of other things you didn't think were served in Japan. The head chef is Italian and all the other chefs go to Italy for training once a year.

SAPPORO Monty Python
B1 Minami 3 Building, West 4, South 3, Chuo-ku, 060-0063 **Tel** *(011) 231-1538*

Blink and you'll miss this tiny, chic French restaurant tucked away in the entertainment district of Susukino. But you'd be missing out on their delectable menu, with a choice of cheese and wines that makes you forget you're in Asia and not Europe. The waiters are absolutely charming, and quality not quantity is the philosophy here. Closed Tuesdays.

SAPPORO Mikuni
Stellar Place, JR tower, Sapporo Station, 2-5, Kita 5 jo-nishi, Chuo-ku, Sapporo, 060-0005 **Tel** *(011) 251 0392*

Located on the 9th floor of the JR Tower, this luxury restaurant has mainly French fare. The view is show-stopping – a panorama of Hokkaido's geometric metropolis, complemented by an elegant interior. If that doesn't justify the price tag alone, the gastronomic delights certainly do, and the sinfully-delicious dessert menu is sure to tempt.

SAPPORO 21 Club
25F Novotel Minami 10-jo, Nishi 6, 064-0810 **Tel** *(011) 561-1000*

This sleek Japanese restaurant is the last word in sophistication; it's also Sapporo's highest, offering some wonderful views. While prices are high, the food is exquisitely prepared, and the *teppanyaki* is worth every penny. There's a fine selection of wines and also wine advisors to help you. The bar offers an elegant location for pre-dinner drinks.

SOUNKYOU Yama no Shokubou
Kamikawa-cho, Sounkyou, 078-1701 **Tel** *(01658) 5-3521*

This small restaurant close to the expansive and breathtakingly-beautiful Daisetsuzan National Park is very popular with the locals and easy on the wallet. It serves tasty *ramen* (noodle soup), curry, and meat dishes that really hit the spot after a hard day's hiking, or even a lazy day soaking in one of the many delightful hot springs in the area.

TOYA NATIONAL PARK Michel Bras
Windsor Hotel, Shimizu, Toyako-cho, Abuta-gun, 049-5722 **Tel** *(0142) 73-1111*

This Michelin-starred restaurant is rated one of the 10 best French restaurants in the world located outside France. With credentials this good, further praise is barely needed but the food is sublime, and the wine list rivals the best that Paris can offer. The view of the beautiful Lake Toya National Park is nothing short of spectacular.

SHOPPING IN JAPAN

Unusual glassware

Shopping in Japan is an amazing experience. With as many traditional arts and crafts products as contemporary and imported items, there is the most fascinating choice imaginable. Equally interesting is the range of shops – from glitzy department stores and huge shoppings malls to roadside stalls and tiny craft workshops. Within 24 hours, the constant greetings of *irasshaimase* (Welcome!) on entering a shop are either driving visitors crazy or have become part of the general background noise. Japan is no longer the most expensive country in the world, but still the price of certain commodities may shock. Some goods made in Japan, such as cameras and other electronic items, are actually cheaper to buy abroad. On the other hand, it is possible to buy original and unusual souvenirs surprisingly inexpensively. For details on shopping in Tokyo, see pages 104–107; for Kyoto, see pages 180–83.

Canal City shopping complex in Fukuoka, Kyushu

SHOPPING HOURS

Supermarkets and department stores are usually closed for just one weekday a month or one weekday every two months – the day varies, depending on local custom. A number of specialty shops – boutiques included – may not open on Sundays and national holidays. Family-run businesses are generally open daily, including Saturdays, Sundays, and national holidays.

Opening hours of most shops are 10am to 8pm. Department stores usually close one hour earlier. Convenience stores – chains such as **Seven-Eleven** and **Lawson's** – are open seven days a week, 24 hours a day. Vending machines *(see p315)* are widespread in hotels and at roadsides, offering drinks, some food, plus batteries, CDs, and other practical items 24 hours a day.

PRICES AND SALES TAX

In department stores and boutiques, and in inner-city areas, prices are nearly always marked in Arabic numerals. In local shops and supermarkets, and in areas where non-Japanese are few and far between, prices may be written only in kanji characters. When shopkeepers are unable to make themselves understood verbally to visitors, they may type the numbers on a calculator, write them down, or sign with their fingers. If you are traveling off the beaten track, it is useful to learn the characters for the numbers one to ten, one hundred, and one thousand, and for the word *yen (see pp412–16)*.

All purchasable items and services are subject to a government-imposed consumption tax of five percent.

The price displayed should by law now include the tax, although in practice this may not be the case.

In the booming 1980s, all prices were fixed, but in more recessive times, the emphasis is on discount shopping, with stores lowering prices to match strong competition. Flea markets and antique fairs are the only places where haggling is accepted as an integral part of the proceedings.

HOW TO PAY

The Japanese yen continues to be regarded as a stable currency, despite various ups and downs since the late 1980s. Cash is by far the easiest method to pay for goods. There need be no anxieties about being given the right change; Japanese are scrupulously honest – especially in handling guests from abroad.

Prices displayed in Arabic numerals in a sweet shop

Inside Mikimoto Pearl shop in Ginza, Tokyo's premier shopping district

It is customary, when paying, for a small tray to be offered; you should place money on it, and your change will be returned without hand-to-hand contact. International credit cards are still surprisingly unpopular in smaller shops. In general, the larger the emporium, the wider the range of international cards taken. VISA, American Express, Diners Club, and MasterCard are the most widely accepted.

RIGHTS AND REFUNDS

Refunds are not encouraged but are legal if the sales slip can be produced, and the item in question has not been tampered with. Some stores give redeemable coupons rather than money, so that they do not lose out. Without a receipt, return is impossible.

TAX-FREE SHOPPING

Japan tax-free shops offer a good range of domestically made and imported brand items all free of the five percent sales tax added elsewhere. You will need to show your passport. Authorized outlets are mainly located in shopping districts and urban areas frequented by tourists, as well as the international airports. The best-known in the capital are the **Tokyo International Arcade** (near the Imperial Hotel) and **Laox** (see p107) for electronic goods; and in Kansai, the **Kyoto Craft Center** (see pp182–3). It is a good idea, however, to compare the prices of goods in these shops with those in

specialty and discount stores, as the latter may work out the same or even cheaper.

In some shops, particularly department stores, you may have to pay the full price for an item, then obtain a refund and customs document from a tax-exemption counter. This document is retained by customs as you leave Japan.

EXPORTING LARGE ITEMS

Most specialty duty-free outlets will arrange packaging of bulky goods for export if required. The same applies to antiques such as *tansu* (chests) and screens. There are also a large number of moving companies that specialize in handling large-size items; shop around in English-language newspapers and listings publications.

COMPATIBILTY OF ELECTRICAL GOODS

Great care should be taken when buying electrical or electronic products. Make absolutely sure that circuits are either compatible with, or can be easily adjusted to, a home country's power system (see p371). Also, the FM radio band is different (from 76 to 90) from that used elsewhere in the world.

Japan uses the NTSC system for video and DVD, which is compatible with Canada, the US, and South and Central America. PAL video systems, used in other parts of Asia, Australia, and Europe, among other places, are available at electronic specialists such as those in the Akihabara district of Tokyo (see p73).

CLOTHING SIZES

Buying clothing in Japan can be a problem. Young people are growing to Western sizes now, but a lot of clothing is still cut for older-style Japanese physiques. That means smaller overall and with shorter sleeves in particular. The range of sizes available tends toward small to medium with a few large (not as large as Western large). Remember to take your shoes off when entering a fitting room.

Men's Suits and Coats

Japanese	S	M	L	XL
US	34	36	38	42
British	34	36	38	42
Continental	44	46	48	52

Women's Clothes

Japanese	7	9	11	13	15	17
US	8	10	12	14	16	18
British	10	12	14	16	18	20
Continental	36	38	40	42	44	46

Shoes

Japanese	23	23.5	24	24.5	25	25.5	26
US men's	–	–	–	–	7.5	8	8.5
US women's	5.5	6	6.5	7	7.5	8	8.5
British	4.5	5	5.5	6	6.5	7	7.5
Continental	36	37	38	39	39	40	40

An elegant display of watches in the window of Tokyo's Wako store

DEPARTMENT STORES

Japan's mainstream department stores often fulfill a remarkable number of functions, housing ticket agencies, art galleries, and currency exchanges, alongside a huge range of consumer goods. Some stores are built over or enclose major train stations, resembling a city in microcosm. The early *depato* developed out of Edo-period kimono suppliers, with stores such as **Takashimaya** and **Mitsukoshi** leading the way. Others were rooted in the fortunes of industrialists seeking in patriarchal fashion to meet the needs of the masses.

Most major stores are laid out in a similar fashion. Food – together with rich pickings of free samples – is usually located in the basement; the first floor is often given over to candies, cosmetics, or accessories; restaurants serving a range of different cuisines tend to be on the top floor; playgrounds for small children are often on the roof. In between are fashion, furniture and furnishings, electrical goods, kitchenware, kimonos and traditional crafts, even pets. Customers tend to ride to the top by elevator and then descend by escalator, browsing and buying en route; Japan calls this the "shower effect." Sales are held in spring, summer, fall, and winter, and there are additional special discount events.

The really top-notch department stores are more specialized. **Matsuya** is associated with upscale fashion brands.

Wako, regarded by many as the most elite department store in Japan, sells expensive jewelry, lingerie, and accessories. At the other end of the scale, Seibu's **Parco** caters to the affluent youth market, housing new-wave fashion and the full range of contemporary arts all under one roof.

Restrooms are often luxuriously appointed with areas for feeding and changing

SHOPPING MALLS AND ARCADES

A Japanese city is not a city without its fair share of malls and arcades. Many date from the postwar period and, being generally located in downtown areas, are old-fashioned in style and appearance. Nevertheless they are where most people eat and play *pachinko (see p97)* in between routine shopping and bargain hunting.

Adjoining Senso-ji Temple in Tokyo *(see pp86–7)* is an old-fashioned arcade of shops selling a mixture of tourist souvenirs and quality traditional crafts. In Osaka, Umeda Underground Arcade is famed.

DISCOUNT STORES AND SUPERMARKETS

In many respects, supermarkets are the same in Japan as elsewhere. A few sections and products may seem strange and exotic, such as the extensive displays of noodles, tofu, *kamaboko* (fish-paste

products), tempura, sashimi, and *bento* (prepared lunch boxes). Under the same roof as the supermarket may be a florist, bakery, dry cleaners, and drugstore *(kusuri)*.

Kinokuniya and **Meiji-ya** supermarkets specialize in high-quality imports. At the other end of the scale, **Jusco** offers economically priced store-brand goods with an emphasis on recycling and environmental concern. **Hundred Yen** shops sell household goods, stationery, toys, cosmetics, and batteries – all at ¥100. **Ito-Yokado**, **Seiyu**, and **Daikuma** cater to families; newcomers like **Aoki** and **Konaka** specialize in men's suits. Being cheap, cheerful, in strong competition, and often near train stations, they are always packed.

ARTS AND CRAFTS CENTERS

Arts and crafts are held in equally high esteem in Japan. A finely lacquered comb is therefore regarded with as much respect as *nihonga* (traditional Japanese painting). Nowhere else in the world can such a wealth of techniques and genuine appreciation of this labor-intensive work be found. There are 2,000 potters in Tokyo alone, and all make a living. Bamboo has 2,000 traditional uses, many of which are still employed for brushes, baskets, tableware, and furniture.

Imaemon pottery from Arita in Kyushu

A basketware shop in Yufuin, Kyushu

The best place to see a full range of what is available nationwide is at a handicraft center. Both Tokyo and Kyoto have excellent craft centers *(see pp106–7 and pp182–3,* with regular demonstrations of traditional arts and crafts as well as items on sale, often at tax-free prices.

Regional arts and crafts centers abound, displaying the work of local artists and artisans. Ask at the nearest TIC for details of local centers. Certain areas specialize in ceramics, *washi* (handmade paper), marquetry, ironware, or textiles, for example. Boutiques mixing indigo-dyed or specialty woven fabrics with other crafts, such as woodturning, glassware, and ceramics, are popular.

Stalls en route to the shrine of Tenman-gu in Dazaifu, Kyushu

A colorful range of food stalls in Nishiki market alley, Kyoto

MARKETS

Food markets provide an insight into the Japanese enthusiasm for food and cooking. The basement food floor of a major department store is a good place to start.

Small local markets, where farmers sell fresh produce, are usually operated by the agricultural cooperatives *(nokyo)*. These markets can be found all over the country and even in inner city areas, since vegetable plots nestle between homes, factories, and *pachinko* parlors.

Markets for manufactured goods flourish in urban wholesale districts, where industries are concentrated, selling everything from kitchenware to TVs.

TEMPLE AND SHRINE STALLS

In these sacred precincts, there are usually a number of stalls selling religious charms and votive plaques. These are reasonably priced and make good souvenirs. Other types of shopping here fall into two categories: flea markets, and traditional goods associated with seasonal festivals and changes of climate. Regular flea markets, which are listed in English-language publications in Japan, provide rich pickings of everything from junk to rare treasures. Items are not as inexpensive as they used to be, but these markets are still cheaper than antique and secondhand shops for kimono, books, and so on.

Many fairs are staged toward the end of the year. Two examples in the capital are Torii-no-ichi at Otori Shrine in mid-November *(see p46)*, and Hagoita-Ichi (Toshi-no-ichi), held December 17–19 at Senso-ji Temple *(see p47)*. New Year decorations to hang above doorways and on gateposts also draw a lot of business. In summer there are often stalls selling potted *asagao* (morning glory) plants, and metal and glass wind chimes *(furin)*, which catch the breeze.

THE JAPANESE ART OF WRAPPING

Japanese culture is quintessentially wrapping based: the body is wrapped and tied into kimono; tasty tidbits are encased in rice, the staple of everyday life, and further cloaked in seaweed to make *onigiri* (rice balls); hand luggage is innovatively wrapped and tied for ease of carrying in a decorative cloth *(furoshiki)*. Shops will almost invariably wrap goods exquisitely in handmade paper *(washi)*, often in several layers. While the beauty, intrigue, and ultimate revelation of such a tradition has obvious appeal – and is ideal when the purchase is a present – the level of waste is high: now even Japanese consumers are beginning to question the custom.

Decorative paper wrapping

Ribbon adorning a packet of spice

A set of chopsticks, boxed

What to Buy in Japan

The abundance of specialty shops and craft outlets in Japan makes shopping a pleasure. Items available range from beautiful handmade crafts to useful everyday objects and kitsch toys. As a result, there should be something for every budget, and many of the most interesting souvenirs are also compact and light to carry home. Tokyo and Kyoto have the widest choice of shops that are used to dealing with foreign visitors, and many towns around the country have specialty craft centers or workshops. If time is limited, visit a large department store or a crafts emporium.

Wooden doll from Miyajima

Origami paper

CERAMICS

Ordinary pottery shops sell a wide selection of attractive bowls, dishes, cups, and sake bottles for everyday use. For a more unique – and expensive – souvenir, visit regions that specialize in pottery *(see p38)*, or a large craft shop, which should stock a good selection of the main regional styles.

Leaf-shaped dish

Vase from Okinawa

PAPER AND CALLIGRAPHY

Traditional Japanese paper *(washi)* is handmade and often dyed in bright colors or embedded with petals or colored flecks. It is available as stationery, or made into boxes and various origami shapes.

Mobile made of paper

Calligraphy Set
An inkstone, water pot, brush, and ink make up a calligraphy set. The components can be bought separately or boxed.

WOOD AND BAMBOO

A huge range of wood and bamboo souvenirs is available. Lacquerware trays, bowls, and boxes can be expensive but make original souvenirs. They need to be kept in humid conditions to last. Wooden combs, boxes, and dolls are also good buys. Large wooden chests, new and antique, are well designed but costly to ship.

Bizen-ware Vase
A form of unglazed earthenware pottery, Bizen-ware has been produced in Inbe (see p210) for almost 1,000 years. Firing at a high temperature produces different surface finishes. Sake bottles, vases, and other storage vessels are popular.

Echizen-ware vase

Umbrella
Made of bamboo and paper, this umbrella is typical of those seen at onsen resorts. These traditional umbrellas are also available from craft shops.

Lacquer bowl

Woven basket

WOODBLOCK PRINTS

Known as *ukiyo-e (see p85)*, woodblock prints are uniquely Japanese mementoes. Antique and original prints are sold in specialty shops and can be very expensive; modern reproductions are widely available and often of good quality.

Woodblock print of Mount Fuji by Takamizawa

Print of a scene in a women's bath house by Yoshiiku

IRONWARE

The center for iron tea kettles *(tetsubin)* in Japan is Morioka in Northern Honshu *(see 277)*. These items were orignally manufactured for use in the tea ceremony. Many are now mass-produced. Nonetheless, they make useful, durable purchases but are heavy to carry home.

Iron tea kettle

TOYS AND LUCKY CHARMS

Decorative figures and toys are enormously popular in Japan, and there are plenty to choose from. Wooden dolls may be expensive as many are handmade and have become collectors' items.

Charms
Charms, such as this classic lucky cat, are often sold at temple and shrine stalls.

Tin robot

CLOTHING AND TEXTILES

Kimonos run into thousands of yen to buy new but will last for years; second-hand ones are more affordable. Light cotton kimonos, known as *yukata*, are also less expensive to buy. Lengths of silk or hand-dyed fabrics are readily available in department stores.

Straw-soled sandals

Kimono

Indigo casual jacket and trousers

SWEETS

All manner of sweets, cookies, and rice crackers can be found in specialty shops and in department stores. You can usually choose from a selection and have your choice decoratively wrapped. Some tourist sites sell their own distinctively shaped sweets.

Fox-shaped sweets from Tsuruoka

Biscuit shaped like a leaf

Boxed Sweets
The Japanese themselves often give boxes of sweets as gifts. These are decorated as characters in a Kabuki play (see p36).

ONSEN

Japan is peppered with volcanic hot springs, known as *onsen*. Communal bathing in these has been a custom for centuries, as a religious ritual (from the Shinto emphasis on purification), health cure, or just for pleasure. Many spa baths tap into natural volcanic activity, taming the thermal waters; some are artificially heated and enhanced with therapeutic

Washing facilities

herbal concoctions. A visit to an *onsen* is an antidote to the hectic pace of urban life, a chance to recuperate after sightseeing or business, and an insight into a soothing and companionable side of Japan. Hot springs are even used by animals: Jigokudani Onsen near Nagano, for example, is popular with wild monkeys, who sit in the pools to keep warm.

Enjoying a cup of sake in a traditional onsen

TYPES OF ONSEN

The variety of *onsen* is phenomenal. They come in every format: natural and man-made; indoors and outdoors; as small as a bath and as large as a swimming pool; lobster-hot and lukewarm; milky and clear; sulfurously foul-smelling and sweetly earthy. Certain chemical compositions in the waters are said to help different ailments, such as arthritis, hypertension, and skin problems.

Outdoor baths are generally rustic, made of wood or stone, and often by a river or the sea. Some are in caves, under jungle canopies, or behind waterfalls, or take the form of thermal mud or sand baths. Many *onsen* are in the mountains: after hiking, a dip in an outdoor pool in deep snow with a mountain view is perhaps the ultimate *onsen* experience. Exotic indoor *onsen* include baths in cable cars.

Many *onsen* operate as hotels, with meals and *onsen* facilities all included in the room price per person. Staying overnight allows you to sample the pleasures of night-

time bathing. Entire *onsen* resorts have been developed so that between baths guests may wander around the town in their *yukata* (lightweight kimonos) or dine on local fare, often excellent. Other *onsen* hotels are in isolated hamlets in spectacular settings. At some *onsen* hotels and public bathhouses it is possible to stay for just a few hours rather than overnight. Fees can be very reasonable for these short visits – from ¥300 to ¥2,000. For details of individual *onsen*, consult a TIC or local tourist office, or *A Guide to Japanese Hot Springs* (see p409). English may not be spoken at *onsen* hotels and local tourist offices; try to have a Japanese-speaker help you book accommodations.

ONSEN ETIQUETTE

Etiquette at *onsen* is similar to that for communal baths in *ryokan (see p297)*. Pools are usually single-sex; women rarely use mixed pools, except perhaps at

night, when mixed bathing is more acceptable. Occasionally people in outdoor pools *(rotenburo)* wear swimsuits, but mostly everyone is naked. Nonetheless, the atmosphere is not sleazy, and visitors need have no qualms.

If you're staying overnight, change into the *yukata* provided in your room; either way, when you reach the baths, leave all clothes and possessions in the changing room. As with any Japanese bath, wash and rinse yourself thoroughly at the showers and taps provided outside the bath and take great care not to get any soap or shampoo in the bath itself.

The small towel provided can be used as a washcloth, draped across strategic parts of your body, placed on your head while in the pool (said to prevent fainting), or used to dry yourself when you emerge.

Keep all jewelry well away from steam, as the minerals can tarnish metal. Pregnant women, babies and young children, and anyone with high blood pressure should not enter the hottest baths without consulting a doctor first.

A steaming sand bath in Ibusuki, southern Kyushu

SELECTED ONSEN AREAS IN JAPAN

There are over 2,000 hot spring areas across the country, concentrated particularly in Kyushu, the Izu Peninsula west of Tokyo, and the mountainous backbone of Northern and Central Honshu.

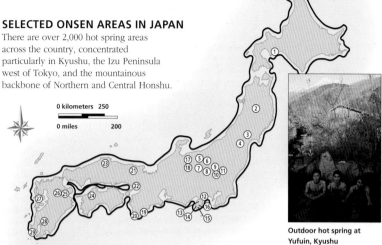

0 kilometers 250

0 miles 200

Outdoor hot spring at Yufuin, Kyushu

KEY TO ONSEN AREAS MAP

① **Noboribetsu**
Hokkaido prefecture. Numerous hotels and huge choice of baths, playfully themed or medicinal. 🛈 *(0143) 84-3311.*

② **Kuroyu**
Akita prefecture. Remote and un-spoiled, with a single thatched inn; inaccessible in winter. 🛈 *(0187) 46-2214.*

③ **Naruko**
Miyagi prefecture. Medium-size *onsen* town known for fall foliage. 🛈 *(0229) 83-3441.*

④ **Zao**
Yamagata prefecture. Popular ski resort and summer hiking base, but not over-commercialized. 🛈 *(023) 694-9328.*

⑤ **Jigokudani**
Nagano prefecture. Famed for *onsen*-loving monkeys; a single, simple inn, plus hotels in nearby villages. 🛈 *(0269) 33-1107.*

⑥ **Echigo Yuzawa**
Niigata prefecture. Traditional resort (on *shinkansen* line); atmospheric setting for Kawabata's novel Snow Country. 🛈 *(0257) 85-5353.*

⑦ **Kusatsu**
Gunma prefecture. Three-minute "time baths" in the scalding water here. Numerous public baths and inns. 🛈 *(0279) 88-0800.*

⑧ **Hoshi**
Gunma prefecture. One lovely tradi-tional *ryokan* with large wooden bathhouse, situated in woodland. *Tel (0278) 66-0005 (ryokan).*

⑨ **Takaragawa**
Gunma prefecture. Perhaps the best riverside pools in Japan, plus a pool for bears; one thatched *ryokan*. *Tel (0278) 75-2121 (ryokan).*

⑩ **Nikko Yumoto**
Tochigi prefecture. Small *onsen* village in Nikko National Park; good hiking. 🛈 *(0288) 54-2496.*

⑪ **Yunishigawa**
Tochigi prefecture. Atmospheric old *onsen* village in remote valley. 🛈 *(0288) 97-1126.*

⑫ **Hakone**
Kanagawa prefecture. Famous old *onsen* town, sprawling up hillside; wide range of inns and baths. 🛈 *(0460) 5-5700.*

⑬ **Shuzenji**
Shizuoka prefecture. Traditional *onsen* town, commercialized but charming; many good inns. 🛈 *(0558) 72-2501.*

⑭ **Osawa**
Shizuoka prefecture. A handful of picturesque *onsen* hotels in rural serenity. 🛈 *(0558) 42-2799.*

⑮ **Odaru**
Shizuoka prefecture. Numerous pools, waterfalls, and caves; several inns. 🛈 *(0558) 32-0290.*

⑯ **Hokkawa**
Shizuoka prefecture. Coastal *onsen* with inns and outdoor baths over-looking the sea. 🛈 *(0557) 23-3997.*

⑰ **Renge**
Niigata prefecture. High in the alps, Renge has a choice of pools around one inn (closed in winter). Ideal for hikers. *Tel (090) 2524-7237 (inn).*

⑱ **Shirahone**
Nagano prefecture. Relaxed moun-tain town near skiing and hiking areas. 🛈 *(0263) 94-2307.*

⑲ **Katsuura**
Wakayama prefecture. An estab-lished resort, with jungle-theme and seaside pools, including a cave-bath. 🛈 *(0735) 52-0555.*

⑳ **Shirahama**
Wakayama prefecture. Popular, coastal resort town with sandy beaches. 🛈 *(0739) 43-5511.*

㉑ **Kinosaki**
Hyogo prefecture. Picturesque old-style town with traditional inns. Tasty crabs. 🛈 *(0796) 32-3663.*

㉒ **Arima**
Hyogo prefecture. Commercial resort with many hotels; pleasantly secluded. 🛈 *(078) 904-0708.*

㉓ **Tamatsukuri**
Shimane prefecture. Japan's oldest recorded hot spring and largest outdoor pool. 🛈 *(0852) 62-0634.*

㉔ **Dogo**
Ehime prefecture. Old-established spa town with classic bathhouse; many inns. 🛈 *(089) 921-5141.*

㉕ **Beppu**
Oita prefecture. One of the world's most thermally active places. Vin-tage complex of hot-spring towns *(see pp228–9).* 🛈 *(0977) 24-2828.*

㉖ **Yufuin**
Oita prefecture. Small craftsy spa town with horse-drawn carriages and very little nightlife. 🛈 *(0977) 85-4464.*

㉗ **Unzen**
Nagasaki prefecture. Bubbling pools in Unzen-Amakusa National Park. 🛈 *(0957) 73-3434.*

㉘ **Ebino Kogen**
Miyazaki prefecture. Beautiful scenery and good hiking by Mount Karakuni. Rocky outdoor pools. 🛈 *(0984) 35-1111.*

㉙ **Ibusuki**
Kagoshima prefecture. Modern resort with tropical atmosphere and hot-sand baths. 🛈 *(0993) 22-2111.*

THEME PARKS

Japan has an astonishing number of theme parks, and Japanese tourists are especially drawn when the theme is new. This has created a lot of competition among managements to come up with fresh and innovative attractions. While many overseas visitors have little interest in this aspect of tourism in Japan, others – especially families and visitors from other Asian countries –

Interactive scientific exhibit

travel thousands of miles to these vast playgrounds. Indeed, some foreigners find the Japanese fascination with theme parks fascinating in itself. Enthusiasts go back again and again, seeking to gain a sense of the outside world in complete security, or in search of an escape from the responsibilities of adulthood in an artificially created, idealized notion of childhood.

HISTORY THEME PARKS

Even those overseas visitors who do not usually visit theme parks may be interested in those devoted to Japanese history and culture. North of Tokyo, the **Nikko Edo Village** has re-created 18th-century buildings and has guides dressed in period costume. Under the same management, **Noboribetsu Date Jidai Mura** in Hokkaido's Shikotsu-Toya National Park has assembled over 90 reconstructed 16th–19th-century buildings from all over the country.

Ise Azuchi-Momoyama Bunkamura is a 16th-century theme park with a reproduction of Azuchi Castle, which used to stand on the shores of Lake Biwa. Near Inuyama, **Meiji Mura** *(see p143)* is an open-air museum that preserves fine examples of Meiji-period architecture. On a smaller scale, **Nihon Minka-en**, between Kawasaki and Yokohama, has local

traditional buildings, including farmhouses, a Shinto shrine, and a Kabuki theater, all in a garden setting.

FOREIGN CULTURE THEME PARKS

These hugely popular theme parks give overseas visitors an insight into the way their own cultures are perceived by the Japanese. For example, **Italian Village** offers horse-drawn carriages, gondola rides and shops selling Italian designer goods. In Niigata in northern Honshu is **Kashiwazaki Turkish Culture Village**. **Tivoli Park** *(see p211)* in Kurashiki is based on Copenhagen's pride and joy. **Porto Europa**, south of Osaka, depicts the flavor of a typical medieval European port. **Tobu World Square** near Tokyo reproduces more than 100 famous buildings from all over the world in miniature. **Nijinosato** in Shizuoka prefecture has Canadian, British, and Japanese villages and a "fairy garden." The

The Dutch-themed Huis ten Bosch park in Nagasaki

attractive **Parque-Espana** in Ise-Shima offers attractions and restaurants with a Spanish atmosphere.

Best of all is **Huis ten Bosch** in Nagasaki *(see p243)*. The whole development is ecologically designed, with faithful reproductions of Dutch architecture. On-site hotels are connected to the sea by inland waterways.

AMUSEMENT PARKS

Since opening in 1983, **Tokyo Disney Resort** has welcomed millions of visitors each year. In 2001 DisneySea joined Disneyland on the outskirts of the capital, east of Daiba, in Chiba prefecture, attracting visitors from all over Asia. A monorail system links the two parks.

In Tokyo itself, **Namco NamjaTown** offers 26 hi-tech virtual reality attractions in themed zones depicting different areas such as European cities; **Toshimaen** is probably the biggest amusement park in Tokyo; **Sanrio Puroland**

Frontage of Frank Lloyd Wright's Imperial Hotel in Meiji Mura, Inuyama

made history as Japan's first completely indoor theme park. North of the capital, **Unesco Village** is (confusingly) a dinosaur amusement park with 250 life-size creatures moving, roaring, and fighting. Attractions include one of Japan's largest merry-go-rounds. **Kinugawa Western Mura** is an American Western theme park town with live shows, country-and-western music, and robots of famous American movie stars.

South of Tokyo, **Yomiuri Land** features the White Canyon, an all-wood roller coaster. **Joypolis**, designed by Sega, has many interactive attractions, including the world's first virtual-reality motion ride.

Yokohama's dockside **Minato Mirai 21** complex *(see p243)* boasts a huge Ferris wheel, capable of carrying up to 480 people at a time.

SCIENCE PARKS

Despite being on the cutting edge of invention, Japan is not well endowed with science parks. Tokyo Bay is now home to **Palette Town** *(see p103)*, which houses several technically based attractions, including Toyota City Showcase, the History Garage, Future World, driving courses, and the E-Com ride. **Space World** is a huge complex in Fukuoka prefecture, with many hi-tech rides. It incorporates a Space Camp where children can experience astronaut training

MARINE THEME PARKS

Hokkaido's **Noboribetsu Marine Park Castle Nixe** offers marine and European themes in whimsical combination. In the Kanto region are **Kamogawa Sea World** and

Viewing turtles in one of Japan's many spectacular aquariums

Yokohama's **Hakkeijima Sea Paradise** – a man-made island with one of Japan's largest aquariums. The highlight of Osaka's Tempozan Harbor Village *(see p203)* is the huge **Osaka Aquarium**, housing 580 marine species. **Marinpal Yobuko** in Kyushu offers a cruise in its "submarine ship" *Zeela*, from which you get a close-up view of the fish through the submerged windows of the vessel. In Okinawa, **Westmarine** offers the same kind of cruise.

DIRECTORY

HISTORY THEME PARKS

Ise Azuchi-Momoyama Bunkamura
1201-1 Oaza Mitsu, Futami-cho, Watarai-gun, Mie-ken.
Tel (0596) 43-2300.

Nihon Minka-en
7-1-1 Masugata, Tama-ku, Kawasaki-shi, Kanagawa-ken.
Tel (044) 922-2181.

Nikko Edo Village
470-2 Karakura, Fujiwara-machi, Shioya-gun, Tochigi-ken.
Tel (0288) 77-1777.

Noboribetsu Date Jidai Mura
53-1 Naka Noboribetsu-cho, Noboribetsu-shi, Hokkaido.
Tel (0143) 83-3311.

FOREIGN CULTURE THEME PARKS

Italian Village
1-15 Minato-machi, Minato-ku, Nagoya.
Tel (052) 655-1800.
www.italiamura.com

Kashiwazaki Turkish Culture Village
Kashiwazaki, Niigata.
Tel (0257) 21-4400.

Nijinosato
4279-3 Shuzenji, Izu, Shizuoka-ken.
Tel (0558) 72-7111.

Parque-Espana
Sakazaki, Isobemachi, Shima, Mie-ken.
Tel (0599) 57-3333.

Porto Europa
1527 Kemi, Wakayama.
Tel (073) 448-0011.

Tobu World Square
209-1 Ohara, Fujiwara-machi, Shioya-gun, Tochigi-ken.
Tel (0288) 77-1000.
www.tobuws.co.jp/default_en.html

AMUSEMENT PARKS

Joypolis
1-6-1 Daiba, Minato-ku, Tokyo.
Tel (03) 5500-1801.
www.sega.jp/joypolis/tokyo_e.html

Kinugawa Western Mura
315-1 Kurihara, Imaichi-shi, Tochigi-ken.
Tel (0288) 21-8731.

Sanrio Puroland
Ochiai, Tama-shi, Tokyo.
Tel (042) 339-1111.
www.puroland.co.jp/spl/english/welcome.html

Tokyo Disney Resort
1-1 Maihama, Urayasu-shi, Chiba-ken.
Tel (045) 683-3777.
www.tokyodisneyresort.co.jp/index_e.html

Toshimaen
Near Toshimaen stn, Tokyo.
Tel (03) 3990-8800.

Unesco Village
2135 Kamiyamaguchi, Tokorozawa-shi, Saitama-ken.
Tel (042) 922-1370.

Yomiuri Land
Yanokuchi, Inagi-shi, Tokyo.
Tel (044) 966-1111.

SCIENCE PARKS

Space World
Kita-Kyushu.
Tel (093) 672-3600.
www.spaceworld.co.jp/english/index.html

MARINE THEME PARKS

Hakkeijima Sea Paradise
Hakkeijima, Kanazawa-ku, Yokohama, Kanagawa-ken.
Tel (045) 788-8888.
http://seaparadise.co.jp/english/english/mokuzi_html

Kamogawa Sea World
1464-18 Higashi-cho, Kamogawa-shi, Chiba-ken.
Tel (0470) 92-2121.

Marinpal Yobuko
Yobuko, Saga Prefecture.
Tel (0120) 425-194.

Noboribetsu Marine Park Castle Nixe
1-22 Noboribetsu Higashi-machi, Noboribetsu-shi, Hokkaido.
Tel (0143) 83-3800.

Osaka Aquarium
Tempozan, Osaka.
Tel (06) 6576-5501.

Westmarine
Naha, Okinawa.
Tel (098) 866-0489.

SPORTS AND OUTDOOR ACTIVITIES

Japan enjoys many traditional sports activities as well as imports from abroad. Some sports that are closely identified with Japan – judo, for instance, which is a matter of extreme national pride at international competition level – have been adopted worldwide. Others, like sumo wrestling, are more exclusively Japanese. It is relatively easy to see most sports in action; participation, especially in some of the martial arts, takes more planning. As competitive and spectator sports, sumo and baseball rank uppermost, with soccer not far behind. Golf and fishing are immensely popular pastimes. With its long coastline, mountainous interior, and range in climate, Japan is also ideal for outdoor pursuits, from water sports to mountain climbing, a perfect complement to the pleasures of urban Japan.

Boating through Takachiho, Kyushu

Sumo wrestlers preparing for a bout, Tokyo

SUMO

A unique mix of sport and ritual, sumo *(see pp34–5)* has had new life breathed into it in recent years by the successes at the highest level of foreigners such as the Hawaiian ex-*yokozuna* (grand champion) Akebono, the Mongolian *yokozuna* Asashoryu and an influx of foreigners at lower ranks.

There are six major tournaments *(sumo basho)* a year, held bi-monthly in four locations: Tokyo (January, May, and September); Osaka (March); Nagoya (July); and Fukuoka (November).

Tokyo *basho (see p110)* are held in the **National Sumo Stadium** (Kokugikan) in Ryogoku *(see p102)*. The venue in Kyushu is the **Fukuoka Kokusai Center**; in the Kansai region of Western Honshu, the **Osaka Prefectural Gymnasium** (Osaka Furitsu Taikukaikan); and in Nagoya, **Aichi Prefectural Gymnasium** (Aichi-ken Taikukan). It is

best to buy tickets in advance, via **Playguide** service centers and other outlets. The most expensive tickets buy a boxed off-area *(masu)* for four near the ring, with *zabuton* (cushions) for seating. While ringside vantage points have the added luster of 100 kg (220 lb) plus of naked muscle and flab landing in the lap, most settle for bench-style seating, rising in tiers.

Each *basho* lasts 15 days. The wrestling starts early morning, a good time to see newcomers in action. Champions compete last, between 5 and 6pm. The Japanese crowds tend to side with winners rather than the underdogs. If you can't make it to see the action live, NHK provides expert TV commentary by native English speakers.

The stables *(beya)* most likely to accept non-Japanese who wish to train in sumo are usually run by foreign stablemasters under the auspices of the **Japan Sumo Association** (Nihon Sumo Kyokai).

OTHER MARTIAL ARTS

These fall into two categories, traditional *(budo)*, and the others. They can be further classified as those involving weapons, and those that are open-handed *(see p35)*. While it is relatively easy to view most sports in action, to be accepted for training in one of the traditional martial arts usually requires personal introductions.

Kendo, under the official eye of the **All-Japan Kendo Association,** is the only form of traditional weaponry practiced widely in Japanese schools and clubs. Championships are usually held in the **Nippon Budokan**, which also has a school.

Judo is the most popular of the open-handed sports. It is also big internationally; many students come to Japan for intensive practice. For all English-speaking services, contact the Department of International Affairs at the **Kodokan Judo Institute** in downtown Tokyo.

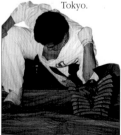

Karate expert breaking roof tiles with one blow of the elbow

Landscaped golf course at the Horin Country Club, Ichihara, southeast of Tokyo

The **International Aikido Federation** promotes the sport according to the ideals of founder Ueshiba Morihei. It welcomes visitors, and classes are often held in the early mornings and late afternoons.

The **Japan Karate-Do Federation** is the official karate organization, but there are many offshoots. The **International Karate Organization**, for example, is eager to promote *kyokushin* karate. The **Japan Karate Association** has weekday classes open to observers. The best time to watch is 7–8pm.

There have been moves in recent years to combine various martial arts, often to extremely violent effect. **World Pancrase Create**, which established its first amateur pancrase *dojo* (practice hall) in 1997, invites interest in this new form of "total fight."

K-1, in which contenders from various martial arts square off against each other, is now a hugely popular sport in Japan. Gloves are worn and attacks are limited to kicking and punching. Often, technique and speed overpower size and strength. The international K-1 Grand Prix is now an annual event.

GOLF

Of the 50 million people who play golf worldwide, 17 million are swinging clubs in Japan. Vistors staying in major hotels should have little problem in finding a game; most have ties to a reputable golf club. The same applies to visiting executives; Japanese corporations consider a game

basic to establishing relationships and will effect all the necessary introductions.

Courses are either private or public. An introduction by a member is essential to gain entry to a private club. If invited, expect to be treated; if reciprocating, expect the day to be very expensive. Public courses are less expensive but often less challenging. The attitude of staff may also be daunting; some welcome non-Japanese players, others may be cautious. JNTO *(see p370)* should be able to recommend public courses. A fun alternative might be to practice at one of the netted driving ranges in urban areas.

For the ultimate treat, book a golf-hotel package, such as offered in Hakone by the **Sengoku Golf Course** in collaboration with the Fujiya Hotel *(see p301)*.

BASEBALL

Japanese baseball is America's national game transplanted. It is believed to have taken root in the 1870s from American expatriates in Yokohama. Pro baseball is organized into two leagues of six teams each: the **Central League** and the **Pacific League**. The season is between April and October.

NHK broadcasts games live on TV, and the seven national sports dailies become increasingly hysterical as the season progresses, especially when the Japan Series gets underway. The spring and summer Koshien high-school baseball tournaments at **Koshien Stadium** in Hyogo Prefecture, hold the nation's attention.

SOCCER

Though played for as long as baseball, soccer has taken longer to capture public interest in Japan. It was not until 1993 that the professional **J-League** kicked off with 10 teams. The opening match between Verdy Kawasaki and Yokohama Marinos played to a capacity crowd at Tokyo's National Stadium. There are now two divisions: J1 with 16 teams, and J2 with 12, each playing a series of round-robin matches.

The **Japan Football Association**, organizes a national league in which amateur teams can also participate. Honours in recent years have been shared between the Kashima Antlers and Jubiro Iwata. The Emperor's Cup (started in 1921) involves more than 80 teams in a round-robin competition.

In 2002, the FIFA World Cup was jointly hosted by Japan and Korea, which helped to increase the game's popularity nationwide.

Team members playing baseball

Hiker resting by a marker post on Mount Fugen, Kyushu

HIKING

Japan is a hiker's heaven. Mountainous and hilly regions, including the many national parks, are crisscrossed with a comprehensive network of trails. Signboards often give precise distances and the average time to be allowed between each stage, but usually just in Japanese.

Much of north and west Japan is covered in deep snow for up to five months a year. Winter and spring hiking should be avoided unless you have an experienced guide and adequate clothing.

Summer and early autumn offer different challenges: extremes of heat and humidity, and thick vegetation that may be difficult to penetrate. But the comfort and clean green of lower slopes, and the wild beauty of many remote places make hiking Japan's most rapidly growing pastime.

MOUNTAINEERING

Chains of peaks run through all four of Japan's main islands. Among the Japan Alps of Central Honshu, for example, many mountains rise steeply to 3,000 m (10,000 ft) and can be as challenging as anywhere in the world. Others are gentler and ideal for less experienced climbers.

Japan's mountains claim fatalities every season. While there is no law forbidding climbing at any particular time, many mountainous areas and peaks have designated climbing seasons – check for dates in advance.

Volcanoes also occasionally take lives; even if an active volcano is not actually in the process of erupting, dangerous gases can be emitted without warning. Check up-to-date safety announcements with local tourist information centers.

There are usually facilities for overnight stays on the foothills and peaks of mountains, though these can be heavily overcrowded. Expect the standard and quality of hospitality in such mountain huts to be variable. Many close outside the climbing season.

SKIING

The great skiing that Japan has to offer is spoiled only by the numbers of people in the most popular resorts. Long lines for lifts are common,

Skiers setting off for the piste at Niseko Ski Resort in Hokkaido

and accommodations are often sold out. Snow is generally of an excellent quality, though, and in most resorts there are courses marked for beginners and intermediates.

Weekend trips, daily excursions, and skiing tours linked to domestic air, road, and rail routes are widely available inside Japan and to many agents abroad. Sometimes these include equipment rental. Large-size ski-boots are hard to find, so check on availability or bring your own.

The most popular areas are in Hokkaido, Northern Honshu (Tohoku), and Central and Western Honshu. JNTO (see p370) publishes a Top 20 ski resorts list, with full details and contact numbers.

WATERSPORTS

In a country with over 4,000 islands and innumerable inland rivers and lakes, water is naturally a favorite playground for the Japanese. Since the sea is often polluted around major conurbations, indoor and outdoor complexes of pools, wave machines, and water slides are popular. Unfortunately many outdoor pools are open for a limited time in midsummer only, coinciding with the time the sea is officially open for swimming from mid-July to the end of August.

Jet skiing, wind surfing, and yachting are all popular. Renting equipment is no problem on good beaches close to major cities; piloted yachts can be chartered from marinas. **Hayama Marina** near Kamakura is classy and expensive. To sail a cruiser in Japan, a specially issued license is necessary. Apply to the **Japan Marine Recreation Association**: a copy of a foreigner's registration card is required.

Many parts of the coastline lend themselves to scuba exploration. Around any developed area, diving can be murky to say the least; by contrast, waters around the islands of Okinawa *(see pp250–59)* are a tropical paradise.

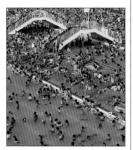

Lively day at the Korakuen swimming pool in Tokyo

ECO-TOURISM

Though Japan lags behind many nations in ecological conservation, concern about the environment has been building since the 1970s, when pollution in many areas reached record levels.

The **Nature Conservation Society of Japan** has a list of accommodations in unspoiled areas, run by people who are concerned with putting guests in touch with nature.

Birdwatching is a very popular activity in Japan. The **Wild Bird Society of Japan**, founded in 1935, has 80 chapters nationwide, each organizing local events.

In areas where commercial whaling was once a way of life, organized whale- and dolphin-watching trips now provide an alternative source of income. The best season in the remote Ogasawara Islands (a 25-hour ferry trip south of Tokyo) is March–April; in Ogata, Kochi prefecture, off the southern tip of Shikoku, the chance of seeing whales between April and October is 80–90 percent.

For visitors looking for action-packed adventure, **Wanderlust Adventures**, in the Kanto area just north of Tokyo, mixes hiking, kayaking, and rock climbing with *taiko* drumming.

DIRECTORY

SUMO

Aichi Prefectural Gymnasium
1-1 Ninomaru, Naka-ku, Nagoya.
Tel (052) 971-2516.

Fukuoka Kokusai Center
2-2 Chikuko-Honmachi, Hakata-ku, Fukuoka.
Tel (092) 272-1111.

Japan Sumo Association
1-3-28 Yokoami, Sumida-ku, Tokyo.
Tel (03) 3623-5111.
www.sumo.or.jp/

Osaka Prefectural Gymnasium
3-4-36 Namba Naka, Naniwa-ku, Osaka.
Tel (06) 6631-0121.

OTHER MARTIAL ARTS

All-Japan Kendo Association
2F Yaskuni Kudan-minami Bldg, 2-3-14 Kudan-minami, Chiyoda-ku, Tokyo.
Tel (03) 3234-6271.
www.kendo-fik.org/english-page/english-top-page.html

International Aikido Federation
17-18 Wakamatsu-cho, Shinjuku-ku, Tokyo.
Tel (03) 3203-9236.

www.aikido-international.org

International Karate Organization
2-38-1 Nishi-Ikebukuro, Toshima-ku, Tokyo.
Tel (03) 5992-9200.
www.kyokushin.co.jp

Japan Aikido Association
www.dokidoki.ne.jp/home2/unoaiki/index.html

Japan Karate-Do Federation
1-11-2 Toranomon, Minato-ku, Tokyo.
Tel (03) 3503-6637.
www.karatedo.co.jp

Japan Karate Association
2-23-15 Koraku, Bunkyo-ku, Tokyo.
Tel (03) 3462-1415.
www.jka.or.jp

K-1 Group
3F 2-18-22 Jingumae, Shibuya-ku, Tokyo.
Tel (03) 3796-5060.
www.so-net.ne.jp/feg/what/index.html

Kodokan Judo Institute
1-16-30 Kasuga, Bunkyo-ku, Tokyo.
Tel (03) 3818-4172.
www.kodokan.org/index.html

Nippon Budokan
2–3 Kitanomaru Koen, Chiyoda-ku, Tokyo.

Tel (03) 3216-5100.

World Pancrase Create
4-2-25 Minami-Azabu, Minato-ku, Tokyo.
Tel (03) 5792-0815.
www.pancrase.co.jp

GOLF

Sengoku Golf Course
1237 Sengokubara, Hakone-machi, Ashigara-Shimo-gun, Kanagawa-ken.
Tel (0460) 4-8511.

BASEBALL

Central & Pacific Leagues
Asahi Bldg, 6-6-7 Ginza, Chuo-ku, Tokyo.
Tel (03) 3572-1673 (Central);
(03) 3573-1551 (Pacific).

Koshien Stadium
1-82 Koshien-cho, Nishinomiya-shi, Hyogo-ken.
Tel (0798) 47-1041.

SOCCER

Japan Football Association
ww.jfa.or.jp
Tel (03) 3830-2004.

J-League
www.j-league.or.jp

WATERSPORTS

Hayama Marina
50-2 Horiuchi, Hayama-cho, Miura-gun, Kanagawa-ken.
Tel (0468)-75-2670.

Japan Marine Recreation Association
Kaiji Bldg, 1-3 Kaigan-dori, Naka-ku, Yokohama.
Tel (045)-201-1222.

ECO-TOURISM

Nature Conservation Society of Japan
2F Mitoyo Bldg, 1-16-10 Shinkawa, Chuo-ku, Tokyo.
Tel (03) 3553-4101.

Wanderlust Adventures
Tel (03) 5211-0473.
@ cbernatt@gol.com

Wild Bird Society of Japan
1F Odakyu Nishi-Shinjuku Bldg, 1-47-1 Hatsudai, hibuya-ku, Tokyo.
Tel (03) 5358-3510.

SPECIAL INTERESTS

Besides the more obvious tourist sights, Japan has many attractions for visitors who wish to learn more about diverse aspects of Japanese culture. Traditional medicine and Buddhist lore, for example, are of great interest to many Western tourists, and various organizations exist in Japan to promote foreigners' understanding of these subjects. Other visitors are more interested in modern Japan and will want to take the opportunity to visit factories or design showcases. Various systems have been developed to facilitate more contact and

A woman practicing moxibustion to improve her health

exchange of ideas between Japanese and overseas visitors. Goodwill Guides are locals, often housewives and retired people, who want to practice and maintain their foreign language skills, and who are willing to show foreigners around the local sights free of charge. Invariably, such individuals are enthusiastic about their own and other people's cultures. Using conversation lounges is an excellent way to establish intercultural friendships, while the Homestay and Home Visit systems offer unique insights into Japanese culture.

Participating in a tea ceremony, often possible via a Goodwill Guide

GOODWILL GUIDES, HOME STAYS, AND HOME VISITS

Established for over 20 years, the **Goodwill Guide** system is made up of Japanese volunteers, registered with JNTO *(see p370)*, all eager to assist visitors from overseas. JNTO has 82 SGG (Systematized Goodwill Guide) groups, which offer local tours in English. JNTO and local TICs have a list of contact numbers, and visitors should contact each SGG group for information. Visitors are requested to pay their guide's expenses.

EIL Japan (the Japanese Association of Experiment in International Living) runs a Homestay Program, which enables people from abroad to stay with a Japanese family for one to four weeks in various locations. Visitors,

who must bear all their own costs, are treated as one of the family and involved in regular daily activities. Contact EIL Japan at least eight weeks before your visit, requesting an application form.

The **Home Visit System** offers the opportunity to visit a Japanese family at home, usually in the evening after dinner. Up to four or five guests are invited at a time. English is spoken by most host families, but some family members may speak other languages. About 800 families are involved, in 13 cities and towns (the scheme excludes Tokyo on Honshu and Kyushu). JNTO overseas offices and local TICs have a list of contact numbers.

CONVERSATION LOUNGES

The basic premise of conversation lounges is to bring together Japanese who want to practice their English and other foreign languages, and visitors from abroad who want to meet Japanese people in relaxed surroundings. Sometimes also described as coffee lounges, these conversation venues can vary in both intent and tone.

Micky House in Shinjuku is free for native English speakers; others can pay each visit. They also have an informal Japanese conversation lounge twice a week. Other venues in Tokyo, such as **Com'Inn**, have different systems of charging. Conversation lounges come and go fairly regularly, or may change direction to become more like language schools; listings magazines are the best source of information for finding up-to-date spots. Be aware that

Japanese woman showing a Western visitor how to play a video game

some lounges operate as commercial matchmaking enterprises – for Western men and Japanese women, rarely the other way around.

SPECIALTY TOURS

Visitors interested in thematic tours rather than the usual kind of sightseeing can try **Sunrise Tours** in Tokyo, operated by the Japan Travel Bureau. A tour might focus on a visit to a calligraphy studio, participation in a tea ceremony, or exploring a downtown area. Sunrise also runs tours specializing in sumo or Tokyo nightlife, including trips to see traditional Japanese theater.

The **Hato Bus Tour Company** has a similar range of half-day, full-day, and nighttime tours for non-Japanese tourists, including a visit to a tea ceremony and a garden tour. **Greyline** runs trips around Tokyo as well as to places such as Mount Fuji and Hakone, and will also arrange private tours tailored to a customer's wishes; the more individual a tour is, the more the cost will be.

State-of-the-art electronics in Tokyo

Traditional Japanese ingredients

In Tokyo, **Mr. Oka's Walking Tours of Tokyo**, which cover historical areas of the city, are regularly advertised in the English-language press. In Kyoto, details about Hirooka Hajime's personally guided tours, **Walk in Kyoto, Talk in English**, are available from hotels and information centers; the tours take place on Mondays, Wednesdays, and Fridays.

In Kyoto you can experience a tea ceremony at **Kyoto International Community House** on Tuesdays at 2pm, or at **Westin Miyako Hotel** every day from 10am–7pm. You will need to make a reservation at both these venues, however, as the tea ceremony is very popular.

FACTORY VISITS

Three automobile manufacturers – **Toyota** (in Aichi prefecture), **Nissan** (in Kanagawa), and **Mazda** (in Hiroshima) – welcome visitors to their various plants. Tours in English can be arranged. The electronics-oriented **Toshiba Science Insitute** in Kanagawa prefecture offers an hour-long tour.

Most tours are on weekdays only, exclusive of national holidays, and it is best to contact the relevant organization in advance.

DIRECTORY

HOME STAYS

EIL Japan
3F Hirakawacho Fushimi Bldg, 1-4-3 Hirakawa-cho, Chiyoda-ku, Tokyo.
Tel (03) 3261-3451.
www.eiljapan.org

CONVERSATION LOUNGES

Com'Inn
5F Arai Bldg, 1-3-9 Ebisu-Minami, Shibuya-ku, Tokyo.
Tel (03) 3710-7063.

Micky House
4F Yashiro Bldg,
2-14-4 Takadanobaba, Shinjuku-ku, Tokyo.
Tel (03) 3209-9686.

SPECIALTY TOURS

Greyline
3-3-3 Nishi-shinbashi, Minato-ku, Tokyo.
Tel (03) 3433-5745.
www.jgl.co.jp/ inbound/index.htm

Hato Bus Tour Company
2-4-1 Hamamatsucho, Minato-ku, Tokyo.
Tel (03) 3435-6081.
www.hatobus.co.jp

Kyoto International Community House
2-1 Toriicho, Awataguchi, Sakyo-ku.
Tel (075) 752-3511.

Mr. Oka's Walking Tours of Tokyo

Tours 7–10pm.
Tel (0422) 51-7673.
www.mroka. homestead.com

Sunrise Tours
Tel (03) 5796-5454 (Tokyo).
Tel (075) 341-1413 (Kyoto).
www.jtb.co.jp/ sunrisetour

Walk in Kyoto, Talk in English
Tel (075) 622-6803.

3F Westin Miyako Hotel
Keage, Sanjo, Higashiyama-ku
Tel (075) 771-7111.

FACTORY VISITS

Mazda
General Affairs Dept, 3-1 Shinchi, Fuchu-cho, Aki-gun, Hiroshima-ken.
Tel (082) 252-5050.

Nissan
6-17-1 Ginza, Chuo-ku, Tokyo.
Tel (03) 5565-2389.

Toshiba Science Institute
1 Komukai-Toshiba-cho, Saiwai-ku, Kawasaki-shi, Kanagawa-ken.
Tel (044) 549-2200.

Toyota
Corporate PR, 1 Toyota-cho, Toyota-shi, Aichi-ken.
Tel (0565) 23-3922.

Illustration of traditional acupuncture points on the body

TRADITIONAL MEDICINE

In the Meiji period, with its emphasis on all things foreign, it became fashionable in Japan to reject traditional healing methods and instead to embrace Western science and medicine. Today, as alternative medicine, including Eastern methods, is burgeoning in popularity in the West, the trend in Japan is also toward a blend of ancient and modern practices.

Natural ingredients prescribed in accordance with traditional Chinese medical custom are known as *kampo*. Ready-mixed and prepared *kampo* products are available from pharmacies, often alongside manufactured prescription drugs. Some restaurants specialize in *kampo* cuisine, designed to balance the metabolism. *Kampo* can also be made up to suit individual needs in specialty stores. In Yokohama or Kobe, Chinatown is the place to go. In Tokyo, **Kampo Museum** has a restaurant and boutique based on *kampo* principles, where customers may consult specialist *kampo* counselors.

Acupuncture and moxibustion, a form of heat therapy, are often used in combination. **Zen Nihon Shinkyu Massage Shikai** in Tokyo and **Meiji University of Oriental Medicine** in Kyoto have information. **Imoto Seitai** practices and teaches traditional manual therapy.

There are numerous other forms of alternative healing derived from Oriental wisdom.

The **Japan Academy of Colorpuncture** uses colored light to restore well-being. **World Kai-igaku Network** helps people to cure themselves. **Lifeforces** offers a range of holistic, complementary therapies including *reiki*, a form of energy healing originally developed in Japan, and *sekhem*, an ancient Egyptian form of energy healing. They also run a free *reiki* share group, where participants can exchange energy, every second and fourth Sunday of the month. The same organizers run **Circle of Light**, which holds a discussion group on the third Sunday of each month to introduce their healing arts to a wider audience.

PILGRIMAGE ROUTES

For many centuries pilgrimages provided Japanese farmers and townspeople with a reason to leave behind work and responsibilities and take to the open road. Nowadays pilgrimages are regarded as a form of spiritual meditation, concerned with making amends and preparing for death. Some non-purists drive or ride the pilgrim routes.

Many of the oldest pilgrimages were connected with a mystical Shugendo cult of mountain worship, which combined elements of Shinto and Buddhism. Its most devout followers, laymen

known as *yamabushi* (mountain priests), still practice in the **Dewa Sanzan** mountains in Northern Honshu (see *p274*). During the Edo period, **Mount Fuji** (see *pp140–41*) became a similar object of worship. Even today, among the thousands of tourists who climb every summer, aged white-clad pilgrims (*henro*) wearing conical straw hats can be seen.

The most famous and demanding route is the **88-Temple Pilgrimage** on Shikoku (see *pp228–9*). The **Western Japan 33 Kannon Temple Circuit** involves visiting temples to Kannon, the goddess of mercy (see *p29*), in Western Honshu. It includes temples in Kyoto, Nara, Ise, and Mount Koya. There is a shorter route for pilgrims in Kamakura (see *pp134–7*), starting a brief bus ride away from the main station and finishing at the temple of Engaku-ji in Kita Kamakura.

Sticks carried by traditional pilgrims

RELIGIOUS STUDIES

Based in downtown Tokyo, the **International Shinto Foundation** was formed in 1994 to disseminate understanding of Japan's native religion. The **Association of Shinto Shrines** publishes a range of free English-language pamphlets and booklets. There are displays on Shinto history and rituals at **Kokugakuin University Shinto Museum**.

Resting pilgrims on the 88-Temple pilgrimage in Shikoku

The **Zen Buddhist Center for International Exchange** provides non-Japanese visitors with access to Zen practices. Their temple, located near Mount Fuji, is remote, with no electricity or telephone. Other Buddhist foundations offering English-language instruction include the **International Buddhist Association**, which conducts a meeting in English toward the end of each month, and **Rissho Kosei-Kai**, which offers dharma seminars four times a year. **Toshoji Temple** holds free *gyoten zazen* (zen meditation) every morning except on Sundays and public holidays. At **Kyoto International Zendo**, just west of the city in rural Kameoka, *zazen* can be practised in tranquil surroundings. Foreigners are welcomed to the temple, main hall, and guest quarters in a traditional farmhouse. A small donation is requested for lodging and meals. A number of temples around the country also offer religious instruction; contact local tourist information offices for more information.

For visitors interested in the fascinating history of Christianity in Japan the **Eastern Cross Museum** in Tokyo displays artifacts from the Keikyo (*keikyo* was the ancient name for Christianity in Japan), Kirishitan, and Kakure Kirishitan eras to the present day, including rare *keikyo* documents, Meiji-era porcelain, and *fumie* – wooden boards on which early Kirishitan were forced to renounce their faith. The same organization also provides useful information on Christian-related sights, including museums and memorial sites throughout Japan, via their website.

The 19th-century Oura church, Nagasaki

DIRECTORY

SURVIVAL
GUIDE

PRACTICAL INFORMATION

From a practical point of view, Japan is much easier for foreign tourists to negotiate than is generally believed. Being unable to speak or read Japanese is rarely a serious problem. Many everyday signs in major cities and at tourist attractions are displayed in Roman script along with Japanese characters. English-speaking locals are generally quick to offer assistance. The infrastructure for tourism (public transportation, accommodations, sight-

Street sign in Japanese and Roman script

北山通り
Kitayama dori

seeing, and so on) is highly developed, because the Japanese are well used to traveling around their own country. Where problems can arise for foreigners, however, is in the surprising contrasts in Japan's unique East-West culture – for instance, the contrast between the ease with which even foreigners can get around on the rail network compared with the difficulty everyone, including the Japanese, has with finding an address *(see p384–5)*.

Picnics in Tokyo's Ueno Park at cherry-blossom time

WHEN TO VISIT

The best times to visit Japan are spring (April and May) and fall (October and November). Temperatures within the country vary widely according to latitude *(see pp48–9)*, but July and August are mostly very humid and better avoided.

Japan has numerous festivals throughout the year *(see pp44–7)*. Cherry-blossom time brings out large blossom-viewing groups who fill the parks day and night, while late summer is a time for local festivals. Peak vacation periods for the Japanese are New Year (December 29 to January 4), "Golden Week" (April 29 to May 5), and the period around Bon, the Buddhist Festival of the Dead (in mid-August). At these times flights and some accommodations are sold out, and some hotels, offices, and tourist attractions may close for up to a week.

WHAT TO BRING

It is a good idea to take a variety of clothing, as modern buildings tend to be overheated in winter and overcooled in summer, while traditional buildings are relatively vulnerable to the elements. The weather can be changeable: an umbrella is more useful than a raincoat,

A colorful display of practical and souvenir fans for sale

especially in midsummer heat. Clothes, even if casual, should be neat, clean, and not too revealing; a short, tight skirt makes it awkward to sit on the floor. Comfortable footwear is a good idea; shoes will be removed frequently, so wear some that are easily slipped on and off, and make sure there are no holes in your socks or tights. Keep luggage to a minimum, and choose items that are easy to carry: stations have many steps and few porters.

Almost anything you need can be bought in Japan, although it may be expensive, and clothes or shoes may be available only in small sizes. Film can be pricey but is reasonable in general discount stores or electrical shops (note that slide film is not usually process-paid); developing is quite cheap, and of good quality, although standard print size is small.

As with any destination, good travel insurance is advisable. If you plan to travel around within Japan, consider obtaining a Japan Rail Pass before you go *(see p389)*.

VISAS AND PASSPORTS

Citizens of most Western countries may enter Japan for short visits as a Temporary Visitor simply with a valid passport. There is no need to obtain a visa. The usual period of stay for a Temporary Visitor is 90 days. Visitors are allowed to enter on this basis for tourism, sports, visiting

◁ **Participant in the Jidai Matsuri (Festival of the Ages), Kyoto**

Film and cameras in a discount camera shop

friends or relatives, study, or business, but may not undertake paid employment in Japan or stay longer than the specified period. (Journalists with US passports are an exception and must obtain a visa before traveling to Japan on business, even for a short stay.)

Citizens of some countries, including the UK and Germany, may extend this 90-day stay by up to another 90 days at immigration offices in Japan (at least 10 days before the original expiration date), but the length of extension is at the discretion of immigration officers.

On the plane you will be given a landing card: you need fill in only the first part, relating to arrival – the second part will be attached to your passport to be completed when you depart. There are no immunization requirements for entering Japan.

Anyone planning on undertaking paid work, long-term study, or voluntary work in Japan should obtain a visa from a Japanese embassy before going to Japan. It is generally not possible to obtain a visa, or change status, once in the country (*see pp376–7*). Foreigners who stay in Japan for more than 90 days must also apply for a Certificate of Alien Registration from the Ward Office of the area in which they are living, within 90 days

Shop selling perfume and cosmetics

of arrival in the country. This certificate, or your passport, must be carried at all times – not doing so can occasionally lead to arrest. Visa-holders who want to leave the country and return within the duration of their visa need to obtain a re-entry permit from an immigration office. Contact the **Ministry of Foreign Affairs** for more visa information.

CUSTOMS

There is no need to fill in a written declaration of your belongings unless you are arriving in Japan by ship, have unaccompanied baggage, or if you are exceeding the duty-free allowances.

Duty-free allowances on entering the country are 400 cigarettes or 500 grams of tobacco or 100 cigars; three 0.76 liter (27 oz) bottles of alcohol; 57 g (2 oz) of perfume; and gifts and souvenirs of a total value up to ¥200,000 (not counting items less than ¥10,000).

Certain articles are prohibited: narcotic drugs or stimulants; counterfeit money; pornography; articles that infringe on patents or copyrights; and firearms and ammunition. Animals and plants are subject to quarantine inspection. There is no limit on the amount of currency that may be taken into or out of the country, but sums over ¥1 million must be declared at immigration.

For guidelines on tax-free shopping in Japan, see page 341. Guns, swords, and some high-quality personal computers require an export license, obtained from the Ministry of International Trade and Industry. Art objects may be subject to restrictions.

FACILITIES FOR DISABLED VISITORS

Facilities for the disabled are of mixed quality. Blind people are well provided for, but the elderly and those in wheelchairs face problems with stations and pedestrian overpasses, as there are endless steps and often no escalator or elevator; the situation is improving, but slowly. Most modern offices and hotels have excellent toilet facilities for the disabled.

FACILITIES FOR CHILDREN

Children are welcomed, and parents can forget their usual worries about safety. Taking children to a restaurant poses no problems, discreet breast-feeding in public is accepted, and baby food, milk, disposable diapers, and boiled water are easily obtainable. Hotels tend to be geared toward adults, but top ones usually offer baby-sitting and nurseries, while at traditional inns a maid may be willing to baby-sit. Many theme parks and museums are great fun for kids, but some very cultured temples and galleries do not allow children. Rush hour travel and very hot *onsen* pools should also be avoided.

Children playing on the sidewalk

Logo of the Japan National Tourist Organization (JNTO)

INFORMATION CENTERS

Outside Japan, tourist information can be obtained from branches of the **Japan National Tourist Organization (JNTO)**. The JNTO has a large range of useful material: general background information, practical leaflets, and brochures on particular locations and specialist interests. The JNTO does not, however, make recommendations or reservations or sell Rail Pass vouchers, but can provide a list of travel agents that do.

In Tokyo, the **TIC** or Tourist Information Center *(see p387)* has knowledgeble staff, and offers information, travel literature, and suggestions on tour itineraries. It also has a counter for the **Welcome Inn Reservation Center** *(see p294)*, where staff will arrange hotel reservations on your behalf at locations throughout Japan. There is no charge for this service.

Information on a local level can be obtained in Japan from the Tourist Information Offices found in almost every town, usually in or near the station; they can often also make hotel reservations. Nearly 100 of these offices are designated **"i"** Tourist Information Offices, meaning they have multilingual staff and carry pamphlets in English. Information on local events is also available from **Information Corner** in Yokohama, Osaka, and Nagoya.

EVENTS INFORMATION AND TICKETS

In major cities, details of attractions and events can be gleaned from local publications such as *Tokyo Journal* and *Metropolis (see p108)*, *Kansai Time Out*, and free brochures – all available at hotels, bookstores, and TICs.

Hotels will usually help reserve tickets for entertainment venues. Ticket-agency booths located in most of the larger cities, inside department stores, convenience stores, and near train stations also book seats in advance and sell tickets up to the last minute. **Ticket PIA** and **CN Playguide** are the main agencies *(see p111)*.

WELCOME CARDS

Several cities have begun to issue a Welcome Card to foreign visitors, and there are now a number of different

ones available. Intended to reduce the cost of a visit, the card can be used to obtain discounts on accommodations, shopping, food and drink, and various other tourist facilities and services. For example, the Tokyo Museum Guide Welcome Card can be used to obtain a discount on the admission price at more than 40 galleries and museums in Tokyo, and the Mount Fuji Welcome Card allows discounts or special services at more than 200 hotels, restaurants, and sights in the Fuji, Hakone, and Izu regions. Obtain these or other cards with a booklet of participating services from a TIC or an **"i"** information center.

OPENING HOURS AND ADMISSION FEES

Temple buildings are typically open from 8 or 9am to 4pm in winter, and until 5pm in summer, though exact times and the number of buildings closed vary widely. Shrines are often open 24 hours. Admission to many temples and shrines is free; others charge a small admission fee, usually between ¥200 and ¥500.

Museums, art galleries, and many other tourist attractions such as technology centers and aquariums are usually open from 10am until 4 or 5pm. Many of these sights are open every day except Monday; when Monday is a

Todai-ji Temple at Nara – like many temples, open longer in summer than in winter

Canal City mall in Fukuoka, containing many shops offering discounts with a Welcome Card

public holiday, they often close on Tuesday instead. Most of these attractions may close for a week or more over the New Year period. Entrance fees to tourist attractions are occasionally under ¥1,000, but are usually more. Certain Kyoto sights – Katsura and Shugaku-in Imperial Villas, for example – require reservations well in advance of visiting.

For shopping hours, see page 348; for banking hours see page 380; and for post offices see page 384.

TIME AND THE CALENDAR

Japan is 9 hours ahead of Greenwich Mean Time and 14 hours ahead of US Eastern Standard Time. There is no daylight-saving time; when countries that use daylight-saving time switch to summer time, the time difference is one hour less.

The Japanese calendar combines the Western system with the Chinese system: years are designated Year of the Tiger, Rabbit, and so on, but they begin on January 1 and not, as in China, in mid-February. Years are numbered both by the

Stamps to mark the 10th year of the Heisei era

Western system and according to the reigning Japanese emperor. The present era, Heisei (meaning "achieving peace"), began when Emperor Akihito came to the throne in 1989, so that year was known as "Heisei 1"; Akihito's father's era was called "Showa." The Japanese system is generally used within the country, especially on official documents, while Western years are used in international contexts.

Misunderstandings about timings and dates are common, and it is advisable to confirm arrangements clearly and, when booking accommodations, to state the number of nights as well as the dates of your stay.

ELECTRICITY

Japan runs on 100 volts, AC – a system similar to that of the US – but the country has two different cycles: 50 cycles in eastern Japan (including Tokyo) and 60 cycles in western Japan. Plugs with two flat pins are standard; this means that appliances that can be used in America can also be used in Japan, but sometimes at a reduced efficiency.

Most British and other European appliances can be used only with transformers suitable for US voltage (which are large and expensive). If in doubt, consult the appliance's instructions.

Some international hotels have two outlets, of 110 and 220 volts, although these accept only two-pin plugs – adapters are available from electrical stores. In older buildings, ceiling lights are often operated by both a switch on the wall and a pull cord on the light itself; each pull of the cord gives a different degree of brightness.

DIRECTORY

JNTO OFFICES OUTSIDE JAPAN

US
One Rockefeller Plaza,
Suite 1250, New York,
NY 10020.
Tel (212) 757-5640.

1 Daniel Burnham Court,
Suite 250C, San Francisco,
CA 94109-5455.
Tel (415) 292-5686.

515 South Figueroa St,
Suite 1470, Los Angeles,
CA 90071.
Tel (213) 623-1952.

UK
Heathcoat House,
20 Savile Row,
London W1S 3PR.
Tel (020) 7734-4290.

Australia
Level 18, Australia Square Tower,
264 George St, Sydney,
NSW 2000.
Tel (02) 9251-3024.

Canada
165 University Ave,
Toronto,
Ontario M5H 3B8.
Tel (416) 366-7140.

OTHER INFORMATION SOURCES

Information Corner
Nagoya **Tel** (052) 581-0100.
Osaka **Tel** (06) 6773-6533.
Yokohama **Tel** (045) 222-1209.

JNTO
www.jnto.go.jp

Ministry of Foreign Affairs
www.mofa.go.jp

CONVERSION CHART

Metric to US/UK Standard
1 millimeter = 0.04 inch
1 centimeter = 0.4 inch
1 meter = 3 feet 3 inches
1 kilometer = 0.6 mile
1 gram = 0.04 ounce
1 kilogram = 2.2 pounds
1 liter = 2.1 US/1.8 UK pints

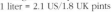

Attitudes and Etiquette

Etiquette is important in Japan – the social lubricant for a crowded community. In recent decades attitudes have relaxed, yet even the most apparently rebellious Japanese won't break certain rules. What constitutes correct behavior often varies according to the situation and status of individuals. Foreigners will be forgiven most gaffes, but good manners will earn you respect. The best approach is to be as sensitive as possible to situations, avoid loud or dogmatic behavior, and follow the lead of those around you.

Paying respects to ancestors at a Tokyo cemetery

Gauze mask, worn to stop the spread of colds

TABOOS

Few allowances are made even for foreigners on certain points, mainly relating to Japanese standards of hygiene. Surprisingly for many foreigners, it is considered unforgivable to get soap or shampoo in a bathtub; washing belongs in the shower area *(see p297)*. It is also a serious mistake to wear shoes indoors, or wear the wrong slippers into or out of a toilet area.

When it comes to table manners, serious errors include touching food in a communal dish with your chopsticks but then not taking it, and shoveling food direct from bowl to mouth. For more about eating etiquette, see pages 318–19.

The major cities now have non-smoking areas (such as Chuo-ku in Tokyo) where smoking on the streets is prohibited – fines will be issued to those caught. Eating on the move is frowned on, at least by the older generation, though eating on longer train trips is fine. Emissions from the body are considered very rude, while anything drawn inward is acceptable. Thus, sniffing is fine, but blowing your nose in public is reviled. Gauze face masks are worn in public both to stop infecting others with, and catching, colds.

THE HIERARCHY

Respect for seniors is fundamental to Japanese society even today. The emphasis on seniority has its roots in both the native Shinto religion (which is based on ancestor worship) and Confucianism (a set of social rules imported from China that reinforced the establishment).

All older people are treated with respect: not only parents, grandparents, company bosses, and teachers but even those a year or two senior in school or employment. The term *sensei* ("teacher") is used for all elders and experts. In the Japanese language, different vocabulary is used to speak to those above and those below, so it is vital for a Japanese to know the relative status of other people; this is one reason why business cards *(meishi)* are so widely used *(see p376)*.

The ultimate parent in such a social system is the royal family: until the end of World War II, emperors were worshiped as the ancestors of the nation. Today, some liberals reject the emperor system and national anthem even as symbols of the country, while right-wing groups fiercely protect the royal family and go so far as physically attacking those who speak out against it. Most people, however, show a lot of respect for the emperor, but stop short of veneration.

BOWING

The traditional greeting in Japan is a bow, its depth reflecting the relative status of participants. Foreigners, however, rarely need to bow – a handshake is fine. In many situations, bows are part of the service, for instance, in elevators, department stores, restaurants, and hotels. They can be ignored or met with a

Bow between business colleagues close in status to each other

brief smile. If you feel the need to bow, hold your arms and back straight, bend from the waist, and pause for a moment at the low point.

BODY LANGUAGE

This is not as sensitive an issue as in many other Asian countries, although it is considered rude to point your feet at people, and it is preferable to avoid wild gesticulation or talking loudly. The Japanese appreciate that sitting on the floor can be a strain for those not used to it, but try not to stretch out your legs. Men may sit cross-legged, while women should tuck their feet to one side.

Personal space is smaller than in the West, and on crowded trains it is worth following the Japanese example and creating a psychological bubble around you by closing your eyes or even taking a nap.

The Japanese practice good posture from childhood: a straight back is respected.

ATTITUDES TO PHYSICAL CONTACT AND SEX

Members of the same sex are physically easy with each other. Don't be surprised if a near-stranger touches you on the arm or massages your shoulders. The atmosphere in single-sex public baths is relaxed. Between the sexes, however (outside immediate family, who often bath together), a public display of contact is very limited. Despite a fashion among some young couples for public passion, most people would not even hold hands in public. Kissing is viewed as purely sexual. A "hello" kiss on the cheek would cause embarrassment, and hugging barely exists.

Skimpy clothing is worn by some girls and will not cause offense, but a shapely or hirsute Westerner in revealing clothes, or topless on a beach, can expect stares and giggles.

In general, sex is seen as free from shame, but something to be indulged discreetly. Shinto emphasizes fertility, and some objects in shrines can be quite explicit *(see p27)*. Homosexual activity, though widely practiced by samurai in the feudal era, on the whole is less openly accepted today than in many Western nations.

Sadly, the sleazier side of the sex trade includes schoolgirl prostitution, and cartoon pornography is widely sold in convenience stores. Nonetheless, everyday life is relatively sanitized, and it is important to remember that geisha *(see p163)* and most bar hostesses are not prostitutes.

SHOES

Shoes are an important element of etiquette. When you go indoors, take off your outdoor shoes and put on slippers, if provided, before you step on to the raised floor. If there are no slippers, or if they are too small for Western feet, go in socks or stockings. The principle is not to contaminate clean interiors with dirt from the outside, so be careful not to rest a shoe on the indoor floor or put a stockinged foot on the dirty part.

The same protocol applies in private homes, temples, and Japanese-style inns *(ryokan)*. In a Western-style hotel, however, "indoors" starts when you enter your own room. If you are unsure where "indoors" begins or, for instance, whether to take your shoes off to enter a restaurant (it depends on the type of restaurant), take your cue from other shoes or slippers in the entrance. (Also place umbrellas in a rack or plastic sleeve if provided at the entrance to the restaurant.)

Traditional footwear neatly lined up on racks outside a temple

Leave shoes neatly, by the step or in a pigeonhole – at an inn, staff may do this for you. To walk on *tatami* matting, remove slippers and go in stockinged feet.

Most restrooms, public and private, have special toilet slippers waiting outside: be sure to change into them as you go in (this is one way people know the restroom is occupied!) and to change back again when you emerge.

ETIQUETTE AT TEMPLES AND SHRINES

The atmosphere in temples and shrines is casual. Visitors should show respect, and not be noisy, but there are few of the taboos found in some other Buddhist nations. Japan is a superstitious society rather than a religious one, its religions mingling unexclusively and priests leading down-to-earth lives.

If you enter buildings in a shrine or temple, except those with stone floors, leave your shoes at the entrance or carry them with you. Plastic bags are often provided for this, especially if you can use a different exit. Some temples allow photography, some only without flash, others not at all. For advice about paying respects in Shinto and Buddhism see pages 26–9.

Fertility statue at Uwajima's Taga Shrine museum

GROUP MENTALITY

One key to understanding Japanese society is its emphasis on the group, which may, for instance, be a family, village, school, company, or the Japanese nation as a whole. Foreigners are likely to gain insight to Japanese group mentality at major tourist sights.

Within a group, peer pressure leads everyone to conform to accepted ways of doing things. A popular saying is "the nail that stands out will be hammered down." Even artists and those on the fringes of society only occasionally show genuine individualism. Foreigners, however, are expected to be more individualistic. The group mentality permeates everything: attitudes and behavior in any situation largely depend on whether the people concerned are inside or outside the group.

HOW THE JAPANESE REACT TO FOREIGNERS

Thanks to a fundamentally courteous culture, visitors meet with warm hospitality. But you will also encounter curiosity and occasional rudeness. Do not be surprised by apparently naive and insular attitudes – Western culture may flood the country but it is filtered and Japanized. Foreigners are still a curiosity in many parts of Japan (especially blondes and black people) and expected to be different. This can often lead to comments that are unintentionally racist. Young Japanese and those who travel abroad are changing the nation's perception of foreigners, but only slowly.

Because of the "them-and-us" group mentality, foreigners *(gaijin)* inevitably remain outsiders however much they are welcomed with warmth and open arms. Anyone who shows sensitivity to Japanese culture, speaks the language well, or is of Oriental racial origin may be accepted to some extent (and will be expected to conform to Japanese ways), but even they can never fully belong.

Group posing for a photograph while on a religious pilgrimage

MEETING JAPANESE PEOPLE

Japanese have a reputation for reserve and politeness, but in fact their social behavior is more complex, dictated by the situation, the place, the people involved, and social expectation. The contrast between, say, the formal etiquette required at a tea ceremony *(see p169)* and the casual abandon expected in a bar, is extreme.

You will find classic manners in hotels, restaurants, and shops, where courteous, efficient service is seen as simply the correct way of doing a job, and not demeaning. The response to waitresses and sales assistants is up to you: some Japanese treat them as invisible, but a token inclination of the head or quiet *"domo"* ("thanks") does no harm.

Sometimes officials such as tour guides seem autocratic, but this is largely due to imperfect English intonation and the expectation of Japanese travelers. If you somehow clash with authority, such as a traffic policeman, use a quiet conciliatory demeanor, not the loud assertiveness that might get results in your own country. This same applies to poor service: complain, but do so quietly and politely. In conversations generally, avoid confrontation and causing loss of face (although this is not as vital as in some parts of Asia). The purpose of conversation for Japanese is not discussion of ideas but building a relationship. Therefore, small talk is important.

Wherever you go, expect to be asked to pose for photographs or to practice English with strangers.

LANGUAGE DIFFICULTIES

Despite the profusion of brand names written in Roman script and often using Western-sounding words, Western visitors may face some language problems outside the main tourist areas. Signs for transportation systems are transliterated in many areas, though inconsistently *(see pp388–91)*.

Helpful sign written in both Japanese and transliteration for English-speaking visitors

Linguistically as culturally, the scope for misunderstanding is vast. The American English taught in schools is heavily weighted to grammar rather than conversation, so few Japanese are comfortable with everyday spoken English. When English is spoken, it is generally pronounced as if it were Japanese, and understood only in this way.

In Japanese all syllables are evenly stressed; no consonant except *n* occurs without being followed by a vowel; *r* and *l* merge into something between, and many words are abbreviated. Thus, for instance, taxi becomes *takushi*, hotel is *hoteru*, Coca-Cola becomes *kora*, and personal computer becomes *pasokon*; London is *Rondon*, New York is *Nyu Youku*, Sydney is *Shidoni*, and Los Angeles often simply *Ros*. For guidelines about pronunciation, see the Phrase Book on pages 412–416.

Further confusion comes from words imported from English that have been changed in meaning, for example *manshon*, not a palatial house but an apartment house; or *roman*, a romance novel. Resulting product names, such as the isotonic drinks Pocari Sweat and Calpis *(see p328)*, and "Japlish" text on t-shirts can be entertaining for visitors.

Even with fluent English speakers, subtleties are often lost in translation. If a Japanese says "yes," it usually means "I understand," not "I agree"; if they say "it's difficult," this means "no." For clarity, avoid negative and either/or questions.

JAPANESE NAMES

The order of Japanese names is traditionally family name followed by given name, as in this book. However, many Japanese automatically reverse this order when giving names to Westerners, so you may need to check which is the "first" name and "surname." Japanese generally call each other by the family name, even if they are quite close friends, but will happily call you by your first name if you prefer.

When speaking to or about an adult other than yourself, add "-san" to their name, which stands for Mr., Mrs., Ms., etc – for instance, Smith-san or John-san. For babies and young girls add "-chan," for young boys "-kun."

GIFT-GIVING

Gift-giving is big business in Japan, one of the most important aspects of etiquette. Any trip means bringing home souvenirs for colleagues and friends, usually something

Box of cookies gift-wrapped first in paper, then cloth

edible. Small gifts may be exchanged at a first business meeting, and if you visit someone's home, never go empty-handed: buy a luxury food item or take a small gift from your home country, especially local specialties and fine teas.

Keep gifts small, to avoid placing obligation on the recipient. Do not expect them to be opened in front of you. Likewise, if someone offers you a gift, it may be best not to open it in front of the giver.

Appearance matters: the Japanese wrap gifts beautifully *(see p351)*. A shop will usually do the wrapping for you, and a carrier bag from an elegant store is also good. Wine, chocolates, or flowers are acceptable gifts, although not the norm, but avoid chrysanthemums, which are used at funerals; do not give four of anything, because in Japanese the words for "four" and "death" sound similar; nor knives, lest they cut the friendship. Be aware that white is the color of mourning (though also worn by brides), and red is for celebration.

TIPPING

Tipping is not necessary anywhere unless stated, and may even cause offense to a proud Japanese. If a receipt or change is placed on a tray, this is through a sense of decorum when handling money rather than the expectation of a tip. When handing over larger sums of money on a more intimate level, for instance, to a guide or babysitter, the custom is to wrap it in an envelope or sheet of paper.

LINING UP AND JAYWALKING

As with so much in Japan, social behavior is full of contradictions. When waiting for a train, people line up neatly *(see pp388–9)* but may resort to pushing and shoving in order to get on. To get off a crowded train, simply push your way out, wordlessly. If you are completely stuck and cannot reach the door in time, call out *"orimass"* ("I'm getting off").

In situations where you want to break into a line – for instance, driving – the key is to catch someone's eye: as long as you are anonymous you can be ignored, but once you are acknowledged you must be treated politely.

As a pedestrian, be careful about jaywalking. It is heavily discouraged and rarely done by the Japanese. If you do it, others may assume you are crossing correctly and follow you unthinkingly, or you may be reprimanded by the police.

Commuters waiting patiently in line on a train station platform

Doing Business and Working in Japan

In business, as in other areas, Japan is a complex blend of hi-tech and old-fashioned. Practicalities are fairly easy in a land that is courteous and technologically up to date. In other respects, doing business in Japan can be a challenge. The structure and culture of business are so different from the West that misunderstandings often arise. With a little luck and planning, it is possible to find work in Japan, although living expenses, especially for accommodations, can be high.

Employees doing communal exercises before starting work

BUSINESS ATTITUDES AND STRUCTURES

Japanese business attitudes are dominated by the long term. This shows in corporate planning and the slow pace of decision-making, as well as individual attitudes. Lifetime employment at a single firm may no longer be the norm, but the company is still a community around which *salarymen* build their lives – if you ask someone what they do, the answer will be not their trade but the company for which they work.

The system is hard for foreigners to break into. Companies tend to be bound together, officially or un-officially, in huge industrial groups *(keiretsu)*, comprising networks of subsidiaries and subcontractors. Japan also has a reputation for protectionism over imports, and, although the situation has eased, there are high import taxes on items relating to industries that the government wishes to protect, such as furniture and medi-cines. Exporting is not so difficult, but dealing with the bureaucracy and paperwork for import and export can be time-consuming. Nonetheless, effort invested in groundwork and building contacts and rela-tionships can pay dividends.

BUSINESS FACILITIES

Most major hotels have excellent business facilities and can provide e-mail and Internet access – often direct from your hotel room – arrange rooms for meetings and conferences, and recommend interpreters. Business services also advertise in Yellow Pages and English-language magazines and newspapers. Outgoing telephone calls from hotels, including e-mail from your laptop, are charged at near-normal rates, without exorbitant surcharges. For details on mobile phones, and fax, e-

mail, and Internet facilities, see page 383. Convenience stores offer inexpensive photocopying and faxing.

BUSINESS CARDS

Known as *meishi*, business cards are an essential part of business and social transactions in Japan. They are vital for learning a person's status as well as their name; bear in mind that job titles may not correspond to Western equivalents, and people may have varied experience within a company. Have a large stock of business cards printed, preferably in English on one side and Japanese on the other. Major hotels and department stores in Japan often provide this service overnight, and Japan Airlines has an inflight service.

The card's design is not important, but avoid rounded corners, as these were tradi-tionally used by geisha and other women in the enter-tainment world, and the implication of frivolity lives on.

Business cards should be treated with respect: when meeting someone for the first time, proffer your card with both hands, and say your name clearly; then hand over the card with your right hand, taking the other person's card with your left. Keep their card in front of you during the meeting. Forgetting their card or putting it in a pocket where it may be crumpled are seen as signs of disrespect to the other person.

NEGOTIATING

Patience and good manners are the keys to successful negotiation in Japan. Japanese who are used to dealing with foreigners will make allowances for Western ways, but to stand the best chance of success it is worth being open to Japanese expectations. Familiarize yourself with the basics of etiquette outlined on

Salaryman relaxing at lunchtime in the park

pages 372–5. Even in hot weather, avoid dressing too informally; arrive for meetings on time or early; speak respectfully; and initially decline the seat of honor (farthest from the door).

Improving personal connections through small gifts or business entertaining is very much part of the system, but overt bribery is not. Japanese companies reach decisions by consensus, so elements of face-saving vagueness or flexibility can be useful. On the other hand, to miminize linguistic confusion it is essential to speak simply and unambiguously. In some situations, an interpreter may help. Be aware, however, that you will not be given a clear "no," even if that is what is meant. Discussion of money is usually left until last and should not be approached too bluntly.

BUSINESS ENTERTAINING

Socializing with business contacts is essential: there is little chance of establishing a good working relationship if you have not built a rapport over a few drinks or a game of golf *(see p359)*. Expect the Japanese to extend the first invitation, and allow them to pay – usually the person who does the inviting picks up the tab. If you would like to return the compliment but are not sure where to take people, ask their advice, or choose a hotel bar (where prices are clearly marked).

Socializing in a bar after work

Conversation can include business matters, but should not be intense. Drunken words or behavior on either side are normal and rarely taken seriously. Although the world of business entertaining is fundamentally male, foreign women are mostly treated as honorary men and, despite the underlying sexist attitudes, should have few problems. For eating and drinking etiquette, see pages 318–19.

Computerized bidding at the Tokyo Stock Exchange

FINDING WORK

Finding work in Japan is not as easy as it was during the economic boom of the 1980s. Most common are English-teaching jobs, which usually require a university degree, and sometimes a TEFL (Teaching English as a Foreign Language) qualification.

The **JET (Japan Exchange and Teaching) Programme** sends college graduates under age 35 to work in Japan, initially for a year, sometimes extendable to two or three. It has over 5,000 participants annually, from 34 countries. For details, contact the Japanese embassy in your country.

There are also limited opportunities in Japan for editorial work, particularly polishing translations of corporate publicity material or technical documents – look for such jobs in Japan's English-language newspapers.

VISAS

Staying in Japan long term generally means qualifying for either a working visa (with a commitment for two or three years working for one firm) or a student visa (which permits you to work part-time). UK, German, New Zealand, Australian, French, Canadian, and Korean citizens between 18 and 30 can also obtain a working-holiday visa, allowing part-time work, for up to a year. Though officially discouraged, it is sometimes possible to enter Japan as a Temporary Visitor and then arrange a job or study course.

LONG-TERM ACCOMMODATIONS

Some apartments can be found at rental rates similar to those in Western cities, but with a lot less space for the money, and the initial start-up costs are extremely high. Cheaper options include "gaijin houses," accommodations for foreigners ranging from pleasant shared apartments for three or four to scruffy hostels with 20 sharing a kitchen. The next step up is a weekly or monthly apartment, at the cost of a budget hotel or less, which is like a regular apartment but requires little or no deposit. In descriptions, room size is measured by the number of *tatami* mats, and apartments may be said to have, for instance, "2DK" – two bedrooms, a dining room, and kitchen.

Long-term visitors outside a "gaijin house" in Kyoto

Personal Security and Health

Hygiene standards are as high as in Western countries, and crime rates are low. Pickpockets occasionally operate in crowds, but bags can generally be put down freely in a store or at a station, and there is little risk in carrying large amounts of cash. *Koban* (manned police boxes) are found in every neighborhood; their presence helps to keep crime down.

A uniformed Tokyo policeman

IN AN EMERGENCY

Emergency calls are free. Your hotel, embassy, or consulate may also be able to help, while Tokyo Police have an assistance phone line for foreign visitors. The **Tokyo Metropolitan Health and Medical Information Center** provides health information; their operators speak English, Chinese, Korean, Thai, and Spanish. In case of translation difficulties during treatment, contact the **Emergency**

Translation Services. Lost possessions are very likely to be returned to you; contact the appropriate local police or transport authorities.

EARTHQUAKES, TYPHOONS, AND VOLCANOES

Each year, Japan experiences more than 1,000 earthquakes large enough to be felt by humans, although most are no more disruptive than the vibrations of a passing truck and are nothing to worry about. Earthquakes are more noticeable in tall buildings, which sway markedly but usually have mechanisms to absorb the motion. In a larger earthquake, especially in an old building, open doors (to prevent them from buckling and jamming) and turn off any gas. Do not go outside, where debris may fall on you, but shelter under something protective such as a reinforced doorway or sturdy table. Don't sleep close to a TV or computer shelf, or next to heavy furniture, such as a wardrobe, not securely fixed to the wall.

Typhoons may cause flooding or landslides, and the worst bring winds so strong that it is wise to stay indoors. The main typhoon season is in September. Active volcanoes usually have fences around them to ensure that no one goes dangerously close. Poisonous fumes occasionally seep from the ground nearby.

THINGS TO AVOID

Paddy fields are areas under cultivation and are private property so you should not walk in them. There are few "off-limits" areas in Japan, but it is advisable to avoid the *yakuza* (mafia, *see p203*), extremist political groups, and some religious sects.

WOMEN TRAVELERS

Official statistics for sexual assault in Japan are very low, and any unwanted propositions from men can usually be shaken off with a simple no. However, groping hands on crowded trains are acknowledged to be a problem, and increasing evidence suggests that sex crimes tend to go unreported or unprosecuted in Japan. Thus, women are best advised to take due care everywhere they go and with whom they associate. Avoid mountain paths after dark and be wary of men outside large train stations who try to initiate a conversation – it may be a ploy for recruiting into the sex trade. On a practical level, tampons are widely available, but the Pill is hard to obtain.

FOOD SAFETY

Food poisoning is rare thanks to good hygiene standards, and an upset stomach is likely to be simply due to a change in diet. The problem, if anything, is over-reliance on science – organic foods are uncommon. Tap water is drinkable throughout Japan, although in cities it may taste chlorinated. Avoid drinking from mountain streams.

Raw fish in sushi and sashimi is not a risk, nor are oysters. *Fugu* (blowfish) is safe provided it is correctly prepared. Only eat raw meat in a good restaurant, and

Schoolchildren practicing earthquake drill

Food stall at in indoor market in Naha, Okinawa

avoid raw bear *(kuma)* and raw wild boar *(botan)* because of risk of trichinosis, borne by parasites. Fruit and vegetables are clean, although insecticides and chemicals are widely applied so it is wise to do as the locals do and peel the fruit.

MEDICAL FACILITES

Facilities are generally as good as in the US or Europe but can be expensive. If you are sick, go to a hospital; for minor problems, consulting a pharmacist is another option.

To find a hospital, doctor, or dentist, contact the International Affairs Division of the prefectural office, the **AMDA (Asian Medical Doctors Association) International Medical Information Center**, or a TIC. The hospitals listed in the directory have some English-speaking doctors. Look, too, for advertisements in foreign-language magazines; international hotels have doctors on call.

Dental care varies in quality and may not meet Western aesthetic standards. Medicines are dispensed at hospitals and pharmacies; a prescription from abroad is more likely to be understood at a hospital. Western brands are available, if expensive, at international pharmacies such as Tokyo's **American Pharmacy**. Contact lenses can be obtained with relative ease,

Sign for a men's public bath

Sign for a women's public bath

and Western-brand lens solutions are very reasonably priced. Japan is big on pick-me-ups containing ginseng, caffeine, and the like, which can work wonders with a hangover. Local mosquito repellents and bite medicines are also good, as are pocket handwarmers *(kairo)*, sold in pharmacies and convenience stores. Chinese herbal medicine is widely available *(see p364)*.

PUBLIC CONVENIENCES

Japanese toilets range from highly sophisticated to very basic. The latter are simple troughs to squat over, facing the end with the hood, making sure nothing falls out of trouser pockets. If squatting is difficult, seek out Western-style toilets; many public facilities, including trains, have both. The usual way of finding out if a cubicle is occupied is to knock on the door and see if anyone knocks back. Toilet paper and hand towels are often not provided, so carry tissues with you.

Older Western-style toilets often have the option of small or large flush. They may also have a panel that, if pressed, plays a tune or makes a flushing sound to discreetly mask natural noises. Newer hi-tech toilets may have heated seats, automatic seat covers, and bidet and hot-air-drying facilities. For protocol on toilet slippers, *see page 373*.

Banking and Local Currency

For visitors used to easy and instant access to cash 24 hours a day in their home country, Japan's banking system can prove frustrating. Japan is largely a cash economy – personal checks are unknown – and cash is still the most popular way to pay for almost everything. After the economic "bubble" burst in late 1989, various scandals resulted in the closure of several banks and financial institutions. A comprehensive restructuring was undertaken and the economy is now recovering.

ATM with signs indicating that it accepts some foreign cards

BANKS AND BANKING HOURS

The nation's central bank, the Bank of Japan (Nippon Ginko), issues newly minted yen currency; it is also the bank of banks, and the government bank. However, this and the prefectural and local city banks are not geared to tourists. Buying yen, exchanging travelers' checks, and any other regular banking transactions may be more easily conducted via major Japanese banks that are authorized money exchangers, such as, **Sumitomo Mitsui**, **Mizuho Bank**, and **Citibank**. Some foreign banks also offer useful services. Note that local banks in rural areas may charge large fees.

Banks open 9am–3pm on weekdays, and close on weekends and national holidays. The exchange rate is posted at about 10am for US dollars, and after that for other currencies. Banks usually exchange currency between 10am and 3pm; some city banks offer exchange facilities from 9am.

Sign for an automatic teller machine (ATM)

TRAVELERS' CHECKS

Although travelers' checks provide a convenient way to carry money around Japan, they are usually accepted only in major city banks and large hotels. Travelex, American Express, and VISA checks are the most widely recognized. It is advisable to bring cash as well as checks, especially if you are traveling away from main tourist centers.

CREDIT AND DEBIT CARDS

International credit cards such as American Express, MasterCard, VISA, and Diners Club are generally accepted by leading banks, hotels, and stores in major cities. There may be a charge to use a credit card. Obtaining cash with credit cards is rarely possible. Even if a machine displays the sticker for your card (e.g. at petrol stations and ATMs), there may be a problem reading it. Many places only accept Japanese-issued cards such as JCB.

CHANGING MONEY

It is possible to change cash and travelers' checks at banks, major hotels (which offer the same exchange rates as banks), *ryokan*, main post offices, and some department stores in cities. Banks and post offices may also offer money transfer facilities. Even leading city banks may be unfamiliar with foreign currency apart from dollars, so be prepared for bank tellers to check with their superiors if they have not experienced such notes before. In city centers, staff may speak English, and forms are often supplied in English – if not, staff will indicate to a customer where to write. Transactions are relatively simple, but usually time-consuming. Always carry your passport as your identity will be checked.

At airports handling international flights, currency exchange counters may be open for longer than regular banking hours; at Tokyo International Airport at Narita, for example, the counter is open from 6:30am to 11pm. It is illegal for public transportation, stores, and restaurants to accept payment in foreign currencies, so a small amount of Japanese yen will be required on arrival to cover immediate needs. It is always wise to obtain cash before traveling in the countryside.

ATM SERVICES

Automatic teller machines are commonly available in large urban areas throughout Japan, although many do not accept foreign credit cards or cash cards. Post Office ATMs are more likely to accept foreign cards; stickers on display inside indicate which cards are accepted. Many convenience stores and supermarkets now have ATMs which stay open all night. Contact your bank or credit card company beforehand for locations of suitable ATMs.

CURRENCY

The Japanese currency is the yen, indicated by the symbol ¥. Coins are minted in denominations of ¥1, ¥5, ¥10, ¥50, ¥100, and ¥500. Bank notes are printed in denominations of ¥1,000, ¥2,000 (introduced in mid-2000), ¥5,000, and ¥10,000. Unused Japanese bank notes (but not coins) can be reconverted to foreign currency at the point of departure; the amount is limited only by the funds carried by the airport exchange center.

JTB COUPONS

Japan Travel Bureau, a specialty travel agency with branches in North America, Europe, Asia, and Australia, sells hundreds of different kinds of coupons that can be exchanged by visitors for services (such as travel, car rental, and accommodations) inside Japan. These can be a convenient means of paying, but work best when combined with a JTB-planned itinerary. Contact a nearby JTB office for further details.

Bank Notes
Each of the banknote denominations carries a portrait of an historical figure, such as the novelist Higuchi Ichiyo, on the ¥5,000 note.

10,000 yen

5,000 yen

2,000 yen

1,000 yen

500 yen

Coins
The denominations of Japan's coins are all marked in Arabic numerals, except for the ¥5. On the reverse side of most of the coins is a flower or plant design; on the ¥10 is a temple.

100 yen   50 yen   10 yen   5 yen   1 yen

Communications

Phonecard dispenser

As befits a country on the cutting edge of technology, the range of communication tools is extensive and state-of-the-art. But with such tools often used all at the same time, noise pollution is quite a problem, especially in busy shopping districts and at major train stations. Public phones are easy to find, though not all are suitable for making international calls. Newspapers and magazines are printed in abundance, and English-language versions are readily available in major cities. The postal system is fast and efficient.

The English-language *Mainichi Daily News* and *The Japan Times*

NEWSPAPERS AND MAGAZINES

The range of newspapers in Japanese is extensive. The most demanding of the reader is *Asahi Shimbun*; the least, *Gendai*, a tabloid containing a fair amount of pornographic material. Somewhere in between, selling around ten million copies daily, is the *Yomiuri Shimbun*. Japanese magazines come and go, seeking to follow news, business, and leisure trends. As for *manga* comic books *(see p25)*, they cover every subject imaginable; the regular bestseller is *Shonen Jump*, aimed at young men.

Four English-language newspapers are printed in Japan. The most widely available is *The Japan Times*; the other three are the *Daily Yomiuri*, the *Asahi Evening News*, and the *Mainichi Daily News*. *The Japan Times* includes a large classified section every

***Tokyo Journal* and *Shukan ST* student paper**

Monday. All are sold at kiosks in train stations, major hotels, and foreign-language bookstores *(see p111)*.

A few English-language magazines are published, often with extensive listings and classified advertisements. These include *Metropolis, Tokyo Journal,* and *Kansai Time Out*. Foreign-language bookstores often stock imported magazines, though these tend to be rather expensive. Newsletters in various languages are produced by community groups all over the country and are widely available.

TELEVISION AND RADIO

NHK is the state broadcaster, running two broadcast and two satellite channels. The nightly 7pm news on NHK has an English-language translation, available on bilingual TVs, which are often found in hotels. Other nationwide networks include Nihon TV, TBS, Fuji TV, and TV Asahi. Cable and satellite are also widely available, as is digital broadcasting on NHK and the other networks. In addition to the usual MTV and CNN, there are many Japanese channels specializing in news, sports, soaps, movies, and so on.

The state radio station NHKFM broadcasts news and mainly classical music.

There are also several commercial radio stations; some, such as J-WAVE and Inter FM in Tokyo, and CO-CO-LO in Central Honshu, offer a choice of programs in English and other languages. Check up-to-date listings pages for frequencies and for times of programs.

A red call box with a gray phone, suitable for international calls

TYPES OF TELEPHONES

The most common public phones are green in color and situated everywhere from stations to inside trains, outside convenience stores, and on street corners. Older versions of the green phones accept ¥10 and ¥100 coins only; newer models take a wider range of coins plus telephone cards. These phones are for domestic calls only.

Gray public phones have an LCD display, a button for converting information into English, volume control (handy in noisy public places), and an emergency button for dialing police, fire, and ambulance *(see pp378–9)*. These phones are the most likely to offer international direct-dialing.

The old-fashioned pink phones still found in many *kissaten (see p317)* are for local calls and accept ¥10 coins only.

TELECOM COMPANIES AND PHONE CARDS

Calls from public phones are automatically connected via **NTT Communications** unless you use a phone card issued by another

Green public phone, the most widespread type

operator such as **Softbank Telecom** and **KDDI**. You usually have to use the appropriate company's access code *(see directory)* when dialing. Softbank Telecom also offers the 0061 Love Love Homecard, which gives you a number that can be keyed in to call abroad from any type of phone (except pink public phones), even mobiles.

Phone cards may be purchased from a wide variety of outlets, including station kiosks, vending machines, and convenience stores.

Beautiful designs on Japanese telephone cards

MAKING INTERNATIONAL CALLS

Some public phones take international credit cards as well as phone cards. As with domestic calls, the call will be routed via **NTT** unless you purchase a phone card issued by one of the other major telecom companies offering international calls. Currently these are **KDDI** and **Softbank Telecom**. The foreign companies MCI World.Com Japan, Global One, and Deutsche Telekom Japan also offer international-only services in Japan.

Dial the appropriate company's access code *(see directory)*, then the country

code, area code (minus any initial zero), then the number. The major companies are in competition, so charges and services are constantly changing; each has a toll-free number for information.

All major hotels offer international direct-dialing. You may be surcharged for calls from your room. **KDDI** and **NTT** offer international collect calls; dial the appropriate access code and then ask the operator to place a collect call. The cheapest times for international calls are from 11pm to 8am daily; the second-cheapest are between 7pm and 11pm.

LOCAL CALLS

The charge for a local call is ¥10 per minute. Use small coins or phone cards in a public phone; unused coins will be returned to you. In this guide area codes are given in brackets; omit the code if calling from inside the area.

MOBILE PHONES

Some foreign mobile phones may be used in Japan via Japanese operators such as Softbank Telecom and Docomo. Check with your mobile operator before traveling. If you are staying for a while, mobiles are cheap to buy and there is a huge choice. For shorter stays, it is possible to rent mobiles from all the big providers through their service desks at Narita and Kansai airports. Some public areas, including bullet trains, have places set aside for mobile phone use.

FAX, E-MAIL, AND INTERNET FACILITIES

Fax machines for public use are located at many convenience stores and at main post offices. Hotels will often have machines available for guests to use, too; they often charge to send faxes but not to receive them.

Internet cafés are rare but can be found in major cities; access is also available in some city halls and public libraries.

INTERNATIONAL DIALING CODES

Use these codes after the international access codes to dial the following countries:
Australia **61**, Brazil **55**, Canada **1**, China, **86**, France, **33**, Germany **49**, Hong Kong **852**, India **91**, Indonesia **62**, Ireland **353**, Israel **972**, Republic of Korea **82**, Malaysia **60**, Netherlands **31**, New Zealand **64**, Peru **51**, Philippines **63**, Russia **7**, Singapore **65**, Spain **34**, Sweden **46**, Switzerland **41**, Taiwan **886**, Thailand **66**, United Kingdom **44**, and US **1**.

MAIL

Post offices (*yubin-kyoku*) and mailboxes in Japan can easily be identified by the character looking like the letter "T" with an extra horizontal bar across the top. Main post offices are usually open 9am–5pm on weekdays and 9am–12:30pm on Saturdays. Smaller post offices may open 9am–5pm on weekdays but are often closed on weekends. Stamps are also sold at some convenience stores and larger hotels. Make sure any mail is addressed correctly and legibly; the postal code is especially important.

International mail is best sent from a main post office. There may be a counter where English is spoken, indicated by a sign. The clerk will weigh the letter to be mailed and sell you the correct stamp. An express mail service is available for more urgent mail inside Japan and abroad; say "express," and staff will stamp it accordingly. EMS is a speedy way to send top priority mail, and has a tracking system. Should an item be especially urgent, send it from **Tokyo Central Post Office**, or **Tokyo International Post Office** (which has an all-night counter).

Items mailed from a mailbox may take slightly longer to reach their destination. Some boxes have two slots; the one on the left is for domestic letters, and the one on the right is for other mail.

Japanese mailbox

Use the right-hand slot for international and express mail. Parcels must be mailed from a post office: fill in the green coupon supplied, but do not attach it to the package; this will be done by staff over the counter. Boxes and bags are available for sending larger items.

COURIERS AND OTHER MAIL SERVICES

Japan is well served with prompt and efficient door-to-door delivery services (*takkyubin*). The best known of these domestic companies is **Yamato**; **Sagawa-Kyubin**, which is based in Kyoto, also serves all of Japan. Small packages can be sent via these courier services from convenience stores; larger items will be picked up at the source. There are also a number of courier services for sending printed materials and packages abroad. **FedEx** and **DHL** are among the best known. **Nippon Courier Services** is also prompt and reliable.

Colorful examples of Japanese postage stamps

Logo identifying post offices and also found on mailboxes

FINDING AN ADDRESS

There are few street names in Japan, and no consistent numbering system for buildings. Indeed, the numbering of buildings in a block is often dictated by the order in which they were built, so finding an address can be a puzzle, even for the Japanese. It is slightly easier in cities such as Nara, Kyoto, and Sapporo, which were built on a grid pattern, as at least the blocks are numbered in sequence. Tokyo, however, was designed in a spiral around the castle and then allowed to develop higgledy-piggledy, in order to confound enemies of the shogunate. Even taxi drivers have a tough time locating addresses in the capital. (All Tokyo sights, hotels, and restaurants listed in this guide are marked on the Street Finder.)

Most Japanese carry name cards with maps. Hotels should provide guests with a map, preferably in Japanese and English, of their location and nearby landmarks.

Addresses in Japanese start with the name of the prefecture, and work backward through various districts to the number of the building. When Japanese addresses are

DIRECTORY

MAIL

Tokyo Central Post Office

2-7-2 Marunouchi, Chiyoda-ku, Tokyo.
Tel (03) 3284-9539 (for domestic mail).
Tel (03) 3284-9540 (for international mail).

Tokyo International Post Office

3-5-14 Shinsuna, Koto-ku, Tokyo.
Tel (03) 5665-4302. (international mail service).
www.post.yusei.go.jp

COURIER COMPANIES

DHL
Tel 0120-39-2580, then press 0.
www.dhl.co.jp

FedEx
Tel (043) 298-1919.
Tel 0120-003200 (toll-free).
www.fedex.com

Nippon Courier Services
Tel (03) 5461-3550.

Sagawa-Kyubin
Tel 0120-14-7070.
www.sagawa-exp.co.jp

Yamato
Tel 0120-01-9625.
www.kuronekoyamoto.co.jp

INFORMATION ON ADDRESSES

Japan Yellow Pages
Tel (03) 3239-3501.
www.yellowpage-jp.com

NTT Town Pages
www.english.itp.ne.jp

written in Roman letters, the order is reversed, so that the block number comes first, following Western convention.

In an address, the first number of, for example, 2-3-4 Otemachi refers to the *chome*, or main block. The second number points to a smaller block of buildings within the original *chome*. The last is the number of the building itself. On city streets, the numbers of the *chome* are given on telephone poles and lamp-posts, reading in this instance 2-3; it is then a matter of finding building number 4.

Local police boxes are used in large part to help people reach their destinations. Officers on duty have maps, and may even call an address to pinpoint the location. Telephone operators will not supply an address, even if a number is known. Consult NTT's **Town Pages**, and **Japan Yellow Pages** (which publishes English-language editions).

JAPAN'S PREFECTURES

The four main islands of Honshu, Hokkaido, Shiko-ku, and Kyushu are divided into 47 areas called *ken* or prefectures. Each prefecture is governed independently under the overall control of central government. The prefectural office is usually located in the largest conurbation, which also has its own city or town office. Honshu's prefectures are grouped into the larger, historical regions of Tohoku, Chubu, Kanto, Kinki, and Chugoku. Tokyo has its own metropolitan government; each of the capital's wards has its own office.

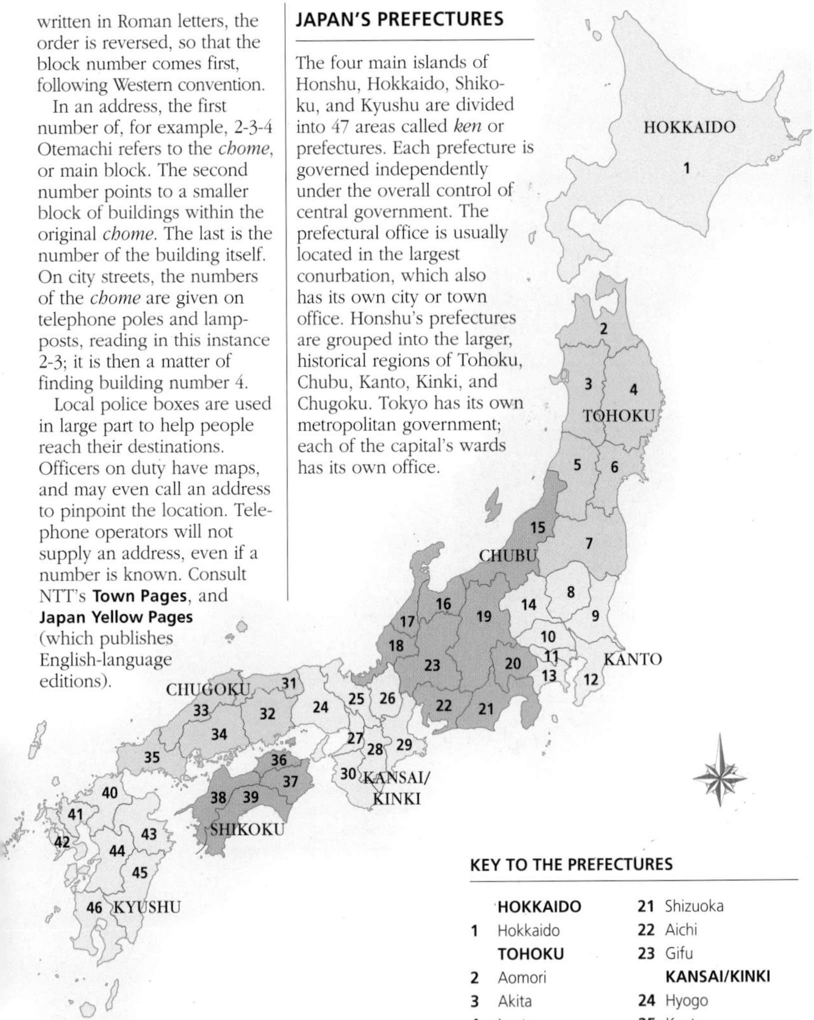

HOKKAIDO

TOHOKU

CHUBU

KANTO

CHUGOKU

KANSAI/ KINKI

SHIKOKU

KYUSHU

OKINAWA ARCHIPELAGO

KYUSHU

OKINAWA

KEY TO THE PREFECTURES

HOKKAIDO	21 Shizuoka
1 Hokkaido	22 Aichi
TOHOKU	23 Gifu
2 Aomori	**KANSAI/KINKI**
3 Akita	24 Hyogo
4 Iwate	25 Kyoto
5 Yamagata	26 Shiga
6 Miyagi	27 Osaka
7 Fukushima	28 Nara
KANTO	29 Mie
8 Tochigi	30 Wakayama
9 Ibaraki	**CHUGOKU**
10 Saitama	31 Tottori
11 Tokyo	32 Okayama
12 Chiba	33 Shimane
13 Kanagawa	34 Hiroshima
14 Gunma	35 Yamaguchi
CHUBU	**SHIKOKU**
15 Niigata	36 Kagawa
16 Toyama	37 Tokushima
17 Ishikawa	38 Ehime
18 Fukui	39 Kochi
19 Nagano	**KYUSHU**
20 Yamanashi	40 Fukuoka

TRAVEL INFORMATION

Most foreigners fly to Japan and then use the country's excellent railroad system. Many of the famous sightseeing areas lie on or near the fast train lines between Tokyo, Osaka, and Fukuoka – visiting such places as Kyoto, Himeji Castle, and Hiroshima is easy, despite the distances involved. Slower trains connect to popular sights such as Nara and Nikko. Local public transportation systems such as subways,

Logo of Japan Airlines

trams, and buses are efficient, but you may need to rent a car to explore remote regions. The **Japan National Tourist Organization** (JNTO) website *(see p371)* provides useful travel information for tourists, including lists of travel agents that can make reservations and sell travel tickets and Rail Pass vouchers *(p389)*. In Tokyo the JNTO also has a Tourist Information Center or TIC, which provides travel information in English.

Japan Airlines (JAL) airplane

INTERNATIONAL AIRPORTS

The usual gateways for foreigners entering Japan are Narita Airport, near Tokyo, which is also called Tokyo New International Airport, and Osaka's Kansai International Airport. Other major airports handling international flights, mainly from Asia, include Naha, in Okinawa; Fukuoka and Nagasaki, in Kyushu; Hiroshima, Nagoya, Niigata, and Sendai, in Honshu; and Sapporo, in Hokkaido.
Japan Airlines (JAL) and **All Nippon Airways (ANA)** are the main airlines of Japan. JAL is particularly popular with foreign tourists.

ARRIVING VIA NARITA AIRPORT

Tokyo's Narita Airport has two terminals connected by a free shuttle bus, which takes about 10 minutes. Narita Tourist Information Offices are located in the arrival lobby of each terminal, and have a multi-lingual staff.
Visitors who have bought a Japan Rail Pass Exchange Order *(see p389)* before arriving in Japan should visit the

Japan Railways (JR) ticket counter. If validated from the day of arrival in Japan, the Pass can be used to make the trip from the airport into central Tokyo by JR train.
Narita Airport is located 60 km (35 miles) northeast of the center of Tokyo, thus the journey by taxi will cost at least ¥22,000. For travelers with heavy or excessive luggage, airport limousine buses are convenient but often slow, depending on traffic conditions. Buses run non-stop to Tokyo, Yokohama, and other nearby airports.
The **Narita Express (N'EX)** train, located beneath the terminal building, travels non-stop and in some luxury to Tokyo station in less than one hour, and then on to Shinjuku and Ikebukuro in the capital, or to

Yokohama and Ofuna, near Kamakura. The Japan Rail Pass can be used on this train, but you will need to reserve a seat (free of charge) at the ticket booth. All signs and announcements for the N'EX are in Japanese and English, and English-language information is available via an onboard telephone service. Remember to reserve a seat when returning to the airport on the N'EX.
Travelers without a JR Pass will find Keisei trains cheaper than the N'EX and almost as fast. The Keisei line connnects with JR at Nippori, with an easy transfer. Board the Keisei Skyliner at Keisei Narita airport station (also below the terminal building); it terminates at Keisei Ueno station, within walking distance of JR Ueno train station and Ueno subway station.
The JR Sobu railway line, which changes name to the JR Yokosuka line at Tokyo station, is the cheapest but slowest form of travel from the airport.

Terminal 2 of Tokyo New International Airport, at Narita

Interior of check-in lobby at Kansai International Airport

ARRIVING VIA KANSAI AIRPORT

Japan's second-largest international airport, Kansai, has direct connections with Europe, North America, and other countries, and is located on a manmade island 5 km (3 miles) off the coast in Osaka Bay. Taxis, limousine buses, and trains are all efficient ways to get into Osaka. There is also a high-speed boat service to Kobe. For Kyoto, Kansai Airport is most convenient. Kansai Tourist Information Office is in the arrivals lobby. For onward journeys by rail, Rail Pass Exchange Orders (*see p389*) may be exchanged at the JR Information Counter, Tis-Travel Service Center, or *Midori-no-madoguchi* (Green Windows, *see p390*).

LUGGAGE DELIVERY

Luggage can be delivered from airports to either a hotel or a private address the following day, and it can be picked up for the return trip. A number of companies offering this service operate counters at Narita and Kansai airports. The basic cost is for one item of luggage weighing no more than 32 kg (70 lb).

DOMESTIC FLIGHTS

The airlines JAL and ANA maintain an extensive network of flights covering the four main islands and many of the smaller ones, too. For trips up to 600 km (350 miles), bullet trains (*see p388*) are often faster and more

convenient than planes. On domestic flights JAL and ANA offer economy seats and, at an extra cost, a "Super Seat" service, which is a combination of first and business class. You can make reservations through a travel agent or directly through the airline's reservation office. For short distances, propeller aircraft are sometimes used.

The domestic "no-frills," low-cost airline **Skymark** was launched in 1998. It operates flights between Haneda Airport (Tokyo), Fukuoka, Tokushima, and Kagoshima.

The runway of Nagasaki Airport, built on the sea

AIRPORT TAX

Passengers traveling from Kansai, Narita, or Fukuoka airports are subject to a Passenger Service Facilities Charge (PSFC). At Kansai this is about ¥2,650 per person, and at Narita and Fukuoka the charge is around ¥2,040 and ¥945 respectively. However, in all cases this tax is conveniently included in the cost of your airline ticket. Other airports do not make this charge.

DIRECTORY

TOURIST INFORMATION

Tokyo office (TIC)
10F Tokyo Kotsu Kaikan Bldg,
Yurakucho, Chiyoda-ku.
Tel (03) 3201-3331.

Narita Airport offices
Arrivals floor, Terminal 1.
Tel (0476) 30-3383.
Terminal 2. *Tel (0476) 34-6251.*

Kansai Airport office
Arrivals floor. *Tel (0724) 56-6025.*

AIRPORT INFORMATION

Narita Airport
www.narita-airport.jp

Kansai Airport
www.kansai-airport.or.jp

AIRLINES

Japan Airlines (JAL)

In Japan:
Tel 0120-25-5931 (toll-free) for international reservations.
Tel 0120-25-5971 (toll-free) for domestic reservations.
www.jal.co.jp

In USA and Canada:
Tel 1-800 525 3663.
www.japanair.com

In UK:
Tel (0845) 7-747-700.
www.uk.jal.com

All Nippon Airways (ANA)
Tel 0120-029-222 (toll-free).
www.ana.co.jp

Skymark
Tel (03) 3433-7670 (Tokyo).

ARRIVING BY BOAT

It is possible to travel to Japan by boat from some parts of mainland Asia, including Pusan in South Korea, and Shanghai in China, from where boats run to Kobe and Osaka. The Far Eastern Shipping Line connects Niigata/Takaoka on the west coast of Japan's Honshu island with the port of Vladivostock in Russia, which is where the Trans-Siberian Railway begins and ends its journey to and from Europe.

Traveling by Train

Tourist train, Nagasaki

Japan's rail system leads the world in terms of safety, efficiency, and comfort. Trains linking major cities tend to have announcements and digital displays running tickertape style in both Japanese and English. In rural areas, the names of train stations may not be given in translation, but railway staff and members of the public generally try to be helpful to foreigners. The Japan Rail Pass is highly recommended. Advice about buying individual tickets and reserving seats is on page 390.

東 口 East

きっぷうりば
Ticket Plaza

本日分・前売分
Today's 新幹線 Advance JR線
Shinkansen JR Line

JAL
ANA
JAS

いらっしゃいませ

Ticket office and advance reservation center at JR train station

THE RAILWAY NETWORK

The Japan Railways Group, known as **JR**, is the main operator. It includes all the *shinkansen* super expresses (bullet trains) and a nationwide network of over 21,000 km (13,000 miles) of tracks. There are also many private railroads linking smaller communities in more remote regions. Often travelers have a choice of lines to the same destination.

THE SHINKANSEN: BULLET TRAINS

The first "bullet train," as it was quickly nicknamed by a marveling media worldwide, drew out of Tokyo Station in 1964, the year of the Tokyo Olympics. Symbolic of Japan's economic recovery and future drive, it became, and remains, a source of national pride.

They are no longer the world's fastest trains, and there are still only a few *shinkansen* lines linking the major cities, but their efficiency, as proved by long-distance journeys timed to the minute,

is legendary. There are four types of *shinkansen* in current use: **Kodama**, which stops at many stations en route; **Hikari**, serving only major stations; **Tsubame** in Kyushu; and **Nozomi**, the fastest and most expensive.

English-language announcements and clear signs make the *shinkansen* an appealing form of transportation for foreigners, often more convenient than flying, though there is surprisingly little space for large suitcases. It is best to

Aerodynamic nose of the fabled *shinkansen*, or "bullet train"

reserve a seat *(see p390)*, as the non-reserved carriages can be very crowded. Reserve a seat well in advance if traveling over a holiday period.

OTHER TRAINS AND LINES

Other major train types include **Tokkyu** ("limited express," the fastest), **Kyuko** ("express"), **Kaisoku** (misleadingly called "rapid"), and **Futsu** local trains.

The main train stations in the Tokyo metropolitan area are all on the JR **Yamanote line**. This loop line is easy for foreigners to use.

Every year there are new train models, including "specials" for tourists; trains with *tatami* flooring; trains with swing seats and panoramic windows; even party trains with karaoke systems.

STATION SIGNS AND FACILITIES

Tokyo's Shinjuku station *(see p93)* is the world's busiest, and several others in Tokyo and major cities are on a vast scale. Finding a particular line or exit during rush hour can be intimidating and exhausting for newcomers with heavy baggage. It is a good idea to find out which named or numbered exit is best for you before arriving at one of the major stations.

The level of signs in English varies greatly. Tokyo's Shibuya station, for example, is a major hub but notoriously bad for navigation. By contrast, Kyoto's new station is geared to tourists, Japanese and foreign, and most of the major tourist destinations are trying to make navigation easier.

Even at large stations, *shinkansen* lines are clearly marked, and other lines are color coded. The yellow bobbles on the floor are intended to help blind people navigate but can be a problem for suitcases with wheels, as is the lack of consistently placed escalators.

Note that trains, especially the *shinkansen*, stop only briefly in order to maintain their timetables. Thus, travelers are encouraged to line up

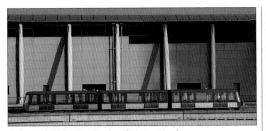

Modern train in the Kansai region of Western Honshu

on some platforms: look out for floor markings relating to each set of doors. There may also be numbers correlating to carriage numbers for trains with reserved seats. Despite these measures, central Tokyo's trains, especially on the Yamanote loop line, often get overcrowded, and white-gloved staff are even employed to help push people in.

Train stations in major tourist areas have baggage lockers and information booths; staff here may speak English and occasionally other languages.

The Japan Rail Pass

ON-BOARD FACILITIES

Services on *shinkansen* and other long-distance routes usually include trolleys for snacks and beverages, and the sale of *bento* lunchboxes and edible *omiyage* (souvenirs). There is often a choice of Western- (sit-down) and Japanese-style (squat) toilets. Toilets and washrooms may be electronically operated, requiring a hand to be passed in front of a panel for flushing, or under a tap to start water flowing.

THE JAPAN RAIL PASS

In a country with some of the world's highest train fares, the Japan Rail Pass is a wonderful deal specially devised for people visiting Japan on tourist visas. However, the Pass must be purchased from an agent abroad, before the visit. It is not for sale inside Japan itself.

The Pass gives unlimited travel on all JR lines and affiliated buses and ferries,

including the N'EX train *(see p386)* from Narita into Tokyo, city-center JR trains including Tokyo's Yamanote loop line, and *shinkansen*, except Nozomi. (If you board a Nozomi, you will be asked to pay for the entire fare.) Subways and private railroads are not included. You may still have to reserve a seat on long-distance trains, but the reservation will be free.

You can choose a 7-day, 14-day, or 21-day Pass, first or standard class. If you intend to travel any greater distance than a return train trip from, say, Tokyo to Kyoto, then the Pass will save money. Showing it to staff at station ticket barriers also saves the hassle of purchasing tickets and negotiating turnstiles with luggage. If you want to explore Japan by train for more than 21 days, or prefer to break up your travels by staying in one place for more than a few days, then consider buying more than one Pass.

JNTO offices *(see p370)* will have a full list of Rail Pass agents in your country (they do not sell Passes themselves).

The agent will issue a **Japan Rail Pass Exchange Order**, usually at a price based on the day's rate of exchange with the yen. This voucher must be exchanged for the Japan Rail Pass proper at designated JR Travel Service Centers in Japan, including Narita and Kansai airports and major train stations. You need to show your passport. When you exchange your voucher for a Pass, you must specify the date on which you wish to start using it; this can be any date within three months of issue of the Exchange Order.

Bear in mind that after the start date of the Pass, its cost cannot be refunded, and neither the Exchange Order nor the Pass can be replaced if lost or stolen.

OTHER PASSES

There are also other less expensive regional rail passes. The **JR East Rail Pass** covers Honshu northeast of Tokyo, and can only be purchased outside Japan. There are two types of **JR West Rail Pass**: the **Sanyo Area Pass** covers the Nozomi *shinkansen*, as well as regular bullet trains from Osaka to Okayama, Hiroshima, and Hakata; the **Kansai Area Pass** includes Osaka, Kobe, Kyoto, Himeji, and Nara. Both can be purchased within or outside Japan.

Most cities have their own special tickets: ask at local TICs or "i" centers. The **Tokyo Free Kippu** covers most of the subway, bus, and tram lines in central Tokyo.

Staffed exit lane for holders of the Japan Rail Pass

DIRECTORY

JR Infoline

(English-language service)

Tel (03) 3423-0111, 10am–6pm daily.

JR East: **www**.jreast.co.jp

JR Kyushu: **www**.jrkyushu. co.jp

JR Tokai: **www**.jr-central.co.jp

JR West: **www**.westjr.co.jp

USING TRAIN TICKET MACHINES

Basic fare tickets for short distances are usually available from vending machines. Some machines accept ¥1,000, ¥5,000, and ¥10,000 notes, and all should supply change. At some stations, maps are provided in English translation, showing in which fare zone your destination lies.

If you are in doubt about the cost of a trip, simply buy a cheap ticket and pay any excess at the destination by using the Fare Adjustment machine near the exit barrier. Some have an English translation facility in the style of an ATM. The machine will supply you with another ticket.

If there is no such machine, or you cannot understand it, the staff will work out the excess for payment. You will not be penalized for having the wrong value ticket.

Vending machines for basic fare train tickets

USING GREEN WINDOWS

Tickets and seat reservations for longer trips can be purchased at *Midori-no-madoguchi* (Green Windows) at JR train stations. You can also buy tickets at Travel Service Centers in the larger stations, and from authorized travel agents. Note that credit cards are not always accepted.

Seat reservations are recommended for most long-distance trips, for a small extra charge or free if you have a Pass. The reservation ticket will bear the date and time of the train and also the coach and seat number. Ask the vendor to point out which numbers refer to each element if you are in doubt. On the platform, find the number that corresponds with the coach number, and line up.

Other Forms of Public Transportation

There are numerous systems of local transportation in the major cities, all of which are efficient, safe, and clean. The only complication for foreigners is in the purchase of tickets: systems vary from city to city, vending machines tend to be only in Japanese, and few staff speak English.

Kagoshima sightseeing bus

SUBWAY SYSTEMS

The Tokyo subway system *(see inside back cover)* is extensive and color-coded on maps to match the color of the cars. The second largest subway system is in Osaka. Yokohama, Fukuoka, Kyoto, Sapporo, and some other cities also have systems. Modes of operation differ slightly.

The JR Rail Pass is not honored on the Tokyo Subway or any other subway tracks. Purchase a ticket from either a vending machine or a ticket window.

Subway ticket vending machines, even in Tokyo, are often only in Japanese. This may seem daunting at first, but with a color-coded transliterated map, such as the one of the Tokyo Subway System at the back of this book, you should find that matching the Japanese characters of your destination with those on the fare chart by the machine is not too difficult. The chart will show in Arabic numerals how much to pay. Press the corresponding fare key on the machine and insert the money. Change will be dispensed with the ticket. As with overland train tickets,

Entrance to subway tracks at Hakata station, Fukuoka

if you are in any doubt about how much to pay, then simply buy the cheapest ticket and pay the excess at the end. The ticket may be punched when passing through the gate, but increasingly more likely has to be put through an automatic machine.

Station names are often displayed on platform signboards in romanized *(romaji)* form as well as Japanese.

All mass-transit systems close at around midnight until about 5am.

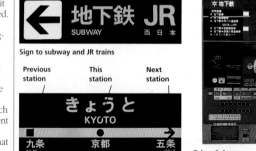

Sign to subway and JR trains

Previous station / This station / Next station

Destination sign on wall of subway platform

Tokyo Subway ticket machine

Interior of public tram in Nagasaki

TRAMS

Hiroshima and Nagasaki still have street cars, or trams; Sapporo retains this mode of transportation, too. Only one tram line remains in Tokyo, the Arakawa *(see p101)*. There are also a few oddities, like the Enoden Railway, at Kamakura, which is part-train, part-tram, sometimes running down the center of the street.

Kochi bus dog logo

Fares and systems for paying on trams differ from city to city; some charge a flat fare, whatever the distance traveled. The fare machine is sometimes manned separately. Follow the example of other passengers as to when to pay, and whether to pay the fare collector or put money into the box.

MONORAIL SYSTEMS

Many cities now operate monorail systems. They are all easy to negotiate and ride. Hiroshima enjoys one such line, which was installed for the Asian Games of 1994. In Tokyo, the monorail from Hamatsucho links with Haneda Airport; the new Yurikamome line links Shinbashi with Tokyo Teleport Town and the far side of the Rainbow Bridge *(see pp102–3)*.

CITY BUSES

Bus depots *(basu noriba)* are often located close to train stations in cities, usually on the same side as where taxis line up. The method of paying fares varies. Some buses are boarded at the front, and the fare – usually a flat rate – deposited into a slot beside the driver. If in doubt, state your destination and offer the driver a selection of small coins to pick out. Disembark from the door in the middle of the bus.

A second system invites passengers to step aboard toward the center or back of the bus; a small machine distributes numbered tickets. The number on this ticket should be matched to a lighted panel at the front of the bus, which shows fares to be paid. If the ticket reads "2," look along the line at the top of the panel and check the sum in yen below the corresponding figure. Drop this amount into the box by the driver when you get off.

Do not step down from either exit until the bus comes to a complete halt, or the doors will not open automatically. When in doubt, observe how local people ride the bus and follow suit.

LONG-DISTANCE BUSES

The efficiency and extent of the rail network in Japan is such that very few foreign tourists attempt to use long-distance buses. However, the bus network is comprehensive, and for those without a JR Rail Pass, a bus is a much cheaper option. While styles and services vary, buses are uniformly comfortable, often with guides, toilets, and even onboard food and beverage services. Local information centers have timetable details, or visit www.jrbuskanto.co.jp.

FERRIES AND TOURIST BOATS

Tickets for most ferries can be bought at the ferry terminal on the day of departure. Usually there is a form to fill in, which enables the ferry company to compile a list of passengers. JNTO's travel manual details the main services. There are many long-distance ferry routes, including to mainland Asia *(see p387)*, but tourists will probably find flying more convenient.

Many boats these days are for tourism purposes only. Flat-bottomed punts are quite popular, with boatmen in traditional clothing.

Gaily painted tourist boat at Matsushima, Northern Honshu

Private Transportation

Japan is an enjoyable and relatively safe country in which to take to the road. In the countryside, renting a car is by far the best and most flexible way to get around. It is also easy and surprisingly inexpensive to rent a vehicle, though the cost of road tolls and parking charges can quickly mount up. Road surfaces and rental cars are generally well maintained. Driving is on the left. The main problem for foreigners on the road is in trying to decipher road signs in already unfamiliar territory. Other problems include such hazards as roads blocked by snow in winter, flooding during the rainy season, and occasional landslides.

Taxi with smartly dressed driver, typical in Japan

TAXIS

All licensed taxis in Japan have green license plates; avoid unlicensed vehicles. A red light on top of the vehicle indicates that it is free. You can flag a taxi or look for a stand – a number of taxi companies operate in each city. Costs are quite high: on a par with, say, yellow cabs in New York. Space for luggage is limited.

The doors of Japanese taxis are operated electrically by the driver from inside; it is not advisable to close or open the taxi door yourself.

Few taxi drivers speak much English. As with finding the location of anything in Japan (see p384), it is best to carry a map marked with instructions in Japanese and the phone number of your destination.

RENTING A CAR

Vehicles are available for rental at ports of entry, from major train stations, and local dealers. Visitors must produce an international driver's license (International Driving Permit) at the car-rental agency. Unfortunately,

some countries, like Germany and Switzerland, have no reciprocal arrangement with Japan for honoring international driver's licenses.

The two largest car-rental companies with English facility are **Nippon Rent-A-Car** and **Nissan Rent-A-Car**. Costs are on a par with the US and Western Europe, in some cases cheaper.

Drivers with rental cars are protected financially from breakdown with insurance. It is a good idea to take out membership of the **Japan Automobile Federation**, which issues a booklet with emergency numbers for foreigners in case of breakdown, and is linked with similar organizations abroad.

ROAD TOLLS

Most national highways are free, but many private roads charge tolls. There is no consistent system of charging: a short distance may cost anything from ¥100 to ¥10,000.

Road sign at a crossing in Kyoto, with some *romaji* transliteration

SERVICING

Fuel is readily available in Japan. The cost of it compares favorably with Europe, but is double the price of Canadian fuel and nearly three times the cost of gas in the US. The international chain ESSO is familiar to drivers in Japan. JOMO is a popular Japanese chain, the name derived from the phrase "Joy of Motoring."

PARKING

Public parking is available – at a price. The general rule is that the closer to any city center, the more expensive

Quiet road in the Mount Aso caldera

parking fees become. To overcome the problem of lack of sufficient space, the Japanese have developed various innovative parking solutions. Lifts and roll-over systems are common; two-car families with only a single parking space often resolve the problem with a two-tier stacking system.

"Beware of bears" road sign in forested mountain region

RULES OF THE ROAD

Japanese drive on the left-hand side of the road. On local roads, the maximum speed allowed is usually 60 kph (37 mph), but may be less, from 30–50 kph (18–31 mph). On highways (expressways) maximum speeds vary from 80–100 kph (50–62 mph). Drivers may not turn left on a red light in Japan, as allowed in some other countries.

While in general the Japanese drive carefully and safely, they have a habit of driving over intersections after a light has turned red. It is not a good idea to follow suit, and vehicles to the front and rear should be observed carefully when approaching traffic lights.

Signs are easier to decipher in cities, but the pressure of traffic and the network of roads, which may include several one on top of another, can be daunting for even the most experienced driver from abroad. A wide berth should be given to dump trucks, whose drivers are paid by the load and are therefore under pressure to drive fast; also watch out for large gangs of notorious *boso-zoku* ("crazy drivers") who gather on weekends in convoys of customized cars and motorcycles, with the sole intention of waking up neighborhoods and causing trouble.

ROAD MAPS

Most foreign drivers rely on *Japan: A Bilingual Atlas*, published by Kodansha International, which gives route maps but does not indicate toll roads or charges. For longer-term visitors who are seriously interested in driving around Japan, Shobunsha's thick *Road Atlas Japan* is the best investment. The atlas can be purchased at specialist travel book stores abroad or any book store in Japan that has a good foreign book section.

RENTING A MOTORBIKE

In the capital, **SCS** (Sato Credit Service) is a motorbike sports shop that specializes in offering rentals. For renting a motorbike outside of Tokyo, check for local motorbike dealers through the nearest Tourist Information Office. A 50cc scooter can usually be ridden on an international driver's license (check your license); anything above this capacity requires an international motorcycle license.

Rickshaw, an old-fashioned mode of transportation

BICYCLES AND RICKSHAWS

The great number of bikes, even in cities such as Tokyo, can be a surprising sight to foreigners with a perception of Japan as a land full of high-tech cars. Rickshaws *(jin-riki-sha)* are also back in fashion in predominantly tourist areas such

Cyclists leisurely cruising down Yufuin's main street

as Kyoto and even Ginza in Central Tokyo. In rural areas, horse-drawn open carriages are common and are popular for weddings.

There are often bicycle rental companies in tourist areas. The main thing to note is that sidewalks are not off-limits to cyclists. Indeed, some towns prefer cyclists to use sidewalks rather than roads, ringing their bells to alert pedestrians. Japanese roads do not have designated cycle lanes, as in China, but there is a good network of cycling paths throughout the country. Bicycles are among the few items that are often stolen in Japan, so be sure to use a bicycle lock if one has been provided.

DIRECTORY

Japan Automobile Federation

3-5-8 Shiba-Koen, Minato-ku, Tokyo 105-0011.

Tel (03) 3436-2811.

www.jaf.or.jp

Nippon Rent-A-Car

Tel (03) 3485-7196.

Nissan Rent-A-Car

Tel (03) 5424-4123.

www.nissanrent.com

SCS

2-1-16 Hakusan, Bunkyo-ku, Tokyo 112-0001.

Tel (03) 3815-6221

☐ 10am–7pm daily.

General Index

Further Reading

Japanese names are given with family name last, as on book covers.

History

Everyday Life in Traditional Japan Charles J Dunn (Tuttle, 1972/1997)

Hiroshima John Hersey (Knopf/Penguin, 1985)

Japan: the Story of a Nation Edwin Reischauer (Tuttle, 1981)

Low City, High City: Tokyo from Edo to the Earthquake Edward Seidensticker (Knopf, 1983)

The Nobility of Failure: Tragic Heroes in the History of Japan Ivan Morris (Tuttle, 1982)

The Pacific War 1931-1945 Saburo Ienaga (Pantheon, 1978)

The Rise of Modern Japan W G Beasley (Weidenfeld and Nicolson, 1995)

A Short History of Japan W G Beasley (University of California Press, 1999)

Tokyo Rising: the City Since the Earthquake Edward Seidensticker (Knopf, 1990)

A Traveller's History of Japan Richard Tames (Windrush, 1993)

The World of the Shining Prince Ivan Morris (Penguin, 1964)

Society and Religion

The Chrysanthemum and the Sword Ruth Benedict (Routledge & Kegan Paul, 1967/Houghton Mifflin, 1989: first published 1946)

A First Zen Reader/A Second Zen Reader Trevor Leggett (Tuttle, 1960/1988)

Geisha Liza Dalby (University of California Press, reissued 1998)

Geisha Jodi Cobb (Knopf, 1997)

The Japanese Woman: Traditional Image and Changing Reality Sumiko Iwao (Harvard University Press, 1993)

Keiretsu: Inside the Hidden Japanese Conglomerates Kenichi Miyashita and David Russell (McGraw-Hill, 1996)

The Land of the Rising Yen George Mikes (Penguin, 1973)

Made in Japan: Akio Morita and Sony Akio Morita (Harper Collins, 1994/E P Dutton (1986)

Pink Samurai: an Erotic Exploration of Japanese Society Nicholas Bornoff (Grafton, 1991)

Religion in Japan ed. P F Kornicki and I J McMullen (Cambridge University Press, 1996)

The Way of Tea Rand Castile (Weatherhill, 1979)

Yakuza David Kaplan and Alec Dubro (Addison-Wesley, 1986)

Zen and Japanese Culture Daisetsu T Suzuki (Princeton University Press, 1970)

Japanese Arts

The Art of Japanese Gardens Herb Gustafson (David & Charles, 1999)

The Art of Zen Stephen Addiss (Harry Abrams, 1989)

Contemporary Japanese Architects Philip Jodido (Taschen, 1997)

Furo: the Japanese Bath Peter Grilli and Dana Levy (Kodansha, 1985)

How to Look at Japanese Art Stephen Addiss (Harry N Abrams Inc, 1996)

Japan Crafts Sourcebook Japan Craft Forum (Kodansha, 1996)

Japan 2000: Architecture and Design for the Japanese Public ed John Zukowsky (Prestel, 1998)

Japanese Art Joan Stanley-Baxter (Thames & Hudson, 1984)

Japanese Country Living Katoh & Kimura (Tuttle, 1993)

The Japanese Film Joseph L Anderson and Donald Richie (Princeton University Press, 1982)

The Japanese Print Hugo Munsterberg (Weatherhill, 1998

The Kabuki Handbook Aubrey and Giovanna Halford (Tuttle, 1990)

Matsuri: the World of Japanese Festivals Villar & Anderson (Shufunotomo, 1997)

Minka: the Quintessential Japanese House Kiyoshi Takai (Tuttle, 1998)

The Noh Plays of Japan Arthur Waley (Tuttle, 1976)

A Taste of Japan Donald Richie (Kodansha, 1985)

The Unknown Craftsman: A Japanese Insight into Beauty Soetsu Yanagi (Kodansha, 1989)

Vanishing Japan: Traditional Crafts & Culture Elizabeth Kiritani (Tuttle, 1995)

What Is Japanese Architecture? Kazuo Nishi and Kazuo Hozumi (Kodansha, 1985)

Sports & Outdoor Activities

A Birdwatcher's Guide to Japan Mark Brazil (Kodansha, 1987)

Grand Sumo Lora Sharnoff (Weatherhill, 1993)

A Guide to Japanese Hot Springs Anne Hotta with Yoko Ishiguro (Kodansha, 1986)

Hiking in Japan Paul Hunt (Kodansha, 1988)

Martial Arts & Sports in Japan (Japan Tourist Board, 1998)

National Parks of Japan Mary Sutherland and Dorothy Britton (Kodansha, 1981)

Travelogues and Memoirs

The Bells of Nagasaki Takashi Nagai (Kodansha, 1984: first published 1949)

From Sea to Sea Rudyard Kipling (Macmillan, 1908)

Glimpses of Unfamiliar Japan Lafcadio Hearn (Houghton Mifflin, 1894: first published 1903)

Home Life in Tokyo Jukichi Inouye (Routledge & Kegan Paul, 1985: first published 1910)

The Inland Sea Donald Richie (Century, 1971/1986)

Japanese Inn Oliver Statler (Picador, 1961/Tuttle, 1973)

Japanese Pilgrimage Oliver Statler (Picador/Morrow, 1983)

Kokoro: Hints and Echoes of Japanese Inner Life Lafcadio Hearn (Tuttle, 1972: first published 1896)

The Old Sow in the Back Room Harriet Sergeant (John Murray, 1994)

Pictures from the Water Trade John David Morley (Andre Deutsch, 1985)

The Railway Man Eric Lomax (Vintage, 1996)

The Roads to Sata: a 2000-Mile Walk through Japan Alan Booth (Weatherhill/Penguin, 1985)

Tales from the Burma Campaign 1942-1945 ed John Nunneley (Burma Campaign Fellowship Group, 1998)

Things Japanese Basil Hall Chamberlain (Tuttle, 1971: first published 1905)

Travelers' Tales Japan ed Donald W George and Amy Greinan Carlson (Travelers' Tales, 1999)

Unbeaten Tracks in Japan Isabella Bird (Virago, 1984: first published 1880)

Fiction

Anthology of Modern Japanese Literature Donald Keene (Tuttle, 1970)

An Artist of the Floating World Kazuo Ishiguro (Penguin, 1986)

Black Rain Masuji Ibuse (Kodansha, 1978)

Botchan Natsume Soseki (Tuttle, 1968)

The Counterfeiter and Other Stories Yasushi Inoue (Tuttle, 1965/Peter Owen 1989)

The Ginger Tree Oswald Wynd (Eland, 1977)

The Izu Dancer Yasunari Kawabata (Tuttle, 1954)

Kitchen Banana Yoshimoto (Faber & Faber, 1988)

The Legends of Tono Kunio Yanagita (Japan Foundation, 1975)

The Makioka Sisters Junichiro Tanizaki (Knopf, 1957)

Memoirs of a Geisha Arthur Golden (Chatto & Windus, 1997)

The Narrow Road to the Deep North Matsuo Basho (Penguin, 1966)

The Penguin Book of Japanese Verse (Penguin, 1998)

The Pillow Book of Sei Shonagon Sei Shonagon (Penguin, 1971)

Shogun James Clavell (Hodder & Stoughton, 1975)

Silence Shusako Endo (Penguin, 1988)

The Silent Cry Kenzaburo Oe (Serpent's Tail, 1988)

Snow Country Yasunari Kawabata (Vintage, 1996/1956)

The Tale of Genji Murasaki Shikibu (Penguin, 1981)

The Temple of the Golden Pavilion Yukio Mishima (Tuttle, 1958; Everyman 1956/1994)

Traveller's Literary Companion to Japan Harry Guest (In Print Publishing, 1994)

Acknowledgments

Blue Island Publishing would like to thank the following people at Dorling Kindersley:

Managing Editor
Anna Streiffert.

Managing Art Editor
Kate Poole.

Editorial Directors
Vivien Crump, Louise Bostock Lang.

Art Director
Gillian Allan.

Publisher
Douglas Amrine.

Production
Marie Ingledew, Michelle Thomas.

The Publishers would also like to thank the following people whose contributions and assistance have made the preparation of this book possible:

Main Contributors
John Benson lives in Kyoto and has written and edited many travel articles and website guides about Kyoto, Osaka, and other parts of Kansai.

Mark Brazil, a biologist, natural history and travel writer, and also film consultant, has lived for extended periods in Hokkaido and is a specialist in the natural history of the island.

Jon Burbank is a travel writer and photographer who lives in Chiba prefecture, to the east of Tokyo, with his family.

Angela Jeffs, a writer and editor, moved to Japan in 1986. She lives in Kanagawa prefecture, southwest of Tokyo.

Emi Kazuko is a writer and broadcaster who moved to London from Japan in the 1980s. She is the author of several books about the cuisine of her home country.

Stephen Mansfield is a travel writer and photographer based in Chiba prefecture, whose works about Japan and Asia have appeared in over 80 publications worldwide.

William F. Marsh, a versatile writer, editor, and filmmaker, sadly died in Tokyo while this book was in preparation.

Catherine Rubinstein is a London-based editor and writer who has lived and traveled for extended periods in Japan.

Jacqueline Ruyak is a travel writer who spends half of the year in the United States and the other half in a thatched farmhouse in the mountains of Northern Honshu.

Additional Contributors
Jane Anson, Harry Cook, Brian Burke-Gaffney, Chie Furutani, Ronan Hand, Saradia Hunnisett, Daniel Inman, David Webb.

Design and Editorial Assistance
Amaia Allende, Annette Foo, Victoria Heyworth-Dunne, Nicholas Inman, Anthony Limerick, Carly Madden, Kate Molan, Helen Partington, Sangita Patel, Samuel Richardson, Lupus Sabene, Conrad van Dyk.

Factchecker
Yumi Shigematsu

Indexer
Hilary Bird

Special Assistance
David Hodgson at the Japan National Tourist Organization, the owners and chefs at Kiku Restaurant in London.

Artwork Reference
Photonica/Amana Images.

Additional Photography
Stephen Bere, Demetrio Carrasco, Ian O'Leary, Martin Plomer.

Photography Permissions
The Publishers thank all the temples, castles, museums, hotels, restaurants, shops, and other sights for their assistance and kind permission to photograph their establishments.

Picture Credits
t=top; tl=top left; tlc=top left center; tc=top center; trc=top right center; tr=top right; cla=center left above; ca=center above; cra=center right above; cl=center left; c=center; cr=center right; clb=center left below; cb=center below; crb=center right below; bl=bottom left; b=bottom; bc=bottom center; bcl=bottom center left; bcr=bottom center right; br=bottom right; d=detail.

The Publishers thank the following individuals, companies, and picture libraries for permission to reproduce their photographs:

AFP: Toshifumi Kitamura-STF 354t; Hwang Kwang 21t; Kauhiro-Nogi-STF 35cb; Ereiko Sugita-STF 57c; Yoshikazu Tsuno-STF 362b; ALAMY IMAGES: Tibor Bognar 13tl; Pacific Press Service/Ben Simmons 323tl; Photo Japan 324br; Popperfoto 112c; Ryofu Pussel 12tl; Darby Sawchuk 111tr; Jeremy Sutton-Hibbert 10cl, 323c, 324cl; Chris Willson 11cl, 325br. ARCAID: Richard Bryant 1988/ Tadao Ando 25cb; THE ASAHI SHIMBUN: 66ca; ASKAEN CO LTD: 196bl; AXIOM: Steve J. Berbow 295b, Michael Coster 34–35, 30b, 169b; Jim Holmes 23tr, 34tl, 38cra, 41tl/crb, 108b, 164-5, 373t; Paul Quayle 29tl, 35bl, 35ca, 102t, 355t. DAVE BARTRUFF: 34tr, 35br, 37bc, 41b, 169t, 259t/c/b, 358b; BRIDGEMAN ART LIBRARY, London, New York, and Paris: British Museum, London, Katsushika Hokusai (1760–1849) *Fuji in Clear Weather* from the series *36 Views of Mount Fuji* pub by Nishimura Eijudo in 1831, 57b; Fitzwilliam Museum, Cambridge, UK, Katsushika Hokusai (1760–1849) *Block Cutting and Printing Surimono*, 1825, 85b; Hermitage, St. Petersburg, Russia, *Fly Eating a Pear* 18th-19th century Japanese netsuke 38tl; Private Collection Ando or Utagawa Hiroshige (1797–1858) *Mountains and Coastline*, two views from *36 Views of Mount Fuji* pub by Kosheihi in 1853, 141c; Private Collection / Bonhams *Satsuma Oviform Vase Decorated with Woman Playing the Samisen*, 19th century, 38br; Victoria and Albert Museum, London, Utagawa Kuniyoshi (1798–1861) *Mitsukini Defying the Skeleton Spectre* c.1845, 85crb; BRITISH AIKIDO FEDERATION 35bc; BRITISH LIBRARY: Maps Collection Maps 63140 (2) *Map of Yedo Japan*, 1704, 57c. CHRISTIE'S: 38dc/cb, 39cl, 51t, 53t, 55cb; 57t, 85t/clb; CORBIS: 59t, 214bl, 255b, 364t; Asian Art and Archaeology Inc 36t, 54ca, 85cla; Morton Beebe S.F. 324tr; Bettmann 28tr; Horace Bristol 29bl; Burstein Collection 52ca; Ric Ergenbright 140tr; Eye Ubiquitous/John Dakers 42–3; Natalie Forbes 281b; Michael Freeman 37t; Historical Picture Archive 141b; Robbie Jack 36br; Kevin R. Morris 359b; Richard T. Nowitz 39br; Philadelphia Museum of Art 58t; Sakamoto Photo Research Lab 193tl; Liba Taylor 372c; Michael Yamashita 12bl, 30tr, 35tr, 38c/bl/br, 43tr/43bl, 140b, 297b, 360b; DOUG CORRANCE: 28ca, 380c. EVOLVER: 368c. MICHAEL FREEMAN: 2-3, 23br, 128; FURUHATA BIJUTSU PRINTING COMPANY: Possesion of Rinno-ji Taiyuin-byo, Nikko, National Treasure, World Heritage 270ca; ZAIDANHOJIN FUSHIN-AN: 169cla. GETTY IMAGES: Stone/Thierry Cazabon 34cb; Stone/ Paul Chesley 25tl, 378b; DAJ 10br, 11tl; Stone/ Charles Gupton 318t, 322cl, 372b; Stone/Will and Deni McIntyre 18cr; Travel Pix 12bl. ROBERT HARDING PICTURE LIBRARY: Elly Beintema 372t; Nigel Blythe 19t, 33tl; C. Bowman 386b; Robert Francis 18b; Gavin Heller 19–21; Christopher Rennie 28–29c, 196tl, 391tr; Paul van Riel 390cl. NIGEL HICKS: 24ca, 27tl, 30br, 31tr/cra, 43cbr, 169crb, 286t, 366–7; HIKONE CASTLE MUSEUM: 54–5; HIMEJI CITY OFFICE: 207b; GEOFF HOWARD: 24bl. JAL AIRLINES: 386c; JNTO: 370t. KOBE CITY MUSEUM: 54cb; KYORYOKUKAI CORP IN AID OF THE TOKYO NATIONAL MUSEUM: 52t, 53c, 63cl, 76, 80c, 81t/ca, 82t/cr/bl/br, 83tl/tr/bl; Important Cultural Properties 50, 52cb, 80bl/br, 81cb/b, 82cl/bl, 83br. LONELY PLANET IMAGES: Phil Weymouth 110tc. MARUHAM CORPORATION: 110cr. NIJO CASTLE: 160t/b, 161tl/bl; MOH NISHIKAWA: 26–27c. ORION PRESS 45b; Angle Photo Library 290tl, 291c; Tori Endo 287t; Asao Fujita 290tr; Masami Goto 291b; Hirohito Hara 30cla; Jyunko Hirai 50t; Masaaki Horimachi 46t, 283b, 286, 291t; Yochi

Kamihara 246–7, 250; Daimei Kato 41tr; Shoji Kato 43tl; Kitakanto Colour Agency 264b; Mitsutoshi Kimura 41tc; Fuji Kogei 40cla; Morita Collection 40t; Hideki Nawate 280; Nigata Photo Library 40cr; Yoshiharu Nuga 40clb; Minoru Okuda 49t; Akinari Okuyama 23tl/bl, 290b; Jiichi Omichi 169cra; Yoshikazu Onishi 258b; Sai 22c; Motonobu Sato 24–5; Shikoku Photo Service 225tl; Koichi Sudo 31tl; Hideaki Tanaka 40bl, 43cla, 204b; Nobuo Tanaka 32cb; Kosuke Takeuchi 42ca; Yoshio Tomii 47b; Tohoku Colour Agency 32cra; Eizo Toyoshima 41cr; Yoshimitsu Yagi 36c; Tomokazu Yamada 288–9; Yuzo Yamada 46b; Hiroyuki Yamaguchi 258t; Kenzo Yamamoto 31clb; Noriyuki Yoshida 16, 30bl, 32t, 40br, 41cl. PHOTOLIBRARY: JTB Photo 12cr; PHOTONICA: Amana Images/Seigo Matsuno 248t; / Ikuo Nonka 47t; /Hiroyoshi Terao 32bl; PICTOR: 42t, 59br; PRIVATE COLLECTION: 3i, 9i, 61, 125i, 293i, 367i. REIMEIKAN COLLECTION, Kagoshima City: 54b; REUTERS: Yuriko Nakao 10tc; SIMON RICHMOND: 32br, 377c; BOARD OF TRUSTEES OF THE ROYAL ARMOURIES: Accession Number XXVIS.158–9 55t; Accession Number XXVIA.20 55ca; CATHERINE RUBENSTEIN: 137cr, 139t, 150t. SHOGAKUKAN INC: publishers of *Big Comic Superior* illustration by Koyama Yuu, Ishikawa Yuugo, Hayakawa Shigei, layout by Norma Takashi & Kachidokii 25bl; SONY CONSUMER PRODUCTS: 24br; Stockhouse, Hong Kong: 58c. TELEGRAPH COLOUR LIBRARY: Tim Graham 358c, 378t; /Bavaria-Bidagentur 376t; Colorific/Jean Paul Nacivet 361t; Michael Yamashita 21c/b, 22br, 34ca, 169clb, 354c; 359t, 387b; Black Star/Patrick Morrow 281t, /Eiji Miyazawa 203bl/br; Matrix/Karen Kusmauski 328tr; /Japack Photolibrary 8–9; /FPG © Travelpix 285b; TOKYO COMEDY STORE: Jun Imai 109br; TREASURES FROM THE TOKUGAWA ART MUSEUM: 54–5b, 56t, 143t. WERNER FORMAN ARCHIVE: 36bl/bcl/ bcr, 37tr, 161tr, /Victoria and Albert Museum, London, 85car.

Front Endpaper: all special photography except MICHAEL FREEMAN Rcr; ORION PRESS: Yoichi Kamihara Ltl; Hideki Nawate Rtr; KYORYOKUKAI CORP IN AID OF THE TOKYO NATIONAL MUSEUM: Rbc.

JACKET Front - 4CORNERS IMAGES: SIME/Sato Hitoschi main image; DK IMAGES: Linda Whitwam clb. Back- ALAMY IMAGES: Eagle Visions Photography/Craig Lovell clb: CORBIS; JAI/Gavin Hellier tl; DK IMAGES: Linda Whitwam cla; Peter Wilson bl. Spine - 4CORNERS IMAGES: SIME/Sato Hitoschi t; DK IMAGES: Demetrio Carrasco b.

All other images © Dorling Kindersley. For further information see: www.dkimages.com

Phrase Book

The Japanese language is related to Okinawan and is similar to Altaic languages such as Mongolian and Turkish. Written Japanese uses a combination of three scripts: Chinese ideograms, known as *kanji*, and two syllable-based alphabet systems known as *hiragana* and *katakana*. These two latter are similar, *katakana* functioning as italics are used in English. Traditionally, Japanese is written in vertical columns from top right to bottom left, though the Western system is increasingly used. There are several romanization systems; the Hepburn system is used in this guide. To simplify romanization, macrons (long marks over vowels to indicate longer pronunciation) have not been used. Japanese pronunciation is fairly straightforward, and many words are "Japanized" versions of Western words. This Phrase Book gives the English word or phrase, followed by the Japanese script, then the romanization, adapted to aid pronunciation.

Guidelines For Pronunciation

When reading the romanization, give the same emphasis to all syllables. The practice in English of giving one syllable greater stress may render a Japanese word incomprehensible.

Pronounce vowels as in these English words:

a   as the "u" in "cup"
e   as in "red"
i   as in "chief"
o   as in "solid"
u   as the "oo" in "cuckoo"

When two vowels are used together, give each letter an individual sound:

ai   as in "pine"
ae   as if written "ah-eh"
ei   as in "pay"

Consonants are pronounced as in English. The letter *g* is always hard as in "gate," and *j* is always soft as in "joke." *R* is pronounced something between *r* and *l*. *F* is sometimes pronounced as *h*. "*Si*" always becomes "*shi*," but some people pronounce "*shi*" as "*hi*." *V* in Western words (e.g., "video") becomes *b*. If followed by a consonant, *n* may be pronounced as either *n* or *m*.

All consonants except *n* are always either followed by a vowel or doubled; however, sometimes an *i* or *u* is barely pronounced. In this Phrase Book, to aid pronunciation, apostrophes are used where an *i* or *u* is barely pronounced within a word, and double consonants where this occurs at the end of a word.

Dialects

Standard Japanese is used and understood throughout Japan by people of all backgrounds. But on a colloquial level, there are significant differences in both pronunciation and vocabulary, even between the Tokyo and Osaka-Kyoto areas, and rural accents are very strong.

Polite Words and Phrases

There are several different levels of politeness in the Japanese language, according to status, age, and situation. In everyday conversation, politeness levels are simply a question of the length of verb endings (longer is more polite), but in formal conversation entirely different words *(keigo)* are used. As a visitor, you may find that people try to speak to you in formal language, but there is no need to use it yourself; the level given in this Phrase Book is neutral yet polite.

In an Emergency

Help!	たすけて！	Tas'kete!
Stop!	とめて！	Tomete!
Call a doctor!	医者をよんで ください！	Isha o yonde kudasai!
Call an ambulance!	救急車を よんでください！	Kyukyusha o yonde kudasai!
Call the police!	警察を よんでください！	Keisatsu o yonde kudasai!
Fire!	火事！	Kaji!
Where is the hospital?	病院はどこに ありますか？	Byoin wa doko ni arimass-ka?
police box	交番	koban

Communication Essentials

Yes/no.	はい／いいえ	Hai/ie.
… not …	・・・ない／ちがい ます。	… nai/ chigaimass.
I don't know.	しりません。	Shirimasen.
Thank you.	ありがとう。	Arigato.
Thank you very much.	ありがとう ございます。	Arigato gozaimass.
Thank you very much indeed.	どうもありがとう ございます。	Domo arigato gozaimass.
Thanks (casual).	どうも。	Domo.
No, thank you.	結構です。 ありがとう。	Kekko dess, arigato.
Please (offering).	どうぞ。	Dozo.
Please (asking).	おねがいします。	Onegai shimass.
Please (give me or do for me).	・・・ください。	… kudasai.
I don't understand.	わかりません。	Wakarimasen.
Do you speak English?	英語を 話せますか？	Eigo o hanasemass-ka?
I can't speak Japanese.	日本語は 話せません。	Nihongo wa hanasemasen.
Please speak more slowly.	もう少し ゆっくり 話して ください。	Mo s'koshi yukkuri hanash'te kudasai.
Sorry/Excuse me!	すみません。	Sumimasen!
Could you help me please? (not emergency)	ちょっと手伝って いただけません か？	Chotto tets'datte itadakemasen- ka?

Useful Phrases

My name is ….	わたしの 名前は・・・ です。	Watashi no namae wa … dess.
How do you do, pleased to meet you.	はじめまして、 どうぞ よろしく。	Hajime-mash'te, dozo yorosh'ku.
How are you?	お元気ですか？	Ogenki dess-ka?
Good morning.	おはよう ございます。	Ohayo gozaimass.
Good afternoon/ good day.	こんにちは。	Konnichiwa.
Good evening.	こんばんは。	Konbanwa.

Good night.	おやすみなさい。	Oyasumi nasai.
Good-bye.	さよなら。	Sayonara.
Take care.	気をつけて。	Ki o ts'kete.
Keep well (casual)	お元気で。	Ogenki de.
The same to you.	そちらも。	Sochira mo.
What is (this)?	(これは)何ですか？	(Kore wa) nan dess-ka?
How do you use this?	これをどうやって使いますか？	Kore o doyatte ts'kaimass-ka?
Could I possibly have ...? (very polite)	・・・をいただけますか？	... o itadake-mass-ka?
Is there ... here?	ここに・・・がありますか？	Koko ni ... ga arimass-ka?
Where can I get ...?	・・・はどこにありますか？	... wa doko ni arimass-ka?
How much is it?	いくらですか？	Ikura dess-ka?
What time is ...?	・・・何時ですか？	... nan-ji dess-ka?
Cheers! (toast)	乾杯！	Kampai!
Where is the restroom/toilet?	お手洗い／おトイレはどこですか？	Otearai/otoire wa doko dess-ka?
Here's my business card.	名刺をどうぞ。	Meishi o dozo.

Useful Words

I	わたし	watashi
woman	女性	josei
man	男性	dansei
wife	奥さん	ok'san
husband	主人	shujin
daughter	むすめ	musume
son	むすこ	mus'ko
child	こども	kodomo
children	こどもたち	kodomo-tachi
businessman/ woman	ビジネスマン／ウーマン	bijinessuman/ wuman
student	学生	gakusei
Mr./Mrs./Ms. ...	・・・さん	...-san
big/small	大きい／小さい	okii/chiisai
hot/cold	暑い／寒い	atsui/samui
cold (to touch)	冷たい	tsumetai
warm	温かい	atatakai
good/ not good/bad	いい／よくない／悪い	ii/yokunai/warui
enough	じゅうぶん／結構	jubun/kekko
free (no charge)	ただ／無料	tada/muryo
here	ここ	koko
there	あそこ	asoko
this	これ	kore
that (nearby)	それ	sore
that (far away)	あれ	are
what?	何？	nani?
when?	いつ？	itsu?
why?	なぜ？／どうして？	naze?/dosh'te?
where?	どこ？	doko?
who?	誰？	dare?
which way?	どちら？	dochira?

Signs

Open	営業中	eigyo-chu
closed	休日	kyujitsu
entrance	入口	iriguchi
exit	出口	deguchi
danger	危険	kiken
emergency exit	非常口	hijo-guchi
information	案内	annai
restroom, toilet	お手洗い／手洗い／おトイレ／トイレ	otearai/tearai/ otoire/toire
free (vacant)	空き	aki
men	男	otoko
women	女	onna

Money

Could you change this into yen please.	これを円に替えてください。	Kore o en ni kaete kudasai.
I'd like to cash these travelers' checks.	このトラベラーズチェックを現金にしたいです。	Kono toraberazu chekku o genkin ni shitai dess.
Do you take credit cards/ travelers' checks?	クレジットカード／トラベラーズチェックで払えますか？	Kurejitto kado/ toraberazu chekku de haraemass-ka?
bank	銀行	ginko
cash	現金	genkin
credit card	クレジットカード	kurejitto kado
currency exchange office	両替所	ryogaejo
dollars	ドル	doru
pounds	ポンド	pondo
yen	円	en

Keeping in Touch

Where is a telephone?	電話はどこにありますか？	Denwa wa doko ni arimass-ka?
May I use your phone?	電話を使ってもいいですか？	Denwa o ts'katte mo ii dess-ka?
Hello, this is	もしもし、・・・です。	Moshi-moshi, ...dess.
I'd like to make an international call.	国際電話、お願いします。	Kokusai denwa, onegai shimass.
airmail	航空便	kokubin
e-mail	イーメール	i-meru
fax	ファクス	fak'su
postcard	ハガキ	hagaki
post office	郵便局	yubin-kyoku
stamp	切手	kitte
telephone booth	公衆電話	koshu denwa
telephone card	テレフォンカード	terefon kado

Shopping

Where can I buy ...?	・・・はどこで買えますか？	... wa doko de kaemass-ka?
How much does this cost?	いくらですか？	Ikura dess-ka?
I'm just looking.	見ているだけです。	Mite iru dake dess.
Do you have ...?	・・・ありますか？	... arimass-ka?
May I try this on?	着てみてもいいですか？	Kite mite mo ii dess-ka?
Please show me that.	それを見せてください。	Sore o misete kudasai.
Does it come in other colors?	他の色もありますか？	Hoka no iro mo arimass-ka?
black	黒	kuro
blue	青	ao
green	緑	midori
red	赤	aka
white	白	shiro
yellow	黄色	kiiro
cheap/expensive	安い／高い	yasui/takai
audio equipment	オーディオ製品	odio seihin
bookstore	本屋	hon-ya
boutique	ブティック	butik
clothes	洋服	yofuku
department store	デパート	depato
electrical store	電気屋	denki-ya
fish market	魚屋	sakana-ya
folk crafts	民芸品	mingei-hin
ladies' wear	婦人服	fujin fuku
local specialty	名物	meibutsu
market	市場	ichiba
menswear	紳士服	shinshi fuku
newsstand	新聞屋	shimbun-ya

pharmacist	薬屋	kusuri-ya
picture postcard	絵葉書	e-hagaki
sale	セール	seru
souvenir shop	お土産屋	omiyage-ya
supermarket	スーパー	supa
travel agent	旅行会社	ryoko-gaisha

Sightseeing

Where is …?	…はどこですか？	… wa doko dess-ka?
How do I get to …?	…へは、どうやっていったらいいですか？	… e wa doyatte ittara ii dess-ka?
Is it far?	遠いですか？	Toi dess-ka?
art gallery	美術館	bijutsukan
reservations desk	予約窓口	yoyaku madoguchi
bridge	橋	hashi/bashi
castle	城	shiro/jo
city	市	shi
city center	街の中心	machi no chushin
gardens	庭園／庭	tei-en/niwa
hot spring	温泉	onsen
information office	案内所	annaijo
island	島	shima/jima
monastery	修道院	shudo-in
mountain	山	yama/san
museum	博物館	hakubutsukan
palace	宮殿	kyuden
park	公園	koen
port	港	minato/ko
prefecture	県	ken
river	川	kawa/gawa
ruins	遺跡	iseki
shopping area	ショッピング街	shoppingu gai
shrine	神社／神宮／宮	jinja/jingu/gu
street	通り	tori/dori
temple	お寺／寺	otera/tera/dera/ji
tour, travel	旅行	ryoko
town	町	machi/cho
village	村	mura
ward	区	ku
zoo	動物園	dobutsu-en
north	北	kita/hoku
south	南	minami/nan
east	東	higashi/to
west	西	nishi/sei
left/right	左／右	hidari/migi
straight ahead	真っ直ぐ	mass-sugu
between	間に	aida ni
near/far	近い／遠い	chikai/toi
up/down	上／下	ue/sh'ta
new	新しい／新	atarashii/shin
old/former	古い／元	furui/moto
upper/lower	上／下	kami/shimo
middle/inner	中	naka
in	に／中に	ni/naka ni
in front of	前	mae

Getting Around

bicycle	自転車	jitensha
bus	バス	basu
car	車	kuruma
ferry	フェリー	feri
baggage room	手荷物一時預かり所	tenimotsu ichiji azukarijo
motorcycle	オートバイ	otobai
one-way ticket	片道切符	katamichi kippu
return ticket	往復切符	ofuku kippu
taxi	タクシー	takushi
ticket	切符	kippu
ticket office	切符売場	kippu uriba

Trains

What is the fare to …?	…までいくらですか？	… made ikura dess-ka?
When does the train for… leave?	…行きの電車は、何時に出ますか？	… iki no densha wa nan-ji ni demass-ka?
How long does it take to get to …?	…まで時間は、どのぐらいかかりますか？	… made jikan wa dono gurai kakarimass-ka?
A ticket to …, please.	…行きの切符をください。	… yuki no kippu o kudasai.
Do I have to change?	乗り換えが必要ですか？	Norikae ga hitsuyo dess-ka?
I'd like to reserve a seat, please.	席を予約したいです。	Seki o yoyaku shitai dess.
Which platform for the train to …?	…行きの電車は、何番ホームから出ますか？	… yuki no densha wa nanban homu kara demass-ka?
Which station is this?	この駅は、どこですか？	Kono eki wa doko dess-ka?
Is this the right train for …?	…へは、この電車でいいですか？	… e wa kono densha de ii dess-ka?
bullet train	新幹線	shinkansen
express trains:		
"limited express" (fastest)	特急	tokkyu
"express" (second)	急行	kyuko
"rapid" (third)	快速	kaisoku
first-class	一等	itto
line	線	sen
local train	普通／各駅電車	futsu/kaku-eki-densha
platform	ホーム	homu
train station	駅	eki
reserved seat	指定席	shitei-seki
second-class	二等	nito
subway	地下鉄	chikatetsu
train	電車	densha
unreserved seat	自由席	jiyu-seki

Accommodations

Do you have any vacancies?	部屋がありますか？	Heya ga arimass-ka?
I have a reservation.	予約をしてあります。	Yoyaku o sh'te arimass.
I'd like a room with a bathroom.	お風呂つきの部屋、お願いします。	Ofuro-ts'ki no heya, onegai shimass.
What is the charge per night?	一泊いくらですか？	Ippaku ikura dess-ka?
Is tax included in the price?	税込みですか？	Zeikomi dess-ka?
Can I leave my luggage here for a little while?	荷物をちょっとここに預けてもいいですか？	Nimotsu o chotto koko ni azukete mo ii dess-ka?
air-conditioning	冷房／エアコン	reibo/eakon
bath	お風呂	ofuro
check-out	チェックアウト	chekku-auto
hair drier	ドライヤー	doraiya
hot (boiled) water	お湯	oyu
Japanese-style inn	旅館	ryokan
Japanese-style room	和室	wa-shitsu
key	鍵	kagi
front desk	フロント	furonto
single/twin room	シングル／ツイン	shinguru/tsuin

shower	シャワー	shyawa
Western-style hotel	ホテル	hoteru
Western-style room	洋室	yo-shitsu

Eating Out

A table for one/two/three, please.	一人／二人／三人、お願いします。	Hitori/futari/sannin, onegai shimass.
May I see the menu.	メニュー、お願いします。	Menyu, onegai shimass.
Is there a set menu?	定食がありますか？	Teishoku ga arimass-ka?
I'd like	私は・・・がいいです。	Watashi wa … ga ii dess.
May I have one of those?	それをひとつ、お願いします。	Sore o hitotsu, onegai shimass.
I am a vegetarian.	私はベジタリアンです。	Watashi wa bejitarian dess.
Waiter/waitress!	ちょっとすみません。	Chotto sumimasen!
What would you recommend?	おすすめは何ですか？	Osusume wa nan dess-ka?
How do you eat this?	これはどうやって食べますか？	Kore wa doyatte tabemass-ka?
May we have the check please.	お勘定、お願いします。	Okanjo, onegai shimass.
May we have some more …	もっと・・・、お願いします。	Motto …, onegai shimass.
The meal was very good, thank you.	ごちそうさまでした。おいしかったです。	Gochiso-sama desh'ta, oishikatta dess.
assortment	盛りあわせ	moriawase
boxed meal	弁当	bento
breakfast	朝食	cho-shoku
buffet	バイキング	baikingu
delicious	おいしい	oishii
dinner	夕食	yu-shoku
to drink	飲む	nomu
a drink	飲みもの	nomimono
to eat	食べる	taberu
food	食べもの／ごはん	tabemono/gohan
full (stomach)	おなかがいっぱい	onaka ga ippai
hot/cold	熱い／冷たい	atsui/tsumetai
hungry	おなかがすいた	onaka ga suita
Japanese food	和食	wa-shoku
lunch	昼食	chu-shoku
set menu	セット／定食	setto (snack)/teishoku (meal)
spicy	辛い	karai
sweet, mild	甘い	amai
Western food	洋食	yo-shoku

Places to Eat

Cafeteria/canteen	食堂	shokudo
Chinese restaurant	中華料理屋	chuka-ryori-ya
coffee shop	喫茶店	kissaten
local bar	飲み屋／居酒屋	nomiya/izakaya
noodle stall	ラーメン屋	ramen-ya
restaurant	レストラン／料理屋	resutoran/ryori-ya
sushi on a conveyor belt	回転寿司	kaiten-zushi
upscale restaurant	料亭	ryotei
upscale vegetarian restaurant	精進料理屋	shojin-ryori-ya

Foods (see also Reading the Menu pp320–321)

apple	りんご	ringo
bamboo shoots	たけのこ	takenoko
beancurd	とうふ	tofu
bean sprouts	もやし	moyashi
beans	豆	mame
beef	ビーフ／牛肉	bifu/gyuniku
beefburger	ハンバーグ	hanbagu
blowfish	ふぐ	fugu
bonito, tuna	かつお／ツナ	katsuo/tsuna
bread	パン	pan
butter	バター	bata
cake	ケーキ	keki
chicken	とり／鶏肉	tori/toriniku
confectionery	お菓子	okashi
crab	かに	kani
duck	あひる	ahiru
eel	うなぎ	unagi
egg	たまご	tamago
eggplant/aubergine	なす	nasu
fermented soybean paste	みそ	miso
fermented soybeans	納豆	natto
fish (raw)	さしみ	sashimi
fried tofu	油揚げ	abura-age
fruit	くだもの	kudamono
ginger	しょうが	shoga
hamburger	ハンバーガー	hanbaga
haute cuisine	会席	kaiseki
herring	ニシン	nishin
hors d'oeuvres	オードブル	odoburu
ice cream	アイスクリーム	aisu-kurimu
jam	ジャム	jamu
Japanese mushrooms	まつたけ／しいたけ／しめじ	mats'take/shiitake/shimeji
Japanese pear	なし	nashi
loach	どじょう	dojo
lobster	伊勢えび	ise-ebi
mackerel	さば	saba
mackerel pike	さんま	sanma
mandarin orange	みかん	mikan
meat	肉	niku
melon	メロン	meron
mountain vegetables	山菜	sansai
noodles:		
buckwheat	そば	soba
Chinese	ラーメン	ramen
wheatflour	うどん／そうめん	udon (fat)/somen (thin)
octopus	たこ	tako
omelet	オムレツ	omuretsu
oyster	カキ	kaki
peach	もも	momo
pepper	こしょう	kosho
persimmon	柿	kaki
pickles	つけもの	ts'kemono
pork	豚肉	butaniku
potato	いも	imo
rice:		
cooked	ごはん	gohan
uncooked	米	kome
rice crackers	おせんべい	osenbei
roast beef	ローストビーフ	rosutobifu
salad	サラダ	sarada
salmon	鮭	sake
salt	塩	shio
sandwich	サンドイッチ	sandoichi
sausage	ソーセージ	soseji
savory nibbles	おつまみ	otsumami
seaweed:		
dried	のり	nori
chewy	こんぶ	konbu

shrimp	えび	ebi
soup	汁／スープ	shiru/supu
soy sauce	しょうゆ	shoyu
spaghetti	スパゲティ	supageti
spinach	ほうれんそう	horenso
squid	いか	ika
steak	ステーキ	suteki
sugar	砂糖	sato
sushi (mixed)	五目寿司	gomoku-zushi
sweetfish/smelt	あゆ	ayu
taro (potato)	さといも	sato imo
toast	トースト	tosuto
trout	鱒	masu
sea urchin	ウニ	uni
vegetables	野菜	yasai
watermelon	すいか	suika
wild boar	ぼたん／いのしし	botan/inoshishi

Drinks

beer	ビール	biru
coffee (hot)	ホットコーヒー	hotto-kohi
cola	コーラ	kora
green tea	お茶	ocha
iced coffee:		
black	アイスコーヒー	aisu-kohi
with milk	アイスオーレ	kafe-o-re
lemon tea	レモンティー	remon ti
milk	ミルク／牛乳	miruku/gyunyu
mineral water	ミネラルウォーター	mineraru uota
orange juice	オレンジジュース	orenji jusu
rice wine	酒	sake
(non-alcoholic)	（甘酒）	(ama-zake)
tea (Western-style)	紅茶	kocha
tea with milk	ミルクティー	miruku ti
water	水	mizu
whiskey	ウイスキー	uis'ki
wine	ワイン／ぶどう酒	wain/budoshu

Health

I don't feel well.	気分がよくないです。	Kibun ga yokunai dess.
I have a pain in …	…が痛いです。	… ga itai dess.
I'm allergic to …	…アレルギーです。	… arerugi dess.
asthma	喘息	zensoku
cough	せき	seki
dentist	歯医者	haisha
diabetes	糖尿病	tonyo-byo
diarrhea	下痢	geri
doctor	医者	isha
fever	熱	netsu
headache	頭痛	zutsuu
hospital	病院	byoin
medicine	薬	kusuri
Oriental medicine	漢方薬	kampo yaku
pharmacy	薬局	yakkyoku
prescription	処方箋	shohosen
stomachache	腹痛	fukutsu
toothache	歯が痛い	ha ga itai

Numbers

0	ゼロ	zero
1	一	ichi
2	二	ni
3	三	san
4	四	yon/shi
5	五	go
6	六	roku
7	七	nana/shichi
8	八	hachi
9	九	kyu
10	十	ju
11	十一	ju-ichi
12	十二	ju-ni
20	二十	ni-ju
21	二十一	ni-ju-ichi
22	二十二	ni-ju-ni
30	三十	san-ju
40	四十	yon-ju
100	百	hyaku
101	百一	hyaku-ichi
200	二百	ni-hyaku
300	三百	san-byaku
400	四百	yon-hyaku
500	五百	go-hyaku
600	六百	ro-ppyaku
700	七百	nana-hyaku
800	八百	ha-ppyaku
900	九百	kyu-hyaku
1,000	千	sen
1,001	千一	sen-ichi
2,000	二千	ni-sen
10,000	一万	ichi-man
20,000	二万	ni-man
100,000	十万	ju-man
1,000,000	百万	hyaku-man
123,456	十二万三千四百五十六	ju-ni-man-san-zen-yon-hyaku-go-ju-roku

Time

Monday	月曜日	getsu-yobi
Tuesday	火曜日	ka-yobi
Wednesday	水曜日	sui-yobi
Thursday	木曜日	moku-yobi
Friday	金曜日	kin-yobi
Saturday	土曜日	do-yobi
Sunday	日曜日	nichi-yobi
January	一月	ichi-gatsu
February	二月	ni-gatsu
March	三月	san-gatsu
April	四月	shi-gatsu
May	五月	go-gatsu
June	六月	roku-gatsu
July	七月	shichi-gatsu
August	八月	hachi-gatsu
September	九月	ku-gatsu
October	十月	ju-gatsu
November	十一月	ju-ichi-gatsu
December	十二月	ju-ni-gatsu
spring	春	haru
summer	夏	natsu
fall/autumn	秋	aki
winter	冬	fuyu
noon	正午	shogo
midnight	真夜中	mayonaka
today	今日	kyo
yesterday	昨日	kino
tomorrow	明日	ash'ta
this morning	今朝	kesa
this afternoon	今日の午後	kyo no gogo
this evening	今晩	konban
every day	毎日	mainichi
month	月	getsu/ts'ki
hour	時	ji
time/hour (duration)	時間	jikan
minute	分	pun/fun
this year	今年	kotoshi
last year	去年	kyonen
next year	来年	rainen
one year	一年	ichi-nen
late	遅い	osoi
early	早い	hayai
soon	すぐ	sugu

Tokyo Subway System

The subway system in Tokyo is fast and efficient. This map shows all the subway lines, plus selected JR (Japan Rail) lines and private rail lines. See the Street Finder maps on pages 114–23 for the location of central subway stations at street level. Many stations have multiple exits; it is often easier to go up to ground level, then orient yourself.

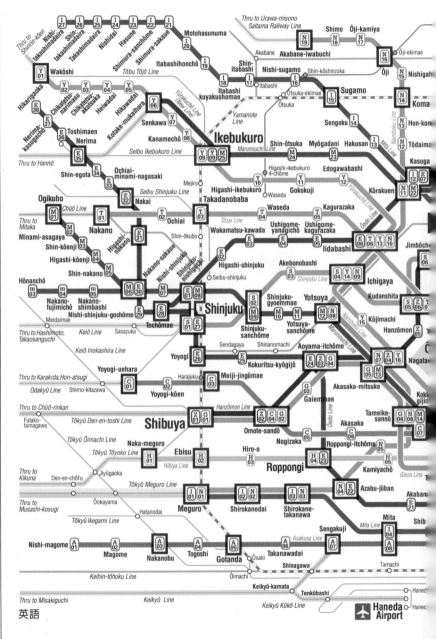

英語